BEHIND AND BEYOND THE METER

BEHIND AND BEYOND THE METER

Digitalization, Aggregation, Optimization, Monetization

Edited by

FEREIDOON SIOSHANSI

Menlo Energy Economics, San Francisco, CA, United States

ELSEVIER

ACADEMIC PRESS
An imprint of Elsevier

Academic Press is an imprint of Elsevier
125 London Wall, London EC2Y 5AS, United Kingdom
525 B Street, Suite 1650, San Diego, CA 92101, United States
50 Hampshire Street, 5th Floor, Cambridge, MA 02139, United States
The Boulevard, Langford Lane, Kidlington, Oxford OX5 1GB, United Kingdom

British Library Cataloguing-in-Publication Data
A catalogue record for this book is available from the British Library

Library of Congress Cataloging-in-Publication Data
A catalog record for this book is available from the Library of Congress

ISBN: 978-0-12-819951-0

For Information on all Academic Press publications
visit our website at https://www.elsevier.com/books-and-journals

Publisher: Brian Romer
Acquisitions Editor: Graham Nisbet
Editorial Project Manager: Leticia Lima
Production Project Manager: Kiruthika Govindaraju
Cover Designer: Mark Rogers

Typeset by MPS Limited, Chennai, India

Contents

Author biographies ix

Foreword by *Andreas Bjelland Eriksen and Ove Flataker,* *The Norwegian Energy Regulation Authority (NVE)* **xix**

Preface by *Dominique Jamme, Commission de Regulation de L'Energie (CRE)* **xxiii**

Introduction by *Fereidoon Sioshansi, Menlo Energy Economics (MEE)* **xxvii**

Part One

Visionaries, dreamers, innovators

1. What lies behind-the-meter and why it matters? 3

   Fereidoon Sioshansi, *Menlo Energy Economics*

2. It is not science fiction: going zero net energy and loving it 31

   Benjamin Schlesinger, *Schlesinger and Associates*

3. Creating value behind-the-meter: Digitalization, aggregation and optimization of behind-the-meter assets 47

   Fereidoon Sioshansi, *Menlo Energy Economics*

4. Customer participation in P2P trading: a German energy community case study 83

   Sabine Löbbe, André Hackbarth, *Reutlingen Univ.,*
   Thies Stillahn, Luis Pfeiffer, *EWS Elektrizitätswerke Schönau eG* and
   Gregor Rohbogner, *Oxygen Technologies GmbH*

5. Aggregators today and tomorrow: from intermediaries to local orchestrators? 105

   Ksenia Poplavskaya, *Austrian Institute of Technology and TU Delft* and
   Laurens de Vries, *TU Delft*

6. Energy communities: a Dutch case study   137

Victor M.J.J. Reijnders, *University of Twente*, Marten D. van der Laan, *ICT Group N.V.* and Roelof Dijkstra, *Enexis Netbeheer B.V.*

7. The expanding role of home energy management ecosystem: an Australian case study   157

Damian Shaw-Williams, *QUT*

Part Two

Implementers & disrupters

8. Behind and beyond the meter: what's in it for the system?   179

Dierk Bauknecht, Christoph Heinemann, Dominik Seebach and Moritz Vogel, *Oeko-Institut*

9. Working backward from behind the meter: what consumer value, behavior, and uncertainty mean for distributed energy technologies   193

Robert Smith, *East Economics* and Iain MacGill, *UNSW*

10. Aggregation of front- and behind-the-meter: the evolving VPP business model   211

Lotte Lehmbruck, Julian Kretz and Jan Aengenvoort, *Next Kraftwerke* and Fereidoon Sioshansi, *Menlo Energy Economics*

11. Platform for trading flexibility on the distribution network: a UK case study   233

James Johnston, *Piclo Flex* and Fereidoon Sioshansi, *Menlo Energy Economics*

12. Smart meters: the gate to behind-the-meter?   251

Carlo Stagnaro, *Istituto Bruno Leoni* and Simona Benedettini, *PwC Italy*

13. D3A energy exchange for a transactive grid   267

Ana Trbovich, Sarah Hambridge, Dirk van den Biggelaar and Ewald Hesse, *Grid Singularity* and Fereidoon Sioshansi, *Menlo Energy Economics*

14. Emerging aggregator business models in European electricity markets   285

Simon De Clercq, *3E*, Daniel Schwabeneder, Carlo Corinaldesi and Andreas Fleischhacker, *Vienna University of Technology*

Part Three
Regulators, policymakers & investors

15. Behind-the-meter prospects: what do household customers' responses to prices tell us?   307

    Bruce Mountain, *Victoria University, Melbourne*

16. Regulating off-the-grid: stand-alone power systems in Australia   317

    Alan Rai, Claire Rozyn, Andrew Truswell and
    Tim Nelson, *AEMC, Sydney, Australia*

17. Distribution network tariff design for behind-the-meter: balancing efficiency and fairness   341

    Tim Schittekatte, *Florence School of Regulation*

18. What market design, fiscal policy, and network regulations are compatible with efficient behind the meter investments?   361

    David Robinson, *Oxford Institute for Energy Studies*

19. Two million plus solar roofs: what's in it for the consumers?   381

    Mike Swanston, *The Customer Advocate, Brisbane, Australia*

20. Will behind-the-meter make a difference?   407

    Fereidoon Sioshansi, *Menlo Energy Economics*

Epilogue by *Jean-Michel Glachant,* *Florence School of Regulation*   **411**
Index   415

Author biographies

Jan Aengenvoort is Chief Communication Officer (CCO) at Next Kraftwerke responsible for public relations and marketing strategy. He has been instrumental in developing NK's marketing message from a small startup into one of the largest VPPs in Europe today. He is an expert on the integration of renewable energies into existing grid structures and energy markets through VPPs and short-term trading.

Jan holds a degree in linguistics and was formerly working as a freelance journalist for several German newspapers.

Dierk Bauknecht is a senior researcher with the Oeko-Institut's Energy and Climate Division. Dierk has led a broad range of national and European projects on the integration of renewables into the power system; the governance of electricity system transformation; infrastructure regulation and smart grids; flexibility options and market design; power system modeling; European renewables policy.

Before joining the Oeko-Institut, he was modeling manager with a UK-based power market consultancy.

Dierk graduated in political science at the Freie Universität Berlin and holds an M.Sc. in science and technology policy and a doctorate from the University of Sussex, United Kingdom.

Simona Benedettini is a senior manager at PwC Italy. Before joining PwC, Simona worked as energy economist for leading industry associations, consultancies, and research institutions.

Simona has published several articles on regulation and competition of the energy sector on academic journals and leading Italian newspapers.

She earned a PhD in law and economics from the University of Siena and has been visiting scholar at the University of Illinois.

Carlo Corinaldesi is working as a project assistant at the Institute of Energy Systems and Electrical Drives in the Energy Economics Group. The current work focuses mainly on aggregation of flexibility in energy management systems and trading wholesale electricity products. Other research interests include the marketing of balancing power, the design of business models and applied game theory.

Carlo Corinaldesi holds a bachelor's degree in energy engineering from the Technical University of Turin and the M.Sc. degree in automation engineering from the Technical University of Vienna.

Simon De Clercq is a consultant in the Grids, Storage & Markets team at 3E. His main fields of expertise are power systems and electricity markets with a strong focus on energy policy. As a consultant he has managed projects on regional renewable energy policy, decarbonization strategies for islands and the role of flexibility in European electricity markets.

Simon holds a bachelor's degree in electromechanical engineering and a master's degree in electrical power engineering, both from Ghent University. He is a certified expert in renewable energy finance from Frankfurt School of Finance & Management.

Laurens de Vries is an associate professor at the Faculty of Technology, Policy and Management of Delft University of Technology. He works in the field of energy market design, analyzing the interrelations between the physical infrastructure, its economic organization and regulation.

Recent research projects involve the design of European balancing markets, the design of direct-current microgrids, and congestion in distribution networks. A second line of research is on how regulation, such as the European CO_2 market, renewable energy policy, and capacity mechanisms, affects investment in electricity generation. He is the coordinator of the European Energy Research Alliance Joint Programme on Energy Systems Integration.

Dr. De Vries has an M.Sc. in mechanical engineering from Delft University of Technology, an M.A. in environmental studies from The Evergreen State College, and a PhD degree from the Faculty of Technology, Policy and Management of Delft University of Technology.

Roelof Dijkstra is a Senior Consultant Sector Strategy at Enexis Netbeheer, one of the biggest Grid Access Providers in The Netherlands.

Roelof is involved in a large scale of project to stimulate the energy transition. One of them is a new price mechanism to stimulate the inhabitants of a district to consume the produced energy at the moment the energy is produced in that district. Another project is to make it possible for a consumer to contract more than one supplier on a connection point.

Roelof studied mechanical and industrial engineering and organizational logistics.

Andreas Bjelland Eriksen is an Adviser at The Norwegian Energy Regulatory Authority (NVE). His responsibilities include topics regarding network tariffs, prosumers, and metering. Through his work, he participates in the Distribution Systems Working Group in CEER.

Mr. Bjelland Eriksen has also served two terms as County Councillor in Rogaland County, during which he was elected deputy chair of the transportation committee.

He holds an M.Sc. in economics and business administration from the Norwegian School of Economics.

Ove Flataker is the Director of The Norwegian Energy Regulatory Authority (NVE).

Prior to working in NVE, Mr. Flataker worked over 20 years with the Ministry of Petroleum and Energy, within electricity and the oil and gas industry. Mr. Flataker's main tasks involved development of the Norwegian electricity market in the 1990s. He has also worked with R&D policy, energy efficiency, full-scale carbon capture and storage, licensing for power plants and grid projects.

Mr. Flataker holds a master's degree in economics and business administration, and a bachelor's degree in Marine Technology.

Andreas Fleischhacker joined the Energy Economics Group at TU Wien as a research associate and project assistant in 2013, where he participates in international and national research projects.

In 2017 he visited MIT/LIDS, MA, United States for joint research. His research interests in energy economics include modeling and optimization of sustainable energy systems under consideration of hybrid grid structures as well as energy sharing concepts for distributed generation.

He received the B.Sc. degree in electrical engineering and the M.Sc. degree in automation engineering from the TU Wien.

Jean-Michel Glachant is the Director of the Florence School of Regulation and Loyola de Palacio Chair at the European University Institute.

He regularly advises the European Commission and various European energy regulators, has been coordinator or scientific advisor of several European research projects, and is a research partner in the CEEPR at MIT, and the EPRG at Cambridge University.

His main research interests are the building of a common European energy regulation and policy, the achievement of the European energy internal market, and the industrial organization and market strategy of energy companies. He has been first Editor-in-Chief of the Economics of Energy & Environmental Policy and Vice-President for Communications of the International Association for Energy Economics. He is the author of numerous books and publications.

He has a master's degree and PhD in economics from La Sorbonne.

André Hackbarth is a researcher and lecturer at Reutlingen University, School of Engineering/Distributed Energy Systems and Energy Efficiency, Germany. His research interests include business models in the energy sector and consumer attitudes, preferences, and decision-making concerning energy-related behaviors and products.

Prior to his current position, he was a research associate at the Institute for Future Energy Consumer Needs and Behavior (FCN) at RWTH Aachen University, Germany.

He is PhD candidate at RWTH Aachen University and studied economics at Heidelberg University.

Sarah Hambridge is the D3A Product Owner at Grid Singularity, pronounced World Economic Forum Tech Pioneer in 2018, and pushing the envelope on decentralized energy markets, peer-to-peer trading, and grid balancing, secured by smart contracts and blockchain technology.

Before joining Grid Singularity, she completed a PhD in electrical engineering at North Carolina State University and has interned at Siemens and Sandia National Laboratories.

Christoph Heinemann is a senior researcher at the Freiburg branch of the Oeko-Institut's Energy and Climate Division. His key activities include the topics integration of renewable energy, flexibility options, regulation, and modeling of the future power system. Before he joining the institute, he worked in the field of smart grids and innovative power products for 2 years.

He studied geography, political economy, and business studies at the University of Freiburg.

Ewald Hesse is cofounder and CEO of Grid Singularity and Energy Web Foundation Council Member. He serves on the advisory board of several startups, including Verv, Kivu Technologies, Leap, and the Scytale Ventures investment fund.

Hesse previously worked as Regional Director for Business Development and Strategy in Southeast Europe at Andritz Hydro. Earlier, he explored technology transfer and joint ventures in China and European automobile sector at Metzler and ABB.

He holds a bachelor's degree in mechanical engineering and project management from the University of Konstanz, Germany. As part of this program, he attended the Polytechnic University in Hong Kong.

Dominique Jamme is managing director at CRE, the French energy regulatory authority. He has a extensive experience in regulation of energy markets. He has held various positions at CRE for more than 15 years, among them director for networks, and was lastly in charge of creating and animating the "prospective Committee" of CRE, gathering experts, academics and companies in order to help CRE imagine the future of the energy sector.

He is a graduate from Ecole Polytechnique Paris and ENSTA Paris.

James Johnston is the CEO and cofounder of Piclo, an innovative technology startup based in London, United Kingdom with a mission to solve the energy trilemma.

Prior to founding Piclo (formally known as Open Utility), James spent 3 years researching building-integrated direct-current microgrids at University of Strathclyde. James is also the founder of Solar Sketch, a design company for the solar industry, and worked as a building services engineer at international engineering consultancy Arup.

James holds a B.Eng. and M.Sc. from University of Strathclyde in mechanical engineering.

Julian Kretz is a project manager in Next Kraftwerke's Business Development Team. He joined the Virtual Power Plant in 2015, working on the improvement of existing products linked to VPPs as well as on the analysis of business cases, market design, and regulatory framework related to market integration of renewable energies. A key subject of his work is the ongoing harmonization of European balancing markets.

Julian holds a Master of Science in Business Administration and Engineering and Electrical Power Engineering from the RWTH Aachen.

Lotte Lehmbruck is Deputy Head of Communications at Next Kraftwerke in charge of communicating the contribution of the company's pioneering work in developing virtual power plants as a central component of the energy transition in Germany and beyond. Among the responsibilities is to translate Next Kraftwerke's business model into plain words. Previously, Lotte was a communication consultant for projects of Federal German Ministries and the European Commission.

She holds a degree as business journalist from the Cologne School of Journalism and diploma in Political Sciences and Economics from the University of Cologne plus a certificate in energy innovation from Stanford University.

Sabine Löbbe is a professor at Reutlingen University, School of Engineering/Distributed Energy Systems and Energy Efficiency, Germany and lecturer in master's programs at the Universities of Chur and St. Gallen, Switzerland. Her consulting company advises utilities in strategy and business development and in organizational issues.

Prior to her current position, she was Director for Strategy and Business Development at swb AG Bremen, project manager at Arthur D. Little Inc., and at VSE AG, Saarbrücken.

She holds a doctorate in business administration from the university Saarbrücken and studied business administration in Trier, Saarbrücken and EM Lyon/France.

Iain MacGill is an associate professor in the School of Electrical Engineering and Telecommunications at the University of New South Wales, and Joint Director for the University's Centre for Energy and Environmental Markets (CEEM). Iain's teaching and research interests include electricity industry restructuring and the Australian National Electricity Market, sustainable energy technologies, and energy and climate policy.

Iain leads research in sustainable energy transformation, including energy technology assessment, renewable energy integration, and distributed energy systems, including smart grids, distributed generation, and demand-side participation. He has published and consulted widely.

Dr. MacGill has a Bachelor of Engineering and a Master of Engineering Science from the University of Melbourne, and a PhD on electricity market modeling from UNSW.

Bruce Mountain is the Director of the Victoria Energy Policy Centre at Victoria University, and the cofounder of retail market data business, [MI] Retail Energy.

He has 27 years of experience as an advisor and researcher on a wide range of issues in the economics of energy and regulation in Australia, Britain, South Africa, and other countries.

He has a PhD in economics from Victoria University, a bachelor's and a master's degree in electrical engineering from the University of Cape Town and qualified as a Chartered Management Accountant in England.

Tim Nelson leads the AEMC's Economic Analysis Division. He is also an associate professor at Griffith University.

Tim joined the AEMC from his previous position as Chief Economist at AGL, one of Australia's largest energy businesses, where he managed the company's public policy advocacy as well as sustainability and strategy. He is a member of Westpac's Stakeholder Advisory Council and the Grattan Institute's Energy Reference Group. He previously held a number of roles with the NSW Government and the Reserve Bank of Australia.

Tim holds a PhD in economics from the University of New England for which he earned a Chancellor's Doctoral Research Medal.

Luis Pfeiffer is part of the team Strategic Business Development at EWS Elektrizitätswerke Schönau eG. He is primarily engaged in the development of innovative energy products for private household customers. The main focus is on the conception of public welfare and sustainable supply models. Energy-Communities and P2P trading platforms play a major role here.

Prior to his position, he worked as an engineer in the design department of a large service provider for large-scale turbo generators.

Luis holds a B.Eng. in mechanical engineering and an M.Sc. in distributed energy systems and energy efficiency.

Ksenia Poplavskaya is a researcher in electricity markets and regulation at the Austrian Institute Technology. She is also a PhD candidate at Delft University of Technology, Faculty of Technology, Policy and Management, where she focuses on agent-based market modeling and optimization of short-term electricity markets and the issues of integrating new actors and technologies into these markets.

In the last 4 years, Ksenia has led and contributed to a number of national and European projects where she explored design questions of interrelated electricity markets, business models of energy system stakeholders and analyzed relevant regulation.

She holds an M.Sc. (Hons) in environmental technology and international affairs from the Technical University of Vienna and the Diplomatic Academy of Vienna.

Alan Rai is a senior economist at the Australian Energy Market Commission and has led various projects, including the integration of renewables into the grid, emissions reduction policies, and reforms to Australia's retail energy markets. He is also a senior research fellow at Macquarie University, and an Industry Fellow at the University of Technology Sydney.

Before joining the AEMC, Alan was at CSIRO Energy, at Macquarie University as an Assistant Professor, and at the Reserve Bank of Australia. Alan holds a PhD in Economics from the University of New South Wales, and a Bachelor of Commerce and Economics (1st Class Honors) from Macquarie University.

Victor Reijnders is a PhD candidate at the University of Twente, The Netherlands. His research mainly focuses on developing and testing new pricing mechanisms for energy communities, as well as creating algorithms for appliances to optimally respond to these pricing mechanisms.

Victor has a B.Sc. and M.Sc. with honors from University of Twente in Applied Mathematics.

David Robinson is a senior research fellow at the Oxford Institute for Energy Studies (OIES). He works primarily on decarbonization with a focus on public policy and corporate strategy in the energy sector.

Before joining the OIES, he led the European operations of NERA and The Brattle Group. He is still an academic advisor to the Brattle Group.

David has a DPhil in economics from the University of Oxford, a master's degree in economic policy and planning from the Institute of Social Studies (Erasmus University) and a Joint Honors BA in economics and political science from McGill University.

Gregor Rohbogner is CEO of OXYGEN TECHNOLOGIES, a startup company, applying a combination of energy informatics, automation and control technology for developing SaaS-products.

Gregor spent 5 years at Fraunhofer Institute for solar energy systems as a project and team leader developing and testing modern control and regulation techniques for decentralized energy systems in the laboratory and field. He has also expanded into advanced distributed optimization algorithms, consensus methods, and multiagent systems in the field of energy and the Fair Merchant Mechanism (FMM).

Gregor studied industrial engineering for automation and control technology at RWTH Aachen University.

Claire Rozyn is a market specialist at the Australian Energy Market Commission. Claire has led various AEMC projects, including work on the regulatory frameworks for standalone power systems, reviews of Australia's east coast and Victorian gas markets, and various matters related to network regulation and system security.

Before joining the AEMC, Claire held the role of senior economist at the Office of Gas and Electricity Markets (Ofgem) in the United Kingdom. Claire holds an economics degree from the University of New South Wales and a postgraduate diploma in economics for competition law from the University of London.

Tim Schittekatte is a research associate at the Florence School of Regulation (FSR). His main research interests include EU electricity network codes, flexibility markets, and distribution network tariff design. He is also affiliated with the Vlerick Energy Center in Brussels.

Before joining FSR in May 2016, he was a visiting researcher at the Grid Integration Group of the Lawrence Berkeley National Lab and a junior economist at Microeconomix in Paris.

He graduated as an engineer from Ghent University, Belgium and completed the EMIN program, an international master in economics. He obtained a PhD in energy economics from University Paris-Sud XI.

Benjamin Schlesinger is the founder of Benjamin Schlesinger and Associates, advising over 600 clients in 30 countries on natural gas and energy commodities, contracting, and pricing over four decades, including leading utility, private power, financial services, trading, producing, manufacturing, and regulatory and educational entities.

Formerly Ben was Vice President of the American Gas Association and member of NYMEX's Natural Gas Advisory Committee. He is a senior fellow and past President of the US Association for Energy Economics and teaches energy economics at University of Maryland's School of Public Policy.

He holds undergraduate degrees from Dartmouth College, and M.S. and PhD from Stanford University in Industrial Engineering.

Daniel Schwabeneder is a researcher at the Energy Economics Group at TU Wien. His research interests in energy economics include the optimization of different flexibility options for the electricity system, including batteries, heat pumps, electric boilers, electric vehicles, demand response, pumped hydro storages, and water reservoirs. Furthermore, he works on the analysis of business models for energy aggregators and develops software tools to model the operation of various flexibility options on day-ahead, intraday and balancing markets.

He holds an M.Sc. degree in Mathematics from the University of Vienna.

Dominik Seebach is a senior researcher with the Oeko-Institut's Energy and Climate Division in Freiburg, Germany. He has proficient expertise in the field of RES-E markets and the role of consumers in the context of environmental additionality in green energy markets.

Previous to his current job, Dominik has been working at ifeu-Institut for Energy and Environment (Heidelberg, Germany) and at the EC DG JRC (Ispra, Italy).

He holds an M.S. in environmental earth sciences (University Bayreuth, Germany).

Damian Shaw-Williams is a researcher with the Institute for Future Environments with Queensland University of Technology. He has over 20 years of experience in the finance sector research and techno-economic modeling of distributed generation and storage.

Prior to joining QUT he worked on the generation, retail and distribution sectors of the energy market, most recently in large-scale generation projects with CS Energy and investment review of distribution network capex projects with Ergon Energy.

Damian holds a BBus (Fin), a MAppFin and has completed a PhD in renewable energy economics with QUT.

Robert Smith has over 25 years of experience working in industry economics, electricity market design, regulation, economic evaluation, and energy efficiency and demand management. Amongst other roles he writes and presents on energy and economics topics under the East Economics name.

His interests include applied economic analysis and understanding how economics, technology, incentives, regulation, and customers' behavior interact to create change.

Robert has a B.Com. in econometrics, a M.Com. in economics from the University of NSW and postgraduate qualifications in finance from the Securities Institute of Australia.

Fereidoon Sioshansi is founder and president of Menlo Energy Economics, a consulting firm advising clients on energy-related issues. For 30 years, he has been the editor and publisher of *EEnergy Informer*, a monthly newsletter with international circulation.

His prior work experience includes working at So. Calif. Edison Co., EPRI, NERA, and Global Energy Decisions, acquired by ABB. Since 2006 he has edited 12 volumes on different subjects including evolution of global electricity markets, distributed generation, future of utilities, and most recently innovation and disruption at the grid's edge.

He has a B.S. and M.S. in civil and structural engineering, an M.S. and PhD in economics from Purdue University.

Carlo Stagnaro is Director of the Observatory on the Digital Economy at Istituto Bruno Leoni (IBL), a Milan-based think tank. Prior to that, he was chief of the Minister's technical staff at the Italian Ministry of Economic Development. He is a member of the editorial board of the journal Energia and a regular columnist to Il Foglio. His publications include Power Cut? How the EU Is Pulling the Plug on Electricity Markets, 2015. Carlo earned an M.Sc. in environmental engineering from the University of Genoa and a PhD in Economics from IMT Alti Studi—Lucca. He is on Twitter@CarloStagnaro.

Thies Stillahn is Head of the team Strategic Business Development at EWS Elektrizitätswerke Schönau eG, a vertically integrated cooperative eco-energy utility in Schönau, Germany, founded in the aftermath of Chernobyl. The work of his team is focused on designing innovative products and concepts for distributed renewable energy systems as well as sustainable mobility.

Prior to his current position he was a project leader in international projects (FP7, Horizon 2020) and consultant for large ICT and utility companies at the Fraunhofer Institute for Solar Energy Systems ISE where he spent 6 years in the field of business models for smart metering and energy management systems.

Thies studied economics (B.A. and M.Sc. degree) with a Major in Strategic Management at the University of Basel, Switzerland.

Mike Swanston heads The Customer Advocate, a consultancy advising regulators and governments on the imperative of a customer focus in meeting the needs of change in the energy industry. A strong supporter of the remarkable shift to customer-owned renewable energy resources, Mike's focus is that customers remain a top priority as networks and markets make the transition to our energy future.

Before forming The Customer Advocate, Mike held executive positions in electricity distribution authorities, including accountability for customer and stakeholder engagement.

Mike holds an honors degree in electrical engineering, postgraduate qualifications in business management and is a fellow of the Institution of Engineers Australia.

Ana Trbovich is cofounder of Grid Singularity and the Energy Web Foundation, accelerating energy transition with blockchain technology. She also serves as Full Professor at FEFA, Belgrade's leading business school, and the European Institute of Innovation and Technology Board Member.

Previously, she actively contributed to Serbia's economic reforms as a nonpolitical high government official, and consulted private and international organizations in public policy and economic development.

She holds a PhD from the Fletcher School, and master's degrees from the Fletcher School and Harvard Kennedy School of Government. She authored publications on good governance, competitiveness, and innovation policy.

Andrew Truswell is a Director at the Australian Energy Market Commission. Andrew's work currently focuses on new technology and business models in the form of stand-alone power systems and embedded networks, and how these impact on consumer protections.

Andrew has previously led a range of AEMC projects, including major reviews of electricity transmission frameworks, gas wholesale market and pipeline arrangements and electricity system security services. He joined the AEMC in 2008, following 8 years at National Grid in the United Kingdom.

Andrew holds a B.Sc. (Hons) in Industrial Economics from the University of Warwick.

Dirk van den Biggelaar is Market Design Engineer at Grid Singularity, engaged in research and development of D3A energy exchange engine's bidding strategies and market structures.

He has acute interest in game theory and distributed optimization in the field of decentralized energy communities, having obtained a bachelor's degree in mechanical engineering and a master's degree in systems and control engineering at Delft University. Before starting at Grid Singularity, Dirk completed an exchange at KAIST University in South Korea and an engineering internship in the Republic of Congo.

Marten van der Laan is a senior business consultant smart energy at ICT Group and USEF Foundation, an international stakeholder group, where he chairs the design team and the review board.

Marten is active in the smart grid domain with experience on Internet of Things technology, integration of renewables in the energy mix, smart energy services, demand response programs, energy communities, and EV smart charging. Previously, he worked as operations manager, consultant, and software engineer in consumer electronics.

He has a master's degree in electrical engineering from the University of Twente and a PhD in mathematics from the University of Groningen.

Moritz Vogel is a research associate at the Freiburg branch of the Oeko-Institut's Energy and Climate Division. His key activities at the Institute for Applied Ecology are located in the areas electricity market design, decentralized energy systems, integration of renewable energies as well as flexibility mechanisms.

He studied environmental sciences at the University of Lüneburg and finished his studies with the Bachelor of Science degree. Afterward Moritz Vogel began the master's studies "Sustainability Economics and Management" at the University of Oldenburg, which he finished with a master's thesis at the German Institute for Economic Research in Berlin.

Foreword

The energy sector is transitioning rapidly. Our common path toward a low-emission future yields an increasing share of intermittent and distributed renewable energy generation. The production of electricity has entered our personal and very visible sphere, be it solar panels on our rooftop, a small windmill in our backyard, and in the case of Norway, an electric vehicle (EV) in the driveway.

In addition, technological developments give us timely access to accurate information like never before. The introduction of smart meters, further described in the chapter by Stagnaro and Benedettini, is turning the distribution grid into a colored box of complex opportunities; unlike the black box of the past where connect and forget was the only option, resulting in investments as the solution to any challenge facing the grid. Distribution system operators (DSOs) are working hard to utilize consumption, production, and technical data to develop better planning tools, and to look at local flexibility markets. Consumers are beginning to understand their energy consumption—if not yet their power consumption—and are looking at how they can reduce their electricity bill while at the same time becoming more environmental-friendly. This is sparking an unprecedented development behind the meter. Third-party actors develop new business models and offer new services and products to consumers and DSOs alike, topics further explored in this volume.

An energy regulation that facilitates efficient market solutions, where possible, and well-regulated natural monopolies, where necessary, is a fundamental prerequisite in this rapidly changing landscape. Overall, the regulation should be technology neutral, avoid hidden subsidies and market distortions, and have a fair distribution of system costs. This will enable the utilization of the most economically and technically efficient solutions.

However, this may not be enough in an energy sector looking to alter its historical ways. Regulators need to work actively to create a level playing field, so that new actors providing system benefits can enter the market. We do not (necessarily) need to rethink everything from existing market designs to metering rules—but rather help those who have new and better solutions thrive in fair and even competition with traditional actors. Our job as regulators is not to ensure that every new initiative succeed or make a profit, but rather to align personal gains with system benefits, so that efficient solutions have the opportunity to develop and prosper. Gaining knowledge on how to do this in a changing energy world will be crucial going forward. Therefore regulators should allow various actors to experiment—for example, through pilot projects and regulatory sandboxes—while at the same time making sure that the knowledge gained from such experiments can be of value to everyone.

The future must be green and digital. However, it is unclear how the various actors in the energy sector will contribute to that future. Will the majority of future solutions be centralized or decentralized? What regulatory developments are required to ensure that all network customers pay their fair share of system costs, while incentivizing efficient sharing of resources? What role will new technologies such as blockchain, vehicle-to-grid, and hydrogen play in an electrified world? This is the fundamental challenge of regulation. The common goals for the future of energy are well known, the solutions or corresponding regulation to get us there are not. Regulation will always lag behind the technological developments. What regulators should ensure is that it lags as little behind as possible.

To achieve this, regulators should ensure that important building blocks are in place. The goal of these building blocks is to allow both old and new actors to prove their economic value to the system. Only then can we put in place a regulation bringing clean energy to all at least cost. At least the following four building blocks will be integral to the system going forward:

- Customers need access to a smart meter.
- Price signals should be cost-reflective, while ensuring a fair distribution of system costs.
- Grid companies must have incentives to postpone or avoid investments, where other measures can ensure sufficient capacity and quality-of-supply at a lower economic cost.
- Rules regarding balancing, data handling, and DSO/TSO (transmission system operator)-coordination will be crucial for the development of behind the meter initiatives.

Customers need access to a smart meter

Information is the new gold, and the best way to extract information about electricity is by installing individual smart meters. The Norwegian smart meter rollout was completed in the beginning of 2019, and we already see DSOs taking advantage of the data, for example, by rotating the placement of distribution transformers. This utilization of information will benefit customers as DSOs solve their tasks more efficiently, which in turn can lead to lower costs for DSOs and tariffs being lower than they otherwise would have been.

We should however not be satisfied. Extracting full value from the smart meters also means helping the consumers gain insights into their consumption data, and, if the consumer allows it, putting these data to use through third-party actors. This could be everything from a simple timer in your EV-charger that reacts to spot-market-prices and tariffs, to an advanced platform for a local flexibility market.

Price signals should be cost-reflective, while ensuring a fair distribution of system costs

Consumers need the services and technology offered from third-party actors to become more active. However, third-party actors will find a hard time creating a valid business model without new and more cost-reflective price signals. To enable new actors that can contribute to a more efficient and cheaper system, end users should be remunerated when making investments that provide an economic benefit. In most countries, this is not the situation today.

On the retail market side a positive development is that consumers are becoming more active participants and are starting to choose (real) spot-price contracts where the price vary per hour. For example, when the possibility to charge your EV when market prices are low, incentivize consumers to choose such contracts and invest in smart equipment.

However, the price signal for the end user is a function of the total cost of energy, including tariffs and levies in addition to the energy (kWh) price. Purely volumetric approaches still dominate tariff structures for small-scale consumers in most countries. These approaches challenge both the utilization of the grid and the cost distribution between grid customers.

Future operational challenges on the demand side are well known. There is an ongoing decoupling between energy and power, which historically have been highly correlated. This decoupling can mainly be attributed to energy efficiency measures, a lack of price signals on power, and more power demanding consumer products. Home charging of EVs is perhaps the major challenge in this regard and threatens to trigger massive investments in the distribution grid if not properly managed. This is particularly true in countries utilizing gas for heating and cooking. The reason for the latter is naturally that fitting EV energy demand (typically around 10 kWh/day) into a grid dimensioned for 3000–4000 kWh/year per household (avg. for continental Europe) will be much more challenging than in a system supplying 16,000–17,000 kWh/year per household (e.g., in Norway or 12,000 kWh in the United States).

A less discussed issue (at least among grid/power engineers and energy experts) is the distribution of system costs. It should not be. Only about one-third of grid costs relate to the short-term operation of the grid. The remaining two-thirds are what economists call residual, meaning that they cannot effectively be assigned to any single consumer. The challenge is how to recover these costs, without distorting the short- and long-term incentives for efficient utilization and development of the grid.

With respect to cost distribution, volumetric tariffs have worked quite well historically. The mentioned decoupling between energy and power is making the current tariff approach less well suited. Paul Simshauser has presented a useful case study of Southeast Queensland.[1] Over a 5-year time frame, the number of household photovoltaics (PVs) increased from roughly none to around one-fourth of household consumers. With a volumetric tariff design, this resulted in an increase in network prices of 112%. Energy efficiency measures, EV charging, etc. create the same challenges everywhere: those who inflict a cost upon the system do not end up paying for it and will, actually, in many cases end up paying less.

Some might argue that there is an inherent trade-off between cost-reflectivity and a distribution of costs perceived to be fair. This might (but not necessarily) be true when investigating a first-best solution, but it can hardly be an argument against shifting from volumetric to more capacity-based tariff structures.

Neither should a more cost-reflective tariff design ruin the possibility of a flexibility market. An efficient flexibility market will likely be the economically cheapest and most reliable way to handle short-term capacity constraints in the grid. However, there will nevertheless be a large share of (fixed) residual costs to be distributed between the consumers. Tariffs that distribute these residual costs to create long-term incentives for adaptation—for example, investing in a steering system to lower the consumer's capacity charge—will enhance the goal of operating with lower capacity margins over time, and thus also increasing the role flexibility markets can play in the future.

[1] Simshauser, P. (2016). Distribution network prices and solar PV: Resolving rate instability and wealth transfers through demand tariffs. *Energy Economics, 54*(C), 108–122.

Grid companies must have incentives to postpone or avoid investments, where other measures can ensure sufficient capacity and quality-of-supply at a lower economic cost

The existing regulations typically favor investments in assets and infrastructure, on which an allowed rate of return can be gained. Moving forward, however, regulators and DSOs must evaluate when network upgrading and expansion can be better addressed through the so-called nonwire solutions, as described in the chapter by Johnston and Sioshansi. Nonwire solutions, such as relieving congestion on the network can, in many cases, defer or obviate the need for expansion and upgrading or limit its scope.

To a certain extent, this is happening already. More and more countries are moving toward a total expenditure (TOTEX) regulation. The next step will be to better align incentives within the regulatory framework, ensuring that grid investments does not yield a higher return than alternative, cheaper measures.

Rules regarding balancing, data handling and DSO/TSO-coordination will be crucial for the development of behind the meter initiatives

For new actors a lack of clear guidelines outlining which party has what responsibility can be a real showstopper. Aggregators need detailed information about consumption to be able to provide their service. If consumers cannot give them access to relevant data, because they do not own it or because the metering infrastructure lack accessibility, aggregators will have a hard time proving their value to the system.

As such, regulators need to pay attention to the difficult details regarding balancing, data handling, DSO/TSO-coordination, etc. For the EU-countries the Clean Energy Package—referenced in a number of chapters—gives some general principles, but there is a significant remaining task in implementing them in practice. This implementation must be solved through a mixture of requirements (e.g., DSOs or a datahub should be required to allow consumers to access and share their data) and pilot projects (e.g., testing how flexibility resources accessed by the TSO in the DSO's grid can be flagged).

These four building blocks do not necessarily include all prerequisites for creating a level playing field, but they at least highlight important features for regulators and other policy makers to consider going forward.

Finally, it is important that regulation is stable, transparent, and predictable. Otherwise, investors might not decide to invest in the market. This should however not hinder regulators from taking a dynamic approach to regulation. Pilots are useful to test the boundaries of the existing regulation but should not be an excuse for not making socially beneficial amendments already today.

We know that a switch from volumetric to capacity-based tariffs will improve system efficiency, although we also would like to further study next-generation (dynamic) tariff designs. Regulators should start by altering regulations in the right direction and then adjust the course as we proceed. Only then can we allow the developments behind the meter to serve their role in a timely and efficient manner.

Andreas Bjelland Eriksen and Ove Flataker
The Norwegian Energy Regulation Authority (NVE)

Preface

Jean-François Carenco, Président of the French energy regulator CRE, has owned a family house for more than 30 years near Montpellier in the South of France. He likes to say that he didn't know where his electricity meter was located in the house until recently when a Linky smart meter was installed. He insists that the energy system, whatever its transformations, must take care of the millions of consumers, residential as well as small and medium-sized enterprises (SMEs), who don't want to (or can't) deal with their energy consumption, other than connect appliances and pay the bill. These consumers probably won't invest much time and money "behind the meter" (BTM) in the predictable future and policymakers must always keep that in mind.

Yet, BTM systems have a decisive role to play in the coming years and decades and this book edited by Fereidoon Sioshansi couldn't come at a better time.

Energy systems all over the world have to change dramatically in order to prevent global warming to get out of control. Fossil fuels must give way to non-CO_2 emitting energies. Regarding electricity, this will materialize through three main changes:

- Replace fossils fuels power plants by renewable ones [mostly wind and photovoltaic (PV)].
- Electrify transport.
- Decarbonize heat supply—and virtually everything else that relies on fossil fuels.

These profound transformations, considered impossible 5 or 10 years ago, have gained full credibility thanks to extraordinary breakthroughs in costs and technologies of PV, wind power, and batteries. It seems the world will finally be able to decarbonize bulk electricity production, as wind and PV are already the most competitive grid-scale technologies.

What can I, a French regulator, offer to put the following chapters of the book into better context? A few ideas come to mind.

Flexibility is the key

Renewable electricity comes with a special feature: it's not dispatchable. Contrary to fossil fuels, nuclear power, or hydroelectricity, one cannot rely on solar and wind power plants to produce when it is needed the most, for instance, in a cold evening in winter. This is annoying because electricity consumption is highly variable and has to be matched by electricity production every second.

Therefore the key notion in electricity systems is now flexibility, which is the ability and the tools needed to adjust electricity production and consumption in real time. Future decarbonized energy systems will have huge flexibility needs, to deal with the variability of renewable sources and the increased role of electricity in the energy mix.

Flexibility resources increasingly lie behind the meter

The high cost of this flexibility could hamper our collective capacity to reach the decarbonization goals. This is where BTM assets and systems enter into play. Technology and innovation now allow to capture and to monetize new distributed means of flexibility, and to tap into existing but ignored flexibility potential on the customer side of the meter.

These new possibilities are made possible by the incredible changes we have all witnessed these last years, notably in digitalization. By aggregating large numbers of small sources of flexibility, it is possible to build and operate "virtual power plants" as flexible and useful for the electrical system as classical thermal or hydro plants. This changes everything. Distributed sources of flexibility, located BTM, will be very diverse and prone to innovators and disruptors: solar roofs, zero net energy buildings, energy communities and collective self-consumption entities, stationary batteries, electric vehicle (EV), etc. All these features, further explored in the book, provide an up-to-date vision of how our energy systems will evolve.

Liberalized markets help but deciding the right market design is complex

BTM developments need regulatory frameworks allowing and encouraging innovation downstream. In this respect, competitive retail markets are obviously favorable, as monopolies usually don't get well with innovation. Transparency on the price of electricity is ensured by wholesale markets for every actor on the value chain. Price variations are huge: average wholesale price in Europe are in the 40–60€/MWh range, but hourly prices can be negative as well as in the thousands of €/MWh. During a recent heat wave in Texas, prices spiked to maximum allowable level of US\$9000/MWh. Flexibility providers can exploit price opportunities and will be more and more able to do so as flexibility needs and price differentials grow.

However liberalized markets have their own complexities and set of difficult questions. For the system to be efficient, economic entities along the value chain have to be exposed to price signals. This is not possible for most small consumers, as they don't want to be exposed to huge and unpredictable price variations.

It turns out that in most European countries, suppliers are not fully exposed to wholesale prices either. With retail competition, each supplier has to be financially accountable for the balance between withdrawals and injections within its portfolio. For the mass market, flow reconstitution is generally based on *profiles*, which represent the collective behavior of categories of consumers. Unfortunately, this destroys any incentive for a supplier to respond to price signals as, whatever the behavior of its individual consumer, the collective profile is used. To recreate the right incentives in the system, flow reconstitution must be based on actual load curves for each individual consumer, which is made possible by smart meters—also covered in this volume.

This is an illustration of a general principle: the market design must convey the right price signals. Every single actor must pay for the costs it creates in the system and symmetrically must be rewarded when it avoids costs as described later.

First, regarding decentralized production and self-production, net metering is not a good thing. Electricity has very different values depending on the time, and it is the same for network costs: as a consumer, you cost a lot to the network when you consume during peak hours, and almost nothing the rest of the time. Allowing consumers to offset their peak hour consumption with anytime production is a bad signal, suppressing any interest to develop battery storage when it would create value for the electric system. Net metering allows residential PV producers to be rewarded even though they don't avoid any network or system costs and basically other consumers are paying for that.

The same idea is true for network tariffs in unbundled systems. Obviously flat volumetric network tariffs aren't good as they don't reflect the strong differentiation in hourly network costs. Moving to pure capacity network tariffs isn't good either as it would reduce incentive to limit consumption, ending up with increased peak consumption and therefore increased network costs. The solution is a right mix between capacity tariffs and time-of-use volumetric tariffs, which requires some sophisticated modeling of networks.

These topics are covered in the third part of the book on regulators, policymakers, and investors. A good market design is essential to make sure that innovation goes in the general interest and that the energy transition can take place at the least cost.

Network operators have to anticipate and innovate

For BTM systems to flourish, "in-front-of-the-meter" operators have to be up to the task. Energy networks are natural monopolies. Even in the most liberalized markets, regulators have to deal with monopolistic network operators, the transmission system operators (TSOs) and distribution system operators (DSOs), which are big incumbents and have a major role to play in fostering innovation and transformation of electric systems, while keeping costs low. A few chapters in the book deal with the interaction between power networks and BTM systems.

One of the most difficult issues is the preference for investment that we see in network operators. This is mainly a cultural as well as a technical issue, because for decades these companies used to build new lines and transformers when faced with congestions on the network. Overinvestment wasn't really a problem because the increase in consumption would eventually justify almost any investment, and also because everyone relied on the network before the rise of prosumers and prosumagers.

But two major trends imply this has to change. First, energy conservation is now an essential part of our future and the financial burden for excessive investment will increase as power consumption stabilizes or decreases. In addition, the growth in intermittent renewable production challenges the way power networks are operated, maintained, and developed. As flows in the network will be much more variable, the solutions can no longer be more infrastructures, which risk being underused most of the time.

Therefore network operators will have to use available resources in flexibility every time it is more efficient than building infrastructure. A few regulatory tools have been identified for this purpose: Totex regulation instead of separate opex and capex regulations, mandatory comparison with flexibility solutions when deciding a new investment in network, incentives on network utilization rate indicators, etc. In more places, regulators now insist on a consideration of the so-called nonwires solutions before granting permission to invest in wires solutions. One desired goal is that TSOs and DSOs set up platforms allowing flexibility providers to bid for their flexibility needs—a topic explored in this volume.

At the same time, BTM innovation questions the very nature of network monopolies, and the traditional boundaries of DSOs and TSOs are becoming less clear than before. The questions are as follows:

- Within distribution grids operated by public DSOs, is it acceptable to allow areas of private networks to develop?
- What to do with off-grid networks? Should they be encouraged? Or tolerated only in special circumstances?
- How does electric mobility, with embedded meters, interact with regulatory regimes where metering is considered a monopoly network activity?

In this time of fake news and widespread confusion between facts and opinions, when scientific consensus is perceived as an opinion among others, this book has the great value of bringing together contributions from various countries and continents on BTM state of the art and perspectives.

BTM can help meet flexibility needs at the least possible cost and therefore is vital to the energy transition. Innovation BTM is a fantastic tool to gain commitment and direct involvement by more and more citizens.

As for Mr. Carenco, he has decided to invest in PV panels on his rooftop. Change is here.

Dominique Jamme
Managing Director, Commission de Régulation de l'Energie (CRE), Paris, France

Introduction

Fereidoon P. Sioshansi
Menlo Energy Economics, San Francisco, CA, United States

Ever since Thomas Edison patented the electric light bulb, the electric power industry has been almost exclusively preoccupied with the *supply side* and the *infrastructure* that resides *upstream* of the customer meter. In fact, up until recently, that is where the industry's reach ended—there was little interest or motivation to go behind or beyond the meter.

This had two important consequences:

- First, it resulted in an *upstream-of-the-meter mentality* not just for those within the industry but also for regulators and policymakers who are responsible for setting tariffs and providing direction as well as for the investment community.
- Second—and far more important—it kept consumers *passive*, totally disengaged and divorced from what was happening upside of the meter and with limited options behind-the-meter (BTM).

In retrospect, this explains many of the challenges facing the industry today as it suddenly confronts the reality of consumers becoming more engaged and more proactive, for example, by becoming prosumers in large numbers in many parts of the world. As the cost of storage continues to drop, as expected, some prosumers may go a step further and become prosumagers.[1] And it is not far-fetched to think of a future with a sizeable number of communities of *nonsumers*—defined as prosumers who generate and feed into the network as many kWhs as are taken out of the network.

That, however, is the beginning of the story of consumer awakening and empowerment. The emergence of new technologies and service options will increasingly enable consumers, prosumers and prosumagers to trade with their peers as the so-called peer-to-peer (P2P) trading schemes proliferate. One prosumer's excess generation during sunny hours of the day, for example, can charge the batteries in the electric vehicle (EV) of a neighbor across the street or across the country.[2]

Moreover, a new generation of smart intermediaries and orchestrators are emerging with business models focused on aggregating large numbers of consumers into large portfolios of distributed generation, distributed storage and flexible loads which can subsequently be remotely monitored, managed and optimized.

---

[1] These issues are extensively covered in Consumer, Prosumer, Prosumager, in a preceding volume published by Academic Press in 2019 and edited by the same editor.

[2] An example of such a trading scheme is described in "My EV, Your PV, or the other way around" in Jan 2019 issue of EEnergy Informer.

These new enablers, assisted by powerful software and relying on artificial intelligence (AI) and machine learning are beginning to offer a myriad of exciting and potentially consequential services made possible through aggregation. By combining the load, distributed generation and storage capacities of large numbers of participants, an aggregator can optimize the performance of the entire portfolio of BTM assets in ways that is not practical or cost-effective for individuals to do on their own—which explains why there has been so little practical and profitable demand response to date.

What has changed? Advancements in technology and dramatic reductions in cost makes it possible not only to communicate with thousands of consumers in real time—say smart meters—but to monitor and remotely adjust individual devices on their premises.

Finally, consumers—or most likely their designated agents—will increasingly be able to access easy to use platforms or electronic marketplaces where a variety of products and services could be bought and sold, with relative ease and at virtually zero cost.

The final frontier, which currently may seem a bit far-fetched, will be the emergence of blockchain technology potentially allowing P2P transactions to take place with speed, ease, high level of security, and—most important—without the costs or involvement of an intermediary or a gatekeeper.

Why focus behind-the-meter?

The short answer is because BTM is the most interesting, unexplored, and potentially fertile area to explore.

How big or important can it be? Very big and very important.

While the "traditional" industry's definition of their business domain typically stopped at the customer meter, there is a universe of possibilities on the *other* side of the meter. While the industry counts the billions it has invested in assets *upstream* of the meter, there is probably as much if not more invested on the customer side of the meter if one counts all the devices that use energy/electricity. Few studies exist on how much may lie BTM—but whatever the number, they are likely to rise.

Consider the following example:

- A prosumager who has invested $40,000 on rooftop solar photovoltaics (PVs), another $30,000 on a distributed battery storage system plus an $80,000 EV in the garage, not an uncommon things in many affluent communities around the world. That is, $150,000 of BTM investments even before counting all the electric and electronic devices in the house—which could easily add up to another $100,000 for an affluent household. A community of such like-minded consumers will be of interest to many aggregators.
- Recent projections by the Bloomberg New Energy Finance showed that by 2030 over 40% of the installed generation capacity in Australia may be BTM.[3] While Australia, Germany, Hawaii, or California may be outliers today, the trend toward self-generation,

---

[3] Australia has passed over two million solar homes by the end of 2018, the highest penetration of residential solar PVs on a per capita basis of any country.

most likely to be followed by distributed storage, is likely to become feasible in other parts of the world.
- For roughly 1 billion people living in developing parts of the world without reliable access to the electricity grid, the pay-as-you-go (PAYGO) model offers a viable option. For these customers, virtually all electrical investments are BTM—since there is no existing grid or upstream infrastructure to speak of.[4]

As the transition to decentralization gains momentum and with the advent of digitalization and virtually universal wireless communications, the opportunities to aggregate and manage BTM assets become not just feasible but increasingly compelling.

What is in this book?

Among the myriad of topics, the book's basic idea is to explore the following:

- What actually lies BTM, today and in the future.
- What can be done with these assets, today and in the future.
- How can individuals, groups, or communities of consumers be aggregated so that their portfolio of BTM assets can be better utilized, today and in the future.
- How can the synergies associated with large pools of BTM assets be optimally utilized to balance load and demand, especially in a future increasingly supplied by variable renewable generation resources.

The book, consisting of 20 chapters, is organized into three parts.

In the book's Foreword, Andreas Bjelland Eriksen and Ove Flataker provide a regulator's perspective on how to treat regulation during a time of rapid change in the BTM space, and describe important regulatory building blocks to enable innovation and new actors contributing to a more efficient utilization and development of the system. Important building blocks include smart meters, cost-reflective tariffs, rules on distribution system operator—transmission system operator (DSO—TSO) coordination, and incentives on the utilization of flexibility services.

Regulation and policy are critical to how much and how fast new innovation and disruption are likely to take place in any given market. A key issue is to align incentives in such a way that both new and traditional actors can prove their value to the system. To facilitate innovation that benefits the system, the regulatory building blocks must also be enhanced by a regulatory sandbox that allows trial.

The authors point out that only if we challenge the current regulatory framework, can we develop future regulatory principles designed to enhance the role of the consumer and facilitate the green transition.

In the book's Preface, Dominique Jamme points out that energy systems all over the world have to change dramatically to prevent global warming to get out of control. Fossil fuels must give way to non-CO_2 emitting energies.

---

[4] PAYGO consumers qualify as "nonsumers" since, by definition, they consume what they can generate and/or store, drawing no net kWhs from the grid.

The author notes that the profound transformation of the energy sector, considered impossible 5 or 10 years ago, has gained full credibility thanks to extraordinary breakthroughs in costs and technologies of PV, wind power, and batteries. It seems the world will finally be able to decarbonize bulk electricity production, as wind and PV are already the most competitive grid-scale technologies.

He rhetorically asks, "What can I, a French regulator, offer to put the following chapters of the book into better context?" followed by a list of observations on what needs to happen.

Part one: Visionaries, dreamers, and innovators

The first part explains why this book is focused on BTM, including opportunities to aggregate and optimize the BTM assets.

In Chapter 1, What lies behind-the-meter and why it matters?, Fereidoon Sioshansi outlines the defining issues of the book, which include (1) what actually lies BTM; (2) what can be done with these assets; (3) how individuals, groups, or communities of consumers may be aggregated so that their portfolio of BTM assets can be better utilized; and (4) how can the synergies of large pools of BTM assets be optimally utilized to balance load and demand, especially in a future increasingly supplied by variable renewable generation resources.

The author points out that while individual consumers can gain by more actively participating in the evolving market, the opportunities expand as large numbers of them join, allowing aggregators or orchestrators to monitor, manage, and optimize their loads, distributed generation and storage, including ever increasing numbers of EVs.

The chapter's main contribution is to outline the exciting range of products, service options, and business models that are emerging to create and successfully monetize the value of the new offerings.

In Chapter 2, It is not science fiction: going zero net energy and loving it, Ben Schlesinger describes the motivation and design features of a custom-built home that aims to cut off the net use of fossil fuels by relying almost entirely on power of the Sun and the Earth—not only to power the house but also to provide as much mobility as possible.

While Schlesinger's zero-net-energy (ZNE) house may not be for everyone or suitable everywhere, it nevertheless demonstrates that the concept works. ZNE homes are moving mainstream as states such as California already require them starting in 2020 for new construction as do many countries in Europe.

The chapter's main intention is to demonstrate that the Sun and the Earth provide more than sufficient free energy to live without fossil fuels, with an estimated 10-year payback, not bad considering that typical houses last 30—50 years if not longer. The question is how widely can this success be replicated elsewhere and what would be the implications of ZNE homes over time.

In Chapter 3, Creating value behind-the-meter: digitalization, aggregation, and optimization of behind-the-meter assets, Fereidoon Sioshansi points out that an increasing number of innovative companies are positioning themselves in the sweet spot where large numbers of BTM assets can be successfully aggregated, remotely monitored, managed, and optimized, reducing energy bills for the participants while delivering valuable services to other stakeholders such as the network operator and/or the wholesale market.

This chapter provides examples of the innovators in this emerging space and how they may further disrupt the traditional relationships between the incumbents and consumers.

While many technical, regulatory, privacy issues have yet to be resolved before successful and profitable players emerge, it is clear that many players are attempting to enter the field by amassing scale while creating and monetizing value, and many of the promising contenders are not from within the ranks of the incumbents.

In Chapter 4, Customer participation in P2P trading: a German energy community case study, Sabine Löbbe, André Hackbarth, Thies Stillahn, Luis Pfeiffer, and Gregor Rohbogner reflect on prosumers' and consumers' motivations for participating in P2P electricity trading and discuss a micro market for realizing such an exchange.

The authors examine the different interests and requirements of prosumer, prosumager, and consumer segments to participate in P2P electricity trading, based on results of a nationwide survey and a local field test. They derive practical solutions for P2P electricity trading and propose different products and services prone to differentiate in a competitive market. These products are a platform-based, distributed, fully automated solution for energy trading and control within the current German environment and regulatory framework. They culminate in a micro market for realizing the P2P exchange.

The chapter's main contribution is to develop valuable BTM P2P electricity trading products and services based on innovative and unique trading algorithms—"fair merchant mechanism"—taking customer preferences into account.

In Chapter 5, Aggregators today and tomorrow: from intermediaries to local orchestrators?, Ksenia Poplavskaya and Laurens de Vries focus on aggregators as actors at the forefront of energy transition that can help unlock value from both the front and behind-the-meter.

This chapter provides a comprehensive overview of aggregator business models in Europe and identifies new opportunities in the evolving and increasingly distributed energy system. It further discusses the reasons for barriers to their market penetration and ways to overcome them underpinned by a critical assessment of the European business model environment.

The chapter's main contribution is to address aggregators' business models at the intersection of market design and regulation. It proposes future value streams from operation of local energy communities, trading platforms, and provision of distribution-level flexibility that would deliver value for their customers and energy system as a whole.

In Chapter 6, Energy communities: a Dutch case study, Victor Reijnders, Marten van der Laan, and Roelof Dijkstra describe a possible concept for a community to operate as one large unit in the electricity system. By this, they form one connection point and have to take care of all aspects of behind-the-meter themselves, including settling mutual transport.

Next to introducing a general framework, this chapter presents preliminary results from a Dutch pilot in which a neighborhood of 47 households operates as one connection point on a transformer, therefor using a capacity tariff. To achieve this, 19 of these houses were equipped with batteries and inhabitants were activated via an app to flatten the overall profile.

The chapter's main contribution is presenting and demonstrating a general framework for a community with energy management systems and batteries, to operate as one connection point and taking care of all aspects of behind-the-meter, now and in the future energy market.

In Chapter 7, The expanding role of home energy management systems: an Australian perspective, Damian Shaw-Williams describes the growing requirements on home energy management systems (HEMS) to realize the potential for BTM infrastructure to be enlisted in the managing of networks.

The author discusses the development of HEMS against the background of the decentralization of energy networks involving a mix of technologies with early adopters and the entry of aggregators existing beside legacy systems. The requirements of balancing load through interactions with the grid, generation, storage, and coordination of smart appliances are discussed. Technical standards regarding data and communications are considered as are security and optimization methodologies.

The chapter's main contribution is the identification of requirements for metering and data infrastructure necessary to access the full range of benefits of optimization of the household's assets and the real-time incorporation of network/aggregator requirements.

Part two: Implementers and disrupters

The second part of the book examines some of the obvious consequences of BTM revolution about to proliferate in many parts of the world.

In Chapter 8, Behind and beyond the meter: what's in it for the system?, Dierk Bauknecht, Christoph Heinemann, Dominik Seebach, and Moritz Vogel analyze current developments behind and beyond the meter from a system perspective: how should these concepts be designed to benefit the power system in general and the integration of renewable energy in particular?

The chapter examines which system implications of beyond-the-meter and BTM approaches should be considered when evaluating such concepts, not the least when designing the regulatory framework. It provides a general overview and looks at two specific cases: BTM self-consumption in combination with batteries as well as peer-to-peer trading of renewable electricity.

The chapter's main conclusions are that BTM and-beyond-the-meter concepts can support the energy transition toward a system based on renewable energies. Yet individual interests and incentives are not necessarily in line with the needs of the overall energy system and political aims. This needs to be reflected in the regulatory framework.

In Chapter 9, Working backward to get behind-the-meter: what customer value, behavior, opportunity, and uncertainty mean for new technology, Robert Smith and Iain MacGill quote Steve Jobs, former CEO of Apple, who famously said, *You've got to start with the customer experience and work backward to the technology. You cannot start with the technology and try and figure out where you are going to sell it.*

The authors note that the excitement of new inventions and ideas tends to make visionaries to envision a future of technological triumphalism where, because the engineering and economics are better, the new will sweep away the old. This top-down approach to the role of technology, it is argued, often becomes unstuck when it confronts customer's complex view of value in usage, a view that already allows diverse energy solutions to coexist.

This chapter looks backward from what customer value, now and in past technologies, to see what this means for future technologies behind and beyond the meter.

In Chapter 10, Aggregation of front- and behind-the-meter: the evolving VPP business model, Lotte Lehmbruck, Julian Kretz, Jan Aengenvoort, and Fereidoon Sioshansi describe advances in remote sensing and AI, which allows large portfolios of assets to be monitored, managed, and optimized with ever more precise granularity making it possible for virtual power plants (VPPs) to scale up while offering valuable services to both the grid operator and major savings and/or additional revenues to participating clients.

The authors describe the experience of Europe's one of the first and biggest VPP from inception to present, including how the company envisions expanding its products while entering new markets beyond.

The chapter's main contribution is to show the extent to which VPPs can grow to offer new services and many of the regulatory and policy barriers that still remain to be resolved before such companies can reach their full potential.

In Chapter 11, Platform for trading flexibility on the distribution network: a UK case study, James Johnston and Fereidoon Sioshansi describe the capabilities of Piclo, a platform that offers visibility on areas where congestion appears on the distribution network and correlates them with flexibility providers in nearby areas.

This allows customers or aggregators with demand flexibility and/or those with storage or any suitable BTM device to mitigate congestion. Examples include large customers with flexible demand, for example, a supermarket warehouses to adjust or temporarily turn off fridges and freezers to reduce demand or a fleet of EVs charging or potentially discharging in response to price signals.

The chapter describes how such flexibility platforms can give distribution network operators enhanced control of local production, consumption, and storage—which will enable further integration of renewables and EVs into the grid in a cost-effective way.

In Chapter 12, Smart meters: the gate to behind-the-meter, Carlo Stagnaro and Simona Benedettini argue that smart meters are the necessary gateway to most BTM services. They point out that smart meters provide real-time consumption data that can be used by other smart devices, appliances, and the essential gateway to any aggregator or optimizer of energy generation, consumption, or storage.

The chapter provides guidelines to understand under which conditions benefits from smart meters are likely to exceed the costs, including how the roll-out of smart meters should be implemented, whether it should be voluntary or compulsory, and who is in charge of deploying and operating the meters.

The authors point out that little use can be made of data per se if customers are not actively engaged and empowered and says this requires institutional reforms.

In Chapter 13, D3A energy exchange for a transactive grid, Ana Trbovich, Sarah Hambridge, Dirk van den Biggelaar, Ewald Hesse, and Fereidoon Sioshansi introduce the D3A, an open source, customizable energy exchange, developed by Grid Singularity with the objective of supporting the Energy Web Foundation's mission to enable a decentralized, digitalized, and democratized energy system.

The authors describe how the D3A optimizes the operation of each grid device through its representative agent, delivering an enhanced understanding of the smart grid mechanics and thereby facilitating a pragmatic adoption of decentralized energy management. The D3A can be used as a tool to configure an optimal market design and make investment and management decisions (currently available as a simulation environment at D3A) and ultimately deployed to operate the modern transactive grid.

The chapter also explores the role of blockchain in establishing a transparent and efficient market structure where all market actors have equal access to flexibility resources.

In Chapter 14, Emerging aggregation business models in European electricity markets, Simon De Clercq, Daniel Schwabeneder, Carlo Corinaldesi, and Andreas Fleischhacker discuss how European electricity suppliers are reacting to the advent of independent aggregators by offering aggregation services alongside their regular electricity supply services.

The authors present two cases of incumbent suppliers who, in search of a more resilient business model, are using the features of the combined supplier—aggregator business model to tap the unharnessed potential of aggregating BTM assets. Good Energy in the United Kingdom is looking to access residential flexibility and activate market participation of household consumers through a home energy management device. In Austria, oekostrom assesses the services it can offer to facilitate the installation of collective solar generation on apartment buildings.

The chapter finds that the combined aggregator—supplier model can bring much-needed innovation to conventional electricity supplier business models by allowing suppliers to diversify their revenue mechanisms and broaden their value proposition.

Part three: Regulators, policymakers, and investors

The third part of the book is mostly focused on the limitations inhibiting further innovation and disruption taking place in BTM space due to regulatory and policy restrictions, limitations, and/or lack of clarity on what can and cannot be done or is allowed in BTM space.

In Chapter 15, BTM prospects: what do customers' responses to prices tell us? Bruce Mountain surveys contemporary evidence, mainly in Australia, of how household customers respond to electricity prices in grid-supplied electricity and how they have responded to opportunities to self-produce electricity behind-the-meter.

The author suggests customer's decisions on BTM production reflect a higher level of engagement and price elasticity, than their decisions about grid-supplied electricity.

On the basis of this evidence he identifies the likely sources of BTM value and concludes that small customers will continue to pursue BTM production and also storage as a substitute for grid supply.

In Chapter 16, Regulating off-the-grid: stand-alone power systems in Australia, Alan Rai, Claire Rozyn, Andrew Truswell, and Tim Nelson discuss the economic and regulatory issues associated with stand-alone power systems (SAPS). The authors discuss and compare the two broad supply models, one where hitherto grid-connected customers continue to be supplied by their local network service provider, and one where a third-party provides service.

The rise of SAPSs raises the question of the extent to which the regulatory framework for grid-connected customers should be applied to SAPS-connected customers and the existing regulations may not automatically apply for a third-party SAPS.

The chapter's main contribution is to discuss how SAPS should interface with the wholesale and retail markets, the various design approaches considered and the related pros and cons of each approach, and the rationale for the preferred approach.

In Chapter 17, Distribution network tariff design for behind-the-meter: balancing efficiency and fairness, Tim Schittekatte describes how current distribution network tariff design is challenged by BTM-technology adoption and provides an analysis of how to enhance current practices.

The author explains how ill-adapted distribution network tariffs can cause over- or underinvestment in BTM technologies leading to an efficiency issue and also cause adverse distributional consequences for passive, sometimes vulnerable, consumers leading to a fairness issue.

The author shows how to redesign the distribution network tariff to better deal with these issues. However, it is found that when only considering "traditional distribution network tariff design options" a trade-off between efficiency and fairness will always exist. Finally, the author argues that the trade-off can be broken—with regulatory fixes to soften the fairness issue without sacrificing efficiency and with tools to improve efficiency beyond network tariff design.

In Chapter 18, What market design, fiscal policy, and network regulations are compatible with efficient BTM investments?, David Robinson examines the welfare implications of consumers moving away from traditional regulated bundled services delivered through the network.

The author points out that if markets, taxation, and regulation motivate *inefficient* BTM activities whose consequence is a loss of social welfare or merely shifts the burden to others, then they should be reformed. He argues that badly designed policies could also discourage efficient investment BTM or motivate inefficient use of the assets. The chapter examines specific market designs, fiscal policy, and distribution network regulations that favor efficient BTM activities and identifies specific BTM activities and business opportunities that are consistent with these new frameworks.

The chapter's main contribution is to identify how such reforms can promote efficient demand-side flexibility, facilitating deep penetration of intermittent renewables and the development of a supply chain of the BTM appliances and services required to support that flexibility.

In Chapter 19, Two million plus solar roofs: what's in it for the consumers?, Mike Swanston points out that the central question is "do *all* customers gain as the BTM revolution revolves around them?", —since not all consumers are likely to become prosumers or prosumagers. Will all gain, or some at the expense of others?

Through the lens of the Australian experience, the chapter examines how typical customers make decisions based on costs, service attributes, and their relations with the incumbents.

In particular, the author explains what has led to over 2 million households and businesses in Australia—roughly 25% of all energy consumers—choosing to invest in rooftop PVs, and possibly moving on to distributed storage, EVs, and so on. The incumbents, regulators, policymakers, and new entrants are attempting to respond to the extreme variability to household usage patterns through new market mechanisms and updated technical connection standards and tariff reform.

In Chapter 20, Will behind-the-meter make a difference?, Fereidoon Sioshansi says that based on the evidence presented in the book, the answer varies depending on where and in what time frame.

The author points out that the longer term impact of BTM investments depends on the relative costs, regulatory policies, and—perhaps most important—on the rapidly improved technologies and equally rapidly fall in costs. As more consumers become prosumers and perhaps prosumagers, the notion of producing, storing, and consuming electricity in a mostly self-contained system may move mainstream, albeit unevenly in different parts of the world.

One thing, however, that is broadly accepted is the fact that consumers have more choices in more places and they are—for the most part—exercising their newfound freedom to move away from the traditional reliance on a single provider for all their needed services. This is a welcomed development encouraging service and product innovation in an industry not known for either.

In the book's Epilogue, Jean-Michel Glachant points out that decentralization, digitalization and what he calls "activation" are the main drivers of change in the BTM space and beyond. He notes that the combination of the three is leading to investment in generation and storage in what he calls "retail-size" units, as described by Swanston in chapter on Australia where roughly a fourth of the consumers have become prosumers by investing in rooftop solar PVs.

Similarly, he notes that the emergence of aggregators and smart intermediaries who can create a portfolio of "retail-size" consumption units and offer their collective response as tradable products in the wholesale market is significant, as is the emergence of trading platforms and blockchain, themes covered in the book.

Glachant, however, admits that many obstacles, complexities, and ambiguities remain, as noted by Sioshansi in Chapter 20, Will behind-the-meter make a difference? But the transition to mastering and unlocking the potentials of the BTM space has clearly begun.

PART ONE

Visionaries, dreamers, innovators

What lies behind-the-meter and why it matters?

Fereidoon Sioshansi

Menlo Energy Economics, San Francisco, CA, United States

1.1 Introduction

This chapter, being the first in the volume, starts with the question that many a reader may legitimately ask upon coming across the book's title—namely, what lies "behind-the-meter" (BTM) and why does it matter? Why devote a whole volume to the topic, and what can be gained from reading such a book? These are perfectly good questions.

As mentioned in the book's Introduction, for most of its history, the electricity sector was defined to cover essentially, if not exclusively, what lies *upstream* of the customers' meter—namely generation assets and the extensive transmission and distribution network that delivers power to customers. A typical textbook might illustrate this traditional utility-centric paradigm as in Fig. 1.1, with customers' meters as the terminal point.

This view, which persists to this day in many a mindset, misses the most important part of the picture, namely, what do customers *do* with the electricity that is finally delivered to their meter—and the ubiquitous electrical sockets that feed the devices that use electricity within their premises.

What customers traditionally did with the electricity, of course, has changed over time as new applications and devices were added, most notably air conditioning, which is now taken for granted in many parts of the world as an essential necessity. But until recently, customers—with a few exceptions—bought all kWhs they used from the network that connects them to upstream generation assets. kWhs consumed equaled kWhs delivered to the meter. Moreover, the vast majority of customers paid for the kWhs delivered based on bundled regulated tariffs, where the term *bundled* in this context means that the tariff included the total cost of all upstream investments such as generation, transmission, and distribution plus costs of retailing services, applicable taxes, and levies.

This picture is beginning to change in some parts of the world as some consumers can generate some or virtually all the kWhs they consume from rooftop PV panels. For these

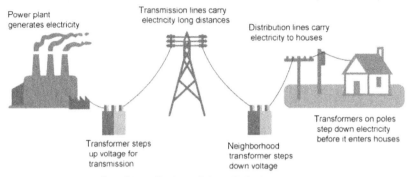

Illustration of the traditional utility perspective

Electricity generation, transmission, and distribution

Source: Adapted from National Energy Education Development Project (public domain)

FIGURE 1.1   Traditional utility-centric paradigm of the electric power sector. Source: *Adapted from National Energy Education Development Project, www.NEED.org.*

prosumers, kWhs consumed no longer equal kWhs delivered and paid for from the network. In fact, in places where net energy metering is available, the prosumers may pay little or virtually nothing for service if their *net* consumption—that is, total kWhs consumed less total kWhs generated and fed into the network—is small or zero. In some cases, prosumers who generated more than they consumed may in fact get a refund from the network operator.[1]

Currently, the number of prosumers is small relative to consumers. But if the relative cost of self-generation is lower than buying bundled kWhs from the network—as it is in places such as Australia[2]—one can expect their numbers to rise.[3] In the state of California, for example, self-generation is expected to reduce the number of kWhs purchased from the grid by an estimated 50 GWh by 2030 as illustrated in Table 1.1. The same phenomenon is already happening in Australia, a country with a population of 24 million with over 2 million solar roofs.

As these examples illustrate, the fact that kWhs *consumed* will no longer equal the kWhs *sold* to customers is not something many utility executives could have imagined a mere decade ago. A decade from now, the phenomenon will be pronounced in many parts of the world as residential, commercial, and even industrial customers generate some of their juice from rooftop solar—or in the case of some large commercial and industrial customers buy it from an alternative source, not necessarily the regulated utility that serves them.

---

[1] The details, of course, vary but in many parts of the United States, for example, most residential customers pay little or no fixed monthly fees, which means that if their self-generation equals or exceeds consumption, their monthly bill may be zero or conceivable negative.

[2] Refer to chapter by Swanston in this volume.

[3] In many parts of Europe, tariffs include hefty levies—sometimes comprising a quarter of the total bill, further incentivizing self-generation.

TABLE 1.1 Not all kWhs *consumed* will be *bought* from the network.

	2018	2030
Consumption	260,000	340,000
Sales	260,000	290,000

CEC projections of *consumption* versus *sales* for California, in GWhs,[4] shows a growing departure between the two over time.
California Energy Demand, 2018-2028 Preliminary Forecast, California Energy Commission, Aug 2017, CEC-200-2017-006-SD.

The next major shock is likely to come from rapid technological advancements in energy storage, not just batteries but all sorts of storage devices and media such as storing hot water or ice for use at a later time. Such opportunities allow some prosumers to become *prosumagers* by storing some of their self-generated power for use at later times, such as after the sun goes down. Again, the economics of such options critically depend on bundled retail prices, including taxes, levies, and other charges that are usually embedded in the tariffs.

If prosumers are offered little or none for the excess generation fed into the network that increases the attractiveness of self-storage. Electric vehicles (EVs) are among the emerging BTM technologies that may act as distributed storage. Their numbers are expected to rise exponentially in many parts of the world over the next decade or two. The storage capacity of several million EVs, if they are aggregated and collectively managed, can serve as a huge storage capacity on a typical network.

Such scenarios are already happening and their impact is beginning to get noticed in places like California or Norway, where the penetration of solar PVs and EVs is high, respectively.

Fast forward, so to speak, and the picture that emerges may look like the one illustrated in Fig. 1.2, where electricity may be generated from solar PV panels on millions of customers' roofs, feeding the network—rather than taking from the network at least on sunny hours of the day—and charging the storage devices while meeting the customers' needs. An example of such a setup is described in the following chapter by Schlesinger. Of course, not all customers would fit this picture, but some could. The point is not how many consumers may turn into prosumers or prosumagers but that the traditional view of the industry is likely to undergo significant change, that is, the contrast between Figs 1.1 and 1.2.

But that is only the beginning of BTM story. Increasingly proactive consumers, prosumers, and prosumagers will begin to engage in other forms of transactions with and among each other in the so-called peer-to-peer (P2P) trading. For example, prosumers may offer their excess solar generation to other consumers and/or EV owners, whether they are across the street or the state. Such transactions, which are currently restricted or

---

[4] According to the CEC's preliminary forecast, the self-generation from solar PVs will amount to 30–35 GWh by 2028 plus over 16 GWh from non-PV self-generation, a number exceeding 51 GWh by 2028. This, of course, may turn out to be an underestimation. Further details may be found at Electricity sales no longer the same as consumption, *EEnergy Informer*, p. 14, Apr 2019 at www.eenergyinformer.com.

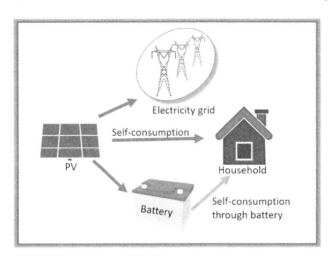

FIGURE 1.2 The emerging picture looks different than the historic one in Fig. 1.1.

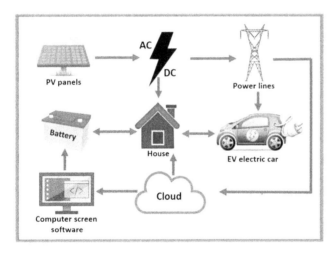

FIGURE 1.3 And the future is likely to be even more radically different than the past.

prohibited by regulations, are likely to grow as regulators allow more types of P2P transactions to take place when it is economical to do so.[5]

Even more interesting—and consequential—developments may be expected with the emergence of smart *intermediaries, aggregators,* and *orchestrators,* topics covered in following chapters, who can combine large numbers of consumers, prosumers, and prosumagers and monitor and optimize the entire portfolio of assets.

This is schematically illustrated in Fig. 1.3, which has no resemblance to Fig. 1.1. It shows a smart intermediary who is monitoring and managing the flows of electrons in a more complex—perhaps convoluted—network. It shows distributed generation and

---

[5] OFGEM, the regulator in the United Kingdom, for example, is considering allowing a single customer to be served by multiple retailers, further describe below.

storage as an integral part of the picture. It shows continued reliance on the network but rather differently than what is shown in Fig. 1.1. It assumes that much of the data and communication between various devices and agents will be handled in the "cloud." In short, a dramatically different picture than Fig. 1.1.

As further described in the following chapters, the preceding scenarios are not science fiction. These are beginning to happen, and the pace of adoption can be expected to accelerate as the technologies improve and their costs continue to decline. Clearly, a lot is happening BTM and it really matters.

The balance of this chapter is organized as follows:

- Section 1.2 provides an overview of BTM generation.
- Section 1.3 describes the fast growth and promise of BTM storage including the expected rise of EVs.
- Section 1.4 explains the attractiveness of aggregation of BTM assets and energy communities.
- Section 1.5 speculates on the applications of stand-alone devices.
- Section 1.6 describes why the time has arrived for regulators to rethink the rules and restrictions pertaining to BTM space followed by the chapter's conclusion.

1.2 Behind-the-meter generation

The most obvious type of BTM asset, of course, is rooftop solar PVs—now ubiquitous on millions of residential, commercial, and industrial roofs around the world. In some jurisdictions, good records are available on how many, what size, and how much output is generated from the rooftop solar PVs, while in other places, the records are spotty or nonexistent, especially for off-grid applications, where there is no requirement to report the existence of the PVs if they are not connected to the network. In Australia, for example, there are reasonably good records available, as further reported in the chapter by Swanston, and there are proposals for strengthening the reporting requirements.

The first question is why do consumers install solar PVs in growing numbers? The answer—the underlying motivation—varies from place to place but is usually driven by the relative cost of buying all kWhs from the grid and paying the bundled regulated tariff versus generating all or most of the kWhs at the premise where they are used. If the bundled retail tariffs are high—as in Australia—and/or include high levies and taxes—as in most parts of Europe—then consumers may be better off to self-generate as further described in Box 1.1 for Australia.

Aside from the economics, some consumers are motivated by other factors such as the fact that they can brag to neighbors that they rely mostly on renewable green energy rather than the dirty brown version provided by the network.[6] Some consumers don't particularly like their local monopoly distribution company and/or don't trust the

[6] The author has heard this argument from numerous solar rooftop owners in Australia, where the bulk of generation in many states comes from coal-fired plants.

BOX 1.1

In Australia, it is not the affluent who go solar[7]

Australia already exceeds 2 million solar roofs and the numbers are rising. That is noteworthy. But what is more interesting about Australia is that the main driver is not generous subsidies, tax credits, feed-in tariffs, or building codes—as in California— but the desire to save money on utility bills. Plain and simple. Moreover, while in many places—for example, California—solar customers tend to be the more affluent living in larger detached homes in up-scale suburbs; in Australia, it appears to be mostly the middle class who go solar.

Retail rates in Australia have risen substantially in recent years—for many reasons—motivating more homeowners to go solar. Moreover, it is mostly the lower and middle-income households who are going solar. For them, electricity bills represent a higher percentage of disposable income, hence the motivation to save by buying less from the grid. This according to data recently released by *Solar Citizens*, an Australia-based solar organization.

As reported in *RenewEconomy* (Feb 26, 2019), *Joseph Scales*, Solar Citizens' National Director said, "People are reaching for ways to get control over their energy costs and for millions of low- and middle-income households, solar is the best way to do that.[8]" Their research concluded "… PV uptake was lowest among the highest socio-economic group and highest among the lowest socio-economic group."

As noted, this is in stark contrast to places such as California, where the typical solar home tends to be a large one with a big roof in an affluent sunny neighborhood. And given the generous net energy metering (NEM) law currently available in California and in a number of other states, customers are paid full retail price for every kWh *injected* into the grid. Unsurprisingly, the more affluent homeowners with big air conditioning loads, pool pumps, and hungry appliances are more likely to invest in solar panels. They can afford to pay for the panels up-front or lease them under a power purchase agreement from the installer. And when they do, they reduce their *net* purchases from the network, lowering their bills and contributing *less* to the upkeep of the grid.

This has led to an outcry that solar PV owners are causing everyone else's bills to rise and that the less affluent nonsolar customers are subsidizing the more affluent solar ones.

In describing why affluent Australians may not be attracted to solar investing, *Bruce Mountain, Victoria Energy Policy Center*'s director speculates that buying solar is probably "not at the top of their (affluent customers' priority) list," adding, "As power bills soar, taking ownership of your electricity usage and buying in the cheaper power (i.e., self-generated) becomes more and more attractive for the less-wealthy — especially as solar prices continue to drop."

---

[7] Refer to In Australia it is not the affluent who go solar, *EEnergy Informer*, p. 15, Apr 2019 at www.eenergyinformer.com.

[8] Refer to https://reneweconomy.com.au/less-affluent-australians-behind-national-solar-uptake-44928/.

BOX 1.1 (cont'd)

According to Mountain, "For most people, if you have a north-facing roof (anywhere in Australia), solar will pay for itself in 5 years or less."

Even more surprising is the finding that those in the lower socioeconomic tiers who are investing in solar panels are in fact helping to reduce electricity prices for *everyone*, including the nonsolar customers. This is rather different than what many studies in the United States have concluded.

According to Scales, "By exporting excess electricity back into the grid, people from lower socio-economic groups are providing a low-cost source of power for everyone else," adding, "Around a third of all households sell electricity back to their retailers at a rate that is lower than the spot market price."

This is clearly different than the current prevailing laws in many US states where the excess solar-generated power injected into the grid gets a credit equal to the full retail price. Since retail prices tend to be significantly higher than average wholesale prices, under prevailing NEM laws, solar customers get a generous credit for all kWhs sold to the grid. According to a blog posted by *Lucas Davis*, a Professor at Univ. of California Berkeley, the average nonsolar California customer is estimated to be subsidizing the average solar customer at roughly $65 per year[9]—not a huge amount, but clearly a questionable one, since it acts as a regressive tax.

But things are apparently different in Australia, according to data from *Solar Citizens.*

"This research totally debunks the myth perpetuated by the coal lobby that household solar drives up power prices − it does the opposite."

"The 2 million solar houses across Australia act like one huge power station generating around 8,900 GWh of electricity in the past year alone − more than any coal fired power station and at much lower cost."

It makes perfect sense, according to Mountain, "The people who economically stand to get the greatest benefit from rooftop solar appear to be installing it in the greatest numbers." ∎

---

retailers—hence are willing to pay a premium to make their own even if it costs a bit more.[10] Others like the fact that they are mostly or partially self-reliant, and so on.

In Germany and a number of other European countries a significant portion of the retail tariffs consists of taxes and levies—which some consumers perceive as excessive. Self-generation allows them to skip paying these taxes and levies.

Whatever the motivation(s), the number of prosumers is on the rise as the cost of solar PVs continues to decline.

---

[9] Refer to blog post by Lucas Davis, Mar 26, 2017, at https://energyathaas.wordpress.com/2018/03/26/why-am-i-paying-65-year-for-your-solar-panels/.

[10] This sentiment is also often heard in Australia.

For an increasing number of commercial and industrial customers, going green offers a marketing advantage—something that may distinguish them from their competitors. In many cases, there is significant peer pressure to go green following the lead of others who have done so. Companies like Walmart, Ikea, Costco, and Amazon, for example, now routinely cover the entire rooftops of their stores and distribution centers with solar panels. But in most cases, they do not have sufficient roof space to generate as much electricity as they consume. Many sign long-term power purchase agreements (PPAs) with renewable developers to provide sufficient green electrons to offset their total consumption.[11]

In such cases, of course, the electrons delivered to customers do not necessarily come from the wind farms or solar parks that they have signed the PPAs with, but they offset the kWhs consumed with green electrons generated somewhere.

This growing phenomenon—while not BTM—nevertheless diverts generation from the traditional utility-owned thermal plants to renewable generation resources, usually owned and operated by independent producers—further diverting sales and revenues from the upstream utility-owned plants.

1.3 Behind-the-meter storage and electric vehicles

The rapid evolution of small-scale or distributed storage is a recent phenomenon, which started with the likes of Tesla offering stand-alone battery packs, called Powerwall, to residential and commercial consumers—as further described in the following chapter by Schlesinger. But batteries are one form of storage. Energy can be stored in a variety of media—such as ice, cold, or hot water—for use at later time. As the cost of such technologies continues to fall, their economic viability becomes more compelling. Moreover, stored energy, like distributed generation, can be aggregated and remotely managed in ways that deliver much better value, given its relatively high costs.

There are several powerful drivers that promise to make distributed storage as ubiquitous as distributed generation notably:

- excess self-generation,
- variable tariffs, and
- rising variable renewable generation.

The first is obvious. During daylight hours on sunny days of the year, any solar roof with decent capacity is likely to produce more than the local demand, especially if the occupants are out midday, as in many residential buildings. If the regulation allows the excess generation to be fed into the grid and offers a decent reward or credit for the hours when the meter is "spinning backwards," the excess midday generation provides a revenue stream for the homeowner or commercial establishment.

But if there are restrictions on how much can be exported and/or very little is paid for it that increases the viability of investing in distributed storage. Currently in California,

---

[11] Refer to SEIA website on corporate PPAs including https://www.seia.org/research-resources/solar-market-insight-report-2019-q2.

the excess can be fed into the network and consumers get a credit equal to the full retail price—making solar PVs a no-brainer for many customers with big monthly bills.

By contrast, in Australia, prosumers get paid the wholesale price for the exported power—which is significantly below retail price. This suggests that many Australian homeowners with rooftop solar will be incentivized to invest in distributed storage.

There are, of course, two other ways to make better use of midday excess energy:

- store it in EVs and
- sell or trade it with a neighbor, across the street, town, or state.

As the technology improves and regulators relax some of the restrictions on sharing and trading electrons among customers, many clever ways to put the excess generation to good use are expected to emerge, including the example in Box 1.2.

Moreover, the distribution companies, who are increasingly confronted with large fluctuations on their networks as further explained in the chapter by Johnston and Sioshansi are eager to make better use of distributed storage on customers' premises as described in Box 1.3.

EVs with their large storage batteries are expected to be a huge source of BTM investments, in time exceeding investments in distributed generation in solar PVs.

There is little disagreement that the number of EVs will rise dramatically over the next decade and beyond (Box 1.4). It follows that more EVs will require more charging stations, and that will increase electricity consumption as the global light-duty car fleet gradually converts to electric over time. The only question is how fast will the transition be.

In a few countries, generous government subsidies are leading to the virtual phaseout of internal combustion engines (ICEs) within the next decade as in the case of Norway. Sweden recently joined Denmark and Norway in proposing a total ban of ICE sales starting in 2030. Other countries and a number of cities have also proposed similar bans by the same time frame if not sooner.

Needless to say, how, when, and where millions of EVs will be charged—and discharged—will determine how well the variable renewable generation from distributed solar as well as utility-scale solar and wind farms will be utilized. As described in Box 1.5, the variability of generation requires far more flexibility on the demand side and all sorts of storage—EVs, hot water storage, and other means of energy storage—will be needed in the years ahead.

1.4 Behind-the-meter aggregation

While individual prosumers and prosumagers, especially those with EVs, can—and increasingly do—play a proactive role in balancing variable generation and load on networks, there is only so much that a single customer can do. Moreover, not all prosumers and prosumagers are sufficiently incentivized to do all that *can* be done. It takes considerable time and effort to monitor prices on the wholesale market, solar insolation, state of charge in a battery, and/or EV or how much energy is stored in the hot water tank.

As several chapters in this book explain, this offers an opportunity for smart aggregators to step in.

BOX 1.2

My electric vehicle (EV), your PV

With so many solar homes and an increasing number of EVs, it is easy to connect the dots leading to new and potentially profitable business models. One such idea was recently outlined by Vincent Schachter, Sr. VP of energy services of eMotorWerks in an interview with *Microgrid Knowledge*—which was reprinted in other media. The basic concept is that EVs, buildings with rooftop solar PVs,[12] and/or distributed storage and smallish microgrids will be key market actors in a future where consumers produce, share, or trade energy, also referred to as peer-to-peer (P2P) trading.

It is not hard to imagine a future where an EV driver could pull up to a small microgrid consisting of one or more connected solar homes, plug-in, and "trade" with the energy sellers within—say homes or buildings that have rooftop solar PVs. Conversely, the EV could discharge some of its excess juice to the homeowners on a cloudy day.

As described in the *MicroGrid Knowledge* article, eMotorWerks and LO3 Energy have joined forces to demonstrate that such a future is feasible.[13] The two companies announced a collaboration in mid-Dec 2018 to test systems and software that will let consumers buy and sell electricity within microgrids using their solar homes and EVs without an intermediary or a central clearinghouse.

The partners wanted to test the feasibility and efficiency of an energy ecosystem where EVs don't just *charge* but also *discharge*, and where future *prosumers* can better control their energy generation, consumption, and storage. The companies said they may test their ideas in New York's famous Brooklyn Microgrid project, where LO3 Energy has already successfully demonstrated a community blockchain scheme. If all goes according to the plan, they hope to develop a trading platform that could be applied to other microgrids and other applications worldwide.

While the basics are intuitive, the scheme quickly gets complicated. To make it work the microgrid will have to integrate eMotorWerks JuiceNet EV charging platform into Exergy, LO3's transactive energy system. The idea is to allow participants to bid prices for buying or selling electricity similar to how traders currently do in competitive wholesale power markets but on a miniscule scale, with solar households and EV owners as traders. Crucially, the idea is to make this possible without a central clearinghouse or an intermediary using a blockchain ledger.

According to Schachter, "This is where the industry's headed … (being) able to leverage EV batteries and flexible resources locally," as explained in his interview with *Microgrid Knowledge*.

---

[12] Refer to My EV, your PV – or the other way around, *EEnergy Informer*, p. 16, Jan 2019 at www. eenergyinformer.com.

[13] At https://microgridknowledge.com/emotorwerks-lo3-microgrids/.

BOX 1.2 (cont'd)

In practice, the EV driver could transact with the small-scale microgrid in a variety of ways. The EV owner can leverage the flexibility inherent in storage capacity of its battery while the PV households can gain an additional source of revenue for the rooftop solar, especially during sunny days where there is generation exceeding demand on the distribution network.

Who buys or sells what will depend on the circumstances, timing, price, location, and congestion on the distribution network. On a cloudy day, for example, the homeowners in the microgrid may be willing to buy energy from the EV. On a sunny day, when the households have excess solar energy, they may offer the EV owner low-cost juice for charging the batteries.

The buyers and sellers would agree on the price for such transactions. This is precisely the idea vouched by the likes of Edward Cazalet who described it in a book titled *Transactive Energy* along with Stephen Barrager.[14] For example, a household might offer to buy energy if it falls below a threshold price. Or the EV owner may say you can use my battery all night so long as it is fully charged by 9:00 a.m. when I leave for work and need the EV's full range for the morning commute. In practice, of course, the communication and the transactions will be automated and algorithm-driven preset by the buyers and sellers using

something like eMotorwerkss JuiceNet smartphone application. In other words the traders would hardly, if ever, be communicating or bidding in real time. Artificial intelligence and machine learning will figure out when to buy or sell and at what price based on behavior patterns, service needs, and other parameters set by the traders in the scheme, observed, learned, and improved over time.

The proposed scheme could mark the next step in the LO3 Energy's Brooklyn Microgrid business evolution, as it demonstrates its platform operating on the microgrid level and/or in new applications.

In an article by *Utility Dive* (Dec 6, 2018) LO3 Energy's CEO Lawrence Orsini said that utilities should see EV charging as another option to "efficiently match local energy supply and demand," adding, that the partnership with eMotorWerks could help to enable "more transactions among other microgrid participants and EV drivers.[15]"

In the *MicroGrid Knowledge* interview, Schachter said, "It's in our DNA to try to optimize the energy related to charging and then to deliver whichever services we can deliver in a given geography that make sense for our customers and partners."

The two companies have decided to collaborate after realizing that their products complement one another. In the microgrid,

---

[14] Barrager, S., & Cazalet, E. (2014). Transactive energy: A sustainable business and regulatory model for electricity. Available from <https://www.amazon.com/Transactive-Energy-Sustainable-Regulatory-Electricity-ebook/dp/B00OW9SFHA>.

[15] At https://www.utilitydive.com/news/lo3-energy-emotorwerks-partner-to-connect-evs-to-microgrids-optimize-rene/543733/.

BOX 1.2   (*cont'd*)

LO3 Energy will provide the financial platform that manages the price signals and P2P transactions while handling energy transactions within the microgrid and between the microgrid and the central grid. Using LO3's mobile app, consumers can decide what they're willing to pay for local energy produced. As in any competitive platform or auction, the supply and demand are matched in real time and highest bid required to clear the market sets the price as in any competitive wholesale market.

The scheme helps with another major EV challenge, namely, managing the stress on the distribution network. Charging an EV, depending on the speed, can be equivalent to the capacity requirements of two to three typical homes to the distribution network. Hence, with millions of EVs added over the next decade or so, the question is, can the existing grid handle the extra load?

The answer depends on the number, timing, and location of EVs, when they are charged, or potentially discharged. It is easy to imagine a scenario where large numbers

EV owners can charge or discharge depending on the prevailing prices. Source: *©Elexon Limited.*

In the meantime, eMotorWerks JuiceNet allows control over the flow of energy. It aggregates supply and demand and makes matches in real time using a cloud-based platform. "We've been on that wave of aggregating demand response with EV batteries for the last couple of years in California. But this is an evolution from the status quo—the ability to do it and then to trade," Schachter said.

of EV owners arrive at home, or work, at more or less the same time and simultaneously plug-in to charge. Under these circumstances, energy management becomes "all about space and time," Schachter said, adding, "It becomes important to monitor, track and control the movement of energy in a granular manner, something the trading platform can do," in the interview.

BOX 1.2 (*cont'd*)

The two companies expect to have demonstration results to show in a year once they work through the logistical details. The scheme offers a lot of potential, which may explain why *eMotorWerks* was acquired by *Enel*. The company made headlines in September 2018 with a 30 MW virtual battery, made up of 6000 EV chargers that it had aggregated for participation in California's wholesale power markets.

There is a lot at stake. Bloomberg New Energy Finance (BNEF), for example, believes that EVs may represent as much as 28% of the global light-duty vehicle sales sometime shortly after 2025. And the Edison Electric Institute, which represents the US investor-owned utilities, projects 7 million EVs will be on the US roads by 2025—up from about 1 million today. With so many EVs expected and millions of PVs already in place, finding better ways to get power-hungry EVs and PVs with surplus energy during sunny hours of the day to trade locally offers a compelling case. ∎

BOX 1.3

Behind-the-meter (BTM) storage on the rise[16]

More utilities around the United States are getting into BTM storage with the approval of state-level regulators, a trend that is expected to accelerate as the cost of distributed storage continues to fall. New Hampshire is the latest to join other states as utilities experiment with new business models in utility-owned, customer-sited battery energy storage pilot projects. And the increasing frequency of service interruptions due to weather-related outages provides additional justification for such efforts.

Liberty Utilities in New Hampshire, for example, has proposed a pilot project among the most ambitious tests of a utility's ability to use BTM battery storage systems. It is the second regulator-approved program for utility ownership of BTM resources in the United States but won't be the last.

The following phases of the scheme could offer opportunities for the *private sector* participation alongside the utility—which explains why solar-plus-storage installers such as Sunrun and ReVision Energy decided *not* to oppose the initial phase of the pilot. As explained to *Utility Dive* (Nov 27, 2018) by Sunrun's Director for Policy and Storage Market Strategy, Chris Rauscher, "The utility's insistence on owning batteries makes it an outlier nationally, but the program as a whole puts Liberty at the cutting-edge on the battery use case.[17]"

Many investor-owned utilities are using batteries to shave peak demand, provide

---

[16] Refer to BTM storage on the rise, *EEnergy Informer*, p. 15, Jan 2019, at www.eenrgyinforrmer.com.

[17] At https://www.utilitydive.com/news/new-hampshire-settlement-moves-cutting-edge-utility-btm-storage-pilot-for/542866/.

BOX 1.3   (cont'd)

grid services, and make utility systems more flexible. But those projects are typically subcontracted to third-party providers.

As in virtually all regulatory-approved pilots of this type, Liberty Utilities must demonstrate to the New Hampshire Public Utilities Commission that the scheme can cut peak system demand *and* deliver a positive net present value to *all* its customers, not just those who participate in the scheme. If the pilot project succeeds as intended, it can lead to bigger pilots and opportunities for third-party providers to offer similar services.

In the pilot's first phase, Liberty Utilities will offer 200 Tesla Powerwalls with each participant taking two batteries along with control software at a heavily subsidized cost of $2,433, or a 10-year lease option at $25/month. The retail installed price of the batteries is currently around $16,500.

The only other regulated US utility with a similar program is Vermont's Green Mountain Power (GMP), which offers a utility-owned, customer-sited battery storage pilot for $1,300 or a monthly fee of $15. GMP's 2000 Tesla Powerwalls are already fully subscribed, and the scheme is reportedly ready for full deployment in 2019.

In both cases the regulators approved the small-scale pilots based on the evidence provided that the schemes can cost-effectively reduce system peak demand with customer-sited batteries. The utilities now have to deliver evidence that the pilots will have positive benefits without increasing rates to nonparticipants. ∎

BOX 1.4

Rapid growth of electric vehicles (EVs) stunning[18]

For some time, there has been speculation about the expected growth of EVs with continuously rising projections of how many may be on the roads in the future. The biggest surprise has been that no matter how big the projected numbers, someone else comes up with an even bigger number and even earlier date. In its latest World Energy Outlook (WEO) released in Nov 2018, the International Energy Agency (IEA), for example, projects that by 2040 half of all global light duty vehicles will be electric—roughly 1 billion of them.

Volkswagen, the world's biggest automaker, for example, expects to offer as many as 70 new electric models by 2028 and produce as many as 22 million EVs over the next decade.

Not surprisingly, both the automakers and oil companies are changing gears. For the former the message is rather unambiguous: phaseout internal combustion engines, while increasing the production of EVs with new models and new features to fit the needs of diverse global consumers. It will be an expensive changeover, but it is inevitable. ∎

---

[18] At https://www.iea.org/gevo2018/ also in Rapid growth of EVs stunning, *EEnergy Informer*, Feb 2019, p. 6, at www.eenergyinformer.com.

BOX 1.5

Fill'er up with solar energy[19]

Among Albert Einstein's many famous quotes is that we can't solve problems by using the same kind of thinking we used when we created them. One of these problems, of course, is what to do with the excess renewable generation, particularly from wind and solar resources—which are cheap and come in great abundance, but not necessarily when or where we need them. As the percentage of such variable renewable resources grows, the grid operators face ever more difficult challenges to absorb them when they are available and replace them with other resources when they are not. It is the proverbial feast or famine problem, the California "Duck Curve."

Severin Borenstein, a Univ. of California, Berkeley professor, who serves on the Board of Governors of the California Independent System Operator (CAISO), is certainly familiar with these issues. But even he was "fascinated" during a recent visit to the CAISO control center in Folsom, CA.

In a blog post on 11 March,[20] Borenstein describes a fairly typical day in the life of CAISO grid operators (accompanying visuals).

It had been a fairly clear and cool day in the Golden State, lots of solar power production and fairly moderate demand. That meant that as the sun set, operators had to ramp up non-solar supply very rapidly. The personnel in the control room

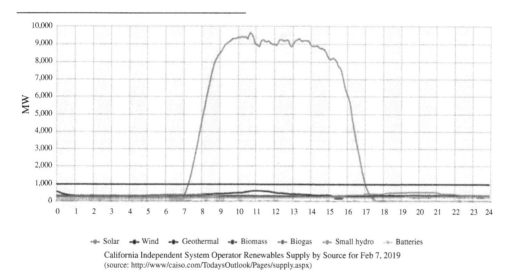

--●-- Solar   --●-- Wind   --●-- Geothermal   --●-- Biomass   --●-- Biogas   --●-- Small hydro   --●-- Batteries

California Independent System Operator Renewables Supply by Source for Feb 7, 2019
(source: http://www.caiso.com/TodaysOutlook/Pages/supply.aspx)

Why isn't California doing more? Source: <*https://energyathaas.wordpress.com/2019/03/11/charging-with-the-sun*>.

[19] Blog posted on Mar 11, 2019, at https://energyathaas.wordpress.com/2019/03/11/charging-with-the-sun/.

[20] https://energyathaas.wordpress.com/2019/03/11/charging-with-the-sun/.

BOX 1.5 (cont'd)

were relaxed and professional, but they were also busy keeping the system in balance as about 8 GW of supply from solar farms—about a third of the total demand CAISO was serving that afternoon—disappeared over the course of a couple hours. (The yellow in figure above is solar.)

That got Borenstein thinking:

In fact, watching the efforts of the CAISO grid operators prompted me to take action to make their lives a tiny bit easier: I reprogrammed our **hot tub** to run its filter

The scene (at CAISO control room) got me wondering again why California isn't doing more to coordinate end-use demand with electricity production from intermittent renewable sources.

There are a myriad of small and large opportunities that can help as Borenstein describes:

cycle in the middle of the day — the so-called belly of the duck — instead of later in the afternoon. If we had a **programmable electric water heater**, I could have also set it to heat during the duck's belly, but we are sadly still combusting natural gas for our hot water and space heating.

Bornstein, like many others, is constantly reminded of the many neglected opportunities for using and/or storing energy during the belly of the *California duck curve* when excess solar energy is available and enormously cheap—so cheap that its price occasionally goes negative.

Likewise, there are equally attractive opportunities to reduce and/or shift usage away from the neck of the duck curve. The daily rise and fall of midday solar generation (visual below) is a challenge, *and* an opportunity.

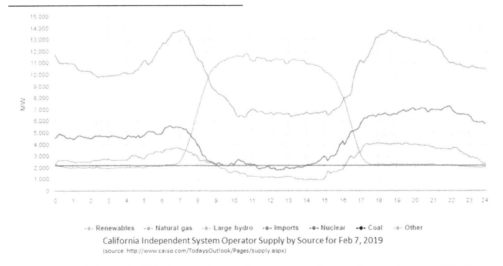

-●- Renewables   -●- Natural gas   -●- Large hydro   -●- Imports   -●- Nuclear   -●- Coal   -●- Other
California Independent System Operator Supply by Source for Feb 7, 2019
(source: http://www.caiso.com/TodaysOutlook/Pages/supply.aspx)

Another typical day at CAISO: feast or famine. Source: *<https://energyathaas.wordpress.com/2019/03/11/ charging-with-the-sun>*.

BOX 1.5 (cont'd)

In his blog, Borenstein wrote:

In discussing the value of such coordination of demand and renewable generation, I've found that there are 3 types of views among the few people who think about such things: naïve, glib, and correct ….

That makes investment in a wind or solar plant more profitable, and that leads to more investment in these technologies. "Shifting my demand is raising profits for wind and solar plants" just doesn't have the same warm and fuzzy feel as 'my

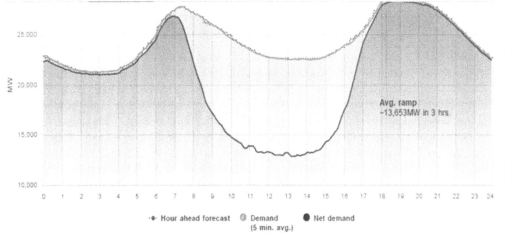

Avg. ramp
~13,653MW in 3 hrs.

•● Hour ahead forecast   ◎ Demand   ● Net demand
(5 min. avg.)

The Duck: CAISO Total Demand and Net (of Solar and Wind) Demand for Feb 7, 2019
(source: http://www.caiso.com/TodaysOutlook/Pages/default.aspx)

Fill up during the valley, avoid the peak. Source: <https://energyathaas.wordpress.com/2019/03/11/charging-with-the-sun>.

Borenstein subscribes to the third, the "correct" option, which he describes as follows:

Shifting your demand from one hour to another, causes prices to rise in hours that get more demand and fall in hours that get less. So, moving your electricity consumption to correspond with production from wind and solar means that those intermittent renewable generators get a larger share of the total revenues paid to producers without changing their production.

electricity comes from a wind or solar plant', but it has more basis in reality.

The variability of renewables is a given—and managing the inevitable fluctuations, such as when the sun goes down—will only get more challenging which is why we need to think creatively—and far more aggressively—about flexible demand, more and better ways to consume and store the excess generation, and clever ways to shift demand. ■

What makes BTM assets even more interesting is the fact that they are getting increasingly smart and increasingly connected—making it easier not only to aggregate but to monitor, manage, and optimize large numbers of them remotely as further explored in Box 1.6.

These technological advancements coupled with cheap sensing and communication creates enormous opportunities for large numbers of consumers with flexible demand to be coupled with equally large numbers of prosumers and prosumagers with storage capacity as further described in the chapter by Lehmbruck et al. and Poplavskaya and de Vries.

BOX 1.6

Amazon and Google in smart home[21]

Recently *The Wall Street Journal* (WSJ) ran a story that predicted that Amazon and Google—and their counterparts in China and elsewhere—would use their fledging home automation empires to eventually expand into the electricity business, perhaps not literally but virtually. In the WSJ's article, Bradley Olson said the two giants "... are taking early steps to expand into the electricity business, as home-energy automation emerges as a rich source of customer data.[22]"

As noted by Olson, "The technology giants aren't interested in selling megawatts — at least not for now. But they are seeking ways to expand their smart speakers, internet-connected thermostats and other devices to harness information on consumers' personal energy use." In other words, access to customer data seems to be the main draw.

Most experts looking into the future of electricity business agree that future homes are likely to have solar panels, electric vehicles, and possibly other forms of storage. In such an environment, companies that can remotely monitor and manage such behind-the-meter devices stand to create and capture value—and new revenue streams.

Both tech giants, who previously made smallish investments, are now poised to expand. In 2014, Google acquired Nest Labs, a maker of smart wireless thermostats, for $3.2 billion. Nest has expanded its product line to include home-security cameras and carbon monoxide monitoring.

Likewise, Amazon's first major investment in the smart home space was the acquisition of Ring, who makes video doorbells, for around $1 billion. Its other investments include Ecobee, a competitor to Nest,

---

[21] At https://www.wsj.com/articles/google-amazon-seek-foothold-in-electricity-as-home-automation-grows-11548604800 also covered in At last: Amazon enters smart home, *EEnergy Informer*, p. 1, Nov 2018 at www.eenergyinformer.com.

[22] Olson, B. (2019). Google, Amazon seek foothold in electricity as home automation grows. *The Wall Street Journal*. <https://www.wsj.com/articles/google-amazon-seek-foothold-in-electricity-as-home-automation-grows-11548604800>.

BOX 1.6 *(cont'd)*

and an alliance with Arcadia Power, an energy efficiency service provider.

Now, both companies are embarking on much more ambitious plans to get into home automation, energy management, and potentially much more.

Amazon's home automation strategy rests on its smart speaker, Echo, and its voice-activated software, Alexa. Various surveys put the US smart speaker penetration levels at around 20% of households with Wi-Fi by the end of 2018, a 50% increase over 2017. That amounts to roughly 19 million homes, dominated by Amazon and Google, with their competing platforms.

Using artificial intelligence (AI) and through machine learning, a smart intermediary can remotely monitor and adjust thousands—or millions—of devices, cycling them on or off in response to fluctuations in renewable generation but without causing any service disruption or inconvenience to the average customer. This is not science fiction and many companies, Amazon and Google included, are likely to scale-up quickly once they put the pieces together.

As an example of what can be done with AI and a portfolio of customers, during a solar eclipse in 2017, Google recruited 750,000 Nest owners to opt an automated program that allowed it to clip roughly 700 MW during the eclipse. It is not hard to imagine what can be done with 7.5 million customers.

Since Amazon started requiring that its chips be embedded in many of the appliances it sells, they are showing up in large numbers of devices—TVs, washers and dryers, washing machines, refrigerators, stoves, home entertainment systems, and everything else. Since these devices are communicating wirelessly with Amazon's Echo, Amazon is in a position to collect and analyze the data.

As it learns more about each household's energy consumption, generation, and storage patterns, it can better manage and optimize everything. And by aggregating large number of homes with multitude of devices, it can begin to manage the entire portfolio of behind-the-meter assets. Virtual power plants and soaking up the midday solar generation are not as farfetched as once believed.

While many see nothing sinister about Amazon's strategy or those of other data-centric companies such as Google, others are concerned about privacy and security of sharing so much intimate granular data with Amazon or—for that matter—anyone.

Other skeptics worry about the potential for the abuse of the information gathered from such devices—including their unintended release into the hands of hackers. ∎

Aside from the strong economies of scale, aggregation offers much better utilization of BTM assets, which would otherwise be poorly utilized, or underutilized as explained.[23]

A variation of the BTM aggregation described in the preceding section is to aggregate large numbers of consumers, prosumers, and prosumagers into a community as described in chapter by Reijnders et al.

[23] Refer to behind-the-meter investments poorly utilized, *EEnergy Informer*, Sept 2018 at www.eenergyinforrmer.com.

A community of like-minded customers, say, a retirement community or private golf course in sunny Arizona, can be designed and built from ground up with a privately owned distribution network, solar roofs, backup generation, and storage, including EVs and electric golf-carts to operate as a semi-independent microgrid.[24] While connected to the network, such a community can store its excess solar generation during midday hours when prices are low, while selling it to the macrogrid after the sunset when they are high.

An energy community offers technical and economic possibilities that are not necessarily available to aggregators who are dealing with multiple customers across a vast distribution network.

In an extreme case, such communities can be turned into virtual *nonsumer* communities where there is little or no net kWh purchase required from the macrogrid. Such a community can—with appropriate design and management—generate as many kWhs as it consumes over a year—but not necessarily during every hour of the year.

1.5 Stand-alone devices: no meter and no grid

Finally, a number of even more exotic forms of BTM devices are appearing, which operate essentially as stand-alone and—in many cases—are not even connected to the network, hence do not even require metering.

Aside from the PAYGO off-grid solar + storage systems, which are proliferating in remote rural areas, mostly in developing countries, these stand-alone devices are showing up in both developing and developed economies in special applications where demand is modest—and can be supplied by distributed generation plus storage.

Such stand-alone devices produce, store, and consume electricity without being connected to the network. For example, a number of bus stops in Zaragoza, Spain have crystalline silicon PV glass panels on the top canopy generating power, which can be stored in batteries under the seats, powering the screens, and providing lighting for the canopy, as illustrated in Fig. 1.4.

Similarly, self-contained, stand-alone applications are popping out in large numbers all over the world, including parking meters, outdoor lights, traffic signals, wireless relay signals, to mention a few (Fig. 1.5).

Many mobile and/or outdoor applications are also emerging with a combination of distributed solar and storage providing basic but limited services—which in some cases may be adequate for delivering limited services, such as for the houseboat in Fig. 1.6.

These developments, namely, advances in technology allowing self-contained mini islands of power generation, storage, and consumption could play an increasing role as the costs of such devices continue to fall (Fig. 1.7). The same pattern is observed with isolated PAYGO solar microgrids and self-contained communities that are increasingly able to provide services with little reliance on the traditional networks.

---

[24] Refer to Sonnen's project in Prescott Valley, AZ, at https://www.utilitydive.com/news/sonnen-prepares-its-next-step-in-aggregating-residential-storage/540760/.

FIGURE 1.4   Self-contained bus stop in Zaragoza, Spain, is a stand-alone, self-contained system, which produces, stores, and consumes electricity. Source: *Photo: Onyx Solar. <https://www.onyxsolar.com/24-projects/solar-pv-canopy/362-photovoltaic-bus-stop>.*

FIGURE 1.5   Increasingly, self-contained devices appear where generation, storage, and consumption are integrated within the same device, often without any connection to the network as in the two examples above parking meter (left) and park light (right) where the top portion of the pole is covered with PV panels with storage device embedded in the pole.

FIGURE   1.6 Self-contained solar plus storage provides basic services in an increasing number of mobile and/or outdoor applications such as houseboats.

FIGURE 1.7 As the costs continue to fall, more applications for self-contained systems will emerge such as the stand-alone EV charging station providing free solar energy in San Francisco.

FIGURE 1.8   Solar electric vehicles. Source: *Sono Motors, sonomotors.com.*

These stand-alone devices are an interesting new phenomenon, which may potentially further divert revenues from the traditional network. They are a special kind of BTM assets where there is no meter.

Other promising stand-alone devices keep coming to the market, including solar EVs, where the exterior of the car is covered with solar PV panels integrated into the surface of the car (Fig. 1.8). These cars can essentially become self-propelling machines so long as they are parked in the sun and do not drive long distances. According to one manufacturer, a typical driver living in a sunny city like Los Angeles or Sydney and driving average commuting distances may only need to charge from the grid on a few occasions in a typical year.

1.6   Regulating behind-the-meter

Regulators increasingly realize that many of the valuable capabilities of the BTM assets are locked up or strictly restricted because of regulatory barriers or restrictions, topics further explored in the third part of this volume.

There are two particular areas limiting further development of the BTM assets:

- allowing P2P trading and
- allowing future consumers to buy—or sell—different services from—or to—different suppliers.

The former should be obvious as discussed above. The latter becomes important as the size and number of BTM devices grow. As illustrated in Box 1.7, some regulators are beginning to consider alternative forms of regulations fit for the BTM-rich future.

Another area requiring innovative regulatory thinking is the dormant demand response business, which has not developed anywhere near its full potential. For example, Wood Mackenzie estimates that the United States alone can have as much as 88 GW of flexible demand in the residential sector by 2023.[25]

BOX 1.7

Ofgem: changing the rules[26]

With all the attention focused on behind-the-meter (BTM) space and the myriad of innovations that promise to deliver new services—not just to individual customers but to aggregation of customers—the frontiers of what can and cannot be achieved are being extended to previously unchartered territory. One promising concept getting traction in some circles is the idea of allowing customers to get services not from one, but multiple suppliers.

Traditionally, customers got electricity service from a single supplier, even when they have retail choice. In fact, in many places, they are obligated by regulation to buy from a single supplier—typically the local regulated monopoly distribution company serving their area—or not at all.

Customers are not only investing in BTM assets but are incentivized to have them aggregated so that they can be better managed and utilized, including virtual power plants (VPPs).

The South Australian Government, for example, recently announced a $100 million program to incent 40,000 residential customers to install batteries in their homes. The fine print in the scheme includes a requirement that all these batteries be registered into a central database allowing a third party to remotely manage and optimize how and when they are charged and discharged, in other words be capable of operating as a VPP.

Across the world, as the proportion of variable renewable generation increases and as more customers install rooftop solar PVs, the opportunities to aggregate and manage these assets increases with tangible benefits for all concerned, including the distribution network operators who can gain from the increased flexibility offered by the VPPs.

---

[25] Refer to https://www.elexon.co.uk/wp-content/uploads/2018/04/ELEXON-White-Paper-Enabling-customers-to-buy-power-from-multiple-providers.pdf also at Single customer buying from multiple suppliers? Why not? *EEnergy Informer*, p. 19, Nov 2018 at www.eenerrgyinformer.com.

[26] Enabling customers to buy from multiple suppliers at https://www.elexon.co.uk/wp-content/uploads/2018/04/ELEXON-White-Paper-Enabling-customers-to-buy-power-from-multiple-providers.pdf.

BOX 1.7 *(cont'd)*

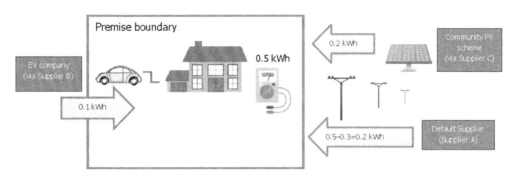

Time has arrived for one customer buying from multiple suppliers. Source: *Elexon, <https://www.elexon. co.uk/ https://www.elexon.co.uk/wp-content/uploads/2018/04/ELEXON-White-Paper-Enabling-customers-to-buy-power-from-multiple-providers.pdf content/uploads/2018/04/ELEXON-White-Paper-Enabling-customers-to-buy-power-from-multiple-providers.pdf>.*

However, the market—particularly BTM market—is rapidly changing and there is a growing belief that customers should have the option to buy—or sell, or trade—their energy from/to multiple suppliers if they wish to do so, say, because this lowers costs or has other benefits. The United Kingdom's energy regulator, Ofgem, has expressed interest in exploring such possibilities.

If this were allowed, customers may decide they want to buy energy to charge their electric vehicles (EVs) from one supplier, while selling or sharing the excess generation from their rooftop solar panels to a neighbor—or whatever. Having the option to buy or sell from/to multiple suppliers would enable a wide range of innovations in the electricity supply market that is currently difficult if not impossible.

Imagine a customer buying

- some of its supply from a community-owned and operated distributed generation and/or battery storage system;
- the juice to charge the EV from an alternative supplier—perhaps an auto company leasing the vehicle and its electricity usage;
- some juice from a third supplier only when prices are low; and
- the balance—residual—of the needs from a fourth supplier at regulated price.

It is not difficult to imagine customers wanting to take advantage of such options as they become available. In a white paper titled *Enabling customers to buy from multiple suppliers*, Elexon[27] points out the following:

---

[27] https://www.greentechmedia.com/articles/read/88-gigawatts-by-2023-u-s-residential-flexibility-on-the-rise#gs.191wdx.

BOX 1.7 *(cont'd)*

- Community-owned distributed generation and storage where the output may be shared among members are already a reality.
- EV manufacturers to offer vehicles on a simple £/mi basis, including all the electricity needed to charge the vehicle (this could be at multiple charging points at different locations, subject to technology solutions to support appropriate measurement at the various locations). This could also apply to future "device as a service" markets for household appliances in "smarter homes" (for example, fridge rental with power included).
- Peer-to-peer trading, for example, a customer buying a neighbor's excess solar energy. This could be facilitated by the development of apps that allow consumers with micro-generation to sell (or give) their excess generation to other nearby consumers (rather than receiving the export feed-in tariff). For example, an app could be designed that allowed consumers to donate their "spill" to local charities, or families in fuel poverty.
- The most interesting is "Rapid switching" where energy is purchased from different suppliers or wholesale energy sources for periods as short as the prevailing settlement period, typically half hourly.

In its white paper, Elexon, sets out a vision for a new market structure which could allow multiple suppliers to deliver energy through a single meter, which is currently impossible to do.

Elexon provides an example of a customer who is purchasing electricity from three different sources A, B, and C as illustrated in the visual.

For the sake of argument, let us say that during a half-hour settlement period, the consumer uses 0.5 kWh of energy as recorded on the meter. Of this, let us say 0.1 kWh was used—and recorded by the EV metering device—to charge the EV, 0.2 kWh was supplied by the community PV scheme and the remaining 0.2 kWh came from default supplier A. In this case the various submeters keep track of the purchases of energy from the EV company, the community PV scheme, and supplier A. It is not rocket science to settle with the three suppliers according to the agreements in place.

To enable customers to buy electricity from more than one supplier, however, not only do regulations have to change, but new arrangements have to be in place to keep track of who bought what from whom and at what price and under what terms and conditions.

The writing is already on the wall. In the United Kingdom, Ofgem has already started an inquiry to examine the pros and cons of such options with regulators in other parts of the world likely to consider similar initiatives. ■

1.7 Conclusion

With the expected growth of distributed generation, storage and EVs consumers will make massive investments in the BTM space in the coming years. These investments plus all the other devices residing in customers' premises can be utilized in promising ways not only to complement the supply-side generation but to make the distribution network to operate more productively and smoothly. Much remains to be done to bring necessary changes including new regulatory thinking about a future where demand finally plays a role in balancing supply and demand in a future dominated by variable renewable generation.

It is not science fiction: going zero net energy and loving it

Benjamin Schlesinger[1,2]

[1]Center for Global Sustainability, University of Maryland Public Policy, College Park, MD, United States [2]Benjamin Schlesinger and Associates, LLC, Bethesda, MD, United States

2.1 Introduction

With the falling costs of solar photovoltaic (PV) panels, geothermal drilling, and battery storage, plus advancements in energy efficiency of buildings, appliances, lighting, and more, it seems increasingly likely that constructing homes or buildings that are zero net energy (ZNE), or carbon neutral, can be cost effective.[1] Moreover, as described in other chapters of this volume, there are increasing numbers of individuals who are sufficiently motivated to go the extra mile, so to speak, to experiment with new ways of making homes more efficient and less energy or carbon intensive. These trailblazers of ZNE homes are not only pushing the envelope on what can be done but are demonstrating to others that it can indeed be done.

Their motivations, of course, vary. Some are seeking lower energy bills—which can be high in places where the retail rates are high or have the potential to grow quickly. Others want to reduce their carbon footprint and may be less focused on a quick payback. Although the number of carbon-neutral homes in the United States isn't known, there are at least 2 million solar homes in Australia (Sydney Morning Herald, 12-2-2018), as further explained in the chapter by Swanston. In California, effective 2020, new residential construction must adhere to CEC 2019 Building Energy Efficiency Standards, which include rooftop solar and significant efficiency measures. Similar regulations are evolving within the EU.

In the light of how important these developments are, this chapter describes an effort to see if a large, single-family home can be built with other priorities in mind, but that is also carbon neutral using best available off-the-shelf residential energy technology as of

---

[1] Carbon neutral and ZNE are different ways of describing essentially the same goals.

2018–19. The discussion reviews goals, design, choices of building materials and equipment, reviews preliminary results after the first year of operation, and offers a few insights about the implications of what might happen if more buildings were built to the same standards. The author is a well known natural gas authority and declaims any effort to suggest that natural gas isn't a vital energy form where it is or can be available. As there was no gas utility service where this new home was built, other energy forms had to be incorporated—so why not a zero-energy house?

This chapter is organized as follows:

- Section 2.2 sets out the rationale for this ZNE project,
- Section 2.3 discusses the scope of the experiment and technology choices,
- Section 2.4 reviews performance in the first year of operation,
- Section 2.5 presents an initial rough-cut economic analysis, and
- Section 2.6 concludes the chapter and discusses implications.

2.2 The lure—"by the way" carbon neutrality

In building this new home in the Mid-Atlantic community of St. Michaels, Maryland, three basic goals were considered and balanced, in the order listed below:

- beauty,
- functionality, and
- environmental compatibility.

The beauty part means living by lovely open water in a Charles Paul Goebel designed home with an Erin Paige Pitts interior—top designers in the business. The functionality goal was pursued by these two wonderful designers, and it also dictated the choice of local builder Paquin Design/Build and their experienced, practical, dogged crew.

Just as most houses are built with nonenergy priorities in mind, like location, rooms, etc., so too this house is not optimized for energy efficiency, insolation, or solar orientation. The effort was to achieve carbon neutrality in an incidental way, that is, just build the house you want and pick the best off-the-shelf energy options currently available. The thought is, if this strategy can succeed in producing carbon neutrality without breaking the bank, then some basic reasons to not address climate change might be eliminated—too expensive, can't afford it, too complicated, not available.

Costs included in this first round of the analysis are those above and beyond what would normally be placed in any code-compliant new home—in many cases, these normal elements would enable the house to save considerable energy. Instead, the lure was to pick the best available, and see if that would achieve carbon neutrality.

2.3 The program defined and implemented

Completed in November 2018, the house is located in St. Michaels, Maryland, a historic fishing, shipbuilding and sailing village located on Maryland's Eastern Shore of

FIGURE 2.1   Views around the house. Source: *Solar PV panel array courtesy Sunrise Solar, 2018.*

Chesapeake Bay, about an hour and a half from Washington, DC, and 2.5 hours south of Philadelphia. The house is situated on open water facing northeast toward the mouth of the Miles River and the Eastern Bay. The structure includes 5140 ft^2 of conditioned living space in a New England style house, with a garage and a driveway, and over 2 acres of lawn. Fig. 2.1 shows the house, the solar array, and a view from the house.

The Mid-Atlantic region where the house is located experiences extremes temperature and humidity, with much colder winters and a lot more rainy days than, for example, Los Angeles (Fig. 2.2). These factors don't bode well for maintaining a carbon-neutral house since natural gas is used heavily in the Mid-Atlantic region in winters for heating and hot water. In addition, rainy days and thick cloud covers greatly reduce solar generation. Snowfalls rarely occur in Los Angeles and snowfall in St. Michaels amount to only about 45% of the Unites States average—so the lack of heavy snow is a positive factor because solar PV panels are clearer during winter than in many other US locations.

The factors highlighted in Fig. 2.2—lower low temperatures and higher highs, and some snowfall (even if only 45% of the United States average)—pose especially important challenges to making any house in the Mid-Atlantic carbon neutral, let alone this house because of its large volume of conditioned space and its two electric vehicle (EV) chargers.

Four core elements were incorporated into the design and construction of the house to try and achieve carbon neutrality—energy efficiency, geothermal energy, solar energy, and battery storage. These are further explained below:[2]

- *Structural energy efficiency.* The house is well insulated but, then again, so too are most new houses. It's constructed with 2 × 6 studs, rather than 2 × 4's, and numerous, large windows (Andersen A-Series) comprise much of the exterior. The purpose of using

---

[2] See also the author's construction-period blog at www.BSAenergy.com/wordpress1.

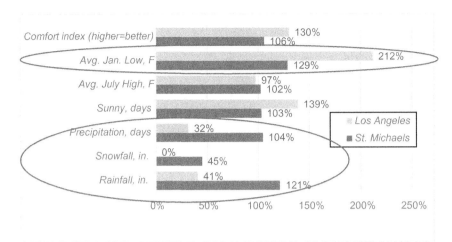

FIGURE 2.2   Climate in St. Michaels, MD versus Los Angeles, CA, as percentage of United States averages. Source: *Benjamin Schlesinger and Associates, LLC, from www.bestplaces.net.*

2×6's and a number of other reinforcing elements was mainly to protect the structure from sharp, sustained winds that emanate from time to time out of the Chesapeake's Eastern Bay, of which the property faces from the north, and other potential damage. Using 2×6 studs also allowed room within outer walls for double insulation, including 2″ of blown-in foam sealant and 4″ of fiberglass batting. Basement cinderblock walls were likewise sealed with 2″ blown-in insulation. Interior walls were insulated with rock wool, principally for sound, but also to improve control of room-specific temperatures. Wherever possible, empty spaces between second-floor ceilings and roofing provided further insulation of heated and cooled (conditioned) living spaces. Most of the energy insulation steps in the house were compliant with code, apart from added interior soundproofing, so none of these items are included in the cost of the energy systems.

- *Geothermal wells and ground-source heat pumps.* Eight 220′ deep geothermal wells were drilled in a rectangular grid beneath the front yard, with a network of 1″ feed pipes to extract and return a liquid glycol mix for heat transfer. Now that the front lawn has grown back, the geothermal wells and piping network can no longer be seen without disturbance to the property. Fig. 2.3 shows the geothermal drill site in front of the house in March 2018. This was a fast and efficient process, albeit a little messy, that derived substantial technology and practice benefits from hundreds of thousands of gas wells drilled not far from the region in the past decade.

Geothermal energy is gathered from the wells and delivered to two 4-t ground-source heat pump systems located inside the house. Developed in a joint project with the US Department of Energy's Oak Ridge National Laboratory and ClimateMaster, the "Trilogy 45" series equipment was selected because it was, and remains as of this writing, the most energy-efficient HVAC/hot water system available for residential use, based on any tech-nology or fuel, according to Energy Star ratings. Their 48.8 SEER rating is achieved

FIGURE 2.3   Geothermal well drilling site.

through numerous internal engineering design and equipment innovations, for example, variable speed fans and motors, and nine subzones throughout the house. By comparison, most other geothermal heat pumps are in the neighborhood of 20 SEER to 30 SEER. The Trilogy 45 heat pump systems are quite large as each includes an 80-gal hot water tank, but they are quiet and draw no outside air, so they're located within the house—one system is in the basement and the other is located in an upstairs closet. Household hot water supply is a byproduct of the Trilogy 45 system, thus no other water heating equipment is needed.

- *Solar PV panels*. Fifty 360-W SunPower PV panels (Model X22-360) are mounted on two nearly flat sections of rooftop and thus generally cannot be seen from ground level. When purchased in 2018, these were the most efficient PV panels available for residential markets in the United States—most other solar PV panels were rated at just below or above 300 W per panel. It was understood that, in order to hide the PV array from view for aesthetic purposes, rather than mount them on slanted sections of the roof, the compromise was that their placement on flat roofing would result in suboptimal performance. In other words a fifty 360-W panel array would optimally generate 18 kWh at peak, but this array will not do so because of its positioning. Nonetheless, the performance in the first year has been impressive, generating an estimated 20 t of carbon offsets in the first 13 months, according to SunPower's estimates, further discussed below.

FIGURE 2.4   Three Tesla "PowerWall 2" batteries on site.

- *Battery storage.* Three Tesla PowerWall Series 2 lithium-ion battery packs are installed in the garage, as shown in Fig. 2.4, to support energy needs of the house. With a combined storage capacity of 40.5 kWh, they store enough electricity to power the house comfortably through the night and, together with the solar PV panels, hopefully refill sufficiently during days, and so continue like this indefinitely. The likelihood of power outages in the vicinity of the house is surely nonzero given the severe winter temperatures and summer storm weather. Consequently, since they were installed in early January 2019, the three PowerWalls have almost always been kept in their emergency backup mode, that is, they're nearly always fully charged. Sure enough, they powered the house seamlessly during five brief power outages through mid-2019. Tesla's PowerWall 2 systems are charged preferentially with solar energy and can be operated in any of several modes other than backup that involve varying degrees and strategies for energy offsets and supply. Since they've so far only provided emergency backup power, however, their costs are not included in the carbon-neutrality analysis herein.[3] Future updates will focus on developing the best strategies to operate the batteries toward the goal of carbon neutrality while still providing emergency backup supplies of electricity.

In addition to the foregoing core energy components—efficiency, geothermal, solar energy, and battery storage—a number of other relevant elements were included and/or remain under consideration, as follows:

- *Deconstruction.* The property in St. Michaels had an older, smaller home already on it, owned by the late Rev. and Mrs. George Evans. Rev. Evans served as Chaplain of the US Marine Corp, and it seemed appropriate to honor his service and homesite in some

---

[3] The comparable installed cost of a gas-fired backup generator for this house would be approximately $10,000.

useful way. Rather than tear it down, therefore, the house was deconstructed, that is, literally dismantled down to (but not including) the floors, siding, and rafters. All were donated to the Choptank Habitat for Humanity. *Note*: Deconstruction is a new field and practitioners are hard to find, and harder to schedule, and hand done, so this process took about a month. The energy consequences of deconstruction are not known.

- *Propane*. Natural gas utility service is not available in St. Michaels. A 500-gal propane gas tank and distribution network are installed on the property, but gas is used almost entirely for nonenergy "cosmetic" purposes, that is, visible-flame appliances: cooktop, barbeque, and fireplaces. Also, the swimming pool is equipped with a propane heater which has never been used (although it might be used in the autumn). During the first year, an estimated 20 gal of propane were burned—all for the above cosmetic uses. Nonetheless, carbon emissions from propane combustion must be added to other carbon emissions caused by the house and its electricity supplies. More on this below. To clarify, for all intents and purposes, apart from cosmetic uses of propane, this is an all-electric house.
- *Swimming pool solar cover*. The property came with a 40′ swimming pool, but it was plastic lined and leaked badly. Rebuilding the pool and coping provided the opportunity to install a sliding pool cover that acts as a heat blanket, hence the loosely accurate "solar cover" term. As evenings cool, the cover is manually closed thus allowing pool water to retain direct solar heat from the previous day. This greatly reduces the need to operate the heater, which is likely to remain unused until the autumn, and then far less than otherwise. Subsequent iterations of this work will quantify the carbon savings of this equipment.
- *EVs*. The homeowners charge their EVs on a regular basis, so the house's garage is equipped with two 240-volt EV charging stations—one 80 amp Tesla wall connector and one NEMA 14−50 outlet. EV charging while at home is included in the numbers in this chapter, which amounted to about 2000−3000 mi of the 12,000 mi driven during the first year as defined in this chapter. EV charging draws a considerable amount of electric power, and this is particularly true for long-range Teslas. St. Michaels is located within the PJM region, and PJM reports fuels used to power the grid on an hourly basis. Numerous analyses have shown that carbon emissions from generating electricity used to charge EVs are lower than carbon emissions from comparable gasoline vehicles—no replication of those studies is presented in this chapter. For purposes of future analyses, therefore, most EV charging is excluded from the analysis of the house's carbon neutrality; instead, electricity used to charge EVs is considered to be an offset to gasoline usage for comparable vehicles.
- *Boating*. Thus far, the owners have not yet purchased a boat, so the house experiences no marine carbon emissions. As the waterfront depth is not sufficient to support a sailboat, the owners are considering a powerboat and are reviewing the options. Ethanol fuel for marine applications is unavailable locally and appears not to be advantageous to common gasoline motors. Biodiesel, on the other hand, operates quite successfully at various mixtures in most diesel engines and is available from agricultural and food processing enterprises in the region. There is a single diesel outboard on the market in the United States, Yanmar's 200 HP Dtorque turbo diesel outboard engine. The owner is continuing to review boat-and-motor options that would

involve the use of biodiesel in this equipment for pleasure craft to prevent the use of marine gasoline.

- *Lawn care.* With more than 2 acres of lawn, the house requires regular lawn cutting and treatment. For the first year a local lawn service has been retained that uses gasoline-powered riding lawnmowers. The owners are investigating the purchase of a lithium-ion battery-electric riding lawnmower that would be used for weekly cutting, for example, a Ryobi 42 in. 100 amp battery unit has recently become available at retail markets. This unit would be charged using the existing NEMA 14–50 outlet installed in the garage.
- *Water and sewer.* The property is served by municipal water and sewer systems and uses an on-site well for irrigation. The latter system draws electric power for an electric pump and, therefore, that demand is a part of the carbon analysis in this analysis.

2.4 Performance analysis: first year

As noted earlier, the overarching aim was to see if the homeowners could achieve carbon neutrality without sacrificing beauty, comfort, quality of life, etc., and without spending a fortune on equipment and installation. To determine if this experiment was successful in the first year, the overall analysis process is as follows (not all steps were completed in the first-year analysis):

1. Determine energy usage and consumption from the local electricity utility.
2. Quantify costs of electricity with versus without energy systems.
3. Assess avoided use of fuels used to produce electricity in the region.
4. Use the foregoing to develop a strategy for managing on-site battery storage.

Two sources of information about the house's on-site energy supply and demand are available:

- *Choptank Electric Cooperative,* the local electricity distributor, provides retail electricity to the house and engages in buyback of excess electricity generated on site. To this end, Choptank has installed a two-way meter. Choptank provides data on electricity quantities supplied, quantities generated, and the net of these two, on a quarter-hourly basis with daily and monthly aggregations. Choptank uses this information for billing purposes, so it provides the backbone data for this analysis. The geothermal wells are unmetered, thus no data are available for geothermal energy generated on site; this factor shows up simply as reduced consumption of electricity, much as insulation.
- *SunPower,* the manufacturer of the house's solar PV panels, provides raw electricity generation data on an hourly basis, with daily and monthly aggregations.

As yet, no further information systems are installed in the house that would add to the foregoing information. The Trilogy 45 installation includes prewiring for portions of an advanced home energy management systems (HEMSs) and incorporates HEMS features for all of its energy components. As described in the chapter by Damian Shaw-Williams, a broader HEMS could make it easier to monitor and optimize more of the house's energy systems, including utilization of batteries and EVs.

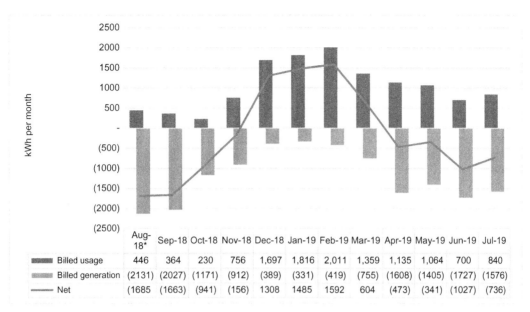

	Aug-18*	Sep-18	Oct-18	Nov-18	Dec-18	Jan-19	Feb-19	Mar-19	Apr-19	May-19	Jun-19	Jul-19
Billed usage	446	364	230	756	1,697	1,816	2,011	1,359	1,135	1,064	700	840
Billed generation	(2131)	(2027)	(1171)	(912)	(389)	(331)	(419)	(755)	(1608)	(1405)	(1727)	(1576)
Net	(1685	(1663	(941	(156	1308	1485	1592	604	(473)	(341)	(1027)	(736)

FIGURE 2.5 Billed electricity usage, generation, and net: first 12 months. Source: *Choptank Electric Cooperative, 2018–2019. Months refer to the preceding sixth day through the fifth day of the month shown. Asterisk denotes the full month consisting of July 12, 2018 through August 5, 2018 plus July 6, 2019 through July 11, 2019.*

Regarding the amount of on-site solar electricity generated, the foregoing two sources of information, Choptank and SunPower, disagree considerably, with Choptank's numbers consistently well below SunPower's. While some losses in conversion from DC to AC may explain part of the difference, other factors may be at work as well. In the discussions on this question with both Choptank and SunPower personnel, it seems possible that Choptank's consumption data might be partly understated so that the net numbers they report appear valid, but not the consumption or generation numbers, that is, some of the generation might be charged against some of the usage. This point remains open but, until it is resolved, this first-cut analysis relies on Choptank's billed kWh numbers, as summarized in Fig. 2.5.

Based on Choptank's numbers and billings summarized on a monthly basis in Fig. 2.5, the house appears to have been carbon neutral on an annual average basis in its first year. In other words, from July 12, 2018 when the solar panels entered service through July 11, 2019, the house generated about 2 MWh more electricity than it consumed for the full year. But Fig. 2.5 also reveals a clear seasonal pattern of electricity consumption and production that is not always carbon neutral in every time period:

- Starting from July 12, 2018, when the 50 solar PV panels went live, electricity generation in the summer and early fall far outstripped power demand in the house, which was mostly for cooling and construction equipment.
- Then, this pattern reversed during peak winter months, when the low sun angle and even some snow cover made solar less effective. Moreover, the 8-well geothermal

energy system was seasonally less productive as well, although the house's ground-source heat pumps still used much less energy than conventional heat pumps while also providing hot water.

- Then in late winter and spring 2019, the solar PV "power plant" was once again outproducing household demand, on average.
- Finally, through midsummer 2019, results were positive although less than expected with frequent thunderstorms, often hazy weather, and greater demand.

Carbon neutrality and electricity net-neutrality are equated in this study because Choptank derives its electricity supply from the PJM grid, which relies on coal and natural gas for a majority of its generation. Although the house has been carbon neutral in the first year, some grid power is required almost daily to keep it powered during peak winter months, as illustrated in Fig. 2.5. At other times, as described above, electricity is typically sold to the grid. Needless to say, if this house were located in Hawaii, Arizona or Iowa, for example, its performance, carbon neutrality, and battery storage–discharge pattern would be substantially different due to the different resource mix, solar insolation, and temperature variations in different parts of the United States. The same, of course, applies to other regions of the world.

Fig. 2.6 is especially interesting because it shows how coal and natural gas are used to produce electricity in PJM broadly throughout the afternoons and evenings during much of the year. This information will be key in formulating a battery deployment strategy that will enable this house to minimize system carbon emissions.

2.5 Rough-cut economic analysis

Initial year cash flows for the carbon-neutrality components of the construction are summarized in Fig. 2.7, which also projects a 15-year cash flow. The payback period is estimated to be about 10–11 years, with a 15-year internal rate of return of 5%. Amazingly, the total outlay for electricity was only $98 in the first year, which consisted of $13 per month fixed charges, minus the net of energy payments between the homeowners and Choptank Electric Cooperative, minus solar renewable energy credits (SRECs) sold. In addition to electricity the homeowners paid $32 for about 20 gal of propane used in cook-tops and occasionally fireplaces. Initial capital costs of $65,966 included solar PV system and upgrade to Trilogy 45 geothermal systems, after federal and state incentives, discussed further below.

How much does a comparable house in the area pay for utility bills? Points of comparison are difficult to define in an internally consistent way.[4] For a first-cut analysis that has meaning in the context of the author's experience, the comparison underlying this analysis is made between the house in this chapter versus the homeowners' previous house in Bethesda, Maryland during calendar years 2017 and 2018. Similar in size, occupancy, weather, and climate, the Bethesda house was built in 1991–92 as a natural gas showcase,

[4] The author declined in this analysis to attempt a with-versus-without carbon neutrality study within the same structure in St. Michaels because this would involve an uncomfortable level of guesswork.

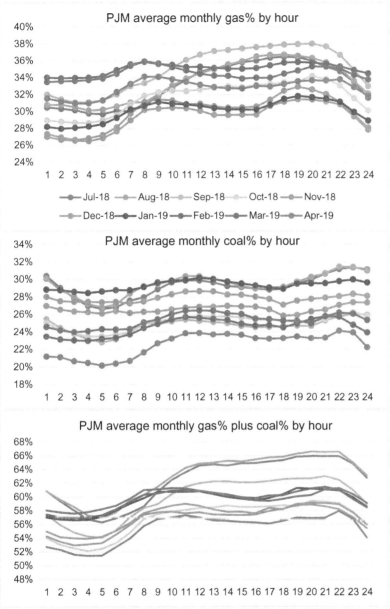

FIGURE 2.6 Analysis of PJM avoided fuels in annual and diurnal cycles in first year. Source: *Benjamin Schlesinger and Associates, LLC, from PJM.*

Source: Benjamin Schlesinger and Associates, LLC, from PJM

with 13 gas appliances, including the only residential compressed natural gas vehicle fill appliance in Maryland, in effort to reduce consumption of electricity and gasoline. The energy and other appliances in the author's Bethesda house were maintained/replaced on a regular basis. Insulation was R30 ceilings, R19 walls, which more than complied with

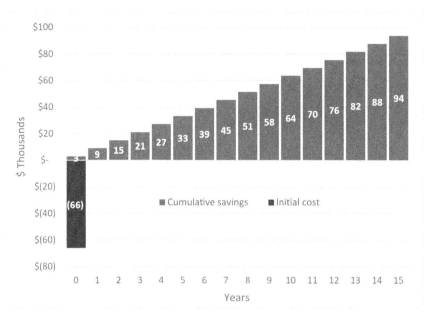

FIGURE 2.7 Cumulative cash flow projection, undiscounted. Source: *Benjamin Schlesinger and Associates, LLC, from Choptank Electric Cooperative monthly bills in St. Michaels, and Pepco and Washington Gas bills in Bethesda, and initial capital expenditures (see text).*

code at the time of construction. All considered, it was felt that the Bethesda house was a suitable comparison for the new St. Michaels house, thus the analysis results (Fig. 2.7) are based on that comparison.

Another meaningful comparison can be made versus energy costs and demand in the older, and 20% smaller, 43-year-old structure which previously stood on the same property. During the 7 months from April to October 2017, between purchase and deconstruction, that house consumed 14,082 kWh of electricity, costing $1892. This contrasts with 4337 kWh costing $91 in fixed charges less sell-backs and SRECs in the new, larger house for the same 7 months as they occurred during its first year. This 95% energy cost savings actually understates the ZNE advantage because, in addition to HVAC, lighting, the nearly all-electric kitchen, and other electricity appliances demand in the new house also included several dozen EV charges in these 7 months, and a far higher occupancy percentage. Outside temperatures and inside energy services were roughly comparable in both time periods. In all, the new carbon-neutral house consumed about 31% of the energy of the older, smaller conventional house, and its energy costs were only about 5% of the costs in the previous house. Because comparable months exclude winter, when the house's energy systems are the least effective (as discussed above), this comparison was not used in the economic analysis in this section. Nevertheless, both this and the preceding comparison points to how high the house's energy costs would be absent its carbon-neutrality features.

In addition, a number of other simplifying—perhaps "heroic" − assumptions underpin this initial analysis:

- Fuel prices and per-unit electricity costs, as well as the $13 monthly utility fixed charges, were assumed to remain constant for the next 15 years, that is, the same as they were in 2018−19. With significant surpluses of both natural gas and coal likely to persist for many years in the United States, this may be a reasonable assumption for a first-cut analysis. In addition, because of the continued outlook for low gas prices, the value of SRECs is assumed to remain constant at their presently depressed levels.
- As mentioned earlier, initial capital costs for SunPower solar PV and ClimateMaster Trilogy 45 geothermal systems in the St. Michaels house include a 30% investment tax credit and $4000 in Maryland Energy Administration grants, including $1000 for the solar energy system and $3000 for the geothermal energy system. The author received these incentives in 2019. This point is discussed further below.
- No degradation in either solar PV panel or geothermal system performance is assumed to take place over the life of the study. Although a 0.8% annual solar PV degradation is reported in older studies, SunPower advises owners of its X22-360 panels to expect annual degradation of 2% in the first year, and less than 0.25% per year afterward through year 25. Degradation information is unavailable for the geothermal systems. Future updates will test this assumption.
- As described above, three Tesla PowerWall 2 batteries were installed in the house in January 2019 and have been used in the backup-only mode since then, providing household electricity in several power outages. One of the goals of this analysis has been to determine the best way to use on-site battery storage to minimize carbon emissions on-grid. PJM's fuel use patterns shown in Fig. 2.6 suggest that one possible way to maximize carbon offset would draw electricity from the batteries as soon as the sun begins to set through till about 10:00 PM, that is, when PJM's generation from carbon fuels appears to be at its highest. Pending a closer analysis of this and other possible strategies, the costs and benefits of on-site battery storage are excluded from this first-cut analysis. During the house's second year, the author plans to test different ways to operate the PowerWall 2 batteries so as to minimize PJM carbon emissions.
- As discussed above, SunPower's electricity production data have been set aside in this first analysis; instead, the analysis relies on Choptank Electric Cooperative's billings and other reports reflecting their data on energy consumption and generation at the house. Further study and discussion with Choptank will hopefully yield a more comprehensive understanding of their information and why it differs so extensively from SunPower's data.
- Finally, as pointed out above, the homeowners often charged their EVs at the house during the first year, including during latter stages of construction on regular inspection visits. Since EV charging equipment was installed in autumn 2018, several EV charges per month have added about 700−800 kWh to billed electricity usage for the first year, a demand that is included in the numbers in Fig. 2.5. That's enough electricity to drive a Tesla roughly 2000−3000 mi—about one-fourth of the author's

annual mileage—the author's remaining EV charges were at his Washington DC area residences and at two Tesla superchargers en route the 90 mi between Washington, DC and St. Michaels.[5]

One potential caveat to this analysis is that the owners received their occupancy certificate in November 2018, partway into the first year as defined herein, that is, the first year of solar and geothermal operations. As construction neared completion in late summer and fall 2018, much of the effort moved indoors, consisting of finishing work inside the structure, thus HVAC and some other electricity demands are fairly similar to occupancy. In addition to HVAC, various power tools, vacuums, and other electric machinery were operated throughout the days, and the crew charged phones and computers in the house; however, there was little nighttime lighting, and the use of the kitchen had not yet begun. Fig. 2.5 shows that monthly electricity consumption during summer 2019 exceeded that of summer 2018, although demand in both summers was especially low for a 5140 ft^2 house. Future updates to this analysis will test the durability of first-year results.

2.6 Conclusion

Going back to the initial question in this chapter, is it possible to build a house that achieves carbon neutrality, and does so in an incidental way, so that, just build the house you want and pick the best off-the-shelf options currently available? First-year results of this analysis suggest the answer is yes, albeit with a 10 + -year payback, subsidies included. Like any analysis, there will be pluses and minuses. All other things equal, there would be a faster payback if/when energy prices are higher and/or with a price on carbon, but a slower payback without subsidies. Faster paybacks will follow as technology improves and equipment efficiencies improve, slower paybacks without geothermal energy from the earth. Faster paybacks with design optimization (pointing the PV panels toward the sun), slower paybacks if we include mobility (but other advantages would outweigh that). Moreover, some efficiency improvements will take place in front of the meter, as the electricity industry enhances the equation by installing renewable, noncarbon supplies for all to use, alleviating some of the householders' burden.

More important, can the author's apparent successful effort at building a carbon-neutral home be extrapolated to the state, the United States, or the world at large? And if it could, what might this imply? The answer may lie less in the numbers in this study and its updates and more on larger processes at work.

First, the issue of high up-front investment costs has plagued the renewables field for decades. Financial models to address the problem abound—utility cost sharing,

[5] There was no attempt in this study to carve-out EV charging from other electricity uses in the new house, so all that electricity demand is included in this analysis, and in Fig. 2.5. Note, the author's EV charges have taken place at various times throughout the day and evening, thus were not exclusively from solar energy; once the batteries are operated in a more concerted way, then EV charging may draw more specifically from solar power.

equipment leasing, vendor sharing/ownership of energy production, government grants and subsidies (which have benefitted this project), and numerous combinations of these and other concepts. Regulatory policies that accelerate the implementation of carbon neutrality can surely advance the field, as they do in California and an increasing number of other places, but some form of assistance will be needed if the timetables are aggressive, especially to enable market penetration at all income levels.

But ultimately, cost reduction is key. One old independent driller, the late Michael Halbouty, who chaired Pres. Reagan's energy transition team in winter 1980–81, was asked what's the best way to cure the nation's then-ailing energy industries. He famously answered with three basic strategies—"Produce, Produce, Produce!" History has shown Halbouty's advice to be literally prophetic for natural gas, and it's now proving true for solar energy and batteries as well, with massive production increases and improvements that are continually lowering PV panel costs and raising efficiencies. For example, SunPower has announced they're offering a 400-W PV panel in 2019— that's an 11% improvement in a single year over their industry-leading PV panels atop the author's St. Michaels house. Likewise, as pointed out earlier, drilling hundreds of thousands of gas wells in the US Shale Revolution have spilled over to benefit geothermal drilling, with lower costs, faster time schedules, and numerous refinements—this doubtless enabled the author's eight geothermal wells to be drilled and completed in about a day and a half, a process that used to take a week. The Halbouty lesson here is that solar and geothermal costs are declining so sharply that, at some point soon, the need for governmental incentives may be obviated, perhaps as early as in the 2–5-year time frame.

Who's leading, who's following? The author's house grabs attention for reasons having really nothing to do with energy. Its impressive solar, geothermal, and energy efficiency advancements are all hidden from sight—what people notice is its design and craftsmanship, inside and out, and the wide water views. In reality, most people look at houses and see things like location, size, structural, and interior design, how close are the schools—and of course the price tag! In fact, how many visitors climb into the basement or utility closets to check out advanced ground-source heat pumps, or up into the attic to observe shell-within-shell blown-in insulation? Not too many, beyond engineers and inspectors.

Can these dots be connected? The author hopes so. Indeed, to create change, as Tesla taught us, you've got to show beauty. Funny little electric cars were pioneering, but limited in demand, except the highly successful hybrid Toyota Prius. On the other hand, Tesla will likely produce its millionth car sometime in early 2020 selling at retail costs at least double that of the Prius. Likewise, the hope is that advanced energy technologies can be placed in houses that people need and like, even if they don't win architectural awards. The point is not only that a carbon-neutral house can be constructed but also a beautiful, livable, affordable house can be built where you want it, that's incidentally also carbon neutral. If and only if that's the case, in this author's view, then carbon neutrality can succeed in becoming a regular component of residential housing. ZNE codes can accelerate the process if they're developed and enforced in a way that engages the industry and pulls all income levels into the future.

One. Visionaries, dreamers, innovators

   The payoff would be grand. Residential structures in the United States alone produce on the order of a billion metric tonnes of carbon dioxide each year, including electricity generation used in homes plus other home energy consumption (EIA 2011, electricity adjusted downward by 20%). Replicating the success in other countries will add to the benefit. Keeping all that carbon out of the atmosphere could be one leg in the many-legged stool that may be needed to avoid, delay, or mitigate a climate disaster.

Creating value behind-the-meter: Digitalization, aggregation and optimization of behind-the-meter assets

Fereidoon Sioshansi

Menlo Energy Economics

3.1 Introduction

The subtitle of this chapter conveniently includes the 4 key words that essentially describes its content, namely:

- Digitalization
- Aggregation
- Optimization; and
- Behind-the-meter assets.

These, of course, are themes that are more extensively covered in subsequent chapters in this volume. And as reflected throughout the book, they capture some of the most important trends that are likely to transform the electric power sector, particularly its downstream segments including the distribution network, electricity retailing and the interface with the end-customers.

As further described in Sioshansi, Brown & Woodhouse[1], digitalization of behind-the-meter assets is likely to define the future winners and losers in the power sector. Digitalization is important because for the first time in the industry's history, utilities — as well as others — can not only remotely monitor and control customers' smart meters, but

---

[1] Consumer, prosumer, prosumager, F. Sioshansi (Ed.), Academic Press, 2019.

can increasingly do the same for individual devices within customers' premises as further described in chapter by Stagnaro & Benedettini.

The significance of digitalization and aggregation of behind-the-meter assets and emerging business models is further described in chapters by Poplavsaya & de Vries and Lehmbruck et al, where it is explained how loads, distributed generation and storage of hordes of customers can be pooled into a massive portfolio, which can subsequently be optimized, the next item on the list.

Optimization of behind-the-meter assets, further described in chapters by Lobbe et al, and Reijnders et al includes early attempts to implement such concepts in practice within energy communities. With so many moving parts in a large pooled portfolio of BTM assets, however, optimization can only be achieved by relying on powerful software including rapidly evolving algorithms using artificial intelligence (AI) and machine learning (ML).

Finally, it goes without saying that the focus of much of these efforts is on behind-the-meter assets — which have traditionally been ignored totally or for the most part by the incumbent utilities, who until recently had a monopoly on generating, delivering and serving customers. They never imagined that their hapless, captive and utterly passive customers would some day have a chance to, for example, generate, store and trade electricity with their peers let alone allowing others to aggregate, monitor and optimize their loads, DG and DS.

As further described in this chapter, peer-to-peer trading has recently been successfully demonstrated to be feasible on a localized distribution network, suggesting that — perhaps in the future — such mostly-autonomous local energy communities may be allowed to pay only, or mostly, for those assets that they utilize and not the rest of it. These are radical ideas not fully understood, let alone accepted by regulators, who, after all, must make sure that the rising numbers of prosumers and prosumagers do not adversely affect the ranks of the traditional consumers who rely on bundled regulated tariffs[2].

Not surprisingly, some incumbents in the industry are facing the grim prospects that many of their customers may part ways, relying on them mostly for reliability and balancing services but not necessarily for delivering many — or any — kWhs.

This chapter's main aim is to explore how value can be created in the process of digitalization, aggregation and optimization of behind-the-meter assets and who are the likely candidates to create, capture and monetize the value.

The balance of the chapter is organized as follows:

- Section 3.2 describes the digitalization of behind-the-meter assets;
- Section 3.3 explains how aggregation and optimization of digitalized BTM assets can create value; and
- Section 3.4 examines a few promising enterprises who are trying to create value by aggregating behind the meter assets followed by the chapter's conclusions.

[2] For further analysis of the likely developments refer to New Business Models in Electricity: the Heavy, the Light, and the Ghost, Nicolò Rossetto, Piero Carlo Dos Reis & Jean-Michel Glachant, June 2019, Florence School of Regulation.

3.2 Digitalization of behind-the-meter assets

Until recently, the best that could be hoped for was for every customer to have a smart meter allowing not only remote reading of the consumption but the ability to introduce real-time pricing (RTP), also known as dynamic pricing[3]. Since electricity prices vary by time of day and location, charging customers for how much, when and where they consume is much fairer and more equitable, topics that are further described in chapters by Stagnaro & Benedettini and Schittekatte, among others.

While smart meters are not yet ubiquitous everywhere, they are becoming more common in more places. But now, advances in information and communication technology (ICT) allow much deeper and more granular penetration — not just to meters but to individual devices within customers' premises, i.e., behind-the-meter assets. In this context, digitalization is not simply connecting gadgets and collecting much more granular data in real-time and location but collecting and analyzing the data and putting it to work to create value and offer new services.

There is universal agreement that the digitalization of the energy sector is likely to lead to new business models and new ways of thinking about delivering highly customized and targeted energy services to individual customers as further described in Box 3.1.

BOX 3.1

Next: Digitalization Of Electricity Sector[4]

Digitalization is the next big thing — in electricity and everything else

Digitalization is the latest buzzword these days. One often hears the term without knowing what it means, why it matters or how it will impact things — such as transactions in the electricity sector among sellers, buyers and — increasingly — between consumers in what is broadly referred to as peer-to-peer (P2P) or transactive trading. Everybody assumes that digitalization is inevitable, that it will improve delivery of services and/or lead to the introduction of new service options that are currently not practical, profitable or both. But beyond such generalities, it is hard to decide what to expect and when.

Jean-Michel Glachant and Nicolò Rossetto, both at the Florence School of Regulation, summarize their thinking in a policy brief, which identifies six fundamental building blocks that they claim will be driving digitalization and that can be used as an analytical compass to map the changes likely to occur in the electricity sector.

---

[3] For literature on RTP and TOU, refer to Ahmad Fauqui under publications at https://www.brattle.com/experts/ahmad-faruqui#publications.

[4] The digital world knocks at electricity's door: Six building blocks to understand why FSR Policy Brief, Jean-Michel Glachant and Nicolò Rossetto, 2018 at https://cadmus.eui.eu/handle/1814/59044.

BOX 3.1   *(cont'd)*

The 6 can be grouped in 3 categories as illustrated in the accompanying visual:

1. Infrastructure changes, which encompass the deployment of proper **digital infrastructures** internal to the otherwise bricks-and-mortar, or in this case poles & wires, networks;
2. Market changes, which include platforms for direct digital production and consumption or for interaction within two-sided markets; and
3. The digital frontier, which encompasses digital communities with dis-intermediated peer-to-peer (P2P) transactions, and virtual resorts with artificial intelligence (AI).

The first building block is the deployment of proper digital infrastructures, i.e., computer terminals, smartphones and telecom networks with the capability to transform data and pieces of information into series of zeros and ones that can be read, processed, combined, stored, transmitted, received and injected into a decision-making process, be it automated or managed by a human.

The second entails the deployment of smart infrastructures internal to bricks-and-mortar networks similar to efforts by airlines to digitalize their otherwise unchanged physical assets and operations. Examples include online sale of tickets and check-in procedures − allowing customers not only to buy and pay for services but to select their seats, pre-order dietary meals, or make sure the kids are seated with their parents without human interface. This, according to Glachant & Rossetto, represents a form of "back-office digitalization", where physical assets and their operation become smarter and may allow better and cheaper delivery of services that already exist today.

For frequent flyers, the airline reservation systems are a marvel to behold − when they work.

Smart infrastructures can also allow the delivery of innovative and highly customized services through transformative digitalization such as fast delivery of online shopping offered by the likes of Amazon and its Prime delivery service − which has

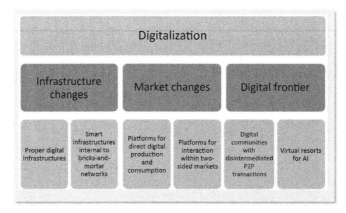

Source: 'Glachant Jean-Michel and Nicolò Rossetto, The Digital World Knocks at Electricity's Door: Six Building Blocks to Understand Why, Policy Brief 2018/16, Florence School of Regulation'

BOX 3.1   (cont'd)

changed customer expectations of what fast delivery is all about. Not surprisingly, Amazon is now entering the smart home space using its wireless Echo speakers and vice-activated Alexa personal assistant.

The third include platforms for direct digital production and consumption, where digital products are directly provided to consumers on platforms such as in Internet search engines, e-mails, instant messaging, data storage, digital maps, e-books, e-journals and online audio and visual products. In this case, consumers access information they need on a convenient platform — sometimes for a fee but most often in exchange for allowing the information provider to collect information on them — a controversial practice.

The fourth form of digitalization may be called platforms for interaction within two-sided markets. These platforms do not necessarily produce anything to be consumed directly but act as *intermediaries* that bring buyers and sellers of goods and services together even if the goods themselves are not necessarily digital.

Glachant & Rossetto distinguish these platforms into 2 categories:

• Low interaction platforms, which operate as a search engine coupled to a home delivery loop, such as Amazon's Prime delivery service, or a direct online service such as Apple Music; and
• High interaction platforms, which represent the backbone of the emerging sharing economy, allowing companies like Airbnb or Uber to thrive. These platforms not only offer useful information — which can be freely searched — but allow transactions such

as booking a room or a ride and paying for the service online, easily and without cumbersome paperwork or an annoying intermediary.

The fifth is what the authors call digital communities with dis-intermediated P2P transactions.

Glachant & Rossetto point out that individuals can eliminate intermediaries and third parties from their direct economic relations or interactions, relying instead on a *community* for the management of a common resource or the trading of a product or service.

Recently, new technologies like the much talked about blockchain, further described in chapter by Trbovich et al, promise to make the possibility of direct P2P trading, without a central clearinghouse or intermediary universal. The beauty of the distributed ledger at the heart of the blockchain technology is its ability to trace all P2P trades to where they originated in the network — allowing the members of the community to verify whether a transaction in fact occurred and keep track of the transactions and the settlement. If the many remaining challenges can be satisfactorily addressed, blockchain technology can revolutionize all sorts of transactions, and not just in the electricity sector. And that explains the excitement and hyperbole.

The final block in the visual above is a virtual resort for artificial intelligence, where individuals surrender their autonomy to the algorithms or the artificial intelligence (AI) that is managing the interactions among the members or visitors in the "resort."

BOX 3.1   *(cont'd)*

Glachant & Rossetto point out a subtle but critical difference between an energy "community" and what they call an energy "resort." In the former case, members of the community – say a retirement or gated community – collectively make the rules and force all newcomers to agree to abide by them. In the latter case, the resort owner/manager makes the rules and enforces them on all visitors. The visitors cannot change the rules. For example, when you visit Disneyland or go to an all-inclusive resort in the Caribbean, you must abide by the rules, say no bathing suit in the formal dining room.

As the authors see it, in such a digitalized "resort" the participants, allow the AI to take the decisions and manage the assets within the boundaries of the resort according to the rules and procedures defined by its developer, operator and manager. And this level of autonomy and centralization allows the developer to better manage and optimize the resort's facilities and assets – just as in a real resort.

While intermediaries are no longer needed in a digital community with disintermediated P2P transactions, a virtual resort with AI promises the replacement of people with machines. In this case, decisions and actions by the users cease to be necessary. Is that utopian or scary?

As more interest is focused on aggregating loads, distributed generation and storage, the aggregation and intermediation become critical and so will the rules and procedures to manage and optimize the portfolio of behind-the-meter assets – a recurring theme in this book. In fact, the virtual resort of Glachant & Rossetto is precisely what Sonnen is trying to do in its retirement community in Prescott Valley in Arizona[5]. By building a community from ground up, Sonnen, and others with similar plans, can manage the energy production, storage and consumption of the entire community including future electric vehicles, which can serve as both load and storage. And that is why having rules for the entire "resort" will be critical to better management of services.

The critical question is what to make of all this, especially the fact that humans may no longer be needed to do anything?

Glachant & Rossetto don't claim to know the full ramifications of digitalization but say the 6 identified building blocks offer a toolkit to identify the key issues at stake and where we might be going in the future by examining the ramifications of each of the 6 – some of which are more compelling and obvious than others.

The authors say digitalization involves transformative changes in the infrastructure and market arrangements that we rely on to produce, exchange and consume a large number of goods and services. In some cases, digitalization may herald the end of the traditional intermediaries and the active role of customers, at least in the way we know it. Artificial intelligence and machine learning is coming.

The 6 building blocks, they say, allow consumers, companies, regulators and policymakers to understand what digitalization entails, and to better prepare and manage the inevitable changes it will bring. ∎

---

[5] Refer to at https://www.prnewswire.com/news-releases/sonnen-powered-mandalay-homes-community-named-top-innovation-in-building-technology-for-2018-300763060.html.

Moreover, as explained in more interesting as consumers become prosumers – by investing in solar self-generation – and prosumagers – by investing in storage – as well as acquiring electric vehicles (EVs), another form of distributed storage.

What sorts of services can be offered and what sorts of value can be generated from digitalization of BTM assets? In a report published in 2017, the International Energy Agency (IEA) provides some answers[6]. Among the most valuable would be the most obvious and pressing, namely the ability to better manage not only how much energy is used by individual customers but by individual assets when and where. This allows for much better balancing of variable load and generation – a problem that is becoming more challenging since more generation will be coming from variable renewable resources.

According to the IEA, among the most obvious and valuable applications of digitalization in the electricity sector is the possibility to engage in demand response or DR. As millions of customers and billions of devices get connected, utilities as well as grid operators can better match supply and demand in real time as explained in Box 3.2.

BOX 3.2

88 GW Of Demand Flexibility by 2023[7]

Wood Mackenzie identifies big potential for DR in the US residential sector

In a recently released report, Wood Mackenzie says the US can have as much as 88 GW of flexible demand in the residential sector alone by 2023. US is currently far from such a target. What will it take to get there? Wood Mackenzie says grid-connected devices can help alter load shape, but the future hinges on customer demand, rate design and – most critically – regulatory incentives that allows the monetization of value.

Wood Mackenzie defines demand flexibility as the "ability of hardware and software to come together to create load shapes that are desired by utilities and market operators," adding, "Flexibility makes it possible to shift demand and harness **distributed resources** for the benefit of the grid, while also creating market opportunities for new types of companies."

It identifies two major trends as the main drivers of residential flexibility:

- First is the growing customer interest in smart home devices, home energy storage and electric vehicle charging, all of which can contribute significantly to flexibility;

---

[6] Refer to https://www.iea.org/digital/, 2017.

[7] Refer to https://www.greentechmedia.com/articles/read/88-gigawatts-by-2023-u-s-residential-flexibility-on-the-rise#gs.20rk97.

BOX 3.2   (cont'd)

- Second are changes in regulation evolving to enable flexibility beyond traditional demand response (DR) programs and new incentives enabling grid-connected behind-the-meter (BTM) devices to respond to price signals.

According to Fei Wang, a senior grid edge analyst for Wood Mackenzie Power & Renewables, "If you can achieve reliability and affordability using behind-the-meter resources, that's a success. But the right incentive framework needs to be there so that utilities can get a return (on their investment)."

The number of customer-sited assets is poised to grow quickly over the next 5 years. Residential energy storage systems and electric vehicle chargers are expected to grow rapidly. These BTM assets have significant potential to alter customer load shapes once enabled by proper regulatory incentives and price signals such as time-of-use (TOU) pricing.

Different types of BTM devices have varying capacities for responding to price signals or commands. For example, distributed energy storage can mitigate peak demand on the distribution network for short durations; distributed solar can be paired with distributed energy resources and smart inverters to respond to events on the grid while smart thermostats can be used to adjust HVAC energy consumption. Another promising area, of course, is EV charging and discharging, which can act as storage or generation depending on the case.

Regulatory incentives and innovative pricing will ultimately determine how many BTM devices respond to price signals on the distribution network as well as prices on the wholesale market. Wood Mackenzie identifies dozens of utilities in the US who have pilot programs that include incentives for investment in BTM devices including solar PVs, EV charging, distributed storage and smart thermostats.

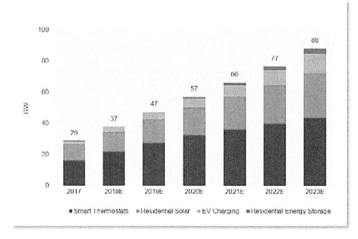

The more connected devices, the more flexible demand *Source: Wood Mackenzie Power & Renewables, GTM Research, Oct. 2018.*

BOX 3.2 *(cont'd)*

As time goes on, other regulatory policies will encourage more BTM assets to be technologically enabled to respond to price signals or commands. California and Hawaii already require distributed solar systems to be equipped with advanced inverter technology, which allows power production to be adjusted in real time. Such requirements will enable BTM devices to provide useful services such as voltage control and frequency stability to the distribution network.

Many BTM devices installed in homes have the potential to provide demand flexibility but are not currently used for such services. Enabling regulation is key to reach the 88 GW flexibility potential identified in the US residential sector, but it will take far more, including powerful software and

appropriate business models that allows for monetization of the value generated. Needless to say, the same applies everywhere, this is not a US-specific potential. At this point, it is not clear if the utilities/distribution companies will be able to capitalize on this enormous potential, or do little and thereby allowing newcomers to steal the show.

Wood Mackenzie says the ubiquity of smart meters and smart BTM devices offers opportunities for utilities to enroll customers in sophisticated load control and demand response programs allowing them to tap into flexibility behind the meter where devices can be remotely monitored and dynamically adjusted without affecting service quality. ∎

Despite the significant potential of demand response, thus far, DR has barely delivered compared to estimates of its expected potential for a variety of reasons further described in Box 3.3. One simple explanation may be that managing usage behind-the-meter has been difficult and expensive. This, of course, is changing.

BOX 3.3

FERC: Not Enough DR[8]

The potential for demand response is enormous and sorely underutilized

According to the Federal Energy Regulatory Commission's annual update on demand response and advanced meters released in mid-Nov 2018, the capability to

manage peak demand in the US wholesale markets grew 3%, roughly 27,541 MW, between 2016 and 2017 while the potential remains largely untapped. FERC also noted wide variations in the amount of demand response (DR) in the regional markets — with some ISOs/RTOs doing a far better job of acquiring and utilizing DR resources

---

[8] Refer to https://www.ferc.gov/legal/staff-reports/2018/DR-AM-Report2018.pdf and EEnergy *Informer*, Dec 2018, FERC: Not enough DR at www.eenergyinformer.com.

BOX 3.3 *(cont'd)*

---

than others. In a few cases, the amount of DR actually *dropped* — moving in the wrong direction.

FERC's report also provides details on the status of **smart meter** penetration across the US. It said that at the end of 2016, nearly half of the meters in the US were advanced with digital two-way communication capabilities. That means that 70.8 million out of 151 million meters in use, a 4% increase from 2015 to 2016.

(MISO) saw the biggest growth of DR in its market, increasing 9.7%, or 961 MW.

The FERC report also assessed the amount of total potential peak savings in the retail market in 2015–16, as well as the amount of DR from residential, commercial and industrial sectors. The total potential peak savings from combined retail DR programs across the country increased by nearly 9%, or 3,050 MW, between 2015 and 2016 with varying levels in different parts of the country.

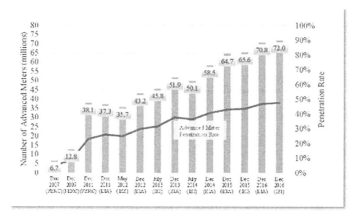

Electric meters getting smarter, slowly *Source: FERC Nov 2018.*

The California Independent System Operator (CAISO), for example, saw demand response participation in its wholesale market fall 2.6%, or by 187 MW, in 2017 while there was even a bigger drop of 6.5%, or 316 MW, in PJM's DR market. In contrast, the Midwest Independent System Operator

Residential demand response programs account for the largest portion of potential peak demand savings from the region encompassing the Western Electricity Coordinating Council (WECC) at 47%, 40% in the Midwest Reliability Organization's territory.

BOX 3.3 *(cont'd)*

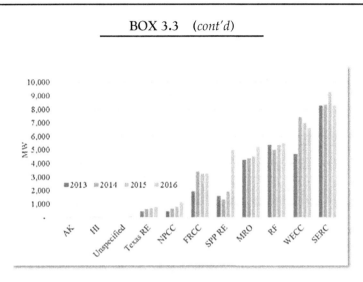

Far more DR potential mostly underutilized across the US *Source: FERC Nov 2018.*

Clearly, what is currently managed is a fraction of the potential for DR. If left on their own, utilities and even market operators do not appear to have sufficient incentives or motivations to capture more of the potential DR that is available — and by all indications cost-effective — in the various markets. Which leads to the conclusion that outsiders and newcomers are more likely to capitalize on the under-utilized DR and demand flexibility opportunities inherent in behind-the-meter assets. Regulations can boost the speed with which they can be managed, and new technologies will allow innovative companies to monetize the value. ∎

Two closely related and equally obvious digitalization applications further highlighted in the IEA report are

- The improved integration of variable renewable generation; and
- Better management of how, when and where electric vehicles (EV) can be charged and discharged.

The former saves fuel, avoids pollution while making better use of variable renewable generation[9].

With millions of future EVs expected in many parts of the world, the storage capacity of EVs offer attractive opportunities for grid-to-vehicle (G2V) and vehicle-to-grid (V2G) applications.

[9] Refer to EEnergy Informer, Apr 2018, RMI: More renewables, more flexible demand at www.eenergyinformer.com.

Increasingly, it is becoming clear that more flexible demand plus far more storage will be needed to maintain grid reliability and balance supply and demand in a future dominated by variable renewable generation.

In summary, the digitalization of behind-the-meter space has barely started suggesting that far more is likely to materialize in the coming years.

3.3 Behind-the-meter aggregation, optimization and value creation

The preceding discussion described some of the ways digitalization of behind-the-meter (BTM) assets can take place and some of the obvious applications. This section describes how value can be created and captured BTM.

The logic and attraction of aggregation should be obvious. The great majority of customers, aside from industrial and some large commercial customers, tend to be small both in terms of the number of kWhs consumed and their capacity requirements. The savings in monitoring and managing their individual usage tends to be small, even more so when looking at individual devices within their premises. Even with the falling cost of ICT, there are transaction costs to recruit customers to participate in, say, DR programs.

The key to unleash the value in most cases is to aggregate large numbers of small to medium sized customers into large blocks of load and capacity, which are worth monitoring and optimizing, as described in Box 3.4.

BOX 3.4

Who Will Capture Value Behind-the-meter[10]

Distributed energy resources growing faster than upstream infrastructure

The evidence that the place to focus on in the future is mostly behind-the-meter (BTM) is gaining momentum. In Sept 2018, Energy Post published an extensive interview with Jan Vrins, Managing Director at Navigant, a consultancy, which echoed many of the same themes. He said the much talked about energy transition, "... has already happened. We have entered a new world in which growth will come from distributed energy resources ..." including BTM products and services such as

- Energy efficiency;
- Rooftop solar PVs;
- EVs;
- Home storage; and
- Microgrids.

---

[10] Refer to https://energypost.eu/exclusive-top-energy-influencer-jan-vrins-navigant-europe-not-looking-enough-behind-the-meter/ and EEnegy Informer, Oct 2018, Who will capture value BTM?.

BOX 3.4   *(cont'd)*

Vrins added:

"Over the next 10 years, distributed energy resources will grow 8 times faster than net central station generation globally. In North America and Europe, growth may be even higher."

Jan Vrins described the rapid changes taking place in the energy market, focusing on what he calls the "Energy Cloud" – a "network of networks" which connects everything to everything else.

According to Vrins, "This development will change our entire energy system, how it's operated, who are the producers, who are the consumers – the whole dynamics. We project that it will create an additional $1.1 trillion in value by 2030 globally."

Clearly, new value is likely to be created – no one can be sure how much – and even more important, who will be able to capture it.

As the global electricity system is becoming more decentralized and more renewable, Vrins worries that, "... there seems insufficient awareness of how the system will change in its totality. Renewable energy is partly centralized generation. But the system will move to decentralization: distribution-level generation and a whole range of products and services behind-the-meter. The value will move downstream."

Vrins said that when he talks to utilities in Europe, "... they often tell me, 'we understand what you are saying, but we don't see business in it.'" He says this is a big mistake – missing the enormous shift in value moving downstream of the meter.

In the case of EVs, Vrins points out, "If all cars in the UK were EVs, together they will have enough capacity to supply the UK, France and Germany with electricity. It's an enormous capacity for storage and even for generation. If I drive home from work with my EV, my battery may still be 90% full. Most EV owners will only need to charge once a week. So this becomes an enormously valuable resource."

He is, of course, not the first to have discovered the enormous potential and perils of millions of EVs that are likely to be added to the distribution networks around the world over the next decade or two. Vrins sees opportunities for what he calls vehicle-to-home integration. "And this becomes even more interesting when you combine it with home energy management systems, including rooftop solar with storage, and demand response systems."

Vrins, like everyone else looking at BTM space, is keen on the potential role of intermediaries, aggregators and enablers – he calls them "orchestrators[11]" – and says this will be "the fastest growing and most profitable business model category across the utility value chain." Few would disagree.

---

[11] Refer to chapter by Poplavskaya and de Vries on "orchestrators".

BOX 3.4   (cont'd)

"The network orchestrator will have the key role of optimizing the use of all the assets in the system ... including linking the platforms with the centralized generation and distribution system."

As is generally agreed, Vrins notes that there will still be a role for centralized assets — the key is to integrate the centralized with decentralized assets in such a way that leads to optimal outcomes. This is particularly true in the developed economies where the existing centralized infrastructure, the gird, is functioning well and has already been paid for.

Who can best perform the crucial role of the orchestrator? Surprisingly, Vrins believes that the orchestrator role can be best performed by vertically integrated utility companies — virtually dead or dying species in Europe and many other competitive markets where regulators have split them apart.

Vrins says that in places where they still exist, as in many parts of the US, "The (vertically integrated) utility company is in the best position to decide, for example, where microgrids should be built and how best to connect them to the centralized system. If everyone makes their own decisions, the result will be suboptimal."

While few disagree with the suboptimal part, not everyone agrees that vertically integrated regulated utilities are the best to perform the critical — and potentially highly lucrative — role of the orchestrator.

There is no question that they *could* play this role, nor any arguments that they have access to lots of useful information on the customers and the intricacies of the distribution network, and that is precisely the reason why many would *not* necessarily want them to assume the role of the orchestrator.

Vertically integrated utilities are not generally known for being innovative or customer-focused, nor fast moving or technology savvy. Why would anyone want to give them a carte blanche to play the orchestrator's role?

In the case of Europe, Vrins says this role could be played by distribution system operators (DSOs), who would also have to be allowed to be active in generation and storage.

What happens to competition? Vrins says that, "... would take place in the products and services offered on the platforms", adding, "You would get a different kind of unbundling: horizontal instead of vertical." The strict unbundling rules in the EU, however, could hamper the development of an efficient "Energy Cloud" system in Europe, according to Vrins.

Vrins observes that over time, "distributed energy resources are becoming baseload and central generation is becoming backup" but says that is *not* how many are looking at it, nor do many "... recognize and capture the value of ... 'non-wire' solutions — local flexibility solutions." ■

There are clear signs that new business models are emerging to take advantage of opportunities in aggregation such as those highlighted in Box 3.5. The key to successful applications is smart software, artificial intelligence and machine learning, tools that allow remote monitoring, management and optimization of large numbers of assets possible.

BOX 3.5

New Business Models At The Grid's Edge And Beyond[12]

Clever entrepreneurs are finding value in most obvious places others missed

Not a day goes by without the news about a new start-up or one that has been around but flying under the radar appears in the press. Energy is a hot topic with lots of venture capital (VC) and other sorts of funding going into promising — and some not so promising — ventures to generate, store, trade or otherwise better optimize and manage its use. With so many to choose from, it is not easy to pick a winner, and in many cases, it is hard to know who the big winners may be.

Three "interesting" businesses are briefly outlined below, not in any particular order.

The first, is Open Utility (now called Piclo Flex, further described in chapter by Johnston & Sioshansi), a London-based start-up that has been around and growing. Its main claim to fame, is to bring a new level of price and cost transparency to the distribution network as well as the opportunity for generators, distribution companies and customers to trace how the power

flows and when and where the network may be congested.

Such information is critical in deciding, for example, when and where electric vehicles may be charged if you are in EV charging business. Similarly, distribution companies are keen to know who is consuming or generating electricity on the network and when. Regulators are increasingly interested to design more granular tariffs that accurately reflect the costs imposed on the network by different customers across the network and at different times.

In April 2018, Open Utility (now called Piclo) announced that it had formed a partnership with Scottish and Southern Electricity Networks (SSEN) to develop a smart grid platform that would offer flexibility services. SSEN maintains the network supplying over 3.7 million homes and businesses in central and southern England and Scotland.

As distributed generation (DG), electric vehicles (EVs), demand response (DR) and energy storage begin to be introduced, giving customers access to new products and services from new providers, the need for a

---

[12] Energy Informer, June 2018, New business models at the grid's edge at www.eenergyinformer.com.

BOX 3.5   (cont'd)

smarter, more flexible and more resilient distribution network rises. Distribution Network Operators (DNOs), Distribution System Operators (DSOs) or distribution companies – the acronyms vary from one place to another, but the fundamentals are the same – are increasingly looking for better ways to manage the flows across increasingly congested networks.

And as new types of services, such as peer-to-peer (P2P) trading and flexibility services evolve, there will be increased need for managing distributed generation and storage with variable demand at a local level. This reduces the need for upgrading the network potentially saving and/or deferring massive investments in so-called grid modernization projects.

The partnership with SSEN will trial Open Utility's Piclo platform, allowing the parties to procure flexible capacity from distributed assets on the network such as batteries and from DR aggregators to meet the *local* needs of customers.

Piclo's platform – like all platforms – offers a matchmaking service allowing localized trading of energy, capacity and other services among customers, generators and providers of flexibility services. Just as Airbnb's platform brings vacationers and homeowners with spare rooms together, Piclo allows participants to register their availability and preferences, and matches them with opportunities and services offered by the DSOs. Platforms will become increasingly critical.

In principle, the platform will unlock new revenue streams for homes, businesses and communities, whilst supporting the growth of DERs on an increasingly decentralized network.

Describing its main business function, James Johnston, CEO of Piclo, said:

> "Unlike other industries like short-term rentals and taxi services, the energy sector cannot be transformed by an online marketplace acting alone, but through meaningful partnerships with incumbents working towards a common goal."

In this context, platforms such as Piclo will increasingly be needed to manage the evolving needs of the distribution networks of the future who will be managing two-way flows and complicated transactions.

Another noteworthy company is OhmConnect[13], whose motto is "Save energy. Get paid." The company's business plan is that simple.

OhmConnect is in the business of encouraging and aggregating the energy-saving decisions of thousands of customers, mostly residential, since individual savings are too small to matter or bother with. The San Francisco start-up claims to have signed up 290,000 customers for its hour-long demand response or DR events. Distribution utilities pay for its services – which is aggregating the response of its entire community of customers at times of high prices.

In describing the company's business model, Curtis Tongue, cofounder of the

---

[13] Refer to https://www.ohmconnect.com.

BOX 3.5 (cont'd)

startup, explains that utilities have, for whatever reason, not managed to do a good job of doing what it does, except for large commercial and industrial (C&I) customers. Tongue says California's 3 large investor owned utilities (IOUs) Pacific Gas and Electric Company (PG&E), Southern California Edison Company (SCE) and San Diego Gas & Electric Company (SDG&E) were initially skeptical about OhmConnect's success but have changed their mind.

Like other enterprises offering similar DR services, OhmConnect monitors electricity prices on the wholesale markets and sends text messages — called *OhmHour* — to its members asking for energy-saving response — that is how the "Save energy. Get paid" works. Many customers can, and apparently do, respond — and get paid.

When customers sign up, they agree for OhmConnect to monitor their home's smart meter — virtually all homes in California now have smart meters. This allows the company to learn about their historical power usage patterns and establish a baseline for how and when they typically use energy.

Not surprisingly, OhmConnect has found that many customers — currently around 20% and rising — prefer to *automate* their response to the OhmHour signals — it is not worth the bother for most to monitor and manually respond given the meager savings. For example, those with smart thermostats such as Nest, can allow OhmConnect to remotely adjust the setting for an hour, the usual duration of an OhmHour. The same could apply to those with electric vehicles (EVs), with the signal warning them not to charge when prices are high, and/or the local network is congested — features that can become far more valuable as more customers invest in such devices.

The company takes a cut on the amount the utilities save — reportedly around 20%. The challenge, of course, is how to grow the customer base from 290,000 to millions — that's where the big payoff is. But, as one would expect, expanding the customer base has not been easy.

According to several articles in the press, the company is becoming more sophisticated in identifying customers who are likely to join and —more important — likely to save by participating in the scheme.

An important factor is that when customers sign up they agree to participate unless they *opt-out*. When an OhmHour alert arrives, customers have to decline, otherwise, it is assumed that they wish to participate. This means that some savings can be eked out of virtually all — and all receive at least a token reward for staying in the scheme. Apparently, customers get hooked to the rewards, even if they are not substantial. Who doesn't like to get something for doing virtually nothing?

Looking for a bigger customer base, the company is looking beyond California. The DR market is potentially huge — Grand View Research says it could be worth $36 billion by 2025. Tongue admitted that, "Consumer awareness is a significant headwind[14]," adding, "Most people are not

[14] Refer to https://www.fastcompany.com/40515338/this-startup-will-pay-you-to-use-less-electricity.

BOX 3.5   *(cont'd)*

aware in California that a company like OhmConnect actually pays out for saving energy. But we do see a lot of the market shifting to an energy sharing model instead of demand response on the commercial side."

If one strategy doesn't pan out, switch to one that does. That is how start-ups fine tune their business plans.

The final "interesting" start-up is another San Francisco-based company called Off Grid Electric[15]. As the name suggests, it offers off-grid solar electricity service as a solution to an unreliable or non-existent grid, mostly in remote and rural areas with little or no existing service. For many of the customers this is the first time they've been able to turn the lights on in their homes. As everyone knows, the first few kWhs of electricity — say to charge your mobile phone — are the most valuable. This typically starts a chain reaction that enables people to achieve other aspirations such as education, access to information, and more productive evenings.

After starting its service in Tanzania, the company has successfully raised additional funding to expand into other countries.[16]

With around 600 million people in Sub-Saharan Africa currently without power — over a billion globally — the off-grid solar market is a booming industry ripe with opportunity. Moreover, the founders of the company are not solely motivated to make money, but to uplift millions of people out of poverty by offering a highly valued service at an affordable price. Their services are aimed to serve the energy needs and income of their clients — they appeal and are affordable to almost any budget.

As described in an article in Bloomberg[17],

"Just as mobile phones bypassed landlines in developing countries, off-grid solar and battery systems are viewed a way to provide power to more than 600 million people in sub-Saharan Africa. The declining price of panels has allowed startups including Off Grid to offer consumers pay-as-you go leasing options that compete in price with traditional kerosene lamps and diesel generators."

According to Xavier Helgesen, co-founder and CEO of Off Grid, "The fundamental economics drive this all," adding, "I keep telling people that an electron from a solar panel is the cheapest electron you are going to find pretty much anywhere in the world."

Off Grid Electric's business model, called pay-as-you-go, is to lease sturdy, stand-alone systems that include solar panels, batteries, lights, mobile phone chargers and selected appliances. The lease model works

---

[15] Refer to https://www.greentechmedia.com/articles/read/55-million-investment-sets-new-record-for-off-grid-service-companies#gs.20z824.

[16] Its backers include a number of impressive brands such as Tesla, Total, Helios Investment Partners, GE Ventures and Electricite de France (EDF).

[17] Refer to https://www.bloomberg.com/news/articles/2018-01-19/san-francisco-startup-nabs-55-million-to-expand-solar-in-africa.

BOX 3.5 (cont'd)

since most customers cannot afford to buy the units outright. Customers make payments with mobile phones — and are cut off if they don't, which tends to encourage regular payments. In most cases, they own the units after 2–3 years of making payments. There is no metering, customers can use as little or as much as their small system provides and they can use it when they want since the battery offers service during nighttime. Thus far, Off Grid serves more than 150,000 homes and businesses in Tanzania, Rwanda, Ivory Coast and Ghana.

more than doubled from 2015 to about 1.5 million homes in October 2017 with more than $200 million in investments in 2016. Itamar Orlandi, an analyst with BNEF said, "Solar and storage kits are playing a transformational role in areas where power is either very unreliable or not available at all, which is the case in vast parts of Africa."

If there is a single common theme among the 3 companies featured here it is that in all cases clever entrepreneurs have found a viable business model built on

Off grid solar *Source: Zola Electric.*

According to Bloomberg New Energy Finance (BNEF), the number of pay-as-you-go home solar systems worldwide has

delivering value in niches where others had missed or did not realize any value existed. ■

While still in their infancy, the indications are that companies engaged in aggregation and optimization of BTM assets are successfully developing and applying viable business models and these developments are beginning to alter how energy services are delivered to customers including a host of new services such as demand flexibility and demand response, which were previously difficult and/or expensive to provide on commercially viable scale. Box 3.6 describes some anecdotal examples of how innovative aggregators are trying to create and monetize value behind-the-meter and how these efforts are likely to alter business fundamentals.

BOX 3.6

Aggregators To Alter Fundamentals Of Electricity Business[18]

Amassing large portfolio of loads, distributed generation and storage is key

If the number of prosumagers grows, as expected, they will no longer be dependent on net kWh purchases from the grid — in fact some may become net exporters. For prosumagers, the critical service provided by the network is no longer *energy* per se but rather balancing services, voltage and frequency support, power quality and, most important, service reliability. After all, prosumagers will not cut the cord as they continue to rely on the network during extended periods when there is no sunshine and their batteries dry up.

This fundamentally changes the value proposition for being connected to the network. It will no longer be about energy, the net kWhs, but about service reliability, not worrying about how much juice is left in the battery before the lights go out. It is the equivalent of *"range anxiety"* for current electric vehicle (EV) owners on a long cross country road trip.

In turn, this requires fundamental new thinking about the *value of service* and how much should prosumagers pay when and if they consume very few net kWhs, if any. In this context, volumetric tariffs make little

sense while reliability of service makes a lot of sense and has a lot of value. The grid becomes a form of insurance and backup for prosumagers who essentially operate their own mini micro-grids.

That, however, is not the end of story as two other developments are rapidly emerging:

- Aggregation and optimization of distributed loads, generation and storage; and
- Intermediation and peer-to-peer trading through open platforms.

The former is already here as businesses emerge to aggregate the distributed loads, generation and storage of multitudes of consumers, prosumers and prosumagers while remotely monitoring, controlling and managing the portfolio of assets in real time. This allows the intermediary not only to optimize the virtual dispatching of the diverse collection of resources but to *monetize* and *capture* their value.

Aggregation and optimization of massive portfolio of behind-the-meter assets is likely to grow as a business opportunity because individual prosumagers will have limited capabilities and/or financial incentives to mess around with capturing the modest value streams of their own mini

---

[18] EEnergy Informer, Apr 2018, Aggregators alter business fundamentals at www.eenergyinformer.com.

BOX 3.6 (cont'd)

micro-grids, creating a huge opportunity for the aggregators.

It is the equivalent of the powerful network effect in social media. Facebook or LinkedIn may not be the best, but who wants to set up a second social network when everyone is already using these? The exponential power of large numbers favors aggregation of massive portfolios. Scale matters.

Numerous companies have emerged in the past few yeas to take advantage of the collective capacity of hundreds, thousands — and in the future possibly millions — of diversified loads, distributed generation and storage. While the business models vary, virtually all are focused on remotely monitoring individual customer loads, generation and storage, managing and optimizing the aggregated portfolio and maximizing the inherent flexibility and diversity of the behind-the-meter assets.

By doing so, they can monetize streams or stacks of value

- By charging customers' batteries when wholesale prices are low, or discharging them when the opposite is true;
- By adding flexibility to loads by scheduling energy intensive devices or operations — say preheating or pre-cooling buildings depending on the prevailing prices; and
- By supporting local distribution networks at times and locations when/where they are stressed.

In theory at least, these and a multitude of other services can be offered at substantial cost savings to participating assets in the portfolio with little or no inconvenience or service degradation.

How? Through remote real-time monitoring of multitudes of devices on customers' premises, which can be analyzed and optimized by software using artificial intelligence (AI) and machine learning (ML). There is no other way to do it — the task gets quickly complicated.

Participating customers define their operating requirements — such as: I don't want the lights to go out during business hours, or the freezer to thaw, or the water storage tank to be empty or overflow, or the elevators to get stuck between the floors, or the warehouse get too cold or too hot. In practice, the software gets to know each customer intimately over time. Some fine-tuning may be required. But once the basic parameters are understood, the software essentially takes over, refining and optimizing so that the customers are not even aware that their operations and equipment are being remotely monitored, controlled and manipulated. Nor do they care that the aggregator is making money off the portfolio, so long as their energy service needs are met at a cost lower than they could do on their own.

The aggregator's business model, of course, is based on sharing a portion of the achieved savings from the optimized portfolio with the participating customers. It is win-win, indeed win-win-win if the benefits to the network are included.

How much can be gained and shared is an open question since many technical, operational, contractual and regulatory hurdles need to be resolved. And there are risks to all parties as investments have to be made in remote sensing, real-time communication, software development as well as taking measures against cyber-security and other risks. Most important, the participating customers have to get comfortable with the aggregators and vice versa.

BOX 3.6 (cont'd)

Opportunities in open platforms allowing peer-to-peer (P2P) trading and transaction energy – are likely to follow along with business models to monetize the value streams. While promising, they are mostly work in progress.

Eventually, the two approaches may merge. While some customers with certain applications – say an independent system operator (ISO) – may prefer to manage their own critical requirements – say optimizing the locational pricing interface with a distribution system operator (DSO) in real-time – using an open platform providing real-time locational price visibility – others may prefer to delegate the implementation details to a platform service provider who is better at it.

On that note, providing real-time locational price visibility on an open or public platform has already emerged as a viable business. Start-ups such as London-based Piclo[19] and its competitors are frantically exploring viable business strategies and service options. The key, as with everything else in business, is to find a way to make the service profitable by monetizing the streams of value in the value chain.

Whether aggregating and optimizing distributed assets or offering platforms with real-time locational price visibility, scale is critical to success since the values derived from individual transactions are likely to be modest at best.

It is fair to say that the focus of action is shifting from managing generation assets – much of it coming from variable renewable generation in the future and thus essentially unmanageable – to managing behind-the-meter assets.

Why has it taken so long for this realization to sink in? Partly because of inertia in an industry that is not used to innovating or taking risks and partly because regulators are even more risk averse – and possibly further behind in acknowledging the changes that are impacting the industry.

This explains why much of the changes expected are not likely to come from within the power sector but from outsiders, start-ups and newcomers who are not encumbered by the industry's lethargic culture or bound by the regulatory status-quo. They will, however, have to learn to deal with both. There is no easy way around that. ∎

While the types of services and how they are offered varies from one application to another, aggregators are increasingly zeroing on a handful of products or services with commercial value, such as flexible demand, frequency control, energy storage and similar services where they can be rewarded by the network and/or the grid operator or, in some cases, products in the wholesale market.

What is attracting many start-ups, of course, is the ability to scale up quickly once a viable business model has been created and the promise of high profit margins that may follow once they reach critical size. Moreover, successful platform operators reportedly manage decent profit margins – at least in other industries –as described in Box 3.7.

[19] Further described in chapter by Johnston and Sioshansi.

BOX 3.7

How to make a profitable business out of a platform or an app?

This was not an easy question to answer before Uber and Airbnb emerged as multi-billion-dollar companies

Recently many successful enterprises have emerged making good money by doing virtually nothing – by relying on others to do the work. For example, consider platforms offering flower delivery. They do not grow the flowers, nor transport them, nor make the flower arrangements, nor bother with the final delivery. They merely collect money and direct others to do the hard work. They need no assets, no hardware, no physical presence – which is why successful ones with massive scale can be enormously profitable. The same goes for airline and hotel booking platform operators, cousins of Airbnb.

Even more striking, however, are food delivery companies such as Just Eat in UK or its counterparts such as GrubHub, Delivery Hero and Takeaway.com. According to an article in the Wall Street Journal[20] (1 Mar 2018), Just Eat enjoys a 20% operating margin for doing virtually nothing. It offers a platform on which customers can order food from participating restaurants. As described in the WSJ article, these intermediaries

> "… make money by charging restaurants a cut of orders placed through their platform. The restaurants, for the most part, handle getting the food to the customer."

Amazing. No kitchen, no cooking, no physical assets, no rent, no hassle, no delivery and a 20% operating margin. Too good to last? The same article points out that, "Traditional platform need to invest in delivery or risk having their lunch eaten."

Delivery, especially for hot and perishable food, is – you guessed it – a capital intensive and low margin business. One option is to find other intermediaries to handle the drudgeries, say Uber Eats or its counterparts. Many restaurant chains, of course, have internalized the delivery service – such as Domino Pizza – where most of the business is take-away.

Why talk about flower or food delivery business in a book focused on the electricity sector? Because platforms will be coming to the electricity marketplace sooner than you may think, and they will eat the incumbents' lunch as has happened in other industries. ■

The difficulty, however, is how to get the "platform-based" business off the ground. The reality is that managing behind-the-meter assets, especially when dealing with millions of small residential customers with small BTM assets, is notoriously challenging. For example, the margins for monitoring and adjusting an electric water heater, is hardly worth the bother. This means that large scale is critical to a viable operation. The only way to succeed if that is all you are doing is to have a million or more customers. But that

[20] Food delivery gets a new threat, by Stephen Wilmot, The Wall Street Journal 1 Mar 2018, refer to https://www.wsj.com/news/author/stephen-wilmot.

means establishing a million accounts, settling and keeping track of millions of transactions — which entail significant transaction costs.

Another way to enhance profitability is to engage in *value-stacking* — which entails gaining the benefits of multiple sources of revenue rather than relying on a single revenue stream. An extreme case of value stacking is described in Box 3.8, where Sonnen, recently acquired by Shell, is developing an energy community with the intent of monetizing value from multiple sources by managing the entire community's loads, distributed generation and storage. For more on community energy opportunities refer to the chapter by Lobbe et al and Reijnders et al.

BOX 3.8

Sonnen To Synergize The Power Of Aggregation[21]

Intelligent storage is the centerpiece of a proposed scheme in Arizona

In mid-October 2017, German-based Sonnen (now part of Shell) announced it was embarking on an ambitious project with an American homebuilder in sunny Prescott, Arizona. The aim is to build a community of 3,000 homes capable to generate, store and share electricity in collaboration with Mandalay Homes. While the initial press release (PR) was rather short on specifics, it is not hard to read between the lines, so to speak. According to the PR, each home in the new community will have solar PVs on the roof plus a battery in the garage enabling every household to produce, consume and/or store most of its own electricity.

But in an added twist, that is common to others in this emerging field including Tesla Energy and Stem, the energy storage systems (ESS) in the homes will be *interconnected* and able to communicate with each other using the same technology that has already been used in similar experiments for power sharing in Germany. Sonnen calls it "sonnenCommunity." Think of it as an intelligent aggregated and enabled peer-to-peer (P2P) trading scheme where the participants are entirely passive. And that is the beauty of the idea: it does *not* require individual households to mess around with their thermostats, PVs, batteries or, for that matter, anything else. Sonnen will manage the whole thing for them.

What is the advantage of this clever twist? It turns the community of 3,000 homes into a virtual power plant (VPP) with an aggregated capacity of 11.6 MW and potential storage capacity of 23 MWh, according to Sonnen.

In this case, the batteries can store energy during peak production times — say sunny days of summer — and feed it back into the grid after the sun has set — and when peak demand typically happens these days.

---

[21] Refer to https://www.prnewswire.com/news-releases/sonnen-powered-mandalay-homes-community-named-top-innovation-in-building-technology-for-2018-300763060.html also featured in EEnergy Informer, Dec 2017, Sonnen: Power of aggregation at www.eenergyinformer.com.

BOX 3.8 *(cont'd)*

In California, for example, the utilities have re-defined the peak demand to be between 6–9 pm, not noon to 2 pm, as it used to be in pre-solar days. What is more, the VPP can offer services to the distribution network or the grid operator, relieving stress at times of peak demand. Schemes such as this will be sorely needed to cure the *California's Duck Curve* problem (visual below) or its equivalents now appearing elsewhere.

In announcing the venture, Philipp Schröder, Managing Director of Sales and Marketing at Sonnen said, "This is the city of the future, a place where all residents produce, store and share their own energy." Setting the PR aside, it is a brilliant idea whose time has arrived. Moreover, with the expected emergence of digitization and big data, the business model is ripe for implementation and scaling up.

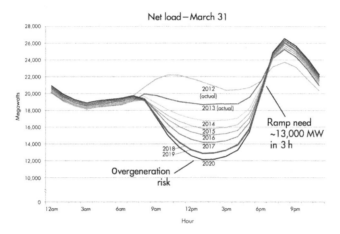

CA Duck Curve. *Source: CAISO.*

Such schemes typically include a smart home energy management system, which optimizes solar power generation, storage and consumption while communicating with the network all the time. There are significant synergies when the load, generation and storage of 3,000 homes are pooled together and collectively managed, optimized and ultimately *monetized.*

While Sonnen's community in Arizona is not unique, it clearly shows the growing role of storage in an integrated energy management system. And if you think aggregating the load, generation and storage of 3,000 homes in a good idea, think how much more can be done with a community of 30,000, or 300,000 or 3 million homes? ∎

3.4 Case study: Voltalis adds value by aggregating devices behind the meter[22]

While there may be many disagreements about the future transformation of the electricity sector, there is universal agreement that most future networks will have increasing amounts of variable renewable generation. And as the percentage of renewables rises above some threshold, say above 50%, the grid operator will be challenged to manage stability and reliability on the network.

In the case of California, it is the well-known *California Duck Curve*[23] — referring to the rapid rise of solar generation when the sun rises in the morning and the equally rapid drop of solar generation at sunset (Fig in box 3.8). In this case, the grid operator must quickly ramp down all dispatchable thermal generation to make room for solar output in the morning, while reversing the process in the evening once the sun sets.

In other countries, notably Denmark and Germany, variable wind tends to play havoc as wind generation rises and falls and cannot always be accurately predicted.

Aside from the challenges of managing the grid's reliability is how to manage large swings in wholesale prices due to supply and demand imbalances, a frequent problem. When generation exceeds load, such as during mid-day sunny hours or windy periods, prices on the wholesale market plunge, frequently going negative. On the other extreme, when there is no sun and/or no wind and demand is at its peak, prices spike. Finding ways to make good use of the price variations may be a challenge to some, but an opportunity for aggregators.

Historically, grid operators maintained a sufficient number of flexible resources, mostly gas-fired peakers, to fill in the voids in the variable renewable generation. These resources are expensive to maintain, are polluting when utilized and cannot perfectly make up for the fluctuations in variable generation. Batteries do a much better job of this but are not currently available in large scale on most networks.

This has created an opportunity for new players who can offer fast response to signals from the grid operator to ramp up or down *flexible demand*. It is nothing new, the essence of demand response (DR) or price-responsive demand — it goes by different names in different places.

But while the basics are well-known and have been tried in many parts of the world, DR has not reached the state of maturity to contribute significantly to stabilize the grid or to substitute for polluting peaking generation. This, however, may be changing for several reasons:

- First, grid operators increasingly need more *flexible* generation and/or *flexible* demand as the percentage of renewables on their networks continues to rise;
- Second, the technology to monitor and manage customer demand continues to improve and the cost of doing this has fallen; and

---

[22] This section is based on an article titled Time is ripe for aggregation of behind-the-meter assets, which appeared in the June 2019 issue of EEnergy Informer at www.eenergyinformer.com. It is based on details provided by Voltalis with special thanks to Pierre Bivas.

[23] Refer to https://www.caiso.com/Documents/FlexibleResourcesHelpRenewables_FastFacts.pdf.

- Third, regulators in more countries are beginning to realize that to maintain the reliability of future networks, new incentives are needed to enable flexible demand, distributed storage, and electric vehicles to more proactively participate in the market.

Among many newcomers trying to fill this void is Voltalis[24], a Paris-based company, founded in 2006, who aggregates and manages behind-the-meter customer assets. It monitors electrical appliances in homes and offices and delivers reliable, dependable, low-cost demand response (DR) services to the grid operator and/or to the wholesale market, as well as in the specific capacity mechanism. The company has attracted roughly 100,000 customers amounting to 300 MW of inexpensive capacity aggregated from roughly a million electrical appliances mainly in homes, but also in commercial premises, offices and various public and municipal buildings (Fig. 3.1).

In describing the company's business model, its founder, Pierre Bivas, says participating consumers essentially get *free* monitoring services and save energy, which reduces their monthly energy bill by up to 15%.

According to Bivas, the benefits accrue to others as well,

> "Companies in the generation business should also benefit from flexible demand participating in the market, as far as these companies adapt their range of assets and strategies. Indeed, DR participation in the market is a way to avoid volatility of prices — which is a risk for all market participants — and also, physically, a way to smoothen load curves, so that generators are used more efficiently. Not to mention that, thanks to DR contributing to the reliability of the power system, it will be easier for generators to get rid of their old, expensive and polluting power plants."

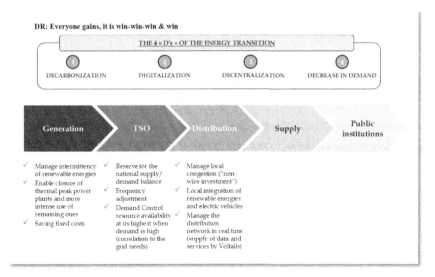

FIGURE 3.1   How Voltalis delivers DR.

[24] For further details visit https://www.voltalis.com.

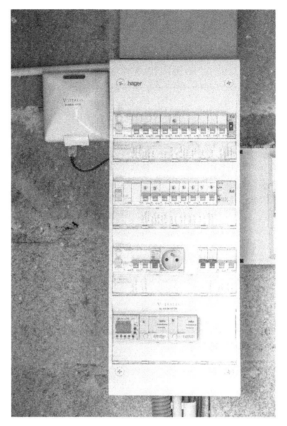

FIGURE 3.2   Typical Voltalis control device installation. *Source" Voltalis.*

Voltalis installs the monitoring devices (Fig. 3.2) and manages them free of charge. Customers share the *flexibility* of their consumption — which Voltalis aggregates and operates at scale without inconveniencing them. It sells these services to the grid operator and/or in the wholesale market, which provides a revenue stream. It is a win-win-win with benefits for all three.

Initially, the French network operator, Réseau de Transport d'Électricité (RTE), agreed to test the scheme's proof-of-concept in a trial. After a successful pilot project, where Voltalis demonstrated that it could effectively and reliably deliver balancing services to the grid, it gained confidence in the DR solution and the underlying technology. Voltalis' distributed demand response accounted for more than 80% of the DR volumes delivered in the French market in 2018.

Moreover, Bivas explains that the scheme also benefits *non-participating customers*, since Voltalis' intervention *reduces* electricity costs for *everyone*. Offering DR is far less expensive than paying generators to provide peaking capacity or flexibility services to the grid, there is less need for polluting generation and/or for grid reinforcements (Fig. 3.3).

So, what's there not to like? As it turns out, the generators, especially those with expensive and inefficient peaking plant, end up losing revenues since their services will not be

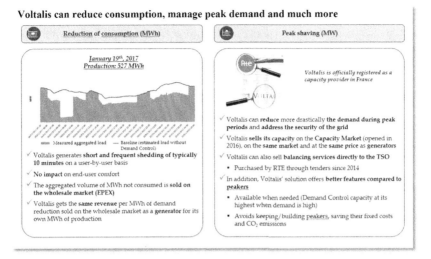

Voltalis can reduce consumption, manage peak demand and much more

FIGURE 3.3   How Voltalis reduces consumption especially during peak demand hours.

needed as often or they won't get paid as much as they used to before DR services became practical and affordable.

Despite occasional skirmishes with the generators who stand to lose as aggregated DR business models proliferate, Bivas is optimistic that Voltalis and others offering similar services will eventually prevail. After all, they offer a superior service at lower cost.

According to Bivas, after years of resistance from the incumbent generators, the French Parliament ruled in favor of the scheme followed, more recently, by supportive directives from the European Commission, who is eager to support the rapid growth of renewables[25].

Now regulators across Europe are receptive to similar business models (Fig. 3.4). Likewise, since 2008 the Federal Energy Regulatory Commission (FERC) has moved in the same direction in the US, forcing organized market operators to acknowledge the growing role of DR and — more recently — storage by allowing them to actively participate in ancillary services as well as in wholesale markets[26].

FERC says demand-side resources should be allowed to participate in markets as an alternative to traditional forms of generation — on their merits and without undue discrimination — based on their net benefits to all consumers.

DR and storage, both newcomers to the electricity business, are slowly finding useful niches in which to operate and generate viable revenue streams. With supportive regulations, far more can be expected in the yeas to come (Fig. 3.5).

---

[25] Art 17 of the recent Directive on common rules for the internal market for electricity (EU) 2019/944.

[26] Refer to FERC Order 745 at https://www.ferc.gov/EventCalendar/Files/20110315105757-RM10-17-000.pdf.

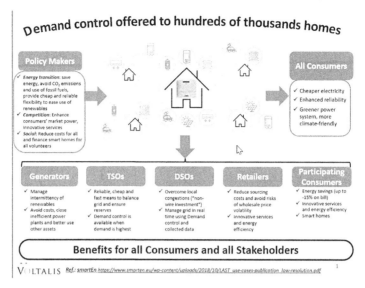

FIGURE 3.4   Aggregators need regulatory support and policy clarity to succeed.

FIGURE 3.5   Voltalis control center. *Source: Voltalis.*

Further elaborating on its business model, Bivas claims that Voltalis is mainly engaged in delivering *demand control* rather than traditional *demand response*,

> "The changes in demand are actually under control, so that they can be delivered in a market — and that the aggregator commits to deliver when he sells in the market, and is responsible for delivering accordingly, exactly as a generator would. Only when this is achieved does demand provide an actual alternative to generation."

One. Visionaries, dreamers, innovators

Moreover, Bivas explains that after working mostly on demand control and reduction, Voltalis has extended its solution to include control of various distributed resources including PVs and EVs so as to provide an overall optimization solutions (Box 3.9).

BOX 3.9

How is Voltalis different than traditional DR providers?

Voltalis claims to be rather different than traditional DR provides in a few subtle but important ways

According to Pierre Bivas, "Our experience suggests that a majority of consumers everywhere will gain from participating in such schemes, even for households who are not tech savvy since the provider will take care of the details."

In contrast to DR providers who primarily focus on aggregating large commercial and industrial (C&I) sector, Bivas believes that the residential and small commercial market offers larger opportunities. A report from the European Commission concluded that the residential is by far the greatest potential for DR, and expected to grow from 120 GW today to 160 GW by 2030. Similarly, studies by FERC[27] and others suggest substantial potential for DR in the residential and small commercial markets in the US.

Moreover, Bivas points out that

- Curtailing a manufacturing plant, for example, comes at a cost, because of the impact on the manufacturing process. This limits how frequently their critical loads may be curtailed. While DR based on HVAC loads in the residential and small commercial is basically energy savings without any change on comfort.

- This means that an aggregator of industrial DR is basically a trader, a middleman between the TSO (for balancing/ancillary services) and the manufacturing industries, who, practically speaking, operate DR in their plants — themselves, rather than the aggregator.

Mathieu Bineau, Voltalis' COO, who is leading the company's expansion, explained that while DR from large industrial customers may be called only in exceptional circumstances — e.g., in extreme peaks or emergency situations — DR as operated by Voltalis can be used daily, to reduce volatility either on the demand side or due to intermittency of renewables. The widespread use of DR increases the integration of renewables.

Both Bivas and Bineau point out that Voltalis is different since it invests in a network of devices to build and manage a large portfolio of distributed assets, which generates sufficient revenues to make it a viable business

Finally, Bivas claims that companies such as Voltalis can offer essentially a service free of charge to end consumers by managing how and when they use energy without inconveniencing them while providing flexibility to the network and the wholesale market. ∎

---

[27] Refer to FERC reports on DR potential in Box 3.3.

Needless to say, Voltais is not alone in trying to create and capture value in the behind-the-meter space. Others are trying similar approaches, which — like ice cream — come in a variety of flavors[28]

A variation of the above are a number of approaches focused on creating semi-independent communities of consumers, prosumers and prosumagers while offering clever ways for them to exchange or trade their surplus generation or storage capacity *locally* so that energy can be locally produced, stored and consumed.

Such schemes, if they can be successfully demonstrated on large scale, can upend customers' traditional interface not only with energy suppliers but also their reliance on the distribution and transmission network. Box 3.10[29] describes one example of such disruptive innovations that may become more widespread once regulation allows local and peer-to-peer trading.

BOX 3.10

Swiss Scheme Demonstrates Successful Peer-to-peer Trading

Trading excess generation to neighbors is no longer science fiction

By now, it is accepted that with the passage of time, more **consumers** will become **prosumers** — that is produce some or most of the kWhs they consume by generating it — typically by investing in rooftop solar PVs. **Australia**, for example, already has over 2 million solar roofs and **California** perhaps approaching a million. Depending on the size and efficiency of the panels and the amount of sunshine, many of these prosumers produce more kWhs than they need for local consumption during the sunny hours of the day.

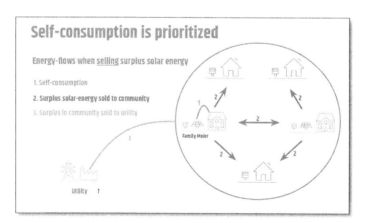

Source: Quartierstrom Project, ETHZ. www.quartier-strom.ch (direct link to the English version of the website ist: https://quartier-strom.ch/index.php/en/homepage/

---

[28] For example visit Voltus (no relation to Voltalis) at https://www.voltus.co and Extensibleenergy at https://extensibleenergy.com.

[29] Energy Informer, July 2019, Swiss scheme, page 16 at www.eenergyinformer.com.

BOX 3.10 *(cont'd)*

The excess generation can usually be fed into the grid — assuming there is a decent reward for the exported power — or can be saved in a storage device for use at later hours, say in a battery, in an electric vehicle (EV), in a hot water tank or similar devices. All of these options are being explored, especially if there are limitation on how much can be fed into the grid and/or if very little is paid for it during the sunny hours, when solar generation has little or no value.

This has led to a new idea. How about selling, sharing or trading the excess generation with a neighbor, perhaps one who can put the excess kWhs to good use, say to run its air conditioner, its pool pump, its Jacuzzi or charge its EV battery.

On the face of it, such peer-to-peer trading has many merits.

- First, it allows the locally generated electrons to be consumed locally — rather than overloading the local distribution network, which was not designed to handle such flows.
- Second, if the neighbors can agree on how much to pay/get for the kWhs

traded, then the retailer and/or the distribution company need not have to worry about such transactions, nor will there be any need for billing and settlements if the neighbors can amiably sort things out.

Complicated it may be but science fiction it is not. As reported in My EV, Your PV, Or The Other Way Around[30], variations of such P2P trading schemes already exist, such as a homeowner with excess solar generation offering some of the excess juice to anyone with an empty EV battery who can simply charge up from a private EV charging station in the driveway. This may not be strictly legal — certainly not encouraged under current regulations — but it is already happening. It is not fundamentally different than setting up a lemonade stand in the driveway. And should regulations allow such practices, it is likely to take off. Australia's 2 million solar PV owners are likely to start experimenting, especially since they are getting very little for feeding the excess solar into the network.

[30] Jan 2019 issue of EEnergy Informer at www.eenergyinformer.com.

BOX 3.10   (cont'd)

Source: Quartierstrom Project, ETHZ. www.quartier-strom.ch (direct link to the English version of the website ist: https://quartier-strom.ch/index.php/en/homepage/

Legal and regulatory barriers aside, how can future prosumers engage in P2P trading? Once the number of traders exceeds two, things get progressively complicated.

How can large number of consumers transact without going through a central clearinghouse – which will add to the costs and complexity? Can a community of like-minded consumers and prosumers set up a local electricity market for trading? Moreover, since the P2P trading makes use of the existing distribution network, how much should they pay so that non-participants are not adversely affected? And most important, how can traders in such a scheme settle among themselves in a way that is fair and reasonable, that is, pays those with excess power according to what they are willing to sell and charges buyers according to what they are willing to buy?

These are vexing questions that keep increasing numbers of researchers, academics and practitioners busy, including a group at ETH Zurich in a project called Quartierstrom[31] – it literally translates as district power in German.

For the demonstration, the researchers recruited 37 households, 27 of them prosumers, with 200 kW of combined solar capacity and 80 kWh of battery storage in Walenstadt, Switzerland. The households are in close proximity of each other and downstream of a transformer. The objective of the experiment was to engage the

[31] Refer to https://ethz.ch/en/news-and-events/eth-news/news/2019/06/quartierstrom-en.html.

BOX 3.10 (cont'd)

participants in local electricity trading without a central authority or clearinghouse, but rather relying on a distributed blockchain technology. The participants in the local market – consumers, prosumers and prosumagers – could trade with one another by setting price limits on how much they were willing to buy or sell for locally produced and consumed electricity.

Moreover, the research team came up with a *bottom-up* grid tariff, where traders would only pay a *reduced* amount for utilizing the *local* grid infrastructure but not the rest of it, that is the portion upstream of the transformer, which they did not use in the experiment.

It must be pointed out that the Swiss legislation – as well as regulations prevailing nearly everywhere else – currently does *not* allow for such a scheme where the local community only pays for the local portion of the network. For such innovative schemes to take place, regulations and tariffs must be modified[32].

The logic of the local grid tariff means that you pay less for the grid if you trade within the community, which incentivizes local generation, consumption, storage and balancing. You pay for what you use. Electrons remain in the neighborhood. Less energy losses, less pollution, less grid congestion. This, of course, does not address the biggest elephant in the room issue, which is who will pay for the grid if local energy communities avoid paying for some of the costs.

The scheme has successfully run since January 2019 without a central authority. It suggests that the idea *can* be scaled up on larger community level, according to Sandro Schopfer, the Quartierstrom Project Lead at Bits to Energy Lab[33], which is part of the Institute of Information Management at ETH Zurich.

In describing the proof of concept, Schopfer said, "Beside demonstrating the technical feasibility of localized trading, the project aimed to illustrate how current tariffs at the local level can be replaced with prosumer-friendly schemes for future ecosystems where localized trading is permitted."

The ETHZ researchers are now looking at a number of other issues including user behavior, acceptance and level of interaction with the system and pricing as well as ways to integrate flexible loads and making battery storage systems not only reduce exports at the household level but also at the community level to achieve higher self-consumption and self-sufficiency at the local community level. ∎

Clearly, as explained in chapters by Lobbe et al and Reijnders et al, the concept of local or community energy is in vogue and with advances in blockchain technology is likely to find new practical applications such as the one described in Box 3.10. Regulators will

---

[32] Andreas Bjelland Eriksen and Ove Flataker, Norwegian regulators, are cognizant of such issues as further explained in the book's Foreword.

[33] Refer to https://im.ethz.ch/people/sschopfer.html.

increasingly be confronted by new challenges on how the costs of the network are to be recovered by consumers, prosumers and prosumagers.

3.5 Conclusions

This chapter described why an increasing number of innovative companies are positioning themselves in the sweet spot where large numbers of behind-the-meter assets can be successfully aggregated, remotely monitored, managed and optimized, reducing energy bills for the participants while delivering valuable services to other stakeholders such as the network operator and/or the wholesale market.

While it is too early to say how widespread and successful they may be, the innovators in this emerging space intend to further disrupt the traditional relationships between the incumbents and consumers.

Many technical, regulatory and privacy issues remain to be resolved before successful and profitable players emerge, but already it is clear that many players are attempting to enter the field by amassing scale while creating and monetizing value, and many of the promising contenders are not from within the ranks of the incumbents.

4

Customer participation in P2P trading: a German energy community case study

Sabine Löbbe[1], André Hackbarth[1], Thies Stillahn[2], Luis Pfeiffer[2] and Gregor Rohbogner[3]

[1]Reutlingen University, Reutlingen, Germany [2]Elektrizitätswerke Schönau (EWS), Schönau, Germany [3]Oxygen Technologies, Freiburg, Germany

4.1 Introduction

In January 2021 the guaranteed fixed feed-in tariffs (FiTs), which were introduced 20 years ago in the German Renewable Energy Sources Act (EEG), will expire for the first renewable energy generation assets. Especially from 2025 onwards, the capacity of photovoltaic (PV) systems that is no longer eligible for EEG support scheme will start to increase dramatically, reaching the peak in 2030–33, that is, two decades after the solar boom period. It is estimated that by 2033 more than one million owners of small-scale PV systems may end up with stranded assets unless they find innovative solutions regarding utilization or sales of their electricity production (PWC, 2018).

A viable option is to turn these prosumers into prosumagers, that is, retrofit PV systems with battery storage, either stationary or in the form of electric vehicles to increase the customers' own consumption or take advantage of price differentials by storing some of the solar generation. Moreover, the rapidly increasing degree of digitalization, smart metering, and control technologies, accompanied by the increasing importance of local or regional production and self-sufficiency on the consumer side, open up further possibilities for innovative utilities to develop solutions for handling the surplus energy of small PV systems. Their market potential are additionally reinforced by the increasing number of households that are willing to forego fixed FiTs for renewable generation assets to be installed, mainly due to greater independence and lesser bureaucracy or taxation issues.

One of these potential options that are also supported by the European Union in the so-called clean energy package (EC, 2018) are local and renewable energy communities, that is, virtual and decentral market places for energy trading and sharing—either with direct peer-to-peer (P2P) transactions or via an aggregator (see, e.g., Löbbe & Hackbarth, 2017; Parag & Sovacool, 2016).

In all of these new local energy exchange services, private households need the support of service providers concerning implementation, platform provision, or regulatory requirements, including trading, billing, and balancing group management. These requirements offer an opportunity for innovative utilities to assist private households in becoming posumagers and/or to successfully trade or share their excess electricity generation.

The main focus of this chapter is to describe the development and practical test of such an energy community in Schönau in Southern Germany. This field test is coordinated and implemented by Elektrizitätswerke Schönau eG (EWS), a citizen-owned energy cooperative and one of the four largest green energy providers in Germany. The EWS project team is complemented by Oxygen Technologies, a software and automation company that contributes the P2P power-trading and control system, as well as Reutlingen University conducting consumer research. The latter aims at identifying private households' motivation and interest in participating in such energy communities and to evaluate attractive potential products and services.

The balance of the chapter is organized as follows:

- Section 4.2 provides a review of research activities and market developments as well as regulatory barriers concerning energy communities.
- Section 4.3 introduces in more detail the EWS energy community field test in Schönau, Germany.
- Section 4.4 covers the results of a Germany-wide survey on households' preferences for energy community characteristics.
- Section 4.5 describes the implications for the design of products and services derived from these results followed by the chapter's conclusions.

4.2 Energy communities: research, regulation, and market developments

4.2.1 Research results regarding energy communities

Scientific research and experimental field tests regarding prosumer-centric energy exchange markets have drastically increased in number in the recent past. Their main focus usually lies in the technological and economic evaluation of the feasibility and efficiency of different electricity market architectures and network or communication designs.

The scientific approaches comprise case studies, optimization and simulation studies, game theoretical concepts, as well as regulatory considerations. In general, the different concepts proposed and discussed in the literature and tested in the field can be differentiated by four major characteristics (see Espe, Potdar, & Chang, 2018; Mengelkamp, Diesing, & Weinhardt, 2019; Sousa et al., 2019):

- Spatial proximity between prosumers and consumers: Either the community is operated without connection to the public grid in the so-called island mode, or the actors are connected through physical or virtual microgrids, eventually enabling system services to the grid.
- Degree of decentralization and micro-market design: In most cases a community manager supervises the energy exchange within the community and mediates between the community and the energy system as a whole. An alternative design permits direct transactions between actors. Thus, peers negotiate and trade electricity with each other directly without centralized control.
- Transaction or exchange mechanism: Auction, direct trading, flexibility market, or others.
- Number and type of market participants needed or analyzed: Aggregators, prosumers, consumers, storages, other energy providers, grid operators, or others.

In conjunction with these diverse approaches and research objectives regarding platform-based energy markets, a plethora of terminologies has emerged including:

- clean energy community;
- community-based market;
- prosumer/energy collective or electricity prosumer community group;
- local energy market (LEM);
- crowd energy; and
- P2P electricity trading.[1]

In general, the underlying concepts are rather similar. However, in the absence of a universal definition, in this chapter, "energy communities" are considered to be virtual and decentral market places, enabling private citizens to trade and share electricity. In these market places, members do not have to be spatially close to each other or be physically connected via a local grid. This may rest upon exchange mechanisms supported by a central aggregator or upon direct P2P transactions. Members may have a say concerning the goals and actions of the community. This definition is in line with the European Directive and the descriptions outlined in Chapter 5, Poplavskaya and de Vries and Chapter 6, Reijnders et al. in this book.

4.2.2 Regulatory restrictions

Today, two main obstacles influence the viability and the success of P2P electricity trading: legal requirements for energy suppliers and the profitability after subsidies. Under the current regulatory regime in Germany, owners of energy generation assets automatically become energy providers if they supply end-customers with electricity. This role

---

[1] For more information, see, for example, Rathnayaka, Potdar, Dillon, Hussain, and Kuruppu (2014), Teufel and Teufel (2014), Ford, Stephenson, and Whitaker (2016), Moret and Pinson (2018), Sousa et al. (2019), and Mengelkamp, Schoenland, Huber, and Weinhardt (2019).

obliges to fulfill numerous legal requirements concerning billing, electricity labeling, reporting, and settlement. Consequently, the transaction costs are prohibitively high for small market players and intermediaries need to be mandated to execute these tasks. Hence, size matters to achieve a break even.

Currently, three options to market electricity from EEG-subsidized assets are available in Germany:

1. claiming the fixed EEG feed-in remuneration,
2. claiming the market premium in the market premium model (MPM),[2] and
3. direct marketing on the electricity wholesale market or over the counter (OTC) without support scheme.

Options 1 and 2, the EEG and the MPM options, require to pool the renewable energy in a separate balancing group. These balancing groups may not be settled with the electricity consumption of other community members prior to marketing it on the wholesale market. Furthermore, this renewable electricity loses its "flag" and turns into "gray electricity". This is a fundamental problem for energy communities, as prosumers are able to supply consumers with energy only if both are pooled in the same balancing group. Thus, the only possibility for prosumers to supply others directly with their electricity is option 3, selling the electricity OTC without support scheme.

However, directly selling electricity from assets can be disadvantageous:

• First, owners of these generation units have to forego the fixed FiT and depend on volatile wholesale market prices—a disadvantage which is obviously not affecting those generation assets that already dropped out of the EEG or MPM regime.
• Second, asset owners are required to quarter-hourly record and account the amount of electricity fed into the grid, which requires sophisticated and comparably expensive metering hardware. However, in the course of the planned smart meter rollout in the upcoming years in Germany, significant cost reductions can be expected.

Thus, the most important target groups for energy communities today are the customers running out of the FiT support scheme and those planning a new installation.

4.2.3 Current market players

Recently, several platform-based local electricity markets and community approaches have emerged around the world (see Park & Yong, 2017; Zhang, Wu, Long, & Cheng, 2017). In the German electricity market a number of players have recently started to commercialize platform-based and partially blockchain-based electricity products with community characteristics. These players are characterized in Fig. 4.1.

A first group of suppliers offer so-called "prosumage" and "self-sufficiency"-oriented products, such as EnBW's "Solar + ", EWE's "myEnergyCloud", and SENEC's

[2] In MPM operators of renewable energy generation >100 kW are not payed a fixed FiT, but a market premium for each kilowatt-hour they feed into the grid and sell on the electricity market. The market premium equals the difference between the technology-specific FiT and the average technology-specific market price for electricity (BMWi, 2019).

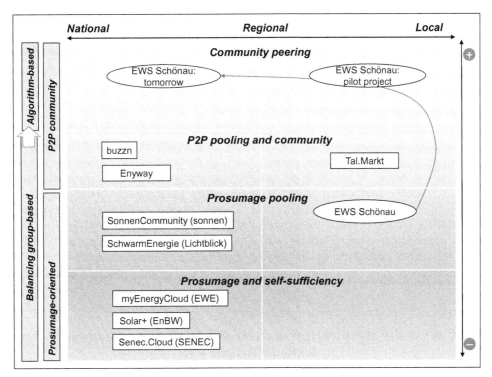

FIGURE 4.1 Selected market players in German P2P electricity markets.

"Senec.Cloud". Prosumagers can deposit excess electricity into a virtual electricity account—for example, in summer—and withdraw electricity if needed—for example, in winter. Each prosumer operates an own account and energy is not transferred between prosumagers. Consequently, there is no interaction within a community as defined in Section 4.2.1. More often than not, all prosumers obtain the same technology, for example, battery storage. The main value proposition of suppliers in this segment generally is to maximize the customers' own consumption.

The second group "prosumage pooling" encompasses prosumager-only communities such as LichtBlick (SchwarmEnergie) and Sonnen (SonnenCommunity). They pool prosumagers in a nationwide community. Currently, suppliers manage these communities centrally with controlling software and a trading algorithm. A so-called community manager delivers additional services such as trading with third parties, providing residual power and managing the balancing group. Customers' batteries often serve to provide ancillary grid services. However, as long as the customers' assets are subsidized via the EEG FiT regime, prosumagers do not supply one another with energy directly, for reasons described in Section 4.2.2, but via trading on the wholesale market. Therefore, prosumager-only communities currently do not constitute communities in the strict sense either, even though their main value proposition is to share excess electricity within the community.

In the third group "P2P pooling and community", suppliers enable consumers to individually select a specific local producer or generation unit who then directly supplies them without intermediary. This incorporates local platforms—such as Wuppertaler Stadtwerke (Tal.Markt)—and national platforms—such as buzzn or Enyway. EWS's activities currently also belong to this group, as described in the following. Consumers obtain digitalized information regarding their chosen producers and assets. An important goal is to establish an emotional connection between consumers and producers. However, the main value proposition for consumers is the liberty to choose and obtain direct supply of renewable energy with proof of origin. Hence, the idea of several members sharing energy with each other does not apply here either.

To summarize, none of the currently existing products and services in Germany offers both aspects, locality and community, as main value proposition. Thus, EWS's energy community field test in Schönau is the first German energy control and trading system which enables a citizen-owned, transparent, digital platform-based, and regional power supply via a prosumer community. It was specifically designed to gain practical experience with the direct marketing of distributed electricity resources. In the next section the field test is outlined.

4.3 Case study: the Elektrizitätswerke Schönau eG peer-to-peer energy community field test

4.3.1 Field test: objectives, partners, and approach

For testing real-time electricity sharing in prosumer communities, EWS (Box 4.1), headquartered in Schönau, started a field test in 2017. EWS customers within the own distribution grid in the small town of Schönau as well as in surrounding grids are participating.

Launched in 2017 with a planned project duration of 5 years, the project serves three main objectives:

1. Continuously test a broad variety of technologies, including generation, storage, and meters from different manufacturers under different conditions, for example, different ages of dwellings and electrical installations and different distribution grid operators.
2. Test the integration of diverse devices into the optimization software of Oxygen Technologies (Box 4.2), which includes the processing, transmission, and forecasting of data, in order to test different energy community models—from centrally controlled to P2P energy exchange.
3. Develop products and services for sharing electricity, compatible with EWS guidelines of being a sustainable solidarity community.

Twenty seven single family houses, a farmer, and four apartment buildings with landlord-to-tenant electricity supply participate in the Schönau field test. They represent 20 prosumers, based on 4 PV assets installed before the year 2000, 4 electric vehicles, 1 agrophotovoltaics system, 8 cogeneration units, 15 battery storage systems, including 11 lithium iron phosphate (LiFePO$_4$), 4 saltwater, and 1 redox flow battery shown in

BOX 4.1

Elektrizitätswerke Schönau eG (EWS)

EWS is a citizen-owned energy cooperative located in Schönau in the Black Forest, Southwest Germany. EWS originated in the purchase of the local power grid by a parents' initiative in the 1990s. Shaken by the Chernobyl disaster in 1986, the initiative took up the fight against the nuclear industry and the monopoly of the local energy supplier. EWS was founded to buy the power grid and to put its operation into the hands of the citizens of Schönau. With the liberalization of the German electricity market in 1998, it became possible to supply customers outside their own service area. EWS seized this opportunity to offer the first nationwide 100% green electricity tariff. Since then, the number of customers continuously increased and EWS developed into a vertically integrated utility. Today, EWS is one of the four largest suppliers of green energy in Germany with over 200,000 electricity and gas customers throughout the country.

In addition to grid operation in Schönau and the nationwide supply of end customers with green electricity, EWS owns and operates several larger wind and PV assets in Southern Germany with an installed capacity of over 20 MW. These include the highest wind farm in Germany at the time of construction in 2017. Moreover, EWS owns and operates several local heating networks, forming the infrastructure to enable a regional and sustainable heat supply, supporting cooperation and engagement with and between the citizens.

The initial vision of a sustainable, climate-friendly, and citizen-owned energy supply is constantly to be transferred to the needs and opportunities of energy transition. Therefore, with the upcoming digitalization, EWS acquired a share in Oxygen Technologies, supporting the access to tools necessary to transfer the idea of decentralized and citizen-supported energy supply into the future electricity market. The Schönau field test is part of EWS's pathway into the future. ∎

Fig. 4.2, as well as more than 35 kWp additional PV installations. All of the households and systems had to be equipped with smart meters and controllers.

Within a cooperation structure depicted in Fig. 4.3 the partners realize the different tasks in the field test. EWS coordinates the project and offers products and services to the customers. Thus, EWS forms the link between customers and various suppliers and service providers. This includes energy data management and energy economics, bundling assets, such as storage technologies from different hardware manufacturers, new intelligent measuring systems to be developed by the measuring point operator, and new software units and data analytics, plus the integration of these components. End customers test these different packages, concepts, and ideas during the field test. Oxygen delivers the fair trade mechanism explained in Section 4.2.3.

To ensure value creation for the customer, participants get involved in continued innovative and explorational workshops. This allows the cooperation partners to learn

---

BOX 4.2

Oxygen Technologies

Oxygen Technologies is a software and automation company offering IT solutions for the digital transformation to both existing and potential future energy providers. The company was founded as a spin-off of Fraunhofer ISE in Freiburg, Germany in 2016. In June 2019 it employed 35 people with a core expertise in energy informatics, technology, and economics. All four company founders hold a majority share and work actively in the company.

Oxygen Technologies offers a peer-to-peer power-trading and control system, including the software. Via the companies' platform ELEMENTS, prosumers and consumers can establish an energy trading community in which every member can directly trade power with each other in an efficiently automated way. Oxygen Technologies provides its ELEMENTS platform as a white label solution to community managers.

The algorithmic basis of their product has been conceived and tested by the Oxygen founders at Fraunhofer ISE in Freiburg. The technology is currently being put into operation with EWS's customers—prosumers and consumers—in the field test. This way, EWS is both investor and customer of Oxygen Technologies GmbH. ∎

FIGURE 4.2   Saltwater battery installation in participating household.

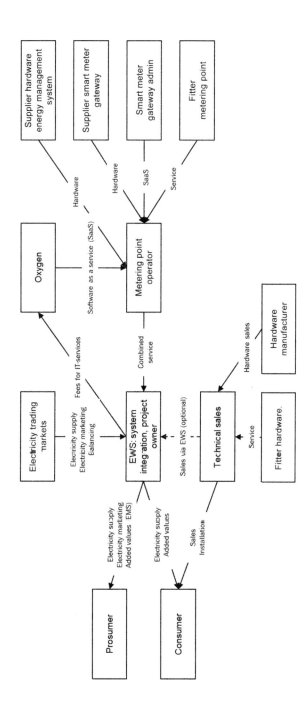

FIGURE 4.3 Contributions of main cooperation partners within the EWS P2P energy community field test. *EWS*, Elektrizitätswerke Schönau eG; *P2P*, peer-to-peer.

from their preferences concerning service packages, data privacy, or data visualization and to exchange experiences (Fig. 4.4).

The Reutlingen Energy Center for Distributed Energy Systems and Energy Efficiency, Reutlingen University (Box 4.3), accompanies the field test with academic research focusing on consumers' preferences and experiences. This comprises the generation of input for and moderation of the aforementioned workshops as well the realization and interpretation of a nationwide survey as described in Section 4.4.

Together with EWS and its cooperation partners, the researchers specify target groups for different products and service bundles and help to define unique selling propositions.

FIGURE 4.4 EWS P2P energy community field test: workshop with prosumers (top), developed ideas for visualization (bottom). *EWS*, Elektrizitätswerke Schönau eG; *P2P*, peer-to-peer.

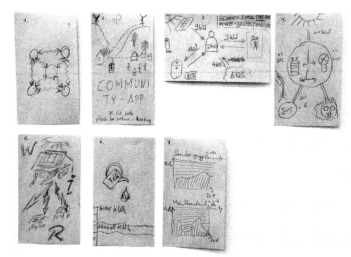

BOX 4.3

Reutlingen Energy Center for Distributed Energy Systems and Energy Efficiency, Reutlingen University

In the Reutlingen Energy Center, 12 professors with a staff of 18 employees teach in a master's program and research on distributed energy systems and energy efficiency. Research is focused on integrated solutions regarding technical, economical, entrepreneurial, and societal issues. Facilities include laboratories such as a virtual power plant, PV, cogeneration and thermal storage, smart metering and smart grids, as well as supporting control and steering devices, software, and IT. Regarding energy economics, the focus is on applied research regarding:

- strategic, organizational, and behavioral issues of energy efficiency;
- prosumage, nonsumage, peer-to-peer-trading, and energy communities; and
- products, services, business models, and strategies regarding distributed energy systems and energy efficiency. ∎

Through the continuous feedback loops customer-friendly products can be developed and simultaneously tested in the field.

EWS's P2P energy community field test started with two **preparatory phases**:

1. In the first phase, prosumers and prosumagers are pooled into a joint balancing group, as described in Sections 4.2.2 and 4.2.3. This allows private customers to supply each other with electricity at balancing group level within the energy community. As pooling small and volatile generation with consumption in a joint balancing group is not common practice, the field test aims at implementing and rigorously testing all processes related to this task.

2. In the second phase, the production and consumption of each customer is recorded at one minute intervals. The data are aggregated and processed in a cloud and returned to the customers via a responsive web app. The choice of information to be depicted and the form of visualization is based on the consumer preferences gathered in workshops and surveys as described in Section 4.4. Thus, the app provides customers with tailor-made information on real-time production and consumption (Fig. 4.5). The users can switch between two views: the minute-based status of their own energy production, storage, consumption, and export to or import from the community, as well as the corresponding data for the community. The objective at this stage is to offer a benefit to participants and to learn about customers' interest in and usage of information regarding energy exchange.

These preparatory phases are followed by three **implementation phases** in which three different community options with varying degrees of decentralization of control are tested (Fig. 4.6).

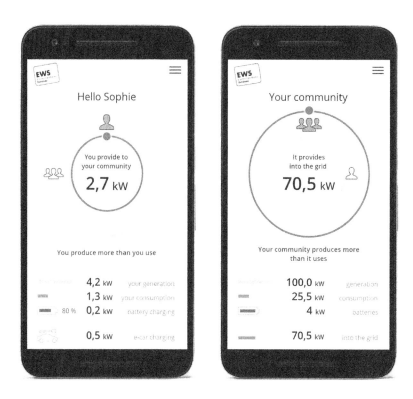

FIGURE 4.5 EWS's P2P energy community field test: mobile app visualization. *EWS*, Elektrizitätswerke Schönau eG; *P2P*, peer-to-peer.

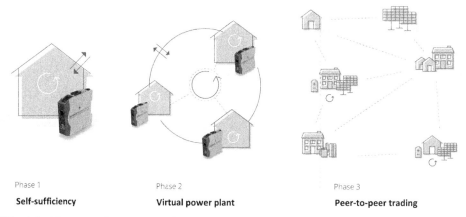

FIGURE 4.6 Three implementation phases in the EWS P2P energy community field test. *EWS*, Elektrizitätswerke Schönau eG; *P2P*, peer-to-peer.

1. **Phase 1, self-sufficiency:** In the first phase, assets installed, such as PV systems, battery storage, and charging stations, are centrally controlled. The underlying optimization logic considers each of the customer's assets independently and maximizes the respective own consumption. Excess production is made available to the community and shortfalls are covered by EWS.
2. **Phase 2, virtual power plant:** In the second phase, the community is optimized as a whole and battery storage systems feed into and out of the grid bidirectionally. Other flexibilities, such as combined heat and power assets and charging stations, are integrated, taking the respective asset constraints into account. The objective is to maximize the community's degree of autarchy or revenues.
3. **Phase 3, P2P trading:** In the third phase, the so-called fair merchant mechanism (FMM) allows optimizing the community without centralized control. Instead, microcontrollers independently communicate from peer to peer, being able to take participants' individual preferences into account. The mechanism is described in Section 4.3.2.

As Fig. 4.6 indicates, the number of communication connections and, thus, the number of data multiplies from phases one to three. To manage this complexity, systems such as the FMM are essential.

4.3.2 Peer-to-peer energy trading: the "fair merchant mechanism"

In Oxygen Technologies' FMM—a P2P power-trading and control system—every member of the energy community can act as a trading partner with equal rights. This enables prosumers and consumers to buy and sell power among each other automatically and without having to involve any middlemen. The FMM auction algorithm was developed at Fraunhofer ISE in Freiburg, Germany and is specifically optimized for the requirements of energy trading. It gets along without a blockchain-based technology.

The data are collected in Oxygen's cloud-based IT platform ELEMENTS, and the status of power demand and supply is updated every minute. The operator, EWS, accesses the platform through a hardware based two-factor authentication. To implement the FMM the ELEMENTS Gates—small embedded computers—are connected to the meter cabinets or straight to the renewable energy units of the respective energy community members. The FMM algorithm is implemented on the ELEMENTS Gates.[3]

Hardware security chips ensure that high IT security standards are met. Furthermore, they are operated in a secure virtual private network and monitored and fed with updates.

Several technologies have been developed to implement a decentralized energy trading system. These include highly performing P2P communication between the ELEMENTS Gates, a consensus procedure, and middleware for communication in the field to implement the various protocols of the energy devices.

---

[3] https://www.oxygen-technologies.de/fair-merchant-mechanism/

A coordinating algorithm determines the physical balance between consumption and generation. Coordination can be centralized and decentralized, with the latter being realized in the P2P concept. As described above, the coordination algorithm is distributed across all installed ELEMENTS Gates in the community members' households. Every minute the ELEMENTS Gates send a bid to the community for the amount of energy needed in the respective household or the amount of energy the household can offer. The bid also includes the demanded or offered price for the electricity. The price for each bid is calculated based on the expected consumption, the fill level in every storage facility, and the prognosis of the available generation units, and other factors. When calculating the bids, the ELEMENTS Gate also considers the customer's preference, such as maximizing own consumption, economic optimization, or maximizing convenience. The community member can communicate this via apps, such as the "EWS-Community-App."

After every ELEMENTS Gate has put forward its bid the clearing algorithm is executed every minute by a stochastically defined decentral ELEMENTS Gate, which produces a uniform exchange price on the community micro-market. Thus, all community members buy or sell energy for the same price. Depending on this clearing price, the ELEMENTS Gates switch generation and storage units off or on, until a new time interval starts to determine and execute selling or buying prices and procedures.

4.3.3 Preliminary experiences

A number of challenges have to be addressed before successfully operating an energy community. Broadly speaking, these challenges can be divided into technical, energy-economic, and communication issues.

The following very practical but crucial technical challenges have been experienced:

1. As some manufacturers do not open up the interfaces to third parties, the external control of these assets is impossible. Consequently, if the IT service provider is unable to remotely read or control data of an asset, this asset cannot be integrated into the central optimizer. Hence, EWS provides its customers with a whitelist of technology to ensure that only controllable assets are installed. Unfortunately, however, through this customers owning assets with closed interface are initially excluded.
2. By German law, electricians are obliged to ensure existing as well as newly installed circuits are state-of-the-art when installing new technology in the electrical system of a customer's home. That is, the electrician can be held liable in the event of any damage related to the electrical home system. Consequently, the electrician normally insists on updating the electrical system before installing new assets, inducing additional expenses for the customer. Ultimately, this may turn out to be a deal breaker for the customer.
3. While guaranteeing a standardized and stable communication via the customer's internet connection, problems may arise due to low data volume capacity, insufficient data throughput, or the customer's interruption of the internet connection resulting in a failure of the communication between the home energy system and the central optimizer.

As far as the energy-economic challenges are concerned, the main problems relate to the interaction between EWS, the respective distribution network operators (DNOs), and the metering point operator (MO)—a fairly new market player who operates the electricity meters in competition. These challenges encompass the following:

1. The re-registration processes for small PV systems: For a PV system to be included in the energy community, it must first be moved from the EEG balancing group to the community's balancing group. To this end, EWS sends a message to the corresponding DNO—a process that is neither automated nor standardized.
2. The transmission of load profile data to the DNOs: After successfully re-registering a PV system to the new community's balancing group, the MO transmits load profile data of the generation asset to the DNO every 15 minutes with a smart meter gateway (SMGW). Since today's SMGWs are at the beginning of technical maturity, data transmission problems regularly occur. For the same reason the SMGW administration software is prone to errors.
3. The complexity of managing the community's balancing group: If the actual energy demand and supply of the many small-scale, weather-dependent assets deviate from the forecast, the energy supplier—EWS—has to pay for the required balancing energy. Therefore, advanced forecasting methods are required. In the worst case, that is, persistent nonmarginal deviations between forecast and actual load, the transmission system operator (TSO) may even close the energy community's balancing group.

Overcoming these challenges of course offers some added value for EWS, as learning to develop energy data and portfolio management in decentralized energy systems is a core competence for the future.

On the other hand, the customers must be informed about the particularities of the specific community and its operating principle in an understandable way. As surveys and everyday practice show, customers express a high trust in EWS which certainly helps to master this challenge.

4.4 Customer preferences: results of a nationwide survey

To obtain a realistic view of the market potential and challenges of energy communities, an online survey was carried out in July 2019 among 1000 private households in Germany. The aim was to analyze consumer preferences regarding energy communities in general and their specific attributes in particular. The results of this survey are supposed to allow the deduction of conclusions regarding products and services in Section 4.5.

The survey was representative of the German population regarding gender, education, and federal state, with the great majority of participants being consumers (95%), of whom roughly 6% are planning to install a power generation asset in the upcoming 2 years. Comparable to the German population, about 5% of the respondents in the survey are prosumers already, of whom 2% are planning to install a further power generation asset in the upcoming 2 years.

Currently, only 3% of the respondents are familiar with the concept of energy communities or know about specific offers that are presently available. This lack of familiarity with the concept is one of the greatest barriers for energy communities and, thus, has to be tackled by EWS's marketing strategy in the future.

Respondents would be most willing to participate if the energy community is operated by a municipal utility, followed by offers from a regional energy provider, eco-energy provider, large, nationwide operating energy company, and energy cooperative, with internet, tech, or telecom companies being the least preferred providers (Fig. 4.7). Since EWS is organized as an energy cooperative, operating as large eco-energy provider with nationwide customer base but also serves as a municipal utility in Schönau itself, thus combining many of the different roles, this result is good news for EWS.

The vast majority of survey participants prefer local or regional energy communities. Respondents would mainly participate if they would not pay more than in their current

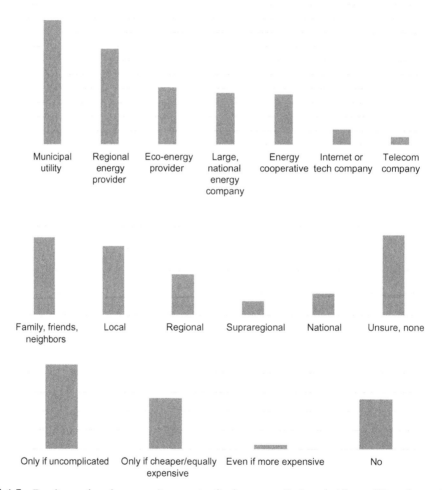

FIGURE 4.7   Results: preferred community operator (top), community type (mid), conditions for participation (bottom)—relative results.

electricity tariff or if the process of changing to this new option would be easy, that is, supported by an all-inclusive care-free package. Only a small minority would switch even if energy communities were more expensive, while about one quarter of the respondents is reluctant to participate in any case (Fig. 4.7).

Moreover, respondents rate costs as being by far the most important factor of energy community services, followed by the availability of a web portal, for example, for billing purposes, the utilization purpose of revenues, for example, distribution to members or donation, the regionality of the energy community, the self-sufficiency or autarchy rate of the energy community, and the codetermination in the energy community.

Compared to those not willing to participate, respondents who are open toward energy communities are higher educated and home owners. They prefer local or regional energy communities and rate the costs, autarchy rate, energy mix, pioneering character, possibility to exchange with other members of the community, and codetermination in the energy community as most important characteristics. They are more interested in energy community product if it is offered by a regional utility, eco-power provider, or energy cooperative and less interested if large national energy companies and municipal utilities are its providers.

These findings are broadly in line with and extending the results of five empirical scientific studies analyzing the motivators of private households to participate in virtual, platform-based energy communities or LEMs. Mainly conducted in Germany and Switzerland (with between 154 and 4148 participants), the main conclusions of these studies can be summarized as follows (Gstrein, 2016; Hackbarth & Löbbe, 2019; Mengelkamp, Schoenland, et al., 2019; Mengelkamp, Staudt, Gärttner, Weinhardt, & Huber, 2018; Reuter & Loock, 2017):

- Energy communities/LEMs are comparably unknown—only about 15% of respondents are familiar with it—but the concept is generally highly endorsed by respondents.
- Except for being middle aged, better educated and living in larger, urban households, interested and uninterested individuals are relatively comparable concerning other sociodemographic characteristics.
- Economic aspects dominate the willingness to participate, although energy community size and locality, comfort, technical security, data privacy, interaction frequency, customization, transparency, supplier, and the electricity source also play an important role in the decision process.
- Intangible values like emotions and trust, community identity, lifestyle, such as sharing or being an innovator, price consciousness, energy consciousness and knowledge, peer effects, and attitudes, such as environmental awareness, technical interest, or independence, are considered to be the most important factors for participation.
- Potential participants are more likely to be prosumers or individuals planning to purchase further technological devices.

EWS is currently developing product and communication strategies based on these findings, differentiated for consumers, prosumers, and those planning to buy decentralized production or storage assets. Obviously, all customer groups demand products and services that are easy to understand and not more expensive than their current electricity supply. Beyond customer surveys, the market for energy community products is being shaped by market actors like EWS. Therefore, strategic perspectives are outlined in Section 4.5.

4.5 Future product development for energy communities

Eventually, managers of smaller utilities might point out: "What do we need energy communities for? We already are one!".

The mission of German local and regional utilities basically is to deliver security of supply, public services, and local welfare for all, which already reflects a specific degree of community spirit. The problem, however, is that innovation and disruption do not stop only because incumbents think they do their best. And in highly competitive markets, such as the German energy market, the decision-making power is with the customers and not the utilities. Thus, innovation challenges solutions that were considered appropriate and sufficient in the past. This is why EWS and their partners work on the aforementioned innovative solutions.

From a technological viewpoint the implementation of local, regional, or national communities is feasible even within the current German regulatory framework—although it is not an easy task. From a marketing viewpoint a customer segment interested in energy community products exists, as the field test, characterized in Section 4.3, and the survey results, described in Section 4.4, demonstrate. Based on these results, products and services can be shaped. The three implementation phases in the EWS P2P energy community field test, developed in Section 4.3, can serve as a structure to develop different products with value propositions for specific target groups and the potential for further differentiation, as described in Fig. 4.8.

4.5.1 Community with focus on individual self-sufficiency

In the first option, EWS controls prosumage assets on the customers' premises centrally, aiming at maximum self-sufficiency. The excess production is made available to the community and shortfalls are covered by EWS. Thus the product encompasses the optimization of own consumption and the delivery of the residual load—prioritizing supply from within the community, if available, before purchasing the remaining load in the wholesale market.

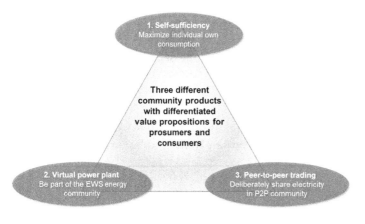

FIGURE 4.8 Main value proposition of the three different community options.

Renewable generation assets, for which the fixed FiT has expired, are able to deliver low-cost electricity which can be redistributed and branded as regional electricity.

The main target group of this product should be "self-sufficient", that is, prosum(ag)ers owning some kind of energy generation and/or storage system who are willing to pay for a certain degree of autarchy and independence.

The benefits for customers encompass cost reduction, since own consumption generally is cheaper than electricity from the grid, the increase of self-sufficiency and independence from large, faceless companies, the participation in an energy community, the possibility to support decentralized, local energy producers, the transparency of energy flows and provenance, and/or the delivery of residual load from regional green electricity.

Moreover, future chances for further differentiation exist, including decreasing costs for smart meters triggered by their rollout in Germany which could enable an affordable infrastructure for a multitude of applications behind the meter, such as smart home, smart living, smart assistance services, and home energy management ecosystems—see Shaw-Williams in Chapter 7 and De Clercq et al. in Chapter 14 for more details. This could especially be attractive for prosumers which usually are technically interested innovators as they installed their PV systems already two decades ago.

4.5.2 Community with focus on virtual power plants

A virtual power plant is designated to optimize the generation portfolio and consumption of community members as a whole so that the community's degree of autarchy or the overall revenue is maximized or the environmental impact minimized, as presented in Chapter 10 by Lehmbruck et al.

The main target group mainly consist of "cooperators", that is, prosum(ag)ers and consumers attracted by engaging in an energy community and interested in the self-sufficiency of the community, the codetermination, and the possibility to exchange with community members.

Possible benefits for customers comprise the support of self-sufficiency within the community, independence from large, faceless companies, as well as the chance for participation and codetermination in an energy community offering a strong community feeling. This might also include an investment of jointly generated revenues in assets for the community. Environmental awareness, regionalism, and community-related topics play a greater role compared to the first product aiming at individual self-sufficiency. However, optimization goals targeting at either autarchy, cost reduction, or environmental impact can serve to attract different target groups.

Chances for further differentiation include flexible production and storage units as well as load management for optimizing balancing costs or offering ancillary services to the power grid. So far, the TSOs manage these ancillary services exclusively. Should comparable market places appear on the distribution grid level, this would open up additional revenue streams and corresponding possibilities for customer differentiation of local energy communities.

Such earnings can either ameliorate the profitability of the service or serve for investments within the community. The latter option would stimulate the installation of new community-owned renewable generation assets and could increase the bond of participants with their community.

Furthermore, this opens up cross-selling potential regarding behind the meter products, such as sale and contracting offers of distributed energy generation and storage units with or without operation and maintenance services. As for today, the margins in these asset-based products and services seem to be more promising than margins in energy sales.

Moreover, the sharing of other goods and services in the neighborhood might be interesting for the target group of local energy communities as well—ranging from sharing of drilling machines to dog sitting or advice regarding energy management to consulting concerning income tax statement procedures.

4.5.3 Community with focus on peer-to-peer trading

Based on a trading algorithm, such as the FMM, implemented on distributed microcontrollers, the community's energy portfolio can be optimized without centralized management.

The target group can be characterized as "liberal ecoinnovators", that is, innovative consumers and prosum(ag)ers with available flexibility in generation, storage, or consumption who are interested in trading and exchange in a community, autarchy and technical innovation, as well as data, system, and cyber security.

The benefit for customers encompasses self-organized energy supply by all community members, transparency, and the possibility to influence the own electricity flow and value. The community no longer needs a central structure, such as a utility or an aggregator, as all activities are P2P-based and as the market-based trading algorithm ensures the most cost-effective supply at all times. It is a decentralized supply system with the highest fail-safe performance, based on entirely decentralized data storage at the customers' sites.

Chances for further differentiation might be found by supporting localized self-supply communities in apartment buildings, such as landlord-to-tenant electricity. This offer might be developed for and in cooperation with communities or housing associations. Already today, tax exemptions support the profitability of such products.

Furthermore, should DSOs develop grid fees with time-dependent price differentiation, thus rewarding producers for feeding electricity into the grid in times of high consumption or low production, this could be utilized as a further incentive to optimize the local energy community. Corresponding revenues could be allocated to the specific customers or be socialized within the community.

4.6 Conclusion

EWS and Oxygen Technologies rolled out an energy community in Germany in summer of 2019. Based on experiences gathered in the Schönau field test, P2P community products shall be launched in the near future.

As market surveys demonstrate, the concept of energy communities still is rather unknown to Germans in general. Hence, energy communities will remain a niche market in the foreseeable future. However, in the next years, energy communities will be of interest to prosumers, especially those owning renewable generation that will phase out of subsidies, as well as those households planning to install renewable generation units. Specific consumer groups willing to pay for self-sufficiency, regionality, transparency, independence, or self-determination should be focused on. Thus, differentiated customer segmentation and strategy development is one of the major objectives at this stage of innovation.

Three promising options for community products were outlined in Section 4.5, that is, first, maximizing individual self-sufficiency, second, becoming part of the EWS energy community acting as a virtual power plant, or, third, sharing electricity in a community that decentrally trades between peers.

All potential customers like to rely on a trustworthy supplier, due to the unfamiliarity and complexity of the product. This opens up a good opportunity for innovative municipal or regional utilities, eco-energy providers, and energy cooperatives. Therefore EWS, enjoying a high credibility and trust in the market and especially among their customers, is in a good starting position to develop these innovative products.

To some extent the economic viability and attractiveness of energy communities will depend on the regulatory framework. The transfer of the European Clean Energy Package into German law should facilitate the possibility to produce and sell own electricity and, thus, support the development of energy communities. As EWS's vision is a citizen-owned and decentral energy supply, preparing for this new framework is a must.

References

BMWi. (2019). *State-imposed components of the electricity price*. Berlin, Germany: Federal Ministry for Economic Affairs and Energy. [Online] <https://www.bmwi.de/Redaktion/EN/Artikel/Energy/electircity-price-components-state-imposed.html>.

EC. (2018). *Renewable energy: Moving towards a low carbon economy*. Brussels, Belgium: European Commission. [Online] <https://ec.europa.eu/energy/en/topics/renewable-energy>.

Espe, E., Potdar, V., & Chang, E. (2018). Prosumer communities and relationships in smart grids: A literature review, evolution and future directions. *Energies, 11*(10), 2528. Available from https://doi.org/10.3390/en11102528.

Ford, R., Stephenson, J., & Whitaker, J. (2016). *Prosumer collectives: A review*. Dunedin, New Zealand: University of Otago.

Gstrein, M. (2016). *Handling the crowd — An explorative study on the implications of prosumer-consumer communities on the value creation in the future electricity network* (Doctoral thesis). Fribourg, Switzerland: IIMT University Press.

Hackbarth, A., & Löbbe, S. (2019). Attitudes, preferences and intentions to participate in peer-to-peer electricity trading: The case of Southwest German households. In *Reutlingen working papers on marketing & management 2019-2*. Reutlingen, Germany.

Löbbe, S., & Hackbarth, A. (2017). The transformation of the German electricity sector and the emergence of new business models in distributed energy systems. In F. Sioshansi (Ed.), *Innovation and disruption at the Grid's Edge—How distributed energy resources are disrupting the utility business model* (pp. 287–318). London, UK: Academic Press.

Mengelkamp, E., Diesing, J., & Weinhardt, C. (2019). *Tracing local energy markets: A literature review*. Karlsruhe, Germany: Research Report, Karlsruhe Institute of Technology.

Mengelkamp, E., Schoenland, T., Huber, J., & Weinhardt, C. (2019). The value of local electricity – A choice experiment among German residential customers. *Energy Policy, 130*, 294–303.

Mengelkamp, E., Staudt, P., Gärttner, J., Weinhardt, C., & Huber, J. (2018). Quantifying factors for participation in local electricity markets. In *Paper presented at 15th International Conference on the European Energy Market (EEM)*, June 27–29, 2018, Lodz, Poland.

Moret, F., & Pinson, P. (2018). Energy collectives: A community and fairness based approach to future electricity markets. *IEEE Transactions on Power Systems*. Available from https://doi.org/10.1109/TPWRS.2018.2808961.

Parag, Y., & Sovacool, B. K. (2016). Electricity market design for the prosumer era. *Nature Energy, 1,* Article number: 16032.

Park, C., & Yong, T. (2017). Comparative review and discussion on P2P electricity trading. *Energy Procedia, 128,* 3–9.

PWC. (2018). *Alte Photovoltaik-Anlagen: Ende der Förderung in Sicht. #energyfacts.* Germany: PricewaterhouseCoopers.

Rathnayaka, A. D., Potdar, V. M., Dillon, T., Hussain, O., & Kuruppu, S. (2014). Goal-oriented prosumer community groups for the smart grid. *IEEE Technology and Society Magazine, 33*(1), 41–48.

Reuter, E., & Loock, M. (2017). *Empowering local electricity markets: A survey study from Switzerland, Norway, Spain and Germany.* St. Gallen, Switzerland: Institute for Economy and the Environment, University of St. Gallen.

Sousa, T., Soares, T., Pinson, P., Moret, F., Baroche, T., & Sorin, E. (2019). Peer-to-peer and community-based markets: A comprehensive review. *Renewable and Sustainable Energy Reviews, 104,* 367–378.

Teufel, S., & Teufel, B. (2014). The crowd energy concept. *Journal of Electronic Science and Technology, 12*(3), 263–269.

Zhang, C., Wu, J., Long, C., & Cheng, M. (2017). Review of existing peer-to-peer energy trading projects. *Energy Procedia, 105,* 2563–2568.

Aggregators today and tomorrow: from intermediaries to local orchestrators?

Ksenia Poplavskaya[1,2] and Laurens de Vries[2]

[1]AIT Austrian Institute of Technology GmbH, Vienna, Austria [2]Delft University of Technology, Delft, the Netherlands

5.1 Introduction

Rapid changes in the electricity sector are creating new challenges and opportunities for market participants. In the European Union (EU), these changes are underpinned by three trends forming the centerpiece of the EU's energy policy:

- Decarbonization drives growing expansion of renewable energy sources (RES) in the electricity grid and markets.
- Decentralization is supported by the push for consumer empowerment and the new opportunities on the demand side.
- Digitalization enables new solutions to connect and coordinate system elements and stakeholders across supply, demand, and grid levels, as further described in Chapter 3.

These trends foster the emergence of aggregators and position them as key enablers that can help unlock value from in front of and behind the energy meter, for example, by pooling consumer loads and small-scale generation or enabling prosumer entry to electricity markets. Yet, so far, their market entry has been a mixed success in the EU countries. The range of value streams that are available to aggregators, consumers and prosumers depends on technical prerequisites, such as availability of smart meters and appropriate communication infrastructure, and also on the market design and the regulatory framework, which create opportunities along with challenges for aggregators.

This chapter reviews the current business models of European aggregators and, based on an assessment of their drivers and barriers, describes how these models may evolve. It then identifies three future value streams for aggregators that would allow them to further exploit the potential of local flexibility options. While this analysis is focused on the EU, similar considerations apply elsewhere: the three underlying trends mentioned above are universal, yet, specific value streams available to aggregators elsewhere will depend on the applicable regulation.

The chapter is organized as follows:

- Section 5.2 describes existing aggregators, their main functions, benefits, and unique selling points.
- Section 5.3 provides the big picture of an aggregator's business model environment. It describes current enabling factors and barriers along with the recent changes in the EU regulatory framework.
- Section 5.4 gives a comprehensive overview and analyzes business models of 26 well-known aggregators across the EU.
- Section 5.5 turns toward the future and explores new opportunities and possible business models for aggregators and the changes required to bring them about followed by the chapter's conclusion.

5.2 The roles of aggregators

A real boost to aggregators in the EU was given by the formal acknowledgment of the crucial role of aggregators in the future electricity markets in the Clean Energy for All Europeans Package (hereafter EU Clean Energy Package), a set of directives and regulations that were adopted in 2018−19. The EU defines an independent aggregator as "a market participant that combines multiple customer loads or generated electricity for sale, for purchase or auction in any organized energy market <...> that is not affiliated to a supplier or any other market participant" [Directive 2019/44/EU, 2019; Art. 2(14−15)]. This leaves a lot of room for aggregators to define their business models.

An aggregator is expected to perform an important social function of empowering consumers and small-scale generators and facilitating their access to the markets. One might argue that if markets were perfect, there would be no need for aggregators. However, in practice, aggregators can perform several functions and even though competitive and transparent markets would allow a more diverse spectrum of providers, aggregation would still remain relevant.

Various studies show that end users generally show a low interest in active management of their assets (cf. Lund et al., 2016). Aggregators' ability to connect their customers' assets to the market at minimal transaction costs is one of their most important *raisons d'etre*. The key consists in using advanced automation solutions to extract value from customer flexibility without affecting their comfort levels or operations.

Second, most demand-side providers would otherwise not enter electricity markets or provide system services since generating value with one's flexibility requires complex decision-making to evaluate different options. It involves a high technical expertise and business acumen to generate meaningful gains. Moreover, it inevitably involves a high administrative and operational effort as well as exposure to market risks. Therefore, even with perfectly

Technological know-how

- ICT-based management and control systems
- IT know-how (software-as-a-service)
- Proof of service
- Monitoring

Business acumen

- Identification of flexibility potential and optimization for customers
- Well positioned to cater to different customer groups
- Electricity market and industry expertize

Scale effects

- Reduced transaction costs
- Reduced day-to-day operational effort
- Intermediation for multiple services
- Risk and complexity management
- VPP functionality (matching and coordination)

FIGURE 5.1 Technological know-how, business acumen, and scale effects form an aggregator's unique selling points.

accessible markets, these actors would be left at the market fringe. Aggregation in turn is a low-margin business; hence, it requires scale and volume to be profitable.

A third benefit is the pooling of resources. In a balanced portfolio, multiple technologies can help overcome each other's technical constraints. As individual small units cannot provide a meaningful system service precisely due to their limited scale, it requires IT knowledge and an advanced communication infrastructure, something that an aggregator brings to the table. This also allows an aggregator to effectively exploit scale effects and thus reduce transaction costs and mitigate risks for individual participants. The value of aggregators stems from their potential to bundle not only different load or generation sources but also different value streams from multiple activities.

The removal of transaction costs through information and communication technology (ICT) solutions, the business acumen, and the benefits of scale effects form an aggregator's unique selling points (USP), as is shown in Fig. 5.1.

Aggregators do not only cater to end users and distributed energy resources (DER), but combine business-to-consumer (B2C) services with business-to-business (B2B) solutions. For instance, they may assist balance responsible parties[1] by optimizing their portfolios and thereby minimizing imbalances. They can help transmission system operators (TSOs) to procure balancing services more cost-efficiently and distribution system operators (DSOs) to manage their local constraints and obtain a better overview of flexibility at lower voltage levels. Utilities (retail companies) may use aggregators' software and virtual power plant (VPP) solutions to tap into their customers' demand response (DR) potential and offer them bundled electricity services.

In sum, aggregators perform multiple functions such as information management by identifying flexibility potential, pooling of heterogeneous technologies with the help of control and communication systems, matching flexibility to specific markets and services,

[1] Balance responsible party refers to an entity responsible for managing imbalances of their balancing portfolio, a virtual group of generation and/or load, and settling the imbalances incurred as a result of deviations from their submitted generation and/or consumption schedules.

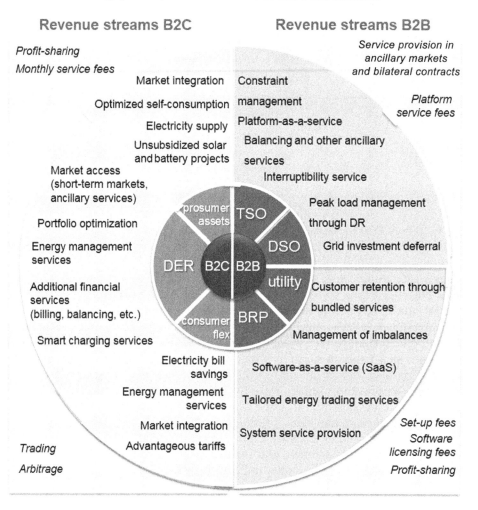

FIGURE 5.2 Potential roles of aggregators, their customer groups (inner circle), value propositions (outer circle), and revenue streams.

and transaction guarantor by bearing responsibility for a reliable service provision (Eid, Codani, Chen, Perez, & Hakvoort, 2015). This position at the intersection of different functions and customer groups creates the intrinsic value of an aggregator role for the system and allows him to obtain several revenue streams. Fig. 5.2 illustrates the roles that aggregators may perform for the various types of actors in the electricity sector. Next to the circle, the main revenue streams in the B2C and the B2B segments are indicated.

5.3 Drivers and barriers

The constraints and enabling conditions that are created by external factors determine the playing field within which an aggregator can develop his business model. The value

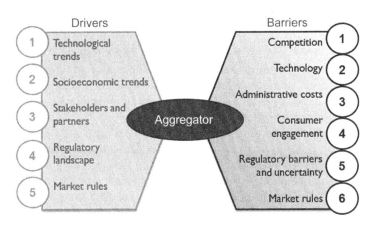

FIGURE 5.3 Drivers and barriers shaping aggregator's business model environment.

that an aggregator can create is a function of the services he can provide and their feasibility in the specific market and regulatory environment. As the latter differs significantly across EU countries, the existing business models are different, too. The factors that shape the external environment can be divided into industry-related factors, regulatory trends, market-related factors, and macroeconomic factors (Osterwalder, Pigneur, & Clark, 2010). This analysis focuses on the first two components to identify current drivers and barriers. Fig. 5.3 provides an overview of the key drivers and barriers, which will be discussed in the remainder of this section.

5.3.1 Drivers

Technological trends: Rapid transformation and decentralization is demonstrated by the intensified use of aggregation or VPP solutions. According to World Energy Outlook 2018, between 2014 and 2017 alone, the volume of aggregation in the EU has grown by over 50% from 12 GW to approximately 18 GW (International Energy Agency, 2018, p. 305). In 2014 utility-owed VPPs accounted for 5 GW as opposed to c. 7 GW of independent third-party owners, whereas in 2017 the volumes amounted to 6 and 12 GW, respectively. About 12.5 GW of the aggregated assets were on the generation side (in the form of VPPs), and 5.5 GW constitutes aggregated demand (International Energy Agency, 2018).

New energy system management tools have opened up opportunities for the demand side, paving the way for prosumers, who are core client segments of aggregators (Fig. 5.2). Electricity itself is only part of the puzzle: other key pieces are communication technology, software and hardware. The aggregator as a new entrant is often more agile and faster at developing technology, which he can either use himself or license to other parties.

Socioeconomic trends: RES-friendly policies and policies encouraging consumer-side participating in the energy system have been shaping the electricity sector. Consumers have been sensitized to the adverse effects of climate change and become aware of the value of environmentally sustainable solutions. "Green solutions" are therefore gaining impetus.

Just like the costs of renewables fell substantially in the past decade, so did the costs of storage. While the development of utility-scale storage facilities slowed down, the installed behind-the-meter (BTM) battery storage capacity grew from a few MW worldwide in 2012 to about 480 MW in 2017 (International Energy Agency, 2018, p. 306), much of this in combination with solar PV.

The stakeholders include not only all types of consumers, prosumers, and small-scale generators but also technology providers and IT companies. Continued success of an aggregator business model relies on smart cooperation across technologies, consumer groups, and industries. This does not only allow exploiting more value sources but also facilitating aggregators' presence in a larger number of countries.

Markets and regulation: The recent adoption of the EU Clean Energy Package galvanized the regulatory landscape in Europe by opening up opportunities for DER and demand to participate in all electricity marketplaces, including ancillary services for the TSO. European short-term electricity markets are being adjusted to account for a growing need for system flexibility, including local flexibility, to offset the challenges of RES integration. As electricity markets become more granular,[2] aggregators not only obtain more trading opportunities for short-term flexibility but also need to determine the value of flexibility in a higher time resolution.

5.3.2 Barriers

The most commonly cited barriers for aggregators and their aggregated resources are formal market entry barriers (Borne, Korte, Perez, Petit, & Purkus, 2018), bid size requirements (Koliou, Eid, Chaves-Ávila, & Hakvoort, 2014; Poplavskaya & De Vries, 2019), restrictions to aggregation (ENTSO-E, 2017), and coordination issues with other market actors (Poplavskaya & De Vries, 2018). In fact, the spectrum of existing hurdles is broader, as is illustrated in Fig. 5.3.

Competition: Incumbent utilities are hot on aggregators' heels, while they often enjoy a better market position along with a well-established customer base. According to Navigant consulting, incumbent strategies include investment, acquisition or partnership with aggregators, technology, and platform providers (Metz, 2018). A number of prominent European supply companies have either engaged in aggregation themselves, for example, Statkraft operates the biggest VPP in Europe, set up or acquired an aggregator, for example, Jedlix is part of Eneco; REstore was acquired by Centrica (see Annex A). Italian Enel acquired a number of companies under its umbrella, a software developer for distributed portfolio optimization, Demand Energy, as well as EnerNOC aggregator (see Annex A) and a provider of charging infrastructure eMotorWerks (Metz, 2018). An example of a supplier-aggregator partnership is an agreement between Innogy and Kiwigrid for joint service development.

Utilities are on the lookout for reliable software platforms to pool consumer renewables and storage assets BTM to tap into the DR potential on a large scale. Platform solutions for market-based service procurement has been under development by both aggregators and software developers as key strategic partners but also are actively explored by utilities such as Enel, Engie, Eon, or Innogy (Metz, 2018). New BTM technologies such as storage,

---

[2] In Europe, EPEX Spot has a liquid intraday market with both continuous trading and hourly or 15-minute contracts.

energy management solutions, electric vehicles (EVs), and digitalization are also considered as ways for incumbent suppliers to retain customers.

Technology: Smart meters is a prerequisite for successful demand-side management and real-time communication. Although smart meter rollout was mandated by the Electricity Directive, practical implementation in most EU countries has been slow: so far, only a few EU countries, Italy, Spain, and the Nordic countries achieved large-scale rollouts (International Energy Agency, 2018). Smart meter standards and functionalities also vary between countries. Other technical challenges are the connection of different technologies, software standards, and required IT expertise. The status of smart meters is addressed in Chapter 12.

Administrative barriers: Engaging large numbers of small customers is likely to be associated with high transaction costs for marketing and acquisition, contract management, customer retention, support, and customized offers. At the same time, high recruiting costs may chip away at the aggregator's profits as employees are required not only to have a solid industry knowledge but also IT expertise.

Consumer flexibility is likely to raise coordination issues with balancing responsible parties and suppliers they signed a supply contract with. Responsibility for potential imbalances is one of the key issues in the aggregator debate in Europe. As most aggregators do not engage in consumer energy supply, they still rely on a supplier to cover—at least partially—their customers' demand. Decoupling energy supply from sale is complicated: if an aggregator would buy prosumers' energy to take it to the market, this would alter their suppliers' schedule, leading to additional imbalance costs. Unless the information exchanges and settlement rules are clearly specified, aggregators will find it difficult to access demand-side flexibility.

Consumer engagement: Currently, most suppliers agree to offtake and remunerate consumers' self-generated energy at a predetermined tariff, but only if these consumers also have a power supply contract with them. This limits consumers and aggregators in several ways. First, consumers have no choice or control over the price they receive for the self-generated energy. For instance, the tariff received is often lower than the price they have to pay for the energy bought from the supplier and does not correspond to the market price. Second, aggregators are unable to offer their service to such consumers as they are virtually "bound" to the supplier.

Instead through an aggregator, a large customer may also decide to participate in the market itself. If a pricing scheme offered by an aggregator is not attractive enough, a prosumer may accept a buyback payment offered by his regular supplier. In Chapter 9, the authors discuss consumer behavior and mention the limitations of rational decision-making. Limitations in consumer engagement in the Australian context are also addressed in Chapter 15.

Regulatory barriers and regulatory uncertainty: Until recently, the participation of demand, aggregated or not, the use of storage for different services and aggregation itself were formally restricted or even prohibited (ENTSO-E, 2017). A lack of markets for most ancillary services in Europe limits the possibility for aggregators to provide them. Only balancing energy is procured competitively (European Commission, 2017), while markets for redispatch or local constraint management are mostly restricted to pilot projects.

Network tariffs are often overlooked as an important factor. High network tariffs on aggregated consumers or prosumers pose a challenge for aggregators to make attractive offers. In most EU countries the energy component constitutes only about a third of a household bill (ACER/CEER, 2018). As a result, potentially minuscule energy savings may make it difficult to convince future customers. Tariffs are not regulated on the EU level but are determined nationally creating large differences.

Since the directives of the EU Clean Energy Package, which define the market rules for aggregators, still need to be transposed into national legislation, there is regulatory uncertainty, which affects the business models of aggregators.

Market rules: As electricity markets were originally designed for large generation units, their rules often discourage or even prevent the entry of smaller, alternative participants. Barriers for the aggregation business are posed by the authorization of independent aggregation itself or by restrictive rules for the underlying pooled resources and their owners. An example is the limited access of DR to European balancing markets. Stringent technical prequalification is necessary to prove the components' ability to quickly react to control signals. Requirements for VPPs are also different and prequalification procedures need to be conducted for each individual country and have different preauthorization periods. Frequency measurement requirements may further block loads from the balancing market. The main barrier identified by Poplavskaya and De Vries (2018) is unit-based prequalification criteria. Pool-based criteria would ease the compliance not only with the technical requirements but also with the required minimum bid size and an aggregator's ability to reliably provide the service.

With respect to market and regulatory challenges the EU Clean Energy Package and EU Network Codes have significantly improved market access for aggregators and provided a clearer regulatory framework for them and their aggregated portfolios. In Section 5.5, it will be discussed how these changes will create new opportunities for aggregators in the future.

5.4 Overview of aggregator business models

This section reviews the business models of 26 prominent independent aggregators in Europe with respect to their portfolios, geographical coverage, ownership models, value streams, innovation, and focus. The results are summarized in Table 5.1. More detailed information about individual aggregators can be found in Annex A.

The overview shows that aggregators are not evenly distributed across Europe. Aggregator hotspots are located in Germany, United Kingdom, and France, the countries with the highest numbers of national aggregators but also where most aggregators operate with 16, 12, and 10 aggregators, respectively. This points to fairly favorable market rules for aggregators. Other aggregator-friendly countries include Belgium, Switzerland, and the Nordics. In turn, aggregation is very much in its infancy in Southern European countries although the recent opening of electricity markets for aggregation is likely to attract new participants in the near future. For instance, Portugal only recently allowed access to independent third-party aggregators whereas Italy allowed for a pilot project with "virtual qualified consumption or generation units" operated by an aggregator for balancing

TABLE 5.1 Overview of European aggregators according to portfolio, geographical coverage, ownership model, value streams, innovation, and focus (parentheses signify planned or pilot activities).

		A1Energy solutions	Actility	BayWa.re	Ecotricity	energy2market	EnergyPool	Enex	Entelios	Enyway	Flexitricity	Group ASE	Jedlix	Kiwi Power	Lichtblick	limejump	Lumenaza	Mark-E	Mobility House	Next Kraftwerke	Noodvermogenpool	Restore	Smart Grid Energy	Sonnen	Sympower	tiko	Voltalis
Portfolio	Generation	✓		✓	✓	✓	✓	✓	✓	✓	✓			✓	✓	✓	✓	✓		✓	✓	✓	✓		✓	✓	✓
	Demand		✓		✓	✓	✓	✓	✓	✓	✓	✓		✓	✓	✓	✓			✓	✓	✓	✓		✓	✓	✓
	Storage			✓	✓	✓	✓	✓	✓	✓	✓		✓	✓	✓	✓	✓	✓	✓	✓		✓		✓	✓	✓	✓
Coverage	Main country	AT	FR	DE	UK	DE	FR	US	DE	DE	UK	ES	NL	UK	DE	UK	DE	DE	DE	DE	NL	BE	FR	DE	NL	CH	FR
	More than one country of operations		✓	✓		✓	✓	✓	✓			✓	✓	✓		✓		✓		✓	✓	✓	✓	✓	✓	✓	
Ownership	Owned by a utility (if not, then independent)					✓	✓	✓	✓		✓		✓		✓	✓		✓				✓		✓		✓	
	Originally from a different sector	✓	✓	✓													✓									✓	
Value stream	Asset management and optimization (day-ahead, intraday markets)	✓	✓	✓	✓	✓	✓	✓	✓	✓	✓	✓	✓	✓	✓	✓	✓	✓	✓	✓	✓	✓	✓	✓	✓	✓	✓
	Balancing and other ancillary services	✓	✓	✓		✓	✓	✓	✓	✓	✓	✓	(✓)	✓	✓	✓		✓	(✓)	✓	✓	✓	✓		✓		✓
	Trading	✓	✓	✓		✓	✓	✓	✓	✓	✓	✓		✓	✓	✓	✓	✓		✓	✓	✓	✓		✓	✓	
	Whitelabel solutions to utilities	✓	✓	✓					✓					✓		✓	✓			✓		✓	✓		✓	✓	✓

(Continued)

TABLE 5.1 (Continued)

	A1Energy solutions	Actility	BayWar.e	Ecotricity	energy2market	EnergyPool	Enex	Entelios	Enyway	Flexitcity	Group ASE	Jedlix	Kiwi Power	Lichtblick	limejump	Lumenaza	Mark-E	Mobility House	Next Kraftwerke	Noodvermogenpool	Restore	Smart Grid Energy	Sonnen	Sympower	tiko	Voltalis
DR (commercial and industrial)	✓	(✓)		✓	✓	✓	✓	✓		✓	✓		✓	✓				✓	✓		✓	✓	✓	✓	✓	✓
Household DR			✓	✓										✓									✓			✓
Electricity supply of end users			✓	✓					✓					✓			✓						✓			
DSO services	✓		(✓)					(✓)		(✓)			(✓)		(✓)			(✓)					(✓)			(✓)
Innovation — Platform/blockchain/P2P offerings		✓			✓	✓	✓		✓	✓		✓	✓		✓	✓		✓	✓	✓	✓	✓	✓	✓	✓	✓
Own hardware/software	✓	✓	✓	✓	✓	✓	✓	✓	✓	✓			✓	✓	✓	✓	✓	✓	✓	✓	✓	✓	✓	✓	✓	✓
Focus — Software development	✓	✓		✓	✓	✓	✓	✓	✓	✓		✓	✓		✓	✓	✓	✓	✓	✓	✓	✓	✓	✓	✓	✓
Customer relationship			✓	✓	✓	✓	✓	✓	✓	✓	✓	✓	✓	✓	✓	✓		✓	✓	✓		✓	✓		✓	✓

AT, Austria; BE, Belgium; CH, Switzerland; DE, Germany; ES, Spain; FR, France; IT, Italy; NL, The Netherlands; P2P, peer-to-peer; UK, United Kingdom; US, United States.

market participation (ARERA, 2017). Meanwhile, no aggregators have been spotted in Eastern European countries or in the Baltic States.

The high interest of sector incumbents in aggregator business model is demonstrated by the fact that 35% of all identified aggregators have been acquired or spun off by large utilities in the last few years (see also Annex A). Other aggregators are newcomers with a core business in a different sector such as IT, for example, A1 Energy Solutions, or technology development, for example, battery manufacturer sonnen.

An important observation from Table 5.1 is that there are only a few examples of aggregators that only use demand or generation assets. Most portfolios include flexibility on both the demand and supply sides, such as Next Kraftwerke, further described in Chapter 10. Moreover, 62% of analyzed aggregators pool storage units. Although over two-thirds aggregate demand, 90% of all DR is still provided by commercial and industrial customers (e.g., EnergyPool, Sympower, and Voltalis). BTM aggregation is its infancy: only German Lichtblick, Mark-E, and sonnen are aggregating household DR. Causes range from a lack of information at the consumer level and limited smart-meter rollout to insufficient investment in BTM technologies needed to create a critical mass of flexibility BTM. Yet, these examples show that BTM and upstream options are not mutually exclusive and viable business models can rely on a combination of the two.

The overview demonstrates the importance of value stacking, that is, generating revenue from multiple value streams on the B2C and B2B sides, for an aggregator's long-term profitability. All analyzed business models included a mix of services. All aggregators are involved in asset management and portfolio optimization. Participation in the balancing market remains the most lucrative revenue stream for over two-thirds of aggregators. The IEA reached a similar conclusion (International Energy Agency, 2018, p. 305). A third of the analyzed aggregators are exploring flexibility provision to the DSO. Yet, since there are no well-established mechanisms nor marketplaces for the provision of DSO services, all the projects are in the pilot phase.

Over 85% of the analyzed aggregators use proprietary soft- and/or hardware for VPP operation, for example, Next Kraftwerke's Next Box, KiWi Power's Fruit, and REstore's and Enel X's software, with 73% of the companies offering it as a white-label solution to other market participants. Such hardware and software can be used by asset owners for a more efficient asset management and schedule optimization and by suppliers for VPP operation, reporting and visualization. A reliable forecasting tool for load, RES generation, and market prices is another factor essential for a successful aggregation business and is often integrated in the software. Next Kraftwerke, tiki, and KiWi Power are among the few aggregators that both commercialize energy portfolios in some countries and develop and provide software- or platform-as-a-service, one of their unique selling points (Fig. 5.1) to other market players in countries where market entry is more complicated. For successful consumer engagement, trust in the service reliability is essential. Particularly for BTM aggregation this implies that outside their home market, aggregators are better off playing the role of service providers and partnering with established local market participants.

Business models typically focus on one of three areas:

- infrastructure management,
- customer relations, or
- product and service innovation (Hagel & Singer, 1999).

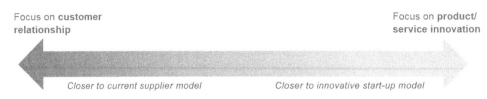

FIGURE 5.4 Aggregator business models can be closer to a traditional supplier or closer to an innovative start-up, depending on whether the main focus is on customer relations or on product and service innovation.

Since in Europe infrastructure management is the prerogative of regulated system operators, aggregators may opt for either of the other two business model types or a combination thereof, which can be illustrated as a scale (Fig. 5.4). The cost structures, value proposition, and revenue streams of a customer-relationship-focused business model are substantially different from a service-innovation model.

Customer acquisition and retention are at the core of the customer-oriented business model and the lion's share of costs stems from marketing and sales. Customer-oriented aggregators compete with incumbent suppliers, even though most aggregators' models do not include electricity supply to final users—only 23% of the analyzed aggregators do (see also Annex A). Customer-oriented aggregators, for example, Flexitricity or Sympower, sell electricity in different marketplaces and offer fixed or dynamic pricing to their—mainly large—customers. Aggregators that focus on product and service innovation have the biggest investment in R&D activities. The main value proposition of aggregators with this model is innovative services. Until recently, product innovation has been a more realistic business model for aggregators due to market entry barriers.

The overview shows that 42% of the analyzed aggregators are exploring new value streams through platform development, Blockchain solutions, and peer-to-peer (P2P) offerings in order to achieve a competitive edge, as further described in Chapter 13. For instance, in exchange for a monthly service charge, EnyWay provides a direct marketplace for consumers and local solar and wind generators to help them switch away from traditional suppliers. EnyWay meets the part of energy demand that could not be covered locally and receives a monthly service charge. Lichtblick provides customers with PV panels dimensioned in a way to cover twice the customer's electricity demand. The customer receives a zero tariff, while Lichtblick sells the other half to the market. Lumenaza offers community management as a service, including Blockchain-based transactions, in addition to traditional energy supply and market positioning of customers' RES. Energy2market also possesses Blockchain expertise, whereas sonnen operates an own platform, sonnenCommunity, for electricity sharing with surplus stored in a virtual electricity pool while offering a special sonnenFlat tariff to flexibility providers.

5.5 New opportunities for aggregators

This section addresses the recent regulatory changes in Europe and how they may impact the business models of aggregators. It will focus on three new trends: energy communities, P2P trading, and the provision of flexibility services for DSOs.

5.5.1 Transformation of the regulatory landscape in Europe

The EU Clean Energy Package and EU Network Codes have made a substantial contribution to regulatory clarity, opening up electricity marketplaces, and creating opportunities for various stakeholders. Most formal barriers to DR and aggregation have been removed: both activities are officially allowed and encouraged (e.g., Directive 2019/44/EU, 2019). The key changes are summarized in Table 5.2 and will be discussed subsequently.

TABLE 5.2 Progress in the European Union (EU) with respect to aggregator business models and value streams.

	Progress	Comments
Short-term wholesale electricity trade		Fully opened to all types of providers, aggregated, or not
		DR formally allowed to participate in the market
		Liquid intraday markets allow flexibility trading close to real time
Balancing markets		Formally opened to all types of providers
		Market rules largely harmonized, balancing products standardized
		Many adjustments to market design are to be implemented before 2021
Incentives for prosumers		Self-generation, consumption and storage are to be encouraged throughout the EU
		As feed-in tariffs are being gradually phased out, stronger incentives for investment in behind-the-meter assets, the optimization of self-consumption, and the involvement of aggregators
		Mechanisms vary nationally (e.g., tax reductions, lower grid tariffs)
Community solutions		Citizen energy communities and renewable energy communities with a broad scope of authorized activities (e.g., shared asset ownership and operation, energy trade) formally introduced in the EU Clean Energy Package
		Rules for peer-to-peer trading platform design and operation remain to be clarified
Network tariffs		Have not been addressed at the EU level; high heterogeneity
		Some tariff reductions for grid-supportive activities exist nationally
		Design of appropriate tariffs for behind-the-meter is urgently needed (see also Chapter 17).
Flexibility for the DSO		DSO is not allowed to own and operate generation assets due to unbundling provisions
		DSOs are encouraged to improve operational efficiency by, e.g., using local flexibility, other than grid expansion, yet no clear mechanisms for procurement
Platform operation		Not explicitly covered in the EU regulation

DR, Demand response; *DSO*, distribution system operators.

The recent developments created opportunities for BTM aggregation. As feed-in tariffs and net metering are being phased out, storage-plus-PV and other BTM flexibility options such as electric boilers and heat pumps offer alternatives for customers to reduce costs by maximizing consumption from own generation. Consumers can also generate revenue by participating in the wholesale and balancing markets or in local trading through an aggregator. Both options are enabled by the EU Clean Energy Package, and a few aggregators have been exploring these value streams (see Section 5.4). The need for system flexibility, especially local flexibility, has been growing strongly. It is likely to continue to increase as higher RES shares increase short-term market volatility and create network congestion. New patterns emerging on the local level in Europe are covered in Chapters 6 and 11.

The EU Clean Energy Package places specific value on community-based solutions. Arrangements in which electricity can be produced, consumed, and shared locally have already been successfully tested in a number of European countries. For instance, Germany implemented its "tenant electricity model" (Mieterstrommodell) that allows landlords to supply tenants with green electricity through an aggregator, for example, German Enyway. Spain has passed its ambitious Royal Decree on Self-consumption in May 2019, both individual and collective (Ministry for the Environmental Transition, 2019). For the first time the package also authorizes P2P trading, which can open up an opportunity for an aggregator as a platform provider. These changes create a chance for an aggregator to turn into a local orchestrator by becoming a community or local flexibility market operator or by offering solutions for P2P trade for prosumers with their BTM assets.

5.5.2 Energy communities

On the consumer side a combination of solar PV with BTM storage or EVs can allow consumers to use self-generated energy more flexibly and to sell their stored electricity at the time when electricity market prices are more attractive. The BTM volume of storage is expected to increase by a factor of 38 in 2025, as compared to 2015, according to Navigant Research (2019).

The EU Clean Energy Package provides for a new approach to consumer participation, which goes beyond the level of individual households. So far, households have been rarely profitable enough for aggregators to make it part of their business models, largely due to a low flexibility volume and often cumbersome arrangements with other market parties (see Section 5.3.2). The focus has now shifted to community-based solutions, which allow aggregators to lower their transaction costs and also to provide different solutions to such communities. The 2019 EU Electricity and the Renewable Energy Directives formalize the concepts of "citizen energy communities" (CEC) and "renewable energy communities" (REC), which are aimed at generating more value locally and at facilitating community-based consumption, sharing and sale of locally produced electricity (Directive 2018/2001/EU, 2019; Directive 2019/44/EU, 2019).

The main features of a CEC include "voluntary and open participation" along with "environmental, economic, or social community benefits" as their *primary* goal. Neither the Electricity nor Renewable Energy Directive limits the area of activities that such communities can undertake. For a CEC, these include "generation, including from renewable sources, distribution, supply, consumption, aggregation, energy storage, energy efficiency services or charging services for electric vehicles" [Electricity Directive, Art 2 (11)].

As a legal entity, an energy community requires a representative. This can be an elected individual or a group of individual shareholders as in the case of a cooperative. An aggregator could represent a CEC or REC in the markets. According to the Directives, the community must maintain its "effective" control for a local economic and environmental benefit, that is, retain the decision-making power. This means that an aggregator acts as a facilitator, responsible for remote control, billing, and use for market participation or grid service provision. Shared use of bulk resources such as a large standalone PV system, battery storage, or a fuel cell could be more attractive than multiple units at individual premises. Another point for an aggregator is that consumers or prosumers will not likely engage in trading and monitoring on a continuous and long-term basis. The first community initiatives show that a lack of sector know-how and IT expertise—two of the main aggregator's unique selling points (Fig. 5.1)—makes it difficult for communities to set up an economically sustainable model (e.g., Dijkstra, 2019).

Educating consumers about the new options that are provided for energy communities by the recent changes in EU legislation is both a challenge and a prerequisite. Community solutions require incentives for consumers to invest in storage technologies and other DER. Such incentives have so far been rather offered by suppliers but may similarly be offered by aggregators. The issues linked to launching energy community projects are further addressed in Chapters 4 and 6.

Importantly, a community scheme would require an aggregator to take over electricity supply and balancing for the community as long as multiple suppliers are not possible within the same community. The aggregator could charge a monthly service fee for its operations or offer community members a beneficial electricity tariff while being in charge of the remaining supply that a community cannot cover locally. Another option would be to set up a profit-sharing scheme with the community where an aggregator is in charge of providing community resources to different markets and services, and the community is able to select its degree of flexibility and level of risk exposure.

Some countries have already eased the conditions for aggregators and active customers. The most recent amendment of the German Renewable Energies Act foresees that prosumers may sell electricity without a supplier license as long as they do so locally as part of the "direct sale" mechanism [Erneuerbare-Energien-Gesetz (EEG), 2017, 2019]. The UK regulator, Ofgem, together with the market operator, Elexon, are investigating the concept of "rapid supplier switching," which would allow procurement of energy from multiple suppliers (ELEXON, 2018). Current market liberalization rules foresee that a consumer may switch supplier at any time. "Rapid supplier switching" involves contracts with several actors at the same time but using their services at different times. The EU regulation does not cover such an option. This arrangement would require a supplier to share his responsibility for a customer's metering point with (an)other market participant(s), for example, a customer's neighbor through a community scheme or an aggregator. Elexon, however, recognized that "the main" supplier should be notified to keep track of energy feed-in and withdrawal to ensure that a supplier does not incur imbalances through other actor's actions.

The financial attractiveness of community-based solutions requires adjustments to the network tariffs. Customers who consume energy locally reduce network stress and may be entitled to lower grid tariffs. For instance, in Austria, the DSOs already started offering reduced network tariffs to energy communities exchanging self-generated energy locally as these minimize the use of the higher voltage levels of the network. Another example from Switzerland is presented in Chapter 3.

The main challenge for an aggregator may be to ensure a sufficient scale. This is why it will remain important that an aggregator offers community solutions only as one of its value streams. The example of the German aggregator sonnen, which successfully set up sonnenCommunity with prosumers, achieved scale by connecting prosumers all over the country. This may mean that to ensure a sufficient scale an aggregator may want to connect multiple communities to extract sufficient value.

5.5.3 Peer-to-peer trading platforms

Energy communities have the option to engage in P2P trading, an example thereof is described in more detail in the Chapter 4. P2P trade is in fact rarely pure, as it tends to make use of the public electricity network. As EU law discourages the building of parallel infrastructure—though does not prohibit it (Van Soest, 2018), peers who trade with each other will still use a DSO's network. Although BTM activities, generation, storage, or sharing was often possible, it tended to exclude the use of the public network rendering community-level P2P trade impossible. Therefore, the main hurdle to a number of prosumers jointly owning and operating a set of PV panels, EVs or a battery storage unit in most EU countries has so far been either lack of legal clarity or outright prohibition.

The EU Clean Energy Package has improved the situation as its provisions can be interpreted to authorize the sale of self-produced electricity regardless of the type of marketplace, organized or P2P. The Renewable Energy Directive Art. 21.2(a) allows the so-called renewables self-consumers to engage in "P2P arrangements." It specifies that P2P trading implies "the sale of renewable energy between market participants <...> either directly between market participants or indirectly through a certified third-party market participant, *such as an aggregator*" [emphasis added] (Art. 2(18)). Indeed, the accounting process, coordination, and balancing still needs to be assisted by a market participant, such as an aggregator.

Transaction platforms are essential enablers of sharing economy (Van Soest, 2018) and are crucial to operationalize P2P trade, monitor and log the exchanges, and automate transactions. Aggregators, many of whom already offer platforms-as-a-service, are well-positioned to offer P2P-enabling solutions, either individually or in partnership with suppliers. The viability of this model is confirmed by the fact that of the aggregators identified in Section 5.4 (Table 5.1), Lumenaza already offers P2P solutions.

Some of the questions concerning P2P trade remain unanswered. For instance, if prosumers decide to go beyond business as usual and sell their production directly to other consumers, they would still be obliged to obtain a supplier license, which requires administrative effort and costs that are too high for households or small commercial customers. The Electricity Directive states that the rights and obligations of a CEC "should apply in accordance with the roles that they undertake, such as the roles of final customers, producers, suppliers or distribution system operators" (Preamble (46) of the Electricity Directive). This provision implies that supplier obligations apply as long as commercial gain is considered the main purpose. This is where an aggregator can help. So far, the schemes where P2P traders do not require a license have mostly been confined to pilot and demo projects, usually combined with grid support services. Besides being mentioned in the Renewable Energy Directive, P2P trade was not directly addressed on the EU level, which can create practical issues and differences in national implementation.

The question of what amounts to commercial activity is more difficult to answer and the only aspect that is clear is that P2P trade is assumed to be conducted by two non-professional private consumers. Yet, it does not, and should not, exclude some sort of profit-making (Van Soest, 2018). Remember that not only households but also commercial customers may engage in P2P trade. A need to make a distinction between different prosumer types, for example, those who occasionally sell their excess energy to a neighbor and "intensive prosumers" who intentionally over-dimension their units with the purpose of market participation, will likely arise (Sia Partners, 2018). The distinction may perhaps be made based on the volume that a renewables self-consumer feeds into the grid, or on the ratio between this volume and his own consumption.

Aside from the CEC context, nothing precludes P2P-trading participants from forming a virtual pool of customers in different locations, which creates a stronger case for an aggregator to operate such a platform. An aggregator may be able to make better use of multiple small BTM resources. Several solutions have already been tested—mostly in pilot projects—such as Blockchain technology and other transaction platforms. At least four of the aggregators reviewed in this chapter are conducting trials of Blockchain applications. Blockchain solutions are also addressed in the Chapter 13. Customizable smart contracts can help take aggregation one step further: they simplify data management, allow dynamic review of transactions, allow prosumers signal their intention to deliver a service, and automatically award transactions. Yet, uncertainty as to how Blockchain and internet of things (IoT) might be regulated in the future, especially with regard to data protection, might delay commercialization.

The success factors of this model are described in Section 5.5.1. The treatment of prosumers engaging in P2P trade as suppliers remains to be clarified along with the design of P2P platforms. Furthermore, if P2P traders are indeed considered suppliers, the licensing procedures must be clarified along with the issue of electricity supply from several suppliers (suppliers, aggregators, and peers).

Consumers' main priorities are ease of use, financial security, and reliability of a service provider (see also Chapter 7). For an incoming aggregator, it is easier to develop a partnership with a trustworthy existing national supply company. This can help to cleanly delimit their activities from those of a supplier and create added value for all participants. In such a model the aggregators' revenue streams may be based on licensing fees and periodic service fees.

5.5.4 Local flexibility for the DSO

European DSOs are particularly affected by the growing shares of small-scale RES at lower network levels. At the same time, they can also benefit from the emerging demand

and supply-side flexibility in the distribution grid. As, due to unbundling requirements, DSOs are not allowed to operate electricity generation and storage themselves, procurement of flexibility from third parties, either bilaterally or through designated marketplaces, may be a solution. Currently, there are aggregators who mostly provide ancillary services to TSOs for balancing purposes. Designated DSO marketplaces have so far been nonexistent. Voltage control is usually provided on a mandatory basis without remuneration (Merino et al., 2016). For this reason, besides balancing, the aggregators that were reviewed in Section 5.4 only participated in pilot projects for constraint management. The business potential in the provision of local flexibility is, for instance, indicated by the takeover of the German aggregator energy2market by one of the largest European utilities, Électricité de France (EDF), which estimated the European flexibility market at 200 GW today and double of this volume in 2030.[3]

Transposing the main features of the multisided platform business model, as presented by Evans, Hagiu, and Schmalensee (2008), to an aggregator case, platform-as-a-service can facilitate interaction among different interdependent customer groups, thereby contributing to a more efficient system operation. This business model is gaining traction in numerous sectors thanks to advancements in information technology. In the electricity sector, 14 out of 26 aggregators already offer platform solutions to utilities and system operators, for example, Voltalis, Restore and KiWi Power. With the aid of an advanced communication infrastructure an aggregator may assist a DSO in voltage control, utilizing free network capacities more efficiently, and shaving off or shifting load peaks.

One of the prerequisites for the success of this business model is a sufficient number of members of one customer group, in this case consumers and prosumers, to ensure participation of other customer groups, such as system operators. This often leads to the need to "subsidize" the first group to attract the second group, which is the main source of revenues for the aggregator. There are a number of ways in which aggregators can "subsidize" consumers and prosumers, such as a free app, energy management tools, or free use of the platform. For instance, tiko and Voltalis provide a free app to customers whereas Jedlix and Mobility House developed their own apps for EV owners (see Annex A).

Some of the concerns that the activities of aggregators raise among existing stakeholders is that they may cause network stability issues and increase imbalance costs for suppliers. An aggregator-operated platform can overcome these concerns by sharing information with other actors and, for example, by supporting system operators to efficiently communicate system constraints. This approach could also help to turn existing suppliers from competitors into partners.

The most recent approaches to market-based procurement of system services for the DSO involved the creation of a dedicated platform or a so-called flexibility market. Main drivers were existing European market operators, EPEX and Nordpool. The former is testing a platform, the EPEX Flexibility Marketplace, in Northern Germany as part of the Enera project which brings together RES operators and VPPs on the one side and system operators on the other side. The main traded product is the "variation of one's consumption or generation profile for each 15-minute period of the day" (EPEX SPOT, 2019). Nordpool partnered with a Nordic supplier, Agder Energi, to set up the NODES platform.

---

[3] https://www.pv-magazine.com/2019/06/14/edf-to-acquire-energy2market/

Entelios is an aggregator that participates in the NODES platform; more aggregators are expected to join (Deuchert, 2019). Yet, an aggregator could operate such a local platform itself as well, as he can provide the main functions: identifying flexibility, pooling resources using own hardware and software and providing flexibility for multiple value streams. The recent experience from the United Kingdom in implementing a platform for trading flexibility is described in Chapter 11.

The multisided platform is the core of the value proposition in this model in which the aggregator's main activities would include identification of flexibility potential, platform management, and operation. The aggregator would act as a market operator or "match-maker" and charge transaction fees. Revenue streams are obtained primarily from B2B customers in the form of set-up and service fees for platform operation, while a critical mass of customers on the other side make the aggregator an indispensable binding tissue for the local system.

So far, platforms are not regulated in the EU. The main challenge to this model is to design and test such a platform-based market, which requires a close cooperation between aggregators and DSOs. However, if the main design rules for platforms are not regulated at the EU level, a high level of heterogeneity among local platforms can be expected, creating difficulties for the participants.

Regulators are pushing DSOs to consider non-wires alternatives before allowing network upgrades, which may foster aggregation and optimization of BTM loads. A UK platform for trading flexibility is described in Chapter 11. A prerequisite for the successful operation of a platform then lies in providing sufficient incentives for DSO(s) to use the platform. Those DSOs that are subject to CAPEX-based regulation may have little incentive to use flexibility markets instead of usual reinforcement measures. Markets catering to the DSO should therefore be formally established and promoted as a means of more efficient network operation.

The analysis above shows that aggregators are most likely to generate more value than costs by capturing and monetizing multiple value streams and catering to multiple customer groups (Fig. 5.2). Obtaining value from multiple sources makes an aggregator less reliant on a particular customer group or activity. Many of the barriers described in Section 5.3 are being gradually lifted thanks to, among others, the adoption of the EU Clean Energy Package, Network Codes, and individual national initiatives.

This discussion, together with the summary in Table 5.2, highlights the issues that still need to be organized or regulated so that more aggregators can find profitable niches. As aggregators are already actively engaged in portfolio optimization and software development, they are well-positioned to harvest value from local resources, either through community solutions or flexibility platforms. These value streams can be exploited in addition to optimized consumption, which is the main driver and a prerequisite for value stacking. It is necessary that the individuals give their permission to use the aggregated resources not only for local trading but also for market operations of an aggregator. This also offers more financial benefits to the participants in the aggregated community pool or flexibility platform.

Aggregators can help to move the sector beyond the traditional mentality of considering electricity in terms of kWhs that are fed into the grid by large companies and withdrawn by consumers. A focus on consumers shifts this view, first toward service and later toward solution-oriented thinking. This is especially true because the shares of BTM technologies are rapidly growing allowing aggregators to offer bundled services. However, the margins appear to be razor-thin, hence scale is critical to profitability.

5.6 Conclusion

Recent changes in technology, regulation, and market design affect the business models of aggregators. This chapter identified new ways in which these business models may evolve and deliver value for aggregators' customers and energy system as a whole. The analysis of the drivers and barriers to their market penetration were underpinned by a critical assessment of the state of European electricity sector regulation, national examples, and a broad overview of business models of 26 European aggregators. Their number will most likely grow given the emergence of prosumers and the growing need for system flexibility, although it is not certain whether they will remain independent. The attractiveness of the aggregator business is high enough for the incumbents to integrate it in their existing activities, as was shown in the analysis in this chapter.

Five factors have so far helped established independent aggregators to maintain a foothold in the market:

- active marketing strategy combined with a positioning as a branch and IT expert;
- speed of innovation and business model agility, that is, adjustment of the business model given the national regulatory context and the needs of the sector;
- value stacking, that is, deriving value from multiple streams and customer groups;
- strategic partnerships that allowed aggregators to expand their activities into new countries; and
- aggregators' own active participation in shaping the policy dialogue and regulatory framework.

These factors will remain relevant in the future as demand for local flexibility continues to grow.

Whether an independent aggregator manages to carve out a niche for himself further depends on the country conditions and the chosen combination of value streams. Their relevance is seen to be growing not only as electricity market participants but also as providers of specialized service offerings for other actors, software-as-a-service, and platform-as-a-service enter the market. The development of community-based solutions, P2P trade, and local energy markets may help aggregators position themselves as local orchestrators.

This chapter explored three future value streams for an aggregator enabled by the recent regulatory changes in the EU and the factors for successful commercial evolution. Through offering their services to local energy communities, aggregators can provide sector knowledge along with technical and financial expertise for such communities to develop. As a facilitator of P2P trade, an aggregator can enable automated transactions, optimized local energy use, and generate savings for consumers. Finally, as a multisided platform operator, an aggregator can provide a service to the DSO and a chance to consumers or small generators to profit from their flexibility. For these models to be successful and replicable, a number of issues such as purchase of electricity from multiple sellers and network tariff schemes must be revised, and more specific rules guiding local energy solutions and P2P trade, the roles and responsibilities involved, as well as the design of multi-sided platforms must be addressed in regulation in more detail.

Whether provided by an independent market player or by an incumbent participant, aggregation is core to the future development of the electricity sector allowing to integrate BTM solutions into the systems and activate consumers.

Acknowledgment

The authors would like to thank Aby Chacko (tiko), Stephan Marty (KiWi Power), and Matthias Dilthey (sonnen) for the discussions that contributed to this chapter.

References

ACER/CEER. (2018). *Annual report on the results of monitoring the internal electricity and gas markets in 2017— Electricity and gas retail markets volume* (p. 35). Agency for the Cooperation of Energy Regulators and the Council of European Energy Regulators. Retrieved from <https://www.acer.europa.eu/Official_documents/ Acts_of_the_Agency/Publication/MMR%202017%20-%20RETAIL.pdf>.

ARERA. (2017). Delibera ARERA 372/2017/R/eel—Approvazione regolamento relativo al progetto pilota per la partecipazione della domanda al MSD. In *Pub. L. No. 372/2017/R/EEL.*

Borne, O., Korte, K., Perez, Y., Petit, M., & Purkus, A. (2018). Barriers to entry in frequency-regulation services markets: Review of the status quo and options for improvements. *Renewable and Sustainable Energy Reviews, 81*, 605–614. Available from https://doi.org/10.1016/j.rser.2017.08.052.

Deuchert, B. (2019). NODES – A new market design to trade decentralized flexibility. In *Presented at the Grid service markets symposium.* Lucerne, Switzerland. Retrieved from <https://gsm450601838.files.wordpress.com/ 2019/07/g0405-is09-20190704-nodes-gsm.pdf>.

Dijkstra, J. (2019). Ameland: frontrunner in the energy transition. Presented at the Grid Service Markets Symposium, Lucerne, Switzerland. Retrieved from <https://gsm450601838.files.wordpress.com/2019/07/ g0201-is15-presentatie_zurich_3-7-2019_without_movie.pdf>.

Directive 2018/2001/EU. (2019). Directive (EU) 2018/2001 of the European Parliament and of the Council of 11 December 2018 on the promotion of the use of energy from renewable sources (recast). *OJ L 328*, 82–209, 21.12.2018.

Directive 2019/44/EU. (2019). Directive (EU) 2019/44 of the European Parliament and of the Council of 5 June 2019 on common rules for the internal market for electricity and amending Directive 2012/27/EU (recast). *OJ L 158*, 125–195, 14.06.2019.

Eid, C., Codani, P., Chen, Y., Perez, Y., & Hakvoort, R. (2015). Aggregation of demand side flexibility in a smart grid: A review for European market design. In *Presented at the 2015 12th International conference on the European Energy Market (EEM 2015).* May 19, 2015, Lisbon, Portugal. <https://doi.org/10.1109/EEM.2015.7216712>.

ELEXON. (2018). *Enabling customers to buy power from multiple providers* (p. 8). ELEXON. [White paper]. Retrieved from <https://www.elexon.co.uk/wp-content/uploads/2018/04/ELEXON-White-Paper-Enabling-customers-to-buy-power-from-multiple-providers.pdf>.

ENTSO-E. (2017). *Survey on ancillary services procurement, balancing market design 2016* (p. 222). ENTSO-E. Retrieved from <https://www.entsoe.eu/Documents/Publications/Market%20Committee%20publications/ WGAS_Survey_final_10.03.2017.pdf>.

EPEX SPOT. (2019). Local flexibility markets: Beyond the status-quo. In *Presented at the Grid service markets symposium.* July 2019, Lucerne, Switzerland. Retrieved from <https://gsm450601838.files.wordpress.com/2019/07/ g0401-is08-epex_spot_local_flexibility_gsm-luzern_04072019.pdf>.

Erneuerbare-Energien-Gesetz (EEG). (2017, 2019). Gesetz für den Ausbau erneuerbarer Energien (Renewable Energies Act, amendment of 2017). In *BGBI. I S.706.*

European Commission. (2017). Commission Regulation (EU) 2017/2195 of 23 November 2017 establishing a guideline on electricity balancing. *OJ L 312*, 6–53.

Evans, D. S., Hagiu, A., & Schmalensee, R. (2008). *Invisible engines: How software platforms drive innovation and transform industries.* Cambridge, MA: MIT Press.

Hagel, J., & Singer, M. (1999). *Unbundling the corporation. Harvard Business Review.* Boston, MA: Harvard Business School Publishing, March-April issue.

International Energy Agency. (2018). *World energy outlook.*

Koliou, E., Eid, C., Chaves-Ávila, J. P., & Hakvoort, R. A. (2014). Demand response in liberalized electricity markets: Analysis of aggregated load participation in the German balancing mechanism. *Energy, 71,* 245–254. Available from https://doi.org/10.1016/j.energy.2014.04.067.

Lund, P., Nyeng, P., Duban Grandal, R., Sorensen, S.H., Bendtsen, M.F., le Ray, G., ... Mac Dougall, P.A. (2016). EcoGrid EU — A prototype for European smart grids. In *Deliverable D6.7. Overall evaluation and conclusion* (p. 92). Energinet.dk.

Merino, J., Gomez, I., Turienzo, E., Madina, C., Cobelo, I., & Morch, A. (2016). *Ancillary service provision by RES and DSM connected at distribution level in the future power system (no. D1.1).* Project SmartNet. Retrieved from <http://smartnet-project.eu/wp-content/uploads/2016/12/D1-1_20161220_V1.0.pdf>.

Metz, A. (2018). *European utilities have increased their activity in new energy platforms.* Navigant Research. <https://www.navigantresearch.com/news-and-views/european-utilities-have-increased-their-activity-in-new-energy-platforms-part-1> Retrieved 02.05.19.

Ministry for the Environmental Transition. (2019). *Real Decreto 244/2019, de 5 de abril, por el que se regulan las condiciones administrativas, técnicas y económicas del autoconsumo de energía eléctrica. In Pub. L. No. BOE-A-2019-5089.*

Navigant Research. (2019). *Residential energy storage: Advanced lead-acid, flow, and Li-ion batteries for residential applications: Global capacity and revenue forecasts* (p. 40) Washington, DC: Navigant.

Osterwalder, A., Pigneur, Y., & Clark, T. (2010). *Business model generation.* Hoboken, NJ: Wiley.

Poplavskaya, K., & De Vries, L.J. (2018). A (not so) independent aggregator in the electricity market: Theory, policy and reality check. In *Presented at the 15th International conference on the European energy market.* June 27, 2018, Lodz, Poland. <https://doi.org/10.1109/EEM.2018.8469981>.

Poplavskaya, K., & De Vries, L. J. (2019). Distributed energy resources and the organized balancing market: A symbiosis yet? Case of three European balancing markets. *Energy Policy, 126,* 264–276. Available from https://doi.org/10.1016/j.enpol.2018.11.009.

Sia Partners. (2018). *Peer-to-peer (P2P) energy: A threat or an opportunity for traditional suppliers ?* Energy Outlook by sia Partners. <http://energy.sia-partners.com/20180911/peer-peer-p2p-energy-threat-or-opportunity-traditional-suppliers> Retrieved 15.04.19.

Van Soest, H. (2018). Peer-to-peer electricity trading: A review of the legal context. *Competition and Regulation in Network Industries, 19*(3–4), 180–199. Available from https://doi.org/10.1177/1783591719834902.

Annex A Overview of business models of European aggregators

Name	Country	Specifics	Business model	Portfolio specifics
A1 Energy Solutions https://www. a1energysolutions. at/	AT	Originally telecom company	• Participation in the AT balancing market • Asset management and optimization • Service provider for suppliers (as VPP operator), municipal utilities and energy-intensive industries • Own communication and data management platform using A1 own network suitable for monitoring • Own hardware, grid control (also as white label) • DR (peak load shaving and shifting) • Acts as its own BRP	Pool of CHP plants, small hydro, heat pumps, emergency power generators, wind, biogas, boilers, etc. Industrial DR, private households with adjustable loads (electric boilers, heat pumps as well as batteries or PV panels)
Actility https:// www.actility.com/	FR; also operates in BE, NL, UK, DE, IT, etc.	Mostly provider of IoT services	• Utility services (e.g., smart meter applications) • IoT network infrastructure and connectivity solutions: ThinkPark Energy platform • Smart energy management for commercial and industrial customers • Demand response facilitator for grid operators	
BayWar.e. https:// www.baywa-re. com/en/	DE; also operates in ES, FR, UK, Scandinavian countries	Spinoff of a trading conglomerate, BayWa	• Optimization of self-consumption for commercial and industrial customers	7000 MW of generation managed worldwide Supply of green electricity to 25,000

(Continued)

(Continued)

Name	Country	Specifics	Business model	Portfolio specifics
			• Energy trading services • Collaboration with EPEX operator of EPEX Flexibility Marketplace in a pilot flexibility platform in northern Germany for TSO/DSO services • Electricity supply of end users	corporate and private customers
Ecotricity https://www.ecotricity.co.uk/	UK	Originally, green energy supplier	• Offers a VPP solution to green energy providers (wind, solar, and green gas), consumers, and storage operators • Green electricity supplier for household and business customers	n/a
Energy2Market (e2m) https://www.e2m.energy	Originally from DE; operates in FI, IT, FR, BE, PL, SE, NO, AT; UK	Planned to be acquired by EDF in 2019	• Portfolio manager and VPP operator for generators, switchable loads, and storage • White-label offers to utilities outside DE • Service provider for balancing energy (FCR and FRR products) • Partners with Swytch, Blockchain-based RES data and incentive platform, Blockchain protocol development for RES monitoring	VPP total capacity over 3500 MW ($\sim$1200 MW of wind, 1600 MW of biomass, $\sim$633 MW of solar, 90 MW of hydro power); industrial loads and storage facilities
EnergyPool https://www.energy-pool.eu/	Originally from FR; also operates in DE, BE, UK, NO, etc.	Strategic partnership with Schneider Electric	• Demand response aggregator of industrial and large commercial consumers for short-term electricity markets, balancing market and capacity market	4 GW of flexible load, 2 GW of generation assets and DER

(Continued)

(Continued)

Name	Country	Specifics	Business model	Portfolio specifics
Enel X https:// www.enelx.com/ en/	Originally: US; also operates in: UK; IT, DE, FR, IR	American EnerNOC acquired by Italian Enel in 2017	• Solution for utilities and system operators: DERMS, and Flexmart VPP platform • DR aggregator for businesses • Energy management and software provider • Proprietary software for asset optimization; customized energy procurement tools • Capacity auction participation in Ireland	Flexible load, storage, and electric vehicles 217 MW demand response in Ireland's capacity auction
Entelios https:// entelios-de-web-test.azurewebsites. net/	DE; also operates in NO, SE, and CH	Acquired by Adger Energi	• Industrial DR aggregation and portfolio management • Flexibility trading on part of the client • Participation in the balancing market and German market for interruptible loads • proprietary Entelios Software Suite and white-label DR-as-a-Service • Cooperates with a flexibility platform operator, NODES, operator to provide DR to German DSOs	Industrial and commercial flexible loads, generation, and storage
Enyway https://en. enyway.com/	DE	Spinoff of Lichtblick	• Prosumer service provider: allows households obtain an own share of a large-scale PV panel for 39€ or 99€ for building costs; Enyway is the operator; Enyway uses Blockchain for assigning shares of PV	Large 1.5 MW PV sharing; operators of 35 solar, wind, and small hydro generators

(Continued)

One. Visionaries, dreamers, innovators

(Continued)

Name	Country	Specifics	Business model	Portfolio specifics
			• Provides and operates an online marketplace for local trading between end users and small-scale RES operators	
Flexitricity https://www.flexitricity.com/	UK	Acquired by Alpiq (Swiss electric utility) in 2014	• Largest UK aggregator of industrial DR • Short-term market trading • Balancing market participation, including short-term operating reserve and capacity market in the UK • Use of Footroom or Demand turn-up to avoid curtailment of wind farms by the TSO • Projects where it provides services for DSOs to refer infrastructure investments	Generation and load: CHP, manufacturing loads, sewage and landfill gas, diesel, small hydro and storage, space cooling and cold storage Portfolio of c. 300 MW
Grupo ASE https://www.grupoase.net/asesor-energetico-grupo-ase/	ES		• Largest aggregator of large-scale industrial and commercial DR in Spain • Portfolio management • Energy service company for large customers	400 large-scale and 1100 medium-scale industrial and commercial clients
Jedlix https://jedlix.com/	NL	Owned by Dutch supplier, Eneco	• Smart-charging platform provider, e-car fleet operator and aggregator, customer app, concludes contracts with car manufacturers • Partners with Next Kraftwerke for TSO services	EV fleet ~6000 cars ~60 MW

(Continued)

One. Visionaries, dreamers, innovators

(Continued)

Name	Country	Specifics	Business model	Portfolio specifics
KiWi Power/ Kiwigrid https:// www.kiwipowered. com/	Originally from UK; also operates in FR, NL, CH, BE, DK, and DE	Engie is a stakeholderoriginally, a technology provider; now focuses on strategic partnerships	• Technology provider (own software and hardware, KiWi Fruit) • Asset management and optimization • Platform-as-a-Service for DER management • Grid balancing, capacity market • Constraint management for system operators • Peak shaving • Service provider for utilities → outside of the UK operates through building partnerships with utilities with local knowledge and expertise • KOMPv2 platform for automated DR • Service provider for other aggregators • Transactive Grid solution (platform) • Flexibility platform operator in Flexhub project • charging pattern optimization/smart charging	>1 GW of connected DER in total; 70 MW of battery systems in the UK, several hundred MW; includes commercial and industrial DR (e.g., from hotel chains, hospitals or industrial customers for AC, heat pumps, refrigeration); bulk and BTM battery storage (for customers with load of 1MW +) and DR, RES, EVs, and charging stations
LichtBlick https:// www.lichtblick.de/	DE		• Independent demand aggregator • Product SchwarmEnergie, including battery, EV, heating, and home appliance aggregation • RES supplier of end users using Lichtblick's components: fixed 0€/month consumption tariff	Biggest solar provider (c. 1,000,000 household customers); flexible loads, battery and thermal storage, and distributed generation Supply of electricity from RES to 70,000 commercial and industrial customers

(Continued)

One. Visionaries, dreamers, innovators

(Continued)

Name	Country	Specifics	Business model	Portfolio specifics
Limejump https://limejump.com/	UK	Energy technology company; acquired by Shell in 2019	• Prequalified participant in UK's frequency response and balancing mechanism • Participation in the UK capacity market • Generation management and forecasting services • Power purchase agreements with RES providers • Project to provide peak load management with batteries for a British DSO	185 MW of energy storage; batteries, chillers, CHP engines, etc.
Lumenaza https://www.lumenaza.de/de/	DE	Software developer	• Platform provider for consumers, suppliers and generators; • Community/P2P trading solutions • "Direct sale" offering to German prosumers • Balancing group management as a BRP • Can act a retail supplier	Projects included aggregation of residential PV and battery storage as well as of wind parks
Mark-E https://www.mark-e.de/	DE		• Electricity supply of end users • Participates in balancing mFRR and aFRR with Mark-E Power Pool of small-scale generation • "Direct sale" offering for RES operators	c. 40% RES; portfolio of 2200 MW 368,000 customers Pool of small-scale generation (of min 500 kW)
Mobility House https://www.mobilityhouse.com/	DE		• EV fleet and load management with own software • optimization of EV charging; V2G solutions	Second-hand car batteries; partners with Nissan: stationary second hand car batteries (13 MWh); 3 MWh

(*Continued*)

(Continued)

Name	Country	Specifics	Business model	Portfolio specifics
			• EV park as mobile storage (project for TenneT DE);—uses Blockchain technology	battery storage sites in NL: 30 MW +
Next Kraftwerke https://www.next-kraftwerke.de/	Originally from DE; also operates in NL, BE, AT, ITA and FR, and CH		• Own software: Next Box • Balancing market participation • Acts as its own BRP • Schedule optimization for asset owners, generators, and consumers • Wholesale market trading with a VPP • In NL partners with AgroEnergy and Tenergy to provide Incidence reserve for the Dutch TSO, TenneT—in NL cooperates with Jedlix for TenneT NL to provide short-term storage from an EV pool • Service provider elsewhere in the world: offers platform/digital solutions for different applications, e.g., NEXTRA (trading and portfolio optimization tool for utilities, BRPs and other aggregators)	c. 6800 MW, 2550 MW of flexibility (c. 7600 units) and over 700 MW of aggregated consumers; RES aggregator in Italy; greenhouse lighting, CHPs or an EV car pool in NL
Noodvermodelpool http://nlnvp.nl/	NL	Acquired by Actility in 2017	• Largest DR aggregator in NL • Prequalified provider of emergency reserve (balancing product) in NL	Includes c. 40 industrial partners from the water industry, hospitals, and data centers

(Continued)

One. Visionaries, dreamers, innovators

(Continued)

Name	Country	Specifics	Business model	Portfolio specifics
Restore https://restore.energy/en/	Originally from BE; also operates in DE, UK, FR, NL	Acquired by Centrica in 2017	• Energy technology provider • Balancing (FCR and aFRR) and capacity market participation with BTM assets of large industrial and commercial clients; • Service to large customers through proprietary software, FlexTreo. • FlexPond platform solution for utilities	Industrial DR (e.g., steel, paper, chemical industry) 2300 MW of aggregated flexibility
Smart Grid Energy https://www.smartgridenergy.fr/	FR		• Demand-side management of commercial and industrial clients • Asset management and optimization of generation • Participation in the FR balancing and capacity markets	Large flexible industrial and commercial load of c. 600 MW (paper, metal, chemical, cement industries, hospitals, logistics centers); rapid reserves 500 MW. Key figure in capacity mechanisms— 1000 MW
Sonnen https://sonnengroup.com/	Originally from DE; also operates in IT, UK	Originally, technology provider (battery manufacturing and EV chargers); acquired by Shell in 2019	• Own technology, sonnenBatterie • Operation of an own platform, sonnenCommunity, for electricity sharing with surplus stored in a virtual electricity pool • Offers a special sonnenFlat tariff to flexibility providers • Aggregated storage used for balancing market participation (prequalified for FCR) • Electricity supply of end users	battery storage: 40,000 household batteries worldwide— 300 MWh combined with smart home management

(Continued)

One. Visionaries, dreamers, innovators

(Continued)

Name	Country	Specifics	Business model	Portfolio specifics
			• participates in pilot project of a German TSO, TenneT, for redispatch using batteries and Blockchain • Pilot project for local congestion management in DE	
Sympower https://www.sympower.net/	NL, FI		• Balancing market participation with industrial demand response	Flexible loads (cooling, heating, ventilation, lighting, and water systems)
tiko Energy Solutions https://tiko.energy/	Originally from CH; active in FR, DE, AT	Shareholders include Swisscom, the biggest Swiss telecom company	• DR aggregator/VPP operator • Technology provider (outside CH) • Micro-local management of household electricity equipment • Balancing service in CH (FCR, aFRR) • BRP services • Partners with conventional power plants • In other countries, active through partnerships: • e.g., FCR provision in DE in partnership with Sonnen	>100 MW: heating/cooling, water boilers, batteries, PV, EV chargers, heat pumps
Voltalis http://www.voltalis.fr/	FR		• Largest aggregation platform for DR • Optimization of self-consumption with Voltalis Box • Ancillary services for the TSO • IoT service provider for utilities and DSO • Home energy management solutions and app	Commercial, industrial and also residential DR (100,000 + individuals connected) 1,000,000 connected appliances: water boilers, electric heating systems, air conditioning, batteries, EVs, and solar PV

AT, Austria; *BE*, Belgium; *BRP*, balance responsible party; *BTM*, behind-the-meter; *CH*, Switzerland; *CHP*, combined heat an power; *DE*, Germany; *DERMS*, distributed energy resource management system; *DK*, Denmark; *DR*, demand response; *DSO*, distribution system operator; *ES*, Spain; *EV*, electric vehicle; *FCR*, frequency containment reserve; *FI*, Finland; *FR*, France; *FRR*, frequency restoration reserve; *IoT*, Internet of things; *IR*, Ireland; *IT*, Italy; *NL*, The Netherlands; *NO*, Norway; *P2P*, peer-to-peer; *PL*, Poland; *RES*, renewable energy sources; *SE*, Sweden; *TSO*, transmission system operator; *UK*, United Kingdom; *US*, United States; *V2G*, vehicle-to-grid; *VPP*, virtual power plant.

Energy communities: a Dutch case study

Victor M.J.J. Reijnders[1], Marten D. van der Laan[2] and Roelof Dijkstra[3]

[1]University of Twente, Enschede, The Netherlands [2]ICT Group N.V., Groningen, The Netherlands [3]Enexis Netbeheer B.V., Groningen, The Netherlands

6.1 Introduction

All around the world, local communities are popping up, which aim to organize their energy production and consumption. Many of these communities do not want to be dependent on large, faceless energy companies. Instead, they believe that there is only one way to become more environmental-friendly; to get, to some extent, independent of the overall energy system by organizing a local energy system where energy is locally produced, consumed, stored, and shared. In 2018 around 500 energy communities were active in The Netherlands alone. Similarly, in other parts of Europe, the number of energy communities has been steadily growing over the years (Stichting HIER Opgewekt, 2019). In many cases, these communities consist of proactive prosumers which want to be part of a decentralized, decarbonized, and digitalized energy system and aim to push the energy transition forward.

The increasing environmental awareness leads to a yearly increase in the share of electric vehicles (EVs), photovoltaic (PV) systems, and batteries owned by households. However, the increase of these assets also introduces problems to the local energy infrastructure, mainly to the electricity system (Koirala, Koliou, Friege, Hakvoort, & Herder, 2016). These problems include voltage and frequency issues, which are often due to the highly synchronized electrical loads and demands. Energy communities may contribute to these problems, but they can also be part of the solution to overcome these problems. If the individual consumers in a community coordinate their energy-related behavior in some way, this can be the starting point for the decentralized optimization of their combined energy profile.

In literature a growing interest in decentralized energy management solutions can be found (Bahrami, Toulabi, Ranjbar, Moeini-Aghtaie, & Ranjbar, 2017; Kaundinya, Balachandra, & Ravindranath, 2009; Thomas, Zhou, Long, Wu, & Jenkins, 2019). An advantage of such decentralized solutions is that they are often still computationally tractable, solve the problems at the place where they occur, retain economic benefits locally, and support the inhabitants in changing their behavior (Koirala et al., 2016; Lu et al., 2011). In general, the concepts that arise in a specific decentralized context may only solve the concrete problem at hand, but these concepts can be copied to other locations. Centralized solutions may, in theory, be able to solve the energy management problem to optimality. However, their solutions are not scalable, especially taking into account the growing number of steerable devices in the electrification at hand and are therefore no longer a suitable option.

As mentioned above, one approach to realize decentralized energy solutions is through a citizen energy community where the members control the community to provide environmental, economic, or social benefits to the community or the local area (European Parliament and the Council of the European Union, 2019). With this, the community members may control the actions of the community themselves or may outsource this control to a third party, for example, an aggregator.

An example of a beneficial decentralized solution is lowering the load on the grid coupling point of an energy community. Lowering this load does not only reduce the transport losses but also unburdens the remainder of the grid. From this reduction, several players in the system would benefit. The network operator could give a discount on the network tariff since the peak load on the coupling point is lower, and therefore the stress on his network would decrease. A lowered stress, in turn, would increase the life span of most assets and lower the need to replace (underground) cables in the (near) future (Groen, 2018). For the energy supplier the energy consumption of the neighborhood becomes more predictable or even "shapable," and the supplier can purchase energy at a lower cost. The supplier may therefore also give the community a discount on their electricity price. These discounts together could stimulate the energy community to reduce its peak loads.

Since a community is set up by its members, the members need to find a way to share the savings they achieve as a community. Next to compensating the individual members, an alternative way may be to use the savings to, for example, buy community-owned solar panels, or to set up a community playground.

Focusing on the shared connection and not on individual households takes a different approach than most other methods to reduce the stress on the grid. In this case the network operator and energy supplier are only concerned with the energy flow on the common connection point, and not with what is happening behind this point. So instead of managing everything behind the meter of a single household, a neighborhood can be aggregated and managed with appropriate methods, such as innovative pricing mechanisms or an energy management system.

This chapter considers a real-world project, called GridFlex Heeten, where a control strategy for a neighborhood is applied, which aims to influence the energy flow at the common connection point of this neighborhood. In the future the concept may be extended to other neighborhoods.

This chapter is organized as follows:

- Section 6.2 considers energy communities and their benefits.
- Section 6.3 describes the mentioned GridFlex Heeten project.
- Section 6.4 analyzes the difficulties to extend energy community concepts.
- Section 6.5 presents the key results of the case study, followed by the conclusions of the chapter.

6.2 Energy communities

Several interchangeable terms with minor differences are used to describe energy communities, and the usage mainly depends on the geographical origin of the publication. The most frequently used terms include the following:

- According to the European Commission, a **Citizen Energy Community** is citizen energy community' means a legal entity that: "(a) is based on voluntary and open participation and is effectively controlled by members or shareholders that are natural persons, local authorities, including municipalities, or small enterprises; (b) has for its primary purpose to provide environmental, economic or social community benefits to its members or shareholders or to the local areas where it operates rather than to generate financial profits; and (c) may engage in generation, including from renewable sources, distribution, supply, consumption, aggregation, energy storage, energy efficiency services or charging services for electric vehicles or provide other energy services to its members or shareholders;" [Article 2 of the Electricity Directive, (European Parliament and the Council of the European Union, 2019)].
- In the same directive the European Commission also speaks about **Renewable Energy Communities**. These can generally be seen as a subset of citizen energy communities, as the members of renewable energy communities need to be located in the proximity of renewable energy projects owned and developed by the community (Roberts, Frieden, & d'Herbemont, 2019). This indicates that there are more stringent requirements to become a renewable energy community.
- **Advanced Energy Communities** is a term mostly used in the United States (Narayanamurthy, 2016). Although being very similar to the European Commission definition, the advanced energy communities focus more on the technologies being used within the community.
- In Japan the term **Smart Community** is used (Japan Smart Community Alliance, 2015). Also here, the Smart Community does not need to be locally operated or owned at all.
- In Australia the term **Community Energy** is defined by Australian Renewable Energy Agency (ARENA) (2015). ARENA takes the definition a bit broader, thereby including any community renewable energy project.

Even though a community focuses on local benefits, it does not mean that all members are situated in that same area. Places and communities are not synonymous—there can rather be multiple overlapping communities in one place (Walker, Devine-Wright, Hunter, High, & Evans, 2010). A citizen energy community is simply a community where citizens own and participate in renewable energy or energy efficiency projects (according to REScoop).

In the context of energy communities, several other concepts are often used. Although these concepts are closely related, they are used in slightly different contexts. Note that some of these concepts are also used in other parts of this book.

- **Energy cells** consist of generators, converters, storage systems, consumers, and connections to electricity, gas, and heat distribution grids on various scales (the size of a house, neighborhood, and city) (Günther et al., 2018).
- **Microgrids** are typically defined as *"electricity distribution systems containing loads and distributed energy resources, (such as distributed generators, storage devices, or controllable loads) that can be operated in a controlled, coordinated way either while connected to the main power network or while islanded"* (Marnay et al., 2015). Here, the focus is more on the controlled operation and on being able to operate in islanded mode. In most cases, there is also a focus on financial benefits.
- A **virtual power plant (VPP)** *"aggregates the capacity of many diverse DERs, it creates a single operating profile from a composite of the parameters characterizing each DERs and can incorporate the impact of the network on aggregate DERs output. A VPP is a flexible representation of a portfolio of DERs that can be used to make contracts in the wholesale market and to offer services to the system operator"* (Pudjianto, Ramsay, & Strbac, 2007). A VPP hereby transcends the microgrid definition by not being bound to the same physical grid, as further described in Chapter 10.

This chapter focuses on citizen energy communities, as further described in the recently adopted Clean Energy Package of the European Union (EU). This new energy rulebook gives an obligation to the EU countries to adapt their legislation to allow for citizen energy communities. Because of this, these communities turn into official legal entities having corresponding rights. With the Clean Energy Package, citizen energy communities obtain rights to

- generate, consume, and sell their own renewable energy;
- share energy within the community; and
- engage in individual and "jointly acting" self-consumption.

The latter, however, is restricted to joint self-consumption in the same building or apartment block. According to the EU legislation, consumers shall have entry to all electricity markets to trade their flexibility and self-generated electricity, and consumers should have the possibility to participate in all forms of demand response. The EU directive has been put into force in June 2019; member states have until June 2021 to implement the directive in their national legislation.

As mentioned before, the definition of citizen energy communities does not imply proximity. As long as there is a legal entity that is owned and controlled by the members, they can be considered to belong to the same community. Together they can aim to control their energy flows to be, for example, energy-neutral over a specific period (e.g., a year) or even energy-independent. However, since these members are not necessarily located on the same part of the grid, the benefits of being energy-independent are not visible when looking at the actual energy flows in the corresponding grids. The transportation losses and the stress on the network could even increase as being an energy-independent community might imply that large amounts of energy are exchanged between different members of the community. As such, it has an advantage if the members of a community are also physically in one area and connected to the same network.

On the European scale, there are thousands of energy communities (Wierling et al., 2018) and over 1,000,000 citizens involved (REScoop.eu, 2018). The organization REScoop. eu is the European federation for renewable energy cooperatives and has a growing network of 1500 European cooperatives. Most are active in production; some examples are

- ODE decentraal in The Netherlands (ODE, 2019) and
- DGRV in Germany (DGRV, 2019).

Others organize the energy supply for their members, such as

- Energie VanOns in The Netherlands (Energie VanOns, 2019),
- COCITER in Belgium (COCITER scrl, 2018), and
- Ènostra in Italy (ènostra, 2016).

Furthermore, EWS in Germany (EWS Schönau, 2019) is active in distribution. More information on EWS and their peer-to-peer energy trading community can be found in Chapter 4 of this book. Additionally, an interesting example of an energy community, which is similar to the considered case in this chapter, can be found in Chapter 3.

This chapter is focusing on energy communities that are physically close to each other. In particular, they should have a common coupling point to the electricity grid by, for example, being connected to the same low voltage/medium voltage (LV/MV) transformer (Fig. 6.1). In this sense, achieving lower peaks as a community actually lowers the stress on the grid.

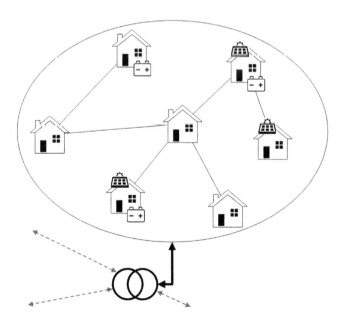

FIGURE 6.1 An energy community located on the same part of the grid with a transformer as a common point of coupling.

The concept of energy communities used in this chapter is closest to the microgrids mentioned above. In literature, much attention is paid to microgrids (Hirsch, Parag, & Guerrero, 2018; Zia, Fahad, Elbouchikhi, & Benbouzid, 2018), whereby a clear distinction is made between islanded, and nonislanded microgrids.

Islanded microgrids are not relying on the main electricity grid (or only very seldom) (Bakar, Hassan, Sulaima, Nasir, & Khamis, 2017; Kaundinya et al., 2009). All energy generation and load balancing have to be done within the microgrid, making it independent and resilient to disturbances in the main grid.

The difference to nonislanded microgrids is that nonislanded microgrids still regularly use their connection to the main grid, although they often limit the power exchange. Becoming an islanded microgrid is not that common since the investment and operating costs are very high. Besides that, there are not many benefits in becoming islanded, and legislation around it is a challenge (van der Mei, Doomernik, & Lalieu, 2019). The energy communities which consist of physically close entities could best be compared to a nonislanded microgrid, although in a community, the members themselves control the community and are less focused on financial benefits.

Like nonislanded microgrids, energy communities may aim to become more independent from the main grid. However, there are also benefits to gain by staying connected to the grid, for example, for offering certain flexibility services to the grid an energy community which can create extra income. An overview of such energy services and flexibility services for communities is given in (USEF, 2019) and further explained in the remainder of this section. In total, seven different energy and flexibility services are distinguished in USEF (Fig. 6.2).

These seven services are the main benefits for forming an energy community, and some of these propositions can be found back in existing projects. The seven energy and flexibility services for communities are as follows:

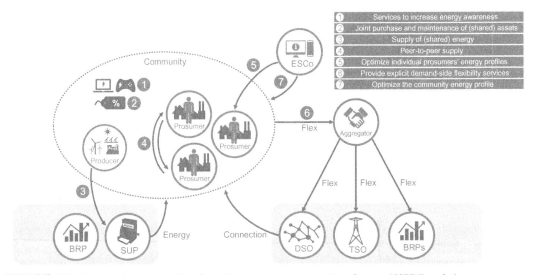

FIGURE 6.2   Seven value propositions for citizens energy communities. Source: *USEF Foundation.*

- **Services to increase energy awareness**. Mostly this includes training and information sharing, but also the use of smart meter data to better understand individual consumption patterns and the impact of renewable generation on the energy balance. In the case that a consumer has rooftop PV installed, he or she will better understand the challenge to reach day−night balance and summer/winter balance.
- **Joint purchase and maintenance of (shared) assets**. Most communities start via shared investments in renewable generation resources like wind turbines or solar farms. Typically, the energy generated by their resources is sold to an energy wholesale market party via a so-called power purchase agreement.
- **Supply of (shared) energy**. Once generation capacity is available, communities can further evolve by organizing self-supply from their resources. To this end, the community should take the electricity supplier role, including the responsibilities related to this (regulated) role, or associate with an existing supplier. Furthermore, the community, as a legal entity, must respect the freedom of individual consumers to choose their supplier without being expelled from the community.
- **Peer-to-peer supply**. A logical extension to self-supply is to facilitate peer-to-peer transactions between the participants. Here, an infrastructure for keeping track of all transactions and setting the prices for electricity must be in place.
- **Optimize individual Prosumers' energy profiles**. In case the participants have a certain degree of flexibility in their consumption and generation, that is, can shape their energy profiles, this flexibility can be used to create added value. The flexibility can be used to optimize the individual profiles towards increased self-consumption, reduced peak load, or in response to dynamic tariffs. This is sometimes referred to as *implicit demand response.*
- **Provide explicit demand-side flexibility services**. The flexibility of the participants can be used to deliver flexibility services to stakeholders in the electricity market. For example, a community can bundle the individual pieces of flexibility into a larger volume and offer balancing services to transmission system operators, congestion management services to grid operators, or trade on the electricity markets. This is sometimes referred to as *explicit demand response.* Typically the flexibility is offered via a market bid, acquired by the counterparty, activated, and settled afterward. The community takes the so-called aggregator or demand−response operator role and (risk) positions in the various markets.
- **Optimize the community energy profile**. Instead of optimizing the individual profile, one could optimize the joint profile. It must be noted, however, that there is not always an economic benefit. This depends on local pricing structures, taxes, and other legislation.

The community may take several roles in the traditional energy field. Taking a supplier or aggregator role, as needed in some of the services listed above, requires a certain level of organization and professionalism of the community as these roles impose a lot of risks and responsibilities. This maturity is also required for taking over some responsibilities of a distribution system operator (DSO), in case the community wants to operate as a microgrid.

TABLE 6.1   Details of Dutch energy communities in 2018 (Stichting HIER Opgewekt, 2019).

Location	Number of communities	Number of citizens	Community solar power (MWp)	Community wind power (MW)
The Netherlands	~500	~70,000	74.5	159

Most often, a community initiative starts with an enthusiastic group of people. However, it seems that it is challenging to ensure continuity. The reasons for this may be that the risks are hard to bear and difficult to share amongst the community members or that the community faces some competition of traditional suppliers who have certain competitive advantages due to their larger size (Seyfang, Park, & Smith, 2013). An example of such an advantage occurs in the case of balance responsibility of a portfolio. This task is typically easier with increased portfolio size. Thus, in the long run, energy communities may need to structure their organization and grow to a critical mass to survive.

Despite all the drawbacks mentioned above, energy communities are emerging and also recently got a dominant position in the European legislation. The underlying motivations for participating in energy communities are the fact that they can take the lead in the energy transition, be in full control, and reinvest all benefits into the community. In 2018 almost 500 energy communities were identified within The Netherlands (Stichting HIER Opgewekt, 2019). This was a 20% growth compared to 2017. Further details can be found in Table 6.1. An example of a Dutch energy community is investigated in depth in the following section.

6.3 Case study of GridFlex Heeten

An example of a citizen energy community is given in the village of Heeten, The Netherlands, where 47 households are organized in a local community. All the households are situated behind a single transformer and are working together to reduce the stress on the local distribution network (Fig. 6.3). Their primary focus is on the reduction of the peaks at the transformer.

To reach their goals the community has initiated the GridFlex Heeten project (GridFlex, 2019), where a consortium of Enexis B.V.(project manager), Endona U.A., Escozon U.A., Enpuls B.V., Dr Ten B.V., ICT Group N.V., and the University of Twente are working together. The partners have the goal of using the flexibility of batteries and the flexibility of the inhabitants of the energy community in combination with novel pricing mechanisms to reduce the overall stress on the network. Lowering this stress would result in deferring or avoiding grid reinforcement, as well as reducing grid losses. This would save costs for the network operator, and indirectly, for the participants as well. Endona U.A. has obtained an exemption on the Dutch energy law for experimenting with different electricity tariffs so that these pricing mechanisms can be validated in this field test.

In the community of Heeten, some of the households have rooftop PV installations, and some are equipped with a 5 kWh battery behind the meter. All households provide access

FIGURE 6.3 An aerial view of the GridFlex Heeten energy community and the neighboring solar park. Source: *Enexis Netbeheer B.V.*

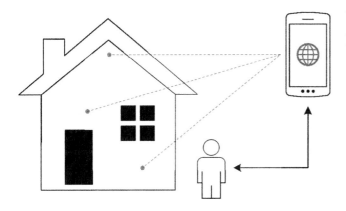

FIGURE 6.4 The inhabitant of a house gets feedback on its consumption via an app.

to their smart meter data and their PV production, giving insight into their local energy streams (Reijnders, Gerards, Hurink, & Smit, 2018). They also receive information about their energy consumption via an app on their phones (Fig. 6.4).

This information consists of their current and past energy usage, split into their gas and electricity consumption, as well as their PV production, standby usage, and self-consumption rate (Fig. 6.5, right panel). The app allows the inhabitants to get a clear view of their energy profiles and peak usage. The batteries are shown as well, so the inhabitants can get a good impression of the battery's behavior (Fig. 6.5, left panel). These households also get a price forecast for the coming 24 hours via the app (Fig. 6.5, middle panel). In this way the inhabitants can shift their energy usage to cheaper timeslots. The prices are

  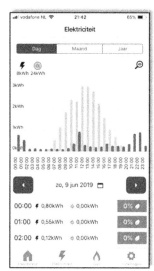

FIGURE 6.5 Overview of the app the inhabitants are using. Source: *ICT Group N.V.*

calculated in such a way that cheaper slots coincide with the periods with low energy traffic on the transformer.

Next to the actively involved participants, another 28 households in the rest of Heeten are only monitored and do not get price forecasts. In this way a change in the behavior of the community compared to this reference group can be detected.

For the pilot the households are not seen as separate entities, but as a whole community located behind one transformer. This is one of the key concepts in this project. All inhabitants behind the transformer are participating and are part of this energy community. In this way, there is one common coupling point over which the connection costs can be calculated.

Traditionally, in The Netherlands, a consumer pays the network operator for his connection (usually a three-phase 25 A connection) and the transport of energy. Network operators calculate their tariffs using an average amount of energy, namely, 3.500 kWh a year, for every consumer with a 3 × 25 A connection. Based on this amount, the total network costs are spread out over all customers. Using the average amount of energy, it means that for a community of 47 households, network operators calculate with an energy usage of 164.500 kWh a year.

In this pilot the connection cost is decoupled from the cost of transport of energy. The consumers pay for their connections as usual. Though for the cost of transport, the community is seen as though they only have one connection. This means that the energy that is transported is measured and calculated on the level of the transformer. In other words, for the transport cost, the energy that stays within the community is not charged, since it is not transported over the transformer. This promotes self-consumption within the whole neighborhood. A similar idea is also mentioned in the ETHZ project in Chapter 3 of this book.

TABLE 6.2 Levels of power demand on the transformer with the corresponding prices for the transport of energy used in the GridFlex Heeten pilot.

Level of demand	Power (kW/15 min)	Price (€/kWh)
Low	0–15	0.01
Medium	15–25	0.05
High	25 and above	0.25

The transport costs for the energy usage of the community are not calculated in the usual way. Each household still pays for the transport of their energy; only the price is different than usual. In the pilot the price of the transport per kWh depends on the total power of the community. This price increases with the power demand on the transformer. This means that every inhabitant of the neighborhood pays the same price per kWh, but the price depends on their behavior as a group.

For the price scheme, three different levels of demand with a corresponding power range on the transformer are defined. This leads to three different prices used (Table 6.2). Since the measurements on transformers take place every 15 minutes, the level of demand is determined by the average power supplied on the transformer in these 15 minutes. Consequently, the costs of transport of energy for a household are calculated by multiplying the energy consumption of the house with the price corresponding to the level of demand on the transformer. Since each household has a different energy usage in these 15 minutes, their costs for that period are different as well.

When switching to a higher level of demand, the price for every kWh increases. For the increase between two consecutive levels, the same factor is used. This implies that the result is approximately a quadratic price function which is known to support the reduction of peaks (Mohsenian-Rad, Wong, Jatskevich, & Schober, 2010). In the case of GridFlex the factor between the levels is 5. This factor, as well as the limits between the levels, is selected by analyzing past energy usage and making sure the prices to be paid by the inhabitants still are reasonable. More specifically, when the needed power for the community is lower than 15 kW, the price for transport is €0.01 per kWh, from 15 kW until 25 kW the price is €0.05 and above 25 kW the price is €0.25 for every kWh that has been transported (Table 6.2).

By using batteries and by shifting the energy consumption of the inhabitants, the community can reduce the costs of transport. The batteries are operated automatically depending on weather forecasts, past energy consumption, and information about the neighborhood. This means that the only influence the inhabitants of the neighborhood have is to change their consumption. As mentioned above, the inhabitants are supported by an app, so they know the expected level of demand on the transformer level (Fig. 6.5, central dashboard). If the inhabitants manage to decrease their energy usage in an expected high demand period, they may drop to only having a medium level of demand. This would amount to paying a factor 5 less for the transport of energy in that period.

The idea behind this pricing scheme is to reduce the transport losses of energy and to reduce the congestion on the grid (with the consequence of reduced investments in the grid). The cost reduction is highest if the community succeeds to reduce the transport of energy to zero, meaning no transport over the transformer. This way, they would even become an islanded microgrid. In this pilot the added value of batteries, along with the inhabitants' willingness to shift their energy consumption, is studied.

In terms of the seven value propositions of USEF (Fig. 6.2), the community in Heeten is an example of a community with collective generation and flexibility from batteries. The flexibility is used in an implicit demand—response scheme on a community level to minimize the joint peak load. This would correspond to the seventh type of energy and flexibility service for communities, as introduced in Section 6.2. Typically, as a side result also the joint self-consumption rate will increase since people want to reduce peaks and keep all energy behind the meter, and therefore also behind the transformer.

By reducing the peaks, the network operator has some benefits as well. The assets in the electricity grid do not age as quickly as they would otherwise, and the costs for maintenance or even replacement can be lowered. Also, there may be fewer voltage problems in the neighborhood, and there might be no need (yet) to upgrade to a more expensive transformer (Groen, 2018). Therefore the network operator can offer some remuneration to the inhabitants, as is done now with the variable transport cost.

In the pilot the added value of the batteries within the pricing scheme has been extensively evaluated. The results of this effort are presented in Section 6.5. However, the pilot is still running, and further data is being collected to get a better understand to which extent the inhabitants are willing to shift their energy consumption.

6.4 Extending the GridFlex concept

In this section the fundamental difficulties for extending the GridFlex concept and other concepts for energy communities are addressed. This includes an analysis of the possibilities in current legislation and some suggestions on how to change this legislation to overcome the problems faced by energy communities nowadays.

The potential to extend the Heeten setup to a general concept for energy communities is mostly dependent on legislation. As per today, the Dutch legislation hampers some of the seven value propositions mentioned in USEF. To some extent, this is due to the composition of energy prices in The Netherlands. It consists of a grid tariff based on the capacity, the supply costs, which is typically a price per day and a price per kWh, and taxes and levies. Based on an annual usage of 3500 kWh, this adds to 0.23€/kWh (Fig. 6.6). There is very little bandwidth in which this electricity price can be varied. The grid costs, as well as the taxes, are regulated, so the only price differences come from the energy supply costs. Likewise, the tariffs for the network operators are regulated. This is all done to provide fair prices to all customers. However, the current system allows no incentives which can be given to customers to change their energy consumption pattern. Up to now, such approaches can only be tested in pilot projects.

Looking at the seven energy and flexibility services from Section 6.2, energy communities today have difficulties to participate in some of these services. Under current Dutch law, these services may not be allowed or not adequately valued. Other services are hardly

2019 energy price in The Netherlands (based on annual usage of 3500 kWh)

FIGURE 6.6 Energy price distribution in The Netherlands.

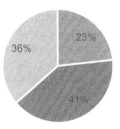

23%

36%

41%

▪ Grid costs   ▪ Energy supply   ▪ Taxes and levies

profitable or can be very difficult to set up. Below, an analysis of the seven services in the current legislation is given:

- **Services to increase energy awareness**. These services are possible. Many pilot projects aim to accomplish more energy awareness. Since customers can opt to read out their smart meter data, individual consumption patterns and information on the energy balance can be extracted, and corresponding information can be passed to the inhabitants. This may lead to increased awareness and therefore often also to higher self-consumption rates. Additionally, it often leads to lower consumption due to more efficient energy usage.
- **Joint purchase and maintenance of (shared) assets**. It is possible to purchase solar or wind installations. For many energy communities, this was the main reason for being initiated. Their advantage is that they do not have to pay tax on the energy they consume annually from their common generation source (Dutch: postcoderoosregeling). However, this scheme does not encourage physical joint self-consumption since the calculations are only on an annual basis.
- **Supply of (shared) energy**. In principle, a community may take the role of the electricity supplier, including the responsibilities related to this (regulated) role. Note that for the latter, it may associate with an existing supplier. However, this results in considerable responsibilities for a community, and it is questionable if any benefits would arise, compared to the larger scale of traditional suppliers.
- **Peer-to-peer supply**. This is not possible in current legislation. For this, all participants would have to obtain permits to sell electricity and would have some balancing responsibility. Prosumers, in general, do not have the amount of production, flexibility, and automation needed for this task. Although some suppliers offer a peer-to-peer proposition to their clients, for a community, this would imply that all members must switch to this particular supplier to make it work.
- **Optimize individual Prosumers' energy profiles**. Grid costs are depending on the capacity of the given connection and by that are fixed. Hence, there is no incentive to

reduce grid usage at peak times. Energy prices are typically determined by fixed tariff or day—night tariff. In the latter case the differences are rather low, and therefore there is no significant reason to optimize the profile for varying energy prices. However, the legislation does allow for optimization. On the other hand, consumers can claim a tax refund for their annual self-consumption. Hence, all consumption up to the level of the production surplus is not taxed (Dutch: salderingsregeling). This means a net-zero energy building would not pay any taxes on its consumption, though they would often cause immense peaks in the network. Note that this scheme does not encourage consumers to optimize direct self-consumption and also ruins the business case for home batteries. Due to the low price variation in combination with the tax refund scheme, there is no financial advantage to store self-generated energy in a battery for later consumption. At this point, people can use the grid as a "battery" without even paying for losses caused by this "battery." Nowadays, only in some particular cases where the battery is used to reduce the grid connection capacity, a beneficial business case is possible. The current regulation of the tax refund scheme will be faded out between 2023 and 2031, meaning the market for batteries might grow.

- **Provide explicit demand-side flexibility services**. Communities who want to participate in explicit demand response are facing high minimum product sizes and need consent from their supplier. This makes it nearly impossible for smaller energy communities to participate in any explicit demand response unless they participate in a larger body.
- **Optimize the community energy profile**. Since currently there are no possibilities within the law to negotiate a specific energy tariff for a community, and the current legislation also does not allow a community to disconnect from the main grid, there is currently no benefit for this service. Possibly when microgrids can go completely islanded, operators would allow them to only pay for their portion of the grid. However, this would be extremely difficult to organize and execute.

Summarizing, today the tax schemes for both individuals and communities are very advantageous to invest in renewable generation, whereas the added value of exploiting the flexibility of energy is almost none.

For the pilot in Heeten an exempt from the law was approved, which allows the community to offer dynamic grid tariffs. Instead of a fixed tariff of 0.52€/day, which results in 0.05€/kWh based on annual usage of 3500 kWh, the community members are offered a varying scheme, as explained in Section 6.3. Without the exempt in the law and the fact that this is a pilot project, these dynamic tariffs would not have been possible. Results on the savings can be found in Section 6.5.

From the perspective of a network operator, giving possible discounts to a community only makes sense if it can be shown that the community reduces the stress on the grid. However, this is only possible if there is some common connection point to the grid by the community. Therefore one of the hurdles of setting up a grid tariff for an energy community similar to the one introduced in this chapter is that the whole neighborhood behind a transformer (or another common connection point) needs to become part of the community. Setting up such a community in an existing neighborhood is therefore very challenging. Most probably, some customers do not want to be included (Bauwens & Devine-Wright, 2018).

However, for newly build neighborhoods, this could be an interesting opportunity. By making the energy community an integral part of the neighborhood, it becomes natural to have the whole neighborhood working together. This also supports the project of 3000 households which is built by Sonnen in Arizona to utilize as a VPP. More information on this project can be found in Chapter 3.

Whether or not the concept of GridFlex is scalable to other communities is mainly dependent on the upcoming legislation in response to the EU directive. However, the outcome of pilot projects like GridFlex could steer the legislation in the right direction. More concretely, based on the experience with the pilot project that suggestions to the current legislation can be made which should make the following aspects possible:

- A clearly defined legal position of citizen energy communities with the possibility to generate, store, and consume electricity, access to all markets and a level playing field with traditional market players.
- A grid tariff scheme where higher community self-consumption and lower peak loads can be compensated.
- An energy pricing scheme where energy transfers within the community have a lower price than energy exchanges across the "borders" of the community.
- A taxation scheme where individual self-consumption and community self-consumption is encouraged. This scheme should consider real-time self-consumption instead of annual averages.

If these aspects are integrated into future legislation, better business cases for energy communities can be made.

6.5 Preliminary results of the case study

One of the crucial questions of the project is to test if household batteries have a significant effect on the total energy profiles of the neighborhood. For this, virtual batteries of 5 kWh were simulated at 24 locations in the local grid and controlled using a smart steering algorithm for the batteries.

The neighborhood was modeled in the open-source Decentralized Energy Management toolkit (DEMKit) (Hoogsteen, 2017; Hoogsteen & Hurink, 2019). DEMKit is a software tool used for decentralized management of energy systems using a model predictive control system. For GridFlex Heeten a model of the neighborhood was set up, and data from the households was used as input. Virtual batteries were then added to this model of the given situation in Heeten.

To analyze the situation in Heeten, load flows were simulated and predicted. In addition, an ADMM type of control (Rivera, Goebel, & Jacobsen, 2016) was used to send steering signals to the virtual batteries. In this control the batteries iteratively send adjusted schedules to lower the expected peaks on the transformer for the coming 24 hours. When an acceptable solution is achieved, the coming period (15 minutes) from the resulting schedule is executed. After that, the process is repeated meaning that new predictions and load flows are simulated, and the control process is iterated.

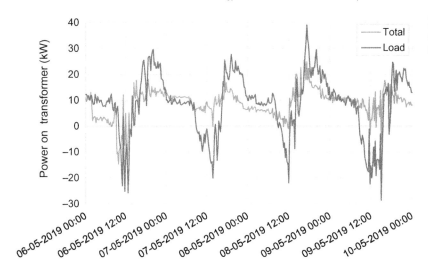

FIGURE 6.7 The effect that batteries have on the peaks.

TABLE 6.3 Usage of each level of demand with and without batteries.

Level of demand	Energy per level without batteries (% of total energy)	Energy per level with batteries (% of total energy)
Low	66.3	81.6
Medium	25.0	17.4
High	8.6	1.0

One of the lessons learned from the case study is that the batteries can have a tremendous effect. Fig. 6.7 shows the resulting peaks of the neighborhood with and without batteries. It can be seen that the peaks have been reduced by up to 36% (from 39 to 25 kW). Using the new payment scheme as described in Section 6.3, the inhabitants together would save 1500€ a year (about 14 % of the total connection and transport costs). Note that this money is provided to the entire neighborhood.

Additionally, information was given to the inhabitants to decrease their energy consumption, as well as to shift their consumption away from peak moments. As the pilot is still running, there are no conclusive results on the effects of the information yet.

For the network operator the situation also improved as the neighborhood only exceeded the 15 kW mark 18% of the time, compared to 34% without using batteries (Table 6.3). While the current peaks do not pose a problem for the present cables and transformer, it is a good indication of what impact batteries could have.

Even though the results achieved with the battery are considerable, this only covers half of what the project aims to research. In the next step, we will analyze how much the inhabitants are willing and able to shift their energy consumption. First meetings with the inhabitants are promising and have shown the interest and willingness for this. This is especially the case when interfaces of appliances like a washing machine or dishwasher can be programed to start at a later time.

Summarizing, the first results show that batteries have a high added value when it comes to relieving stress from the grid, given some smart steering can be used. The influence of the flexibility of the inhabitants on the energy profile of the community still is unclear.

6.6 Conclusion

Energy communities are on the rise in Europe. A reason for the growth in the number of energy communities can be found in the motivation of prosumers to take the lead in the energy transition and to be in full control, and the fact that benefits may be reinvested into the community. Additionally, seven energy and flexibility services for energy communities are listed in this chapter, which may allow additional benefits to be achieved for the inhabitants of the community.

However, many barriers are still to be overcome for energy communities to achieve these benefits. Next to the need for a structured organization and a sufficient scale to withstand the competition of more prominent players, energy communities are still very uncommon and up to now have hardly any options to attain savings. The latter problem stems from the main barrier for energy communities, the current legislation. Luckily, the new EU directive makes citizen energy communities an official legal entity, implying that energy communities are getting a position in legislation. However, their exact rights and duties are still to be determined. With proper price schemes from suppliers or network operators and the legal options to apply them, significant savings can be acquired when the community is controlled in a smart way, as is demonstrated in the case study of this chapter.

The mentioned case study applies a dynamic community grid tariff as implicit demand response, in combination with batteries, to research the effect they have on the peaks of the community. This approach is specifically created for energy communities that have one common coupling point to the distribution grid. Simulations for the given case study identified several key benefits, including lowering the peaks at the transformer by 36% and potential savings of 1500 €/year in grid costs for the inhabitants.

It is still to be seen if the upcoming legislation in response to the new EU directive will allow copying concepts like GridFlex Heeten to other neighborhoods as well. Hopefully, the outcome of pilot projects like GridFlex Heeten will steer the legislation in the right direction.

To conclude, based on the experiences and results achieved within the GridFlex Heeten project, a lot can be expected from energy communities in the coming years.

References

Australian Renewable Energy Agency (ARENA). (2015). *Community energy.* <https://arena.gov.au/where-we-invest/community-energy/>.

Bahrami, S., Toulabi, M., Ranjbar, S., Moeini-Aghtaie, M., & Ranjbar, A. M. (2017). A decentralized energy management framework for energy hubs in dynamic pricing markets. *IEEE Transactions on Smart Grid, 9,* 6780–6792.

Bakar, N. N. A., Hassan, M. Y., Sulaima, M. F., Nasir, M. N. M., & Khamis, A. (2017). Microgrid and load shedding scheme during islanded mode: A review. *Renewable and Sustainable Energy Reviews, 71,* 161–169.

Bauwens, T., & Devine-Wright, P. (2018). Positive energies? An empirical study of community energy participation and attitudes to renewable energy. *Energy Policy, 118,* 612–625.

COCITER scrl. (2018). *Comptoir Citoyen des Energies.* <https://www.cociter.be/> Accessed 25.07.19.

DGRV. (2019). *Die Genossenschaften.* <https://www.dgrv.de/> Accessed 25.07.19.

Energie VanOns. (2019). *De energie van de toekomst is groen én lokaal.* <https://energie.vanons.org/> Accessed 25.07.19.

ènostra. (2016). *Energia Rinnovabile e Sostenibile.* <https://www.enostra.it/> Accessed 25.07.19.

European Parliament and the Council of the European Union. (2019). *Directive (EU) 2019/944 of the European Parliament and of the Council of 5 June 2019 on common rules for the internal market for electricity and amending Directive 2012/27/EU.* European Union.

EWS Schönau. (2019). *atomstromlos. klimafreundlich. bürgereigen.* <https://www.ews-schoenau.de/> Accessed 25.07.19.

GridFlex. (2019). *Duurzamer dan duurzaam.* GridFlex Heeten. <https://gridflex.nl/> Accessed 25.07.19.

Groen, M.C. (2018). *Assessing the effect of smart reinforcement alternatives on the expected asset lifetime of low voltage networks.*

Günther, L., Garzon-Real, J., Zdrallek, M., Wolter, D., Lucke, N., & Benthin, J. (2018). Residential quarters as innovative energy cells. In *CIRED workshop 2018.* Ljubljana.

Hirsch, A., Parag, Y., & Guerrero, J. (2018). Microgrids: A review of technologies, key drivers, and outstanding issues. *Renewable and Sustainable Energy Reviews, 90,* 402–411.

Hoogsteen, G. (2017). *A cyber-physical systems perspective on decentralized energy management.*

Hoogsteen, G., & Hurink, J.L. (2019). *DEMKit.* <https://www.utwente.nl/en/eemcs/energy/demkit/#more-information-and-projects> Accessed 20.08.19.

Japan Smart Community Alliance. (2015). *Smart community Japan's experience.*

Kaundinya, D. P., Balachandra, P., & Ravindranath, N. H. (2009). Grid-connected versus stand-alone energy systems for decentralized power—A review of literature. *Renewable and Sustainable Energy Reviews, 13,* 2041–2050.

Koirala, B. P., Koliou, E., Friege, J., Hakvoort, R. A., & Herder, P. M. (2016). Energetic communities for community energy: A review of key issues and trends shaping integrated community energy systems. *Renewable and Sustainable Energy Reviews, 56,* 722–744.

Lu, S., Samaan, N., Diao, R., Elizondo, M., Jin, C., Mayhorn, E., ... Kirkham, H. (2011). *Centralized and decentralized control for demand response. ISGT 2011* (pp. 1–8). IEEE.

Marnay, C., Chatzivasileiadis, S., Abbey, C., Iravani, R., Joos, G., Lombardi, P., et al. (2015). Microgrid evolution roadmap. In 2015 *International* symposium on smart electric distribution systems and technologies (EDST) (pp. 139–144). IEEE.

Mohsenian-Rad, A.-H., Wong, V. W. S., Jatskevich, J., & Schober, R. (2010). *Optimal and autonomous incentive-based energy consumption scheduling algorithm for smart grid. 2010 Innovative Smart Grid Technologies (ISGT).* IEEE.

Narayanamurthy, R. (2016). *Advanced energy communities: Grid integration of zero net energy communities.* Electric Power Research Institute, Inc.

ODE. (2019). *ODE decentraal.* <https://www.duurzameenergie.org/> Accessed 27.07.19.

Pudjianto, D., Ramsay, C., & Strbac, G. (2007). Virtual power plant and system integration of distributed energy resources. *IET Renewable Power Generation, 1,* 10–16.

Reijnders, V. M. J. J., Gerards, M. E. T., Hurink, J. L., & Smit, G. J. M. (2018). Testing grid-based electricity prices and batteries in a field test. In *CIRED workshop 2018.* Ljubljana.

REScoop.eu. (2018). *Renewable Energy Cooperative.* <https://www.rescoop.eu/> Accessed 25.07.19.

Rivera, J., Goebel, C., & Jacobsen, H.-A. (2016). Distributed convex optimization for electric vehicle aggregators. *IEEE Transactions on Smart Grid, 8,* 1852–1863.

Roberts, J., Frieden, D., & d'Herbemont, S. (2019). *Energy community definitions*. Compile.

Seyfang, G., Park, J. J., & Smith, A. (2013). A thousand flowers blooming? An examination of community energy in the UK. *Energy Policy, 61*, 977–989.

Stichting HIER Opgewekt. (2019). *Hét kennisplatform voor lokale duurzame energie-initiatieven*. <https://www.hier-opgewekt.nl/> Accessed 25.07.19.

Thomas, L., Zhou, Y., Long, C., Wu, J., & Jenkins, N. (2019). A general form of smart contract for decentralized energy systems management. *Nature Energy, 4*, 140.

USEF. (2019). *USEF white paper: Energy and flexibility services for Citizens Energy Communities*. <www.usef.energy>.

van der Mei, A., Doomernik, J. P., & Lalieu, L. (2019). The perfect storm for monopoly grids: The dual disruptive impact of distributed generation and local competition. In *CIRED 2019*. Madrid.

Walker, G., Devine-Wright, P., Hunter, S., High, H., & Evans, B. (2010). Trust and community: Exploring the meanings, contexts and dynamics of community renewable energy. *Energy Policy, 38*, 2655–2663.

Wierling, A., Schwanitz, V. J., Zeiß, J. P., Bout, C., & Candelise, C. (2018). Statistical evidence on the role of energy cooperatives for the energy transition in european countries. *Sustainability, 10.9*, 3339.

Zia, M., Fahad, E., Elbouchikhi., & Benbouzid, M. (2018). Microgrids energy management systems: A critical review on methods, solutions, and prospects. *Applied Energy, 222*, 1033–1055.

The expanding role of home energy management ecosystem: an Australian case study

Damian Shaw-Williams

Queensland University of Technology, Brisbane, QLD, Australia

7.1 Introduction

From prosumer to prosumager, a household's ability to optimize energy use and cost has the potential to revolutionize the management of networks. The rise of smart appliances has greatly increased both the scope for optimization behind-the-meter (BTM) and its complexity. Smart plugs have accelerated this trend; however, the entry of new providers to the market has seen a proliferation of components and protocols. Already significant security vulnerabilities have been identified, and with the continued risk of fragmentation, these security and privacy vulnerabilities could impact the rate of uptake if not addressed.

The home energy management systems (HEMS) of a prosuming smart house must incorporate a wide range of forecasting, scheduling, and real-time communications across multiple stakeholders. These growing capabilities of HEMS place it as the key enabler of the digitalization, aggregation, and optimization of the BTM environment and a means to unlocking network efficiencies through the optimization of the aggregated household sector.

This chapter looks at how the role of HEMS has evolved from early energy monitoring schemes and how the advent of the smart home has seen a multitude of new entrants providing controllable appliances to be connected to networks. Privacy and security concerns are considered as well as the risks of continued fragmentation and how they can be mitigated.

The balance of this chapter is organized as follows:

- Section 7.2 provides a background of the development of HEMS.
- Section 7.3 considers how security and privacy vulnerabilities can be addressed.
- Section 7.4 details the risks of fragmentation and potential solutions.
- Section 7.5 outlines digitization of the grid through smart meters and the Australian context followed by the chapter's conclusions.

7.2 Developments of home energy management systems

An increased focus on household energy efficiency and reduction of energy costs has seen the rise of HEMS. HEMS are defined as providing monitoring, control, and automation through the use of sensing, measuring, smart appliances, enabling information communications technology (ICT) and control functionality (Asare-Bediako, Kling, & Ribeiro, 2012). Historically HEMS have progressed from basic energy monitoring facilities that improved a household's energy awareness and enabled manual time-shifting of discretionary household loads. The primary motivations have been the householders desire to manage cost exposure and the network operators desire to manage network peaks.

A study by Beudin et al. found that in a review of 36 studies reviewing the potential efficiency gains of HEMS an average cost reduction of 23.1% and peak reduction of 29.6% (Beaudin & Zareipour, 2015). However, subsequent studies showed that the initial enthusiasm subsided as the novelty wore off. Similarly, a survey-based study of Australian householders found that an initially high level of engagement gave way over time to disinterest, neglect, and in certain cases, technical malfunction (Snow, Buys, Roe, & Brereton, 2013). Similarly, a paper by Hargreaves, Nye, and Burgess (2013) found that though equipped with greater awareness of their energy usage some households realized the limits of their energy saving potential and disengaged. More recent studies such as the chapter by Mountain reach similar conclusions, namely, limited ability of the average consumer to actively engage or respond to price signals.

Early forms of controllable appliances have been those adapted for participation in demand management (DM) schemes. Traditionally in Australia this has taken the form of control over household water heating systems, pool pumps, and more recently air-conditioners. In the Australian context, Energex, a South East Queensland distribution utility, has a scheme that utilizes over 50,000 air-conditioning units to assist with managing peak demands. All major brands of air-conditioners available in Australia now have this capability. Additionally, the rapid increase in the number of photovoltaic (PV) installations in South-East Queensland has seen the repurposing of the traditional hot water DM scheme to the absorption of surplus PV generation during the day (Swinson, Hamer, & Humphries, 2015). This is a common approach in similar climates with ample solar resource such as southern California, which must also balance widespread air-conditioner use and a residential peak that occurs in the evening.

These early controllable appliance programs were enabled by a physical Demand Response Enabling Device (DRED) built into the appliance. Audio Frequency Load Control signals are sent via the electricity network to electric hot water systems on controlled load, switching them off during peak times as required. Approximately 59% of residential customers on the Energex network (around 770,000) have an electric hot water system. However, these bulky, space-consuming solid-state technologies are giving way to more compact, wireless, and efficient embedded or chip-based systems.

With the widespread adoption of household PVs, uptake of battery energy storage systems, and the increasing diversity of smart appliances, the scope for household optimization has greatly expanded its potential for network management. The resulting capabilities have seen the suite of HEMS functions now extending to interaction with utility demand response programs, home automation services, personal energy management, data analysis and visualization, auditing, and related security services (Bojanczyk, 2013). Specifically, the HEMS ecosystem comprise sensors, monitors, interfaces, appliances, and devices networked together to enable automation as well as localized and remote control of the domestic environment (Wilson, Hargreaves, & Hauxwell-Baldwin, 2017). A suite of capabilities that mirrors that of aggregators and network operators that are adapting from centralized models. An example of the diversity of market participants supplying this ecosystem is illustrated in Fig. 7.1.

There are a wide range of HEMS controllers/hubs ranging from the simpler energy monitoring through to algorithmic optimization, for example, HomeSeer through its HomeTroller product provides control of light switches, thermostats, door locks, audio/video equipment, cameras, garage doors, water valves, and energy monitors. Notably hardware interfaces (Z-Wave, Insteon, UPB, X10, etc.) are not included which illustrate the need for awareness of the range of standards used by manufacturers. Insteon provides a

FIGURE 7.1 Categories of smart home element suppliers. Source: *European Commission [Digital Transformation Monitor. (2017). Smart home: Technologies with a standard battle. In D. T. Monitor (Ed.), Digital transformation monitor (p. 4). Brussels, Belgium: European Commission (Digital Transformation Monitor, 2017)].*

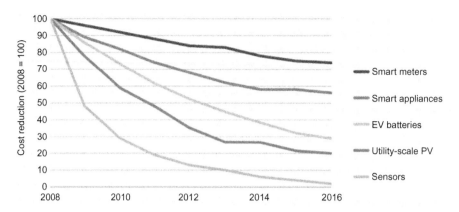

FIGURE 7.2 Unit costs of key emerging electricity technologies. Source: *IEA digitizing energy report [International Energy Agency. (2017a).* Digitalization & energy *(p. 76). Paris, France: International Energy Agency (International Energy Agency, 2017a)].*

range of controllable appliances and the Hub Central Controller which can control up to 40 appliances and integrates with Amazon Alex and Google Home; however, optimization capability is not included. While HEMS such as CarbonTrack provides monitoring and appliance control and optimization through timers and algorithms and can be integrated with Amazon Alexa.

There has been rapid growth in the broader smart appliance market, an International Data Corporation (2019) report forecasts spending on smart appliances to reach $61 billion globally in 2019, whilst another International Data Corporation report forecasts the smart home market to be nearly 1.3 billion devices by 2022 (Loucks, 2018). The increased competition in the market has seen a dramatic reduction in appliance costs and greater functionality. The decrease in unit costs of over 40% for smart appliances is as shown in Fig. 7.2, and it is estimated that 10% of homes will be "smart" by 2025 (Anonymous, 2017).

There is a distinction to be drawn between HEMS and home automation systems, such as Amazon Alexa and Google Home, whereby lighting, climate, and appliances can be managed for household convenience and comfort; goals that may at times be at odds with energy efficiency. However, this increasing product range of controllable networked smart appliances, when home automation is integrated with HEMS, increases the potential gains of optimization (Fig. 7.3).

Home automation received initial impetus with the release of Amazon's Alexa voice-controlled assistant in 2014, followed 2 years later by Google's Home and then Apple with the launch of HomePod in 2017 (Deagon, 2018). A recent report has found 100 million devices with Alexa installed have been sold, and there are also more than 28,000 smart home devices compatible with Alexa, made by more than 4500 different manufacturers. Google has reported that it expects to hit 1 billion Google Assistant compatible devices in 2019 (MT Newswires, 2019).

The constant connectivity of controllable appliances is not without its costs in the form of standby power. An International Energy Agency (2017b) report forecasts unmanaged standby of controllable appliances globally could waste around 740 TWh per year by 2025,

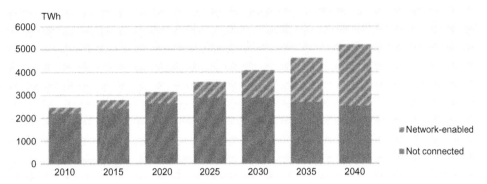

FIGURE 7.3 Household electricity consumption of appliances and other small plug loads. Source: *National Institute of Standards and Technology. (2018a). In: US Department of Commerce (Ed.).* Smart grid interoperability and cybersecurity workshop *(p. 9). Washington, DC: US Government (National Institute of Standards and Technology, 2018a).*

equivalent to the current annual electricity consumption of France and the United Kingdom combined. Fig. 7.4 illustrates both the issue of growing appliance-driven demand and the means to address it through optimization via its controllability, which when able to be utilized for network management purposes provides significant opportunities for efficiencies.

7.2.1 Home energy management systems optimization potential

The majority of HEMS currently on the market provide a link to cloud-based data repository that is accessed by an app. They, in the main, rely on user intervention to manage energy use in response to alerts regarding use, generation, and or market pricing information. However, the expanding range of controllable appliances and digitalization of energy services provides the basis for automation and optimization of the BTM ecosystem. These advanced HEMS controllers will enable consumers to automate the balancing of priorities and so avoid the pitfalls of waning enthusiasm.

To realize the optimization potential of the growing HEMS ecosystem, it requires automation and sophisticated scheduling algorithms that incorporate a wide range of usage and sensor data. Uncertainties of household appliance operation and intermittency of solar generation must be incorporated as well as minimizing energy costs, without compromising household customer comfort (Chen, Wei, & Hu, 2013).

There is a rapidly expanding body of work looking at HEMS optimization methodologies. In previous studies, researchers have either utilized predictive energy management or focused on real-time energy management. The former category uses the historical data to predict the electricity consumption to find out the optimum strategy to control the electrical appliances. The second category uses the real-time algorithms to control the thermal devices or shift the controllable devices to meet the dual aims of minimizing energy costs and managing peak demand (Shakeri et al., 2017).

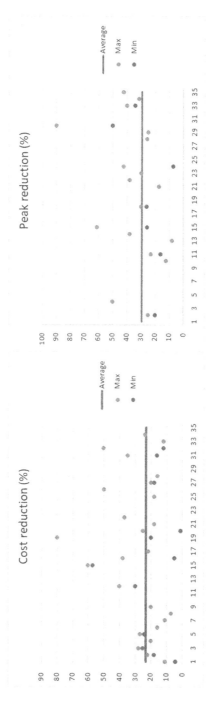

FIGURE 7.4 Range of study results by cost and peak reduction. Source: *Graphs compiled on data sourced from Beaudin, M., & Zareipour, H., 2015. Home energy management systems: A review of modelling and complexity. Renewable and Sustainable Energy Reviews 45, 318–335.*

There have been a number of studies looking at the benefits on smart home optimization primarily through the metric of reduction in energy costs. The primary focus has been the optimization scheduling function with various methodologies applied to the operating algorithm. In studies by Shakeri et al. simulation results indicate, similarly to Voltalis as discussed in Chapter 3, that the proposed system is able to reduce energy costs from between 15% and 20% without sacrificing the user's comfort. The proposed algorithm receives the price information from the utility company in advance and purchases the electricity at off-peak hours and utilizes the battery as well as manages the temperature of the thermal appliances during peak hours (Shakeri et al., 2017, 2018).

A paper by Chen et al. (2013) proposed a deterministic linear programming–based scheduling scheme that achieves up to 45% monetary expense reduction, and the proposed stochastic design scheme achieves up to 41% monetary expense reduction. Similarly, a paper by Izmitligil and Ozkan modeled a main controller that manages power resources, appliances, and plug in hybrid electric vehicles (PHEVs) based on a solution of a mixed integer linear programming problem with defined smart and energy-efficient operation constraints based on pricing, supply, and preference. The HEMS provided a 48%–68% reduction in electricity expenses (İzmitligil & Apaydn Özkan, 2018). Further, Mohsenian-Rad, Wong, Jatskevich, Schober, and Leon-Garcia (2010) studied DM through the scheduling of appliances and found a reduction in energy costs of 18%.

As renewable penetration increases, the complexity of grid management increases due to volatile climatic factors, system noise, line losses, and behind the meter activities. While much BTM optimization research has focused on the reduction of household energy costs, there is also significant potential for aggregations of prosuming households to be enlisted in managing the network. The potential of demand response (DR) may exceed that of aggregated household benefits given the network capital efficiencies in deferred augmentation and reliability (Shaw-Williams, Susilawati, & Walker, 2018).

As aggregators enter the market, they will provide the coordination of resources of growing pools of prosuming households that will enable them to access DM and ancillary services markets, in sufficient numbers to revolutionize network management (Damisa, Nwulu, & Sun, 2018). Additionally, there is great potential for improvements in reliability as found in the study by Alowaifeer, Alamri, and Meliopoulos (2018) where they found that the installation PV + ESS (energy storage system) with HEMS to 1 feeder out of 11 affected the reliability of the system. For instance, loss of load probability reductions of 2.12% is shown in the HEMS only scenario and 8.77% in the HEMS–PV–ESS scenario.

7.2.2 Automation the key for home energy management systems optimization of the smart home

Many environmental and usage factors can affect a household's energy use resulting in a high degree of short-term stochasticity. Similarly, the potential intermittency of renewable generation requires the incorporation of weather and demand forecasting capabilities resulting in a significant increase in data volumes and analytics. Such forecasts are essential for appliance scheduling, generation scheduling, and battery utilization (Adika & Lingfeng, 2014). Further, as studies have shown where energy management systems are reliant on householders acting, the benefits can be short-lived as people become bored with it. Hence, automation utilizing artificial intelligence (AI) and machine to machine (M2M) communication will be the key to managing the expanded data requirements and achieving optimization benefits.

Network operators must consider the potential resources of households whether pooled with an aggregator or direct contractual relationships. The potential of the aggregated household sector to contribute to DM and network stability is significant. However, the increase in capabilities makes the problem-solving in this domain an increasingly complex task. The challenge of balancing increasing amounts of renewable energy generation and consumption in real time, and forecasting demand and planning for energy system requirements in the future, creates an enormous opportunity for machine learning (ML) (Song, Qin, & Salim, 2017; Tayal, 2017).

To fully realize the benefits of automation, it will require the use of distributed intelligence and analysis at each network layer and local area. This will require the efficient allocation of computational resources required at each level based on the complexity of the local area balancing solution. Through these means a more decentralized and responsive network, better able to respond to local conditions than traditional centralized command and control approaches, is possible, as discussed in more detail by Johnston and Sioshansi in Chapter 11.

7.2.3 Increasing home energy management systems reach through retrofitting with smart plugs

For appliances without built in communications the ubiquity of "smart plugs" means that even "dumb" appliances can be monitored and controlled and thus optimized Smart plugs are "designed as plug-in adapters that act as an intermediary between the device and the power source" (Blanco-Novoa, Fernández-Caramés, Fraga-Lamas, & Castedo, 2017). Previously basic smart plugs provided the means to record appliance energy use and communicate it with the local HEMS controller. Now smart plugs can receive a signal to schedule appliance operation as well as minimize standby energy use. By optimizing the portfolio of appliances, generation and storage a household can implement chosen priorities whether they be cost minimization or householder comfort.

There are a large number of manufactures of smart plugs, including Belkin, Sonoff, TP-Link, Edimax, Wemo, Xiamo, Anker, iHome, and GE. Smart plugs use networking protocols such as Wi-Fi, Zigbee, Z-Wave, WeMo, Bluetooth, Thread, and other protocols. The components differ across manufacturers posing a challenge to developers of monitoring applications (Mtshali & Khubia, 2019).

Digital assistants like Amazon's Alexa, Google's Home, and Apple's HomePod are able to control smart plugs via voice-activated commands. However, not all plugs are compatible with all platforms giving rise to additional compatibility layers such as IFTTT—"if this, then that." IFTTT is a free service that can connect a wide variety of internet-connected apps, services, and devices (Duffy, 2018). Hence, standardization is key to minimizing the need for additional layers of control.

The range of smart plugs and their providers illustrates both the opportunities to extend the potential benefits of HEMS through increasing home automation as well as some of the challenges in the form of security and market fragmentation.

7.3 Smart home security and privacy vulnerabilities

With the advent of smart appliances and a digitalized grid, significant data protection and privacy questions have arisen. The growth in data relating to energy use will enable comprehensive behavioral profiles to be developed. Analysis of electricity consumption patterns a granular level can result in revealing private information such as occupancy or socioeconomic status (Asghar, Dán, Miorandi, & Chlamtac, 2017). Even in advance of smart appliances in a number of countries, there has been a push back on the roll-out of smart meters by some consumers due to concerns about the real-time nature of the data that is able to be captured (Horne, Darras, Bean, Srivastava, & Frickel, 2015; Snow, Radke, Vyas, & Brereton, 2014).

More recently, privacy concerns have also been raised with voice-activated home automation systems. There are a number of cases where privacy has been breached, such as randomly recording conversations and sending a transcript to a random contact (Sam Wolfson, 2018). As the quantity and diversity of energy use data that is recorded and passed back to the respective companies' servers increases so does the potential for privacy and security breaches.

The diversity of control and communications software and standards deployed already in smart appliances has been identified as a cybersecurity weakness (Constantin, 2016). Specifically, issues arise due to the need to exchange high volumes of data in real time over public networks (Mai & Khalil, 2017). Where smart plugs are utilized to merge a home automation system with HEMS it exacerbates the range of security and privacy concerns. That many smart devices need internet connection in order to work makes them prone to network-based attacks, which unfortunately can compromise the privacy of the home users.

A study by Zhen et al. found commonly available smart plugs can be vulnerable to (1) device scanning attack, (2) brute force attack, (3) spoofing attack, and (4) firmware attack (Zhen et al., 2017). These vulnerabilities can be ascribed to the insecure communication protocols and lack of device authentication on smart plugs. Further, a review by consultants at SoftScheck found that a widely available smart plug could be reverse engineered to enable access to an outside party due to a lack of authentication (Stroetmann, 2018).

Compared to device hardware and firmware, the communication protocols with the controlling app can be a crucial vulnerability. An analysis by Junior, Melo, Lu, d'Amorim, and Prakash (2019) of 96 IoT devices and the 36 respective controlling apps found that 50% of the apps did not use proper encryption techniques. There is the ongoing need to balance the capabilities offered by gathering more detailed data to billing, operations, and value-added services and maintaining a secure digital environment.

From the regulatory perspective, in the EU the focus has been heavily on data protection. The European Data Protection Supervisor has issued an opinion on the usage of smart meters' data, stating "Stakeholders must be aware that processing of personal data in the context of smart grids/smart metering will have to fully comply with the national legislation transposing the relevant EU legislation, including Directive 95/46/EC, and—to the extent applicable—the e-Privacy Directive" (Office of the European Data Protection Supervisor, 2012).

Solutions identified in previous studies have focused on technological innovations, design approaches, organizational approaches, and stakeholder communication (de Wildt, Chappin, van de Kaa, Herder, & van de Poel, 2019). Specifically, technical innovations include intrusion detection systems, encryption as explored in more detail by Kaftwerke in Chapter 10, access control systems, antimalware software or firewalls, and aggregation of data with optimal practice to incorporate a range of these solutions. Similarly, the study by Zhen et al. (2017) suggested the following defense strategies:

- secure communication protocol—secure encrypted communication protocols, for example, DTLS, TLS/SSL, and HTTPS;
- mutual authentication between plugs and servers;
- intrusion detection system—to identify extensive scanning attacks;
- anti-bot mechanisms—for example, CAPTCHA; and
- data integrity—message authentication codes.

7.4 The potential for smart home appliance fragmentation

The trade-off between functionality, convenience, and security is a delicate balance. Researchers have found an overwhelming majority of consumers wanted systems to be "designed to be reliable, easy to use, controllable, and easy to over-ride" and "guarantee privacy, confidentiality, and secure data storage" (Wilson et al., 2017). However, the range of new entrants into smart home technology has increased the potential for fragmentation which if left unaddressed could obstruct the realization of optimization benefits of the smart home ecosystem.

Within the smart home the leading protocols are Zigbee and Z-Wave, and the newer Thread, use low-energy radio waves to communicate in a mesh as opposed to more energy intensive WiFi or short-range Bluetooth. Zigbee was built from the ground up as an open standard under the control of the Zigbee Alliance and is present in many products; however, Z-wave has a broader penetration in Australia (Blichert, 2018). The protocols are defined methods for transmitting information and if a manufacturer deviates from these specifications, their products may not be able to communicate with products or platforms. As the area develops there is tension between competing platforms adding functionality and the interoperability of equipment.

A range of services are aiming to cross these divides through interoperability solutions such as IFTTT (Duffy, 2018). The interoperability features will no doubt become increasingly important; however, it provides another layer that can potentially be vulnerable to security breaches.

In a familiar case of standards lagging the development of a new market, it is hoped that by the development of interoperability standards, the scope for consumer confusion and barriers to optimization will be reduced. Standardization of protocols will assist with the willingness of customers to adopt as well as reduce security vulnerabilities.

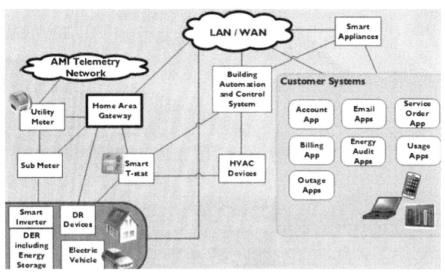

FIGURE 7.5 Emerging household ecosystem. Source: *National Institute of Standards and Technology. (2018c). In: US Department of Commerce (Ed.).* Smart grid interoperability and cybersecurity workshop *(p. 107). Washington, DC: US Government (National Institute of Standards and Technology, 2018c).*

In the United States the body charged with the development of such standards is the National Institute of Standards and Technologies (NIST) within the US Department of Commerce. The National Institute of Standards and Technology (2018b) has primary responsibility to coordinate development of a framework that includes protocols and model standards for information management to achieve interoperability of smart grid devices and systems.

NIST is currently developing the newest iteration of the relevant standard NIST Framework and Roadmap for Smart Grid Interoperability Standards, Release 4.0. The draft conceptual model includes new features, including a focus on intelligent distribution systems incorporating improved controllability and empowered customers domain where operations and intelligence across a diversity of household ecosystems as illustrated in Fig. 7.5.

While such standards are voluntary, they result from industry collaboration and provide a means for new market entrants to ensure compatibility in product development.

7.5 Grid digitalization progress

To fully realize the benefits of a smart grid, whereby the network itself can generate, store, and shift energy and managing network stability, using the full range of grid-connected equipment and appliances requires real-time automated solutions. In order to provide this platform, ICT infrastructure must be embedded in the network. Such infrastructure opens the way for third-party aggregators to coordinate distributed demand response and network support services.

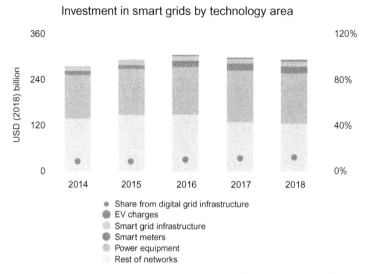

FIGURE 7.6 Investment in smart grids by technology area. Source: *International Energy Agency. (2019). Tracking clean energy progress (p. Tracking Clean Energy Progress (TCEP) assesses the status of 45 critical energy technologies). Paris, France: International Energy Agency (International Energy Agency, 2019).*

A report by the International Energy Agency found that smart grid investments rose 10% in 2018; however, investment in these technologies remains low compared to investment in traditional infrastructure as shown in Fig. 7.6. The report goes on to note that despite initial enthusiasm for smart grids, there now appears to be a slowdown in the adoption of microgrids and virtual power plant (VPP) with no expansion in 2018. The report notes that further efforts are needed to implement regulatory frameworks that recognize and reward investment in new digital technologies and in other "nonwire" alternatives to traditional electricity grid extensions.

In Australia, Northeast Group estimates investments in smart grid infrastructure reaching USD6.1 billion between 2017 and 2027 (Northwest Group, 2018). South Australia remains at the forefront of the energy transition in some respects, with one of the highest proportions of renewable energy incorporated into their network and a 50,000 household VPP underway. Western Australia, an large islanded network unconnected to the national energy market (NEM), has a range of programs underway, including trials of microgrids, distributed energy generation, behind the meter software and systems, demand side management, stand-alone power systems, and advanced metering infrastructure (Tayal, 2017), and as outlined in more detail in Swanston in Chapter 19.

For all sectors of the energy network, digitalization provides opportunities to improve performance for the benefit of individual companies, the system as a whole, energy consumers, and the environment. The connectivity component of digitalization has the potential to reshape the power sector by connecting power supply with key demand sectors as illustrated in Fig. 7.7.

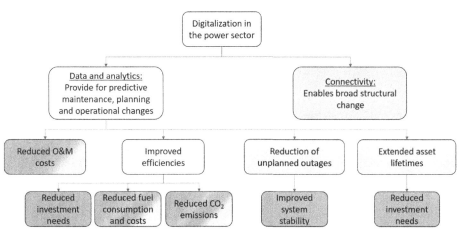

FIGURE 7.7 Impact of digitalization on electricity sector assets. Source: *International Energy Agency. (2017a). Digitalization & energy (p. 76). Paris, France: International Energy Agency.*

7.5.1 Smart meter roll-out the basis for growth of aggregation and optimization

The optimization capabilities in HEMS have developed rapidly and are outstripping those of the network beyond the meter. For the full potential of the aggregated and optimized household sector to be realized, the fundamental requirement is the rapid transition to smart meters. Smart meter adoption as discussed by Stagnaro et al. in Chapter 12, is the foundation for the transition to smarter and more efficient networks. The smart grid will be based on real-time monitoring and multidirectional communications between prosuming households and aggregators/network operators. Globally there have been great strides in the roll-out of smart metering, with China is approaching full deployment, and Japan, Spain, and France are poised to achieve full roll-outs in the next few years. In the United States and the European Union, smart meters have been deployed in over half of the market, Fig. 7.8 illustrates the regional progress to date.

In Australia, there are roughly 3.3 million smart meters installed across the national electricity market, of which 2.8 million are in Victoria, out of 13.6 million meters in total, accounting for less than a quarter of all electricity meters (Latimer, 2018). In Fig. 7.9 the expected replacement rate of legacy meters can be seen.

The roll-out however was not without issues which may have delayed adoption in other Australian states. The State Government of Victoria mandated the roll-out of smart meters in 2006 and was to be paid for by cost pass through to customers; a review in 2011 found that the cost had blown out from $319 million AUD to $2.2 billion (The Victorian Auditor General, 2015). However, the program has resulted in 98.62% of targeted sites having a smart meter, and 86.5% of those delivering data remotely. The AG went on to

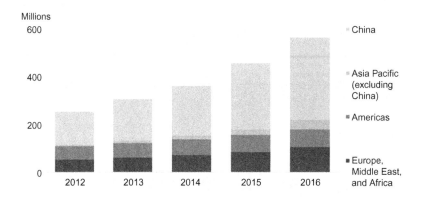

FIGURE 7.8   Acceleration of smart meter installations. Source: *International Energy Agency. (2017c).* Energy efficiency 2017 *(p. 59). Paris, France: International Energy Agency (International Energy Agency, 2017c).*

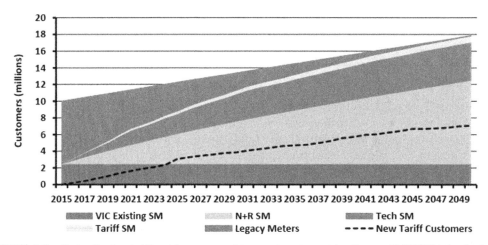

FIGURE 7.9   Cost reflective tariff uptake compared to smart meter uptake. Source: *ENERGEIA for the Energy
Networks Association. (2016). Network transformation roadmap: Work Package 5 — Pricing and behavioural enablers, network pricing and incentives reform (p. 44). Energeia (ENERGEIA for the Energy Networks Association, 2016).*

find that the project suffered from its mandatory nature, lack of explanatory efforts to
inform the public and lack of clarity regarding the benefits. However, the report concluded that the benefits as outlined in the original are unlikely to be realized; however, the
infrastructure is now in place for technological developments and innovation the benefits
of which were not available when the project was conceived. The aggregation of the
household sector for generation, storage, and network management would be a prime
example of such innovation.

7.5.2 Preparing Australian networks for the transition

Australia, while leading the world in the rate of residential PV adoption, is lagging when it comes to adapting networks to provide the flexibility through monitoring, control and communications that would allow effective network optimization. A recent report by the World Economic Forum benchmarked Australia 43rd out of 115 on their energy transition index, and 28th out of 32 developed countries (World Economic Forum, 2019) (Fig. 7.10).

In efforts to spur the uptake of distributed energy technologies Australian regulators are considering approaches to reducing barriers to entry for new service providers. With enhanced data capabilities, aggregators will be able to provide access to a wider range of incentives for households' distributed resources (Shaw-Williams et al., 2018; Shaw-Williams, Susilawati, Walker, & Varendorf, 2019). With sufficient metering and connectivity, aggregated entities will be able to participate directly in wholesale markets, demand response and ancillary markets. These additional potential revenue sources will assist in bringing solutions to market that can more closely align incentives with beneficial investments.

The primary barrier to new entrants and enhanced network capabilities is within network constraints. The AEMO and ENA Open Networks Program (AEMO & Energy Networks Association, 2018) attempts to provide a framework to identify new market structures and digitalization platforms that would facilitate the transition. The capabilities required to integrate data and operations of customers and the network are illustrated in Fig. 7.11.

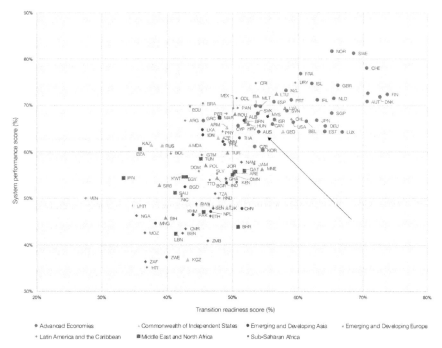

FIGURE 7.10 ETI 2019 Performance/Readiness matrix by country. Source: *World Economic Forum. (2019). Fostering effective energy transition insight report (p. 22). World Economic Forum.*

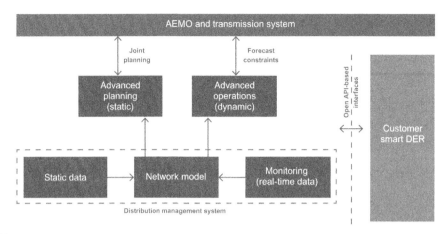

FIGURE 7.11 Capabilities required to dynamically manage DER. *DER*, Distributed energy resources. Source: *AEMO & Energy Networks Association. (2018). Open energy networks. Melbourne, Australia: Australian Energy Market Operator, p. 18 (AEMO, 2018).*

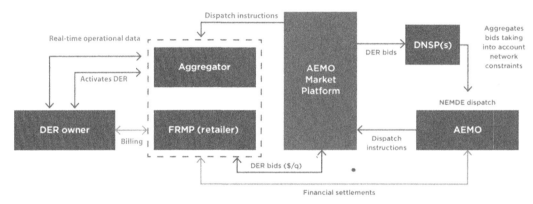

FIGURE 7.12 Proposed AEMO central platform. Source: *AEMO & Energy Networks Association. (2018). Open energy networks. Melbourne, Australia: Australian Energy Market Operator, p. 27 (AEMO, 2018).*

One such structure proposed is that of a single integrated platform; AEMO central platform and optimizing dispatch considering transmission and distribution network constraints as shown in Fig. 7.12.

In this structure AEMO provides a centralized platform that as the interface for aggregators to bid distributed resources directly into markets. Network operators would also be connected to the platform for greater visibility of network conditions.

7.6 Conclusion

With the growing capability in homes and in network management, there is great scope for real-time automated systems interacting on both side of the meter to provide economic benefits to all stakeholders. However, network optimization capabilities in Australia are lagging behind those of households creating a barrier to increased network efficiencies. Smart homes significantly add to potential DM and network support capabilities. In the absence of political direction, networks are reactive to changing conditions that are driven by household investment decisions. This is expected to continue with household uptake of smart home devices driven by continued energy price increases.

As aggregators increase their presence in energy networks as discussed in by Poplavskaya and de Vries in Chapter 5 and Lehmbruck et al. in Chapter 10, they will provide the impetus for the uptake of enhanced automation and data-driven solutions. Monitoring and coordinating aggregations of prosuming smart homes in real-time while participating in wholesale markets is a complex set of operations and will drive automation. Currently network operators are confronted with a wide range of devices and protocols and exploding data quantities that require significant investments in data analytics and ML. This fragmentation of device ecosystems poses potential vulnerabilities in terms of network security and potential privacy concerns which already has the attention of regulators.

HEMS are emerging that are better able to manage consumption and generation patterns in response to automated instructions or remote signaling. As the spread of PV, batteries, smart devices, and advanced HEMS continues, it is crucial that standards and protocols covering interoperability and standardized communications formats are developed in order to realize the full benefits on offer.

There needs to be significant political investment in driving the energy transition as a key national priority. With the goal of maximizing distributed renewable generation in the network, the network stabilization capabilities afforded by a network of smart prosuming households is essential. The economic benefits on offer of significantly improving energy efficiency through the reconceptualization of the network as a platform with low barriers to entry of new players and innovation are well proven, painfully obvious and should be pursued as a matter of urgency.

References

Adika, C. O., & Lingfeng, W. (2014). Autonomous appliance scheduling for household energy management. *IEEE Transactions on Smart Grid, 5*, 673–682.
AEMO. (2018). *Integrated system plan.* Melbourne, Australia.
AEMO & Energy Networks Association. (2018). *Open energy networks.* Melbourne, Australia: Australian Energy Market Operator.
Alowaifeer, M., Alamri, A., & Meliopoulos, A. P. S. (2018). *Reliability and cost impacts of home energy management systems* (pp. 1–6). IEEE.
Anonymous. (2017). Study: Global smart home market to exceed $14 billion in 2017. *Appliance Design, 65*, 6–7.
Asare-Bediako, B., Kling, W. L., & Ribeiro, P. F. (2012). *Home energy management systems: Evolution, trends and frameworks* (pp. 1–5). IEEE.
Asghar, M. R., Dán, G. R., Miorandi, D., & Chlamtac, I. (2017). Smart meter data privacy: A survey. *IEEE Communications Surveys & Tutorials, 19*, 2820–2835.
Beaudin, M., & Zareipour, H. (2015). Home energy management systems: A review of modelling and complexity. *Renewable and Sustainable Energy Reviews, 45*, 318–335.

Blanco-Novoa, Ó., Fernández-Caramés, T. M., Fraga-Lamas, P., & Castedo, L. (2017). An electricity price-aware open-source smart socket for the internet of energy. *Sensors (Basel, Switzerland), 17*. Available from https://doi.org/10.3390/s17030643.

Blichert, F. (2018). *Zigbee vs Z Wave: Which is best for your smart home?* DGiT.

Bojanczyk, K. (2013). *Redefining home energy management systems green tech media.*

Chen, X., Wei, T., & Hu, S. (2013). Uncertainty-aware household appliance scheduling considering dynamic electricity pricing in smart home. *IEEE Transactions on Smart Grid, 4*, 932—941.

Constantin, L. (2016). *Hackers found 47 new vulnerabilities in 23 IoT devices at DEF CON.* Computerworld.

Damisa, U., Nwulu, N. I., & Sun, Y. (2018). Microgrid energy and reserve management incorporating prosumer behind-the-meter resources. *IET Renewable Power Generation, 12*, 910—919.

de Wildt, T. E., Chappin, E. J. L., van de Kaa, G., Herder, P. M., & van de Poel, I. R. (2019). Conflicting values in the smart electricity grid a comprehensive overview. *Renewable and Sustainable Energy Reviews, 111*, 184—196.

Deagon, B. (2018). *Amazon fulfilling smart home dream with ring buy, alexa growth.* Los Angeles, CA: Investor's Business Daily, Inc.

Digital Transformation Monitor. (2017). In D. T. Monitor (Ed.), *Smart Home: Technologies with a standard battle* (p. 4). Brussels, Belgium: European Commission.

Duffy, B. M. J. (2018). Ziff Davis LLC. PCMag Digital Group. IFTTT. PC Mag.

ENERGEIA for the Energy Networks Association. (2016). Network transformation roadmap: Work Package 5 — Pricing and behavioural enablers, network pricing and incentives reform (. 44). Energeia.

Hargreaves, T., Nye, M., & Burgess, J. (2013). Keeping energy visible? Exploring how householders interact with feedback from smart energy monitors in the longer term. *Energy Policy, 52*, 126—134.

Horne, C., Darras, B., Bean, E., Srivastava, A., & Frickel, S. (2015). Privacy, technology, and norms: The case of smart meters. *Social Science Research, 51*, 64—76.

International Data Corporation. (2019). *IDC forecasts worldwide spending on the internet of things to reach $745 billion in 2019, led by the manufacturing, consumer, transportation, and utilities sectors.*

International Energy Agency. (2017a). *Digitalization & energy* (p. 76). Paris, France: International Energy Agency.

International Energy Agency. (2017b). *Digitalization & energy* (p. 113). Paris, France: International Energy Agency.

International Energy Agency. (2017c). *Energy efficiency 2017* (p. 59). Paris, France: International Energy Agency.

International Energy Agency. (2019). *Tracking clean energy progress* (p. Tracking Clean Energy Progress (TCEP) assesses the status of 45 critical energy technologies). Paris, France: International Energy Agency.

İzmitligil, H., & Apaydn Özkan, H. (2018). A home energy management system. *Transactions of the Institute of Measurement and Control, 40*, 2498—2508.

Junior, D. M., Melo, L., Lu, H., d'Amorim, M., & Prakash, A. (2019). *Beware of the app! On the vulnerability surface of smart devices through their companion apps.*

Latimer, C. (2018). *What's so smart about electricity smart meters? The Sydney morning herald.* Sydney, Australia: Fairfax Ltd.

Loucks, E. (2018). The appliance revolution. *Kitchen & Bath Business, 65*, 18—19.

Mai, V., & Khalil, I. (2017). Design and implementation of a secure cloud-based billing model for smart meters as an Internet of things using homomorphic cryptography. *Future Generation Computer Systems, 72*, 327—338.

Mohsenian-Rad, A., Wong, V. W. S., Jatskevich, J., Schober, R., & Leon-Garcia, A. (2010). Autonomous demand-side management based on game-theoretic energy consumption scheduling for the future smart grid. *IEEE Transactions on Smart Grid, 1*, 320—331.

MT Newswires. (2019). *Market chatter: Amazon says more than 100 million devices with Alexa sold.* Bethesda, MD: MT Newswires.

Mtshali, P., & Khubia, F. (2019). *A smart home energy management system using smart plugs* (pp. 1—5). IEEE.

National Institute of Standards and Technology. (2018a). In: US Department of Commerce (Ed.). *Smart grid interoperability and cybersecurity workshop* (p. 9). Washington, DC: US Government.

National Institute of Standards and Technology. (2018b). In: US Department of Commerce (Ed.). *Smart grid interoperability and cybersecurity workshop* (p. 7). Washington, DC: US Government.

National Institute of Standards and Technology. (2018c). In: US Department of Commerce (Ed.). *Smart grid interoperability and cybersecurity workshop* (p. 107). Washington, DC: US Government.

Northwest Group. (2018). *Australia—Smart grid.* US Department of Commerce.

Office of the European Data Protection Supervisor. 2012. In: Office of the European Data Protection Supervisor (Ed.). *Opinion of the European Data protection supervisor on the commission recommendation on preparations for the roll-out of smart metering systems*. Brussels, Belgium: European Union.

Sam Wolfson. (2018). Amazon's Alexa recorded private conversation and sent it to random contact. *The Guardian*.

Shakeri, M., Shayestegan, M., Abunima, H., Reza, S. M. S., Akhtaruzzaman, M., Alamoud, A. R. M., ... Amin, N. (2017). An intelligent system architecture in home energy management systems (HEMS) for efficient demand response in smart grid. *Energy & Buildings*, *138*, 154–164.

Shakeri, M., Shayestegan, M., Reza, S. M. S., Yahya, I., Bais, B., Akhtaruzzaman, M., ... Amin, N. (2018). Implementation of a novel home energy management system (HEMS) architecture with solar photovoltaic system as supplementary source. *Renewable Energy*, *125*, 108–120.

Shaw-Williams, D., Susilawati, C., & Walker, G. (2018). Value of residential investment in photovoltaics and batteries in networks: A techno-economic analysis. *Energies*, *11*, 1022.

Shaw-Williams, D., Susilawati, C., Walker, G., & Varendorf, J. (2019). Valuing the impact of residential photovoltaics and batteries on network electricity losses: An Australian case study. *Utilities Policy*.

Snow, S., Buys, L., Roe, P., & Brereton, M. (2013). *Curiosity to cupboard: Self reported disengagement with energy use feedback over time*. Association for Computing Machinery (ACM).

Snow, S., Radke, K., Vyas, D., & Brereton, M. (2014). *Privacy in the new era of visible and sharable energy-use information*. ACM (The Association for Computing Machinery).

Song, H., Qin, A. K., & Salim, F. D. (2017). *Multi-resolution selective ensemble extreme learning machine for electricity consumption prediction*. (pp. 600–609). Springer Verlag.

Stroetmann, L. E. (2018). *Reverse engineering the TP-Link HS110*. SoftScheck.

Swinson, V., Hamer, J., & Humphries, S. (2015). Taking demand management into the future: Managing flexible loads on the electricity network using smart appliances and controlled loads. *Economic Analysis and Policy*, *48*, 192–203.

Tayal, D. (2017). Achieving high renewable energy penetration in Western Australia using data digitisation and machine learning. *Renewable and Sustainable Energy Reviews*, *80*, 1537–1543.

The Victorian Auditor General. (2015). In: The Victorian Auditor General Office (Ed.). *Realising the benefits of smart meters*. Melbourne, Australia: Victorian Government Printers.

Wilson, C., Hargreaves, T., & Hauxwell-Baldwin, R. (2017). Benefits and risks of smart home technologies. *Energy Policy*, *103*, 72–83.

World Economic Forum. (2019). *Fostering effective energy transition insight report* (p. 22). World Economic Forum.

Zhen, L., Junzhou, L., Yiling, X., Chao, G., Kui, W., & Xinwen, F. (2017). Security vulnerabilities of internet of things: A case study of the smart plug system. *IEEE Internet of Things Journal*, *4*, 1899–1909.

PART TWO

Implementers & disrupters

Behind and beyond the meter: what's in it for the system?

Dierk Bauknecht, Christoph Heinemann, Dominik Seebach and Moritz Vogel

Oeko-Institut, Freiburg, Germany

8.1 Introduction

This chapter looks at current developments behind and beyond the meter from a system perspective: How should these concepts be designed to benefit the power system in general and the integration of renewable energy in particular? What should be the main principles and priorities? Which effects should be considered in the design? What are potential pitfalls?

The concepts described in this book offer a range of opportunities in the energy sector: on the one hand, for individual consumers and their role in the sector as well as companies and their business options; on the other hand, for the transition of the sector as a whole toward a system based on renewable energy. A renewable and decentralized energy system entails a range of challenges, including investment challenges, issues of participation and acceptance as well as the question of how a system with millions instead of hundreds of power plants can be coordinated. All these challenges clearly make it worth thinking about concepts like the ones described in this volume.

At the same time, the various behind-and-beyond-the-meter (BTM) concepts have different characteristics, such as

- level of optimization
- optimization goal (self-consumption, efficiency, etc.)
- role of network requirements
- integration of market signals

179

As a result, the various concepts can also exhibit significant differences with regard to system-wide objectives. Especially if one sees BTM concepts as a way to facilitate the transition to a renewable energy system, the concepts can differ in the way they enable such a system at least cost. Therefore it is important to have a framework in place to evaluate the various concepts. This chapter presents key issues that should be included in such a framework. It does so by providing a general overview and by looking at two specific cases.

The chapter is organized as follows:

- Section 8.2 provides an overview of the various criteria that need to be considered when evaluating behind-and-beyond-the-meter concepts. It focuses on their contribution to the development of the power system as a whole, rather than on the perspective of individual companies or prosumers. This can also provide the basis for adapting the regulatory framework, for which key principles are presented. The regulatory framework needs to both enable individual business cases and incentivize individual market participants to contribute to system objectives.
- Section 8.3 presents a closer look at two concepts: self-consumption and district solutions in Germany on the one hand, and peer-to-peer (P2P) trading on the other hand, followed by the chapter's conclusions.

8.2 Behind-and-beyond-the-meter concepts—evaluation criteria from a system perspective

As a starting point, key objectives for the design of power systems are to provide electricity in an environmental-friendly way, at low costs and with a high supply security. From the perspective of an energy transition toward system based on renewable energy, which is the key challenge in today's power system, the question is how such a renewable system can be achieved at least cost, while maintaining security of supply. What has also become increasingly important as a key objective is a system that enables participation of consumers and citizens.

This chapter spells out what needs to be considered when designing BTM concepts in order to contribute to these overall system objectives. This also provides the basis for regulatory principles that can align these system requirements with individual business models.

The energy transition to which BTM concepts can contribute is about replacing a system based on fossil and nuclear generation with renewable generation. However, what should be kept in mind is that the overall level of electricity consumption and thus efficiency still play a major role. "Too cheap to meter" still does not work even in a renewable system, and such a system is indeed only feasible if the demand for renewable generation can be reduced to the extent possible. Especially in a system with electric vehicles, hydrogen production based on renewable electricity, etc., the demand for electricity would skyrocket if efficiency potentials were not exploited.

BTM typically also involves some kind of digitalization, which as a direct effect typically entails additional power consumption. However, even without BTM concepts, it can be assumed that a renewable and more decentralized system generally requires a smarter infrastructure. Still, the infrastructure needed for BTM concepts should be as efficient as possible. Besides the power consumption, this is also a resource issue, for example, regarding the resources needed for battery storage compared to grid extension.

While BTM concepts can entail additional power consumption, they can also help reduce it. This can result not only from visualizing energy consumption and other feedback systems, but also more generally from an increased awareness of BTM consumers for power consumption and the fact that electricity does not simply come out of the plug.

For example, Darby, Strömbäck, and Wilks (2013) have modeled demand flexibility in six EU countries based on a meta-analysis of demand reduction from 100 pilots and experiments with feedback and dynamic pricing. They find that an average 9% reduction of the yearly electricity consumption can be achieved with in-home displays and approximately 5% with informative billing and online feedback. Taking into account that project participants typically show stronger reaction, the authors expect an overall reduction potential of around 3%. A crucial question for the assessment of this dimension of smart grids is how these savings compare with more conventional, less technology-based demand reduction instruments, such as consumer advisory programs, support for more efficient appliances, and product labeling (Almeida, de Fonseca, Schlomann, & Feilberg, 2011). Also, it is worth assessing if electricity consumption can be reduced over a longer period and beyond the pilot project.

These results from "smart grid" projects also provide some evidence concerning BTM concepts. They show that demand can be reduced to some extent, but complementary instruments are still necessary. It is also highly relevant that BTM concepts do not only just focus on on-site generation and storage but also on how demand can be reduced in the first place. If prosumers invest all their money in generation and storage and do not have anything left for more efficient appliances, BTM falls short of its potential.

Once demand reduction is taken care of, a further key issue is developing renewable and replacing conventional generation. How can the concepts covered in this book contribute to this objective?

The most important task is to expand renewable capacity in line with climate targets, etc. Whether or not this generation is used behind the meter or traded on a P2P platform is only secondary from this perspective. In other words, the overall investment in renewables is the key issue, and not so much how and by which consumer this electricity is used. Distributing generation from existing capacity between consumers in different ways is only a zero-sum game and should therefore not be the key objective of BTM concepts.

As a consequence, a crucial question is how BTM concepts can help expand renewables capacity, that is, how they affect investment decisions. Such concepts can make the investment in renewables financially more attractive, for example, because prosumers can save network tariffs. In the case of rooftop photovoltaic (PV), this does not only imply that additional capital can be used for renewables (RES) investments but also means that additional rooftop space is made available for renewables. Considering that space is likely to become a bottleneck for the energy transition in many countries, this is highly relevant. Again, what is most important from a system perspective is that the full rooftop potential is used instead of optimizing the capacity according to local needs, thereby potentially "wasting" rooftop space.

In terms of economics the question is whether the savings by BTM users and the reason for why it becomes attractive for them to invest in renewables actually reflect system costs. If this is not the case, and if the economics are mainly due to the way network tariffs and other fees are regulated, then this can be considered a hidden subsidy as described by Schittekatte and Robinson in this volume on the challenges of network tariff design. This can be justified in order to promote renewable generation. However, if there is a political case for such a subsidy, it is preferable to set up or maintain an explicit and transparent financing mechanism for renewables rather than supporting them via network regulation, etc. Such financing mechanisms have worked very well in many countries in expanding renewable capacity. The feed-in scheme applied in Germany and many other countries is a case in point. Besides investments in new capacity, BTM concepts can also provide a solution for plants that drop out of financing schemes, for example, after 20 years of operation in the German case (see chapter by Löbbe et al. in this volume).

Besides economic motivation for investing in additional renewable capacity, for example, due to "grid parity," the fact that generation is not fed into the grid but consumed on-site may be an additional motivation for some consumers to invest and may thus increase their willingness to invest. In Germany, for instance, a significant number of people prefer their power supply from regional sources (Schudak & Wallbott, 2018). However, further evidence is needed to assess to what extent regional supply can trigger additional investment in practice. There are also some indications that independence from the system can be a driver for battery adoption (Kalkbrenner, 2019). Yet from a system perspective, this is only useful as long as batteries are actually required for energy transition. This issue will also be discussed in the case study in Section 8.3.1.

When it comes to participation, the concepts set out in this book typically increase the number of actors that have an active role in the power system. This mainly means that the stakeholders themselves invest in generation and flexibility, become active market participants, and have more choice as to how they want to organize their electricity supply. This should not be confused with a higher level of democratic participation but can still be beneficial. What is important is that a higher level of participation can help increase acceptance of the energy transition in general and can facilitate individual investment decisions in particular.

In terms of efficiency and designing a low-cost renewable system, behind-and-beyond-the-meter concepts may offer new opportunities for some market participants but may still make the overall system more expensive if not designed in the right way.

On the one hand, BTM concepts lead to a higher demand for flexibility if generation and demand are matched locally. On the other hand, as a result of more local dispatch of flexibility, BTM concepts can reduce the demand for transporting electricity via the grid. The key question is how the cost differences between these two infrastructures compare. Note that if BTM concepts reduce grid usage, this does not imply that the grid capacity, which is the cost driver for the grid, is reduced by the same extent, if people still rely on the grid as back-up capacity. If they do not pay for this backup, this simply means that other people have to pay for it.

The network is a relatively cheap source of flexibility and is often considered as the first flexibility option that should be used and a no regret strategy (Bauknecht et al., 2016;

Schmid & Knopf, 2015). However, load management that can be provided by prosumers offers a relatively cheap source of flexibility and the costs of battery storage keep decreasing so that local balancing may become cheaper than grid usage.

Yet, even in this case, it is important to understand how BTM concepts are implemented and what their "objective functions" are, that is, how they optimize generation, flexibility, consumption, and network requirements. An analysis of a broad range of energy management systems (EMS) has shown that there are significant differences in their objective function (Bauknecht et al., 2017). It is concluded that "depending on the specific EMS approach an increased supply of flexibility for the overall system or additional need for flexibility may follow" and "there are both EMS that ignore grid requirements and systems that explicitly enable interaction with the distribution system operator" (p. 13−14). As for the point made above about efficiency, there are also differences in the extent to which they address demand reduction.

Overall system requirements should be taken into account in the design of BTM concepts. Again, this requires a regulatory framework that enables and rewards concepts that are not just behind-the-meter but also include the big picture. If local flexibility is built up as part of BTM concepts, these should also be offered to the market and not just used locally. This presupposes market rules that allow small-scale flexibility options to participate, for example, via aggregators. Moreover, network constraints should be taken into account when operating local storage and load management. If there is no appropriate regulatory framework, system costs could even increase as a result of prosumage despite the overall increase in flexibility (Neetzow, Mendelevitch, & Siddiqui, 2019). If the objective is to maximize self-consumption and to become as independent from the system as possible, this can mean that local flexibility such as battery storage is used even in times when there are no grid bottlenecks, while at the same time the household flexibility is not used to support the grid in times of network constraints. As for network regulation, it should provide a level playing field for both network expansion and making use of flexibility options, which can reduce the need for network expansion.

Moreover, as for security of supply, the key question is if this is provided in a decentralized way or on a system level. New opportunities on the local level and behind the meter can also give rise to local security of supply concepts. For example, there are various RD&D activities on islanding in Germany. This, however, will further increase the required capacities and thus overall costs.

In terms of replacing conventional generation with renewables, it is also important to note that conventional generation can provide a significant amount of flexibility in the transition toward a renewable system, that is, conventional plants can reduce their generation in times of high renewable feed-in and vice versa. This reduces their full load hours. As soon as local flexibility from battery storage and load management is used as an alternative flexibility option, there is less pressure on conventional plants to provide flexibility and they can increase their generation. This would be an unintended side effect of using local flexibility. Yet what needs to be kept in mind is that flexibility options like storage and corresponding business cases need to be built up even before large capacities are needed, as it may otherwise be too late to develop the technologies at a later stage from scratch.

Next to these infrastructure costs, economic efficiency also depends on how the market functions and whether new market participants can increase competition and market liquidity.

8.3 Case studies: evaluating behind-the-meter approaches

Based on the general overview on evaluation criteria for BTM concepts from a system perspective, what they can contribute to the energy transition and where problems can occur, this section takes a closer look at two specific concepts: self-consumption and district solutions in Germany in Section 8.3.1 and P2P trading in Section 8.3.2.

8.3.1 Behind-the-meter self-consumption in combination with batteries—a German case study

8.3.1.1 Self-consumption in Germany

In Germany self-generation and self-consumption represent a possible behind-the-meter business case for households and other electricity consumers (see also chapter 4 Lobbe et al). This has been fueled by two developments. In recent years electricity prices in Germany increased for households. At the same time, a cost decline of PV power plants was driven by the Renewable Energy Support System (EEG, 2017). With lower levelized cost of electricity (LCOE) generation, feed-in tariffs have been reduced and have fallen below the electricity consumer prices. Grid parity of self-consumption was reached. Fig. 8.1 shows this development.

Today consumers can decrease electricity costs and hedge against increasing electricity prices in the future by investing in generation and storage technology and by consuming their own electricity behind the meter. This is also economically feasible due to the German regulation, which does not charge certain electricity price components on self-consumed electricity (Bundesnetzagentur, 2016).

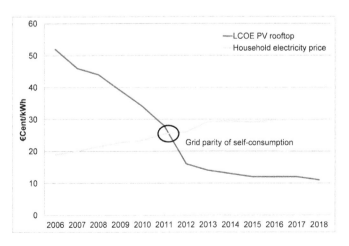

FIGURE 8.1 Grid parity for PV in Germany. *PV*, Photovoltaic. *Source: Own depiction based on Fraunhofer-Institut für solare Energiesysteme. (2019). Aktuelle Fakten zur Photovoltaik in Deutschland, Freiburg. <https://www.ise.fraunhofer.de/content/dam/ise/de/documents/publications/studies/aktuelle-fakten-zur-photovoltaik-in-deutschland.pdf> Accessed 24.07.19 (Fraunhofer-Institut für solare Energiesysteme, 2019).*

The share of self-consumption can be increased by combining PV modules with battery storage. Thereby electricity that is fed into the grid in times of low consumption can be stored and consumed at a later point in time. As a consequence, the installation of batteries has increased in Germany (ISEA RWTH Aachen, 2018). This business case can lead to an increase in investment in these technologies and thus support the development of renewables that is needed for the energy transition.

8.3.1.2 Behind-the-meter storage application examples

Besides the self-consumption use case, other, more complex use cases are discussed for electricity storage in Germany. The Oeko-Institut analyzed different storage application scenarios where the self-consumption use case was extended to an urban district. An optimization model was applied to quantify the effects of storage and self-consumption.

Looking at these use cases from the system perspective set out in the previous section, this analysis reveals interesting differences between the various concepts.

For new city districts integrated energy concepts are proposed by planners (see, e.g., DENA, 2015 for a proposal of an emission neutral district energy concept). These concepts combine electricity generation and consumption of different residents and businesses. This also includes new applications like heat pumps, electric mobility, and battery storage (see, e.g., Thomann, 2017). Instead of utilizing batteries individually, one storage plant is applied to maximize the district's overall self-consumption.

Some actors call for the regulatory rules that are applied to household self-consumption to be extended to such community concepts to support this business case (Gaudchau, Resch, & Zeh, 2016). In other words, they would like to broaden the definition of self-consumption. In Switzerland research projects go even a step further and comprise larger numbers of consumers and PV generation behind one meter. Here, all consumers that participate in this so-called Eigenverbrauchsgemeinschaft (self-consumption community) benefit from self-consumption behind the meter (TN Advanced Energy Concepts, 2018). From a regulatory point of view this is not possible in Germany. Self-consumption is currently only possible for households (Bundesnetzagentur, 2016) and apartment buildings (Bundestag, 2017), but not for districts which are supplied by a public electricity grid.

Our modeling exercise shows that by combining different consumers and PV generation of a whole district, the share of self-consumption within this district is higher than in single households that self-consumed PV generation. This increase of the self-consumption rate is due to the larger electricity demand in the district in relation to the rooftop area available for PV-electricity production. This is particularly the case for districts that consist of many multistory residential buildings with a small rooftop area compared to the consumption in the flats of the building.

The self-consumption rate can be increased further if the district's load curve consists of different load profiles because there are different types of consumers, that is, the demand from households and commerce is mixed. In this case the electricity demand is distributed more evenly over time. As a result, self-generated electricity can almost always be used to cover the local demand.

TABLE 8.1 PV capacity, storage capacity, and self-consumption rates for different scenarios.

	Household	Residential district	Mixed district
PV capacity	7.5	100	135
Electricity consumption	4.750	140.400	486.195
Self-consumption rate without storage (%)	50	40	30
Storage size (kWh)	6	100	135
Self-consumption rate with storage (%)	80	60	31
Storage full load hours	275	248	53

From Oeko-Institut.

The application of electricity storage (prosumager) can further increase self-consumption in a residential or mixed district. However, it does not lead to a comparable increase of self-consumption as in households. This is caused by the large electricity demand that, in the majority hours, exceeds generation.

The reduced need for flexibility such as storage, if more generation options and different loads are combined, can be seen from Table 8.1. The table depicts the results of three scenarios that include a household, a residential district, and a mixed district, which consists of several households and commercial consumers. The PV capacity and consumption of the household are the smallest. The ratio between these two, however, is the largest among all scenarios. This is caused by the large rooftop area for PV in comparison to the consumption. When it comes to the residential district and the mixed district this ratio is much lower. The storage load hours that are depicted in the table act as an indicator for the economic feasibility of the storage plant. From the perspective of individual consumers the use of storage (battery) is especially reasonable for households, as it increases the self-consumption rate from 50% (without storage) to 80% (with storage), and the storage full load hours are high.

However, there is much less need for storages from a system perspective as soon as the grid is being used to distribute the excess energy from PV rooftop generation. This effect is shown in the mixed district scenario, which shows low storage full load hours. Fig. 8.2 shows that a storage plant within a mixed residential and commercial district will hardly be used outside summer time when PV generation will be peaking. During winter most of the PV generation will be directly used by the loads within the district.

Overall, in this example using a storage plant in individual households seems to make sense, while in mixed districts, a storage plant looks like a bad investment. Does this mean that small-scale storage applications should be facilitated? The viable self-consumption business case, which can be reasonable on an individual basis, is hardly cost efficient from a system's point of view. From a system-efficiency perspective optimizing a larger area and using the electricity grid to balance demand and supply will reduce the need for storage capacity. This is in line with the rationale for combining a large number of different consumers in one electricity system in the first place.

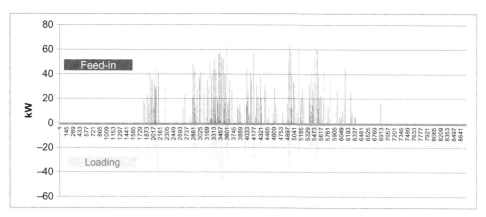

FIGURE 8.2   Storage usage in a district with residential and commercial loads. Source: *Own modeling results Oeko-Institut.*

Furthermore, the storage full load hours act as an indicator for storage losses. If a battery is used frequently to maximize self-consumption, the amount of energy that is lost through storing increases. Storage losses of modern batteries account for about 10% losses of energy. These storage losses are especially high in the household scenario and lower in the mixed district scenario due to the frequent use in the former. Therefore a system that favors storage and self-consumption over grid expansion and electricity transmission with lower energy losses than batteries has higher energy needs that need to be satisfied by additional electricity generation. In case this is provided by fossil power plants, the CO_2 emissions could increase due to this effect.

Those negative effects of implementing storages could be partly overcome by making use of demand-side management options instead. If demand-side flexibility is being provided by aggregating and managing, for example, heat pumps, electric vehicles, and other large-scale loads within a district, behind-the-meter concepts could help to make use of otherwise idle distributed flexibility potential. However, from the systems perspective, flexibility should be used in an optimal way for the whole system in order to lower overall CO_2 emissions and therefore not be limited to the districts needs for maximizing self-consumption.

8.3.2 Peer-to-peer trading of renewable electricity

P2P trading is a contractual and administrative development which allows producers and consumers to conclude bilateral contracts for the supply of electricity, thus challenging the intermediary role of traditional utilities in centralized electricity systems (Bauknecht et al., 2019). The increasing relevance of this approach is triggered by recent technical developments in the field of digitalization. Smart meters allow for the monitoring of small-scale transactions by real-time metering of consumption and production, and technologies like blockchain can be used as a facilitator for decentralized transactions and smart contracts. Thus these technologies can enhance individualized and decentralized markets and the active participation of small-scale actors.

As outlined above, the relevant question in terms of system design toward a sustainable electricity system is the potential contribution of such an evolving trading approach to such a system transition.

- Does it support the substitution of fossil and nuclear fuels by the increased deployment of renewables (or by increased efficiency)?
- Can it reduce the cost of such an electricity system while maintaining security of supply?
- Can active participation of consumers increase acceptance of the energy transition, thus facilitating its realization?

Any such assessment of potential effects should bear in mind that available studies for Germany and Switzerland have indicated that electricity, to a large extent, has been a low-interest product so far, which does only attract little individual interest and involvement by consumers, (Demarmels, Schaffner, Kolberg, & Janoschka, 2013; Reichmuth, 2014). This means that in order to trigger relevant contributions to the energy transition, either the interest by consumers has to increase significantly, or consumers have to be attracted by relevant financial advantages. This may be supported by the general decrease of administrative barriers, for example, through regulatory provisions or a strong role of aggregators and other service providers.

8.3.2.1 Support the substitution of fossil and nuclear fuels?

P2P trading generally allows producers to meet highly individualized needs and preferences by consumers. It has therefore the theoretical potential to tap an increased willingness to pay by these consumers. This opens up an additional revenue stream for these producers. However, this does not necessarily mean that further electricity from renewables (RES-E) is brought into operation. As for RES-E which is subject to public subsidies, it might result either in overfunding of the specific plants (i.e., windfall profits for the plant operator) or in a shift of cost from the subsidy scheme to the individual customer. However, generation from renewables will not increase in this case. As for RES-E plants which are operated beyond public support schemes, an important framework condition is that RES-E is capital intensive but has low operational cost. Therefore once a RES-E plant has been built and put into operation, the production of electricity is rarely limited by the current wholesale electricity price (as it is the case, e.g., for a thermal plant). Extra short-term revenues for the plant operator would only increase RES-E production in cases where the operational cost of a plant is hardly covered by the respective market value on wholesale markets. In such a case the added revenues actually could make the operation economically viable and can avoid an early shutdown of the plant. This is a realistic case, for example, for renewable plants in Germany and Austria for which the period of public support ends after 20 years. For those plants the plant operators have to choose between a shutdown of the plant, repowering, or an appropriate marketing approach (like P2P?) in order to extent the period of operation of the existing plant (Linkenheil & Küchle, 2017; Wallasch, Lüers, & Rehfeldt, 2016; Quentin, Sudhaus, & Endell, 2018).

Decisions on the installation of new renewable plants strongly depend on the bankability of each individual project. This in turn is mainly influenced by sufficiently reliable revenue streams in a limited payback period. For the case of Europe, public support schemes have guaranteed such stable conditions in many countries in recent years, while the revenue expectations on wholesale markets have not provided sufficient investor confidence so far. Is this likely to change with new P2P markets emerging?

Irrespective of P2P markets, financing conditions for renewables are about to change due to reduced LCOE for renewables and often assumed increasing cost of electricity on wholesale markets in Europe. In such a world, long-term power purchase agreements by commercial consumers or by utilities with clear arrangements on the electricity price are discussed as a promising future solution to finance renewables beyond public support schemes (see, e.g., DENA, 2019; Capgemini & RE100, 2018). However, a major feature of digital P2P trading platforms is to facilitate highly flexible supply contracts on a small scale rather than long-term obligations covering the major production share of entire plants or wind farms. Although P2P-market places in principle could also facilitate long-term contracts with stable financing conditions, it does not seem to be the most suitable instrument in order to incentivize new renewable plants.

A further challenge of the energy transition is that increasing shares of intermittent technologies, namely, wind and PVs, have to be integrated in energy systems by different options for flexibility, like demand-side management and storage. In principle, P2P platforms can be used to offer flexible tariffs, which stimulate demand-side management. However, from a system point of view it is not sensible to synchronize a consumer's demand with the production profile of a specific plant. The unique ability of a P2P platform to allow for such a direct relationship therefore is not a key selling point It is rather crucial that the demand of consumers can respond to the needs of the overall electricity system—or of the respective local or regional subsystem in case of grid congestions. P2P trading could be based on tariffs, which provide suitable local or regional price signals; but there is no obvious added value compared to a similar tariff, which could be offered by a local utility in a traditional contractual arrangement.

In the end, the added value of P2P trading platforms in terms of additional integration of renewables could be very generally an increased involvement by consumers. This can be assumed to lead to a higher commitment and motivation to tap flexibility and efficiency potentials on the level of individual consumers.[1] However, the use of smart technologies, particularly blockchain mechanisms, which are based on proof-of-work, can cause high electricity consumption for the underlying computing work. Therefore any increase in efficiency has to compensate this added electricity consumption before it can contribute to an overall increase of system efficiency.

8.3.2.2 Reduction of the overall system cost?

In terms of cost effects, increased market shares of P2P platforms will have effects in different dimensions. As a direct effect parallel markets will inevitably distract participants from a central market place. As long as P2P markets are only a minor niche, this might have a negligible effect, but in principle it reduces liquidity on markets. So what will be the development in these different markets?

[1] The positive effect of increased involvement of consumers has been documented by Roth, Lowitzsch, Yildiz, and Hashani (2018), who showed that coownership in renewables increased the willingness of consumers to adjust their consumption behavior depending on the respective production levels.

In central competitive wholesale markets, the loss of renewable shares to P2P markets will probably result in an increased price level as renewables generally have a downward impact on wholesale prices. This effect is increased by the generally reduced market liquidity. In P2P markets the price for electricity will be even higher than in standard wholesale markets (like the central power exchange). If this is not the case, there is hardly an incentive at all for renewable producers to participate in such markets.

From the perspective of end consumers the wholesale price of electricity only makes up for a minor share of the price they have to pay for their electricity.[2] However, also in P2P arrangements standard services like balance group management, provision of balancing power, and billing have to be provided and paid for. As a result, P2P-platform operators and other service providers have to take over the role of classical utilities to some extent and will ask for an appropriate financial compensation. Also, grid fees and other public charges might be similar to a traditional supply contract. Thus for end consumers it might only be financially beneficial to participate in a P2P-arrangement if the lower administration and system cost compared to a standard tariff by a utility overcompensates higher prices for electricity on wholesale markets.

8.3.2.3 Increased acceptance of the energy transition?

As outlined above, a major characteristic of P2P platforms is that it allows consumers to become highly involved in "their" electricity supply. This obviously has the potential to increase the general acceptance for the energy transition, although reliable empirical evidence on this still has to be provided. It can be assumed that increased acceptance should reduce resistances and not-in-my-backyard activities and could therefore contribute to the development of more renewable electricity plants. However, this seems to be mostly promising if P2P markets strongly focus on local and regional markets so that acceptance is particularly achieved amongst the same group which is actually affected by new plants and other infrastructure.[3]

8.4 Conclusion

Behind-and-beyond-the-meter concepts can support the energy transition toward a system based on renewable and more distributed energies. A system with more decentralized generation also requires innovative decentralized solutions. Yet there are also significant differences between the concepts and the way in which they contribute to system objectives. Moreover, individual interests and incentives are not necessarily in line with the needs of the overall energy system and political aims. As a result, there could be potential effects of BTM concepts that may not help or even hamper the energy

---

[2] Ecofys (2016) showed for EU Member States for the year 2015 that in average the energy price component of the retail price of electricity for households was only roughly one-third of the overall price, with taxes and levies and network tariffs also adding up for roughly one-third each.

[3] Describe in Chapter 4, such an application of a P2P approach within an energy community. It is remarkable that the described value propositions of this approach also focus on the possible individual benefits but do not emphasize claims on a system wide benefit.

transition. This needs to be reflected in the design of these concepts as well as the regulatory framework.

From a political perspective the challenge is to both open up the space for innovative concepts that are needed for the energy transition and at the same time give these developments some direction. It is important to test a broad range of concepts that can facilitate the energy transition. Yet, as soon as they are applied at a larger scale, they should be in line with system requirements as laid out in this chapter.

In order to develop and demonstrate innovative concepts and evaluate their effects, including the testing of future regulatory options, real-world laboratories, regulatory sandboxes, and regulatory innovation zones will become increasingly important. Such demonstration projects are not just about testing the technology, but also about how it works in a real-world context, how the technology interacts with different stakeholders, what its various side effects are, and what the effects of different regulatory option are. Developing various innovations and combining them into a system that works and fulfills ambitious political targets does require new innovation instruments.

It is clear that a broad range of different innovative concepts is needed to explore what is possible and what works. Yet it is also clear that only some of these concepts will succeed. The selection process should not just be left to the market. Rather, it should be guided by system view and a system vision and principles that are derived from that. The energy transition is about combining bottom-up innovation activities with top-down policy-making.

References

Almeida, A., de Fonseca, P., Schlomann, B., & Feilberg, N. (2011). Characterization of the household electricity consumption in the EU, potential energy savings and specific policy recommendations. *Energy and Buildings,* *43*(8), 1884–1894.

Bauknecht, D., Bracker, J., Flachsbarth, F., Heinemann, C., Seebach, D., & Vogel, M. (2019). *Customer stratification and different concepts of decentralization.* In: Sioshansi (Ed.)., Consumer, Prosumer, Prosumager: How Service Innovations will Disrupt the Utility Business Model, pp. 331–352. Academic Press.

Bauknecht, D., Burger, V., Ritter, D., Vogel, M., Langniß, O., Brenner, T., Chvanova, E., & Geier, L. (2017). Bestandsaufnahme und orientierende Bewertung dezentraler Energiemanagementsysteme. In *UBA Climate Change 16/2017.* Öko-Institut; Dr. Langniß Energie&Analyse, Dessau-Roßlau. <https://www.umweltbundesamt.de/sites/default/files/medien/1410/publikationen/2017-05-30_climate-change_16-2017_dezentrale-ems. pdf> Accessed 05.03.18.

Bauknecht, D., Heinemann, C., Koch, M., Ritter, D., Harthan, R., Sachs, A., et al. (2016). *Systematischer Vergleich von Flexibilitäts- und Speicheroptionen im deutschen Stromsystem zur Integration von erneuerbaren Energien und Analyse entsprechender Rahmenbedingungen.* Freiburg, Darmstadt: Öko-Institut; energynautics GmbH. <https:// www.oeko.de/fileadmin/oekodoc/Systematischer_Vergleich_Flexibilitaetsoptionen.pdf> Accessed 19.01.17.

Bundesnetzagentur. (2016). *Leitfaden zur Eigenversorgung.* Bonn. Accessed 10.07.19.

Bundestag. (2017). *Gesetz zur Förderung von Mieterstrom und zur Änderung weiterer Vorschriften des Erneuerbare Energien-Gesetzes: Mieterstromgesetz.* Accessed 11.07.19.

Capgemini & RE100. (2018). *Making business sense: How RE100 companies have an edge on their peers: Energy Transition & Profitability.* Capgemini; RE100. Accessed 06.09.19.

Darby, S., Strömbäck, J., & Wilks, M. (2013). Potential carbon impacts of smart grid development in six European countries. *Energy Efficiency, 6,* 725–739.

Demarmels, S., Schaffner, D., Kolberg, S., & Janoschka, A. (2013). *Ökostrom oder Naturpower?: Handlungsempfehlungen für eine verständliche Marketingkommunikation von Stromprodukten aus erneuerbaren Energien.* Luzern: Hochschule Luzern.

DENA. (2015). *Der Königspark: ein CO$_2$ neutrales Quartier entsteht*. Berlin. Accessed 29.07.19.

DENA. (2019). *Dena Marktmonitor 2030: Corporate Green PPAs: Umfrage zu Perspektiven nachfragegetriebener Stromlieferverträge bis 2030*. Deutsche Energie-Agentur GmbH.

Ecofys, Fraunhofer ISI, CASE. (2016). *Prices and costs of EU energy: Final report*.

EEG. (2017). *Gesetz für den Ausbau erneuerbarer Energien*. Erneuerbare-Energien-Gesetz (EEG).

Fraunhofer-Institut für solare Energiesysteme. (2019). *Aktuelle Fakten zur Photovoltaik in Deutschland, Freiburg*. <https://www.ise.fraunhofer.de/content/dam/ise/de/documents/publications/studies/aktuelle-fakten-zur-photovoltaik-in-deutschland.pdf> Accessed 24.07.19.

Gaudchau, E., Resch, M., & Zeh, A. (2016). Quartierspeicher: Definition, rechtlicher Rahmen und Perspektiven. *Ökologisches Wirtschaften, 31*, 26–27.

ISEA RWTH Aachen. (2018). *Wissenschaftliches Mess- und Evaluierungsprogramm Solarstromspeicher 2.0: Jahresbericht 2018*. Aachen: ISEA RWTH Aachen. Accessed 15.04.19.

Kalkbrenner, B. J. (2019). Residential vs. community battery storage systems – Consumer preferences in Germany. *Energy Policy, 129*, 1355–1363. Available from https://doi.org/10.1016/j.enpol.2019.03.041.

Linkenheil, C.P., & Küchle, I. (2017). *Wirtschaftlichkeitsuntersuchung von Post-EEG-Anlagen*. Energy Brainpool.

Neetzow, P., Mendelevitch, R., & Siddiqui, S. (2019). Modeling coordination between renewables and grid: Policies to mitigate distribution grid constraints using residential PV-battery systems. *Energy Policy, 132*, 1017–1033. Available from https://doi.org/10.1016/j.enpol.2019.06.024.

Quentin, J., Sudhaus, D., & Endell, M. (2018). *Windenergieanlagen—Was tun nach 20 Jahren?* Berlin: FA Wind. Accessed 06.09.19.

Reichmuth, M. (2014). *Marktanalyse Ökostrom: Endbericht. UBA-Texte 04/2014*.

Roth, L., Lowitzsch, J., Yildiz, Ö., & Hashani, A. (2018). Does (Co-)ownership in renewables matter for an electricity consumer's demand flexibility?: Empirical evidence from Germany. *Energy Research & Social Science, 46*, 169–182. Available from https://doi.org/10.1016/j.erss.2018.07.009.

Schmid, E., & Knopf, B. (2015). Quantifying the long-term economic benefits of European electricity system integration. *Energy Policy, 87*, 260–269. Available from https://doi.org/10.1016/j.enpol.2015.09.026.

Schudak, A., & Wallbott, T. (2018). Verbrauchersicht auf Ökostrom: Ergebnisse einer repräsentativen Verbraucherbefragung im Rahmen des Forschungsvorhabens "Marktanalyse Ökostrom und Herkunftsnachweise". *Climate Change 10/2018*. Dessau-Roßlau. <https://www.umweltbundesamt.de/sites/default/files/medien/1410/publikationen/2018-09-10_climate-change_10-2018_kurzstudie-oekostrom.pdf> Accessed 02.05.19.

Thomann, R. (2017). *C/sells goes Franklin: Sektorkopplung am Beispiel einer modernen Quartiersentwicklung*. Mannheim: MVV. Accessed 10.07.19.

TN Advanced Energy Concepts. (2018). *Eigenverbrauch von PV-Strom: Barrieren und Lösungen*. Feldmeilen: TN Advanced Energy Concepts. Accessed 24.07.19.

Wallasch, A. K., Lüers, S., & Rehfeldt, K. (2016). *Weiterbetrieb von Windenergieanlagen nach 2020*. Varel: Deutsche WindGuard. Accessed 06.09.19.

Working backward from behind the meter: what consumer value, behavior, and uncertainty mean for distributed energy technologies

Robert Smith[1] and Iain MacGill[2]

[1]East Economics (Oknamé Consulting), Sydney, NSW, Australia [2]UNSW, Sydney, NSW, Australia

"You've got to start with the customer experience and work backward to the technology. You cannot start with the technology and try and figure out where you are going to sell it." Steve Jobs, when questioned about which technologies were best.

9.1 Introduction

Technology on the supply side of the electricity industry has been surprisingly stable since Edison's Pearl Street power station began operation in New York in 1882. The technology innovation "war of the currents" settled remarkably quickly into progress primarily through scale—larger power plants and higher voltages—rather than radical new technologies. Business model innovation also settled surprisingly quickly. Metering improvements allowed Edison to move away from his early "pay by the light bulb" approach for an electric lighting service to consumption tariffs (of US24c/kWh in the late 1880s). From there the meter became not only the standard "interface" between the industry and the consumers it served but also a barrier between the supply side of the industry and the customer experience.

New supply technologies did arrive. Nuclear generation in the 1960s promised much, still supplies around 10% of global electricity, but is now a falling share of increasing demand. The power sector's second century has seen open and combined cycle gas turbine generation take off and, more recently, global investment in utility renewable wind and solar generation overtake other technologies (IEA, 2019). In networks, high-voltage

DC is now competing with traditional AC for new long distance transmission and smart meters, and ICT more generally, are now changing utility operations. Competition, and hence new business models built around customers rather than consumers, is now being championed by progressive electricity industry jurisdictions. And yet much of the world's electricity industry faces the challenges of technological disruption and climate change in the 21st century still as effectively monopolies, with similar fossil fuel generation, one-way-flow transmission and distribution, "dumb" meters and consumer interfaces that characterized the early 20th century.

Behind the meter on the demand side of the industry, electricity consumers have seen a different story. There has been an almost continuous stream of new electricity consuming technologies flowing into homes, businesses, and industries since the early days of electrification. Some of the original demand technologies have remained largely unchanged over time—resistance bar radiators, hot water systems and irons, and, until recently, the incandescent light bulb. Most of them however are entirely new or changed beyond all recognition, notably ICT. And these are now being joined by behind the meter distributed energy technologies, including rooftop photovoltaic (PV) systems, smart appliances, and battery energy storage systems that are potentially viable alternatives to the existing utility supply arrangements. Even the meter itself has been transformed with smarts and communications.

Optimism seems warranted where, for example, in Australia residential PV ownership jumped from nothing to approaching 25% of households in a mere decade, as discussed in Swanston's chapter. So unsurprisingly technology innovation advocates are shifting their focus to opportunities in the dynamic "behind the meter" sector.

This chapter advises care in accepting these grounds for optimism, before throwing caution to the emerging distributed energy technology winds. The excitement of new energy inventions and ideas tends to make people envision a future of technological triumphalism. Because the engineering and economics of these options are looking increasingly attractive from an advocate's perspective in front of the meter, it seems natural to assume that they will also do so from the consumers' perspective behind the meter and therefore new technology will sweep away the old. But this top-down view risks becoming unstuck when faced with consumers' complex bottom-up views of value from behind the meter.

Consumers' view of value underpins their behavior, allows diverse solutions to coexist, and shapes the role of technology in use. This chapter looks backward from consumer's energy behavior behind the meter to see what this may mean for technologies like distributed generation that can appear compelling when viewed from in front of the meter.

Read the augury for energy and the signs foretell of a new system where centralized generation is dead and distributed energy is king. The problem is that, while it may well be true in the long term, in the short term this not only overestimates the near future but also ignores the past and underestimates the present.

Today it feels like change is ubiquitous, faster, and more dramatic than ever before. But this is a long-standing view that feels so true only because we have not lived through the changes of the past. The current shift to LED lighting from compact fluorescent lamps (CFLs) and incandescent feels rapid but is less momentous than the shift from the light of an oil lamp to the bulb incandescent (Nordhaus, 1998). Moving to transport dominated by electric vehicles (EVs) or automated connected electric shared (ACES) vehicles will feel momentous but is a less fundamental shift than moving from the horse to the automobile (Gordon, 2016). Indeed, ACES will see a return of the functionality of semiautonomous oxen and horses carts that was lost in the move to the automobile.

The future impact of distributed generation and storage will change the well-being of the consumer, now being termed "prosumer" given they produce as well as consume, but it is almost certainly going to have less impact on lifestyles than the arrival of the grid and the subsequent inventions at the birth of electricity (Smith and MacGill, Rosling and Nordhaus). As living standards have risen the marginal contribution of each new technology to lifting individual well-being becomes less as "we contrast the hyperactive pace of innovation at the current time with its apparently weak impact, judging by the slow pace of TFP (Total Factor Productivity) growth" (Gordon, 2016).

Increasingly, as wealthier individuals (Clingingsmith, 2015) in a wealthier world (Rosling), consumers faced with distributed energy choices can not only afford to make the financial decision to invest in better solutions but also to base their energy decisions on broader criteria than financial necessity. Or, as they can and do, choose to purchase instead "high-involvement" products like cars, appliances, clothing, and holidays.

This chapter questions the contention that the current combination of economics and engineering drivers, seen from in front of the meter, are necessarily sufficient to drive adoption behind the meter. Financial viability, expressed as "grid parity" or a short investment payback point, seems to be a necessary condition to trigger the rise of the prosumer but is likely to underestimate the complexity of present consumers' behavior that constrains the widespread adoption of distributed generation and distributed energy solutions.

It is not that consumers as potential prosumers are not rational, it is that they are rational based on their own terms, on what they choose to value. The "attention economy," the "experience economy," the "connected economy" the "weightless economy," and the prospect of a "postscarcity economy" are all concepts that attempt to highlight newer, alternative views of how consumer's wants now stretch beyond the simple functional and financial. And this realization needs to be factored into how a new distributed energy world is shaped and developed, perhaps, as discussed in this book, by automation, aggregation and intermediaries or perhaps by something unexpected.

Understanding how new energy technologies, new markets design, new business models, and new value propositions will shape the future is crucially dependent on what is valued in the mind of the customer behind the meter. This chapter explores these questions and is organized as follows:

- Section 9.2 looks at the components that underlie energy technology adaption and choices.
- Section 9.3 looks at what consumers' current technology choices look like and what this suggests about future choices.
- Section 9.4 looks into the consumer's mind and the values that drive choices followed by the chapter's conclusions.

9.2 Hardware, software, and orgware meet wetware: the mind behind the meter

What people mean by technology has proven rather difficult to define in widely agreed terms. This "science of practical arts" has complex dimensions, such as those captured in

IIASA's (2019) conceptual model of technology which highlights the immaterial as well as material aspects of technology; that *technology = hardware + software + orgware*.

The supply infrastructure required to run electricity networks is generally seen in physical terms as the technology hardware, the power stations, poles, and wires that deliver kilowatts to behind the meter where they can do work for consumers. Current hardware technology developments, discussed in accompanying chapters in this volume, present a strong case for distributed generation's growing engineering and economic advantages and potential from:

- falling costs for distributed generation particularly renewable
- falling costs for energy storage
- reduced physical size and scale of technologies
- reduced economies of scale with larger utility-sized technologies
- falling cost and rising capability in information/data collection and analysis
- falling cost and rising capability in data storage and management
- stagnant or escalating real cost in key established centralized technologies
- environmental policies for addressing climate change and other sustainable energy challenges.

Added to this is the recognition that software also needs to be in place, the knowledge, processes, and experience required to ensure hardware can be used to support successful change. Blockchain and P2P trading, discussed in Chapters 13 and 4, respectively, and home energy management systems (HEMS), discussed by Shaw-Williams in Chapter 7 are examples of innovation supported by enabling technology software.

Next there is the orgware, the institutional foundations, rules and regulations that support the operation of the electricity network. Less obvious to the end use customer, these components can have the most critical impact in shaping future possibilities. As discussed in the chapters that make up part three of this book, Regulators, policy makers and investors, a lot is happening in the traditionally slow moving orgware space. The New York State Reforming the Energy Vision (REV) and the UK regulator OFGEM's RIIO (*Revenue = Incentives + Innovation + Output*) framework are examples of ambitious attempts to shift the regulatory playing field for distributed energy options. REV in particularly has impressive aims to "reorient the electric industry and the ratemaking paradigm toward a consumer-centred approach that harnesses technology and markets" (NYPSC, 2014).

Yet progress in each of these technology aspects can have impact in different areas. Small-scale PV and li-ion battery systems are seen as changing technology behind the meter but, as the ultimate scalable energy technologies, utility-scale applications also benefit from the falling costs and increasing performance of these technologies just like distributed applications. Furthermore, both utility-scale technology "software" and electricity industry "orgware" are still largely tailored to utility-scale technologies and managed in a highly structured and professional way due to the essential role that the electricity industry plays in society. For technological change to support energy transitions a mix of factors need to be in place.

The IIASA argues that four "grand" patterns characterize technological change for energy transitions:

- "... no individual technology, as important as it may be, is able to transform whole energy systems that are large and complex [and] technologies operate more effectively as families or as 'gangs' and not as individuals. Because of clustering and spillovers, it is very difficult to dislodge a dominant technological regime."
- "any new technology introduced is initially crude, imperfect, and very expensive. Performance (the ability to perform a particular task of delivering a novel energy service) initially dominates economics as a driver of technological change and diffusion. In other words: attractiveness beats cheap, at least initially."
- "the history of past energy transitions highlights the critical importance of end-use (i.e. consumers, energy demand) that dominates technology applications. Historically energy supply has followed energy demand in technology applications, and energy end-use markets have been, and remain, the most important market outlets for new energy technologies. In other words: new energy technologies need to find consumers, and better many of them."
- "Finally, fourth, the process of technological change (from innovation to widespread diffusion) takes considerable time: as a rule many decades, and rates of change become slower, the larger the energy system (components) affected." (Grubler, 2012).

So while change is occurring across the electricity sector's hardware, software, and orgware, uncertainty remains as to "the how" and "the when" and so what the future will look like.

A map for forecasting the inevitable penetration of new behind the meter technology seems to exist in the historical "S-curve" adoption rates for new technology as reproduced in Fig. 9.1, compiled across a broad breath of industries, products, and services by the McKinsey Global Institute. On closer scrutiny, however the map is not entirely clear. The time for S-curve adoption rates to reach a 100% saturation stretches from less than 5 to more than 40 years with individual curves exhibiting a set of slopes, shifts, dips, overshoots, and wiggles that for forecasting purposed are more a muddle than a model.

What in retrospect looks like a reliable pattern of adoption useful for prediction is really more of narrative that a roadmap. Things that eventually succeed start growing slow, pick up speed and become widespread then eventually reach an asymptotic saturation acceptance level where growth subsides. But even within the fast and slow case range of this story plotted in the McKinsey's technology adoption trend curves, fast can take 4—15 years and slow 15—45. Within the data curves plotted some items already show 10% adoption in year 0 and others grow "of the chart" beyond a 100% "full adoption potential." And missing are those technologies that failed to make the graph, that started up the curve, fell off or leveled out at low adoption rates, and were superseded by events. Which S-curve path energy prosumers will chose to take from behind the meter is a story yet untold.

There is optimism that behind the meter supply technologies can progress faster along this curve. Research by Gross et al. (2018) found that some selected electricity generation technologies had far longer commercialization time periods (four decades) than energy end use and consumer products (under 30 years, better but still nearly a generation). These findings are supported by other studies, including Lund (2006), which confirm

Historic adoption curves for technological innovations

Adoption trend by technology[1]   Fast case ▬▬▬   Slow case ▬▬▬

Percentage of full adoption potential

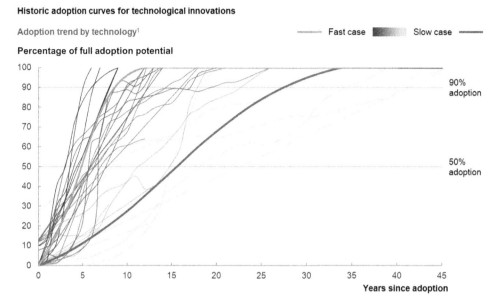

1 Technologies considered include airbags, antilock braking systems, cellphones, cloud CRM, cloud ERP, cloud SCM, color TVs, copper production through leaching, dishwashers, electronic stability control, embolic coils, Facebook, instrument landing systems, laparoscopic surgery, Lithium-ion cell batteries, microwaves, MRI, online air booking, P2P remote mobile payment, pacemakers, PCs, smartphones, stents, TVs, and VCRs.

FIGURE 9.1   S-curve adoption technology rates. Source: *McKinsey Global Institute, 2017.*

uncertainty in the timing, indeed the actual final success, of early stage energy technologies on both sides of the meter.

With the best efforts of modern science, economics, engineering, and management and marketing, the drivers of consumer behavior, particularly with adoption of new technology, remain complex and, despite the wisdom of YouTube gurus, largely unforecastable.

Even a high-level view of consumer behaviors suggests that a lot is going on behind the meter that is not driven by simplistic functional engineering and economics. While this has been well acknowledged in the literature (e.g., Minghui and MacGill, 2019), there has been less progress on successfully integrated that understanding into market uptake and energy technology innovation models.

So the future lies in the consumer's wetware; and what goes on in the mind of the consumer that may cause them to choose to be involved as a prosumer.

9.3 Diversity and difference behind the meter

In previous work the authors (Smith & MacGill, 2014) have demonstrated that, once considered as a whole, the majority of the investment in the electrify grid is done by consumers and the largest part of the industries value chain is behind the meter. The meter is the midpoint not the end point of the value chain for electricity customers with the top being the well-being, quality of life, or satisfaction that is felt by end consumers. For an

TABLE 9.1 Penetration rates of different household energy sources in NSW, Australia.

	East Sydney (%)	West Sydney (%)	Gosford (%)	Hunter (%)	Riverina (%)	North Coast (%)	All regions (%)
Households that use mains gas	54	43	28	36	57	2	44
Households that use cylinder gas	3	6	15	8	11	28	7
Households with controlled load electricity	30	48	63	58	47	78	43
Households with solar PV	12	23	22	27	31	34	19

Frontier Economics. (2016). Determinants of household energy consumption. In: A report prepared for the Independent Pricing & Regulatory Tribunal *(Frontier Economics, 2016).*

average residential customer this investment is probably 60% of their energy service cost but, like most else behind the meter, varies widely because customers' values and behaviors differ.

Sitting behind the meters of otherwise similar residential customers are different household energy sources that coexist in different mixes.

Table 9.1 shows how even within the one city, Sydney, east is east and west is west. Customers' use of mains gas, controlled load hot water, and solar PV shares differ significantly within the Sydney urban area. Move to NSW's regional areas and the differences expand, bottled gas share of usage rises, penetration of solar PV increases, and big penetrations of controlled load electricity are common, especially in the North Coast where mains gas is not an option. The strong penetration of PV is a pointer to a distributed energy future, as described in the chapter by Swanston, but the other energy source choices, while explainable, also point to the variety that can exist across consumers' basic choices of well-established energy technologies in mature markets.

The factors determining residential energy demand mix and growth can be very context specific, including complex drivers from climate, demographics, housing stock, building types, and household appliances and behavior. Moreover, in the last decade advances in energy-efficient technologies for lighting, ICT, space heating and cooling, in the kitchen and water heating have changed customers usage. Together with other energy efficiency−oriented policy efforts such as building standards, this has led to falling residential electricity demand in a multitude of places across the globe (Lim et al.). In Australia over a century of continuous residential electricity demand growth has now been replaced by almost a decade of decreasing demand, much of it through regulation and not initiated by the consumers who ultimately benefit.

Energy efficiency regulation has had substantial success. The Australian Equipment Energy Efficiency program estimates that since its start the phase out of incandescent light bulbs, combined with lighting in state-based energy efficiency schemes, saves around 2.4 TWh of electricity each year, equal to the annual electricity use of 400,000 Australian homes. An average household saves $70 per annum and the cumulative national savings

TABLE 9.2   Simple comparison of the lifetime cost of the common light bulb (undiscounted cash flows).

650–850 lumens light	Incandescent	CFL	LED
Watts used (W)	60	14	7
Average cost per bulb ($)	1	2	4
Average life (h)	1200	8000	25,000
Bulbs per 25,000 hours	21	3	1
Bulb purchase cost ($)	21	6	4
Electricity cost ($)	495	116	58
Cost over 20 years ($)	516	122	62

Source: *Adapted from published figures and prices in from retailers and manufacturers specifications.*

are estimated as $A5.5 billion. As the simple example in Table 9.2 shows, paybacks for more efficient lights should be compelling, yet in 2009 when the phase out started it came as a surprise. There was no momentum for a ban and no one predicted a major market-based shift in consumer behavior away from incandescent bulbs, despite the fundamental financial benefits of more efficient lighting (see Jaffe and Stavins (1994) on the energy paradox).

A simple functional view of a product, even one as clear and straightforward as a light bulb, is not enough as "technology does not just offer a set of limited functions it provides a vocabulary of elements that can be put together—programmed—in endless novel ways for endless novel purposes" (Arthur, 2009).

People's houses are full of energy used for novel purposes. Sparklers, fireworks, and candles, once the makers of fortunes in gunpowder or from the harvesting of spermaceti oil from whales, remain as household energy sources for novel ceremony and celebration purposes. Even as digital solutions are everywhere replacing the mechanical, fashion and prestige mean that the self-winding wristwatch persists not as a decision based on function, low price, or energy efficiency but because watches tell more than time (Coates, 2002), they make a statement about their owners.

Even odder and more novel energy types exist within small niches in houses—bioluminescence, phosphorus matches, springs, stored hydro and compressed air. Adding to these in-house sources of energy is the trend to outsource traditional household energy consumptions through embodied energy that enters the home. Pre-cooked home meals, takeaway, and home delivery (both traditional and linked to the connected share economy such as Uber Eats) are all options that shift the usage and economics of household energy consumption as embodied kWh that now bypass the meter. In one lifetime Australian's have lifted their spending on meals prepared outside the home from one in four food dollars to now spending one in three (ABS).

The price and embodied energy gap in prosumer home production can be enormous. Take, for example, the first part of Amory Lovins' "cold beer and hot shower" concept of energy services. The average retail price of beer in Australia is $12.81 a litre, the bulk of which is $2.62 for tax and excise and $7.21 of retailing margins. Freight and marketing, brewery capital and wages add up to another $2.92 to which need to be added materials and packaging at 40 cents a litre. And ingredients? A litre of beer, not yet cold enough for Amory, uses only 18 cents of ingredients a litre, about 1.5% of the retail cost. Meanwhile, all up the prosuming home brewer's beer cost less than a dollar a litre. A potentially compelling financial proposition, a tax avoidance scheme and an environmentally sound decision with reduced packaging, recycled containers, and reduced transportation "beer miles."

So how many canny home brew beer prosumers are there in Australia? Home brew accounts for only 2.2% of all beer drunk (ACIL Allen, 2019) suggesting that there is more to be considered and valued than price in a home brewers glass of prosumer porter. For the average Australian household these prosumer spent decisions are around the same for alcohol as domestic fuel and power (including gas as well as electricity) as historically electricity and alcohol costs are roughly equivalent shares of customer's budgets for those who drink (ABS).

Where consumer's strong choices align with policy aims, like for Ben Schlesinger in Chapter 2, who has invested heavily in his zero net energy (ZNE) house not because of any mandates but because of what he values, change is easier. But where policy change is not supplemented by strong support in consumer values, as with the Californian Commission requirement that all new residential buildings be ZNE starting in 2020, incentives via price signal or enforcement need to be effective.

Price signals are a key part of the customers' decisions but can be complicated to see and understand as discussed by Mountain in Chapter 15, Schitterkate in Chapter 17 and Robinson in Chapter 18.

The price signals that come with different residential energy option are diverse, not all of which are passed on to customers or recognized by customers, as shown in the Fig. 9.2 graph of network distribution and retail electricity cents/kWh charges. With deregulation and full retail competition it can be difficult to even decide what the "normal" price of electricity is. The darker bar in Fig. 9.2 shows how a "standing" offer retail price for a residential customer compares to the other price signals being provided by the supply side of the industry.

Around a standing offer retail price of about 30 cent a kWh a confusion of prices signals are available, including distribution charges aimed to drive demand management behaviors. At the top end, at 50 cents per kWh, a retail peak electricity tariff means that a twin bar 2000 W electric heaters, sold in large numbers for $A15 whenever the weather gets cold, has a $1.00 an hour peak usage charge. Nor are huge price differentials isolated to grid electricity prices. A quick comparison shows that, as large-scale household storage batteries to support distributed generation are slogging their way down the cost curve with Solar PV toward grid parity, their smaller brethren survive and prosper as immoderate c/kWh charges.

The common AAA battery working way in remote controls, toys, and touches comes at a comparative exorbitant cost when viewed in c/kWh terms—over 100 times a standard mains electricity tariff. Other less common battery types cost even more, as shown in Table 9.3, also see Schlesinger (2010). Odd looking when presented in these term, to the customer this is normal. People don't think in terms of cost per kWh, or in energy units at all, rather they look at the service delivered and the value they ascribe to it.

Residential electricity charges 2019 -$A in cents/kWh

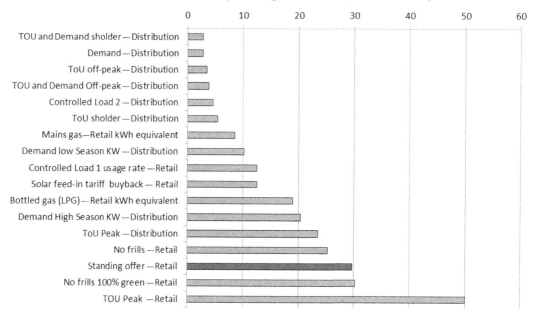

FIGURE 9.2   Residential kWh distribution and retail price signals for Sydney. Source: *(Canstar blue, 2019; Ausgrid, 2019)*.

TABLE 9.3   Simple comparison of the kWh cost of household batteries.

	Energy (single cell)	Cost per cell A$	Cost per kWh (A$)
	Wh	$A	$kWh
AAA cell	11.7	$0.50	$43
AA cell	4.275	$0.50	$117
D cell	25.5	$3.00	$118
C cell	11.7	$3.00	$256
9 Volt	5.13	$6.00	$1,170

Adapted from published figures and prices in from retailers and manufacturers specifications.

   While the batteries are a comparatively small ticket items in household budgets, the apparently "irrational" anomalies in customers' treatment of energy cost are not limited to the small stuff. The most fuel-efficient and cost-effective cars are not the most popular— sports, SUV, and luxury cars abound. Even where prudent and rational choices are taken, in buying a smaller car or perhaps a hybrid, the complex set of status, statement, "do good" and signaling "doing good" are all part of the decisions. Tesla anyone? And all these decisions reflecting the values and choices of customers come with costs and price signals that would seem to struggle against an overly simplified rational external view of customers' preferences.

Recognizing that what a customer values may not be based only on functionality or straight price comparisons is not the same a criticizing the customer. Using heuristics and rules of thumb to assist in making decisions is a valid approach as are customer's choices based on tastes. Something as functional as thirst lends itself to customers' value judgments between a sugared, carbonated, caffeinated soft drink, a prosumer porter, and a glass of wine or water from at tap or from a bottle. Yet the marketing of cola drinks has been shown to change the way the brain responds (Kühn & Gallinat, 2013) and wine appreciation can be driven more by what goes on in the mind than what is done to the grapes (Lecocq & Visser, 2006)—which leads us to look inside the customer's mind.

9.4 A bumpy look into the consumer's mind

So what is going on inside consumer's heads? Phrenology once saw over 40 forces at play shaping behavior and choices, mixing the lower sentiments common to man and animal, such as amativeness, acquisitiveness, and philoprogenitiveness, with superior sentiments like benevolence, conscientiousness, hope, and wonder. In economic terms these are proxies for what drives people's preferences, the things that determine the utility that someone gets from a good or service. Put another way the ultimately value of energy, even in Avory Lovins' terms after it has been converted into a "hot shower and cold beer," only exists in the mind of the consumer (Fig. 9.3).

A hundred years on from the heydays of phrenology, other approaches have superseded reading head shapes and bumps to determine what makes us tick. Modern day mind readers management consultants Bain & Company use a copyrighted Value Pyramid, shown in Fig. 9.4, where Maslow meets Michael Porter, to delve where the phrenologists failed. In Bain & Company's consulting overlay 30 values take the place of sentiments and the division between lower animal and higher superior has been expanded to four areas.

In Bain & Company's categorization a narrow "before the meter" view of a prosumer's value from new distributed energy solutions will tend to concentrate on the lower level functional values and benefits such as reduces cost, makes money, informs, and perhaps reduces risk (of outages). However, prosumers, who needs to take time and effort to manage their energy production and use, may simultaneously experience mixed or negative functional values such as avoiding hassles, simplifies, and risk shifting from the grid to the customer rather than reducing. Yet emotional and life-changing values, such as those supporting environmentally responsible choices (badge value, provides hope, affinity/belonging, and heirloom), can drive potential prosumer energy decision that may not appear sound on purely "functionally" grounds.

The Australia Energy Consumer sentiment survey provides some glimpse on what of customers' report they think about mains electricity and new technology. With overall satisfaction with electricity substantially lower than for comparable utilities and services, Fig. 9.5 shows electricity consumers appear to be a group primed for change. Yet these

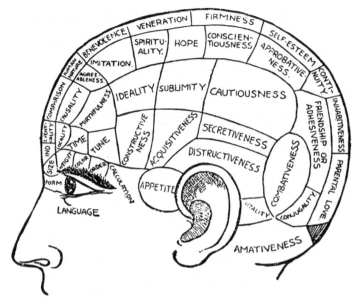

FIGURE 9.3   Phrenology. Source: *Google open licence.*

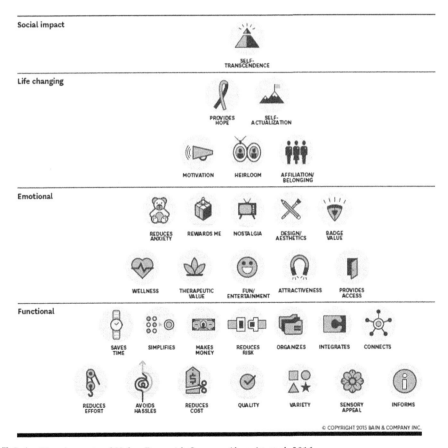

FIGURE 9.4   The elements of Value Pyramid. Source: *Almquist et al. 2016.*

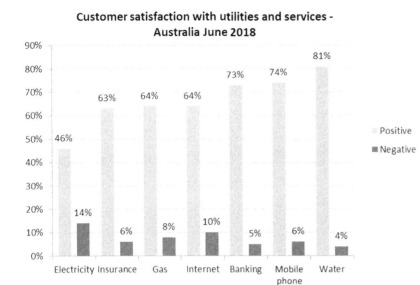

Customer satisfaction with utilities and services - Australia June 2018

FIGURE 9.5 Australia Energy Consumer sentiment. Source: *Australia Energy Consumer sentiment survey June 2018.*

same customers also have low confidence in technology with less than half confident that the market will deliver technological advances to manage their future energy costs. And this confidence is borne out in the natural experiment that has occurred with Australian residential consumers' experience with smart meters in the Eastern states.

In NSW, where installation for residential consumers is optional, smart meters penetration and usage rates have remained relatively low. In the bordering state of Victoria where smart meters are mandatory, reported penetration is high (although reported as less than actual 100% ownership), but still relatively few people see their smart meters as a tool for managing costs, as shown in Fig. 9.6. This implies that lifting from a reported 26% smart meter ownership in NSW to a reported 78% in Victoria (100% with mandatory installation) still sees over two-thirds of customers passive and not responding to the price signals and information provision available from smart meters, further discussed in Chapter 12. If this basic lift in technology, the cost of which is bundled and hidden in electricity tariffs, is not getting used as expected by the majority of Victorian consumers, then it is likely that the higher cost investment in a prosumer lifestyle may also struggle to find acceptance. The natural experiment suggests regulation is not enough; technology is not enough; pricing signals are not enough; and that something else is needed to bring customers along on the journey (Lovell, 2018). Yet technology optimism remains rife.

The expected revolutionary future possibilities for distributed generation and the prosumer seem to borrow technology optimism from the past experience in computing, where small, personal and distributed solutions appear to have triumphed over the large and centralized.

The shift from room-sized IBM mainframes to Digital Equipment Corporation (DEC's) "minicomputers," Apple's personal computers, to smart phones, and now ubiquitous computer connection pointing to the "internet of everything" seems to be following a technologically predetermined downsizing path for end users (even as the cloud grows

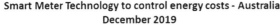

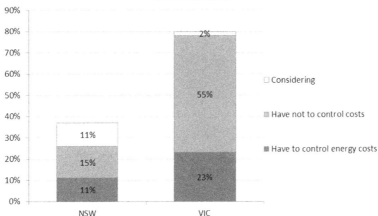

FIGURE 9.6 Australia Energy Consumer reported views on smart meters. Source: *Australia Energy Consumer sentiment survey December 2018.*

overhead). A downsizing path analogous to the current moves to renewable energy and distributed generation that is taking energy behind the meter and away from the centralized grid. Yet even Moore's law's breathtaking, continuous, and seeming endless improvement in the engineering and economics of semiconductors does not make a product immune to the lens of customer value.

Steve Job's lesson of "start with the customer experience and work backward to the technology" is about looking through the customer value lens. Decades before, in 1977 speaking to the World Future Society, Ken Olsen, founder of DEC, also challenged the technology lead view with "There is no reason anyone would want a computer in their home." Listed now as one of history's worst predications (Chaline, 2011), in context he was actual saying a wiz-bang technology that exists and may work will only be adopted into people's homes if it does things that customers value (see Grubler, 2012)—start with the customers' experience. Most recently, technology mogul Bill Gates has expressed strong views about energy futures and the future of batteries driven again by using the customer value lens rather than by following the technology drivers of change (Smith, 2015).

There is growing evidence, building on the apparent failures of some early and very promising BTM technologies to takeoff as might have been expected, about the relevant contribution of a technology-centered approach toward development rather than more user-centered framing (Wilson, Hargreaves, & Hauxwell-Baldwin, 2015). There is an appreciation of the key role of early adopters and the early majority (perhaps 50% of the consumer market), not just the leading innovators (technology enthusiasts) group as key drivers of success in technology innovation. Late majority (conservatives) and laggards (skeptics) will, of course, have to be dragged across the line by their faster moving peers (Coskun, Kaner, & Bostan, 2018). However, like the S-curve this not a predetermined path. Some work exploring the motivations of early movers in particular situations has highlighted the complexity of their expectations—as one example, dual-income families and single individuals had more interest in appliances that can be remotely controlled than housewives did, given more flexible routines. Autonomous appliances were seen as useful in some regards but also posing risks and even threatening family roles and identity (Coskun et al., 2018). Much more to be done before we can safely call a BTM technology revolution that sweeps the old industry away.

Where should we look to find the sizzle needed to sell with a BTM technology steak? The answer may be found in packaging the technology to fit the values and the desires customers already have. The best recent example is Tesla. Technologically advanced yes, geek chic certainly, but it is the value from the emotional engagement pyramid level that makes the product economically viable. Previous attempts at EVs have been earnest, dour, and disappointing. The Tesla approach was to deliberately start with performance and brand building and move backward from customer desire to mass production viability. Reaching beyond the traditional EV markets of government subsidized sales, the techno geek and the accountant, Tesla models operating settings include emotionally engaging "insane" and "ludicrous" modes. Now Tesla faces more challenges in moving to the next step, to win over customers in the mass market and bring with it a transformation of both our transport and electricity sector to eventual create the real success, EV as normal.

9.5 Conclusion—waking sleeping beauty

Approaches to designing of a new energy future are largely driven from in front of the meter, by economists, engineer, technologists, and policy makers. The rapidly improving capabilities and costs of energy generation and storage technologies, aided and abetted by ICT, have created the possibility for a distributed energy future run by the prosumer. This has caused a rethink of the hardware and software of the new system supported by orgware—how institutional relationships work. What is not sufficiently considered is the wetware—what goes on in the mind of the consumer that may cause them to choose to be involved as a prosumer.

From an austerely financial and functional standpoint, looking from in front of the meter, odd behaviors seem to exist behind the meter. The underpinning reasonable assumption behind the adoption rated of new technologies is that consumers are rational and will choose the best option, based on what is in their own best interests. Yet this requires a detailed understanding of customers own best interests and ability to judge.

This is not to say that the energy consumer, the potential prosumer, is immune to pull of the engineeringly sound and economically rational. Rather these are necessary but not sufficient conditions to enable the switch from a centralized to a distributed grid world.

Products do not jump off the shelves based on inherent virtue —they need to be sold.

Other chapters in this book, for example, by Mountain, argue that consumers have a hard time deciding or making decent choices as it is. And the world is going to get more complicated when consumers are confronted with new and more complex investment decisions in DG, distributed storage, peer-to-peer trading or allowing an aggregator to monitor and manage their devices—the types of decisions Ben Schlesinger had to make while building his ZNE house in Maryland, as described in Chapter 2. Fortunately, this may not matter. Multiple values drive customers' choice of everything from beer to cars. The take up of Solar PV has benefited from an inherent sexiness that solar hot water and controlled load never achieved. Don't ignore human nature, recognize, and work with the way people are.

This book explores how digitalization, automation, aggregation, and optimization of BTM assets are doable and will deliver major benefits. This chapter is cautioning that doable is only part of the challenge. This is not to say that consumers are too complex or fickle or irrational or value the wrong things or whatever to make decent decisions. Rather the major benefits of BTM change need to be clear to customers and customers' view of major benefits may not be the same as the industry's.

As Schlesinger puts it in Chapter 2, "indeed to create change, as Tesla taught us, you've got to show beauty." Not marketing spin, spending to create the perception of value, rather it is being awake to the beauty that is there in "behind the meter" technology and having the faith that customers, when shown, will awake to it and value it as well.

References

ACIL Allen Consulting. (2019). *Economic contribution of the Australian Brewing Industry 2017—18 from producer to Consumer.*

Almquist, E., Senior, J., & Bloch, N. (2016). The Elements of Value Understanding the 30 elements of value for consumers can help companies gain an edge. *Harvard Business Review.* August.

Arthur, W. (2009). *The nature of technology, what it is and how it evolves.* Free Press.

Ausgrid Network Price List 2019—2020, 2019. <https://www.ausgrid.com.au/Industry/Regulation/Network-prices> Accessed 08/2019.

Australian Bureau of Statistics. (2017). 6530.0 — Household expenditure survey. In: *Summary of Results, 2015—16.* Australia. <https://www.abs.gov.au/Ausstats/abs@.nsf/0/16D1D54EA86276D0CA2581990017282E? OpenDocument>.

Canstar blue. (2019). <https://www.ausgrid.com.au/Industry/Regulation/Network-prices>. Accessed 07/2019.

Chaline, E. (2011). *History's worst predictions and the people who made them.* Chartwell Books.

Clingingsmith D. (2015). *Negative emotions, income, and welfare.* Department of Economics Case Western Reserve University.

Coates, D. (2002). Watches tell more than time: Product design, information, and the quest for elegance. McGraw-Hill.

Coskun, A., Kaner, G., & Bostan, İ. (2018). Is smart home a necessity or a fantasy for the mainstream user? A study on users' expectations of smart household appliances. *International Journal of Design, 12*(1), 7—20. (2018).

Downes, S. (2019). Electricity price rises & changes Canstar blue. <https://www.canstarblue.com.au/electricity/electricity-price-changes/> Accessed 07/2019.

Frontier Economics. (2016). Determinants of household energy consumption. In: *A report prepared for the Independent Pricing & Regulatory Tribunal.*

Gordon, R. J. (2016). *The rise and fall of American growth the U.S. standard of living since the civil.* Princeton University Press.

Gross., R., et al. (2018). How long does innovation and commercialisation in the energy sectors take? Historical case studies of the timescale from invention to widespread commercialisation in energy supply and end use technology. *Energy policy, 123,* 682—699.

Grubler, A. (2012). Grand designs: Historical patterns and future scenarios of energy technological change. In A. Grubler, F. Aguayo, K. S. Gallagher, M. Hekkert, K. Jiang, L. Mytelka, L. Neij, G. Nemet, & C. Wilson (Eds.), *Historical case studies of energy technology innovation in: Chapter 24, the global energy assessment.* Cambridge, UK: Cambridge University Press.

International Energy Agency (IEA). (2019). *Tracking clean energy progress.* <www.iea.org/tcep> Accessed 09/2019.

International Institute for Advanced Systems Analysis (IIASA). (2019). *What is technology?* <http://www.iiasa.ac.at/web/home/research/researchPrograms/TransitionstoNewTechnologies/What-is-Technology.en.html> Accessed 09/2019.

Jaffe, A., & Stavins, R. (1994). The energy paradox and the diffusion of conservation technology. *16 Resource & Energy Economics., 91*, 92–94.

Kühn, S., & Gallinat, J. (2013). Does taste matter? How anticipation of cola brands influences gustatory processing in the brain. *PLoS One, 8*(4), e61569. Available from https://doi.org/10.1371/journal.pone.0061569.

Lecocq, S., & Visser, M. (2006). What determines wine prices: Objective vs. sensory characteristics. *Journal of Wine Economics, 1*(1), 42–56. Available from https://doi.org/10.1017/S1931436100000080.

Lovell, H. (2018). The promise of smart grids. *Local Environment.* Available from https://doi.org/10.1080/13549839.2017.1422117.

Lund, P. (2006). Market penetration rates of new energy technologies. *Energy Policy, 34*(17), 3317–3326.

McKinsey Global Institute, 2017, McKinsey Global insights "The Future of what works: automatic, employment and productivity, full report" January 2017 "Historical adoption curves for technological innovations". https://www.mckinsey.com/ ∼ /media/mckinsey/featured%20insights/Digital%20Disruption/Harnessing%20automation%20for%20a%20future%20that%20works/MGI-A-future-that-works-Full-report.ashx Accessed 11/2019.

Minghui, E., & MacGill., I. (2019). Consumer-centric service innovations in an era of self-selecting customers. *Consumer, Prosumer, Prosumager: How Service Innovations will Disrupt the Utility Business Model, 127.*

New York Public Service Commission. (2014). *Reforming the energy vision staff, report and proposal.*

Nordhaus W. (1998). Do real-output and Real-wage measures capture reality? The history of lighting suggests not. *Crowles Foundation paper No. 975.* Yale University.

Rosling, H., et al. (2018). *Factfulness: Ten reasons we're wrong about the world—and why things are better than you think.* Flatiron Books.

Schlesinger, H. (2010). *The battery, how portable power sparked a technological revolution.* Smithsonian Books.

Smith, D. (2015). *How to think like Bill Gates.* Michael O'Mara Books Ltd.

Smith, R., & MacGill, I. (2014). Revolution, evolution or back to the future? Lessons from the electricity supply industry's formative days, Chapter 24. In F. P. Sioshansi (Ed.), *Distribute generation and its implication for the Utility Industry.* Elsevier, Academic Press.

Wilson, C., Hargreaves, T., & Hauxwell-Baldwin, R. (2015). Smart homes and their users: A systematic analysis and key challenges. *Personal and Ubiquitous Computing, 19*(2), 463–476.

10

Aggregation of front- and behind-the-meter: the evolving VPP business model

Lotte Lehmbruck[1], Julian Kretz[1], Jan Aengenvoort[1] and Fereidoon Sioshansi[2]

[1]Next Kraftwerke, Köln, Germany [2]Menlo Energy Economics, Walnut Creek, CA, United States

10.1 Introduction

The increased penetration of renewables in the energy mix means that balancing supply and demand in real time is becoming more of a challenge for grid operators as they more frequently face periods when there is too much generation and too little load or vice versa. With the rapid growth of distributed generation, most commonly from rooftop solar PVs and on- and offshore wind turbines, the problem of balancing supply and demand is becoming even more problematic. At times of excess renewable generation, prices in the wholesale market plunge or occasionally go negative. In an increasing number of places, some of the excess solar and/or wind generation must be curtailed—simply because there is no easy way to use it, not enough transmission capacity is available to transport and/or not enough capacity is available to store it for use at later time. These issues are extensively covered in the literature and need not be further amplified here.

Moreover, the traditional means of balancing supply and demand—where dispatchable generation was adjusted up or down to follow the load are not practical when the bulk of generation is no longer dispatchable, nor even fully predictable. This growing challenge, in a nutshell, is what has resulted in the rising interest to better manage inherent flexibilities in demand to better follow variable renewable generation—whether from utility-scale sources or small-scale distributed generation or storage.

Virtual power plants (VPPs) are among the promising ways that variable generation and flexible demand may be optimally balanced in the future, the topic of this chapter, which is organized as follows:

- Section 10.2 outlines the historical VPP business model referring to Next Kraftwerke, among the oldest and most successful of European VPPs;
- Section 10.3 explains how the original business model has changed and is evolving in response to technological innovations, changes in regulations and the changing demands of the grid operators;
- Section 10.4 speculates how the VPP business model is likely to mature as customers become more proactive and more inclined to participate in VPPs because the rising variable energy generation increases the revenue stream embedded in the behind-the-meter assets followed by the chapter's conclusions

10.2 Original VPP business model

There are probably as many definitions of VPPs as there are VPPs. This chapter, however, uses Next Kraftwerke or NK among the earliest and one of the biggest and most successful of the European VPPs, as a case study. As it happens, NK is expanding its business model both geographically and by offering new innovative services as the regulatory environment evolves and as new opportunities are identified and captured.

Box 10.1 provides an overview of NK, as it will be called in the balance of the chapter, how it was founded and what it originally set out to do as captured in an interview with the firm's CEO, Jochen Schwill, in April 2018[1].

The company, which was founded in 2009, reached commercial breakeven point in 2013, expanded into Belgium and Austrian markets in 2014 followed by France, the Netherlands, Poland, Switzerland and Italy in 2015-17 period and by beginning of 2019 grew in size to manage nearly 6.8 GW of capacity as illustrated in Fig. 10.1.

Other NK key statistics are shown in Table 10.1, suggesting continuous growth on multiple dimensions.

Similar to all VPPs, NK provides a range of products and services in multiple markets to multitudes of stakeholders as outlined in Fig. 10.2. The company has fine tuned its offering over the years in response to changing demands and changing regulatory policies. Moreover, it offers slightly different offering in different markets based on what is needed, what is legally permitted, who else is offering similar services, cost and profit margins. Its portfolio of services continues to grow as it enters new markets.

NK uses machine-to-machine (M2M) communication to transfer signals, data and operational commands between the control system, individual assets, the TSOs and the power exchange. An algorithm calculates each individual asset's schedule of operation with the objective to run the assets optimally. That means to optimize revenues for the clients by taking into account the individual restrictions of each asset. It does all this without owning

---

[1] The full text of the interview may be found at The Beam Magazine https://medium.com/thebeammagazine/towards-a-more-democratised-energy-world-3ffc26281285

BOX 10.1

Genesis of Next Kraftwerke

The CEO of NK, Jochen Schwill, describes the company's history in an interview in April 2018, excerpts from which are reproduced blow.

Q: Where does the idea of Next Kraftwerke come from?

When Hendrik Sämisch and I were working on our PhD theses, we were wondering how the increasing share of intermittent renewable energy in the system could be balanced in the future. This is when we started thinking about flexibility and how we would be able to quickly balance the volatile influx of renewable energy.

Q: Where does your commitment to sustainable energy come from?

In the beginning, we were not thinking explicitly about renewable energies as providers of flexibility. We even started the virtual power plant (VPP) by hooking up emergency generators. However, the deeper we got into the matter, the more it became clear to us that renewables are the future—and not only from a business point of view. As citizens, we owe it to society to think about sustainable solutions. So, we started to think about connecting renewable energy units to our virtual power plant and it turned out that some of them are great providers for flexibility. This shows that renewables are competitive and can level out the imbalances they cause.

Q: What is your definition of a democratized energy world? And how is Next Kraftwerke contributing?

In the end, the key issue is participation. So, from our point of view, a democratized energy world is an energy world in which more and more players can participate. This development has already started. These days, it is not a privilege of huge energy companies to build power plants and produce power, because the costs to do that have drastically been reduced. It is not necessary anymore to spend billions of Euros on new power plants—as they are doing for example at Hinkley Point. Our mission is to provide the opportunity for smaller producers to take part in a market which has been inaccessible for them before, and we foster the expansion of renewable energy power plants by providing flexibility.

Q: How would you explain the concept of your virtual power plant to someone who never heard of it?

We digitally connect small- and medium-sized power producing as well as power consuming units and, in doing so, aggregate their performance. We then sell the power at the electricity markets and feed it into the energy system to stabilize the grid. To be clear, we do not own one single unit, but with our technology and the consent of the owners, we can ramp the units up and down as if we were a real power plant. To put it into perspective, we have aggregated an overall capacity of 3400 MW[2]. This is the capacity of two large coal-fired power stations. However, we are almost 100% renewable.

---

[2] The number has grown to 6.800 MW by mid 2019

BOX 10.1   (*cont'd*)

Now, let's dig in a bit deeper into the flexibility issue. Roughly 1000 MW^3 of our capacity are flexible and we provide this flexibility to the energy system—just like a huge battery would do. That means, with our technology we can very quickly feed in power, let's say if a shortage of wind and solar power occurs, but also, if there is too much power, for example when a storm brings in heavy winds, and the system needs to be relieved. We can do that, because we connect units that have flexibility. For example, every Combined Heat and Power unit (CHP) has flexibility, even the backup capacity unit in the local supermarket; most run-of-river hydropower stations have flexibility. Also, many power consumers can provide flexibility to the system if they are flexible when to consume power. In all of those cases flexibility is a byproduct. The units were not built to provide flexibility to the market. They primarily serve others purposes, producing power or heat or whatever. And this is where Next Kraftwerke steps in. We tap flexibility potentials for and with our clients, because they are usually too small to provide flexibility to larger systems like the grid on their own. Shifting production or consumption into times when flexibility is needed makes economic sense and contributes to more efficiency in the system.

Q: How optimistic are you about meeting the demand for electricity using renewable energy by 2050 in Europe?

We are optimistic it is going to work out. Photovoltaics and wind are already the cheapest producers of energy. Why should anyone in 2050 think about other options? We also try to do our share. Since batteries are, still, very costly and thus, storing power is not yet an affordable option in many cases, we keep focusing on providing flexibility and shifting electricity to keep the grid stable. This way we want to support the feed-in of renewables, fuel their expansion and thus, contribute to a greener future in energy.

Q: What would you say is unique about your business?

It is not cheap to build new power plants. And it costs millions of Euros to build battery storage. STEAG, a German utility, invests 100 million Euros into six battery systems amounting to 90 MW. In contrast, we provide a very cost-efficient way to provide flexible power. We were able to aggregate hundreds of megawatts of flexibility for less than 10 million euros.

Q: What were the biggest initial hurdles to building Next Kraftwerke and how did you overcome them?

Legislation was a huge hurdle in the beginning. When we started, there was no legislation regulating what virtual power plants were allowed to do and what not. Luckily, in Germany, legislation changed in our favor with Germany's 2012 Renewable Energy Source Act (EEG), since then renewables were allowed to participate in the market and offer their flexibility for the first time. This is also why legislation is always a key factor for us when thinking about expanding to other countries.

---

^{3} 1,500 MW by mid 2019

BOX 10.1 *(cont'd)*

Q: What do you attribute your success to?

To our team! When the EEG changed in 2012, we became an energy trader overnight. We figured out a way to do it and now we are experts in short term trading. We were able to do it, because we are not afraid of change. We actually like it. We constantly work on further establishing the flow of electricity, data, and ideas to find the best solutions for our clients, a sustainable business and 100% green energy in the future.

Q: How do you believe evolving technology will impact the way we do business in energy over the next 10 years?

10 years ago there wasn't even an open market for control reserve. So, I am very cautious to predict what will happen in the next 10 years. However, I am sure whatever will happen, we will adapt to it. ∎

Milestones

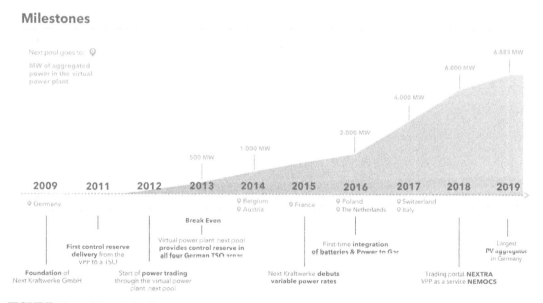

FIGURE 10.1   Historical milestones in NK's first decade. Source: *NK*.

any of the assets that it monitors and manages. To do this, however, it needs the consent of the owners to operate the assets according to the pre-determined schedules and other instructions. For maximum security, the whole server infrastructure operates on redundant systems.

As with all VPPs and aggregators, the business is focused on assembling a large portfolio of assets — in-front of the meter generation resources as well as behind-the-meter loads — which can be remotely monitored and managed (Fig. 10.3). In the case of NK, the

TABLE 10.1 Key data for NK.

Key Data

Sales	Employees	Subsidiaries
627,7 Mio € (2018)	155	10
Aggregated Power	Aggregated asstes	Power delivery
7.142 MW	8.109	140 GWh
R1	R2	R3
57 MW	943 MW	1.652 MW

NK data as of mid 2019.

What does a VPP offer?

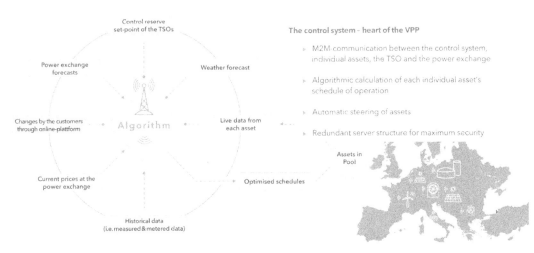

Control reserve set-point of the TSOs

Power exchange forecasts

Weather forecast

Changes by the customers through online-plattform

Algorithm

Live data from each asset

Current prices at the power exchange

Optimised schedules

Historical data (i.e. measured & metered data)

The control system - heart of the VPP

▸ M2M-communication between the control system, individual assets, the TSO and the power exchange

▸ Algorithmic calculation of each individual asset's schedule of operation

▸ Automatic steering of assets

▸ Redundant server structure for maximum security

Assets in Pool

FIGURE 10.2 What products and services does NK offer? Source: *NK*.

portfolio of assets under management includes a variety of load and generation resources with highly uncorrelated patterns of consumption and generation. This diversity of flexible loads and generation allows NK to create value and monetize it.

Who is taking part

Asset types in a virtual power plant

▸ Biogas
▸ Solar
▸ Wind
▸ Hydro power
▸ CHP
▸ Renewable power plants
▸ Power-to-X
▸ Power consumers
▸ Utilities/aggregators
▸ Batteries
▸ Emergency power generators

Interfaces/technologies

▸ Next Box
▸ Protocol interfaces
▸ APIs

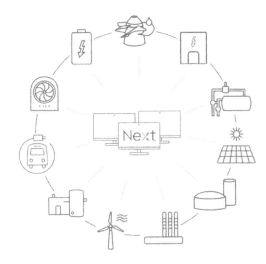

FIGURE 10.3   Who participates in VPP schemes? Source: NK.

Since NK has amassed a multitude of assets the resulting portfolio includes a diverse set of flexible loads, adjustable generation and storage, which means that if one unit unexpectedly shuts down or does not respond to commands, others can substitute to produce the desired outcome. This makes the scheme highly reliable, which is especially important when providing ancillary services.

Intelligent software is at the core of NK's business as with all VPPs. As schematically shown in Fig. 10.4, NK's software allows services to be delivered to clients or particular tasks to be performed as required.

To transmit the data and commands NK relies on the Next Box, a system specifically designed to remotely control the assets by transmitting information directionally via GPRS[4]. Using the Next Box, NK is able to automatically regulate the power-producing and power-consuming assets through its central control system.

To prevent inadvertent tampering data is encrypted in the Next Box. At each access point, the SIM cards must be authenticated so that they can join the closed user group. The SIM cards do not have any access to the Internet outside of the closed user group, which makes data transmission even more secure. Once it is in NKs control system, the data is decrypted.

Moreover, the Next Box is individually configured for the type of asset in the VPP portfolio, for example, district heating units, gas or water storage or pumping and so on. For every asset in the portfolio, a specific timetable or operational restrictions are programmed, so that each asset can always operate under optimal conditions both technically and economically.

[4] GRPS is general packet radio service

The platform for the digital energy world

Operating a power plant without owning any assets

▸ Aggregation of decentralized renewable energy assets through a central virtual platform

▸ More than 8100 assets with more than 7100 MW capacity

▸ Intelligent steering of all networked assets with automatic M2M communication

▸ Grid stability: ensuring that production and consumption are harmonized

▸ Offering access to various markets (i. e., spot exchange and ancillary services)

FIGURE 10.4   Intelligent software: the VPP engine. Source: *NK*.

To successfully manage power supply and demand in real-time, NK has developed a dedicated algorithm, which collects and computes data from various sources such as operational data from NK's VPP, current weather and grid data as well as live market data. The accumulated data allows NK to trade power with the highest profitability on day-ahead and intra-day while participating in real-time reserve markets.

Using intelligent algorithms, the control system can creates individual schedules for flexible assets allowing production to meet demand with higher revenues for the plant operators. Based on price signals, flexible power generators such as CHPs can be ramped up and down precisely to the quarter of an hour. Conversely, consumers with flexible demand such as industrial pumps can be operated on optimized price schedules by shifting their heavy consumption to periods when electricity is cheap and demand is low.

This is a valuable service on networks with large penetration of variable renewable generation, such as in Germany or Denmark, allowing the VPP to help stabilize the power grid even before the use of balancing services become necessary.

If an imbalance on the grid is imminent, the signals from the system operators are processed in the central control system and directly converted into control instructions for the pre-qualified units in the portfolio. Consequently, the VPP can effectively help to keep the grid in balance by delivering frequency control reserves, for example. In the event of an unexpectedly high feed-in, it is also possible to shut down assets within seconds and thus avert critical grid situations. These are among the valuable services that a typical VPP can offer and for which it collects revenues.

Grid stabilizing flexibility
How even small assets can provide grid stabilizing flexibility

Overview

▸ As a cluster, assets execute the TSO signal within seconds
▸ All control reserve products for all TSO regions in Germany with an available flexibility of: R1: **57 MW**, R2: **943 MW**, and R3: **1652 MW**

Benefits

▸ Our Next Pool stabilizes grid frequency and prevents blackouts
▸ The revenue is split between the asset owner and Next Kraftwerke

Through the Virtual Power Plant, Onno Wilberts and Guido Koch, owner of a biogas plant in Reventlind, Lower Saxony (Germany), have been providing grid stabilizing flexibility since 2012.

0 MW

FIGURE 10.5   Grid stability offerings: Sough after by grid operators. Source: *NK*.

To reiterate, the hallmark of all VPPs, NK no exception, is to

- Stabilize demand and/or relieve stress placed on the grid;
- Deliver bill savings and/or offer additional revenues to consumers with flexible demand; and/or
- Increase the value of generation for clients with flexible generation assets.

An example of how NK delivers useful services is illustrated for a client with a flexible biogas plant who is able to follow signals provided by NK, which allows better frequency control on the network.

In 2011 Onno Wilberts and Guido Koch were pioneers in the German biogas industry[5]. Their objective was to build a biogas power plant that can help stabilize grid frequency and follow a peak-load operation schedule that is tied to the wholesale price of power on the network. Today, the power plant is controlled via the Next Box, and its power production is adjusted up and down as often as 20 times a day. The power plant can be controlled in 15-minute increments based on current prices on the spot market. Also the transmission system operator benefits from valuable control reserve services offered by the flexibility of the biogas plant. NK bids the unit's output in the auctions for ancillary services and then automatically ramp the unit up or down accordingly creating value for the client, for the grid operator and for NK.

---

[5] further details may be found at https://www.next-kraftwerke.com/company/case-studies

Flexible power rates

How power consumers can benefit from fluctuations on the power exchange

Overview

▸ Consume power when the demand at the power exchange is low and power costs less
▸ Price forecasts in different time intervals available:
  Variable power rate "Best of 96" (with a granularity of up to 15 min)
  or time zone based "Take your Time"

Benefits

▸ Harmonizing supply and demand of power for the entire system
▸ Saving up to 30 % on energy costs

FIGURE 10.6   Pumping loads offer exceptional flexibility. Source: *NK.*

This is schematically shown in the Fig. 10.5 where the gray line shows the call from the transmission system operator (TSO), the green line is the feed-in profile of the biogas unit, which follows the demands of the TSO.

The biogas plant offers an average electric capacity of 1.2 MW, while the installed capacity is nearly 4 MW. Additionally, the power plant's storage encompasses 14,000 m^3.[6] With the power plant's immense flexibility, it can help compensate for short-term fluctuations in the output of wind and solar plants on the network.

By combining the fluctuations on the price of power, and the inherent flexibility of the power plant itself, Wilberts and Koch can create additional value and gain additional revenues. It is win-win-win. They decide how much power to produce based on the electricity prices while taking advantage of the flexibility of the biogas plant, for example, when repair or maintenance work needs to be done on the network.

Among its many products, NK offers control reserve products for all TSO regions in Germany and elsewhere in Europe.[7]

Another example of how NK is able to create and monetize value is illustrated in Fig. 10.6, where a client with major pumping loads can take advantage of typical daily

---

[6] In most cases — as in this one — the biogas is stored under the roof of the fermenters so no external gas storage is needed for providing flexibility to spot and control reserve markets. If longer-term flexibility is needed, an external gas storage would be helpful, however, few biogas plants have them.

[7] Control reserve products differ greatly from country to country. R1, R2 and R3 are the European classifications for the different control reserve products, R1 being instantaneous frequency control; R2 has to pitch in within 30 seconds and R3 within 5 minutes. NK offers an available flexibility of 57 MW for R1; 943 MW for R2 and 1,652 MW for R3.

and hourly fluctuations in wholesale prices. As shown, this client was able to shift most of its heavy pumping loads to times when wholesale prices are low—saving significant sums in electricity bills without any loss in productivity or disruptions to service[8].

In this case, the control of the client's pumping stations—roughly 0.5 MW—has been connected to the NK's network since 2015. The system continuously receives new electricity prices for feeding into the network and automatically selects the cheapest quarter of an hour to pump the rainwater back into the North Sea. This has enabled the client to reduce its energy bills by around 30% compared with the historical practice, which did not take the variable price of electricity into account. The successful scheme works without adversely affecting the client's critical pumping operations—draining the low-lying marshland is a top priority, but the pumping times can easily be shifted. In this case, NK does not decide or dictate when pumping should take place but gives the client the optimal schedules for pumping based on the prevailing wholesale prices. The client decides whether to follows the suggested schedule or not.

In another interview in April 2019 in Box 10.2, NK's CEO Schwill further explains what NK is, what it does and how it has evolved over time.

10.3 Changing times, changing needs, changing business models

More recently, NK—and one suspects other VPPs as well—have modified their original business models based on the changes in the environment while expanding both the scope of their products and services as well as their geographical footprint attracted by promising opportunities beyond their original base[9].

In case of the NK, this evolution is manifested in at least three dimensions:

- New services and products;
- New partners and affiliations; and
- New markets and geographic territories.

Unsurprisingly, NK has identified energy storage as a natural extension of its original business model. The company has started to add value to its portfolio and its services by including more storage in its offerings when and where this makes sense.

As an example, Box 10.3 describes one interesting project where the value of services provided by NK are significantly enhanced by including storage—in this case in the form of batteries in electric automated guided vehicles (AGV) at a shipping port in Hamburg, Germany.

The rapid growth of electric vehicles (EVs)—a major behind-the-meter asset—creates vast opportunities for VPPs to develop and offer new products aimed at better management of when the EVs are charged and potentially discharged, and where, to reduce additional stress on the aging and often fragile distribution network.

---

[8] For another case study on a similar client, refer to: https://www.next-kraftwerke.com/company/case-studies/variable-electricity-tariff

[9] For further reading on the changing VPP services and business models refer to VPPs add value to behind the meter, EEnergy Informer, May 2019 and NK: Emerging VPPs, EEnergy Informer, Nov 2018.

BOX 10.2

What are the advantages of VPPs[10]?

The CEO of NK, Jochen Schwill, provides an updated description of the company in an interview in April 2019, excerpts from which are reproduced blow.

Q: How would you define a virtual power plant and what are its advantages?

We digitally connect small and medium-sized energy consumers, producers and storage systems in our Next Pool, aggregating their capacity. Electricity producers include biogas plants, cogeneration systems, photovoltaic installations, and hydropower and wind power plants. We use parts of the aggregated capacity to supply transmission system operators with control reserve, thus stabilizing the grid. In addition, we directly market the regular electricity generated by all of these systems via the energy exchange, and we optimize plant production by regulating it in response to the energy exchange's price signals. The idea is to produce electricity when the price is high because the supply is low, and to consume electricity when the price is low because of low demand and high generation. This allows us to balance the fluctuations resulting from the volatile feed-in levels typical for renewable energies and to optimize profits for our customers, who can earn additional income thanks to the optimized operation. As a result, renewable sources of energy become more economical, which in turn boosts their deployment and speeds up the energy transition. Providing more flexibility also boosts efficiency, which benefits the system as a whole.

Q: In which countries outside of Germany does Next Kraftwerke operate? How do the framework conditions differ?

We have operations in Belgium, France, Italy, the Netherlands, Poland, Austria and Switzerland. To be able to operate in any given country, their regulations must allow plant pooling and the market there must allow us to participate as an aggregator.

Q: Who are your customers?

We have a wide range of customers, such as biogas plant operators whose plants we control in response to energy exchange prices, PV project developers, and utilities who commission us with their portfolio management. In the Netherlands, we offer control reserve from lamps in greenhouses. We are in collaboration with the water management association Deich- und Hauptsielverband Diethmarschen to optimize the pumps' energy consumption in relation to energy exchange prices. We offer other energy companies access to our NEMOCS platform to enable them to create their own virtual power plants.

Q: Would you say that the interconnection of different generating installations can be primarily seen as a marketing strategy for green electricity?

Our pool almost exclusively consists of renewable energy systems. We specialize in providing the system with "green" flexibility. The flexibility arising from exploiting the existing potential of renewables is incredible.

---

[10] The interview appears at https://www.thesmartere.de/en/news-press/news/expert-interviews/expert-interview.html?tx_news_pi1[news] = 3287&cHash = beb4692b7655170687f039d405083d66

BOX 10.2 *(cont'd)*

Q: **How do the investment options for cogeneration, biogas, photovoltaic and wind power plants differ?**

The difference lies in the degree of flexibility offered by each of these types of power sources, as well as the regulatory conditions for each of them. Solar power systems, for instance, are not allowed to provide any control reserve.

Q: **How does this interconnection work in practical terms, or in other words, what are the preconditions for the joint control of generating installations?**

Our Next Box was created to connect the large number of small and medium-sized systems with each other. It is a remote control unit that links the systems within the Next Pool with our control system. The plant data is encrypted and sent to our control system via a specially secured GPRS connection. The Next Box is designed according to the grid code provided by the transmission system operators to ensure the highest possible level of security. The Next Box is a machine-to-machine component which sends information about the operation of the decentralized systems to the control system. Data is also transmitted in the opposite direction: The Next Box is able to control the startup and shutdown of electricity generation plants, for example. The signal for such an action comes for the algorithm created specially for our central control system. Depending on the type of system, the Next Box and the algorithm are parametrized individually, which allows gas, heating and water storage as well as timetable restrictions to be programmed so that the unit can always operate under optimal conditions, both technologically and financially.

Q: **What role do storage systems play in virtual power plants and what types of storage systems does Next Kraftwerke use?**

The importance of storage systems is growing steadily. However, they are still expensive, which means that there isn't much choice on the market yet. Virtual power plants provide opportunities for marketing electrical energy from batteries in different markets in order to boost earnings, which can then be rechanneled into financing aspects. So even though there aren't many, there are some batteries in our pool. Let me give you two examples: Next Kraftwerke and Jedlix—an electric vehicle aggregator and smart charging platform provider—have launched a joint pilot project which will deliver secondary control reserve through electric vehicle batteries. The project is part of a larger pilot project commissioned by TenneT. The transmission system operator is testing the technical feasibility of secondary control reserve delivered by new technologies.

And then there is the FRESH collaboration project, focused on flexibility management and new ideas for providing control reserve for heavy goods vehicles in ports. Hamburger Hafen und Logistik AG is using automated guided vehicles (AGVs) at the Altenwerder container port in Hamburg for moving shipping containers between the quay cranes and the storage blocks. The fleet of around 100 heavy goods vehicles is being completely converted to vehicles running on lithium-ion batteries. The idea is that vehicles that are being charged or on standby will soon be used to provide control reserve. The primary focus is on the supply of primary control reserve. Next Kraftwerke's involvement in the project comprises the development of concepts for fleet prequalification and the charging system of AGVs as well as marketing the control reserve power. ∎

BOX 10.3

New value proposition: Storage[11]

Next Kraftwerke is joining Hamburger Hafen und Logistik AG (HHLA), the OFFIS - Institute for Information Technology, and the University of Göttingen in a project called FRESH (visual below). With FRESH, the project partners are trying out new ideas for balancing services provided by batteries in electric automated guided vehicles (AGV) at the Hamburg shipping port.

Terminal Altenwerder (CTA), located in the Port of Hamburg, shipping containers are moved between quay cranes and storage blocks using AGVs as shown in the photo. This fleet of around 100 heavy goods vehicles is currently being converted to run on lithium-ion batteries. Vehicles that are being charged or on standby will soon be used to provide control reserve. Initially, the fleet

Source: © HHLA.

HHLA is a European transport and logistics company, which operates container terminals in the ports of Hamburg, Odessa and Tallinn. At the HHLA's Container

will mainly be used for supplying primary control reserve, but additional control reserve forms and the provision of flexibility will also be explored.

---

[11] Article available at https://www.next-kraftwerke.com/news/fresh-ideas-for-electrifying-port-logistics

---

BOX 10.3 *(cont'd)*

"FRESH" project: control reserve provided by batteries in electric automated guided vehicles

Source: *NK.*

For the project, Next Kraftwerke is developing concepts for the fleet's prequalification to provide control reserve as well as the charging system of the AGV, and trades the control reserve power. In order to provide control reserve, the charging stations will be connected to the virtual power plant using the Next Box, a bidirectional remote-control unit developed by Next Kraftwerke. When calculating the available control reserve, the project partners have carefully weighed important factors. Placing the batteries' capacity on the control reserve market requires a high degree of reliability, but providing control reserve cannot hinder the terminal's logistical operations. A prognosis algorithm calculates the potential amount of power that can be put up for bidding based on estimates of the vehicles' operating and standby times. To continually improve these forecasts, the project partners are using a range of tools that include deep learning, a form of machine learning. Redundancies built into the charging

stations ensure that reliable control reserve is always available. Theoretically, the AGV fleet could supply up to four megawatts of control reserve to the power trading markets.

According to Alexander Krautz, Team Manager of Innovation & Development at Next Kraftwerke, "We are really looking forward to working with HHLA on this unique project. The digitalization and electrification of the logistics industry – with its high energy needs and special considerations – are a challenge for our power system. But they also provide new possibilities when it comes to optimization and stability."

Boris Wulff from CTA's terminal development at HHLA: "Electric drive technology is not some futuristic vision for us. It's something we've been using for quite some time, and we want to expand on our pioneering role in this field. The FRESH project is one more way of pursuing that goal. With Next Kraftwerke, we're glad to have such an experienced partner by our side." ∎

BOX 10.4

VPPs get into EV charging business[12]

In early 2019, Next Kraftwerke and Jedlix, an electric vehicle (EV) aggregator and smart charging platform provider, have launched an international pilot project to deliver secondary control reserve (aFRR) through the batteries of electric cars. Tendered by Transmission System Operator (TSO) TenneT, Next Kraftwerke and Jedlix have been selected for the pilot project that will see TenneT assess the technical feasibility of aFRR delivered by new technologies.

The project is expected to run for two years, during which Next Kraftwerke and Jedlix provide aFRR through Jedlix's EV fleet using the company's smart charging solution. Next Kraftwerke provides the interface to the TSO TenneT and markets the aggregated energy in TenneT's reserve control auctions, while Jedlix steers the charging of EV's over-the-air via its platform. Jedlix establishes the connection by linking its system to Next Kraftwerke's remote control unit Next Box. In doing so, the Jedlix fleet can be controlled by Next Kraftwerke's central control system. This enables real-time data exchange between the Jedlix fleet and Next Kraftwerke, while also making it possible for the Jedlix fleet to receive setpoints from Next Kraftwerke that change the EV's power consumption.

Jedlix vehicle drivers will be introduced to the service through a user interface app, which Jedlix offers to all EV drivers in The Netherlands. By taking part in the pilot, all EV drivers can get rewarded for making the car's flexibility available whenever it is being charged at the driver's home. By connecting the EV to the Jedlix platform, Jedlix can receive user charging preferences and establish a live connection with the EV, making sure they are charged smartly. Depending on the charging preference, each EV can provide either positive or negative control reserves. Jedlix will be able to combine user preferences, car data, and charging station information for a continuous forecast of the available capacity. This is then used by Next Kraftwerke in the bidding process. To level out any potential unavailability of the EVs, Next Kraftwerke and Jedlix pool the EVs with other assets in the Next Pool such as greenhouse lighting, wind, and solar plants, and biogas- as well as greenhouse CHPs. ∎

An example of how NK is capitalizing on this important and growing market is provided in Box 10.4.

10.4 Future of VPPs

As we approach the decade of 2020s, VPPs, NK included, are looking into new opportunities, new offering, new services, new partnerships, new value streams, and new markets to continue their expansion.

[12] Article available at https://www.next-kraftwerke.com/news/next-kraftwerke-jedlix-launch-initiative-to-use-electric-car-batteries-for-grid-stability

One of the underlying drivers for future growth of VPPs is that as customers become more proactive and as the percentage of the variable renewable generation increases, the potential revenue streams of the assets embedded in a VPP's portfolio increases. This means that the services provided by VPPs become more valuable to utilities, to grid operators, to distribution network operators and, of course, to participating customers. The future growth of VPPs—and all behind-the-meter aggregators—is driven by the increased need for flexibility to balance supply and demand in real time. Since in the future more of the generation will come from variable renewable resources, more demand flexibility will be required, and this is the area all VPPs and demand-side aggregators are likely to focus on. Another growth area for VPPs is to offer their powerful software as a service to others who may not have their own.

That is why NK has introduced NEMOCS[13], a VPP-as-a-Service product. For the clients of NEMOCS NK is the software-as-a-service-provider. The client has to close contracts with the owner of the distributed assets and profits from NK support and knowledge while using NEMOCS as the solution to aggregate and manage the units.

In this context, NK is no longer the VPP *operator* but rather the VPP *provider*. The clients, using NK's intelligent software and expertise can provide a range of services in a given market, for example,

- Improved forecasting capabilities resulting in improved trading margins by relying on live-data coming from renewables installations;
- Improved aggregation of distributed loads and/or generation to provide control reserve to the grid; and
- Improved scheduling of distributed fleets of generation, consumption, and storage to enhance wholesale market profitability[14].

As an example, Box 10.5 describes a recent venture with Haezoom in South Korea where NK is capitalizing on its NEMOCS, its software product.

The expansion of NK's business in overseas markets is largely driven by its powerful software NEMOCS, which is increasingly offered in the form of software-as-a-solution basis. This is mainly due to the fact that the company cannot duplicate or clone its own VPP business model globally in a short amount of time mostly because of the very different regulatory rule and market structures in different parts of the world. Like many other start-ups, NK is limited by its limited scale. This has led to the decision to play the role of *facilitator* rather than *operator*. Similar strategies are in play in the US and elsewhere with many companies focusing on offering software, platforms, and services to others who then make good use of such expertise in given markets.

An example of NK' successful entry into the software business may be found in Box 10.6, which describes the company's foray in to the UK market.

As the preceding example explained, NK continues to identify and expand its offerings in Europe as well as markets overseas where opportunities can be identified.

---

[13] Refer to https://www.next-kraftwerke.com/products/vpp-solution for further details

[14] Refer to https://www.next-kraftwerke.com/products/vpp-solution

---

BOX 10.5

Software as a service[15]

NEMOCS, Next Kraftwerke's VPP-as-a-service solution, is making its debut in South Korea with solar energy company Haezoom using it to monitor and control their assets. Haezoom specializes in maximizing solar energy efficiency through data and IT-related technologies. Using Next Kraftwerke's VPP-as-a-service solution, Haezoom will obtain live data from their assets enabled to operate them according to grid situations and fluctuating decentral power supply, also encompassing a curtailment option through the central control system of NEMOCS.

NEMOCS optimizes operation of power-producing and consuming units. It can connect thousands of assets, process their data in real time, and execute operational commands if needed. This allows clients to set up their own virtual power plant without costly infrastructure investments. Jochen Schwill, founder and CEO of Next Kraftwerke said, "NEMOCS incorporates ideas and features from our own IT experts and power traders. We are happy to share our experience and expertise with international partners, especially with a company as progressive as Haezoom."

Jongkyu Kim, CTO at Haezoom said, "As the first registered power aggregator in South Korea, we are planning to operate VPPs with [...] NEMOCS, combined with our solar forecasting technology using the newly launched Korean satellite Chollian-2A. We chose [...] NEMOCS because we are convinced that the VPP approach is the most promising way to deal with decentral renewable energies in a more liberalized market [...] and we trust in Next Kraftwerke's decade-long IT and power market experience. [...]." ∎

In May 2019, for example, NK released a statement describing its latest venture with Tohoku Electric Power Co in Japan as further explained in Box 10.7.

Moving forward, NK, like all players in the VPP and behind-the-meter aggregation space, agree that regulation is key to their expansion and commercial success. The energy sector traditionally is highly regulated to ensure the security of supply and to keep the playing field level for all consumers, not just those who may participate in VPP or other non-traditional schemes. For NK to be able to grow and expand its operations it needs clear market rules on the new role of aggregators including further clarity on the following:

- Are aggregators allowed to enter the energy market?
- Which services are allowed to be delivered by an aggregator?
- Which data security regulation applies for aggregators?
- How do decentralized generators, demand response consumers, and storage units need to be tested by TSOs to deliver control reserve?

---

[15] Article at https://www.next-kraftwerke.com/news/south-korean-pv-company-haezoom-signs-nemocs-contract

BOX 10.6

New offerings in new markets[16]

British green electricity company Ecotricity is the first client to implement NEMOCS, Next Kraftwerke's new software-as-a-service solution. The German virtual power plant operator recently introduced NEMOCS to third parties as a way to network and optimize operation of power-producing and consuming units.

NEMOCS can connect thousands of assets. Their data is processed live, and NEMOCS can execute operational commands if needed. It provides the user with

select the ones available to provide frequency response or balancing reserves and dispatch them in case of a call from the TSO. NEMOCS allows third parties, such as electricity suppliers and utility companies, to set up their own virtual power plant without investing in costly infrastructure while counting on the support, service, and experience of Next Kraftwerke.

Image address
https://www.next-kraftwerke.com/wp-content/uploads/Ecotricity-VPP-NEMOCS.jpg

Ecotricity's VPP & NEMOCS control system working together

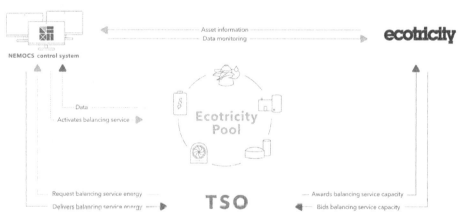

Source: *NK.*

real-time operational data from the networked units to optimize their power production and consumption. Choosing from the many networked units, NEMOCS can

Ecotricity is the UK's first green electricity company, providing thousands of clients in the UK with green energy from its own wind turbines and other renewable energy

[16] Article at https://www.next-kraftwerke.com/news/ecotricity-selects-next-kraftwerkes-nemocs-to-build-virtual-power-plant

---

BOX 10.6   (cont'd)

producers. NEMOCS will help Ecotricity to optimize its units' production and storage as well as its forecast and dispatch by providing it with real time operational data from the units connected. Mark Meyrick, Head of Smart Grids, from Ecotricity: "We have been watching Next's activities in the flexibility space for a while and are big admirers of what they've achieved. As a result we're very happy and excited to be partnering with such an innovative organization who match our pioneering values and commitment to renewable energy, to deliver this innovative project, which will help enable our aspirations in the storage space, amongst other benefits" ■

BOX 10.7

Japanese utility Tohoku utilizes NEMOCS to set up virtual power plant[17]

Japanese electric utility Tohoku Electric Power Co., Inc. (Tohoku EPCO) and Next Kraftwerke have agreed to a strategic partnership in a virtual power plant (VPP) demonstration project utilizing NEMOCS. It is the first time that Next Kraftwerke has concluded a basic agreement with a Japanese power utility. Tohoku EPCO is the fourth-largest electric utility in Japan in terms of revenue, servicing 7.6 million individual and corporate customers in six prefectures in the Tōhoku region and the Niigata prefecture.

Tohoku EPCO launched the VPP demonstration project in April 2018, and has been working since to remotely control and aggregate power-producing assets distributed throughout the regions, making them function as if they were a single power plant by utilizing IoT and other new information technologies. The energy resources include generators and batteries owned by local governments, companies, households of customers, and others. Through the demonstration project, Tohoku EPCO aims to commercialize the VPP and to develop new services in the future. In order to realize this, Tohoku EPCO wants to further enhance its VPP-related knowledge and technology, such as the ability to control energy resources accurately and precisely. Now, cooperating with Next Kraftwerke and utilizing its knowledge and technology, Tohoku EPCO expects to accelerate the commercialization of the VPP and the development of new services.

Tohoku EPCO plans to verify the feasibility of commercializing the VPP and developing new services utilizing Next Kraftwerke's experience systems with the

---

[17] Press release issued on 23 May 2019 may be found at www.next-kraftwerke.com/wp-content/uploads/Nemocs-Tohoku-Japan-VPP.jpg

---

BOX 10.7   (cont'd)

aim of expanding the alliance to include power trading and ancillary services.

According to Alexander Krautz, Head of Innovation & Development at Next Kraftwerke,"Given the expansion of distributed energy resources in Japan, we are very happy to cooperate with Tohoku EPCO utilizing NEMOCS, our software-as-a-service solution, in pursuing its goal of developing new digital business models to strengthen its position as an innovative integrated energy company." ∎

To speed up this process, NK increasingly opts to not build up own subsidiaries in overseas countries but rather to play the role of a solution provider in a partnership with local market players that have an established knowledge on the regulatory ins and outs.

Another opportunity may be to eventually expand into the residential sector when it becomes economical to do so. NK currently does not integrate residential assets into its VPP portfolio since it is not cost efficient due to higher transaction costs and lower flexibility volumes. It only operates on a business to business level. The assets have to have a minimum size of 100 kilowatts to be integrated into the pool.

In an interview with Clean Energy Wire[18], NK's CEO Hendrik Sämisch, described his vision for the future of NK as follows:

> We have already expanded our market in Europe — we offer market access for renewables as well as power generation forecasts, and experience a rising demand for solutions to control renewables in order to balance the grid, and to understand what will happen in the power market in the hours to come. The increasing rollout of renewables poses many questions for grid operators in countless countries that need answering: Where does the power come from? Where does it go? What will happen in four hours? — and we're happy to assist them by saying: 'We can tell you how much power renewables generate this very second at each grid intersection, we can visualize the process, and we can forecast what will happen in four hours.' These issues will become increasingly important in every country on earth within the next five years and we want to provide answers by using our technology.

10.5 Conclusions

Virtual power plants and other aggregators and optimizers of behind-the-meter assets have emerged in recent years due to the rising demand for flexibility to balance supply and demand in real-time on networks increasingly inundated with variable renewable generation. As more markets aim for very high percentage of renewable generation,

---

[18] https://www.cleanenergywire.org/news/start-next-kraftwerkes-renewable-virtual-power-plant-stabilises-grid

balancing supply and demand while maintaining reliability becomes more challenging, and more expensive.

The traditional solutions—adding more storage and more transmission capacity—help but can only go so far. In many networks, increasing amounts of renewable has to be curtailed due to limitations to integrate them and/or result in drops in wholesale prices, which occasionally go negative. This explains the focus into making demand more flexible and more responsive to price.

In the meantime, generation is becoming decentralized with more households, businesses adding solar PVs on rooftops. As electric vehicles move mainstream and as the price of distributed storage falls, there is near universal agreement that the next big—and challenging—frontier is how best to aggregate, monitor and optimize large portfolios of behind-the-meter assets. This, more than anything else explains the rise of VPPs and aggregators in general.

The example of NK, featured in this chapter, points to the progress that has been made to date and identifies some of the remaining challenges.

11

Platform for trading flexibility on the distribution network: a UK case study

James Johnston[1] and Fereidoon Sioshansi[2]

[1]Piclo, London, United Kingdom [2]Menlo Energy Economics, San Francisco, CA, United States

11.1 Introduction

Trading platforms are the latest craze as more products and innovative services can be bought, sold, or traded online, with the products or services often delivered by others. What makes trading platforms especially powerful, and potentially profitable, is that— once the basic proof-of-concept has been demonstrated—they can be easily scaled-up using cloud-based services.[1] The business model is asset light and since the services or products are typically made and/or delivered by others, the platform operator can quickly scale up, move to new markets, or go global.

As they grow, they gain from powerful *network effects*, which means that the successful ones attract ever-larger numbers of customers and providers—hence become more valuable, more popular, and more profitable. This explains the dominance of a handful of big platforms in any given market or business segment—say Uber and Lyft in ride-hailing business, Airbnb in hospitality or eBay, Grubhub, and PayPal in their respective domains—all household names by now.

While many examples of successful platforms may be found in other industries, there aren't too many in the electricity sector—until now. As further explained in this chapter and others in this volume, one reason is that the electricity sector has not fully embraced digitalization of its products and services to date, nor has it made significant progress in capitalizing on opportunities to create and monetize value in this space.

The hesitancy on the part of incumbent distribution and retailing businesses provides an opportunity for newcomers—start-ups and others not necessarily affiliated with the

---

[1] Refer to Chapter 3.

incumbents—to develop platforms that could be used by the incumbents *and* their customers or others.

This chapter explains how and why trading platforms can be successfully deployed to offer valuable products and services in the electricity sector including a case study of Piclo, a London-based start-up that has successfully developed and demonstrated a particularly promising application.

The balance of the chapter is organized as follows:

- Section 11.2 explains what makes trading platforms special.
- Section 11.3 describes the rising complexities of managing increasingly convoluted flows of electrons on aging distribution networks that were not designed to handle the new demands placed on them with the rise of distributed generation (DG), electric vehicles (EVs), and other behind-the-meter assets.
- Section 11.4 introduces the rising interest in so-called nonwire solutions or nonwire alternatives (NWAs).
- Section 11.5 describes a case study of Piclo, a start-up that has successfully developed a platform for trading flexibility on the distribution network in the United Kingdom followed by the chapter's conclusions.

11.2 What's special about trading platforms?

The short answer is that electronic trading platforms are essentially substituting for physical markets where goods and services have traditionally been bought and sold. In today's digitalized world of e-commerce, buyers and sellers gather at *electronic* marketplaces where goods and/or services are offered and can be bought and sold without physical interface, paid for using credit cards or through other means such as electronic fund transfers. The goods or services, depending on the specifics, can be physically shipped or delivered by the same or other service providers. In the case of Amazon the same company that manages the platform usually—but not always—also handles the final delivery. In the case of Uber or Airbnb, they rely on others for delivery of services—none of which they own or operate. In the thriving food delivery business, platform operators do not own restaurants, do not cook the food, and in most cases do not even deliver the food—all of which are handled by others.[2] Ditto for flower delivery business.

In typical applications the platform operator displays the products or services, their availability, price, means and terms of delivery, and usually handles or manages the transactions including settlement and back-office services. But it *generally* does *not* produce or deliver the goods or services—tasks that are done by others. In most cases, it collects a fee for facilitating the financial as well as the physical aspects of the transaction. Even if the fees for individual transactions are modest, the large volume of transactions on a popular platform can generate large revenues and, usually but not always, decent profit margins.

---

[2] Domino Pizza may be an exception, cooking and delivering the goods. But as it turns out, they are facing stiff competition from others as the food delivery business moves to third parties.

What typically help platforms to become successful are the two underlying features of their business model, which are

- asset light and information or data heavy and
- they can scale up quickly and easily.

These two attributes mean that once the platform operator has built a critical mass of users, it can quickly gain scale through network effects, generating significant liquidity and delivering value to all market participants.

Platforms are fairly new in the electricity business. Part of the explanation may be that the utility business is highly fragmented and heavily regulated; hence, developing a successful platform in one country or state cannot necessarily be extended to another place with different players, regulations, market characteristics, and tariffs. Despite these challenges, a number of profitable niches are being explored[3] as described in the chapter by Lehmbruck and others.

11.3 Complexities of managing convoluted flows on aging distribution networks

The rapid rise of DG and EVs is already placing increased demand on networks that were not designed to handle bidirectional flows—in the case of DG—or massively rising and concentrated demand—in the case of EVs.

In Great Britain the demand for electricity is projected to grow significantly to 2050. In some scenarios, it is projected to grow more than 50%—an increase from 292 TWh today up to 440 TWh by 2050.[4]

Unfortunately, these developments are taking place at a time when, in many parts of the world, the distribution networks are rapidly aging and in need of major upgrades and/or modernization.[5]

The combination of the rising complexities of managing increasingly convoluted flows on aging distribution networks—which were not designed to handle the new demands places on them with the rise of DG, EVs, and other behind-the-meter assets—has resulted in the proverbial perfect storm. Some of the issues are

- what to do with the aging infrastructure that is expensive to maintain and upgrade;
- how to manage increasingly complicated follows on the distribution networks originally designed for more predictable one-directional flows;
- how to relieve increasing pockets of congestion on the distribution network on specific locations and times due to the rise of behind-the-meter generation and EVs; and
- how should regulators decide the best course of action given the often missing incentives for distribution network operators (DNOs) who traditionally have

---

[3] For example refer to Trading platforms & VPPs find profitable niches. *EEnergy Informer.* (2018). Available from <www.eenergyinformer.com>.

[4] National Grid. (2019). *Future energy scenarios (community renewables scenario).* National Grid.

[5] Utility Infrastructure Investment To Soar. *EEnergy Informer.* (2017). Available from <www. eenergyinformer.com>.

depended on investing in network upgrades instead of looking for smarter ways to better utilize the existing network through the so-called non-wires alternatives (NWAs) or non-wires solutions, further described below.

Under prevailing regulations in the United States and many other countries, DNOs make money by making investments in hardware on which they can earn a regulated rate of return. All else being equal, they have strong motivations to invest, upgrade, modernize, and replace assets whether or not such investments are fully justified. This leads to a never-ending game of cat-and-mouse between the regulated DNOs and the regulators. If the latter is not alert, competent, and vigilant, the former would rather invest more than may be absolutely necessary.[6]

In Great Britain the regulator, Office for Gas and Electricity Markets (Ofgem), operates a different model called RIIO or Revenue = Incentives + Innovation + Outputs, which is an approach for regulating the amount that monopoly networks can earn from charging customers to use the network. This model is a performance-based framework, which provides the DNOs with more freedom than some of the other simpler models as described above.[7] The RIIO framework provides GB DNOs with quite a bit of freedom to choose exactly how they will operate the networks, which partially explains why DNOs in the United Kingdom are taking a lead in the development of nonwire solutions as outlined in the next section.

11.4 Nonwire solutions to network upgrades

As mentioned in the preceding section, even when the distribution network is stressed or congested, generally not *all* parts of the network are necessarily overstressed at *all* times. In fact, most networks are only overextended during *certain hours* and only in *certain locations*. This means that there is no need to upgrade the *entire* network just to relieve congestion at particular places and only at certain hours.

This realization explains the rising interest in so-called *nonwire solutions*, which offer less expensive ways to relieve localized and sporadic congestion on the network without upgrading the entire network, which can be rather expensive.

For example, the UK Power Networks, the largest DNO in the United Kingdom published their need for nonwire solutions in their Flexibility Roadmap in October 2018.[8] They outlined four specific use cases for nonwire solutions as outlined in Table 11.1.

Traditional substation reinforcement was straightforward when long-term forecasts of incremental demand were predictable. With the transition toward decentralized energy,

---

[6] Grid modernization a euphemism for network gold plating. *EEnergy Informer*. (2017). Available from <www.eenergyinformer.com>.

[7] https://www.ofgem.gov.uk/network-regulation-riio-model

[8] *UK power networks flexibility roadmap*. (2018). Available from <http://futuresmart.ukpowernetworks.co.uk/wp-content/themes/ukpnfuturesmart/assets/pdf/UKPowerNetworks-FlexibilityRoadmapLaunchSlides.pdf>.

TABLE 11.1   Excerpt from UKPN Flexibility Roadmap: DSO flexibility needs and products summary.

Flexibility products	Reinforcement deferral	Planned maintenance	Unplanned interruptions	
			Prefault response	Postfault response
Value drivers	The present value of deferring capital expenditure	Managing unplanned interruption risk during planned maintenance	CI and CML incentives	Avoided cost of temporary generation and potentially CMLs
Procurement type	Competitive tenders or administratively set prices if low liquidity		Framework agreement. optional updating of pricing through contract	
Procurement lead time	6 months ahead and 18 months ahead	Case specific 1−12 months	DER applies if eligible	
Payment	Availability and utilization		Utilization only	
Contract term	1−4 years	Monthly or seasonal	Framework agreement	

CI, Customer interruption; CML, customer minutes lost.
UK Power Networks Flexibility Roadmap, published online October 2018.

net demand on the grid is far less predictable with a conflict between energy efficiency, renewable energy, and electrification of heat and transport, and increased digital demand. In this context, three issues need to be examined:

- reinforcement deferral
- planned maintenance
- unplanned interruptions

The first refers to the fact that deferring long-term decisions—distribution assets have planned lifetimes of 40 years—frequently makes sense to avoid ending up with "stranded" oversized grid assets in the future. DNOs want to have an "option" for flexibility in heavily constrained areas, which can be called on when thermal or voltage limits in substations are breached. The value driver for UK DNOs is the present value in deferring or potentially avoiding capital expenditure. The logic of reinforcement deferral, however, is universal and not limited to the UK DNOs.

The second refers to works that are focused on maintaining the security of supply standards before reinforcement works are complete. In this case the value driver is reducing the risk of unplanned interruptions, further explained below.

The final requirement is for unplanned interruptions, both pre and postfault. In this case, flexibility contracts are used to manage networks during abnormal conditions, for instance, when a fault leads to a localized blackout and the neighboring network has to compensate. In this case the value driver is reducing the customer interruption and customer minutes lost, two incentives applicable to DNOs in the United Kingdom. Similar schemes, of course, apply elsewhere.

In this new landscape, there is a need for an open and transparent market for flexibility services that creates a level playing field for all energy technologies and services to be traded and procured competitively. In the United Kingdom's case, competition is encouraged by the UK government's Department for Business, Energy & Industrial Strategy (BEIS)[9] and Ofgem as one of the guiding principles in their Smart Systems and Flexibility Plan.[10]

The network companies in GB have responded to BEIS and Ofgem with a commitment to procuring flexibility for nonwire solutions. The Energy Networks Association (ENA), the trade association of the GB energy networks, has outlined 6 key principles for delivering nonwire solutions.[11]

1. *Champion a level playing field*: ENA's electricity network members will facilitate and provide convergence and standardization across their customers.
2. *Ensure visibility and accessibility*: Removing barriers and enabling all customers to access and provide services to multiple markets
3. *Conduct procurement in an open and transparent manner*: A definition of common methodologies for all network operators to follow and be transparent about the criteria used in decision-making
4. *Provide clarity on the dispatch of services*: Setting the decision-making criteria underpinning the dispatch of services
5. *Provide regular, consistent, and transparent reporting*: Monitoring and reporting to give confidence to the public. All decisions and reasonings will be readily available.
6. *Work together toward whole energy system outcomes*: Facilitate, coordinated and efficient arrangements, which benefit households and businesses. Ensure that changes deliver the best outcomes for everyone on a whole energy system basis.

It must be noted that the nonwire solutions—sometimes called NWAs—has become a hot topic among many regulators in the United States, Europe, and Australia with the rise of DG, storage, and EVs stressing segments of the network at certain times. Regulators in the state of New York and California (Box 11.1), for example, have ongoing proceedings to examine less expensive nonwire solutions before allowing DNOs to invest huge sums in indiscriminate upgrading of the entire network. Similar initiatives are pursued elsewhere following similar approaches.

11.5 Case study: Piclo flexibility trading platform

Having described the concept of nonwire solutions, this section describes a case study of Piclo,[12] a London-based start-up who has successfully developed a platform for trading flexibility on the distribution network and has demonstrated its functionality in a trial with the six DNOs in the United Kingdom.

---

[9] https://www.gov.uk/government/organisations/department-for-business-energy-and-industrial-strategy

[10] Ofgem. *Upgrading our energy system: Smart systems and flexibility plan.* (2017). Ofgem.

[11] ENA. (2019). *Our six steps for delivering flexibility services.*

[12] https://piclo.energy

BOX 11.1

How does California handle nonwire solutions

The California Public Utilities Commission (CPUC) expects the regulated utilities to examine all cost-effective *nonwire solutions* before allowing them to invest large sums on upgrading the distribution network—that is, the *wires alternative*.

The nonwire solutions proceedings affecting the state's two large investor-owned utilities, PG&E and SCE, may be found at

- PG&E Non Wires Solutions RFOs
  - 2018 RFO—*RFO Site, Webinar for Stakeholders during RFO Initiation*
  - 2019 RFO—*RFO Site, Webinar for Stakeholders during RFO Initiation +*
- SCE RFO for Non Wires Solutions
  - 2019 RFO (open)—https://www.sce.com/procurement/solicitations/didfrfo

- SCE's Advice Letter to CPUC describing their process—https://www1.sce.com/NR/sc3/tm2/pdf/3904-E.pdf
- The proceeding related to planning and evaluation of Integrated Distributed Energy Resources (DERs) may be found at
  - https://apps.cpuc.ca.gov/apex/f?p = 401:56:0::NO
- and
  - http://docs.cpuc.ca.gov/PublishedDocs/Efile/G000/M281/K395/281395288.PDF

A number of other states have also established similar proceedings to consider nonwire solutions. ∎

Until recently, National Grid ESO, the transmission system operator in GB was effectively the only buyer of flexibility. In 2018/19 the ESO procured or facilitated approximately £1.2 billion ($1.45 billion) of flexibility services for national balancing.[13]

With the transition to a decentralized energy system and the growing need for nonwire solutions, the six DNOs that operate the 14 licensed distribution areas in Great Britain are joining National Grid ESO as buyers of flexibility (Fig. 11.1). Under this context, these DNOs are transforming into distribution system operators (DSOs) and playing an active role in the smart management of distribution networks.

Piclo's vision is of an independent marketplace where thousands of small-scale assets or organizations that generate their own energy or reduce consumption on-demand, can trade flexibility to manage local network constraints, and help to defer expensive reinforcement (Fig. 11.2).

The benefits of building an open digital platform for trading flexibility are specific to different users but cumulatively help the energy network to transition toward the goal of a decarbonized system with an increasing number of proactive consumers, prosumers,

---

[13] National Grid ESO. (2019). *Monthly Balancing Services Summary 2018/19*. National Grid ESO.

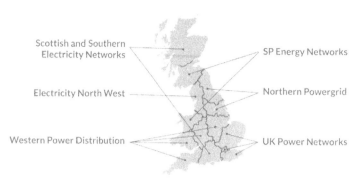

FIGURE 11.1 GB DNOs and the 14 licensed distribution network areas. *DNO*, Distribution network operator. Source: © *Piclo 2019.*

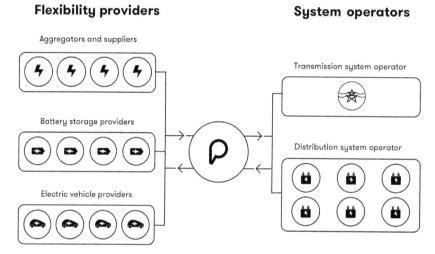

FIGURE 11.2 Piclo flexibility marketplace structure. Source: *Flexibility & Visibility—Piclo White Paper (accessible online: https://piclo.energy/about)* © *Piclo 2019.*

and prosumagers with all sorts of behind-the-meter devices—topics extensively covered in other chapters in this volume.

Piclo believes that the use of its platform will benefit the following:

- flexibility providers
- system operators
- the whole system

In the first instance, a platform for flexibility opportunities nationwide, regardless of size or location of the stakeholders, offers significant benefits to providers of flexibility services. Standardization of data, simplification of search, and transparent commercial terms unlock the potential of providers that do not have the resources for bilateral contract negotiations.

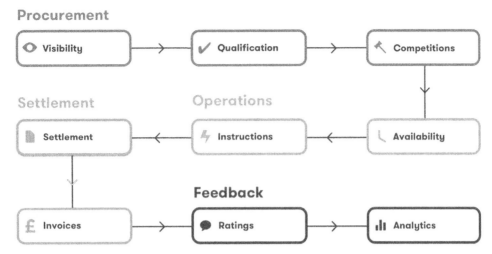

FIGURE 11.3   The stages of procuring flexibility services. Source: *Flexibility & Visibility—Piclo White Paper (accessible online: https://piclo.energy/about)* © *Piclo 2019.*

In the second instance, system operators (both distribution and transmission) can access a liquid market where it is possible to source flexibility with highly specific locational, technical, and temporal requirements.

Finally, the whole system gains from the enhanced visibility, transparency, and multi-buyer coordination offered by a single platform such as Piclo. Flexibility can be scaled-up to support low-carbon technology at a lower cost to consumers.

To test its platform, Piclo launched a trial of an online marketplace for local flexibility in September 2017 with funding from BEIS Energy Entrepreneurs Fund[14] and sought to demonstrate that a digital procurement platform could

- improve transparency and visibility,
- increase participation, and
- reduce the administrative costs associated with procuring flexibility.

To deliver an end-to-end flexibility service, as envisioned by Piclo, many subfunctions have to be successfully delivered including those outlined in Fig. 11.3. In the trials, Piclo focused on developing procurement solutions in the first three boxes, namely,

- visibility
- qualification
- competitive procurement of services using the Piclo platform

---

[14] The Energy Entrepreneurs Fund is a competitive funding scheme to support the development of technologies, products and processes in energy efficiency, power generation and storage. The overall aim of the BEIS Energy Innovation Program is to accelerate the commercialization of innovation cheap, clean, and reliable energy technologies by the mid-2020s and 2030s.

FIGURE 11.4   Screenshot of Piclo Flex with an example published need for nonwires solutions to address reinforcement deferral. Source: *Flexibility & Visibility—Piclo White Paper (accessible online: https://piclo.energy/about)* © *Piclo 2019.*

All six of Britain's DNOs participated in the Piclo Flex trial to learn about the practical steps needed to procure flexibility via a platform. This allowed them to gather tangible evidence for the ENA pan-industry Open Networks Project and demonstrate their "flexibility-first" commitment.[15]

A critical component of the trial was to provide market visibility of nonwire solutions. In the trial, Piclo Flex provided the DNOs with a platform to publish their flexibility needs in a standardized format, including highly specific locational, technical, and temporal requirements as illustrated in Fig. 11.4. In total, Piclo signposted a demand for 456 MW of flexibility across 73 constraint zones.

This is the first time that nationwide flexibility data from multiple DNOs have been available via an open, online platform and represents an opportunity for energy suppliers, aggregators, and demand-side response technologies to consider the potential of their assets beyond the traditional model of procurement. While the initial successful trial was conducted in the United Kingdom, there is no reason a similar platform cannot perform similar functions in other markets, say in California or Australia—places where many of the same issues prevail.

---

[15] ENA Flexibility First Commitment: http://www.energynetworks.org/assets/files/ENA%20Flexibility%20Commitment%20Our%20Six%20Steps%20for%20Delivering%20Flexibility%20Services.pdf (June 2019).

TABLE 11.2 Snapshot of capacity uploaded by distribution network operators (DNOs) during Piclo Flex trial, 2019.

DNO	Flex requirements uploaded	Total capacity advertised (MW)
UK Power Networks	28	103
Scottish and Southern Electricity Networks	6	50.5
Electricity North West	5	8.4
SP Energy Networks	11	116
Northern Powergrid	10	12.5
Western Power Distribution	13	165.4
Total	**73**	**455.8**

© *Piclo 2019.*

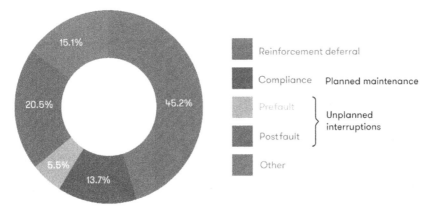

FIGURE 11.5 Breakdown of flexibility requirements during Piclo Flex trial, 2019. Source: *Energy on Trial—Piclo White Paper (accessible online: https://piclo.energy/about)* © *Piclo 2019.*

In the case of the United Kingdom trial, depending on the local context of the network and constraints, there was a significant variance in the need for flexibility advertised by the DNOs as illustrated in Table 11.2.

In this case, out of the 73 constraint zones, the type of requirement for flexibility varied, but the single greatest need was for reinforcement deferral—in 45.2% of the cases—as illustrated in Fig. 11.5. This demonstrates the potential for DNOs to utilize flexibility services to reduce the short-term costs associated with increasing capacity. This is a common phenomenon in nearly all cases, not just in the United Kingdom.

Data uploaded during the trial of flexibility competitions revealed large variations in the scale of individual competitions posted by the DNOs. The variations ranged from 0.2 MW advertised for compliance on winter weekday evenings in Reed in Hertfordshire to 72 MW for unplanned interruptions—one of two similar requirements—in South Hampshire as illustrated in Fig. 11.6.

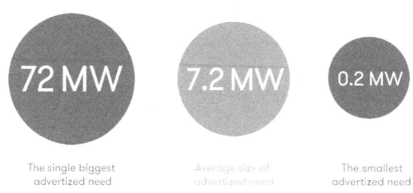

FIGURE 11.6   Data from Piclo Flex trial, 2019. Source: *Energy on Trial—Piclo White Paper (accessible online: https://piclo.energy/about)* © *Piclo 2019.*

This means that the types of potential solution could also be very different. A low level of need such as 0.2 MW could be met on a hyper-local level by around 50 residential batteries, for example. This could be met by the massive expected growth of batteries in both residential and utility-scale applications in the coming years. At the other end of the scale, a 72 MW requirement would need close to 20,000 residential batteries to meet such a demand. This makes it much more likely that this demand would be met by a small number of utility-scale batteries or generators.

Another valuable service offered by the Piclo's platform is providing visibility of matched assets. Piclo Flex also enables flexibility providers (Flex Providers) to publish the location and connection voltage of their assets. The system matches active assets with new demand as it's published, creating ongoing opportunities for them to be leveraged to minimize bottlenecks across the network. This is particularly useful for providers with assets in multiple locations, saving time that would otherwise be spent proactively seeking out and reviewing invitations to tender from more than one DNO.

The platform also supports flexibility providers to

- determine if their assets are in a location that's likely to qualify for competitions in constraint management areas, now or in the future (Fig. 11.7);
- obtain data to support a business case for developing new assets; and
- earn income to supplement or replace government incentives to promote the uptake of renewable and low-carbon electricity generation technologies.

This two-way visibility of both flexibility assets and network needs has the potential to stimulate debate in the energy industry and inform decisions that will support the transition toward a zero-carbon economy and shape the energy system of the future.

Of the 4.4 GW of flexibility assets registered on Piclo Flex by mid-June 2019, behind-the-meter residential batteries were the most numerous, almost 2000 individual units (Fig. 11.8). However, collectively these behind-the-meter assets only contributed a very small share of the total of flex capacity registered on the platform to date, roughly 0.17%. This demonstrates that although an individual residential battery unit may be hugely

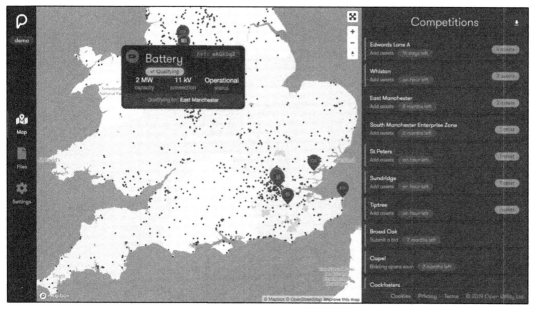

FIGURE 11.7   DNO flexibility needs matched with flexibility assets, demo data. *DNO*, Distribution network operator. Source: *Flexibility & Visibility—Piclo White Paper (accessible online: https://piclo.energy/about) © Piclo 2019.*

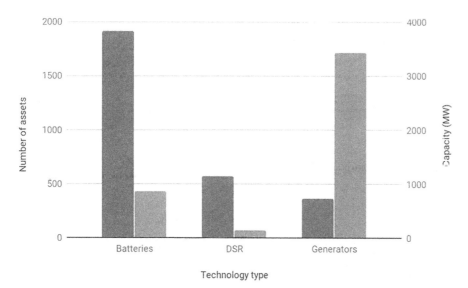

FIGURE 11.8   Capacity and number of assets by technology type registered on Piclo Flex by mid-June 2019, excluding speculative assets. Source: *Flexibility & Visibility—Piclo White Paper (accessible online: https://piclo.energy/about) © Piclo 2019.*

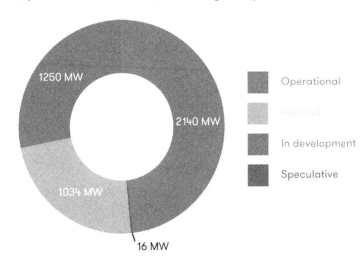

FIGURE 11.9 Status of assets by capacity, in MW, registered on Piclo Flex by mid-June 2019. Source: *Flexibility & Visibility—Piclo White Paper (accessible online: https://piclo. energy/about)* © *Piclo 2019.*

impactful to the economics of an individual household, it is only when millions of these batteries are deployed that they can have a meaningful impact on national energy markets.

Larger batteries—1 MW + size—contributed a more significant 842 MW while thermal generators contributed the most with 3429 MW or 77% of the total capacity. Only 141 MW of behind-the-meter demand-response (DR) systems on commercial and industrial sites have been registered on Piclo to date. This reflects only about 14% of the 1 GW of industrial DR currently active in the United Kingdom.[16]

The type of generator was not captured by Piclo in the trial data. However, many are likely to be traditional "gensets" powered by gas or diesel, supplemented by combined heat and power systems, waste-to-power systems, and wind farms.

As the United Kingdom moves toward a net zero-carbon economy, operators of fossil-fuel power gensets may need to adapt their business plan. According to scenarios created by National Grid,[17] the biggest growth areas are likely to be batteries (growing from 1.8 GW in 2019 to 19 GW by 2050), and vehicle-to-grid technologies (there are only a handful of deployments in 2019 but could grow to 10 GW by 2050).

In addition to the type of assets, Piclo observed an interesting trend where Flex Providers uploaded significant capacity from assets that were yet to be operational (Fig. 11.9). Almost half of the total capacity—48.2%—uploaded during the trial was already operational, but the remaining capacity was split between assets that were "planned" (23.3%) or "in development" (28.2%). Transparency over the best locations to build new assets is essential for flexibility investors and developers. They use Piclo Flex to quickly assess whether new sites will be applicable for nonwire solution contracts, which can be stacked on top of other flexibility contracts from National Grid and therefore can have a significant impact on the profitability of an asset.

[16] National Grid ESO. (2019). *Future energy scenarios.* National Grid ESO.

[17] National Grid ESO. (2019). *Future energy scenarios (community renewables).* National Grid ESO.

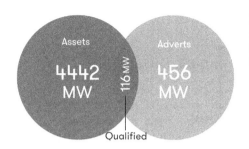

FIGURE 11.10 The capacity of assets uploaded and advertised for flexibility competitions from Piclo Flex trial, 2019. *Source: Flexibility & Visibility—Piclo White Paper (accessible online: https://piclo.energy/about)* © *Piclo 2019.*

The opportunity for assets to pass the "prequalification" stage of flexibility competitions means that those that are inplanning, or purely speculative, can gauge suitability for providing flexibility services for future needs and plan future investment accordingly.

The huge opportunity for providers of flexibility is best demonstrated by looking at the number of unmatched assets to adverts from DNOs. This demonstrates that of 4442 MW of assets uploaded, just 116 MW qualified for active competitions during the trial (Fig. 11.10). And on the other side of the transaction, 340 MW of advertised flexibility need were not matched with eligible assets during the same period.

Platforms like Piclo can play a key role in increasing the number of qualified assets in future auctions. By providing transparent access to data on available competitions, platforms can help spur investment in assets that are situated in the right locations.

As new adverts for DNO flexibility are added over time, Piclo can automatically notify owners whose fixed assets prequalify for new competitions and will expedite the matching process and support those flex providers to extract additional value efficiently from underutilized assets.

Crucially, however, the gap can also be closed by proactive flexibility providers who understand the huge potential of the platform and locational flexibility competitions. The winners will be those that seize on the opportunities that the market reveals, investing in emerging business models or spinning out new ones to capitalize on the growth in demand for flexibility services.

Piclo, for its part, is trying to expand on its existing strengths as further described in Box 11.2, excerpted from a Press Release dated 4 July 2019.[18]

11.6 Conclusion

Piclo has played a pivotal role in establishing a market for DNO flexibility in the United Kingdom. However, the market is still new and fragmented, and there are many barriers to participation by flexibility providers. The highly locational aspect of DNO flexibility requirements is challenging. Until recently there has not been a strong revenue signal for placing flexible assets in specific locations. For existing assets, it is effectively a postcode lottery.

[18] https://connect-world.com/piclo-announces-milestone-auction-result-with-uk-power-networks/

BOX 11.2

Piclo Announces Milestone Auction Result with UK Power Networks

ρ piclo®

Piclo's smart energy platform has been used at a commercial scale for the first time in UK Power Networks' recent flexibility auction. Contracts have now been signed with AMP Clean Energy, Limejump, Powervault, and Moixa to deliver 18.1 MW of flexibility.

First announced on the 15th May, UK Power Networks held the first auction for flexible power, contracting 18.2 MW within their distribution network. This auction was the first commercial use of Piclo's smart energy platform, representing a significant milestone for both Piclo and UK Power Networks. The contracts are collectively worth £450,000 but have helped defer network reinforcement costs.

Following on from this successful first auction, Piclo has secured an ongoing commercial agreement with UK Power Networks to support them deliver their future auctions. This is Piclo's second commercial agreement following the signing of Scottish and Southern Electricity Networks was announced in March this year.

As Piclo continues to rapidly grow, they are actively seeking more flexibility partners across the United Kingdom, expressions of interest from potential international clients, and software developers to help support this exciting period for the business.

Sotiris Georgioupoulos, Head of Smart Grid Development at UK Power Networks said

"Flexibility offers a wealth of opportunities for the energy resources connected to our network like wind and solar plants, but also demand side response to help us create an open, transparent and accountable new market for their services."

"All of the bids we accepted in this tender round met our robust economic criteria to ensure they will benefit our customers by offering lower costs in comparison to the traditional approach of building new assets. The UK is a world-leader in Smart Grid technology and Flexibility has a key role to play as we move towards a decarbonized, decentralized and digitized network that will offer significant benefits to our customers." ∎

As demonstrated in the Piclo Flex case study, there was a big difference in the level of need of flexibility between the six GB DNOs. The need for flexibility is heavily dependent on the context of the grid as well as historical and forecast demand usage. The value pool available to flexibility providers is also highly dependent on the location and nature of the DNO need. However, with the rollout of EVs in the future, it is generally anticipated that DNOs universally will need to procure flexibility across their networks at peak times.

Traditional behind-the-meter assets are expected to enjoy a significant role in the market for flexibility, but so too will assets that are mobile. Mobile generators and transport assets including EVs have the potential to earn revenue from their capacity to store energy. "Vehicle to grid" technology, for example, enables EVs to adopt smart-charging methods to utilize low-cost and renewable energy when it is available and earn revenue by feeding energy back into the grid to help balance the system.

Residential battery systems and prosumers have similar potential and companies that effectively manage these assets on behalf of households can use flexibility and peak-time management payments to incentivize new customers. Households that produce and store their own energy can use payments from flexibility services to plug the gap left by regular feed-in-tariffs for solar generation.

As shown in the Piclo Flex case study, the organizations that facilitate the unlocking of DG from homes across Britain have much to gain. But consumers will benefit, too, as they support the growth of renewables while improving returns on their own smart energy technology investments. Soon, a majority of homes will not just consume electricity, they will be generating, storing, and selling it too, becoming part of a wider decentralized network of clean energy providers.

Looking internationally, there is a big opportunity for DNOs and regulators to copy this successful approach adopted in the United Kingdom. The use of trading platforms can help lower barriers for entry, standardize flexibility requirements, and drive investment signals to the right locations of the grid.

If successful, the prize could be huge. Behind the meter flexibility assets from California to Canberra could be providing critical services to their local distribution network, supporting the ongoing decarbonization of energy grids without sacrificing reliability of the network and at lowest cost to bill payers.

Smart meters: the gate to behind-the-meter?

Carlo Stagnaro[1] and Simona Benedettini[2]

[1]Istituto Bruno Leoni, Milan, Italy [2]PwC Advisory, Rome, Italy

12.1 Introduction

Innovation in metering has historically been a powerful force behind electricity restructuring. In the industry's early stage, the impossibility (or excessive cost) of measuring, monitoring, and metering the real-time flow of electricity was one of the reasons that made vertical integration a practical need. By the same token, new metering technologies and digitalization were among the factors that enabled the industry reform, vertical disintegration, and competition (Kiesling, 2009). As the economic and institutional foundations of electricity systems dramatically changed since the 1980s, so did end-use meters. A first wave of innovation came with automatic meter reading (AMR), that is, the ability of the meter to collect consumption, diagnostic and status data, and transfer them to a central unit where data are processed in due course. A second wave was due to the development of advanced metering infrastructure (AMI), that is, a two-way communication channel that does not only provide frequent reading of consumption but also enables the consumer to turn into a prosumer or prosumager (Alejandro et al., 2014). The introduction of smart meters has been instrumental to open the door to a number of applications, at or behind the meter, that include (but are not limited to) retail competition, the injection into the grid of excess power generated from rooftop solar or other in situ renewable sources, real-time energy pricing, demand-response, and other forms of asset aggregation and management (Sioshansi, 2019).

This chapter is concerned with the features, the role, and the further evolution of smart meters in the context of rapid technological change and the rising interest in monitoring and managing behind-the-meter assets. Energy decentralization and distributed generation make it possible—and perhaps increasingly profitable—to switch off the grid

Behind and Beyond the Meter
DOI: https://doi.org/10.1016/B978-0-12-819951-0.00012-8

251

(Sioshansi, 2016, 2018). However, most consumers still remain connected to the grid, because going off grid is either too costly, not reliable enough, or not feasible at all. Smart meters are a crucial device for those who remain dependent on a grid for a share of their energy consumption and/or for selling excess power from their own generating equipment.

Even though not all behind-the-meter services rely on smart meters, the latter provide the precondition for most of them to actually take place. Smart meters perform three key functions:

- Provide legally valid measures of (close to) real-time energy flows.
- Allow asset aggregation and load shifting, insofar as the impact on actual energy consumption of such practices should eventually be reconciled with the meter's reading of total energy consumption at any given point of time.
- Manage energy flows to and fro the point of delivery, with particular reference to distributed generation and the provision of flexibility services.

These points hold true both in the case that smart meters can measure the individual consumption of each asset behind the meter, and if they can only take trace of total, aggregated consumption.

The balance of this chapter is organized as follows:

- Section 12.2 after the Introduction describes the features, diffusion, and trends in the adoption of smart meters, with a focus on the European Union.
- Section 12.3 explains the alternative business models under which smart meters or similar devices can be expected to spread.
- Section 12.4 asks whether—in a world of smart appliances and (potentially) smart users—there is still a need for a standardized device whose functions can be performed by other devices that are becoming ubiquitous (such as Google Home or Amazon Alexa), particularly in the context of competitive retail markets for electricity.
- Section 12.5 further explores these issues, with regard to the potentialities of the consumer's evolution in prosumer or prosumager.
- Section 12.6 summarizes and concludes.

12.2 What makes a smart meter smart?

A smart meter relies on a so-called AMI, a two-way communication system that involves both physical flows of energy and communication and data exchange between the customer (via the meter) and the utility or the network operator. Coupled with other devices (such as smart sensors, distributed control technology, and asset aggregators behind the meter) that may allow grid management and control. A smart metering system consists of four components (Uribe-Pérez, Hernández, de la Vega, & Angulo, 2016):

- a smart metering device (smart meter)
- a data gathering service (data concentrator)
- a communication system used for data flow
- a centralized management and control system (control center)

The architecture of smart metering system is not the focus of this chapter (for greater detail or for information concerning the several types of smart metering systems, see EEI, 2011). The key takeaway is that smart metering requires large investments both in equipment, software, and cybersecurity. Understanding the functionalities of smart meters, though, is relevant as long as they may complement, or promote, the developments of services behind the meter.

The European Union, which introduced a plan to achieve coverage of at least 80% of its population by 2020, identified 10 common minimum functionalities that smart meters must ensure. These can be grouped in five main categories (EC, 2014):

- consumer (provide readings directly to the consumer and/or third parties update readings *at least* every 15 minutes)
- metering operator (remote readings, two-way communications, provide frequent enough readings for grid control)
- commercial aspects (support advanced tariff systems, remote on/off control supply and/or power limitations)
- data protection
- management of distributed generation

These functionalities lay the basis for the development of behind the meter. The main reason for this is that both physical (energy) and financial (billing) transactions require a legally valid reading. Each and any measure made behind the meter should be reconciled with the total consumption measured by the meter itself. To the extent that behind-the-meter services leverage upon load shifting, demand variations (in response to price or nonprice incentives) should be certified. Although disintermediation is looming (e.g., through blockchain-based applications, see Andoni et al., 2019 and also chapter by Trbovich et al.), many utilities and possibly most regulators are still likely to rely on "official" readings for dispute settlement. Hence, while it may well be the case that behind-the-meter eventually skips the meter altogether, it is likely that for some time the meter will remain the gate to access to further services. A relevant technological, commercial, and regulatory question is *if* and *how* meters are (or can become) smart enough to accommodate these evolutions. Their ability to increase the frequency of readings, getting closer and closer to the real time, is obviously a key variable along this evolutionary path. Even more so, a major issue is whether smart meters will be able to measure the consumption from individual assets, rather than total consumption at the point of delivery.

Smart meters are being introduced because they provide a response to a number of issues concerning the upstream, but they can fertilize the development of the downstream, too. As Sioshansi argues in Chapter 1, the development of the electricity sector has been largely driven by the needs of the upstream (and, one might argue, the supply side). Quite often, regulation has been "acquired by the industry and [has been] designed and operated primarily for its benefit," to paraphrase Stigler (1971, p. 3) (see also Kiesling, 2010). Institutional, technological, and commercial innovation have progressively liberated the customer and opened the box of the downstream, also thanks to the recognition that there are both an immense opportunity for value creation *and* an active consumer/prosumer/prosumager can align her own interests with the broader interest of achieving greater sustainability. Within this context of emergence of new actors, new technologies, and new

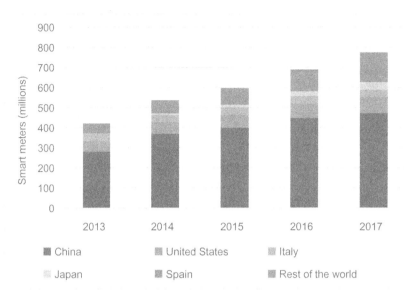

FIGURE 12.1 Global cumulative smart meter installations. Source: *Own elaboration on data from IEA. (2019).* Smart grids. Tracking clean energy report *(IEA, 2019).*

business models, smart meters occupy the peculiar position of serving both the interests of the upstream (by allowing a better management of generating assets and networks) and the downstream (by reducing transaction costs, making information available, and improving the development of behind-the-meter management).

This explains the observed and expected growth in the number of smart meters around the world (Fig. 12.1), with China making the lion's share followed by the European Union and North America. At the beginning of 2019, over 513 million smart meters had been already installed in China, accounting for 64.3% of global installations. Western Europe and North America followed, with 14.1% and 11.6% of global smart meters, respectively (Kelly & Elberg, 2019). Many of these meters are still based on the AMR technology, although second-generation meters, based on the AMI technology, are being rolled out around the world and, in some cases, are already taking over the older devices as they are ageing (as is the case of Italy, among other countries—see Stagnaro, 2019).

The growing diffusion of smart meters is a fact. The question, then, becomes, Which business models are most appropriate to take the most advantages out of the investment? How can this trend promote (or hinder) behind-the-meter businesses?

12.3 Business models for (and behind) smart meters

Why do countries install smart meters? The above-described dynamics is led by a plurality of drivers. In countries where retail competition is not allowed, such as China, investments in smart meters may respond to the need of a better coordination of decentralized assets by suppliers and/or grid operators, or even to the pursuit of unclear private interests (Lin & Purra, 2019). In other places, such as the EU and the United States, it is generally intended to simultaneously promote greater consumer empowerment and environmental goals, including energy efficiency, renewable generation, and load optimization (Accenture, 2013).

Several countries or states made the rollout of smart meters a political priority. For example, the EU set in 2012 a target of 80% of smart meters by 2020. Broadly speaking, two main approaches can be identified: rollout by distribution system operator(s) (DSOs) and rollout by suppliers. Table 12.1 illustrates the state-of-the-art situation in Europe.

As Table 12.1 shows, most EU member states do regulate metering (20 out of 27), rely on the DSOs for either implementation and ownership of smart meters (21) or meter data management (18), and finance the metering investment and operation costs entirely or largely via the network tariff (16). Likewise, in the United States smart meters are mostly installed by DSOs, which are often part of vertically integrated groups (retail competition is not always allowed for small customers in America) (Balmert & Petrov, 2010; Cooper, 2017). The experience with smart meter deployment and funding by suppliers (rather than by DSOs) has not been fully satisfactory. Most notably, the UK program incurred in cost overruns, delays and difficulties with interoperability, which is a crucial feature of smart meters in a competitive environment (CMA, 2016; NAO, 2018). Economic analysis suggests that a regulated monopoly might be the most effective landscape both for meter operation and data management, although these functions need not to be performed by the same subject and the latter might be awarded via tender (Cervigni & Larouche, 2014).

As smart meters are installed and operated by a third party, the issue of the nature, ownership, and management of data becomes relevant—especially in the light of potential developments behind the meter, which may rely on those same data (see the discussion below). A smart meter can (and does) perform two functions, which are instrumental, if not strictly necessary, for behind-the-meter: (1) it provides frequent (or even real-time) readings of the total consumption (although most of the current meters cannot measure consumption from individual assets) and (2) it makes available a (quasi) real-time load curve, allowing real-time pricing and other applications.

These features are crucial for behind-the-meter to flourish because

- Individual asset management must result in individual consumption changes that, when aggregated, match total consumption as measured by the meter. That is particularly important when behind-the-meter services produce load shifting: while alternative devices may manage smart appliances within the home in order to provide network balancing services or other valuable services, their effect must be recorded by a meter before it is actually recognized as "true." This is even more important, as assets behind the meter do not just demand but also generate and/or store, energy (see Section 12.5).
- One powerful incentive to the management of assets behind the meter comes from price incentives that—in turn—require real-time pricing. To any practical purpose it is quite hard to practice real-time pricing without a reliable, legally valid reading of real-time consumption.
- Smart meters may also perform a key function in promoting the smart management of distributed generation and the provision of flexibility services to the balancing markets.

TABLE 12.1 Smart meter deployment in the European Union.

Country	Rollout of smart metering by 2020 status	Expected diffusion rate in 2020 (%)	Metering market	Deployment strategy	Responsible party—implementation and ownership	Responsible party—access to meter data	Financing of rollout
Austria	Wide scale (80% or more)	95	Regulated	Mandatory	DSO	DSO	Network tariff + metering
Belgium	No wide scale	NA	Regulated	NA	DSO	DSO	NA
Bulgaria	NA	NA	NA	NA	NA	NA	NA
Croatia	NA	NA	NA	NA	NA	NA	NA
Cyprus	NA	NA	Regulated	NA	DSO	DSO	NA
Czech Rep.	No wide scale	1	Regulated	NA	DSO	Central hub	NA
Denmark	Wide scale (80% or more)	100	Regulated	Mandatory	DSO	Central hub	Network tariff
Estonia	Wide scale (80% or more)	100	Regulated	Mandatory	DSO	Central hub	Network tariff
Finland	Wide scale (80% or more)	100	Regulated	Mandatory	DSO	DSO	Network tariff
France	Wide scale (80% or more)	95	Regulated	Mandatory	DSO	DSO	NA
Germany	Selective rollout	23	Competitive	NA	Meter operator/DSO	Meter operator/DSO	NA
Greece	Wide scale (80% or more)	80	Regulated	Mandatory	DSO	DSO	NA
Hungary	NA	NA	NA	NA	NA	NA	NA
Italy	Wide scale (80% or more)	99	Regulated	Mandatory	DSO	DSO	Network tariff
Latvia	Selective rollout	23	Regulated	Mandatory	DSO	DSO	Network tariff + DSO resources
Lithuania	No wide scale	NA	Regulated	NA	DSO	DSO	Network tariff
Luxembourg	Wide scale (80% or more)	95	Regulated	Mandatory	DSO	DSO	Network tariff
Malta	Wide scale (80% or more)	100	Regulated	Voluntary	DSO	DSO	Network tariff
The Netherlands	Wide scale (80% or more)	100	Regulated	Mandatory with opt-out	DSO	DSO	Network tariff

Country	Rollout scale	%					
Poland	Wide scale (80% or more)	80	Regulated	Mandatory	DSO	DSO	Network tariff
Portugal	No wide scale	NA	Regulated	NA	DSO	DSO	Network tariff + DSO
Romania	Wide scale (80% or more)	80	Regulated	Mandatory	DSO	DSO	Network tariff
Slovakia	Selective rollout	23	Regulated	NA	DSO	DSO/Central hub	Network tariff + DSO
Slovenia	NA	NA	NA	NA	NA	DSO	NA
Spain	Wide scale (80% or more)	100	Regulated	Mandatory	DSO	DSO	Network tariff + SM rental
Sweden	Wide scale (80% or more)	100	Regulated	Voluntary	DSO	DSO	Network tariff + DSO resources
United Kingdom	Wide scale (80% or more)	100	Competitive	Mandatory	Supplier	Central hub	Suppliers

[a]https://ses.jrc.ec.europa.eu/smart-metering-deployment-european-union, last accessed on 12 July 2019.
From EU Commission Joint Research Center.[a]

The amount of data that a smart meter collects, and its ability to perform two-way communications, including on/off control supply and power limitations, pose an obvious issue of cybersecurity (Halim, Yussof, & Ruzli, 2018; Tweneboah-Koduah, Tsetse, Azasoo, & Endicott-Popovsky, 2018). Whoever is in charge of installing and operating smart meters, within whatever institutional framework, should be required to make sure that both data and communications are managed properly. The same applies to alternative devices that may complement, bypass, or substitute smart meters.

Another data-related issue is even more relevant, as far as behind-the-meter is concerned: who *owns* the smart meter data? What can (and cannot) be done with these data, under which limitations, and to what purposes? Customers themselves are often more concerned about the commercial use that could be made of their own data, than aware of the opportunities they themselves might exploit (DECC, 2012).

Things are rapidly changing, though, and the right of the customer to access, use, and share her data easily is ranking higher and higher as a goal of energy policy. A precondition thereof is data interoperability; another one is the deployment of user-friendly data exchange platforms. While several models are emerging and it is not obvious which one will work best, policy-makers should strike a balance between data protection and privacy, on one hand, and the possibility to actually exploit the power of data and their information content, on the other hand (ASSET, 2018; CEER, 2016a).

From that point of view, even the most stringent privacy regulations—such as the GDPR in the European Union[1]—tend to allow or even promote the use of consumption data to improve the customer's welfare, provided that she has direct access and control over data and that the latter are not used without (or outside) her consensus. Under GDPR's Article 20, the data subject "shall have the right to receive the personal data concerning him or her, which he or she has provided to a controller, in a structured, commonly used and machine-readable format and have the right to transmit those data to another controller." That implies that smart meter-generated data must be made available to the consumer/prosumer/prosumager, who in turn has a right to share them with third parties.

The same obligation is recognized in the EU's energy regulation. Under the so-called Third Energy Package, which currently in force when this chapter is being written, customers "are entitled to receive all relevant consumption data."[2] This provision has been strengthened within the process of reforming electricity market design in the European Union. A new directive, amending the Third Energy Package, has been adopted in 2019, that shall be transposed in the national legislation of all EU member states by December 31, 2020.[3] Under the new framework, "final customers are entitled to receive all relevant demand response data or data on supplied and sold electricity free of charge at least once every billing period if requested by the customer." They are "entitled to delegate to a third

---

[1] General Data Protection Regulation, Regulation (EU) 2016/679.

[2] Directive 2009/72/EC, Art.3(5).

[3] Directive (EU) 2019/944.

party the management of the installations required for their activities, including installation, operation, data handling and maintenance, without that third party being considered to be an active customer."[4]

12.4 The elephant in the smart meter's room: the customer

The rationale behind the installation of smart meters lies in the capability to collect and transfer a growing number of data. Given today's technological achievement, that is relatively easy. What makes the large cost of smart meter rollout pay off, though, is not data per se, but the use that can be made of data. This is also a reason why smart meters are a valuable subject within a book that is dedicated to what may and does happen below the meter. In fact, smart meters may well turn out to be useless—if devices behind the meter can provide better, more reliable, more granular, and legally valid information. Unfortunately, as of now only consumption as recorded by the meter can be the basis for billing, and only certified meters can provide the readings that are required to confirm that load has been shifted and devices have been turned on or off in order to comply with the orders of an aggregator. In other words, for devices and behaviors to develop behind the meter, the meter must be smart enough to (1) match and verify consumption data and (2) allow changes in the demand for physical delivery of energy to be recorded, certified, and accounted for by network operators.

While smart meters play a crucial role today, one might wonder whether they will remain as important as they are now in the future. The answer depends much on technological evolution and on whether meter operators will have enough incentives to improve their functionalities. The aggregate data from the meter is necessary for billing as well as for a certified measure of total energy flows. But demand aggregators and other actors in the behind-the-meter world are more interested in measuring power consumption/production from individual assets. One may speculate that either the meters of the future will develop the ability to measure total as well as individual flows, or they will be progressively displaced by more efficient devices—in which case, utilities and regulators will eventually have to give up the "natural" monopoly feature of the metering service, although meters will remain for some time the main source of information regarding the large bulk of customers who are mere "consumers" of energy.

Smart meters enhance small customers' participation in the market, both at the retail and (directly or indirectly) wholesale level. As Glachant (2019) argues, a few conditions are to be met thereof:

First, the wholesale time pricing has to be shared by consumption units in the very same timeframe to permit a rationale retail response. Second, the consumption devices have to be controllable and monitored within the same time frame. And then, third, ICT has to ensure fully interactive communications in two directions (from wholesale to retail and the other way around). Furthermore, rules at both electricity system operation (at distribution and transmission level) and wholesale market operation have to be adapted to welcome consumption variations as offers taken into account into the wholesale equilibrium.

[4] Directive (EU) 2019/944, Art.13(3) and Art.15(2).

Smart meters provide a response to the points 1 and 3 raised by Glachant: they allow wholesale and retail markets to share the same timeframe and provide a two-way communication system. They may not necessarily be able to control devices behind the meter directly—which is where aggregators enter into play. Yet, the relevant issue here is that aggregators or other forms or remote control would have their way paved by a legally recognized device that can measure and record consumption frequently enough.

Two issues should be explicitly dealt with in this context. The first is dynamic pricing (Dutta & Mitra, 2017; Nicolson, Fell, & Huebner, 2018). A smart meter is the gate toward dynamic pricing which, in turn, is a major driver of behind-the-meter asset aggregation. In fact, if prices cannot be designed in a cost-reflective way, the customer has little or no incentive to manage her consumption in order to provide services in the wholesale markets. For that to happen, the utility or the aggregator should keep trace of the variations in the consumption profile as compared with a counterfactual, but such variations should also be verified. Experiences with dynamic (or even real time) pricing are becoming more common around the world, with particular regard to the United States and the European Union (Hu, Kim, & Byrne, 2015; Kessels, Kraan, Karg, & Maggiore, 2016). In the EU, utilities are offering dynamic pricing in seven member states (Estonia, Finland, Sweden, Spain, The Netherlands, Denmark, and the United Kingdom), while Spain set a regulated default dynamic pricing contract. Dynamic pricing generally results in lower consumption and load shifting, although the evidence on the magnitude of this effect is nonconclusive (EC, 2019). Dynamic prices are only observed in the jurisdictions that have deregulated (or are in the process of deregulating) retail electricity prices.

A secondo issue follows. Smart meters shall pay off, and behind-the-meter aggregation may further gain, insofar as the customer understands that she may be an active part of the system and engages (directly or indirectly through applications or third parties) into the play. There is a large body of literature regarding both the drivers of customer engagement (CEER, 2016b) and the policies that may be employed to promote an active demand (Crampes & Waddams, 2017; Littlechild, 2019; Stagnaro, Amenta, Di Croce, & Lavecchia, 2018). Drawing implications from the abovementioned literature is well beyond the scope of this chapter. Moreover, there seems to be no conclusive evidence of what actually works, nor any agreed-upon textbook approach to the regulation of retail markets. Yet, retail competition may be an important condition to enhance behind-the-meter, along with other features, including fast and reliable billing and switching procedure as well as a plurality of offers and actors. All of this can hardly be achieved without an effective and efficient metering system, of which smart meters are a defining component.

12.5 The smart meter meets the prosumer

A prosumer retrieves both energy from the grid and self-produced energy from rooftop solar panels or other generating devices, while injecting into the grid the power in excess of her need. A prosumager owns a storage facility, too, that allows her to create more value from her self-generated energy and consumption behavior. More opportunities for value creation may stem from the participation in wholesale markets or peer-to-peer trading, which can be leveraged upon by technological startups as well as by more established digital platforms.[5]

The potential business models that prosumers and prosumagers may develop rely on trust-worthy and legally valid recordings of the energy flows to and from the meter. Such flows can be, and often are, recorded by other devices, provided by startups or by large digital companies. For example, several nontraditional operators have recently entered energy markets, including Google Nest in partnership with the San Francisco–based startup OhmConnect,[6] GE Solar and BlackRock,[7] and the Japanese company ENERES that is partnering with DER and AutoGrid to start the world's largest behind-the-meter virtual power plant in Japan.[8] By the same token, Amazon is partnering with traditional utilities by offering the capabilities of its Alexa-enabled devices in France,[9] Italy,[10] the United States,[11] and elsewhere. Not all of these technologies possess the capability of measuring energy flows, and none would have legal validity in doing so without obtaining adequate recognition, but their functionalities may be rapidly improved, if there is a market demand.

Nontraditional operators may either partner or compete with utilities. Devices like the above-mentioned ones have (or may develop) the capability of measuring (and managing) consumption (or production) from individual assets. These data may be used to achieve one or more of the following goals:

- making monetary savings by improving the load profile forecasts and allowing a better performance of energy suppliers in the wholesale and balancing markets;
- saving energy through a better understanding of the consumption of individual assets and/or coordinating the load request from home appliances with the production of rooftop solar;
- minimizing the environmental footprint by shifting the load request from the public network to the hours when the renewable contribution is greater and/or the carbon content of the kWh is lower;[12]
- relying on peer-to-peer energy trading to meet specific energy needs that can be easily shifted in time.

---

[5] See, for example, EEnergy Informer, June 2019; De Clercq, G. (2 August 2018). Run your dishwasher when the sun shines: Dynamic power pricing grows. *Reuters.com*.

[6] https://www.greentechmedia.com/articles/read/nest-and-ohmconnect-partner-to-bring-grid-responsive-smart-thermostats#gs.rka8vl

[7] https://www.pv-magazine.com/2019/07/18/blackrock-goes-behind-the-meter-with-ge/

[8] https://www.smart-energy.com/industry-sectors/business-finance-regulation/japan-developing-worlds-largest-behind-the-meter-der-system/

[9] https://www.edfenergy.com/smart-home/voice-controlled-energy

[10] https://up.sorgenia.it/it/quanta-energia-ho-consumato-i-clienti-sorgenia-lo-chiedono-ad-alexa

[11] https://www.directenergy.com/alexa-skills

[12] Interestingly enough, as electricity generation becomes increasingly decarbonized, energy saving is no longer necessarily correlated with carbon reduction. Under this perspective, energy efficiency policies should be redirected in order to reflect this new fact. See Campbell (2019).

These goals—which are not necessarily consistent with each other and may depend on the customer's preferences—may either be met through partnerships between traditional utilities and digital companies, or by the latter alone if and when they will enter the business of selling energy. Only time will tell whether these devices (and the underlying business models) will eventually bypass the existing meters—or these will become able to interact with such devices or individual appliances.

On top of the large digital platforms' ventures into the energy markets, smaller actors are gaining ground. Startups, smaller, more innovative utilities, and new digital platforms are increasingly entering energy markets in order to harness the vast amount of value that stands behind the meter. Different business models are emerging, too, thanks to the interaction between what Rossetto, Dos Reis, and Glachant (2019) have called "the heavy, the light, and the ghost," that is, the physical assets that are employed to generate electricity (the heavy), the digitalization of retail-size units (the light), and regulated grids (the ghost). Smart meters lie at the center of this change as well as the underlying evolutionary process, insofar as they provide the data upon which the entire system is predicated to work.

Prosumers and prosumagers—as well as any other form of aggregation involving assets behind the meter of electric vehicles—require that two elements are provided in order to orderly engage in power trades: information and communication technologies and optimization techniques (Zafar et al., 2018). These elements are a prerequisite but are by no means sufficient. While there may be alternative ways to equip prosumers and prosumagers with *information* and *connectivity*, smart meters and the connected system (hardware and software) may hardly be ignored, insofar as they respond to the needs of the grid while also potentially empowering the demand side. Again, it should be emphasized that smart meters are more important for what they *may* and for what they *do* deliver. Smart meters deliver more accurate and frequent readings that smooth, simplify, and make more reliable the procedures for billing, switching, and, in the case of prosumers or prosumagers who sell power to the grid, metering the flow of energy (with the aim of valorizing it and/or recognizing guarantees of origin and the like). At the same time, smart meters may deliver a flow of data that consumers/prosumers/prosumagers (or third parties on their behalf) can use to make a more efficient use of their assets behind the meter, be them generating- or consuming-units.

A prosumer without a smart meter can sell her excess power to the grid; if she evolves into prosumager she can also manage it more efficiently. But only when she becomes equipped with a smart meter, she can take control of her own generated power—either directly or by relying on third parties—and move up on the evolutionary ladder to get involved into wholesale markets. Smart meters may not be enough, but they are a practical requirement to allow decentralized assets to be valorized within centralized markets (Bashir, Smits, & Nelson, 2019; Bauknecht et al., 2019). Of course, the issue remains open whether smart devices will eventually bypass smart meters—or smart meters will take over these devices by providing the functionality of monitoring individual assets. However, in the short run, billing and network operations will rely on the measures from certified meters. For behind-the-meter to develop, frequent readings and two-way communications may not be necessary, but they are surely useful. To borrow again from Rossetto et al. (2019), smart meters belong to the ghost: shall they move toward the light?

12.6 Conclusion

Smart meters are not (yet?) part of the behind-the-meter universe, but they are the gate that needs to be entered in order to unveil the potential for asset aggregation. Smart meters—or, to be more precise, AMI, of which the meter is the "last mile"—set the ground for a competitive environment to develop, where the customer becomes active and, if equipped with generating or storage assets, evolves into prosumer or prosumager. There may be alternatives to smart meters to take advantage of digitalization in grid operations and in the supply of electricity, but large scale rollout of smart meters appears to date as the safest and most cost-effective way. Accordingly, smart meters are regarded as a powerful enhancer of renewable integration into the grid, commercial innovation in the supply of energy to customers, and eventually decentralized demand−response programs (Cretì & Fontini, 2019; Cooper, 2017). In a way, smart meters are one of the many evolutionary triggers that allow electricity system to become increasingly decentralized and idle capacity to be used more and more efficiently. The emergence of behind-the-meter is due to the competing forces of liberalization, digitalization, and decarbonization—each of them being a different face for the broader concept of technological change. Smart meters lie at the center of these forces, as they unleash the power of data by making them available to grid operators, professional suppliers, and customers and aggregators alike.

The importance of smart meters for the development of behind the meter aggregation depends upon two features of them: (1) the production of data and (2) the technical and legal verification of such data. While the former may be provided by alternative means (e.g., blockchain-based technologies or other smart devices), the latter will hardly be achieved outside of the regulated realm as long as the natural monopoly remains as a defining feature of power grid and inspires its regulation. Remarkably, this remains true regardless to whether smart meters are operated by the grid operator itself, or by third parties such as energy suppliers or others. What really matters is that data are recognized as valid by those who are in charge of grid operation, and that they can be legally enforced—a feature that soon or late alternative devices might eventually gain, but that is not behind the corner given the regulatory complexity thereof and the likely resistance from traditional utilities.

As soccer coach Vujadin Boskov once famously said, "penalty is when referee whistles." The same is true for electricity system and explains why the road to behind the meter starts at the meter—the smarter, the better.

References

Accenture. (2013). *Realizing the full potential of smart metering.*

Alejandro, L., Blair, C., Bloodgood, L., Khan, M., Lawless, M., Meehan, D., et al. (2014). Global market for smart electricity meters: Government policies driving strong growth. In: *Office of industries working paper, ID-037.* US International Trade Commission.

Andoni, M., Robu, V., Flynn, D., Abram, S., Geach, D., Jenkins, D., ... Peacock, A. (2019). Blockchain technology in the energy sector: A systematic review of challenges and opportunities. *Renewable and Sustainable Energy Reviews, 100,* 143−174.

ASSET. (2018). *Format and procedures for electricity (and gas) data access and exchange in Member States. Final report.*

Balmert, D., & Petrov, K. (2010). Regulatory aspects of smart metering. In: *Issue paper*. ERRA Licensing and Competition Committee.

Bashir, S., Smits, A., & Nelson, T. (2019). Service innovation and disruption in the Australian contestable retail market. In F. Sioshansi (Ed.), *Consumer, prosumer, prosumager*. London: Academic Press.

Bauknecht, D., Bracker, J., Flachsbarth, F., Heinemann, C., Seebach, D., & Vogel, M. (2019). Customer stratification and different concepts of decentralization. In F. Sioshansi (Ed.), *Consumer, prosumer, prosumager*. London: Academic Press.

Campbell, A. (2019). *Redirecting energy efficiency policies for the climate. Energy Institute blog.* UC Berkeley.

CEER. (2016a). Review of current and future data management models. In: *CEER report, C16-RMF-89-03*.

CEER. (2016b). CEER Report on commercial barriers to switching in EU retail energy markets. In: *C15-CEM-80-04*.

Cervigni, G., & Larouche, P. (2014). *Regulating smart metering in Europe: Technological, economic and legal challenges.* CERRE.

CMA. (2016). *Energy market investigation. Final report.*

Cooper, A. (2017). *Electric company smart meter deployments: Foundation for a smart grid.* The Edison Foundation – Institute for Electricity Innovation.

Crampes, C., & Waddams, C. (2017). *Empowering electricity consumers in retail and wholesale markets.* Centre on Regulation in Europe.

Cretì, A., & Fontini, F. (2019). *Economics of electricity.* Cambridge: Cambridge University Press.

DECC. (2012). *Smart metering data access and privacy.* Undertaken by Navigator.

Dutta, G., & Mitra, K. (2017). A literature review on dynamic pricing of electricity. *Journal of the Operational Research Society, 68*(10), 1131–1145.

EC. (2014). Cost-benefit analyses & state of play of smart metering deployment in EU27. In: *SWD(2014) 189 final*.

EC. (2019). Energy prices and costs in Europe. In: *SWD(2019) 1 final*.

EEI. (2011). Smart meters and smart meter systems: A metering industry perspective. In: *EEI-AEIC-UTC white paper*.

Glachant, J.-M. (2019). New business models in the electricity sector. In: *EUI working paper, RSCAS 2019/44*. European University Institute.

Halim, F., Yussof, S., & Ruzli, M. E. (2018). Cyber security issues in smart meters and their solutions. *International Journal of Computer Science and Network Security, 18*(3), 99–109.

Hu, Z., Kim, J.-h, & Byrne, J. (2015). Review of dynamic pricing programs in the U.S. and Europe: Status quo and policy recommendations. *Renewable and Sustainable Energy Reviews, 42*, 743–751.

IEA. (2019). *Smart grids. Tracking clean energy report.*

Kelly, M., & Elberg, R. (2019). *Global AMI tracker 2Q19*. Navigant Research.

Kessels, K., Kraan, C., Karg, L., & Maggiore, S. (2016). Fostering residential demand response through dynamic pricing schemes: A behavioural review of smart grid pilots in Europe. *Sustainability, 8*(9), 929–951.

Kiesling, L. L. (2009). *Deregulation, innovation and market liberalization.* London: Routledge.

Kiesling, L. L. (2010). The knowledge problem, learning, and regulation: How regulation affects technological change in the electric power industry. *Studies in Emergent Order, 3*, 149–171.

Lin, K.-C., & Purra, M. M. (2019). Transforming China's electricity sector: Politics of institutional change and regulation. *Energy Policy, 124*, 401–410.

Littlechild, S.C. (2019). *Replacing the tariff caps and protecting vulnerable customers by harnessing the competitive process.* University of Cambridge – Energy Policy Research Group.

NAO. (2018). Rolling out smart meters. In: *Report by the Comptroller and Auditor General, HC 1680*.

Nicolson, M. L., Fell, M. J., & Huebner, G. M. (2018). Consumer demand for time of use electricity tariffs: A systematized review of the empirical evidence. *Renewable and Sustainable Energy Reviews, 97*, 276–289.

Rossetto, N., Dos Reis, P.C., & Glachant, J.-M. (2019). New business models in electricity: The heavy, the light, and the ghost. In: *Policy brief, 2019/08*. European University Institute.

Sioshansi, F. (Ed.), (2016). *The future of utilities: Utilities of the future.* Atlanta, GA: Elsevier.

Sioshansi, F. (Ed.), (2018). *Innovation and disruption at the grid's edge.* Atlanta, GA: Elsevier.

Sioshansi, F. (Ed.), (2019). *Consumer, prosumer, prosumager.* London: Academic Press.

Stagnaro, C. (2019). Second-generation smart meter roll-out in Italy: A cost-benefit analysis. In: *Paper presented at the Power summit 2019 conference.* Held in Florence on 20–21 May 2019.

Stagnaro, C., Amenta, C., Di Croce, G., & Lavecchia, L. (2018). Managing the liberalization of Italy's retail electricity market: A policy proposal. In: *EUI Working papers, RSCAS 2018/45*. European University Institute.

Stigler, G. J. (1971). The theory of economic regulation. *The Bell Journal of Economics and Management*, 2(1), 3–21.

Tweneboah-Koduah, S., Tsetse, A. K., Azasoo, J., & Endicott-Popovsky, B. (2018). Evaluation of cybersecurity threats on smart metering system. In S. Latifi (Ed.), *Information technology — new generations. Advances in intelligent systems and computing* (pp. 199–207). New York: Springer.

Uribe-Pérez, N., Hernández, L., de la Vega, D., & Angulo, I. (2016). State of the art and trends review of smart metering in electricity grids. *Applied Sciences*, 6(3), 68.

Zafar, R., Mahmood, A., Razzaq, S., Ali, W., Naeem, U., & Shehzad, K. (2018). Prosumer based energy management and sharing in smart grid. *Renewable and Sustainable Energy Reviews*, 82(1), 1675–1684.

Further reading

IEA. (2017). *Market report series. Energy efficiency 2017*.

D3A energy exchange for a transactive grid

Ana Trbovich[1], Sarah Hambridge[1], Dirk van den Biggelaar[1], Ewald Hesse[1] and Fereidoon Sioshansi[2]

[1]Grid Singularity, Berlin, Germany [2]Menlo Energy Economics, San Francisco, CA, United States

13.1 Introduction

As devices in homes and offices acquire digital identity and connectivity that enable analytics and automated transactions based on predetermined preferences, opportunities for peer-to-peer (P2P) transactions among consumers, prosumers and prosumagers and/or their agents, intermediaries and aggregators multiply. In such a future, devising how billions of energy market actors will be able to transact in a way that is cost and time efficient, secure, and trusted is a formidable undertaking.

Blockchain technology offers the promise to enable the prospect of managing multitudes of transactions in the energy space without an intermediary or a central clearinghouse and in a way that gives all market actors an equal opportunity, for instance, to source flexibility. A frequently cited example is a solar generation on rooftop selling its surplus to a neighbor with an empty electric vehicle (EV) battery. Currently such P2P transactions are rare mostly because regulation does not allow customers to transact with each other directly and partly because, until now, we did not have effective means to trace the trading from source to sink and settle in an efficient and scalable manner.

Forecasts suggest that global blockchain technology revenues will experience massive growth in the coming years, with the market expected to exceed $23.3 billion by 2023.[1] This explains the interest and the rush to develop practical applications that are quickly scalable and will address pressing needs such as charging of millions of EVs as they move

---

[1] *Statista.* (2019). Available from <https://www.statista.com/statistics/647231/worldwide-blockchain-technology-market-size/>.

from one location to another, charging and potentially discharging as they go. Currently, the settlement process for such an application is fairly taxing. Other useful applications include demand response and improved management of distributed energy resources (DERs) or trading of carbon certificates in a market with an emissions trading scheme.

An organization developing the critical core operating framework to accelerate the commercial application of blockchain-based applications for the energy industry is the Energy Web Foundation (EWF), assembling over 100 energy and blockchain affiliates to date.[2] The EWF ecosystem comprises both large global corporates and startups innovating in this rapidly growing market segment.

In June 2019, EWF launched the first public, open source, energy enterprise blockchain, owned and managed by the *community* rather than one organization. Several EWF affiliates have deployed commercial blockchain-based applications on the Energy Web Chain, while many are testing and developing additional decentralized applications or dApps.

This chapter explores the recent developments in energy innovation based on the nascent blockchain technology and examines many of its purported benefits and challenges. In particular the chapter examines the D3A application, developed by Grid Singularity as an open source, customized energy exchange, which is currently available as a web-based digital grid market simulation.

The balance of the chapter is organized as follows:

- Section 13.2 provides a primer on blockchain technology, including its promise and challenges, specifically focusing on the electric power sector.
- Section 13.3 introduces D3A, an open source energy exchange engine, enabling a future transactive grid—from simulation to deployment, followed by the chapter's conclusions.

13.2 A primer on blockchain technology: the promise and the challenges

The rise of Bitcoin and the emergence of crypto-currency or token economy[3] in recent years have triggered excitement and heightened interest in the potential applications of blockchain technology in a range of industries, including energy. Considering the concurrent energy sector digitalization endeavors, one can plausibly imagine a future where virtually all consumers have not just smart meters, but also smart connected devices behind-the-meter which can be individually or collectively monitored and remotely managed. Moreover, as extensively covered in other chapters in this volume, the technology will enable engaged consumers, prosumers, and prosumagers, most likely assisted by intermediaries or aggregators, to interact or trade among themselves in a way that is not recognized or allowed by current regulation.

---

[2] The Energy Web Chain White Paper is available at https://energyweb.org/reports/the-energy-web-chain/.

[3] See, for instance, Voshmgir, S. (2019). *Token economy: How blockchains and smart contracts revolutionize the economy.* Berlin: BlockchainHub Berlin.

In such a future, all stakeholders in the energy community—be it prosumers with solar photovoltaic installations (PVs), prosumagers with storage and/or EVs, or intermediaries, including those with smart software and platforms who manage aggregated portfolios of loads, generation, and storage—may wish to engage in direct transactions with one or multiple energy actors and communities. For example, a prosumer may wish to sell the excess generation from rooftop solar panels to another member of the energy community, perhaps an EV owner.

The two parties in such a transaction may wish to trade electrons at times and prices they deem appropriate, not necessarily following the prevailing regulated tariffs. Since the numbers of such transactions could be substantial, each potentially using a price that differs from others, the traditional means of tracing the amount, location, and price to reach settlements will not be able to handle the volume of transactions. The legacy accounting and back-office methods are likely to be highly restrictive in terms of types and level of services offered. Indeed, their limitations in managing an increasing volume of DERs, compounded by smart devices, have already become apparent, leading many energy experts to seek local energy management solutions.[4]

Blockchain technology promises to solve the increasingly complex problem of managing a distributed energy market. Blockchain's main attraction is that it can facilitate multiple transactions among a large number of agents in a secure and trusted fashion. It is a decentralized software platform that does not rely on a central clearinghouse, such as a bank, a utility or other intermediary. As a result, it is an agile solution for business models in value chain management and automation, including new models based on P2P transactions.[5]

The blockchain's principle current technical challenge lies in its limitations to handle large volumes of transactions in real time, which is reflected in the transaction cost and speed. There are, however, several significant initiatives under way, developing scaling solutions that are likely to resolve this limitation, with major progress expected in the near future.[6] The mechanism to manage the cost of transactions is already available, and it is particularly applicable on public networks that use proof-of-authority mechanism, relying on a decentralized network of known legal entities rather than energy intensive machine computations to validate transactions.[7]

---

[4] See, for instance, Li, Z., Shahidehpour, M., & Liu, X. (2018). Cyber-secure decentralized energy management for IoT-enabled active distribution networks. *Journal of Modern Power Systems and Clean Energy*, 6(5), 900–917. <https://doi.org/10.1007/s40565-018-0425-1>; Ahsan, U, & Bais, A. (2017). Distributed big data management in smart grid. In: *Wireless optical communication conference (WOCC) 2017* (pp. 1–6). IEEE.

[5] For a review of blockchain technology application in industry, see Morabito, V. (2017). *Business innovation through blockchain; the B3 perspective*. Springer International; Swan, M. (2015). *Blockchain: Blueprint for a new economy*. O'Reilly Media Inc.

[6] See for example, the Polkadot Network, https://polkadot.network/technology/; for a broader overview of this issue, see the Blockchain Innovation in Europe. (2018). *European Union blockchain observatory & forum report*. Blockchain Innovation in Europe. Available from <https://www.eublockchainforum.eu/sites/default/files/reports/20180727_report_innovation_in_europe_light.pdf>.

[7] Hartnett, S. (2019). *How to manage transaction costs on public blockchains; lessons from Ethereum and the Energy Web Chain*. Energy Web Foundation Blog. Available from <https://energyweb.org/2019/04/01/how-to-manage-transaction-costs-on-public-blockchains/>.

Since the first analysis published by the German Energy Agency DENA in 2016,[8] the scope of research investigating the applications of blockchain technology in the energy sector has been rapidly expanding. Amongst the most comprehensive recent surveys of this nascent technology is an article by Adoni et al. titled Blockchain technology in the energy sector: A systematic review of challenges and opportunities, which appeared in the February 2019 issue of Renewable and Sustainable Energy Reviews.[9] After examining 140 energy blockchain projects and startups, the authors concluded that blockchain can

> "... benefit energy system operations, markets and consumers" because it offers "disintermediation, transparency and tamper-proof transactions, but most importantly [...] novel solutions for empowering consumers and small renewable generators to play a more active role in the energy market and monetize their assets."

Others have also identified a number of early trials for blockchain technology, including implementation of several small-scale demonstration projects.[10]

The Adoni et al. article and others describe the genesis of the blockchain and its rapid evolution in the past few years. In addition to identifying applications with significant potential, researchers also identify many hurdles that remain to be resolved. In addition to the technical challenges, the most perplexing question concerns regulatory compliance. Shipworth et al., for example, discuss a wide scope of regulatory challenges,[11] extending from observing the more general data access and protection policies, to considering changing legacy system laws regulating energy trading.

In their extensive review, Adoni et al. (2019) identify the following areas as likely candidates for practical *near-term* applications in the energy sector:

- billing
- sales and marketing
- trading and markets
- automation
- smart grid applications and data transfer
- grid management
- security and identity management
- sharing resources
- competition
- transparency

These are general categories, with multiple applications in each area, many of which are described in the accompanying chapters in this volume, including aggregation and

---

[8] Burger, C., Kuhlmann, A., Richard, P., & Weinmann, J. (2016). *Blockchain in the energy transition a survey among decision-makers in the German energy industry*. DENA. Available from <https://www.dena.de/fileadmin/dena/Dokumente/Meldungen/dena_ESMT_Studie_blockchain_englisch.pdf>.

[9] Article may be found at https://www.sciencedirect.com/science/article/pii/S1364032118307184.

[10] GIZ and Florence School of Regulation. (2019). *Blockchain meets energy: Digital solutions for a decentralized and decarbonized sector*, GIZ and Florence School of Regulation.

[11] Shipworth, et al. (2019). In F. Sioshansi (Ed.), *Consumer, prosumer, prosumager*. Academic Press.

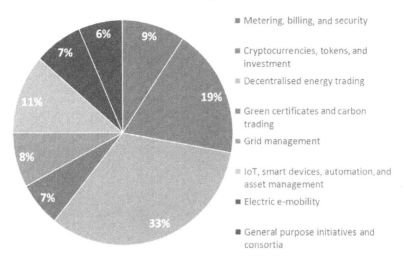

FIGURE 13.1   Blockchain use case classification. Source: *Adoni, et al. (2019). Blockchain technology in the energy sector: A systematic review of challenges and opportunities.* Renewable and Sustainable Energy Review.

optimization of behind-the-meter assets, P2P power trading, virtual power plants, management of EV charging networks, energy communities, and so on. In their survey paper, Adoni et al. provide a breakdown of the categories of applications they found in their research of the field shown in Fig. 13.1.

The debate in the energy blockchain arena is evolving rapidly, moving from the initial awareness of blockchain technology benefits to selecting the most practical near-term applications and the timeline for commercial deployment. Given the growing body of literature on blockchain technology, this chapter will focus on the novel technology's most auspicious applications in facilitating P2P energy trading.

In its second annual survey of energy blockchain startups released at the Event Horizon, energy blockchain's annual summit in June 2019 in Berlin, P2P trading was highlighted as the most popular industry application among the startups followed by Internet-of-Things and security management as illustrated in Fig. 13.2.[12]

Europe is currently the dominant location for energy blockchain companies hosting 24 of 40 startups featured in the report, with a strong presence in Germany, Switzerland, and Spain as shown in Fig. 13.3.[13]

While use cases from these reports are indicative of early development stage applications, only the future will tell which categories will be successfully implemented and eventually grow to become dominant in the years ahead.

Renewable energy certification (REC) applications were first to reach the market. The commercialization of these first market applications has been catalyzed by the creation of

[12] *Event horizon energy blockchain startups who-is-who.* (2019). Available from <https://eventhorizonsummit. com/data/uploads/2019/06/EnergyBlockchainStartupsReport_EventHorizon2019.pdf>.

[13] *Event horizon energy blockchain startups who-is-who.* (2019). Available from <https://eventhorizonsummit. com/data/uploads/2019/06/EnergyBlockchainStartupsReport_EventHorizon2019.pdf>.

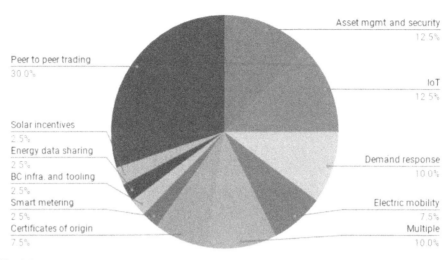

FIGURE 13.2   Energy blockchain startups area of operation. Source: *Event horizon energy blockchain startups who-is-who 2019.*

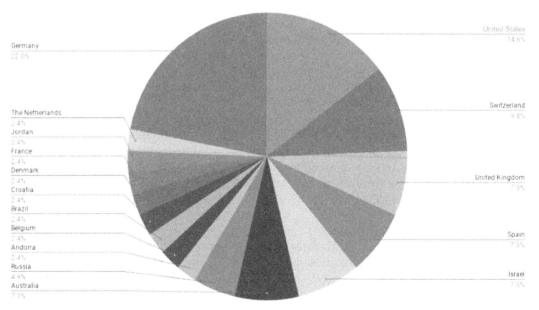

FIGURE 13.3   Energy blockchain startups location. Source: *Event horizon energy blockchain startups who-is-who 2019.*

a shared blockchain technology platform with enhanced functionality for energy industry applications, provided by the EWF.[14] Most energy industry blockchain applications plan to use this platform as noted in the Event Horizon report cited above.[15] And while the REC applications were the first to reach the market, the most transformative applications are likely to be in the area of P2P trading.[16] The next section describes the D3A, an open source energy exchange engine[17].

13.3 D3A energy exchange engine—from simulation to deployment

Since the first successful demonstration of the technology in the Brooklyn Microgrid pilot of a neighborhood energy trading platform and Grid Singularity's research on energy blockchain use cases with a live demonstration of a direct smart meter payment at the MIT Media Lab in February 2016,[18] P2P energy projects have proliferated globally.

Countries like the United Kingdom and Austria have initiated so-called *regulatory sandboxes* to examine the practical implications of blockchain-enabled energy trading,[19] with a particularly strong encouragement provided to energy-related blockchain development in Australia and Asia.[20] Yet, while most of the early P2P applications have opted for a closed-source approach, Grid Singularity, a company that cofounded EWF to accelerate sector development by streamlining and enhancing the underlying operating environment, prefers an open source, modular energy exchange development via D3A.

The D3A is an open source, energy exchange engine that enables its users to model, simulate, and deploy an energy exchange in a local community either as a decentralized exchange or in a centralized fashion. The European Union's Regulation on wholesale energy markets integrity and transparency defines an energy exchange as

---

[14] Deign, S. (June 20, 2019). The energy sector gets its first custom-built blockchain. *Green Tech Media*. Available from <https://www.greentechmedia.com/articles/read/the-energy-sector-gets-its-first-custom-built-blockchain?
utm_source = google&utm_medium = organic&utm_campaign = google_news#gs.r8dj1a>

[15] *Event horizon energy blockchain startups who-is-who*. (2019). Available from <https://eventhorizonsummit.com/data/uploads/2019/06/EnergyBlockchainStartupsReport_EventHorizon2019.pdf>.

[16] For a review of energy blockchain applications in development, see https://energyweb.org/dapps/.

[17] As D3A is still under development, the information contained herein may also be modified with time, with continuous updates available in the D3A wiki, accessible from the d3a.io home page.

[18] Lacey, S. (February 2016). The energy blockchain: How Bitcoin could be a catalyst for the distributed grid. *Green Tech Media*. Available from <https://www.greentechmedia.com/articles/read/the-energy-blockchain-could-bitcoin-be-a-catalyst-for-the-distributed-grid#gs.r9uyqc>.

[19] *Peer-to-peer trading, renewables and blockchain: What's inside Ofgem's 'Regulatory Sandbox'*. (2017). Available from <https://smartgrids.no/peer-to-peer-trading-renewables-and-blockchain-whats-inside-ofgems-regulatory-sandbox//>.

[20] https://asia.blockchain2energy.com/news-updates/2018/10/16/expert-interview-vinod-tiwari

... a multilateral system operated and/or managed by a market operator, which brings together or facilitates the bringing together of multiple third-party buying and selling interests in wholesale energy products — in the system and in accordance with its non-discretionary rules — in a way that results in a contract, in respect of the wholesale energy products admitted to trading under its rules and/or systems.[21]

Depending on the application, the D3A exchange can be operated by a single operator, a group of operators or be completely decentralized. In case it is configured as a decentralized exchange, it could be based on smart contracts, which contain the market logic required to match or clear trades. This option eliminates conflict of interest in that all market participants enjoy the same market access. Bids and offers are supplied to the market based on device trading preferences and matched or cleared according to the smart contract, which could run on a decentralized blockchain-based platform, specifically the Energy Web Chain.

If the D3A is deployed to facilitate a local distributed energy exchange, the traditional roles of the distribution system operator (DSO), which manages the connection to the power grid, and the utility, as a provider of energy, would continue to be required to integrate the local energy market[22] with the wider grid network.

The one important differentiation is that a utility would no longer be the only market actor with which a household exchanges energy, but one of many. In a local energy market or community, households can trade both with neighboring households and the utility, rather than exclusively with the utility. In addition to deriving benefits from local trade, the community is also furnished with an efficient platform to offer energy services to the outside grid. Hence, the local community becomes a grid-edge source of flexibility to decrease stress on the wider distribution grid, as discussed by Mendes et al.[23]

For example, neighborhoods with large capacities of flexibility assets such as EVs, energy storage devices, or flexible loads can be paid to provide their capacity outside of the community to another community. If a neighboring community has too much solar production and not enough consumption, for example, the D3A local community can consume or store the excess generation and, if stored, sell it either back to the community or use it locally at another time. The DSO benefits from a D3A exchange as well, by opting to participate in the local community market to source flexibilities in order to manage congestion when required. Johnston and Sioshansi cover similar examples of trading flexibility on the distribution network in this volume.

The role of the D3A software in facilitating local energy community (LEC) objectives to reach cost efficiency and self-sufficiency based on renewable energy resources with

[21] Regulation No 1227/2011 of the European Parliament and of the Council of 25 October 2011 on wholesale energy market integrity and transparency (REMIT), available at https://www.emissions-euets.com/remitrecordswholesaleenergymarkettransactions.

[22] For more on local energy markets, see Interreg Europe. (2018). *A policy brief from the policy learning platform on low-carbon economy.* Available from <https://www.interregeurope.eu/fileadmin/user_upload/plp_uploads/policy_briefs/2018-08-30_Policy_brief_Renewable_Energy_Communities_PB_TO4_final.pdf>.

[23] Mendes, G., Nylund, J., Annala, S., Honkapuro, S., Kilkki, O., & Segerstam, J. (2018). Local energy markets: Opportunities, benefits, and barriers. In: *Paper No. 0272, CIRED Workshop*, Ljubljana. Available from <http://www.cired.net/publications/workshop2018/pdfs/Submission%200272%20-%20Paper%20(ID-21042).pdf>.

optimal integration in the wider energy system is termed "Community-as-a-Service." D3A can also be used in other use cases. Exemplary use-cases to which D3A provides a solution include the following:

- microgrid management such as in "Community-as-a-Service" noted above;
- decentralized aggregation;
- energy access; and
- forecasting tool to simulate effects of different energy regulation and/or incentive programs.

By opting to operate the D3A smart contracts on a blockchain platform, the D3A could facilitate settlement of transactions in hierarchies without a centralized controller, from the bottom up. This means that energy trades happen at the lowest layer first, such as inside a home, and then have the opportunity to buy or sell at the next layer up, such as between homes on a street.

These trades are stored on a public ledger, allowing for modular scaling of grids and plug and play interoperability in compliance with the relevant legislation. This means that different grid layers, organized by markets, can seamlessly connect and trade with each other in the D3A structure. Hence, the D3A allows energy devices of arbitrary scale to trade with their peers on a scalable market platform resulting in local energy management and grid balancing.

The D3A exchange engine is available as an open source software under a General Public License (GPL GNU v.3) that allows free access and use as long as the final product is also open source, with any modifications requiring permission and any closed-source product development requiring a license.[24] In turn, the D3A user interface was created to allow users without programming skills to interface with the D3A exchange engine through a user-friendly web application, available as a beta version at d3a.io. Energy companies and consumer groups can use the D3A to

- model and simulate a market, thereby facilitating investment and other strategic business decisions;
- deploy the D3A exchange engine to efficiently operate a decentralized and distributed smart grid.

Another important feature of the D3A is that it allows the grid to be organized into areas to mimic the physical grid setup. For example, household devices can be initially grouped into a household area, which are in turn grouped into higher level areas such as neighborhoods, districts, or regions. Since the grid is already organized by different voltage levels, the hierarchies of areas in the D3A reflect the different voltage levels of the modeled grid.

Similarly, markets can be established in each area, or node, in the hierarchical tree. Hence respective grid costs can be calculated in each market. This type of structure enables grid operators to source flexibility for the targeted congestion management or frequency balancing.

---

[24] The D3A source code and more information about the GPL v.3 license is available at the Grid Singularity GitHub Repository, https://github.com/gridsingularity/d3a.

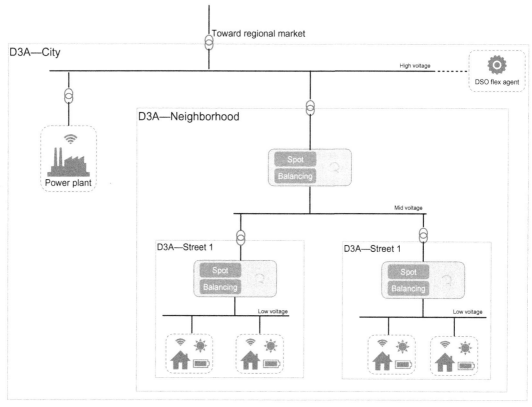

FIGURE 13.4 The D3A hierarchical grid structure shows how markets can be organized and stacked according to the grid voltage levels. Source: *Grid Singularity.*

Market participants are denoted by agents, which represent devices or act virtually to place bids and offers between markets as illustrated in Fig. 13.4, which provides an example of a grid configuration. In this example, each area, such as a street or a neighborhood, contains device agents, which represent energy assets, or other areas, which are subareas. Conventionally, areas represent different voltage levels of the grid. In each area, a market is created. The two street markets in Fig. 13.4 interact through a neighborhood area market, which is connected to a city. A utility is a participant in the city area market. A DSO is present to buy flexibility for its congestion management program. This simple illustration shows how an actual city block or entire city can be modeled by using D3A in a hierarchical way.

Similarly, Fig. 13.5 shows a configured grid example as it may be visualized using the D3A interface, with circles configured by a user to represent areas, and diamonds to represent devices.

In this example, markets are represented as circles and devices as diamonds. Devices trade with each other and with other markets inside a parent market. In this way energy trading can be organized into groups or communities by registering devices in their

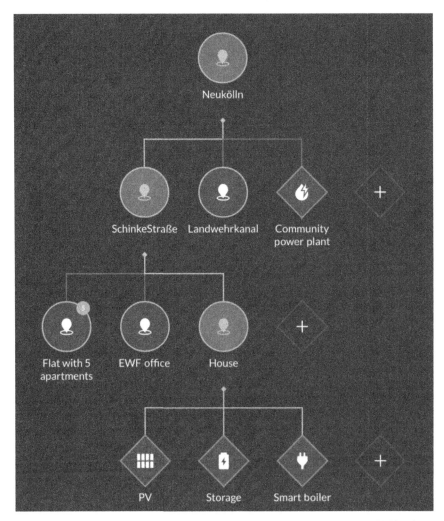

FIGURE 13.5 An example grid configuration using the D3A user interface. Source: *Grid Singularity (d3a.io).*

allowed markets. These markets are then stacked to allow intra-market trading across the entire grid infrastructure, while prioritizing trade in the bottom layer of the markets first.

As these simple examples illustrate, the D3A design considers the following requirements:

- support for the physical grid;
- open market access including scalability and interoperability; and
- regulatory compliance.

These requirements are currently being met by various market actors. No single market actor is able to fulfill all three requirements, but the D3A in its final form will strive to

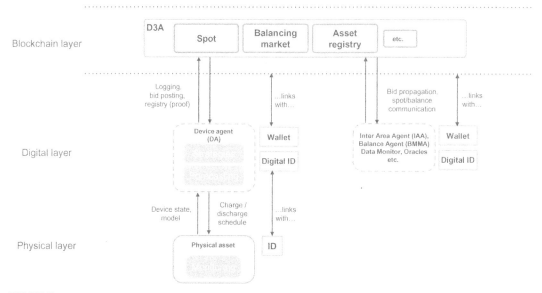

FIGURE 13.6 The D3A architecture connects physical devices to blockchain-enabled energy markets through a digital ID. Source: *Grid Singularity.*

create customizable exchanges in which the physical grid is modeled and maintained, markets are open, scalable, and interoperable, and transactions are compliant with the prevailing regulation. In some cases, compliance with regulation could even be automated by integrating regulatory requirements in the exchange smart contracts.

Broadly speaking, the D3A architecture consists of three layers, as shown in Fig. 13.6:

- a physical layer at the bottom;
- a digital layer in the middle; and
- a blockchain layer at the top.

At the physical layer, the device state of an energy asset is monitored by its device agent. The device agent consists of software, which runs a forecasting module and a price strategy that creates bids and offers for each market interval. The agent communicates its bids or offers to the local D3A market inside the blockchain layer at the top, where bids and offers can match in the spot or balancing markets. While device agents are linked to physical assets, nonphysical agents serve to propagate bids and offers, or to buy balancing reserves.

As schematically shown, the D3A architecture connects physical devices, at the bottom, to the higher layers by first linking physical assets to a digital ID. This connects the physical layer of a device to the digital layer where it can be represented by a device agent. The device agent then interacts with energy markets in the blockchain layer as it supplies offers and bids into the markets. As trades are scheduled in the D3A spot and balancing markets, the device agent communicates the trade plan back down to the physical devices.

In the D3A exchange, energy prices are established by bids and offers, which are issued by the trading strategies of participating energy devices. A trading strategy defines either the willingness to pay or willingness to sell of a certain amount of energy, indicating to the market the price at which the device would accept a trade at a certain time.

The users can, to a certain extent, determine which devices can do what, when or at what price. For example, the user can designate a device as critical, meaning it must run at all times and at any price. Other devices, however, may run only when prices fall/rise below/above a certain threshold.

For instance, consider typical appliances inside a house. Not all devices need to be on at all times. Currently, most consumers are passive price takers and their devices generally do not adjust their demand or pattern of consumption in response to high local energy prices, congestion on the network or periods of high greenhouse gas emissions. They can, however, benefit from lower prices, for example, during sunny or windy periods when renewable generation is plentiful. Or they can avoid periods where emissions are high. Such flexibility, if automated, aggregated, and optimized, can make the entire network to operate more efficiently, at lower costs and with lower emissions.

On the other hand, as already mentioned, some devices may be critical, in which case the user can designate them as price taking load in which case they would continue to operate even when prices spike.

The key point, however, is that many nonessential, and thus flexible, loads can be adjusted, rescheduled, postponed, or curtailed. As noted previously, a smart boiler can reschedule its heating to an earlier or later period, provided the water tank is sufficiently insulated. This flexibility margin creates significant space to trade strategically, aiming for the best price, lowering the customers' energy bills while helping the network run more efficiently.

As noted in other chapters in this volume, what is required is built-in intelligence that sends signals to various devices and records their response without any human interaction. All this can be preprogramed, for example, by indicating that the hot water tank can be heated when prices fall below a given level or the heat pump stops running when prices rise above a given level, or the batteries in the EV can be charged—or potentially discharged—at preset prices. D3A aims to make it easy to allow these types of interactions or trading.

Fig. 13.7 depicts a LEC deploying the D3A exchange and its DSO connection point to the grid. It illustrates how the homes inside of a community can trade with each other while also trading with the utility through an aggregate connection in their local market to the utility.

As illustrated, the energy exchange engine provides a trading platform or market for the local community where individual households can connect and trade amongst each other. The community maintains its connection to the grid, and the D3A exchange engine allows trades to be settled between the community and the utility.

When following basic economic reasoning, in wholesale electricity markets energy is purchased first from the least expensive power source using the merit order up to the most expensive power source. A similar concept can be used in a local market as well. In a local market, local producers are in competition with each other and the utility who sells at a price that is known by the community. Considering grid-parity of solar panels, it is

DSO connection point

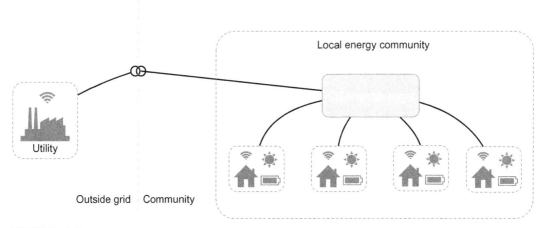

FIGURE 13.7   Grid layout of a LEC deploying a D3A energy exchange engine. *LEC*, Local energy community.
Source: *Grid Singularity.*

assumed that the levelized cost of solar energy is lower than the price of energy imported from the utility.

The levelized cost of energy (LCOE) is the minimum price for which a device should sell energy to break even within the predicted lifespan of the device.[25] To be competitive, local producers will never set their prices lower than their own LCOE or higher than the prices offered by the utility. This creates internal competition among local producers, which can drive down the prices of locally produced energy when there are many local energy sources, and vice versa.

This means that solar assets, for example, can sell energy for prices below the utility or grid flat rate, creating value for other residents in the community who can buy solar energy and also save on their energy bills. In many cases, the feed-in tariff or the rate that the utility would buy energy from solar producers is much lower than the flat consumption rate, allowing the solar producers to make more income by selling locally than to the utility. Such developments, which can be facilitated by implementing P2P trading, are also explored by Schittekatte as well as Robinson in this volume, among others.

Setting aside the equity and regulatory issues aside, however, it is exactly these dynamics that provide guidance to flexible devices in the community in shifting their demand. These devices will attempt to acquire energy when prices are low. In a local market, where inflexible buyers only passively benefit from an occasional drop in prices below the utility price, flexible devices will actively try to reschedule their demand toward periods with high local energy availability, thereby reducing the energy mismatch of the community.

This is yet another example of how the D3A exchange engine can bring lower prices and more competition to both wholesale and retail markets while incentivizing local

[25] For more, see Sayigh, A. (Ed.). (2012). *Comprehensive renewable energy* (p. 37). Amsterdam: Elsevier, Ltd.

energy management, balancing, and congestion relief on the distribution network. These positive outcomes reduce the burden of grid operators, provide better prices for consumers and homeowners, and increase the uptake of variable renewable sources by allowing the market to balance them.

In general, when aiming to maximize revenue, the price is initially set high, and if the offer is not accepted, the price is lowered. The process is repeated until an offer is accepted, or until the price is lowered below the set minimum sale threshold. For example, a PV would start offering its energy at the market maker rate or flat rate of the utility. A customer might buy the energy at that price or a cent below. If, however, there are no buyers in the market, the PV would start lowering its offer. Each time the PV lowers its offer, there is an opportunity for a buyer to accept it. The PV would lower its offer until it reaches its calculated LCOE, which is the lowest value it can sell and break even on investment costs.

Certainly, the PV might choose to sell lower than its LCOE as opposed to not selling at all. These parameters, such as the initial selling price and the rate at which a price is decreased, can be determined using a simple methodology, or according to more sophisticated models, which, for example, use forecast weather conditions to predict market prices. The example given is for a pay-as-offer market, but other market types such as pay-as-clear and pay-as-bid are also available when using the D3A software.

Initial pilots conducted by the Grid Singularity, including operating simulations of aggregate data provided by the Groene Mient LEC,[26] result in clear benefits to D3A implementation. Interestingly, in Chapter 14 of this volume, De Clercq et al. also advocate "dynamic allocation," albeit suggest that a shared energy resource such as a communal battery be operated by the utility that would share the benefits with the community. As noted above, the D3A could be implemented by a single operator such as a utility, but it could also be applied as a decentralized energy exchange, enabling the same high level of self-sufficiency but with the additional benefits of transparency.

In summary, a decentralized energy exchange gives devices and households control over their energy preferences and therefore their bids and offers, which directly determine the cost of energy in the community. This process enables more collaborative and transparent billing compared to a centralized controller, which optimizes the community as a single entity.

The more flexible the community is, both in terms of consumption preferences and the energy resources, the more value is added by the D3A. Significant improvements can be observed even for inflexible energy communities, which will be proved in future investigations of Community as a Service D3A use case.

The D3A exchange engine is a shared, mid-layer platform, intended to engage technology providers and other parties to integrate software and hardware solutions to cocreate the smart-grid of the future. A notable example includes smart device strategies described above. While the D3A already bolsters some default strategies, more rigorous strategies provided by third parties specializing in this field will further enhance its functionality. Users will have the option to test and compare diverse device strategies, optimizing deployment.

---

[26] *Groene Mient Project Internet Portal.* <http://www.groenemient.nl/project/>.

Moreover, in the D3A simulation environment, a power flow analysis can provide insight on heat losses, congestion, and voltage and frequency imbalances throughout the market hierarchy, similar to grid management tools owned and operated by DSOs, transmission system operators (TSOs), and utilities today. Based on such analysis, transmission costs modeling, tertiary reserves balancing system, or even an ancillary services market can be tested. Primary and secondary balancing also have the potential to be accounted for.

Additionally, taxation and grid fees can be set at each area to influence market prices such that, for example, local energy trade can be incentivized. Hence, the D3A will enable users to fully customize the grid infrastructure and layout of their use case and market system, from the device level to the transmission level. In this manner, the D3A brings some of the core technical processes of the grid to the local level, allowing for grid balancing to be directly placed in distributed grids, incentivizing household devices and assets to participate in and be responsible for their own energy balance.

When fully developed, the D3A will be able to facilitate

- various commodity markets, such as a spot market;
- balancing capacity market for the tertiary balancing reserve; or
- flexibility market, as found in wholesale energy markets today, further described in chapter by Johnston and Sioshansi in this volume.

These markets will be accessible by device agents that are registered in the device registry of each respective market and connect each physical device to their market as shown in Fig. 13.6. Fundamental market design choices, such as market clearing intervals, market type, and pricing will all be configurable features provided by the D3A energy exchange.

Finally, market parameters, including local taxes or levies, grid fees, and device registry criteria, can be customizable for each market. These features allow D3A energy exchanges to be applied for a variety of grid operators and communities at various grid levels. These customization features allow the D3A to be deployed on the distribution level, providing access to household assets, while also providing the opportunity to use the D3A as an administrative platform for DSOs, TSOs, and regulators to create and manage these markets.

Simulation of the features mentioned above examined the feasibility or efficacy of a select market structure, helping grid operators and communities to decide how to proceed with their future investment and/or more optimal use of energy resources. These conclusions are summarized on the D3A interface results page (www.d3a.io), along with comprehensive data and graphs to help the user understand the inner workings of their simulated use case.

The D3A simulation environment first provides insights into the feasibility of a configured grid or a choice of devices operating in a select market segment. Second, it creates a rationale for the most optimal energy exchange deployment. Once deployed, the D3A facilitates energy access, market flexibility, as well as improved grid balancing and fine-tuning of market regulation.

Fig. 13.8 illustrates D3A development plans. The available D3A beta version currently facilitates simulation of multiple scenarios, with additional features in development

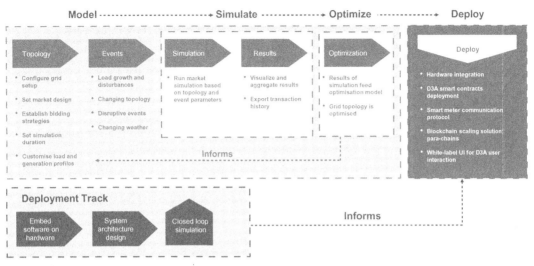

FIGURE 13.8   Development of the D3A, from simulation to real-world implementation. Source: *Grid Singularity.*

leading to an option to deploy and provide "Community-as-a-Service," as well as other energy services as described above.

The open source nature of the D3A software facilitates integration of third party solutions such as device trading strategies, continually improving the functionality of both the D3A exchange and the related software solutions. Similarly, hardware manufacturers can provide diverse physical models of energy assets, which also enhance the effectiveness of the assets.

Researchers and other contributors also play a role in fine-tuning the D3A market design parameters, including algorithms to calculate and manage congestion and economic parameters to determine the return on investment for a certain energy asset.

The D3A is currently being used to simulate Community as a Service projects such as Groene Mient in various global locations. The next steps are to optimize the market simulations and settle on a custom market design, which will be delivered as an exchange engine to each of these areas. Next Grid Singularity is teaming up with deploy vendors and hardware companies to deploy the D3A exchange engine in pilot projects in these locations, with a plan in mind to scale commercially shortly after. The first pilot projects are expected to start in 2020.

13.4 Conclusion

The D3A energy exchange described in this chapter institutes a novel market design that harnesses many of the behind-the-meter opportunities, in significant part by integrating and enhancing other innovative hardware and software solutions. By fostering open source developments, the D3A codebase will ultimately yield the technology to efficiently run a decentralized and distributed smart grid, enabling control and financial settlement for energy resources of any size and type. Its development will accelerate other complementary blockchain products, ranging from device registries to home management devices.

Looking ahead, the energy blockchain innovators will

- increasingly integrate researchers from other fields, namely, artificial intelligence and data science;
- continue to be dependent on core blockchain layer advancements, with the question of scale or transactions throughput particularly impacting P2P applications;
- place a renewed focus on hardware integration both in terms of appliance digital functionality and openness of information gateways like smart meters;
- seek additional development financing to reach commercialization, targeting strategic corporate and venture capital; and
- advocate for a more agile regulatory involvement to mainstream the successful testbed solutions.

Emerging aggregator business models in European electricity markets

Simon De Clercq[1], Daniel Schwabeneder[2], Carlo Corinaldesi[2] and Andreas Fleischhacker[2]

[1]3E, Brussels, Belgium [2]TU Wien, Wien, Austria

14.1 Introduction

European electricity retailing has seen significant changes in the past decade, fueled by two trends. On one hand, a rapid increase in behind-the-meter distributed generation and storage is threatening business as usual for electricity suppliers. Self-consumed electricity reduces the amount of power sourced from the grid, and in competitive markets, suppliers compete to maintain their revenues and sales margin. On the other hand, the digitalization of behind-the-meter assets allows incumbent market players to expand their services but also creates an environment where newcomers can innovate, and peer-to-peer interactions are possible. These can potentially allow customers to operate more autonomously and eliminate their dependency on conventional electricity supply. Meanwhile, regulatory frameworks across Europe are giving consumers a more central role in the energy system to support the transition toward a competitive, sustainable, and affordable energy system. These changes are putting pressure on the conventional business models of electricity suppliers, leading them to consider the sustainability of their current modus operandi.

Traditionally, supplier business models rely on the bulk sale of electricity for their profitability. The traditional value proposition is based on a margin per unit sale of electricity with the objective to maximize sales quantities (Hall & Roelich, 2016). This stands in contrast to the trend toward an energy efficient and sustainable society. Incumbent suppliers are therefore looking for alternate ways to create value.

Not only retail markets are affected. The large-scale increase of variable renewable energy sources is causing power system flexibility requirements across the continent to increase (Sharifi & Yamagata, 2016). Provision of flexibility services was traditionally reserved for large-scale thermal units. Recently, the increase of distributed assets and advanced control through communication technologies has allowed another market role to emerge, that of an energy aggregator. An aggregator combines multiple assets in a single portfolio and optimizes the portfolio's market participation, competing with conventional units on long-term, short-term, and reserve markets (Pause & Wimmer, 2018).

Aggregation can create and offer value both to upstream and downstream market participants (BestRES.eu, 2019). Downstream, aggregators can maximize revenue and reduce costs for industrial, commercial, or domestic customers who own generation and storage units or can offer demand response. For upstream market players, such as large electricity generators, Balance Responsible Parties (BRPs), Distribution System Operators, or Transmission System Operators, aggregators can optimize portfolios and manage system balancing and congestion. Evidently, aggregation blurs the previously well-defined borders between the upstream and downstream of an electricity system: the role of an aggregated portfolio is determined by its function in the system, rather than the individual units of which it consists.

As stated by Poplavskaya and de Vries, aggregators are optimizing the operation of power systems in those places where conventional market mechanisms fail. As listed by Burger, Chaves-Ávila, Batlle, and Pérez-Arriaga (2016) and applied by Schwabeneder, Corinaldesi, Fleischhacker, Lettner, and De Clercq (2019), this can lead to several system benefits:

- economies of scale
- economies scope
- competition and innovation
- deployment of automation technologies
- closing information gaps
- engaging agents for system operations

Aggregation can be considered as a system function and is not tied to a specific type of market participant; an energy supplier, an external third-party or a prosumer with a large number of behind-the-meter assets, can all perform aggregation functions. In unbundled markets across the world, two main emerging business models can be identified that are trying to capture a share of the value created by aggregation:

- Existing suppliers combine the aggregator role with their supply activities as a way to reinvent themselves to better engage with customers.
- Independent aggregators—often new market participants—are taking the most profitable customers of existing suppliers away by aggregating and managing their behind-the-meter assets.

Poplavskaya and de Vries cover several types of independent aggregators. Independent aggregators have received a significant amount of attention, as they have been able to rapidly take up a significant role in European markets. Without owning any assets, they are competing with some of the biggest utilities in the continent. As "virtual utilities," they have increased competition and allowed a wave of innovation to sweep across the electricity sector. Moreover, Poplavskaya and de Vries identify that this has been possible through advanced IT expertise, agile business models, and active participation in pushing the regulatory framework.

However, independent aggregators are not the only actors that are looking to offer this system function. The aggregator and supplier role can be combined to include supply and aggregation services as a single package. This combined model presents several inherent advantages over the independent model:

- Suppliers have an existing portfolio of consumers with whom they have built trust and developed a customer relationship. They furthermore have direct channels to reach them. Traditionally, large suppliers have a large market share that can consist of a significant percentage of the national supply market.
- Combing electricity supply with aggregation services reduces the complexity of coordination between different actors. For customers, the advantage is that they have a single point of contact—and single bill—for the offered services. There is also no need for financial settlement between aggregators, suppliers and BRPs, and the interests from an aggregator and supplier point of view can be aligned.
- The combined role increases economies of scope: bundling services reduces the business costs—such as customer acquisition, customer service, and local control—compared to the situation where these services are carried out by independent actors.
- EU policymakers have understood the importance of a level playing field for independent aggregators and European directives have been put in place to remove the existing barriers to their operation (Wimmer & Pause, 2019). However, European provisions on aggregation have not yet been incorporated into the national legislation of all EU member states. Offering aggregation services alongside supply services is still most compatible with the current market setup in Europe and therefore faces the least barriers (NordREG, 2016) and (Verhaegen & Dierckxsens, 2016).

Regardless of the organizational setup of an aggregator, the size of the aggregated assets is an important parameter. Aggregation of industrial electricity generation and demand has happened for several years (Verhaegen & Dierckxsens, 2016) and is a place where independent aggregators have performed well. As a large share of the low hanging fruits—flexible medium to large scale generation and consumption units—have already been aggregated, market players are moving deeper into the demand side, and exploring the possibilities behind the meter (Glachant, 2019). In theory, aggregation of small-scale assets can offer the same benefits as aggregation of large-scale assets. Though, building a portfolio of small aggregated assets faces several barriers:

- Higher transaction costs are inherent to smaller assets: aggregating hundred 1 MW behind-the-meter units, with different owners, technical configurations, and communication protocols, will require a significantly higher connection cost than a single 100 MW asset.
- Smaller assets have lower legal metering requirements, which means that in the case of monitoring and control, an additional metering device needs to be installed. This cost needs to be directly recovered through the offered aggregation services.
- Current tariff designs for small consumers in many European countries are still volumetric, which do not remunerate flexibility.
- Another problem, explained by Smith and MacGill in this volume, is the limited ability or interest of domestic customers to engage or understand price signals.

This chapter discusses two European electricity suppliers that are looking behind the meter for new value streams. They explore how they can use the combined supplier—aggregator role to simultaneously futureproof their business models and overcome the barriers for the aggregation of residential consumers. For each of the suppliers, the building blocks of their new business models are reviewed to identify how they can create value for themselves and their customers in the respective regulatory environments.

The rest of this chapter is organized as follows:

- Section 14.2 discusses Good Energy, a renewable electricity supplier operating in the United Kingdom that is looking to overcome barriers to access residential flexibility and activate market participation of household consumers.
- Section 14.3 covers oekostrom, an electricity supplier in Austria that assesses the possibilities of providing services to customers in apartment buildings to facilitate the installation of collective solar generation, followed by the chapter's conclusions.

14.2 Behind-the-meter flexibility of residential loads: Good Energy, the United Kingdom

Good Energy is an electricity and gas supplier operating in the UK powering homes and businesses with 100% renewable electricity.[1] They have a portfolio of over 1400 UK generators and own and operate two wind farms and eight solar farms. Good Energy serves more than 250,000 domestic and business customers (BestRES.eu, 2019). The basis of Good Energy's business model is that of a traditional "green supplier": they sell green electricity at a competitive price. By offering locally produced, independent, or community-owned power production they target price-sensitive residential customers and larger businesses willing to promote their social corporate responsibility.

Aware of the potential value that lies behind their customers' meters and trying to stay ahead of the developments in the UK retail market, Good Energy is involved in several innovation projects. Previously, Good Energy collaborated with technology provider Piclo—discussed by Johnston and Sioshansi in this volume—to set up Britain's first online peer-to-peer marketplace for renewable electricity. In this project, finding ways to engage domestic customers was key. One of the main findings has been that "the most significant untapped potential to break market inertia in the domestic sector lies with the availability of granular, half-hourly data." (Open Utility, 2018). To further develop how customer engagement and real-time consumption data can improve their current business model, Good Energy set up a new project called the Home Innovation Trial.

In the investigated new business model, Good Energy shifts from being an electricity supplier toward an energy service provider. They provide customers with a home energy management device that performs live-monitoring and sends real-time information signals on electricity consumption.

The Home Innovation Trial consists of four phases, as shown in Fig. 14.1. After the trial's setup, the first implementation stage starts, Energy Basis. During this stage,

[1] https://www.goodenergy.co.uk/

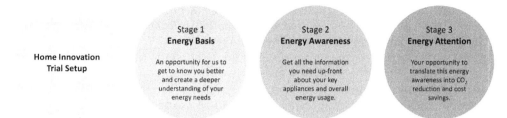

FIGURE 14.1   Stages of the Home Innovation Trial.

customers' baselines electricity consumption data is collected to create a reference tool. Participants do not have access to this data. In the second stage, Energy Awareness, the impact of primary intervention is identified by assessing the participants' behavior to real-time information on their electricity consumption and the associated impact on the electricity bill. In the final stage, Energy Attention, the impact of secondary intervention is identified to analyze participants' responsiveness to infographics, therefore aiming to close the gap between the reference tool and the saving potential calculated in Energy Basis.

Lobbe, in this volume, identifies that cost is one of the most important decision criteria for prosumers and consumers. Whenever electricity demand is low and production from variable renewable energy sources with low short-run marginal cost of electricity like wind and solar photovoltaic (PV) is high, power on short-term markets is cheaper (Sensfuß, Ragwitz, & Genoese, 2008). During hours of high demand and low renewable energy production market, prices are more expensive. Consuming electricity at times of high renewable production can therefore, in theory, reduce the cost of electricity. A limitation to access the economic potential of residential flexibility, however, is that the settlement of residential loads in the United Kingdom still happens based on generic load profiles, and not on half-hourly consumption measurements (Elexon, 2018). This means that any change in residential consumption is seen relative to the household's generic load profile, instead of the household's actual consumption. Time-of-use tariffs can partially translate the time-dependency of electricity prices to residential consumers, though do not represent the complete price volatility of today's and future electricity markets.

Faced with this limitation, Good Energy specifically chose not to use an automated home energy management system. Automated home energy management systems—as covered in this volume by Shaw-Williams—maximize a household's flexibility, but at the same time, do not allow to specifically assess how customers can be engaged to change their consumption behavior. Good Energy instead decided to use a home energy management system that monitors the household consumption and relies on interaction with the consumers through a mobile app to cause shifts in energy consumption.

Good Energy's collaborated with Green Running,[2] an external technology provider, to provide the home energy management technology. Green Running's Verv is a home energy management system that does nonintrusive load monitoring: it disaggregates a household's consumption into the consumption from individual appliances based on a

[2] https://www.greenrunning.com/

reading of the household's main electricity cable. Data processing occurs using artificial intelligence in a connected hub. A mobile application informs the residents of the real-time electricity consumption and cost (Green Running, 2018).

Limited by the lack of dynamic tariffs, customers on static time-of-use tariffs are currently the most interesting as flexibility test cases. Good Energy therefore decided to work with participants that are on an Economy 7 or Economy 10 tariffs. These are consumers with either 7 or 10 hours of off-peak electricity. Ideal participants are E10 customers as they have tariffs that provide 10 hours of off-peak electricity split between night, afternoon and evening, and therefore provide more incentive and flexibility for participants to shift their consumption. Fig. 14.2 illustrates the E7 and E10 tariff structures.

In order to select an appropriate participant base for the trial, Good Energy segmented its Economy 7 and Economy 10 customers into demographic types based on information on affluence, likelihood of having an internet-enabled phone/tablet and interest in new technologies. As this trial is based on engagement, selecting the right customers was important. This is an advantage of the combined supplier–aggregator model: Good Energy was able to preselect the trial participants from its several thousand customers. They consulted their customer base through a survey to identify the households that were most interested in the service. The final set of participants were self-selected to make sure there were motivated to engage with the Verve device. At the beginning of Stage 1—Energy Basis, a total of 43 Verv devices were installed in as many households across England.

In the Energy Basis phase, the Verv device monitors the households' electricity consumption and disaggregates it per device. In the Energy Basis stage there is no interaction: households are not informed of their consumption. An example of the data monitoring by the Verv device for a single household over 1 day (48 settlement periods) is shown in Fig. 14.3.

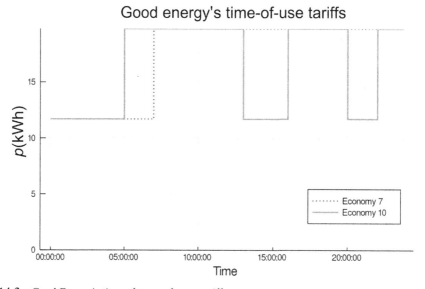

FIGURE 14.2   Good Energy's time-of-use end-user tariffs.

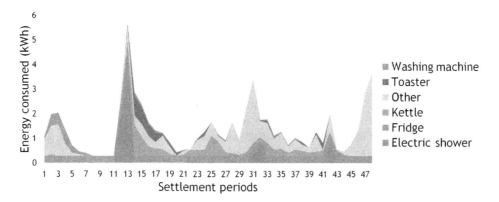

FIGURE 14.3 Time series of consumption per appliance per settlement period. *From De Clercq, S., & Guerrero, C. (2018a). Monitoring and performance evaluation of the real-life pilot projects. In: BestRES project Deliverable D4.4.*

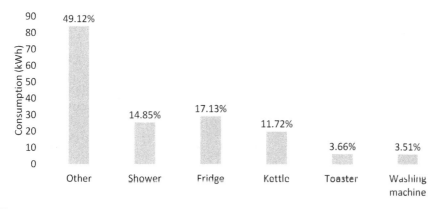

FIGURE 14.4 Consumption breakdown per appliance. *From De Clercq, S., & Guerrero, C. (2018a). Monitoring and performance evaluation of the real-life pilot projects. In: BestRES project Deliverable D4.4.*

The Verv device is able to categorize almost 50% of the consumption, as shown in Fig. 14.4.

After collecting baseline data in Stage 1, Energy Basis, participants entered Stage 2, Energy Awareness. During this stage, the consumption information collected by the Verv device could be accessed by the households through the main Verv app. This includes real-time cost and energy information on home appliances.

The monitoring results did not show an unambiguous effect of the closed information gap. Compared to Energy Basis, Good Energy found that there is generally a reduction of electricity consumption of the entire portfolio. However, seasonal variations in electricity demand are not accounted for. There are households with a reduced peak consumption compared to Energy Basis, but this does not hold true for all of them.

The level of engagement with the participants was stepped up when the trial entered Stage 3, Energy Attention. Infographics were sent to the participants with the objective to give them further insights on their energy behavior. The infographics contain information such as the appliances that were most used in a 1-month period, the household's percentage peak and off-peak consumption per appliance, etc.

Based on the response on the infographics, Good Energy clustered consumers in different groups: those that show awareness of the difference between the peak and off-peak tariffs, and those that do not. The identification considers that households in the first group do not have much more additional load to flex and will therefore not be able to benefit as much as the second group from Verv's real-time information.

The trial results indicate that the immediate effects of engagement-based control are limited: consumers show interest in their electricity consumption data but do not necessarily act accordingly. By providing statistics on household energy consumption, disaggregated per device, consumers become more aware of the cost associated with different appliances in their home. However, the trial results do not indicate that this has a significant effect at a portfolio level.

The impact on cost and revenue is however only one aspect of the business model. Good Energy also identified other benefits that the Verv device can offer. By actively engaging with the customer, a better customer–client relationship is built. The home energy management device is a versatile channel to reach consumers—one that can be used to build trust—which in a later stage can be used to introduce more direct ways of control. On the back end, Good Energy developed an app analytics platform to understand the participants' engagement with the Verv app better. The platform tracks user's interaction with the Verv app and is used to measure user engagement and retention. Data analysis allows to analyze and interpret participants' energy needs and behavior to gain customer insights.

To assess the full business model potential, simulations are conducted that quantify the possible benefits of end users. Two use cases are defined. In the Status Quo use case, end users are charged a two-level time-of-use tariff, as in the trial. In the Advanced use case, they pay an hourly varying price for electricity, as they would under a dynamic time-of-use tariff that is linked to the electricity price on the day-ahead market. The two end-user tariffs, consisting of a supplier tariff, network charges and fees, are illustrated in Fig. 14.5.

The simulations consider a household with various domestic white goods, like a fridge, a microwave or a washing machine. For each of these technologies, certain flexibility characteristics are assumed. In the model, the electric loads of devices like the fridge can be shifted by 30 minutes and the washing machine can be turned on at any time between 08:00 a.m. and 08:00 p.m. Furthermore, all loads react automatically to price signals with the objective to minimize the household's electricity bill. The simulation uses real-life measured data of a household to simulate the effect of flexibility activation on the cost to the customer.

The simulation results are shown in Fig. 14.6. In the Status Quo use case, a cost reduction of about 1% can be achieved by shifting loads from the high-price to the low-price tariff period. Since most load types can only be shifted by 30 minutes and there are only two price levels, the amount of shifted energy is limited. In the Advanced use case, customers

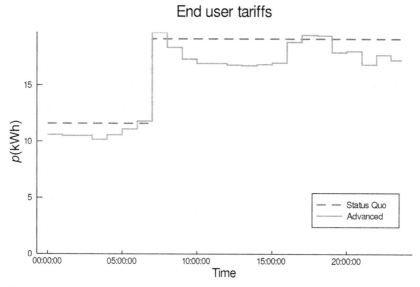

FIGURE 14.5   Total end-user tariffs in the Status Quo and in the Advanced use case for one exemplary day.

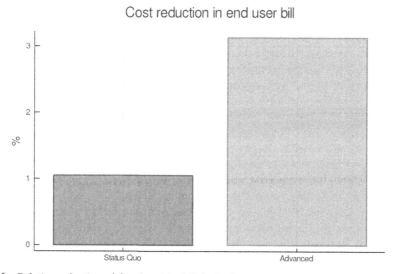

FIGURE 14.6   Relative reduction of the electricity bill for both use cases.

have a more dynamic price and therefore more possibilities to reduce their bill by load shifting. Hence, a slightly greater cost reduction is achieved: approximately 3%.

It is doubtful whether these price differences would convince customers to change their behavior or switch supplier. Even in the dynamic use-case, the simulation results indicate only a reduction of up to 3%, which is a small difference compared to the price differences between UK residential electricity suppliers. Direct control of more appliances would be a way to increase the amount of activated flexibility. Automated control of several households can enable additional remuneration mechanisms for residential flexibility, through for example participation in additional markets as an aggregated portfolio.

Based on these simulation results, it is possible to assess the total potential value of domestic flexibility in the United Kingdom. The annual household expenditure on electricity is 17.7 billion £ (21.5 billion $) in 2018 (Department for Business, Energy, & Industrial Strategy, 2018). Upscaling the potential savings for end users to a nationwide implementation would yield total savings in residential electricity bills of 177 million £ (215 million $) in the Status Quo use case to 531 million £ (645 million $) in the Advanced use.[3]

14.3 Collective distributed generation in apartment buildings: oekostrom, Austria[4]

oekostrom is a green electricity supplier operating in Austria that currently supplies 100% renewable electricity to about 52,000 customers across the country. It is involved in different parts of the electricity value chain, including power production, trading, sales, and energy services. It was founded in 1999 with the aim to support the development of sustainable energy in Austria (BestRES.eu, 2019). Its business model is similar to Good Energy's: retailing green and local electricity to eco-sensitive residential, commercial, and industrial customers. Their pricing is cost-driven in order to be competitive in the Austrian electricity market, though oekostrom clients tend to be willing to pay more for Austrian green power. Besides retailing, oekostrom has a significant portfolio of mainly hydro, wind, and solar power generation.

In 2017, changes in the Austrian regulatory framework on electricity set out new rules for the installation of collective electricity generation units. The Amendment of the Electricity Management and Organisation Act 2010 from July 26, 2017 includes several provisions to promote community generation facilities. The topic of community production facilities is specifically regulated; the amendment states that "network access beneficiaries shall have the right to operate collectively-owned generation assets, as long as the end consumers is not restricted from choosing its supplier."

This regulatory change can be seen in the context of a larger trend across Europe. At the end of 2016, when the European Commission proposed the Clean Energy Package, the concept of energy communities was introduced to give consumers and communities a more central role in European electricity markets. Community energy is not at all new in the EU—in fact an important share of renewable generation across the continent is owned

---

[3] When quoting these values, it is important to note that a linear scale-up is a rough estimate. If the entire domestic electricity demand reacts on the same price predictions, this will influence the actual market price, similar to the economic self-cannibalism of storage on power markets (Dallinger, Schwabeneder, Lettner, & Auer, 2019).

[4] https://oekostrom.at/.

by communities—but the directive guarantees that community energy is translated to the regulatory framework of all member states.[5]

Prompted by the opportunities presented by the regulatory changes, oekostrom decided to investigate how they can use their role as electricity supplier to facilitate community-shared PV schemes in apartment buildings. The shift toward this new business model aims to unburden the residents of their responsibilities regarding the PV installation.

Self-consumption, or consuming PV generation behind-the-meter where it is produced, remains the most lucrative remuneration of residential solar PV. This is the case in Europe, but also in for example Australia, as discussed by Swanston in this volume. Electricity that is locally produced and consumed never crosses into the utility grid and is therefore not registered by the electricity meter. This means that the saved cost is equal to the electricity retail price, which in some European countries can be up to 33 ¢/kWh (Eurostat, 2019). An important premise for this remuneration scheme is that the generation is allocated to a single metering point. This does not pose a problem for single-family dwellings, where the PV installation is connected behind the meter. For apartment buildings, aggregating the consumption of the individual apartments inherently increases the self-consumption of the locally produced PV power and thus improves the asset's economic performance. However, the organizational setup for apartment buildings is more complicated. Individual metering of the PV installation is necessary, and the allocation of the generation to the individual owners needs to be contractually defined.

The complexity of self-consumption on apartment buildings is not the only barrier to the installation of PV installation on those roofs (De Clercq, Schwabeneder, Corinaldesi, Bertetti, & Woyte, 2018):

- There has to be an agreement, often with absolute majority, between the individual apartment owners of the building. Reaching such an agreement can be a troublesome process that, to be successful, requires strong backing from the building's residents.
- Apartment buildings are often inhabited by tenants rather than homeowners, which complicates the decision process. The beneficiaries of the installation—the residents who pay the electricity bill—are not necessarily the owners of the building and are therefore unlikely to invest in collective infrastructure.
- Financing of a dwelling in a building with a collective installation can also cause problems: it is possible that mortgage lenders do not accept a collectively owned installation on the mortgaged property.

As a result of these barriers, the enormous potential of PV installation on urban roofs of apartment buildings has remained largely untapped.

Since October 2001, the Austrian electricity market is open for competition, which means that every consumer has the right to freely choose their supplier (E-Control, 2011). Four organizational schemes for collective PV installations that respect this requirement can be identified (PV-gemeinschaft.at, 2019).

---

[5] A case study of a community energy project in The Netherlands is covered in more detail in this volume by Reijnders, van der Laan and Dijkstra.

- In a first possible implementation scheme, the building owner takes the initiative to finance and operate the collective PV system. The produced electricity is part of the building's collective infrastructure and is used to supply individual apartments and the building's shared facilities. The building owner has a contract with an electricity supplier who buys the excess electricity production.
- In the second model, the role of financer and operator of the installation is taken up by a resident association that consists of the building's residents. Unlike in the previous case, participation in the scheme is voluntary. The electricity is allocated to the participating apartments.
- In the third scheme, a supplier—let us say oekostrom—acts both as an electricity supplier and as an external party that finances, installs, and operates the PV system. It leases a right-of-use for self-consumption to the building's residents. Independently of the resident's incumbent supplier, oekostrom supplies the participating residents with locally produced electricity and is either paid per kWh produced or a fixed amount per period for the use of the installation. This price is below the price of regular electricity supply. The resident's electrical demand that is not covered by PV installation is supplied by the resident's regular supply company, which can be oekostrom but not necessarily. oekostrom receives the revenue from the electricity that is not consumed locally and fed into the grid.
- The fourth scheme is similar: instead of only acting as a third-party financer, oekostrom finances, installs and operates the installation, and provides PV power at a lower cost only to the building's residents that have a supply contract with them. Organizationally this simpler, but it limits the potential scope of the business model.

In the first two organizational schemes, the possible role of oekostrom is limited to buying the excess PV power and supplying the remaining electricity demand of individual apartments. The potential of the third and fourth model is much larger: oekostrom takes ownership of the PV plant, supports the residents to overcome the identified organizational barriers, and in return oekostrom receives a compensation for their services. This can cover the reduction in supplied energy that they face. From a supplier's point of view, the third scheme can be preferred: as the economic performance of the business model increases with an increase in participants, it maximizes the addressable market.

As the generation of the PV plant is shared between the consumers, an allocation method has to be defined between the participants. There are two possible allocation methods in line with the current Austrian regulation (Austrian Federal Chancellery, 2017):

- Static allocation: Every consumer owns a fixed share of the collective solar PV. The production is allocated among consumers according to the shares. In this case, generation cannot be traded between the inhabitants of the apartment house. If the generation exceeds consumption, it is fed into the grid.
- Dynamic allocation: Consumers are allowed to trade energy locally. Electricity will only be sold to the grid in case the aggregated consumption of all participating apartments is lower than the power generated by the collective PV installation. This allocation hence maximizes the installation's self-consumption.

In order to decide on a strategy regarding the apartment building market, oekostrom is interested to know more about the potential of the business model. What value proposition can it offer to those customers? What pricing makes this economically viable? What is the total potential of the Austrian market?

As a first step to answer these questions, a typical apartment building in Austria is analyzed. Fig. 14.7 shows a typical apartment building, consisting of four consumers—three apartments and the communal consumption—and a collective PV installation. In the example, the individual apartments are supplied by three different suppliers. Individual metering occurs for the general consumption, the three apartments and the PV installation.

Fig. 14.8 shows the difference between the two allocation methods that were previously introduced. It uses an exemplary case: PV generation of 12 kWh—represented by the blue squares—is either allocated statically (left) or dynamically (right) to the four consumers. Costumer load is shown as gray squares. Static allocation allocates equal shares of the generation to the consumers, whether the energy is consumed—black framed—or not—red framed. As the red framed production is not consumed by the household to which it is allocated, it is sold back to the grid, regardless of whether other apartments in the same building have a demand for it. Dynamic allocation redistributes the locally generated electricity to neighboring consumers, as indicated by the arrows. In the figure, the local excess

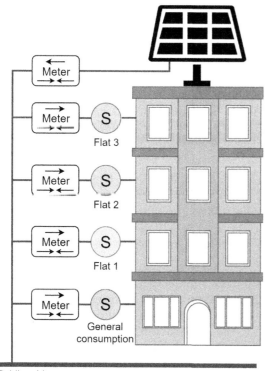

FIGURE 14.7   Typical apartment building with three flats and a photovoltaic power plant.

Public grid

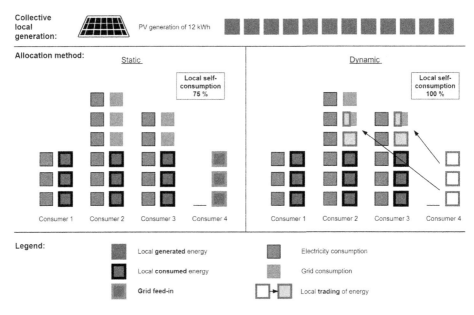

FIGURE 14.8   Example of a static (left) or dynamic (right) allocation.

of PV generation from consumer 4 is dynamically allocated to the remaining flats. As a result of this redistribution, the self-consumption of the PV production increases from 75% to 100%.

While blockchain can be a facilitator to allow units to trade their solar allocation between themselves—as for example done by EDF in a trial in the United Kingdom —also a conventional ledger can be used to keep track of the simultaneity of production, consumption, and allocation.

The following example considers an apartment building in Vienna that consists of 10 flats. Three cases are compared as follows:

• There is no PV generation available: the building's total electricity demand is supplied from the grid.
• The apartment building has a collective PV installation and the generated electricity is statically allocated to the 10 flats.
• The apartment building has a collective PV installation and the generated electricity is dynamically allocated to the 10 flats.

The total electricity costs of the entire building are simulated for each case.

Fig. 14.9 shows a breakdown of the apartment building's total electricity bill for the different cases. The collective PV plant allows a cost reduction of 10% under static allocation and 14% under dynamic allocation compared to the case without PV generation. Increased self-consumption leads to a reduction of the energy component, grid component, and tax component of the grid procurement cost. The PV installation has a corresponding capital and maintenance cost that is smaller than the reduction in grid procurement cost.

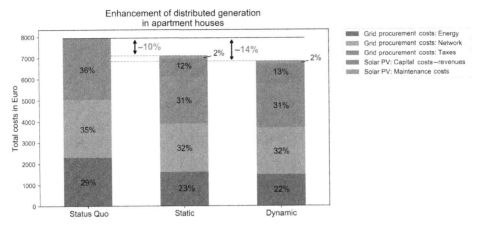

FIGURE 14.9 Total costs of the apartment building without (Status Quo) and with collective PV (static and dynamic allocation). *From Schwabeneder, D., Corinaldesi, C., Fleischhacker, A., Lettner, G., De Clercq, S., & Efthymiou, V. (2018). Quantitative analysis of improved BMs of selected aggregators in target countries. In:* BestRES project deliverable 3.3.

Other case studies with larger rooftop areas show that the dynamic allocation method provides incentives for larger and more efficient use of PV systems. The dynamic allocation method more appropriately reflects the physical power flows and consistently increases the created value for the participating actors.

The simulation results indicate that in the situation where behind-the-meter generation is installed, suppliers face a reduction in revenues from grid-procured energy sales. In the case that the behind-the-meter units are owned and operated by that supplier, this situation can be reversed: a revenue sharing model determines how the cost reduction caused by the PV installation is distributed between the consumers and the supplier.

If in the previous example it is assumed that the supplier owns and operates the PV installation, it is possible to determine the supplier's minimum and maximum revenue considering the following:

- The supplier's revenue loss due to behind-the-meter generation needs to be compensated.
- The apartment building's total electricity bill is not allowed to increase compared to the Status Quo case.

In this exercise, the supplier's profit is the difference between the revenue from selling electricity to the customers on one hand, and the cost for sourcing this electricity and investing in the PV installation on the other hand.

Fig. 14.10 shows the revenue range for the supplier. The brown bar indicates the minimal additional revenues that are necessary to cover the loss in electricity sale and the green bar shows the maximum of the supplier's revenues without increasing the overall costs to the apartment building.

The results show that—driven by the low cost of PV technology and the saved procurement cost—the analyzed aggregation-supplier model can increase a supplier's revenues in

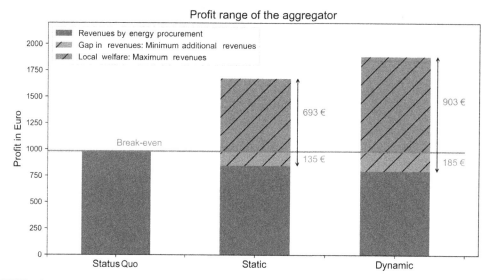

FIGURE 14.10   Profit analysis of the energy aggregator. *From Schwabeneder, D., Corinaldesi, C., Fleischhacker, A., Lettner, G., De Clercq, S., & Efthymiou, V. (2018). Quantitative analysis of improved BMs of selected aggregators in target countries. In: BestRES project deliverable 3.3.*

both the static and the dynamic cases. If well marketed, these results indicate that the business model can unlock a significant number of rooftops for self-consumption.

As was done by De Clercq and Guerrero (2018b), it is possible to quantify the potential amount of PV generation that this business model could introduce in the Austrian market. Based on national statistics of the Austrian building stock, a complete rollout of the business model could add 2.2 GW to the country's generation portfolio. Considering that the solar installed capacity in Austria is 1.4 GW (IRENA, 2019), this is a substantial amount that leaves little doubt about the business opportunity that the business model presents.

The impact of this business model in terms of revenue is also significant. About 2.3 million households in Austria may use collective generation in future (Statistics Austria, 2019). As stated by the Association of Austrian Electricity Companies (2019) average electricity costs are 21.7 ¢/kWh. The total potential of this business model is thus between 132 and 290 million € (145 and 319 million $) in Austria, if collective solar PV in combination with dynamic allocation is implemented on a large scale.

As can be expected based on these results, the implementation of this business model in Austria is quickly gaining pace, reflected in an increasing number of projects across the country. Fig. 14.11 gives an overview of the national track record, with larger installations catering to larger buildings. In the future, it is expected that the number of projects will increase. The value created in the business model, particularly under dynamic allocation, will continue to convince companies to adopt business models that cater to this business segment. As the sector gains experience, implementation will be improved, and operational barriers reduced.

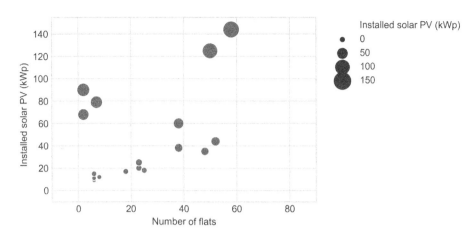

FIGURE 14.11 Collective PV projects implemented in Austria. *Adapted from* PV-gemeinschaft.at. *(2019).* Mögliche Umsetzungsvarianten für PV-Gemeinschaftsanlagen. *<http://pv-gemeinschaft.at/umsetzungsvarianten/>* *Accessed 02.07.19.*

14.4 Conclusion

At its outset, this chapter discusses the emergence of two different types of aggregation business models across European electricity markets. On one hand, independent aggregators are new market entrants that combine smart IT solutions and a deep understanding of electricity markets to offer flexibility services both upstream and downstream of power systems. On the other hand, several incumbent suppliers, faced with a developing retail market, are combining their supply activities with aggregation services to diversify and improve their business models.

The chapter presents two cases of incumbent electricity suppliers who, in search of a more resilient business model, are using the features of the combined model to overcome the barriers of aggregating behind-the-meter assets.

The results of the case studies indicate that the combined supplier–aggregator model presents viable business opportunities. In power systems that are transforming to become more sustainable and efficient, it allows suppliers to diversify their revenue mechanisms and broaden their value proposition.

The results from Good Energy's case indicate that the potential to provide cost reductions using residential flexibility is limited. Nonetheless, the business model leads the way to activate assets behind-the-meter and adds several features to regular electricity supply. Static time-of-use tariffs are an enabler for residential load shifting, and dynamic time-of-use tariffs that are indexed to the electricity market would further encourage customers to make maximum use of their available flexibility. Under the current market settlement rules, direct cost reductions are not the main driver of the business model. Instead, it allows to address new market segments, gather detailed customer data and establish a direct channel to engage with customers.

In oekostrom's case, financing and operating collective PV infrastructure on apartment buildings can become a source of revenue that compensates a potential revenue reduction due to behind-the-meter generation. Revenue sharing is an important topic that needs to be addressed: the cost of the provided service needs to cover both the investment and operational cost of the PV installation and the supplier's revenue loss, while the price to the customer should not increase. The discussion identifies a large potential market, which is reflected in an increasing number of projects across the country. For oekostrom, the business model allows to specifically target residents of apartment buildings as an additional customer segment.

In the discussed cases, suppliers offer a combined set of services to create a one-stop-shop for residential consumers. Both business models are, however, only a first step toward aggregation of residential consumers. It is possible to imagine a portfolio of aggregated households or apartment buildings equipped with behind-the-meter assets that are centrally controlled to optimize electricity consumption and production on a portfolio level. This would maximize the amount of additional value that is created.

Market players such as electricity suppliers, independent aggregators, and technology providers will continue to investigate the most viable strategies to digitalize, aggregate, optimize, and monetize what lies behind and beyond the meter. While only the future can tell which models will be most successful, at least one thing is clear: if incumbent suppliers do not innovate, someone will do it for them.

Acknowledgments

The results described in this chapter have been obtained in the framework of the BestRES and PVP4Grid projects, cofinanced by the European Commission, under H2020 Programme, grant agreements no. 691689 and no. 764786. Detailed information on the projects are available on the project websites: http://bestres.eu and https://www.pvp4grid.eu/. The authors would like to thank the contributions from all project partners and in particular Danelle Veldman (Good Energy) and Maximilian Kloess (oekostrom) to this research.

References

Association of Austrian Electricity Companies. (2019). *LAND AM STROM—Jahresbericht Oesterreichs Energie 2018*.
Austrian Federal Chancellery. (2017). *Federal act providing new rules for the organisation of the electricity sector: ElWOG 2010*.
BestRES.eu. *BestRES project website (H2020 project)*. (2019). <https://bestres.eu> Accessed 07.07.19.
BSW. *PVP4Grid – PV-Prosumers4Grid (H2020 project)*. (2019). <https://www.pvp4grid.eu/> Accessed 09.07.19.
Burger, S., Chaves-Ávila, J. P., Batlle, C., & Pérez-Arriaga, I. J. (2016). *The value of aggregation in electricity systems*. MIT Centre for Energy and Environmental Policy Research.
Dallinger, B., Schwabeneder, D., Lettner, G., & Auer, H. (2019). Socio-economic benefit and profitability analyses of Austrian hydro storage power plants supporting increasing renewable electricity generation in Central Europe. *Renewable and Sustainable Energy Reviews, 107*, 482–496. Available from https://doi.org/10.1016/j.rser.2019.03.027.
De Clercq, S., & Guerrero, C. (2018a). Monitoring and performance evaluation of the real-life pilot projects. In: *BestRES project Deliverable 4.4*.
De Clercq, S., & Guerrero, C. (2018b). Life cycle analysis (LCA) of the improved business models. In: *BestRES project Deliverable 3.5*.

De Clercq, S., Schwabeneder, D., Corinaldesi, C. Bertetti, O., & Woyte, A. (2018). How to create value through aggregation: A business model review for multiple regulatory environments in Europe. In: *Proceedings of the 8th international workshop on integration of solar power into power systems.*

Department for Business, Energy & Industrial Strategy. (2018). *Total household expenditure on energy.*

E-Control. *10 Jahre Energiemarkt Liberalisierung.* (2011). <https://www.e-control.at/documents/1785851/1811255/bericht-10-jahre-energiemarktliberalisierung.pdf/418f0056-6db6-4b87-a835-091d1f512c9a?t=1413905309588>.

Elexon. *Load Profiles and their use in Electricity Settlement.* (2018). <https://www.elexon.co.uk/documents/training-guidance/bsc-guidance-notes/load-profiles/>.

Eurostat. *Electricity price statistics—Statistics.* (2019). <https://ec.europa.eu/eurostat/statistics-explained/index.php/Electricity_price_statistics> Accessed 7.25.19.

Fleischhacker, A., Radl, J., & Lettner, G. (2019). *PV prosumer guidelines Österreich.*

Glachant, J. (2019). New business models in the electricity sector. In: *European University Institute Working Paper RSCAS 2019/44.*

Green Running. *Verv VLUX whitepaper – The evolution of energy.* (2018). <https://vlux.io/media/VLUX_Whitepaper.pdf>.

Hall, S., & Roelich, K. (2016). Business model innovation in electricity supply markets: The role of complex value in the United Kingdom. *Energy Policy, 92,* 286–298. Available from https://doi.org/10.1016/j.enpol.2016.02.019.

IRENA. *Renewable capacity statistics 2019.* (2019). <https://www.irena.org/-/media/Files/IRENA/Agency/Publication/2019/Mar/IRENA_RE_Capacity_Statistics_2019.pdf>.

Nordic Energy Regulators (NordREG). (2016). *Discussion of different arrangements for aggregation of demand response in the Nordic market.*

Open Utility. (2018). *A glimpse into the future of Britain's energy economy.*

Pause, F., & Wimmer, M. (2018). The impact of the CE4AE-Package on legal and regulatory problems for aggregators, encountered in the BestRES project. In: *BestRES project Deliverable.*

PV-gemeinschaft.at. (2019). *Mögliche Umsetzungsvarianten für PV-Gemeinschaftsanlagen.* <http://pv-gemeinschaft.at/umsetzungsvarianten/> Accessed 02.07.19.

Schwabeneder, D., Corinaldesi, C., Fleischhacker, A., Lettner, G., & De Clercq, S. (2019). Assessment of the value of aggregation. In: *BestRES project Deliverable 5.1.*

Schwabeneder, D., Corinaldesi, C., Fleischhacker, A., Lettner, G., De Clercq, S., & Efthymiou, V. (2018). Quantitative analysis of improved BMs of selected aggregators in target countries. In: *BestRES project Deliverable 3.3.*

Sensfuß, F., Ragwitz, M., & Genoese, M. (2008). The merit-order effect: A detailed analysis of the price effect of renewable electricity generation on spot market prices in Germany. *Energy Policy, 36*(8), 3086–3094. Available from https://doi.org/10.1016/j.enpol.2008.03.035.

Sharifi, A., & Yamagata, Y. (2016). Principles and criteria for assessing urban energy resilience: A literature review. *Renewable and Sustainable Energy Reviews, 60,* 1654–1677. Available from https://doi.org/10.1016/j.rser.2016.03.028.

Statistics Austria. *Wohnungs- und Gebäudebestand.* (2019). <https://www.statistik.at/web_de/statistiken/menschen_und_gesellschaft/wohnen/wohnungs_und_gebaeudebestand/index.html> Accessed 09.07.19.

Verhaegen, R., & Dierckxsens, C. (2016). Existing business models for renewable energy aggregators. In: *BestRES Project Deliverable 2.1.*

Wimmer, M., & Pause, F. (2019). Enabling European legal and regulatory framework for business models for renewable energy aggregation. In: *BestRES Project Deliverable 5.3.*

PART THREE

Regulators, policymakers & investors

Behind-the-meter prospects: what do household customers' responses to prices tell us?

Bruce Mountain

Victoria Energy Policy Centre, Melbourne, VIC, Australia

15.1 Introduction

This chapter seeks to contribute to the book by exploring contemporary evidence of how household electricity customers have responded to electricity prices in the way they consume and in some cases also produce electricity. The focus of this exploration is to inform speculation on where the value in behind-the-meter or BTM is to be found for household customers.

But first, what is BTM? The scale and rate of change in the electricity sector means that jargon often runs ahead of commonly understood meaning. Here we define "BTM" as follows: *"BTM refers to technology-driven step changes in consumption, production and storage behind the customers' electricity meter."* A few more restrictions are appropriate: the reference is mainly to small customers whether households or businesses. And of course, "step change" is not discrete, but turning off the lights when one leaves a room is a BTM action but is surely not what is commonly understood by "BTM."

Step changes in consumption (leaving aside those associated with BTM changes in production) might be associated with the application of communication and control technologies to automate changes to the use of electrical devices BTM in a way that substantially reduces (or shifts) consumption but not at the expense of any loss of utility by the customer.

Inevitably definitional endeavors become complex. Using technology to identify the core contemporary BTM technologies classified as consumption, production, and storage helps to narrow the discussion:

- **consumption:** internet-enabled devices that can be coordinated automatically to shift or reduce consumption in a way that does not entail the loss of utility,

- **production:** rooftop solar, and
- **storage:** batteries of various types and thermal storage (hot water).

This "BTM" technology specification provides clarity on the focus of this chapter: what can we learn from the way customers respond to prices in understanding Australian customers' likely demand for BTM technologies?

The main argument developed in this chapter is that the evidence in Australia suggests that households are not able to easily engage in grid-supplied electricity markets. Yet in the way they have invested in their own rooftop photo-voltaic (PV) production; the evidence suggests that customers are engaging successfully in BTM production opportunities. This suggests that customers are likely to continue to seek opportunities to reduce their reliance on grid-supplied electricity and to profit from BTM opportunities to substitute, arbitrage over time, and reduce consumption.

This chapter is organized as follows:

- Section 15.2 examines contemporary evidence of the way that household customers have responded to prices in their consumption and production decisions.
- Section 15.3 draws on the observations in Section 15.2 to speculate on the value that BTM has for small electricity users in Australia followed by the chapter's conclusions.

15.2 Do customers respond to electricity prices?

This section surveys evidence on customers' response to electricity prices in four areas

- the outcomes for households in Victoria when they switch their retailers (relative to the outcomes for households that do not switch)
- the response of households in Victoria to time-of-use tariffs
- the installation of rooftop PV for households in Australia
- half-hourly charges for households in Great Britain

The focus of this section is drawn general conclusions about how customers respond to prices they pay for grid-supplied electricity, and how they have responded to the opportunity to produce their own electricity through rooftop PV.

15.2.1 Do Victoria's households leave less money on the table when they switch electricity retailers?

Governments, regulators, and customer advocates in Australia—and elsewhere—have urged customers to switch retailers to get better deals. Customers have responded, and switching rates are high. A common view is that over almost a decade of unregulated competition a two-tier market has evolved, in which "switchers" avoid the "loyalty tax" paid by "remainers."

Mountain and Rizio (2019) examined 48,000 Victorian household electricity bills that were uploaded to Victorian Government's price comparison website in late 2018 to compare outcomes for switchers and remainers. The typical remainer left $281 per year

(20% of their bill) on the table (in other words if they had been successful in finding the best deal they would have paid $281 per year less). However, after controlling for various factors, those customers that had switched retailer in the previous 12 months only left $45 less on the table than those who had not switched.

The study concluded that customers mostly search for lower prices but that discounts that are not as they seem—many customers with no or low discounts were actually paying less than customers with much higher discounts. In addition, poor advice from price comparison service providers also explains part of the market's failure to give most customers the lower prices that they seem to be searching for.

While Australia's governments have recently introduced a variety of regulatory changes to improve customers' engagement with retail markets, the evidence of their difficulty in successfully engaging in grid-supplied markets will impact their relative perception of the value from BTM alternatives.

15.2.2 The response of households in Victoria, Australia, to time of use electricity tariffs

In the context of the Victoria Energy Policy Centre's research program, the Government of Victoria provided us with 50,000 bills (in PDF format) that customers had uploaded to the Victoria Government's price comparison website (https://compare.energy.vic.gov.au/) over the period from July 2018 to December 2018.

Customers were encouraged to use the Government's price comparison site through the payment of $50 if they consulted the site, although they were not required to upload their bills in order to receive the payment. Customers who had uploaded their bills agreed that the anonymized data from their bills could be used for research.

In this sample, there were 2805 households on two-rate time of use tariffs without rooftop PV and another 3993 households on two-rate time of use tariffs with rooftop PV. The peak rate starts at 7 a.m. and ends at 11 p.m. during weekdays, with the remainder at off-peak. Most customers on-peak/off-peak tariffs will have been shifted onto them by their retailers who in turn were responding to tariff structure changes initiated by the customers' network service provider.

There is no control on either peak or off-peak rates and the 19 different retailers in our sample charged a wide range of peak and off-peak rates. For all those customers on these tariffs, we analyzed the difference between their peak and off-peak rates and for each customer the proportion of their consumption that was during the peak period and the proportion that was during the off-peak period. The market was segmented to distinguish those that had their own rooftop solar (PV) from those without (since PV only produces during daylight hours and daylight hours occur at peak times for 5 of the 7 days in a week). Scatter plots showing the relationship between the proportion of consumption during peak periods (as proportion of all consumption) on the x-axis versus the difference in peak and off-peak prices on the y-axis are shown in Fig. 15.1, for households with solar, and Fig. 15.2, for households without solar.

These charts show that there is clearly no relationship between the difference in the peak and off-peak prices and the proportion of consumption in peak versus off-peak

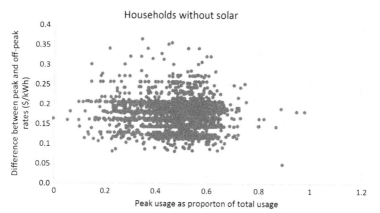

FIGURE 15.1 Prices versus volume, households without solar.

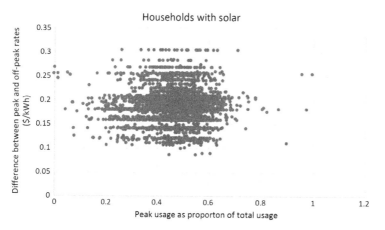

FIGURE 15.2 Prices versus volume, households with solar.

periods. Pearson correlation coefficients and econometric analysis confirmed that there is not a statistically significant relationship between peak and off-peak prices and the proportion of consumption in peak periods.

This result is much as might be expected. In the case of the author's own house, one of the only loads that might easily be shifted into off-peak periods is the automatic dishwasher. In the author's case, each such shifted wash would save around 18 cents or $18 per year but would result in a nontrivial loss of utility (unpacking the dishwasher at times not necessarily of choice). It might be suggested that other households might have greater opportunity to shift consumption from day to late at night without loss of utility but if so, the figures suggest that this is not the case.

There are of course many factors that are likely to affect the way that customers respond to time-varying prices. The outcomes found in this analysis of actual bills in Victoria seems to be different to the outcome of various experiments (see, e.g., Faruqui & Sergici, 2013), although consistent with behavioral economics analyses (see e.g., Hobman, Elisha, Stenner, & Meikle, 2016; Pollitt & Shaorshadze, 2011; Schjneider & Sunstein, 2017) and with more general analysis (Joskow, 2012).

15.2.3 The installation of rooftop PV in Australia

Our solar study (Mountain & Kars, 2018) undertaken for Solar Citizens analyzed the electricity bills in 2018 of 10,051 households in the contestable retail markets in Victoria, New South Wales, Queensland and South Australia. Of the 10,051 households, 2062 had installed rooftop PV. A histogram of the average annual electricity prices (cents per kWh before general sales tax (GST)) of grid-supplied electricity purchased by these households is shown in Fig. 15.3.

The average cost of electricity produced by rooftop PV ranges between 4 and 8 cents per kWh. The 10−19th percentile range of the variable price of grid-supplied electricity is 16−40 cents per kWh, and feed-in prices are typically around 9 cents per kWh. This means that in all but a few households, the installation of rooftop PV will pay for itself over its lifetime, and in most cases payback periods will range between 4 and 8 years. The economics of rooftop PV is affected by the amount of electricity displaced (since grid purchase prices are typically much higher than grid sales prices displacing grid supply is far more beneficial to households than grid export). Although there are scale economies in rooftop PV, the difference in the gains between displacement and export means that maximum benefit depends on grid consumption at the times that sun shines, and of course solar radiance.

Observations from these data suggest consumers have responded rationally to price signals, in their investment in rooftop PV, in particular,

- Households with higher consumption were more likely to install PV than households with lower consumption.

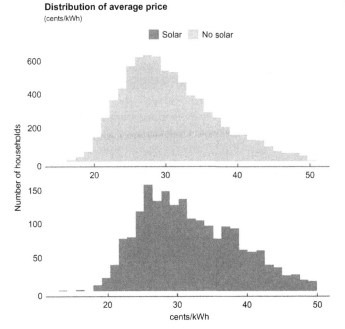

FIGURE 15.3 Histogram of average prices (cents per kWh) before GST.

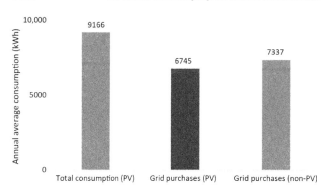

FIGURE 15.4 Residential PV production, export, and self-consumption.

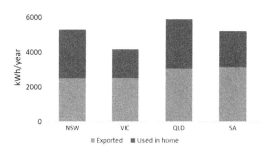

FIGURE 15.5 Residential PV production, export, and self-consumption.

- Regional differences in typical PV system size reflect regional differences in solar radiance and grid consumption.
- The installation of PV was proportionately the highest in households most likely to value the benefits from it.

On the first of these, the analysis shows a direct relationship between electricity consumption and rooftop solar installation. Fig. 15.4 shows that the average annual consumption of electricity of households that installed PV including the consumption provided by their own PV was 9166 kWh, compared to 7337 for households without PV. The median in both cases was lower but the median for households with PV was still higher than for households without PV. After accounting for demand met from their own PV production, households with PV purchased less electricity from the grid than those without PV.

Evidence for the second observation—that regional differences in typical PV system size reflects regional differences in solar radiance and grid consumption—can be seen in Fig. 15.5. This shows the amount of electricity produced by rooftop PV that was used in the home, and the amount of electricity produced by rooftop PV that was exported.

The following is notable in this chart:

- Victoria's households have smaller PV systems than in other states. This is consistent with its relatively lower variable grid charges in Victoria, the lower grid purchases, and poorer solar radiance in Victoria.
- Victoria's households also use proportionately less of their PV relative to households in other states. This reflects relatively higher feed-in rates in Victoria, relative to the variable charges in retail offers than in other states.

TABLE 15.1 Relationship between house value, socioeconomic decile, and rooftop solar PV proportion.

Socioeconomic decile	Property value	Rooftop PV as percentage of all customers in decile
1	$465.089	30
2	$452,841	22
3	$477,171	30
4	$589,010	26
5	$582,951	26
6	$647,968	29
7	$770,425	25
8	$838,482	22
9	$1.015.555	18
10	$1,279,862	13

- Households in Queensland, the state with the best solar insolation, had the largest rooftop PV installations.
- Households in SA, which has the highest grid prices, use proportionately more of the solar PV that is produced on their roofs than households elsewhere.

These observations are consistent with a rational assessment by households of the economics of PV and grid supply.

Evidence to support the third observation (the installation of PV was proportionately the highest in households most likely to value it) can be found in the proportionate uptake of rooftop solar in each of 10 socioeconomic deciles (as defined by the Australian Bureau of Statistics). In each of these deciles the median value of the houses with rooftop PV (by scraping data from real estate websites using the household address) was established. The result is shown in Table 15.1. This shows that proportionate rooftop PV uptake is inversely related to socioeconomic decile and property value. This is consistent with a hypothesis that those most likely to value the benefit from rooftop PV are also those most likely to have invested in rooftop PV.

15.2.4 Half-hourly retail charges for households in Great Britain

Energy supplier, Octopus Energy started offering an electricity plan (Agile) to households in Great Britain with half-hourly energy charges and presented an analysis (see Octopus Energy, 2018) of the responses of its first 47 customers. Agile's half-hourly prices reflect the prices of the electricity that Octopus buys in the day ahead market but are capped at 35 p/kWh. Agile customers are able to check energy prices for the following day online and through the Octopus app at 4:30 p.m. every day.

While just a small sample, 28% showed a statistically significant change in peak time usage, dropping peak usage from 16% to 11.5% of their daily consumption.

Overall, peak use was reduced by 28.19%, while electric vehicle (EV) drivers reduced peak consumption even further, by 47%. The study is currently being expanded to 800 customers.

While merely an initial investigation from a small number of customers, it does show strong customer response particularly from customers with EVs, to much cheaper prices in the early mornings. In correspondence with us, Octopus suggested the size of the customers' response to prices depended on price differences, how the prices are communicated to the customers (Octopus use bills, online dashboards, and emails) and the extent of automation in switchable loads.

The Octopus experience is indicative of the sort of commercial arrangements needed to motivate customers to respond to changes in prices for grid-supplied electricity.

15.3 Where does behind-the-meter value lie?

Having regard to the observations in the previous section, we speculate here on the origin of BTM value to small customers in the Australian market. The value arises when BTM provides the opportunity for customers to pay less for the same amount of electricity or, alternatively, when they obtain more benefit from less grid-, or BTM, supplied electricity. It is argued here that the five main sources of BTM intrinsic value in declining order of importance are as follows:

- Supply substitution
- Exports
- Arbitrage
- Reduced consumption (other than supply substitution)
- Autonomy and independence

These are briefly described in the following sections.

15.3.1 Supply substitution

Supply substitution refers to the value that customers are able to derive from the substitution of higher priced grid-supplied electricity with much cheaper PV BTM. Typically, per kWh consumed, PV offers a two- to threefold reduction in the price of around 40% of a typical customers' annual electrical consumption. As such this is certainly the largest source of BTM value currently and explains the uptake of rooftop PV in Australia. Since PV prices continue to decline and grid prices continue to rise, supply substitution is likely to continue to grow and thus we suggest is likely to remain the largest source of BTM value. Load diverters or similar load control devices (such as for water or space condition) further improve the prospects for supply substitutions.

15.3.2 Exports to the grid

For typical households around 70% of rooftop PV production is exported to the grid. While grid export prices are typically only around half or less variable grid purchase prices, exports add value at around half or less the rate of supply substitution, but since export volumes are typically more than own use, exports to the grid provide in aggregate around as much value as supply substitution. The possible development of decentralized markets may mean a deeper pool of potential buyers of rooftop PV production. However continued expansion of grid-scale and distributed PV might mean a reduction in prices for production exported to the grid.

15.3.3 Arbitrage

The primary source of arbitrage value is the ability to charge a BTM battery with solar produced electricity and use the stored electricity to substitute for grid supply. Continued expansion of solar production will improve the economics of arbitrage further by reducing the opportunity cost of foregone exports. Continued reduction in battery costs, improvement in functionality will increase the scope for arbitrage. The prospect of charges for network access for grid will further reduce the opportunity cost of foregone exports. While battery costs are currently such that arbitrage is ranked the third highest source of BTM value to households, it may quite possibly increase above export value particularly if continued rapid expansion of distributed and grid PV depresses export prices.

15.3.4 Reduced consumption other than supply substitution

Appliance efficiency improvements and better building insulation promise reduced energy consumption for the same or greater utility. While there is nothing intrinsically "BTM" about this—efficiency improvement is continuous—step-change technology improvements have occurred in the last decade (light emitting diode (LED) lighting and heat pump space conditioning). It is difficult to anticipate where further step-change reductions will occur, but considering the relative inefficiency of Australian household electricity consumption, we posit efficiency improvement is likely to be a reasonably important source of BTM intrinsic value.

15.3.5 Autonomy and independence

Many households express a preference for greater independence from grid-supplied electricity. There may be various reasons for this including mistrust of the (grid supply) electricity industry and preferences for self-produced renewable electricity. We are not aware of any surveys of buying decisions that would inform the question of the extent to which the desire for autonomy and independence has affected purchase decisions and will affect BTM development in future. It is likely to be more important to early adopters but is unlikely to be a significant factor in purchase decisions for most customers.

15.4 Conclusion

Surveying the Australian evidence finds that households have responded in a way that reflects a sophisticated understanding of their own (pecuniary) interests in respect of rooftop solar. But on the other hand, households have not generally engaged effectively with retail markets either in selecting cheaper offers when they switch or in moving their consumption to times of the day when it is cheaper. In Britain, Octopus's Agile production is an example, albeit still small scale, that customers' demand can become elastic to half-hourly retail prices when effort is made to communicate prices and automate customer responses.

At the risk of reading too much into the limited evidence, it is suggested that customers can be expected to respond more strongly to pecuniary incentives in their decisions to invest in and then operate BTM technologies, than they respond to pecuniary incentives to change their suppliers or the time profile of their grid-supplied demand. It is this greater engagement in BTM that underlies the expectation that customers will continue to pursue opportunities to replace more expensive grid-supplied electricity with cheaper rooftop PV production. It is also suggested that grid exports are valuable to households and will motivate continued PV uptake, and in the same way, arbitrage through storage will become increasingly valuable. Efficiency improvement and the desire for independence and autonomy will continue to motivate BTM investment, but less so than through the certain financial gains available from supply-substitution, exports, and in due course also arbitrage through storage.

References

Faruqui, A., & Sergici, S. (2013). Arcturus: International evidence on dynamic pricing. *The Electricity Journal, 26*(7), 55−65. Available from https://doi.org/10.1016/J.TEJ.2013.07.007.

Hobman, E. V., Elisha, R. F., Stenner, K., & Meikle, S. (2016). Uptake and usage of cost-reflective electricity pricing: Insights from psychology and behavioural economics. *Renewable and Sustainable Energy Reviews, 57*, 455−467. Available from https://doi.org/10.1016/j.rser.2015.12.144.

Joskow, P. L. (2012). Creating a smarter U.S. electricity grid. *Journal of Economic Perspectives, 26*, 29−48. Available from https://doi.org/10.1257/jep.26.1.29.

Mountain, B.R., & Kars, A. (2018). *Using electricity bills to shine a light on rooftop solar PV in Australia: A report for solar citizens*. Melbourne.

Mountain, B.R., & Rizio, S. (2019). Do Victoria's households leave less money on the table when they switch electricity retailers? In *Working paper 1909*. Melbourne. <https://docs.wixstatic.com/ugd/cb01c4_8babedb580d44-ca080fefea8b2ae8b0b.pdf>.

Octopus Energy. (2018). Agile octopus: A consumer-led shift to a low carbon future. London.

Pollitt, M.G., & Shaorshadze, I. (2011). *The role of behavioural economics in energy and climate policy*.

Schjneider, I., & Sunstein, C. R. (2017). Behavioral considerations for effective time-varying electricity prices. *Behavioural Public Policy, 1*(2), 219−251. Available from https://doi.org/10.1017/bpp.2017.2.

Regulating off-the-grid: stand-alone power systems in Australia

Alan Rai, Claire Rozyn, Andrew Truswell and Tim Nelson
AEMC, Sydney, NSW, Australia

16.1 Introduction

A stand-alone power system (SAPS) is an off-grid electricity supply system that is not physically connected to the main electricity grid. SAPS encompass microgrids, which supply electricity to multiple (nongrid-connected) customers, and individual power systems (IPSs), which relate only to single customers.

New technologies using distributed energy resources (DER) can mean better quality services for customers. Advances in solar power and batteries are making it possible to supply customers at the end of the line in a better and cheaper way. Importantly, the value to consumers from the use of these new technologies need not be dependent on where they are located relative to a customer's meter, that is, whether they are in front of or behind a customer's meter.

Generally, SAPS comprise solar photovoltaic (PV) panels, lithium-ion batteries, an inverter, and a backup diesel generator. The falling costs of renewable generation and battery storage, at both the utility and small scales, are making SAPS an increasingly viable option for supplying electricity to customers located in high cost-to-serve areas of the grid. The deployment of SAPS to these customers can have benefits for the entire community, through reduced network costs, and hence reduced network prices and cost savings to all consumers.

In addition to network costs and prices the benefits of SAPS also relate to safety and reliability. Many areas in which microgrids and IPS are being considered are in fringe-of-grid areas subject to extreme weather such as storms and wildfires, and/or rough terrain. This often results in low levels of reliability for customers. The use of SAPS in these areas

Behind and Beyond the Meter
DOI: https://doi.org/10.1016/B978-0-12-819951-0.00016-5

can therefore both increase reliability and reduce costs. Australia, with its large geographic area and relatively low population density, is at the cutting edge of these developments.

There are two broad drivers of the provision of SAPS:

1. Local network service provider (LNSP)-led SAPS—Under this approach the operator of a distribution network (termed the "local network service provider" or LNSP) is responsible for electricity supply to existing distribution network-connected (i.e., "grid-connected") customers using a SAPS. In this LNSP-led model the grid connection is then severed by the LNSP.
2. Third party–led SAPS—Under this approach a party other than the LNSP (i.e., a "third party") provides a SAPS to supply electricity to customers. A third party–led SAPS can emerge in one of two ways:
   a. The ownership and operation of an existing LNSP-led SAPS is transferred (i.e., sold) to a third party. This party includes operators of other distribution networks (termed non-LNSP-led SAPS).
   b. Grid-connected customers choose to go off-grid using a party other than the LNSP.

These different drivers are important in that it is the party driving the transition to SAPS that will ultimately determine the issues that need to be addressed by regulators, including the extent and form of regulation (if any) necessary to support the transition.

Australia's delegated law-making body, the Australian Energy Market Commission (AEMC) (2019a,b), recently considered these issues in a review of SAPS. The decision on whether or not SAPS assets should be considered as "front-of-meter" or "behind-the-meter" was, to some extent, a policy decision influenced by the existing regulatory framework. Specifically, requiring LNSP-led SAPS to be located in front of a customer's meter enabled the AEMC to define, and therefore treat, the service provided by LNSPs to customers using SAPS assets the same as the service provided by LNSPs to customers using the grid, that is, a supply of electricity to the customer's meter. This decision provided the foundation for a number of decisions made by the AEMC in developing the regulatory framework for LNSP-led SAPS in the National Electricity Market (NEM), including in respect of SAPS. However, this distinction may not be appropriate in all contexts (e.g., third party–led SAPS), and in all jurisdictions, and should be considered carefully on a case-by-case basis.

To this end, matters that have more traditionally been associated with "behind-the-meter" technologies nevertheless remain important and relevant in the context of SAPS, which may, at least physically, be located in front of a customer's meter.

As SAPS supply increasingly becomes a cost-effective alternative to standard supply, this chapter focuses on two key questions facing regulators:

1. Should the regulatory framework for grid-connected customers apply in full to SAPS-connected customers, particularly where the SAPS is provided by the LNSP?
2. Should the regulatory framework for SAPS-connected customers be the same regardless of which party (i.e., the LNSP or a third party) provides the SAPS?

Drawing on AEMC (2019a), this chapter discusses why the answer to this question is "yes"—that is, why the regulatory framework for LNSP-led SAPS supply should broadly emulate the existing regulatory framework for grid supply.

The proceeding sections describe how we arrived at this answer by exploring the interface between LNSP-led SAPS with competitive wholesale and retail markets, the key design features of a regulatory framework for SAPS, and the related pros and cons of the different regulatory approaches.

This chapter also discusses why the answer to the second question is somewhat equivocal, drawing on recent AEMC (2019b) work on third party–led SAPS.

While this chapter explores these questions specifically in the context of Australia, the broader issues considered are relevant to regulators elsewhere, and hence the lessons learned from the Australian experience are universal.

The chapter is organized as follows:

- Section 16.2 discusses four models of electricity supply, and the drivers of expected future uptake of SAPS drawing on Australia's experience.
- Section 16.3 outlines the barriers to the uptake of SAPS.
- Section 16.4 discusses the AEMC's review of the regulatory framework for SAPS.
- Section 16.5 discusses the five dimensions of a regulatory framework for LNSP-led SAPS, including the various options for a SAPS service delivery model and the AEMC's preferred design.
- Section 16.6 summarizes the key considerations in a regulatory framework for third party–led SAPS, including the reasons why this framework may differ from that established for LNSP-led SAPS.
- Section 16.7 sets out the chapter's conclusion.

16.2 Stand-alone power systems as a cost-effective model of supply

There are four models of electricity supply to consumers (see Fig. 16.1):

1. supply via an interconnected grid (i.e., "grid-supply" or "standard supply");
2. supply via an embedded network which, in turn, is connected to an interconnected grid;
3. supply via a microgrid, which may or may not be isolated from the interconnected grid as described elsewhere in this volume; and
4. supply via an IPS, which only provides electricity to the customer in question.

16.2.1 Falling costs of stand-alone power system

The increasing viability of SAPS as a cost-effective electricity supply model is driven by the falling costs of DER, especially battery storage. Mountain and Swanston discuss price drivers in Australia elsewhere in this volume. Between 2010 and 2017 the price of lithium-ion battery batteries in Australia fell by 79% (BloombergNEF, 2018). Capital costs for a fully installed residential storage system are expected to fall by 58% by 2030 (Fig. 16.2).

While SAPS are currently most viable for customers located in higher cost-to-serve areas, projected declines in the costs of DER are likely to further improve the economics of SAPS, making them increasingly viable even in lower cost-to-serve areas. BloombergNEF (2018)

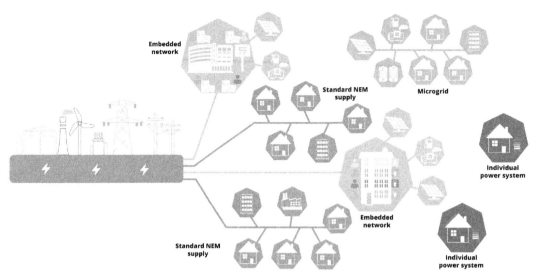

FIGURE 16.1 Four models of electricity supply. Source: *Courtesy of the Australian Energy Market Commission (AEMC) (May 2019a). Review of the regulatory frameworks for stand-alone power systems − Priority 1, Final report. Sydney: Australian Energy Market Commission, Figure 1.1.*

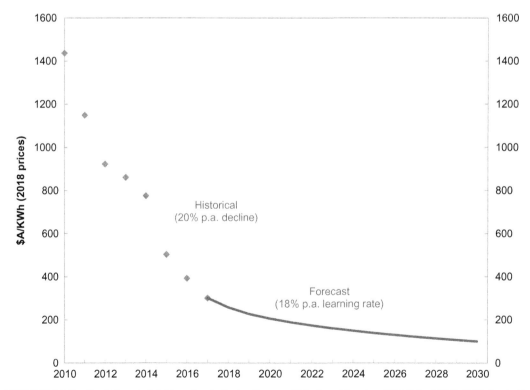

FIGURE 16.2 Capital cost of lithium-ion batteries. Source: *Data from BloombergNEF (May 2018). 2018 Australia behind-the-meter PV and storage forecast. Sydney: Bloomberg New Energy Finance.*

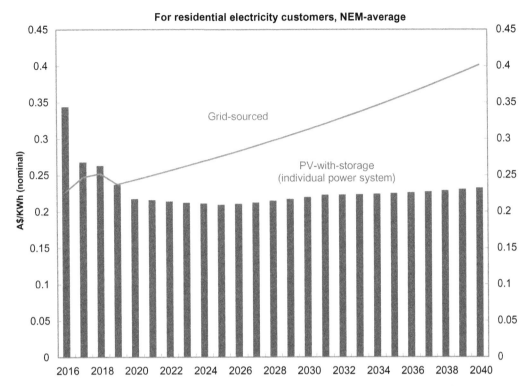

FIGURE 16.3 LCOE of alternative models of electricity supply. *LCOE*, Levelized cost of electricity. Source: *Data from BloombergNEF (May 2018). 2018 Australia behind-the-meter PV and storage forecast. Sydney: Bloomberg New Energy Finance.*

estimates that IPS comprising PV-with-storage is likely to achieve socket parity with grid-sourced electricity for residential electricity customers in 2019 and remain cheaper thereafter. In 2020 PV-with-storage is forecast to have a levelized cost of electricity of $0.22/kWh, 10% lower than grid-sourced electricity prices (Fig. 16.3).[1]

Due to both the limited experience with SAPS to date and the significant number of factors that influence the costs of a SAPS—such as the size of the system, accessibility of the location, solar resource availability, and the level or variability of energy demand—it is difficult to estimate the levelized cost of SAPS. This is especially the case for microgrids. In addition, the desired level of reliability can have a significant impact on costs.

Nevertheless, in Australia, available information indicates that the numbers of customers identified as candidate sites for LNSP-led SAPS is likely to be up to 10,000 in the NEM, and up to 15,000 customers in the wholesale electricity market (WEM), over the next decade (Fig. 16.4). While this represents only 0.1% of the 9 million customers in the NEM, and 1.5% of the 1 million customers in the WEM, the declining costs of DER is

[1] The grid-sourced prices in Fig. 16.3 average across both high and low cost-to-serve areas. Thus, according to BloombergNEF, socket parity has already been achieved in high cost-to-serve areas.

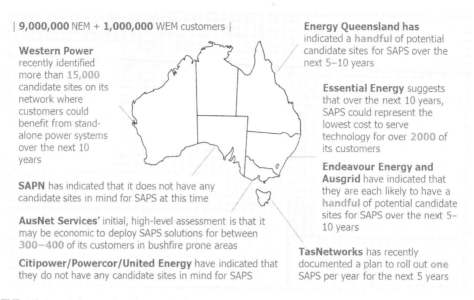

| 9,000,000 NEM + 1,000,000 WEM customers |

Western Power recently identified more than 15,000 candidate sites on its network where customers could benefit from stand-alone power systems over the next 10 years

SAPN has indicated that it does not have any candidate sites in mind for SAPS at this time

AusNet Services' initial, high-level assessment is that it may be economic to deploy SAPS solutions for between 300–400 of its customers in bushfire prone areas

Citipower/Powercor/United Energy have indicated that they do not have any candidate sites in mind for SAPS

Energy Queensland has indicated a handful of potential candidate sites for SAPS over the next 5–10 years

Essential Energy suggests that over the next 10 years, SAPS could represent the lowest cost to serve technology for over 2000 of its customers

Endeavour Energy and Ausgrid have indicated that they are each likely to have a handful of potential candidate sites for SAPS over the next 5–10 years

TasNetworks has recently documented a plan to roll out one SAPS per year for the next 5 years

FIGURE 16.4 Likely uptake of LNSP-led SAPS. *LNSP*, Local network service provider; *SAPS*, stand-alone power system. Source: *Courtesy of the Australian Energy Market Commission (AEMC) (May 2019a). Review of the regulatory frameworks for stand-alone power systems – Priority 1, Final report. Sydney: Australian Energy Market Commission, Figure 2.2.*

likely to make this supply model an increasingly viable alternative to standard supply into the future. As Swanston notes in Chapter 19 of this volume, more than 2 million Australian households have already installed solar PV as a partial grid-substitute.

16.2.2 Customer density, cost-to-serve, and reliability

Generally, cost-to-serve is inversely related to customer density, the number of customers per kilometer of network line.

In Australia, distribution network areas with lower than average customer densities tend to have a higher than average annual cost-to-serve (Fig. 16.5). For the 2011–17 period the highest cost-to-serve network area in the NEM had an average annual service cost of around $2000 per customer, with density of less than 10 customers per network line km. In contrast, the lowest cost-to-serve area had an average service cost of around $500 per customer, with a customer density of 70 customers per network line km. As in other countries, customer density is lowest in the regional and remote areas of Australia.

For grid-connected customers, there is also a clear relationship between customer density and reliability of electricity supply. Distribution networks with lower customer density tend to exhibit poorer reliability outcomes.

In Australia, network areas with lower customer densities tend to be associated with longer average system interruptions and with more frequent service interruptions (Fig. 16.6). The top chart shows that, between 2011 and 2017, the duration of supply

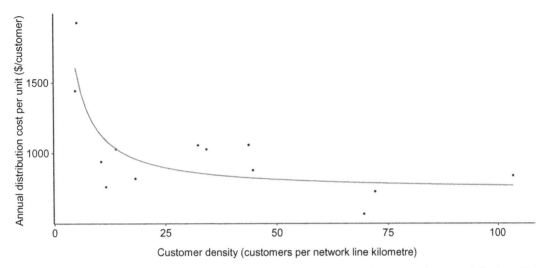

FIGURE 16.5   Customer density and distribution cost-to-serve (2011–17). Source: *Courtesy of the Australian Energy Market Commission (AEMC) (May 2019a).* Review of the regulatory frameworks for stand-alone power systems – Priority 1, Final report. *Sydney: Australian Energy Market Commission, Figure 2.3.*

interruptions in the lowest density distribution network areas are, on average, over five times longer than the duration of interruptions in the highest density areas. Over the same period the bottom chart shows that the number of supply interruptions in the lowest density areas is, on average, four to five times higher than the number of supply interruptions in the highest density areas.

It is worth noting that Figs. 16.5 and 16.6 do not reveal the intra-network variability in cost-to-serve and reliability. As would be expected, locational variations in reliability outcomes may exist within a distribution network, driven by many factors, including geography, climate patterns, and terrain. Although remote areas are typically likely to be associated with lower reliability and high costs-to-serve, it is possible that more densely populated areas (with better, but still below average, reliability and lower costs-to-serve) have a higher total cost associated with poor reliability outcomes. In this context the economic case for SAPS may not necessarily be limited to more remote areas.

16.2.3 Global research on off-grid supply

Australia's experience is not unique. Given that it can be costly to provide electricity via the grid in low-density areas, and that the costs of off-grid system components have dropped sharply in recent years, it is not surprising to find global examples where it is more cost-effective to supply electricity via off-grid systems than to maintain and replace existing links to the grid. Bauknecht et al., for example, discuss the costs and benefits to the broader electricity system of new and emerging technologies in Chapter 8.

In a 2017 report by the International Renewable Energy Agency (IRENA) (2017), IRENA found that by 2025, autonomous renewable mini- or microgrids will be able to provide

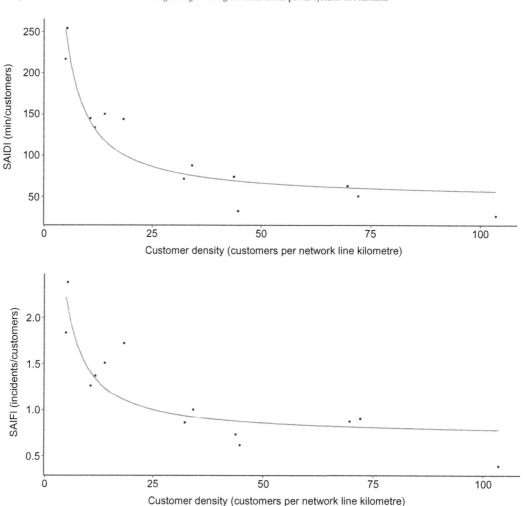

FIGURE 16.6 Customer density and network reliability (2011−17). Source: *Courtesy of the Australian Energy Market Commission (AEMC) (May 2019a).* Review of the regulatory frameworks for stand-alone power systems − Priority 1, Final report. *Sydney: Australian Energy Market Commission, Figure 2.4.*

both basic and high tiers of service at competitive prices, leading to the significant commercialization and deployment of these technologies to remote areas globally. Further, as the costs of these systems decline, renewable mini-grids will increasingly be able to compete with extensions of main grids. By 2035, these systems will be a cost-competitive option, even in areas close to the main grid.

This report indicates that the deployment of high-service microgrids (providing continuous power) is currently "mature" in Canada and the United States, and in parts of East and South Asia and Oceania, and "emerging" in many other jurisdictions (IRENA, 2017).

Consistent with IRENAs findings, various other studies also suggest that, as the cost of SAPS decline, these technologies will become more cost-effective than grid-sourced electricity for electrifying rural areas of South-East Asia (Kaundinya, Balachandra, & Ravindranath, 2009; Palit & Chaurey, 2011).

These findings highlight the significant opportunities available to jurisdictions from developing appropriate regulatory settings to allow the efficient use of SAPS to supply customers.

16.3 Barriers to the realization of the benefits of stand-alone power system

The previous section indicates that some customers in the low-density areas of the grid may be good candidates for SAPS, when considering both price and reliability of electricity. If these customers move from grid supply to SAPS supply, the total costs of providing distribution services to all customers, including those SAPS customers, could be lower, and the customers who move off-grid may have greater reliability. Additional benefits such as reduced wildfire risk and improved land amenity may also arise.

Achieving the benefits of SAPS, however, requires identifying and, where possible, removing any barriers to the roll-out of these systems to customers: by the competitive market in the first instance and by network businesses in the second.

16.3.1 Barriers to provision of stand-alone power system by the competitive market

While customers are generally free to move to off-grid supply at any time, they are unlikely to do so unless provided with the appropriate incentives. The incentive issue is likely to be relevant in jurisdictions with requirements or policies designed to charge similar groups of grid-connected customers—for example, residential customers—the same rates for electricity. This is commonly known as postage stamp pricing.[2] If the price of off-grid supply exceeds the cross-subsidized price of grid supply, a grid-connected customer has no financial incentive to move off-grid. Instead, these customers are likely to retain their grid connection even where a SAPS solution would provide a more cost-effective alternative.

This is illustrated in Fig. 16.7, where Line A indicates the per-customer cost to provide electricity via the national grid; it varies with customer density. The dashed line, Line B, indicates the prices paid by grid-connected customers, on the basis that electricity costs are averaged across all customers in the distributor's area, and location-specific cost differences are not passed through. Line C indicates the per-customer cost to provide electricity via off-grid supply; for this illustration, it is assumed this does not change with customer density—unlike grid supply costs.

In the low customer density area on the left of the graph, the gap between Line A and Line C indicates the potential savings from moving these high-cost customers from grid

---

[2] Some jurisdictions also have subsidies for remote customers (AEMC, 2019a). Even in jurisdictions without explicit subsidies or postage-stamp pricing, there is a lack of sufficiently location-specific network pricing, for historical and other reasons. Instead, all customers of the same type (e.g., residential) in a distribution network area are charged the same network prices.

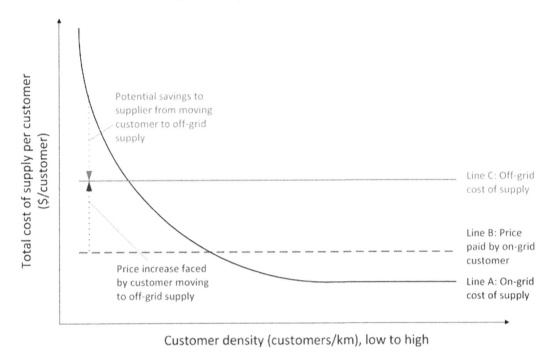

FIGURE 16.7 Stylized example of barriers to uptake of a SAPS. *SAPS,* Stand-alone power system. Source: *Courtesy of the Australian Energy Market Commission (AEMC) (May 2019a).* Review of the regulatory frameworks for stand-alone power systems − Priority 1, Final report. *Sydney: Australian Energy Market Commission, Figure 2.9.*

supply to off-grid supply. Note that if these savings were achieved, Line B—prices paid by all customers—may decrease marginally. However, Line C is higher than Line B, so these customers would pay more if they chose to move from grid supply to off-grid supply and would have no incentive to do so if they were paying for an off-grid system themselves.

Over time, Line C is expected to fall as off-grid supply components continue to get cheaper. This means the potential savings from moving high-cost customers to off-grid supply will increase. However, as long as Line C remains higher than Line B, customers have no financial incentive to move off-grid. This is despite the overall system costs being lower if they did so.

In the context of a third party−led SAPS the bigger of the two barriers relates to cost. A grid-connected customer that chooses to go off-grid chooses to pay the SAPS price instead of the grid-connected price, and thereby forgoes any cross-subsidy that may be present. The barrier in relation to regulated revenues and assets is nonexistent as a third party−led SAPS is not a regulated service.

While it would be economically efficient to implement a cost-reflective network pricing regime to improve the locational signals provided to customers, the experience in Australia is that policy makers have been reluctant to do so, particularly given the implications this would have for some residential customers.

In Australia, governments' desire to maintain postage-stamp pricing across certain groups of customers—irrespective of where they are located and therefore their cost-to-serve—means that alternative arrangements are needed in order to be able to capture the benefits provided by the use of SAPS for electricity supply. Concern about the fairness of tariffs for electricity is discussed by Schittekatte in Chapter 17.

16.3.2 Barriers to the provision of stand-alone power system by local network service providers

The regulatory frameworks governing electricity supply have traditionally been designed on the understanding that generators, transmission systems, and distribution systems are connected to each other to form the integrated electricity systems and associated markets seen across the world today. The result, however, is that the application of these frameworks to isolated systems is not necessarily straightforward and in some cases may be inhibited by earlier assumptions regarding the "connectedness" of the assets necessary to supply electricity to customers.

In Australia, certain definitions within the national energy laws and rules effectively preclude network businesses from recovering expenditure on SAPS from regulated revenue on the basis that SAPS assets and associated services cannot provide "distribution services" as currently defined in those instruments.[3] Restrictions of this nature mean that network businesses are unlikely to install SAPS assets themselves, or to purchase SAPS services from the competitive market, in order to supply electricity to customers even where SAPS would provide an efficient alternative to grid-supply. Kuiper discusses regulatory governance in a future where half the energy consumers are also energy producers in Chapter 20.

16.4 Designing a regulatory framework for stand-alone power system—the Australian experience

As explained above, in the light of the falling costs of new technologies using DER, regulators around the world, including in Australia, are focused on ensuring customers that remote and regional areas are able to benefit from the falling costs of renewable generation and batteries.

16.4.1 Australian Energy Market Commission review of the regulatory framework for stand-alone power system

In 2018 the AEMC was asked by the Council of Australian Governments' Energy Council to review the regulatory arrangements for SAPS in the NEM. The review was triggered by concerns that the current regulatory frameworks inhibit the use of SAPS where these would represent a more efficient solution to supply some customers.

---

[3] This is a consequence of the fact that the national regulatory framework for energy, the national energy customer framework (NECF), applies only to customers connected to the interconnected system (i.e., the NEM) and do not apply to customers supplied by systems outside the NEM.

The first priority for the AEMC was to develop amendments to national energy laws and rules to allow currently grid-connected customers to be transitioned to SAPS supply by their LNSP. In Australia, LNSPs are already developing plans to utilize SAPS solutions as an efficient alternative to supply certain existing customers. In some cases, projects are very advanced and could be completed almost immediately upon changes to the regulatory frameworks being implemented.

As a second priority, the AEMC was asked to review the regulatory frameworks for SAPS provided by parties other than LNSPs. There have long been isolated electricity supply systems in Australia, largely microgrids supplying remote towns in Queensland and South Australia. For historic reasons, these systems have been regulated on a state, rather than national, basis. Falling technology costs and increased sustainability concerns in some communities suggest a greater likelihood that new systems may now be established, calling into question the suitability of existing laws and regulations in this changing environment.

16.4.2 Criteria for assessing a potential regulatory framework for stand-alone power system

The AEMC's primary objective in relation to its first priority (LNSP-led SAPS) was to develop a regulatory framework to allow LNSPs to transition customers to SAPS supply where it is economically efficient to do so, while maintaining appropriate consumer protections and service standards.

In considering the potential regulatory arrangements to achieve this objective, the AEMC was guided by the national energy objectives—specifically, the national electricity objective (NEO) and the national energy retail objective (NERO).[4] While both these objectives are phrased in terms of achieving economic efficiency in the long-term interests of consumers, the latter includes an additional consumer protections test that requires any reforms to existing retail arrangements to be compatible with the development and application of consumer protections for small customers.

The consumer protection test is important in which any assessment of potential regulatory arrangements to accommodate SAPS requires more than just an economic assessment (i.e., cost-benefit test); there is also the need to consider the potential impact on consumer regulatory protections (to the extent that such impacts cannot be quantified and captured within a cost-benefit test).

To inform its assessment the AEMC identified five key criteria, drawing on principles of good market design and best practice regulation:

- *Facilitating competition and consumer choice*—Competition is a key driver of productivity and efficiency in markets, driving lower prices and improved choices for consumers in the long run. Regulatory arrangements for SAPS should facilitate competition and choice, with readily available clear, timely, and accurate market information.

---

[4] In considering the need for, and design of, potential reforms, the AEMC is guided by the NEO, NERO, and the national gas objective, depending on the fuel type and market under consideration. For more details, see https://www.aemc.gov.au/regulation/regulation.

- *Promoting efficient investment and allocation of risks and costs*—The regulatory framework for SAPS should encourage innovation and promote efficient investment in network infrastructure and the supply of energy services, as well as continuing to remain fit-for-purpose if and when the penetration of LNSP-led SAPS increases. Economically efficient outcomes are most likely to arise where risks and costs are appropriately allocated to the parties best placed to manage them, and transaction costs are minimized.
- *Appropriate consumer protections and compliance mechanisms*—Where SAPS supply is provided as a regulated LNSP-led service at the same price as paid by grid-connected customers, protections should be no less stringent than the relevant protections provided to grid-connected customers. However, there may be instances where SAPS-connected consumers may be willing to forgo some protections in return for lower prices. A similar trade-off could be made between price and reliability.
- *Clear, consistent, and transparent regulatory arrangements*—The regulatory framework for SAPS needs to be transparent and result in predictable outcomes for all participants and should provide a clear, understandable set of rules to encourage effective participation in the market.
- *Regulatory arrangements that are proportionate*—Regulatory frameworks should balance the costs of regulatory arrangements with their expected benefits and be fit for purpose. Where arrangements are complex to administer, difficult to understand, or impose unnecessary risks, they are less likely to achieve their intended ends, or will do so at higher cost.

While these criteria were identified by the AEMC as being appropriate within the Australian context, they are also likely to be relevant in other jurisdictions where an economic assessment of potential regulatory arrangements for SAPS is necessary and/or appropriate.

16.5 Key design choices for a regulatory framework for stand-alone power system

The regulatory framework for SAPS incorporates the arrangements by which LNSPs would decide to transition a customer(s) from standard supply to SAPS supply, and the subsequent arrangements for the ongoing supply of electricity to those customers, including the allocation of roles and responsibilities and the application of consumer protections.

To this end the AEMC identified five dimensions of the regulatory framework for LNSP-led SAPS (AEMC, 2019a) (Fig. 16.8).

This section focuses specifically on the "SAPS service delivery" dimension, and discusses a number of illustrative options considered by the AEMC as part of its recent work to develop a regulatory framework for SAPS. These options are differentiated by their approach to setting the price charged to the customer-facing party—the retailer—for the energy it delivers to the SAPS customer.

There are, however, a number of design elements common to all of SAPS service delivery options considered by the AEMC. These common elements are represented by the four

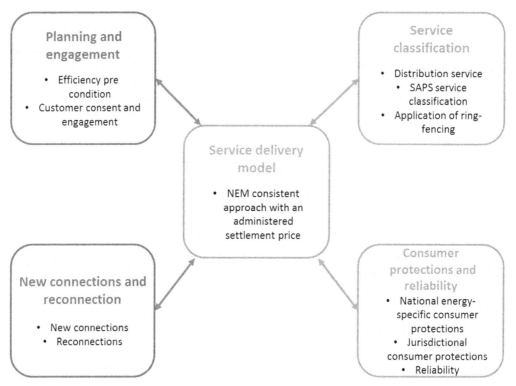

FIGURE 16.8   Five dimensions of a regulatory framework for LNSP-led SAPS. *LNSP*, Local network service provider; *SAPS*, stand-alone power system. Source: *Courtesy of the Australian Energy Market Commission (AEMC) (May 2019a)*. Review of the regulatory frameworks for stand-alone power systems — Priority 1, Final report. *Sydney: Australian Energy Market Commission, Figure 2.*

outer dimensions shown in Fig. 16.8 and include matters such as the setting and measurement of reliability standards, the rights of reconnection, the approach to the classification of SAPS services.[5]

16.5.1 Service delivery models for local network service provider-led stand-alone power system

Unlike P2P or aggregation models (Chapters 4 and 10), a SAPS service provided to a customer(s) incorporates a suite of activities and services, including local generation services, network services, and retail services, as well as supporting services such as metering. Over time, SAPS models may evolve further in the wake of home automation and other smart digital technologies (Shaw-Williams discussion of this in Chapter 7). This raises questions of how to define and allocate responsibility for these services, including

[5] A brief summary of the AEMC's position in respect of these common elements is provided in Section 5.2.

the interaction between the contestable and regulated elements of a SAPS, and the extent to which this should differ from what occurs in the NEM.

Consumer prices, whether in a SAPS or the NEM, consist of three components:

1. Network—the cost of transporting electricity from generators to consumers;
2. Generation—the cost of generating electricity; and
3. Retail—the cost of retailing energy, including billing, and metering.

A SAPS can therefore be considered as having three elements:

1. distribution system—that is, the poles and wires components of a SAPS—which provides a distribution service;[6]
2. generating system(s), an input to the distribution system—for example, the solar PV panels, battery packs, and diesel generators; and
3. retail system, which provides various retail services—for example, customer management, billing, metering, new in-premise energy management systems—and directly interfaces with SAPS customers.

In the NEM the latter two elements are contestable and subject to modest economic regulation.[7] The former is subject to various forms of economic regulation, including price or revenue caps and connection obligations.

In respect of SAPS the degree of contestability in the provision of, in particular, the retail and generation services may not be consistent with the competitive conditions in NEM, especially for IPS and small-scale microgrids.

To this end a key issue to consider when designing a regulatory framework for SAPS is which of the three elements—that is, generation, network, and retail—should be considered contestable and, therefore, which of the three elements would benefit from arrangements that continue to promote the development of effective competition.

Incorporating effective competition is generally the preferred means of achieving efficient, lowest cost service provision. The level of competition associated with different SAPS service delivery models can be shown along a competition continuum shown (Fig. 16.9).

In terms of the retail component, if "competition in the market" for provision of retail services is workable and effective, then it may be sensible to extend, where possible, existing retail arrangements[8] to SAPS customers. AEMC (2019a) referred to this approach as the "NEM consistency model" of SAPS service delivery.

Under this model, LNSP-led SAPS services would be delivered using existing wholesale energy market arrangements, including the market operator's (Australian Energy Market

---

[6] In the case of an IPS, the distribution service would consist of the wiring from the generation assets (e.g., rooftop PV and battery storage) to the customer's meter box.

[7] For generation, regulations include caps on wholesale prices and controls on how generators bid into the market; for retail, regulations include various consumer protections and, increasingly of late, retail price caps.

[8] These arrangements include the choice of retailer, choice of retail offer, and access to retail competition, in those jurisdictions of the NEM with retail market contestability.

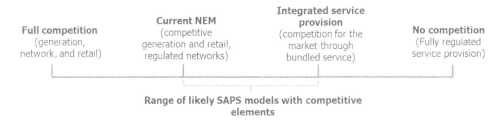

FIGURE 16.9   SAPS competition continuum. *SAPS*, Stand-alone power system. Source: *Courtesy of the AEMC.*

Operator: AEMO's)[9] settlement system. This approach makes it feasible for the SAPS retail service to be provided by competing grid retailers, thus allowing SAPS customers to

- maintain their relationships with existing retailers;
- retain their existing retail offers; and
- maintain access to retail market competition.

This model would help to ensure that customers transitioned to SAPS were "no-worse-off" in terms of the consumer protections, including price, they receive following a transition to SAPS. Crucially, it would also negate the need for LNSPs to seek, and relevant customers to provide, explicit consent for the transition to SAPS.

In terms of the generation component, if competition in the market for retail services is workable and a NEM consistent approach to service delivery is considered possible, there are two approaches to pricing the generation element of a SAPS:[10]

1. using wholesale prices for the NEM (i.e., a price that varies every 5 minutes), perhaps for the NEM region in which the SAPS is located or
2. using predetermined prices.

AEMC (2019a) referred to the first option as the "NEM consistency (wholesale price) model" and the second as the "NEM consistency (administered settlement price) model."

In contrast, if competition in the market for the provision of retail services is not considered workable, it may be sensible to pursue a SAPS service delivery model which uses "competition for the market" to allocate a provider of each (or both) of the SAPS retail and generation services. Further, if both competition in and for the market for the provision of generation and/or retail services is not considered workable, allocating the relevant LNSP responsibility for all SAPS functions may be warranted.[11]

---

[9] AEMO performs a number of gas and electricity market, operational, development, and planning functions. Among other things, it manages the NEM.

[10] Note that the two approaches to pricing generation under a NEM consistent model are relevant whether or not competition is workable in the provision of SAPS generation.

[11] In this case, an LNSP would then be free to outsource any or all of these functions and subfunctions—including the retail function—but would remain responsible for ensuring compliance with all SAPS regulations.

Both of these approaches are referred to broadly as the "integrated service delivery model" (AEMC, 2019a). Under this model a new retailer role and a regulated retail price would need to be established for SAPS customers.

A brief overview of these models is provided next.

16.5.1.1 National Electricity Market consistency model with National Electricity Market wholesale spot prices

Under this pricing option the retailer would be charged the NEM wholesale spot price for the energy it delivers to the customer, using existing wholesale electricity market arrangements, including AEMO's settlement system. The financial flows between the various parties are shown in Fig. 16.10.[12]

Retailers would aggregate their SAPS and NEM customer loads and hedge the price and volume risks with NEM-domiciled generators.

The key feature of the NEM consistency model is that the retailer—customer relationship would not need to change between grid and SAPS service provision. This provides a simple and straightforward means of ensuring that grid-customers being transitioned to SAPS will be no-worse-off in respect of the consumer protections they receive, including the price they pay for energy, because they will continue to receive energy in the same way contractually with their retailer. Importantly, this outcome negates the need for LNSPs to seek, and relevant customers to provide, explicit consent for the transition to SAPS.

The fundamental issue with the NEM consistency option, however, arises from the inherent expectation that retailers would continue to manage price risk by hedging their overall customer load—including SAPS customer load—through financial contracts with generators in the NEM. If the penetration of SAPS customers increases substantially and generation from the NEM is replaced by generation from SAPS, it may become increasingly difficult for NEM generators to provide sufficient financial derivative contracts to address the spot price risk of total demand (i.e., demand for hedges to cover grid and SAPS customer load). A mismatch between the demand for hedging contracts and supply of those hedges would therefore be expected to increase the costs of hedging and reduce overall contract market liquidity.

16.5.1.2 National Electricity Market consistency model with administered wholesale prices

Under this model the retailer would be charged an administered, SAPS-specific, settlement price for the energy it delivers to the customer. Existing wholesale electricity market

---

[12] Upon transitioning from the NEM to the SAPS, the customer would continue to pay their existing retailer (under their existing retail contract). The retailer in turn would forward the network charges to the LNSP and would settle the energy delivered to SAPS customers with AEMO at the wholesale spot price. The SAPS generator would receive an energy payment from AEMO also at the wholesale spot price, plus a make-whole payment from the LNSP consistent with the contractual arrangements for SAPS generation services between the LNSP and the SAPS generator.

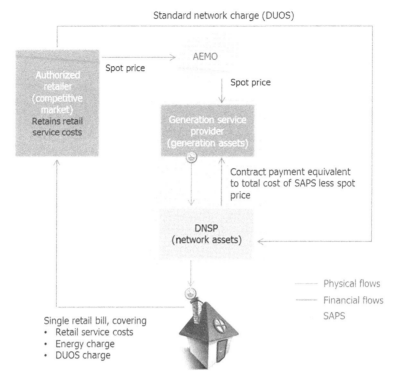

Standard network charge (DUOS)

AEMO

Spot price

Spot price

Authorized retailer (competitive market)
Retains retail service costs

Generation service provider (generation assets)

Contract payment equivalent to total cost of SAPS less spot price

DNSP (network assets)

Physical flows
Financial flows
SAPS

Single retail bill, covering
• Retail service costs
• Energy charge
• DUOS charge

FIGURE 16.10   The NEM consistency (wholesale spot price) model. *NEM*, National Electricity Market. Source: *Courtesy of the Australian Energy Market Commission (AEMC) (May 2019a). Review of the regulatory frameworks for stand-alone power systems − Priority 1, Final report. Sydney: Australian Energy Market Commission, Figure A.1.*

arrangements, including AEMO's settlement system, would be used, amended as necessary to provide for the SAPS-specific settlement price.

In contrast to the previous model [NEM consistency (wholesale spot price)], this model would remove retailer risk associated with price volatility in the spot market and therefore also the need for retailers to hedge SAPS customers' load with NEM generators (AEMC, 2019a).

16.5.1.3 Integrated service delivery model with regulated retail prices

In this model a regulated retail price would be established. The retailer would be charged a wholesale energy price calculated as the regulated retail price less the standard network charge less the SAPS retailer's margin, agreed in advance in its contract with the LNSP. Fig. 16.11 shows an integrated delivery model where the generation and retail functions are provided by the same party.

This model makes it feasible for SAPS customers to be, on average, no-worse-off in respect of the price each customer pays (or at least is offered) for energy relative to equivalent grid-connected customers, where it is not possible or appropriate to preserve SAPS customers' access to the competitive retail market.

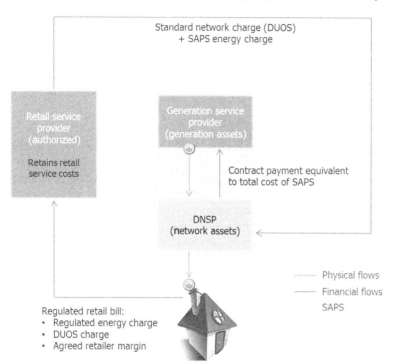

FIGURE 16.11 Integrated service delivery model. Source: *Courtesy of the Australian Energy Market Commission (AEMC) (May 2019a).* Review of the regulatory frameworks for stand-alone power systems — Priority 1, Final report. *Sydney: Australian Energy Market Commission, Figure A.2.*

Importantly, these arrangements would operate outside existing NEM wholesale market arrangements and associated contract markets. This removes the risk of any reductions in derivative contract market liquidity as well as any unintended distortions in the wholesale market arising from retailers seeking to hedge SAPS customer loads with generators that are located outside the SAPS.

16.5.1.4 Australian Energy Market Commission's preferred model

Of the three service delivery models noted above, we prefer the second one: a NEM consistent approach that utilizes an administered settlement price charged to retailers for the delivery of energy to SAPS customers.

By utilizing existing wholesale market arrangements, including the settlement system, the Commission's recommended model will facilitate a seamless transition to SAPS. In doing so, this model negates the need for LNSPs to seek, and relevant customers to provide, explicit informed consent for the transition.

Further, by emulating the conditions under which a customer would be supplied if they were connected to the grid, this model also provides a simple and straightforward means of ensuring that grid-customers transitioned to SAPS will be no-worse-off in respect of the price they pay for energy. It also avoids the need for potentially complex and costly retail price regulation.

16.5.2 Other features of the local network service provider-led stand-alone power system regulatory framework

This section briefly describes the common features of a SAPS regulatory framework as identified by the AEMC (2019a), including the AEMC's proposed recommendations in respect of each dimension.

16.5.2.1 Service classification

Supplying electricity to customers via poles and wires connected to the national grid is a core network service for which LNSPs can generally expect to earn regulated returns for the provision of these services to customers. A key question when designing a regulatory framework for SAPS is therefore whether the provision of SAPS services by LNSPs constitutes a "core network service" and, if so, whether there are any regulatory barriers to its classification as such.

In the context of the NEM the AEMC recommended changes to the national energy law and rules to broaden the definition of "distribution services" to include SAPS services, thereby enabling LNSPs to utilize SAPS where efficient, and to fund these services through their regulated revenues in the usual way.

16.5.2.2 Planning and engagement

The objective of a regulatory framework for LNSP-led SAPS should be to achieve an outcome, whereby LNSPs pursue and develop SAPS only where these provide a more efficient model of supply for customers than continuing to provide them with standard supply via the interconnected grid. The need to establish an economic test to determine whether a SAPS model of supply provides an economically efficient alternative to standard supply for some customers is therefore a key consideration when designing a regulatory framework for SAPS.

In the NEM, SAPS solutions will effectively be treated the same as any other nonnetwork option within the existing network planning and investment frameworks. To this end the AEMC concluded that the existing regulatory investment test for distribution (the RIT-D) and associated process will apply to SAPS.[13]

To recognize the importance of effective and timely engagement between LNSPs and affected parties including potential SAPS customers and the local public, the AEMC also recommended LNSPs carry out a comprehensive program of information provision and consumer engagement where SAPS supply is identified as being the most efficient means of continuing to supply a customer with energy. MacGill and Smith talk about consumer value and behavior in relation to new technologies more broadly in Chapter 9.

16.5.2.3 New connections and reconnection

As noted in Section 16.3, postage stamp pricing policies and associated cross-subsidies can have the effect of removing any incentive for existing grid-customers in high

[13] The RIT-D is an economic cost-benefit assessment. For SAPS options not subject to the RIT-D (which would generally be because a financial threshold is not met), there is no requirement for LNSPs to undertake a cost-benefit assessment, consistent with the existing approach for all projects not subject to a RIT-D.

cost-to-serve areas to move to off-grid supply provided by a competitive provider, even when there may be economic benefits for consumers overall.[14] In contrast, new customers without an existing grid connection are likely to have a financial incentive to obtain off-grid supply from the competitive market, in particular where regulatory frameworks require these customers to pay the full costs of establishing a new grid connection—quite costly for customers in certain remote and rural regions. In this context a key question for policy makers is whether LNSPs should be permitted to provide new connections via SAPS.

The AEMC concluded that customers seeking a new connection would be unable to connect to a new SAPS provided by their LNSP, thereby preventing these customers from accessing cross- or direct subsidies arising from LNSP supply while also promoting competition in the provision of SAPS by third parties.

16.5.2.4 *Consumer protections and reliability*

A key issue for the development of a regulatory framework for SAPS relates to the energy-specific consumer protections applicable to customers receiving supply via SAPS. Consideration needs to be given to whether the full suite of consumer protections afforded to grid-connected customers are appropriate for all types of SAPS and/or whether additional consumer protections may be required.

The AEMC followed a general principle that energy-specific consumer protections for customers transitioned to SAPS supply by their LNSP should be equivalent to those for grid-connected customers. To this end the AEMC recommended that the existing energy-specific consumer protection framework applicable in the NEM, including jurisdictional consumer protections and reliability of supply obligations, be extended to customers supplied by LNSP-led SAPS.

16.6 Considerations for the regulatory framework for third party–led stand-alone power system

The discussion in this chapter is predominantly related to LNSP-led SAPS, that is, a SAPS where the LNSP owns and operates at least the network component (and possibly also the generation and retail components). This section provides a brief overview of how a regulatory framework for third-party SAPS may be less extensive than for LNSP-led SAPS.

There are two key differences between LNSP-led SAPS and third party–led SAPS:

1. *The lack of need for consent and the choice available to customers.* Customers being considered for transition to an LNSP-led SAPS supply are not choosing to move off-grid for their own reasons. Rather, they are customers identified by an LNSP as those who could be more efficiently supplied via SAPS for the benefit of all customers. In

---

[14] For this reason, it may be efficient to allow LNSPs to facilitate the provision of SAPS as a regulated service to existing grid-connected customers, where competition is not practicable and off-grid supply is cheaper than maintaining a grid connection.

contrast, customers transitioning to a third party—SAPS are more likely to be doing so by choice.

2. *The lack of postage-stamp pricing for customers who voluntarily choose to go off-grid.*
Customers who choose to move off-grid in favor of receiving supply via a third-party SAPS are unable to access the cross-subsidies resulting from postage stamp pricing or other policies which are available to customers supplied by LNSP-led SAPS. This means that

   a. supply from an IPS would likely be comparable in cost to supply via a third-party microgrid and

   b. customers would have the choice to request a connection offer from the local LNSP.

The degree of customer choice and, consequently, the need to develop specific arrangements to ensure the long-term interests of consumers—for example, through consent requirements—are key considerations when designing an appropriate regulatory framework for third-party SAPS.

The scope and breadth of potential SAPS is large, with many variations likely in the size of the systems, as well as ownership structures and operating models. Consequently, a one-size-fits-all approach to their regulation may not be appropriate. Instead, regulatory arrangements should follow the principle of proportionality.

Given the likely variation in the size of third-party SAPS, a tiered regulatory framework may be appropriate. AEMC (2019b) proposed the following three tiers (see "categories" in Fig. 16.12):

- Category 1: These SAPS have the largest number of customers and/or the largest loads and could be determined by a form of coverage test to determine whether the competition within the SAPS would be efficient.
- Category 2: This includes systems bigger than category 3 and SAPS where competition is not considered efficient. The threshold between categories 2 and 3 might be based on the number of small customers and/or the size and complexity of the system.

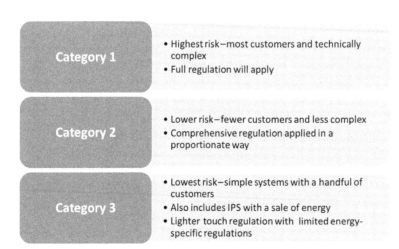

FIGURE 16.12 Proposed tiered framework for third-party SAPS. *SAPS,* Stand-alone power system. Source: *Courtesy of the Australian Energy Market Commission (AEMC) (June 2019b).* Review of the regulatory frameworks for stand-alone power systems — Priority 2, Draft report. *Sydney: Australian Energy Market Commission, Figure 1.*

- Category 3: This includes systems with a sale of energy and/or more than one customer but fewer customers than category 2. This category could also include microgrids with only large customers.

The proposed regulatory framework for third-party SAPS in the NEM is less developed than for LNSP-led SAPS and continues to evolve.

16.7 Conclusion

The falling costs of new technologies, including DER resources, are giving rise to new electricity supply models that are challenging the traditional, and increasingly narrow, architecture of energy markets worldwide. Traditional assumptions around the connectedness of the infrastructure necessary to supply electricity to customers, and the consequent charging structures these assumptions have long underpinned, have left regulators grappling with questions around how best to lawfully capture all of the benefits available from implementing alternate models of supply.

As the Australian experience demonstrates, revising regulatory frameworks in the wake of the increasing viability of SAPSs will enable the range of benefits associated with SAPS supply—including higher levels of service and reliability for SAPS customers and, crucially, lower the costs of supply to these customers and to everyone else—to be achieved.

Acknowledgment

We thank Alisa Toomey and Lily Mitchell for assistance with this chapter. All views, errors and omissions are the responsibility of the authors, not the AEMC.

References

Australian Energy Market Commission (AEMC). (2019a). *Review of the regulatory frameworks for stand-alone power systems - Priority 1.* Sydney: Australian Energy Market Commission, Final report, 30 May.

Australian Energy Market Commission (AEMC). (2019b). *Review of the regulatory frameworks for stand-alone power systems − Priority 2.* Sydney: Australian Energy Market Commission, Draft report, 27 June.

BloombergNEF. (2018). *2018 Australia behind-the-meter PV and storage forecast.* Sydney: Bloomberg New Energy Finance, May.

International Renewable Energy Agency (IRENA). (2017). *Innovation outlook: Renewable mini-grids, summary for policy makers* (p. 12) International Renewable Energy Agency.

Kaundinya, D. P., Balachandra, P., & Ravindranath, N. H. (2009). Grid-connected versus stand-alone energy systems for decentralized power − A review of literature. *Renewable and Sustainable Energy Reviews, 13,* 2041−2050.

Palit, D., & Chaurey, A. (2011). Off-grid rural electrification experiences from South Asia: Status and best practices. *Energy for Sustainable Development, 15*(3), 266−276.

Further reading

IEA. (2018). *World energy outlook 2018 − Executive summary.* New York: International Energy Agency, November.

Distribution network tariff design for behind-the-meter: balancing efficiency and fairness

Tim Schittekatte

Florence School of Regulation, Florence, Italy

17.1 Introduction

This chapter revolves around the design of electricity distribution network tariffs for residential consumers.[1] Consumers pay distribution network charges to contribute to the recovery of the costs of the distribution network, which delivers electricity locally. ACER and CEER (2018) report that distribution network charges represent on average about one-third of the electricity bill (after value-added tax (VAT)) in the EU. Extremes are Norway (Oslo) where distribution charges represent about 50% of the bill and Italy (Rome) where distribution charges only represent 15% of the bill.[2]

Until recently, distribution network tariffs were designed in a simplistic way in most countries. The more electricity you consumed, the more you contributed to the recuperation of the cost of the local network, that is, distribution charges were mainly accounted for volumetrically. This arrangement was deemed fair as high usage, and thus higher network contributions correlated rather well with more affluent consumers. Further,

---

[1] This chapter is based on the PhD thesis of the author (Schittekatte, 2019). The author would like to acknowledge the feedback and support from the editor, Nicolò Rossetto, Valerie Reif and Leonardo Meeus.

[2] In this chapter an unbundled distribution system operator (DSO) is assumed for which the costs are recovered by the distribution network tariff as is the case in the EU and some states in the United States. This contrasts with a monopolistic vertically integrated electricity company bundling generation, transmission, distribution, and retail for which the final electricity tariff covers all these activities together.

such charges were predictable, simple, and, anyhow, most meters were only capable of measuring the cumulated consumed volume.[3]

Back then, consumers were fully reliant on the supply from the monopolistic utility for their kWhs. All changed with the uptake of more affordable residential solar photovoltaic (PV) panels. With volumetric network charges in place, consumers installing PV panels significantly reduce their net volume of electricity consumed. As such, they contribute a lot less to the recuperation of network costs. However, these so-called prosumers tend to rely on the network as much as they did before. This reality remained salient until suddenly PV uptake accelerated in recent years and finally ignited the network tariff debate in Europe and the United States. As noted in Chapter 19 by Swanston, Australia is even more advanced. Given these developments, two issues emerged: an efficiency and a fairness issue.

First, there is an efficiency issue. With solar PV installed on your roof and volumetric network tariffs, you cannot only offset paying for the production of electricity, but you can also avoid paying for the network. If you generate electricity with your PV panel, you will offset the need to produce that electricity centrally. Thus it does make sense that with a PV panel on your roof, you will have to pay for fewer kilowatt hours centrally produced.[4] However, in the majority of cases, your PV panel will not reduce the need for the local network. Networks are dimensioned for peak requirements, which often do not change by having a PV panel on your roof. As such, volumetric network tariffs are an implicit subsidy for PV adoption, that is, the savings from installing residential solar PV are a lot higher than the reduction in system costs such investment causes.

Second, there is a fairness issue. Some consumers have to pay a lot fewer network charges by installing solar PV, while the total network costs to be recuperated remain more or less the same. That can only mean that other consumers have to contribute more. In other words, volumetric network charges cause cross-subsidies between PV and non-PV owners. Actually, with increasing PV adoption, more network costs are shifted to non-PV owners. Thus one can reason that all consumers will adopt solar PV in the end. However, some consumers will not be able to make the move. They are uninformed, do not own a roof, or have limited financial possibilities.

It is important to note that besides solar PV, we are currently also witnessing the breakthrough of other behind-the-meter (BTM) technologies such as batteries, heat pumps, and electric vehicles (EVs). The adoption of these technologies makes distribution network tariff design even trickier as consumers cannot only self-produce but also better control when they withdraw and inject electricity in the grid.

This chapter attempts to answer the following question: *"In this new world with consumers having several BTM options, how can we re-design the distribution network tariff in a way that it is efficient and fair?"* To do so the chapter is organized as follows:

[3] Enabling more advanced network tariffs is one of the important drivers to install smart meters. Smart meters are covered in more detail in Chapter 12 by Stagnaro and Benedettini.

[4] You will pay for less kWhs of electricity produced but that does not always mean that the total cost of the supplied electricity will be lower.

- Section 17.2 focuses on how to use the network tariff to signal the cost of future grid investments to grid users.
- Section 17.3 discusses how to recuperate the residual grid costs as it is well known that cost-reflective network tariffs alone do not lead to full grid cost recovery.
- Section 17.4 looks at how the issues discussed in Section 17.2 and 17.3 interact and finds that a trade-off between efficiency and fairness exists.
- Section 17.5 discusses elements that could affect this trade-off in either way.
- Section 17.6 introduces innovative approaches to improve the trade-off and is followed by the chapter's conclusions.

17.2 Signaling future grid costs: it's all about cost-reflectiveness

As described in the introduction, until recently, residential consumers were fully reliant on the grid for their electricity needs. There was simply no other option. At the same time, consumers were often quite unaware of how much electricity they were consuming at what time. To say the same thing in the words of an economist, the consumers' elasticity was very low. The distribution network tariff had a purely allocative objective, recuperating all the network costs in an acceptable way.

The situation is changing as many consumers can now invest in BTM technologies to fulfill at least a part of their electricity needs. At the same time, smart metering and digitalization allow for easier monitoring of electricity consumption. In other words, consumers are more elastic; they can react the way the network is priced. We can expect "price reactiveness" to increase even more in the future with the introduction of house automation, artificial intelligence, and internet of things as, for example, discussed in Chapter 3 by Sioshansi. If consumers start reacting to the way the grid is priced, it becomes costly to have a badly designed network tariff design in place.

In this context, the key issue is the cost-reflectiveness of a network tariff. In short, with a cost-reflective network tariff, one pays the price of one's own actions. In theory, by having a cost-reflective tariff in place, consumers are informed about whether to use the network at a certain time or whether to change their consumption behavior. For example, when a prosumer uses zero net kWhs from the grid, it does not imply that she is not responsible for any network costs. It all depends on when exactly the prosumer injects and withdraws electricity from the grid. The idea is that a cost-reflective tariff will lead to an efficient outcome. A (cost-)efficient outcome is one in which the cost-reflective network tariff leads to the overall lowest final cost for serving the electricity needs of all consumers. If network charges are not cost-reflective, consumers will not see the correct trade-off between utilizing the network or adjusting their consumption at a certain point in time. Two situations can occur.

First, the network tariff can be too low, meaning that the consumers' actions inflict more cost than the network charges they would have to pay. This means that we end up in a situation with an overly expensive grid as the consumers are not incentivized enough to adapt their actions, leading to a higher total system cost. An example would be that consumers who have an intelligent heating system driven by a heat pump command their house to be heated at moments when the electricity (including the grid) is priced cheaply even when the network is close to congestion. If many consumers act similarly, it would eventually mean that the network needs to be expanded. In this case, it will be hard for a regulator to protect passive consumers from the actions of prosumers. All consumers will have to pay back the cost of this (avoidable) network expansion through the network tariff. No expansion would have been needed, or the expansion could have been delayed if the network tariff had been cost-reflective. In this case, a cost-reflective network tariff would incentivize the consumer to program their heating at times when the utilization of the grid was low.

Second, the network tariff can be too high, meaning that the consumers' actions inflict less cost than the network charges they have to pay. Using the same example, consumers could opt for gas heating instead of electric heating although electric heating would have been a cheaper option if network charges had been cost-reflective. The electricity network could accommodate the extra load without problems, under the condition that the heating would be correctly programmed. This would mean that we end up in a situation with overpriced actions by the consumers and an underutilized grid. This would again lead to a higher total system cost for the final energy service than when the network tariff had been designed properly. Similarly, too high network tariffs can also overincentivize self-generation. This then leads to prosumers (overly) avoiding paying for network charges and passive consumers paying a bigger share of the network charges.

So what does such a cost-reflective tariff look like in theory? For example, the Utility of the Future report by the MIT Energy Initiative (2016) explains that the main cost driver of an electricity network, whether it is distribution or transmission, is the coincident peak demand over an element [see also, e.g., Burger, Schneider, Botterud, and Pérez-Arriaga (2019)].[5] High loads or generation can cause this peak demand. A line or feeder is dimensioned to cope with the maximum power in kW or MW it is expected to carry resulting from the simultaneous electricity usage of many users at a certain point in time. This is very similar to highways or telecom lines. Therefore a cost-reflective distribution network tariff consists of a forward-looking peak-coincident capacity charge. The peak-coincident charge should be computed as the incremental cost of the network divided by expected load growth, the so-called long-run marginal cost (LRMC) of the network. Easier said than done. Several implementation issues make the introduction of this network tariff proposal difficult in practice. Two issues are covered here: a lack of information and regulatory constraints.

First, a lack of information. LRMC pricing is not so easy to implement in distribution grids. Gómez (2013) describes the distribution networks as follows: *"A friend of mine who worked in a distribution company likened electric power generation and transmission to a bull and distribution to a beehive. Whereas generation and transmission comprise comparatively few and very large-scale facilities, distribution involves a much larger number and wider variety of equipment and components."* In other words, it is hard to get a complete picture of the distribution network. There is a lack of information about the real-time network flows requiring significant investments in IT infrastructure in most countries. Without this information, it is almost impossible to reflect the grid costs in the network tariff truly, as it is not clear what is really going on in the network.

---

[5] Besides the coincident peak demand, other cost drivers could, for example, include losses or the penetration of solar PV, which might induce bidirectional flows and thus requires investment in additional electronics (e.g., protection and voltage regulation) in the grid. For more information, see also the Future of Solar Report by the MIT Energy Initiative (2015) and Chapter 9 of IEA (2016).

BOX 17.1

Proposal for the implementation of cost-reflective distribution network tariffs in Australia[6]

Passey et al. (2017) analyze several distribution network tariffs proposals that include variations of capacity-based network charges. The authors develop a method to assess visually how cost-reflective a particular capacity-based network tariff is. In this box, two extremes are highlighted. First, a "standard" capacity-based network charge as proposed in 2017–18 for South Australia Power Networks. Each household gets charged according to its individual monthly measured peak demand averaged over a half-hour period. Also, a minimum charge of 1 kW applies to those consumers with a lower peak usage during that month. Second, a more sophisticated capacity-based

charge is introduced for which each household gets charged depending on its power usage during the half-hour in which the monthly system peak occurs. Only summer and winter months are taken into account as in those months the annual peaks occur. There is no minimum charge. Table 17.1 gives an overview of the difference between the two distribution network tariff designs.

Using data from 3876 Sydney households, Fig. 17.1 shows the mapping of how much consumers pay in terms of network charges (vertical axis) versus how much they contribute to the network cost (horizontal axis) for the two network tariff proposals. The contribution to the network cost

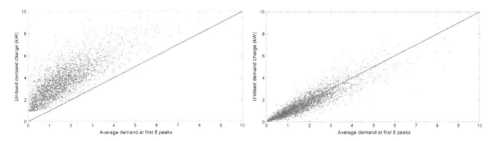

FIGURE 17.1 Mapping of what consumers pay in terms of network charges (vertical axis) vs their contribution to the network cost driver (horizontal axis). Left: standard demand charge and right: peak-coincident demand charge. Source: *From Passey, R., Haghdadi, N., Bruce, A., & MacGill, I. (2017). Designing more cost reflective electricity network tariffs with demand charges.* Energy Policy, 109, 642–649.

In Box 17.1, practical examples of implementations of cost-reflective distribution network tariffs are given. Different implementations of capacity-based charges are being tested in the example described in the box.[7] Capacity-based charges are a popular

---

[6] In the US context a capacity-based charge is often referred to as a demand charge.

[7] This box is based on the work of Passey, Haghdadi, Bruce, and MacGill (2017). For more details, please see the original paper.

BOX 17.1   (cont'd)

TABLE 17.1   Specifications of implementations of two capacity-based network tariffs.

	Standard capacity-based charge (left)	Peak-coincident capacity-based charge (right)
Minimum kW charge	Yes (1 kW)	No
Timing measurement	No specific timing, individual peak	At the time of the monthly network peak
Months	Every month	Only winter and summer months

is proxied by the average demand at the time of the eight highest system peaks in that year. The left graph shows the results for the standard capacity-based charge $(r = 0.80)$, while the right graph shows the results for the more sophisticated implementation $(r = 0.92)$. It is clear that the more sophisticated implementation better aligns what a consumer pays with the costs he/she causes.

Please note that this exercise purely shows how to target the cost driver better but does not conclude on the ideal magnitude of the charge. It goes without saying that also the calculation of the magnitude of the charge, which depends on the long-run marginal cost of the network, is a very difficult exercise. ■

alternative to volumetric charges. With a capacity-based charge a consumer pays distribution charges according to its peak consumption (in kW). The idea is that as network costs are driven by the peak demand, we charge consumers according to their individual peak demand. However, it is not so easy to implement a cost-reflective capacity-based charge.

Second, regulatory constraints. Even if all network information is known, it does not mean that all this information can be used. A fully cost-reflective network tariff would need to have a very fine locational and temporal granularity. In the extreme case, in order to apply it perfectly, it would almost be a user-by-user tariff. Regarding location, generally, a network tariff per region or DSO area is applied in Europe (European Commission, 2015). This is mostly done for reasons of acceptability and simplifies the administrative work. For example, imagine that you live in a district that did not see an update of grid infrastructure in the last decade and local demand is increasing. If a cost-reflective network tariff with very fine locational granularity would be applied, it is possible that grid tariffs suddenly become substantially higher at peak times in your neighborhood. This would happen to incentivize grid users to adjust their electricity consumption at times when the grid is stressed. Another district could have been upgraded just a couple of years before the implementation of this new network tariff. This district could then constantly see low grid charges, as there is ample spare capacity in the local network at all times. Choices of the DSO in the past, on which affected grid users had little influence, cause the difference in grid charges. Regarding the timing, peak prices would have to be announced ex ante or accounted for ex post. If they are announced ex ante, it could happen that the expected peak differs from the realized peak. If they are accounted for ex post, consumers' bills could become unpredictable. MacGill and Smith also argue in Chapter 9 that the average consumer might find it difficult to deal with the complexities and uncertainties related to tariffs.

Besides implementation constraints, there is the fact that purely cost-reflective charges do not guarantee complete cost recovery of the efficiently incurred grid costs [see, e.g., Borenstein (2016), MIT Energy Initiative (2016), Ofgem (2017)]. A cost-reflective network charge sends a signal to the grid user to make optimal use of the network, leading to a cost-efficient outcome for all. However, efficiency is decoupled from another objective, namely, the recovery of all grid costs in the shorter term. In reality, there will always be residual grid costs. These residual costs are sunk, that is, investments done in the past to meet the future electricity demand. The total amount of sunk costs to be recovered is unaffected by the way the network is utilized. Therefore we need to complement a cost-reflective tariff with another charge to recuperate these sunk costs. This leads us to the next section in which the second part of the distribution network tariff design problem is discussed.

17.3 Sunk grid costs: it's all about cost-recovery

There is little discussion in literature and practice about allowing the DSO, the company responsible for maintaining, developing, and operating the distribution network, to recuperate its "efficiently incurred grid costs."[8] The question on how to incentivize the monopolistic DSO to run the grid efficiently and how to calculate the efficiently incurred costs is out of the scope of this chapter.[9] Instead, this section looks at how to recuperate these costs through the network tariffs.

How can we design a complementary charge in a way that it does not interfere with the cost-reflective signal of the forward-looking charge? In theory, the best way to design such minimally distortive charge is by applying Ramsey pricing.[10] With this approach the residual costs are assigned to consumers according to their elasticity to price. Inverse proportionality is followed; this means that a higher proportion of the costs is allocated to those

[8] The DSO can own the distribution network assets. Alternatively, these assets can also be owned by third parties (often municipalities) but managed by the DSO. In some jurisdictions, the DSO is referred to as the distribution network operator.

[9] For more information on incentive regulation of distribution grids, see, for example, Gómez (2013). A more recent detailed description of incentive regulation of electricity network companies can also be found in Rious and Rossetto (2018a, 2018b).

[10] Ramsey was the first to derive the formula for optimal taxation (Ramsey, 1927). Allocating sunk network costs is a very similar exercise as taxation. In both cases a lump sum of money needs to be recuperated, and the way this money is recuperated should have a minimum impact on the existing incentives. Exceptions are Pigouvian and possibly "sin" taxes for which the main objective is not to recuperate money but to discourage an activity.

consumers who change their consumption behavior the least in response to price changes. As such, the way the total grid costs are recuperated modifies as little as possible the optimal outcome compared to when consumer decisions are subjected solely to cost-reflective charges.

Although efficient, there is a critical issue with Ramsey pricing. Namely, it is often perceived as unfair as it discriminates users on the basis of their elasticity to prices [see, e.g., Neuteleers, Mulder, and Hindriks (2017)].[11] For example, network tariffs can be designed as such that two consumers who share the same load profile but have a different willingness to pay for electricity pay a different share of the residual grid costs.[12] As mentioned above, the lower the elasticity, the higher the contribution to the residual grid costs. In the case of network tariffs, consumers with very low elasticity and thus bearing most of the residual grid costs would often be passive consumers with little possibilities other than the grid to be supplied from electricity. Besides, to implement Ramsey pricing, the price-elasticity of the different consumers needs to be estimated. This is not easy to do. Therefore strictly applying Ramsey pricing is unattainable in practice.

Schittekatte, Momber, and Meeus (2018) test the relative performance of different tariff designs other than Ramsey pricing to recuperate sunk grid costs. Imagine a scenario where the grid has been overdimensioned, while the load is reducing. In this scenario, little grid costs can be reflected by a network tariff, and the share of sunk grid costs from past investments that need to be recovered is significant. The paper shows how efficiency and fairness issues differ from one network tariff to another tariff and how these are impacted by the investment cost of BTM technology. In the paper the increase in network charges paid by passive consumers compared to a baseline is used as a proxy for fairness. The reason for this is that when we redesign the network tariff, we do not start from scratch. There is a tariff in place, and consumers can perceive an increase in what they pay for the network (in the extreme case: "bill shocks") to be unfair when this increase is neither caused due to a change in their consumption behavior and nor due to a change in the overall cost of the network. Box 17.2 discusses the approach of the British regulator, Ofgem, for the design of the charge to recuperate residual grid costs.

17.4 Combining the two: trade-off between efficiency and fairness

In the previous two sections the analysis was split up between designing a cost-reflective forward-looking network charge and designing a complementary charge to recover the residual costs. In this section, both problems are combined, and it is shown how they interact. The results described in Schittekatte and Meeus (2020) are used to illustrate this analysis. Supporting documentation can be found in the paper.

Fig. 17.3 shows the results. All results are relative to the reference which is the "as-it-used-to-be-scenario," that is, no consumer installs any BTM technology and the network

[11] However, unfair does not imply unlawful.

[12] With "the same load profile" is meant that two grid users consume the same amount of electricity at the same time.

BOX 17.2

Ofgem's proposal for the recuperation of residual grid costs[13]

Ofgem (2018) recognizes that the electricity sector is changing and that action needs to be undertaken to ensure that network charging works in the interest of current and future consumers as a whole. The redesign of charges to recuperate residual costs is one part of the exercise. The total residual grid costs for transmission and distribution networks charges are estimated to be about £4bn/year in Great Britain. Ofgem's assessment on how to redesign the charges consists of two parts: a qualitative part and quantitative part. In the qualitative part, Ofgem identifies three guiding design principles: reducing harmful distortions, fairness and proportionality, and practical considerations. These three principles lead Ofgem to four basic options for the design of the residual network charge. Finally, two candidate designs were brought forward in Ofgem's public consultation:

- **Fixed charges.** There is a strong theoretical basis for fixed charges, as they cannot be easily avoided other than by disconnecting from the grid. The fixed charge would differ per consumer segment, for example, the voltage level of the connection
- **Agreed capacity charges.** These would be assumed or "deemed" for households and microbusinesses and based on

specified capacity levels for other customers. Agreed capacity charges allow for greater differentiation between types of consumers, particularly at domestic, extra-high voltage, and transmission level, and have thus fewer step-changes in charges for different groups. However, as they are based on capacity, there could still be some scope to take action to reduce the contribution to residual charges.

Fig. 17.2 is an outcome of the quantitative part of the consultation. It shows the impact of the two charging proposals compared to the baseline for different types of domestic consumers. The baseline is volumetric charges.

First, the upper four consumer types. It is obvious that with the two proposals, higher consuming users see reductions in their charges, and low-consuming users will see increases. This increase for low-consuming users is the reason why fixed charges are often deemed unfair. The reduction for high-consuming users is most under fixed charges.[14] High-consuming users, who often also have higher capacity needs, will most likely contribute more under agreed capacity charges than under fixed charges.

Second, the results for lower four consumer types illustrate the impact of certain

---

[13] This box is based upon a consultation of the "Targeted charging review: minded to decision and draft impact assessment" by Ofgem (2018).

[14] The "economy 7" consumer types are consumers that opted in to pay less for electricity during the night. Often they are high-consuming users. In Ofgem's consultation, economy 7 consumers are considered as a different consumer segment. Thus they pay a different fixed charge.

BOX 17.2   (cont'd)

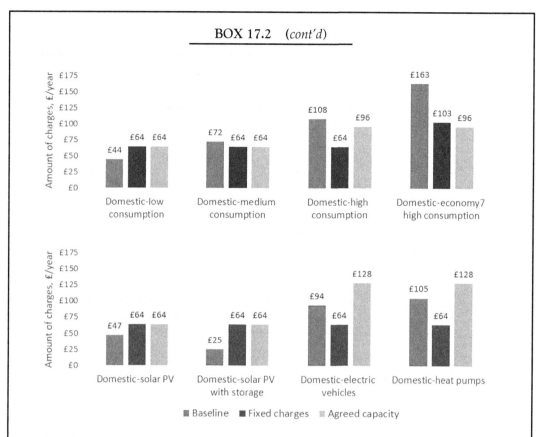

FIGURE 17.2   Financial impact of the two proposals versus the baseline (volumetric charges) on different consumer groups. Source: *Based on Ofgem. (2018). Targeted charging review: Minded to decision and draft impact assessment. In* Public consultation.

BTM technologies on residual contributions.[15] Solar PV and battery users will see increased charges in all cases. This is because, currently, the use of these technologies substantially decreases the volumetric residual charges. The opposite holds for consumers with electric vehicles and heat pumps. Under fixed charges, these users significantly reduce their residual charges.

However, under agreed capacity charges, these users can see an increase in contributions to the residual grid costs as electric vehicles and heat pumps have high-capacity requirements.

Besides distributional consequences, the quantitative assessment also estimates the system benefits. By reforming residual charges, Ofgem estimates that with both of

---

[15] The consumption of all considered consumer types, prior to the adoption of the different BTM technologies, is assumed to be equal to that of an average domestic user.

BOX 17.2   (cont'd)

the candidate options, the potential net system benefits to 2040 are in the range of £0.8—£3.2bn and benefits to consumers as a whole in the range of £0.5—£1.6bn. Fixed charges are Ofgem's preferred option, even though it is acknowledged that fixed charges have a negative distributional impact on smaller consumers. The main reason for preferring fixed charges is the fact that there is still a distortion present with agreed capacity charges. ■

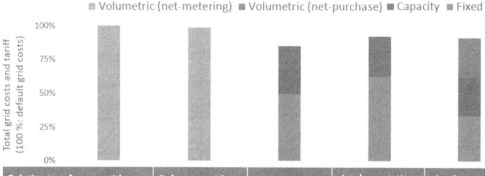

Volumetric (net-metering)   Volumetric (net-purchase)   Capacity   Fixed

Relative to reference without active consumers:	Reference with active consumers	Theory	Implementation issue	Implementation issue + fairness
System costs	+ 3.4 %	− 1.4 %	− 0.3 %	+ 0.1 %
• Total grid costs	−1.4 %	− 14.6 %	− 7.5 %	− 8.5 %
• Total energy costs	− 41.6 %	+ 1.7 %	+ 0.7 %	− 5.6 %
• PV investment	5 kWp	0 kWp	0 kWp	0.7 kWp
• Battery investment	0 kWh	2.7 kWh	1.8 kWh	2.0 kWh
Network charges passive consumer	+ 78.0 %	+ 12.6 %	+ 15.6 %	+ 10.0 %

FIGURE 17.3   Network tariff design and results under different assumptions. Source: *Own image.*

charges are volumetric. There are five key assumptions. The implications of the last two assumptions are further discussed in Section 17.5.

- Some of the future grid investments can be influenced by the way the grid is used: other investments are made in the past, and their costs are sunk. This depends on the grid investment cycle we are in and how local demand evolves. In this example the assumption is that the grid costs consist originally of 50% prospective (variable in the mid- to long term) and 50% sunk grid costs.
- 50% of the consumers are active who react rationally to the way the grid is priced. Active consumers follow their self-interest, that is, if it makes sense for them to invest

in BTM technology to lower their total costs to serve their electricity needs, this is what they will do. The considered BTM technologies are solar PV and batteries. The other 50% of the consumers are passive. They are uninformed about the possibility to invest in BTM technology. They either do not have the financial means, are strongly risk-averse, or simply do not have space. Fifty percent of the active consumers might seem quite a lot today. With dropping costs in distributed energy resources (DER), rising electricity bills, digitalization, and more climate awareness, a proportion of currently indifferent passive consumers might turn active.

- Active consumers consume slightly more electricity than passive consumers (before active consumers are enabled to install solar PV and batteries). This statement is a simplification of reality, but evidence is found in the literature. Borenstein (2017) analyses Californian data and finds that the income distribution of solar PV installations is heavily skewed toward the wealthy but adds that the gap is narrowing with time. It is also found that PV adopters have slightly higher energy consumption levels and peak demands. Similarly, Hledik, Faruqui, Weiss, Brown, and Irwin (2016) analyze data from Great Britain and confirm that lower income consumers are also smaller consumers of electricity, although the correlation appears to be somewhat limited. In this example, it is assumed that in the reference scenario, the network charges paid by the passive consumers are 33% lower than the network charges paid by the typically more affluent active consumers with high consumption levels.
- Positive externalities from solar PV adoption due to the replacement of polluting generation plants are not accounted for.
- The recuperation of taxes and levies does not interfere with the analysis. Often, these charges are also recuperated volumetrically.

The first result (column 1) shows the reference network tariff, that is, volumetric network charges with net-metering, with active consumers being able to install solar PV and batteries. As also described in the introduction of this chapter, the results show there is a clear case to redesign the network tariff that was historically in place. Active consumers are strongly incentivized to invest in solar PV, as by doing so, they can avoid paying for energy and grid charges. The overall expenditure on energy costs does indeed decrease strongly, but grid costs decrease very little. Due to the misalignment of the active consumers' private incentives and the overall system, a 3.4% increase in system costs compared to the baseline (in which no consumer can invest in BTM) results. Also, active consumers significantly lower their grid charges, but the grid costs do not lower proportionally. Therefore these grid costs are shifted to passive consumers and a significant fairness issue results.

The second result (column 2) shows the theoretically best solution that leads to the most (cost-)efficient solution, that is, with the lowest system costs. It is assumed that the capacity-based charge is a perfect proxy for the grid cost driver. The resulting network tariff consists of a fixed charge to recuperate the sunk grid costs and a capacity-based charge to align grid benefits with consumer benefits.[16] It can be seen that when having a perfect

[16] Fixed network charges are deemed nondistortive as full grid defection is not considered. Also, the formation of energy communities that could lead to difficulties with the implementation of fixed network charges is not considered in this example. For more information on energy communities, see Chapter 6 by Reijnders et al. in this book.

proxy for the network cost driver, a system cost reduction can be achieved. Active consumers install a battery to lower their grid charges, and by doing so, they also lower the overall grid costs.[17] The network charges for the passive consumers increase due to the introduction of the nondistortive but regressive uniform fixed network charge. This is a similar dynamic as can be seen for the low-consuming users in Fig. 17.2 within Box 17.2.

The third result (column 3) shows the impact of having more realistic assumptions about the implementation of cost-reflective network charges. We know from Box 17.1 that it is hard to implement fully cost-reflective capacity-based charges. Even if the individual peak demands of consumers are reduced, it does not mean that the future investment costs reduce proportionally.[18] To avoid overincentives in reducing one's individual peak demand, the most cost-efficient solution is to reduce the magnitude of the capacity-based charge. However, cost recovery needs to be respected; thus the fixed charges need to increase. Compared to results with a perfect proxy for the grid cost driver, the efficiency decreases, and the fairness issue aggravates. This result illustrates how implementation issues with cost-reflective tariffs interact with fairness issues caused by the nondistortive recuperation of residual costs with fixed network charges.

The fourth result (column 4) shows what happens when capping the increase in network charges for passive consumers as a high increase in network charges for certain consumer groups is deemed unfair. Suddenly, a three-part network tariff combining fixed, capacity, and volumetric charges, results, even though in theory, volumetric charges are not part of an optimal distribution network tariff design.[19] The result nicely illustrates the trade-off between efficiency and fairness. By introducing a volumetric network charge with net-purchase at the expense of the unpopular high network fixed charge, some efficiency is sacrificed for fairness.[20]

Paradoxically, in this example, with a regulatory toolbox limited to volumetric, capacity, and uniform fixed charges, the rise of active consumers enabled to invest in solar PV and batteries results in a sort of "prisoner-dilemma." Namely, a situation that is worse both from the system (+0.1%) and passive consumer (+10%) perspective when compared to the reference case without active consumers. The next section discusses two important assumptions that could lead to an under- or overestimation of this trade-off. Anyhow, it is clear that we need creative tools to break the trade-off. These tools are discussed in Section 17.6.

---

[17] A small increase in energy costs results due to energy losses of the battery.

[18] A reduction of 1 kW individual peak is assumed to results in a 0.75 kW reduction in the investment need, which is most probably an optimistic assumption. A similar reasoning holds for time-of-use network tariffs. Lowering one's peak during a "peak time block" will not always result with a one-on-one reduction in the overall (local) network peak.

[19] With volumetric network charges with net-purchase, consumers are charged for the network according to their gross electricity withdrawal.

[20] More specifically, in this example, the increase of network charges for passive consumers is reduced with 5.6% points at the expense of a 0.4% point increase in system costs.

17.5 Under- or overestimation of the trade-off: taxes & levies and carbon pricing

At the beginning of this chapter, it was stated that about one-third of the bill consists of network charges in the EU. Another third consists of energy costs. The last third of the bill consists of all types of taxes (other than VAT) and levies. However, the consumer sees the electricity bill as a whole. The latter two components can make the efficiency versus fairness trade-off in recuperating network cost more complicated or easier than was depicted before.

First, more complicated. The recuperation of taxes and levies is not very different in nature from the recuperation of residual grid costs. A lump sum of money needs to be recuperated, and the responses of consumers to the way their contributions are charged have little impact on the total money to be recuperated.[21] Thus the optimal way from an efficiency point of view would be to recover a major part of the taxes and levies through fixed charges. However, doing so would increase the magnitude of the fixed charge even more in the final bill. This severely further complicates the efficiency and fairness trade-off.

Second, easier. Electric energy, the commodity, is priced in €/kWh. For domestic users, energy prices in the bill can closely follow the wholesale electricity price (real-time energy prices) or be more static. It depends on the available offers of the retailer, the preference of the consumer, and the available meter. The relevant issue here is the magnitude of the final energy price. In theory the marginal cost of the most expensive generating unit sets the electricity price per time unit. The marginal costs should internalize all costs, including the cost of carbon. However, due to political feasibility, often the carbon price, if there is any carbon price at all, is a lot lower than the societal cost of carbon (Borenstein & Bushnell, 2018). In other words the final electricity price in the wholesale market is often too low when compared to the average social marginal cost per kWh. A remedy for this can be to recuperate some of the residual grid costs through volumetric charges to make up for the "too low" electricity price. In other words, by getting two wrongs, we can actually get it right. This makes the trade-off between efficiency and fairness a bit easier as the magnitude of fixed charges, needed to recover all grid costs, would reduce.[22]

---

[21] Batlle (2011) argues that, in some cases, levies to recuperate renewable subsidies can be charged in a cost-reflective manner. Namely, in the context of renewable targets as a proportion of total electricity consumption, a cost-reflective allocation of the cost of renewable support policies would entail a volumetric charge calculated as the product of the percentage renewable target and the extra cost of generation from renewable sources. This method does not guarantee full recovery of all levies.

[22] Borenstein and Bushnell (2018) did an analysis of the current tariffs and carbon prices for all states in the United States. They found that for some states indeed the overly volumetrically charged residual costs more or less make up for the "too low" electricity price. However, this does not always hold. For other states, the final €/kWh charge (summing up all volumetric charges plus the energy price) in the bill is either "too high" (e.g., California) or "too low" (e.g., North Dakota) when compared to the average social marginal cost per kWh.

17.6 Breaking the trade-off

This section is split up into two parts. First, tools to improve efficiency beyond network tariff design. Second, regulatory fixes to remedy fairness concerns without sacrificing efficiency.

17.6.1 Tools to improve efficiency beyond network tariff design

As discussed in Section 17.2, truly cost-reflective distribution network charges are hard to implement. Other mechanisms could complement network tariff design to unlock consumer flexibility to make better use of the existing distribution grid and limit costly reinforcements. Three mechanisms of particular interest are identified: smart connection agreements (SCAs), local flexibility markets, and distribution locational marginal pricing (DLMP).

First, a SCA implies that grid users have interruptible connections rather than conventional noninterruptible or firm connections. SCAs would mainly apply to new connections for distributed generation such as a wind power plant connected to the distribution network. The idea is that grid users engaging in an SCA have to pay fewer grid charges because they allow the DSO to curtail their connection a predetermined number of times. By limiting these connections at times of possible network congestion, the DSO can avoid or postpone reinforcement. Thus a win−win situation results. Anaya and Pollitt (2015) show that the smart connection option is by far the best option when compared with firm connections. Furusawa, Brunekreeft, and Hattori (2019) describe the current implementations of SCAs in Germany, France, and Great Britain. The advantage of SCAs is that DSOs have more certainty about the available flexibility and can easily use the SCA to solve local issues. The disadvantage of an SCA is that they can create barriers to offer services in other markets, for example, balancing or capacity markets. This is true because the service provider with the SCA is not sure that the delivery of the service will be possible. Its availability is a function of the needs of the DSO. However, solutions are being developed to overcome such issues, for example, by making connection agreements tradable.

Second, flexibility markets are markets in which distribution-connected units offer their flexibility to DSOs (and/or transmission system operators (TSOs)). These markets are still quite nascent in Europe. Schittekatte and Meeus (2020) discuss four pilot projects in Europe, implementing flexibility markets. Piclo Flex, described in greater detail in Chapter 11 by Johnston and Sioshansi, is one of them; the others are Enera, NODES, and GOPACS. It is shown that the implementation of the platforms differs in many ways. Importantly, some platforms (Enera, NODES, and GOPACS) focus on short-term (intraday) trading of flexibility, while Piclo Flex is mostly focused on reservations ahead of time. Also, projects differ in the sense that on the same platform only DSOs (Piclo Flex); DSOs and TSOs (Enera); or DSOs, TSOs, and other market parties (GOPACS and NODES) can trade flexibility. An advantage of flexibility markets over network tariffs or SCAs is that prices are determined in a market-based way instead of administratively. This way the value of flexibility is revealed. Difficulties with flexibility markets are entry barriers for smaller players. However, aggregators can solve that problem by bundling grid users with

BTM resources, as also described in Chapter 5 by Poplavskaya and de Vries. Another difficulty is that as grid problems are local, there might not always be a market that is liquid enough. Lastly, network tariffs and SCAs can interact with the profitability and even the possibility of offering flexibility services.

Third, a more futuristic idea is to implement DLMP as described in the Utility of the Future report by MIT Energy Initiative (2016). At transmission-level in some states in the United States (e.g., PJM, CAISO, and ERCOT), there is nodal pricing implemented, that is, accounting for network constraints within the wholesale energy market. DLMP implies doing the same at distribution-level. Currently, DLMP is not implemented anywhere. There are serious practical implementation challenges to overcome to allow DLMP to work. Obtaining all necessary information and the computation is challenging. Also, there are several institutional complexities with DLMPs as described in Hadush and Meeus (2018). Therefore these authors discuss an alternative to deal with congestion in distribution grids, namely, tradable access rights between TSOs and DSOs or other borders in the distribution grid.

17.6.2 Regulatory fixes to remedy fairness concerns without sacrificing efficiency

Even though uniform fixed charges are a nondistortive way to recover sunk grid cost and taxes and levies, they have socially adverse distributional impacts that we cannot ignore. Some recent papers are looking at how to design nondistortive charges that limit the distributional impact. Most proposals include differentiated fixed charges. But differentiated based on what? The idea is that we need to find a proxy that leads to a fairer sharing of the burden, while the proxy should be hard to game.

Batlle, Mastropietro, and Rodilla (2018) propose moving residual costs in the bill to a differentiated fixed charge that is based on the historical consumption of each customer. The core idea behind their proposal is to allocate costs based on backward cost causation. Namely, when these costs were incurred, they certainly had a cost driver (i.e., peak demand). The differentiated fixed charge should be based on a sufficiently large number of years in order to avoid distortions. Solutions to practical implementation issues such as switching of house ownership and calculating the charge for new houses are discussed in the paper. Another interesting paper in this regard is the work by Burger, Knittel, Pérez-Arriaga, Schneider, and vom Scheidt (2020). They test the calculation of differentiated fixed charges based on historical consumption patterns [as in Batlle et al. (2018)], geography or customer income.[23] The option of introducing opt-in low-income programs to mitigate the impact of increased fixed charges is also contemplated. Even though not free from flaws, the authors argue that having differentiated fixed charges, whether based on historical consumption, geography, or income, are better than low-income programs because such programs historically have very low opt-in rates due to uninformed consumers.

---

[23] They give the example of a "review period" of 10 years for the fixed charges based on historical consumption patterns.

A more extreme proposal, as also discussed in the Utility of the Future report by MIT Energy Initiative (2016) is to allow for the under-recovery of the grid costs as full cost recovery leads to inefficiencies. Not recovered residential network costs would have to be recuperated through other means than the electricity bill. An alternative could be to let taxpayers pay for these costs, as is done for roads in some countries.

17.7 Conclusion

This chapter discussed how the traditional distribution network tariff design is challenged by BTM-technology adoption and provides an analysis of how to enhance current practices. If network tariffs are not properly redesigned, the energy transition will be more costly and raise more fairness concerns than should have been the case. It is shown that with a regulatory toolbox limited to simple volumetric, capacity, and uniform fixed charges, it is hard to come up with an efficient and fair network tariff. Both objectives interact and a trade-off seems to exist. The conclusion is that we need creative tools to break the trade-off between efficiency and fairness in distribution network tariff design. Two types of tools are identified: tools to improve efficiency beyond network tariff design and regulatory fixes to remedy fairness concerns without sacrificing efficiency.

First, cost-reflective network tariffs are hard to implement. They should have a very fine locational and temporal granularity. In the near future, network tariffs that have an element of time-variation and vary depending on the exact location are definitely possible and encouraged. However, it is very likely that at least part of the efficiency gains of truly cost-reflective network tariffs will be missed out due to implementation issues. Therefore complementary mechanisms are needed to unlock flexibility at the distribution grid. Three identified complementary mechanisms in this chapter are SCAs, local flexibility markets, and distribution location marginal pricing.

Currently, regulators are experimenting with SCAs and divers pilots implementing flexibility markets are popping up. Regulators will have to learn from these experiences in order to adapt the regulations to enable successful models to scale up. The interactions between these mechanisms and network tariff design need deeper analysis and are a very promising research topic. Also, in order to make more advanced cost-reflective network tariffs and complementary flexibility mechanisms work, there will be a greater role for automation, aggregation, and innovative solutions from retailers as the complexity and the speed of the price signals is hard to manage for individual consumers.

Second, even though uniform fixed charges are a nondistortive way to recover the residual sunk grid cost, and taxes, and levies, they have adverse social distributional impacts that we cannot ignore. Innovative proposals to lower distributional impacts include the recuperation of part of the network costs through differentiated fixed charges. In that regard, it is obvious that it will be a big challenge for regulators to come up with proxies for differentiated fixed network charges that are understandable and acceptable for consumers. Raising awareness among consumers to get public support will be the key. At the same time, beyond being fair, network tariff choices need to be consistent and stable enough to minimize uncertainty.

Or, will the politicians make it easier for the regulators by moving part of the "hard to allocate sunk grid costs" from the electricity bill to general taxation? As, for example, is done with road infrastructure, where not all costs are recovered by tolls. However, no general taxation is without distortions. This will for sure be an important debate in the future. Similarly, it is not so obvious that subsidies for renewables should be recuperated through the electricity bill as is done in most countries today. Besides creating difficulty in how to design the charges, high levies for electricity and low prices for other (fossil) energy carriers also unjustifiably hinder the electrification of transport and heat and the efficient development of power-to-X technologies.

References

ACER & CEER. (2018). Electricity and gas retail markets volume. In *Annual report on the results of monitoring the internal electricity and gas markets in 2017*.

Anaya, K. L., & Pollitt, M. G. (2015). Options for allocating and releasing distribution system capacity: Deciding between interruptible connections and firm DG connections. *Applied Energy*, 144, 96–105.

Batlle, C. (2011). A method for allocating renewable energy source subsidies among final energy consumers. *Energy Policy*, 39(5), 2586–2595.

Batlle, C., Mastropietro, P., & Rodilla, P. (2018). Redesigning residual cost allocation in electricity tariffs: A proposal to balance efficiency, equity and cost recovery. In *Working paper IIT-18-119A. Version of 24 November 2018*.

Borenstein, S. (2016). The economics of fixed cost recovery by utilities. *Electricity Journal*, 29(7), 5–12.

Borenstein, S. (2017). Private net benefits of residential solar PV: The role of electricity tariffs, tax incentives and rebates. *Journal of the Association of Environmental and Resource Economists*, 4(S1), S85–S122.

Borenstein, S., & Bushnell, J. (2018). Do two electricity pricing wrongs make a right? Cost recovery, externalities, and efficiency. In *Energy Institute at Haas WP 294. Version of September 2018*.

Burger, S., Knittel, C., Pérez-Arriaga, I., Schneider, I., & vom Scheidt, F. (2020). The efficiency and distributional effects of alternative residential electricity rate designs. *The Energy Journal*, 41, 199–239.

Burger, S., Schneider, I., Botterud, A., & Pérez-Arriaga, I. (2019). Fair, equitable, and efficient tariffs in the presence of distributed energy resources. In F. P. Sioshansi (Ed.), *Consumer, prosumer, prosumager. How service innovations will disrupt the utility business model* (pp. 155–188). Academic Press.

European Commission. *Study on tariff design for distribution systems*. (2015). Available from <https://ec.europa.eu/energy/sites/ener/files/documents/20150313%20Tariff%20report%20fina_revREF-E.PDF>.

Furusawa, K., Brunekreeft, G., & Hattori, T. (2019). Constrained connection for distributed generation by DSOs in European countries. In *Bremen energy working papers, no. 28*.

Gómez, T. (2013). Electricity distribution. In I. J. Pérez-Arriaga (Ed.), *Regulation of the power sector* (pp. 199–250). Springer.

Hadush, S. Y., & Meeus, L. (2018). DSO-TSO cooperation issues and solutions for distribution grid congestion management. *Energy Policy*, 120, 610–621.

Hledik, R., Faruqui, A., Weiss, J., Brown, T., & Irwin, N. (2016). The tariff transition: Considerations for domestic distribution tariff redesign in Great-Britain. In *Volume I – Final report for citizens advice*.

IEA. (2016). *Re-powering markets: Market design and regulation during the transition to low-carbon power systems*.

MIT Energy Initiative. *The future of solar energy*. (2015). Available from <https://doi.org/10.1002/yd.20002>.

MIT Energy Initiative. (2016). A comprehensive and efficient system of prices and regulated charges for electricity charges. In *Utility of the future. An MIT Energy Initiative response to an industry in transition* (pp. 75–136).

Neuteleers, S., Mulder, M., & Hindriks, F. (2017). Assessing fairness of dynamic grid tariffs. *Energy Policy*, 108, 111–120.

Ofgem. (2017). *Targeted charging review: Update on approach to reviewing residual charging arrangements*. Available from <https://www.ofgem.gov.uk/publications-and-updates/reform-electricity-network-access-and-forward-looking-charges-working-paper>.

Ofgem. (2018). Targeted charging review: Minded to decision and draft impact assessment. In *Public consultation*.

Passey, R., Haghdadi, N., Bruce, A., & MacGill, I. (2017). Designing more cost reflective electricity network tariffs with demand charges. *Energy Policy, 109*, 642–649.

Ramsey, F. (1927). A contribution to the theory of taxation. *Economic Journal, 37*, 4–61.

Rious, V., & Rossetto, N. (2018a). Continental incentive regulation. In L. Meeus, & J.-M. Glachant (Eds.), *Electricity network regulation in the EU: The challenges ahead for transmission and distribution* (pp. 28–51). Edward Elgar Publishing.

Rious, V., & Rossetto, N. (2018b). The British reference model. In L. Meeus, & J.-M. Glachant (Eds.), *Electricity network regulation in the EU: The challenges ahead for transmission and distribution* (pp. 3–25). Edward Elgar Publishing.

Schittekatte, T. (2019). *Distribution network tariff design and active consumers: A regulatory impact analysis* (Ph.D. thesis). Université Paris-Saclay. Available from <https://tel.archives-ouvertes.fr/tel-02099785/>.

Schittekatte, T., & Meeus, L. (2020). Distribution network tariff design in theory and practice. *The Energy Journal* (in press).

Schittekatte, T., & Meeus, L. (2020). Flexibility markets: Q&A with project pioneers. *Utilities Policy* (in press).

Schittekatte, T., Momber, I., & Meeus, L. (2018). Future-proof tariff design: Recovering sunk grid costs in a world where consumers are pushing back. *Energy Economics, 70*, 484–498.

Further reading

Johnston, J., & Sioshansi, F. P. (2020). Platform for trading flexibility on the distribution network: A UK case study. In F. P. Sioshansi (Ed.), *Behind and beyond the meter: Digitalization, aggregation, optimization, monetization.* Academic Press.

MacGill, I., & Smith, R. (2020). Working backwards to get behind the meter: What customer value, behavior, opportunity and uncertainty mean for new technologies. In F. P. Sioshansi (Ed.), *Behind and beyond the meter: Digitalization, aggregation, optimization, monetization.* Academic Press.

Poplavskaya, K., & De Vries, L. (2020). The evolving role of aggregators: From intermediaries to orchestrators? In F. P. Sioshansi (Ed.), *Behind and beyond the meter: Digitalization, aggregation, optimization, monetization.* Academic Press.

Reijnders, V., van der Laan, M., & Dijkstra, R. (2020). Energy communities: A Dutch case study. In F. P. Sioshansi (Ed.), *Behind and beyond the meter: Digitalization, aggregation, optimization, monetization.* Academic Press.

Sioshansi, F. P. (2020). Creating value behind-the-meter: Digitalization, aggregation and optimization of behind-the-meter asset. In F. P. Sioshansi (Ed.), *Behind and beyond the meter: Digitalization, aggregation, optimization, monetization.* Academic Press.

Stagnaro, C., & Benedettini, S. (2020). Smart meters: The gateway to behind-the-meter? In F. P. Sioshansi (Ed.), *Behind and beyond the meter: Digitalization, aggregation, optimization, monetization.* Academic Press.

Swanston, M. (2020). Two million plus solar roofs: What's in it for the consumers? In F. P. Sioshansi (Ed.), *Behind and beyond the meter: Digitalization, aggregation, optimization, monetization.* Academic Press.

What market design, fiscal policy, and network regulations are compatible with efficient behind the meter investments?

David Robinson

Oxford Institute for Energy Studies, Oxford, United Kingdom

18.1 Introduction

The framework of markets, fiscal policies, and regulations designed for liberalized electricity systems last century are now obsolete due to the penetration of intermittent renewables, the development of distributed energy resources (DER), and the growing importance of behind the meter (BTM) investments. This chapter argues that liberalized power sectors require a new framework. The focus is on getting prices right to encourage efficient BTM decisions. That means eliminating price distortions from existing regulatory and fiscal regimes, and creating or changing markets to reflect the new economic and technological conditions.

The chapter draws on experience in the European Union (EU), especially Spain, to illustrate the problems and identify reforms. Many countries, certainly all of the countries in the EU, share with Spain the challenge of making this transition within a liberalized industry structure. The chapter is organized as follows:

- Section 18.2 introduces the analytical framework.
- Section 18.3 summarizes key features of the Spanish electricity system related to renewable energy and BTM investment.
- Sections 18.4–18.8 identify fiscal, regulatory, and market design problems that will either motivate inefficient BTM decisions or stop potentially efficient BTM activity altogether. For each the chapter proposes reforms to improve price signals.
- Section 18.9 concludes the chapter.

18.2 Getting the prices right: economic efficiency and behind the meter decisions

In the early 1990s the overriding goal of electricity sector liberalization was to create new institutional arrangements

> "that provide long-term benefits to society and to ensure that an appropriate share of these benefits is conveyed to consumers through prices that reflect the efficient economic cost of supplying electricity and service quality attributes that reflect consumer valuations." Joskow (2006).

The liberalized industry structure[1] was designed so that prices would reflect the efficient economic cost of supplying electricity, with three specific efficiency objectives.

- *Operating efficiency.* Energy-only markets were designed to provide incentives to replicate the existing cost-based merit order dispatch, using a price-based dispatch to ensure that the cheapest generator available at any time was dispatched.
- *Allocative efficiency.* As part of the liberalization process, governments largely dropped price controls on electricity. This led to the end of most subsidies and cross-subsidies as generators and retail suppliers tried to avoid selling at a loss. As a result, prices tend to reflect marginal costs.
- *Dynamic efficiency.* A key aim of liberalization was to transfer investment risk to investors, so as to sharpen the incentives to efficiency. Prior to liberalization, investment decisions were typically made centrally by government or regulated monopolies, while the costs and risks were passed to consumers. In many cases, this led to expensive and inefficient decisions for which consumers had to pick up the bill. Liberalization aimed to stop this sort of situation from arising again.

Liberalized markets in the EU have functioned reasonably well on the first two types of efficiency and much less well on the third type. There has always been a concern about "missing money," that is the inability of the "energy-only" electricity market to generate sufficient revenue to recover investment costs. In many countries, this led to capacity remuneration mechanisms to provide supplementary income. When climate change became an important policy objective, after 2000, governments were increasingly reluctant to leave investment decisions to the market. Government support led to rapid penetration of solar- and wind-based electricity, contributing to the decline in the cost of those renewables. This penetration broke "energy-only" markets, which were designed for technologies with significant marginal (mainly fuel) costs, not for technologies with zero, or very low, marginal costs. The penetration of renewables is driving short-term energy prices down to levels that make investment in renewable and conventional generation unattractive in the absence of government support. There is apparently no exit strategy for continued subsidies and government control over investment (Keay, 2016).

---

[1] The structure included (1) vertical separation of competitive businesses (generation and retail) from network monopolies; (2) horizontal restructuring to ensure competition in generation; (3) integration of transmission with system operations; (4) creation of a wholesale spot energy and operating reserve market; (5) network regulation to enable open access; and (6) an independent regulator (Joskow, 2006).

The accelerated decentralization of the electricity sector is introducing an additional dilemma. DER are key to renewable penetration and electrification, for instance through rooftop solar, battery storage, heat pumps, and more flexible consumption. On the other hand, current electricity markets, fiscal policy, and regulations do not provide efficient price signals for DER/BTM investment and operations.

This chapter proposes a return to the basic idea behind liberalization: providing price signals to motivate efficient decisions. It focuses primarily on the price signals that influence decisions by consumers or intermediaries such as retailers and aggregators. It identifies problems with existing markets, regulation, and fiscal policy and proposes reforms to provide more efficient price signals.

18.3 Spain's changing approach to renewables and behind the meter investment

Spain is currently undergoing a process of reform to support accelerated decarbonization and decentralization of the power sector. It may be helpful to provide some background on Spain's policies toward renewables and DER.

First, until 2018, Spain experienced two fundamentally different policies toward renewable energy. Starting soon after 2000, the policy was to promote investment in renewable power through regulated tariffs and other incentives. The policy was very successful in attracting investment in solar and wind power, especially under the Socialist Government between 2004 and 2011. However, the regulated revenue entitlements, especially for solar power, were unsustainable. These costs contributed to an electricity tariff deficit of over €25 billion,[2] a financial liability for future electricity consumers. In 2012 the new government, led by the conservative *Partido Popular*, introduced legislation to stop the tariff deficit from growing further. The new regime, which applied to existing renewable assets and new ones, was supposed to ensure that owners of renewable assets received no more "incentives" than were required to obtain a "reasonable" rate of return on investment, assuming efficient investment and operations. The change involved a reduction in annual support costs of about €2.3 billion for existing assets (a reduction of approximately 20% on average). This led to over 30 challenges in international arbitration tribunals; Spain faces potential payments of over €7 billion for economic damages.[3] The government also froze the development of new renewable projects for 5 years. In 2017–18 the government held auctions for about 8 GW of renewable power in order to meet the European 2020 target of 20% renewable energy as a share of total energy consumption.

Second, until recently, renewable support focused almost exclusively on large-scale capacity. There was no effort to encourage investment in rooftop solar or other DER. Indeed, the legislation introduced in 2012 was deliberately designed to discourage the development of rooftop solar by households, with the government arguing that distributed

[2] This is really a debt that reflects accumulated annual deficits between, on the one hand, regulatory entitlements (distribution, transmission, financial support for renewables, and many other policies) and, on the other hand, collected revenues.

[3] "España acumula condenas por 740 millones y litigios por otros 8.100 millones por el recorte a las renovables", David Page, *El Independiente*, 11 de julio 2019.

generation favored the wealthy and, if subsidized, could contribute to a new tariff deficit. The most controversial measure was to impose a so-called "sun tax" on the owner of the embedded generation. The payment appears to be a tax on own-generation, but it is calculated so that all consumers, with or without rooftop photovoltaic (PV), pay the same amount to finance network costs and policy-related costs, which are discussed in Section 18.4. The only exception to this rule applied to consumers with contracted capacity below 10 kW. The "sun tax" was just the most visible disincentive for own-generation; others included complicated authorization procedures with heavy penalties for noncompliance. Not surprisingly, until very recently, there was virtually no investment by small consumers in rooftop solar or other DER.

Third, in 2018, a new Socialist Government introduced legislation to stimulate the development of rooftop solar and other DERs. This reversal was largely due to the change in government, but also to the falling cost of rooftop solar, growing public opposition to the "sun tax," and the fact that new European legislation was being prepared that would give consumers far greater freedom to produce their own electricity. The new Spanish legislation eliminated the "sun tax" and introduced a regime enabling consumers (individually or collectively) to install rooftop solar and batteries for their own use and for the (limited) sale of surplus electricity to the system. The government also drafted a Climate Change and Energy Transition Law and submitted a draft National Energy and Climate Plan to the European Commission. At the time of writing, neither the draft law nor the plan was yet final, but they send a signal in favor of renewable energy and BTM investment. For instance, the draft plan foresees investment in 6 GW of renewable power per year from 2021 to 2030, including a significant amount of distributed generation by consumers. It also foresees 5 million electric vehicles (EVs) by 2030 and an ambitious improvement in the efficiency of buildings. Both the Spanish legislation and the transition plan coincide well with European legislation[4] that promotes active participation of consumers in electricity markets and protects their right to develop DER BTM.

To summarize, Spain has opened the door to the development of rooftop solar and other BTM investment and it is very hard to imagine that the door will close because European legislation now clearly supports this development. However, existing fiscal, regulatory, and market structures do not provide efficient price signals to investors in BTM assets. Consequently, there is a material risk that investments will occur that are not economic and that consumers and their agents will not have incentives to use BTM resources efficiently. There is also a risk of slowing efficient investment BTM, for instance in heat pumps and EVs. It makes sense to try to fix the problems now to ensure that BTM investments are beneficial for investors and more generally for society.

The next sections examine five policy challenges that need to be addressed to provide price signals for efficient BTM decisions.

- fiscal policy reform to encourage efficient BTM investment;
- redesigned access tariffs to encourage consumers to make efficient use of networks, while allocating the cost of system expansion to those who cause it.

---

[4] Known as the Winter Package, which was passed in June 2019.

- establishing new markets enabling BTM assets to contribute to managing local distribution network congestion;
- enabling BTM assets to participate in all markets for energy and services; and
- defining a new market design "vision" for a future decarbonized and decentralized electricity sector.

18.4 Reforming fiscal policy

Governments almost everywhere have used electricity tariffs as a revenue collection mechanism to finance public policies. The EU's accounting of electricity costs distinguishes three cost categories: (1) taxes and levies, (2) energy, and (3) networks. Of the first, taxes, like value added taxes (VAT), fund general government expenditure, whereas levies usually fund specific policies, such as the promotion of renewables.

As Fig. 18.1 shows, Spain (ES) is among the EU countries with the highest share of taxes and levies. In 2017 the latter accounted for almost 50% of the electricity price for residential consumers. Other countries, notably Denmark and Germany, had even higher shares of taxes and levies. Between 2008 and 2015 the share of taxes and levies rose substantially in the EU, from 28% to 38% of the average final residential tariff. The most substantial increase reflected financial support in the EU for renewables and combined heat and power (CHP), which together rose on average from 14% to 33% of taxes and levies over the same period. Fig. 18.2 illustrates the increase in taxes and levies in Spain from 2008 to 2015, especially to support for renewables/CHP.

The result is that electricity prices today in many European countries are much higher than the costs of generating, transmitting, and retailing electricity. This creates an incentive for consumers to generate their own electricity to avoid paying taxes and levies. In Spain, for instance, residential consumers that generate their own electricity can potentially save over 25% of the price of delivered electricity, even without selling excess own-generated electricity to the system. This reduces substantially the pay-back period on investment in rooftop solar generation.

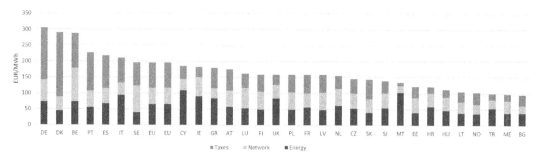

FIGURE 18.1 Household electricity prices in 2017, EU Member States. Source: *From EC (2019).* Commission Staff Working Document, Accompanying the document: Report from the Commission to the European Parliament, the Council, the European Economic and Social Committee and the Committee of the Regions: Energy prices and costs in Europe, *European Commission, COM (2019)1 final.*

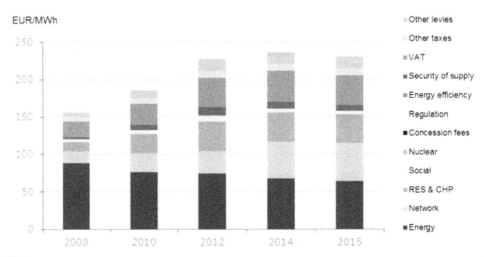

FIGURE 18.2 Composition of Spanish household electricity prices 2008–15. Source: From *EC (2016).* Commission Staff Working Document, Accompanying the document: Report from the Commission to the European Parliament, the Council, the European Economic and Social Committee and the Committee of the Regions: Energy prices and costs in Europe, *European Commission, 30 November 2016, COM (2016) 769 final.*

This incentive for self-generation in European countries is analogous to those described in other chapters of the book. Swanston, for example, explains that over 2 million Australian households have gone solar, mostly to avoid paying high bundled tariffs. Schlesinger explains the trend toward zero net energy consumption in the United States. In most cases, avoiding high prices seems to be a strong motivation.

Who can blame consumers for wanting to pay less? The problem is that, when high prices reflect taxes and levies, the bypass is usually uneconomic from a system perspective, potentially creating serious problems and policy reversals.

- *Inefficient price signals encourage uneconomic bypass.* From a system perspective the cost of rooftop renewables with developed distribution grids is typically higher than the cost of large-scale wind or solar, even after taking account of the reduced system losses and other possible benefits of distributed generation. Where incremental costs are lower for renewable electricity generated within the existing system, tariffs that do not reflect that difference will encourage uneconomic bypass of the system, raising system costs. Of course, consumers may choose to generate their own electricity for other reasons. Nevertheless, they should be given accurate information about the incremental costs of the alternatives. Section 18.8 explains how the "two market model" offers an alternative means of acquiring renewable electricity.

- *This fiscal policy could discourage decarbonization via electrification.* The rising fiscal burden on electricity is at odds with the policy aim of decarbonization through electrification. Take transport, for example. In Spain, as in most of Europe, the fiscal burden on transport fuels has been fairly steady over the past 20 years while CO_2 emissions from transport have been rising. During the same period the fiscal burden on electricity has risen substantially and CO_2 emissions from electricity have fallen, mainly due to the penetration of renewables. Consequently, electricity is becoming relatively more expensive compared to fossil fuels used in transport and in other end markets (heating and industry). This could slow the process of decarbonization through electrification (Robinson, 2017; Robinson, Llamas, López-Otero, & Rodrigues, 2019).

- *Potential political reversal?* If a growing number of consumers does not pay the levies, then who will? One possibility is that poorer citizens—who could not afford to invest in solar panels—will subsidize wealthier households. A second possibility is that the government could force the electricity companies to swallow the costs. A third is that the government would find itself with a new "tariff deficit." All of these concerns help to explain the origins of the "sun tax." As explained earlier, the effect was to discourage decentralized energy generation. However, the new Spanish legislation faces the same problem. If the missing tax and levy revenue becomes substantial, one cannot rule out that a future government will reintroduce some version of the "sun tax." Spain is not the only system facing this problem. In California, for instance, the generous net energy metering law allows solar customers to be subsidized by the nonsolar ones, and the former tend to be more affluent. In all countries, it is politically very difficult to withdraw a benefit of this kind. It would be better to avoid or minimize the distortion from the outset.

What can be done to resolve this problem? The following four solutions are all worth considering, with the first being superior to the others but very difficult to implement. The likely outcome will probably be some combination.

- *Pass levies to the government budget.* The first solution is to finance (at least some of) the policy costs through the government budget. For instance, in Spain, half of the costs of subsidizing electricity on the islands is recovered through a levy on electricity sales throughout the country. The other half is already included in the government budget, so there is no reason in principle why the rest should not be. The largest share of the levies finances the "extra" renewable costs that cannot be recovered through sales in the energy market. Financing these costs through general taxation is justified on the grounds that revenue is financing a public good. In the words of Newbery (2015),

   "It thus follows that the revenue needed to finance renewables and other public goods should come from general taxation raised in the least distorting ways consistent with distributional objectives – either through income taxes or a uniform rate of VAT, and not by selectively charging single products like electricity."

   In practice, governments in Spain and in most countries are reluctant to pass policy costs from the electricity price to the budget since this either creates a larger government deficit or requires the introduction of politically sensitive measures to raise taxes in other ways.
- *Spread the levy costs more widely.* A second solution, which is a variation on the first, is to share some of the policy costs within the energy sector, in particular through an additional levy on oil and gas products. The argument for sharing in this way is that investment was undertaken to meet the European goal of 20% renewables as a percentage of energy (not electricity) consumption. This solution meets understandable

resistance from the oil and gas industry. The oil industry argues that their tax burden is already very high and there is much debate about whether their taxes cover all environmental externalities.

- *Limit the potential for a tariff deficit.* A third option, which has been adopted by the government, is to limit the freedom of consumers to sell excess self-generated electricity. By legislating that consumers may not be net sellers to the system (i.e., their bills will always be equal to or greater than zero), the government mitigates the potential size of a new tariff deficit. However, the system still loses levy revenue. Furthermore, this measure does nothing to address the other concerns, notably the disincentive for electrification.

- *Collect the remaining levy costs in a connection charge.* To the extent that these measures leave policy costs in the electricity tariffs, the aim should be to minimize the distortions they create. The best way to do this would be to recover the policy costs through a fixed charge for all consumers connected to the system (regardless of their BTM assets). The challenge is to decide the basis for setting that charge for different consumers, bearing in mind that the charge does not reflect the incremental costs of the system. It makes little sense to set a higher connection charge for consumers with rooftop solar. Rather, it would be better to choose a mechanism designed to distort investment or consumption decisions as little as possible, subject to equity concerns. Finally, a high fixed connection charge could motivate disconnection from the system, with all the problems this would entail; that risk reinforces the case for eliminating levies from the tariff or reducing them as far as possible.

Other countries finance public policies in different ways. In the United States, for instance, investment and production tax credits have been a means of financing renewables. However, most countries in Europe have relied heavily on levies on residential electricity tariffs. Almost everywhere, when consumers find that they have the opportunity to bypass these levies, they have a clear incentive to do so even when this creates costs for society as a whole.

18.5 Redesigning access tariffs

Before liberalization, network pricing was not a problem. Electricity companies needed to make a margin over their overall costs and it did not matter greatly where the costs arose. With liberalization, it became critical to understand the costs involved in the now separate functions of transmission and distribution and to reflect them properly in prices. With the challenges of decarbonization and decentralization, network tariffs have become much more complex.

There are many important issues in defining network prices today.[5] The analysis below deals at a high level with two of these issues: temporal signals and the recovery of fixed costs.

[5] See Keay and Robinson (2017a) for a fuller analysis of the main policy issues related to network pricing, notably the importance of location signals.

Currently, regulated network, or access, tariffs in Spain include a fixed component related to the consumer's contracted capacity (per kW) and a variable component related to consumption (per kWh), with some time-of-use (ToU) and seasonal variations.[6] The current tariff design is problematic for at least four reasons.

- *Inefficient signals for network investment.* The fixed component reflects a consumer's contracted capacity, not the consumer's demand at times of *coincident system peak*. Consequently, tariffs do not provide signals to lower demand at system peak and therefore do not help to reduce or postpone future investment.
- *Inefficient signals for use of uncongested capacity.* Neither the fixed nor the variable elements of access tariffs provide a sharp enough signal to use the network when it is underutilized. This indirectly leads to greater use of the network during peak periods.
- *Uncertain recovery of fixed network costs.* Consumers are now aware that their contracted capacity is greater than the capacity they require, which leads to a decline in contracted capacity. The resulting loss of revenue will get worse as consumers develop distributed generation along with storage. Furthermore, while most network costs are fixed, a significant share of revenue comes through the variable charge, which makes the revenue streams vulnerable to the loss of throughput resulting from distributed generation.
- *Discourages investment in EV networks.* The high fixed element of the tariff discourages investment in EV charging networks mainly due to the difficulty of recovering those fixed costs from the low volume of EV charging in the early years following investment. We understand Tesla chose not to develop a network in Spain at least partly for that reason.

There are various reasonable alternatives to this tariff structure. The analysis below considers two possibilities: one based almost entirely on fixed payments for contracted capacity (kW) and the other based solely on variable payments for energy actually sold (kWh). Both extremes are unlikely today, but the analysis helps to understand the pros and cons of the alternatives and the direction of change.

The aim of the access tariff design should be to use the existing network efficiently, especially using it during periods when it is not congested; make efficient investment decisions; provide the basis for recovering investment costs; support efficient electrification; and be sensitive to equity considerations.

18.5.1 Fixed charging approach

Under this model, fixed costs are recovered through a fixed charge based on contracted capacity (per kW) and variable costs through a variable component (per kWh). Since 80%−90% of network costs are fixed, under this model the fixed component is the main source of revenue. To provide temporal signals, this model has different fixed charges reflecting anticipated peak and off-peak conditions. Supporters of this kind of model argue that it (1) promotes electrification, notably heat pumps, because of low variable charges;

---

[6] Although access tariffs in Spain also collect taxes and levies, these were discussed in Section 18.4. They are not addressed again here.

(2) is predictable, similar to flat tariffs used in telecom, and therefore easy for consumers to understand; (3) involves no price shocks; and (4) facilitates investment in EV charging networks due to the low off-peak fixed charge. On the other hand, this model raises some concerns.

- In most countries, it is politically unacceptable to levy a large fixed charge on small consumers if this means that poor consumers will be penalized. There is a debate about whether the poorest really are penalized. They may consume a lot of electricity due to bad insulation and old radiators. Wealthier people may have alternatives that reduce electricity consumption from the system, including self-generation, gas and gasoil. In any case, the solution for energy poverty is a combination of direct public support, as well as more efficient buildings and heating systems (e.g., heat pumps).
- If the payment is based on contracted capacity, consumers will reduce the amount they contract, reducing the potential to recover fixed costs. This could be addressed by an annual regulatory "true-up," although these are often politically difficult to implement. In any case, incentives to reduce the need for capacity are welcome.
- The fixed payment provides no basis for reflecting actual use of the network, especially at peak times. (Smart meters are able to monitor this time-differentiated use in 15 minutes periods.) This problem could be addressed by measuring actual use during periods of congestion, but this would eliminate the advantage of price stability and require a completely different system.
- This model does not reflect the increasing uncertainty about when the network will be congested, especially as a result of the growing penetration of intermittent renewables and BTM activity. If the tariff is set annually based upon a historic contribution to the system peak, it will not reflect actual congestion.
- High fixed charges could also encourage consumer disconnections, with all the problems that would entail.

18.5.2 Variable charging approach

A second approach is a tariff structure that recovers most or all costs through a variable payment related to volume (kWh) and the ToU. Endesa has made a proposal along these lines, as reflected in Fig. 18.3. They use a road traffic light analogy to identify three periods (p1-red, p2-yellow, and p3-green). The tariff reflects the average capacity used in each period, which is equivalent to the energy consumed in each period.

- *Green-light hours* account for 70%−80% of hours, when congestion on the distribution and transport network is very low. For these the variable charge would be very low to encourage utilization of the network and to lighten congestion in other hours.
- *Yellow-light hours*, possibly 15%−20% of the total, correspond to times when congestion on the network is moderate, and variable charges would be somewhat higher than during the green-light hours.
- *Red-light hours*, around 5%−10% of the time, correspond to heavy congestion on the distribution system, when variable charges will be significantly higher.

	Time period
	P1 P2 P3

Mainland system		1	2	3	4	5	6	7	8	9	10	11	12	13	14	15	16	17	18	19	20	21	22	23	24
Monday to Friday on working days	January																								
	February																								
	March																								
	April																								
	May																								
	June																								
	July																								
	August																								
	September 1–15																								
	September 15–30																								
	October																								
	November 1–15																								
	November 15–30																								
	December																								
Weekends and holidays																									

	Time periods		
	P1	P2	P3
Number of hours	672	1479	6609
Share of hours	7.70%	16.90%	74.40%

FIGURE 18.3 From Endesa proposal for a time-differentiated variable access tariff in Spain.

These tariffs reflect low short-run marginal costs as well as congestion costs, which vary by time period, in addition to allowing for fixed cost recovery. They aim to provide signals for efficient use of the network and encourage a shift from red-light peak hours to green off-peak hours. They are consistent with the development of EV networks and incentivize EV charging during green hours. However, there are a number of possible concerns.

- If poorer consumers need more electricity, especially at times of system peak, this system would penalize them. On the other hand, it would benefit the poor who do not consume much electricity, or consume it off-peak. As mentioned above, energy poverty is a policy issue that is best addressed by providing direct subsidies to the poorest consumers, rather than distorting the price signals, and through better insulation and the installation of more efficient equipment, such as heat pumps.
- Fixed cost recovery is at risk since success in reducing congestion will lower revenues. This problem applies to both models and is not a reason to discourage efficient use and development of the network.
- The system may be too complex, with consumers not understanding its implications or, more importantly, reacting negatively when electricity bills jump to reflect seasonal peaks. Consumers are familiar with peak pricing, for instance with airlines, but not for electricity. This can be addressed through education but will take time. More importantly, retail companies and aggregators may offer bundled prices that differ from the access tariffs so that consumers do not have to worry about network tariffs.
- Although this model would support the development of EV networks and off-peak use of EVs, it would raise the price of electricity used in red periods, including by heat pumps. On the other hand, it would encourage the use of batteries to store electricity

during green periods. Indeed, this network pricing structure would provide commercial opportunities for the retail company or aggregator.
* Endesa's initial proposal sets ToU tariffs in advance and does not reflect real-time congestion, so it is not as efficient as it could be. A "dynamic" variation of this model, also proposed by Endesa, would allow access charges to vary in real time to reflect actual congestion on the system. Although that would increase price volatility and might elicit negative consumer reactions to changes in price, the dynamic model offers further commercial and trading opportunities for intermediaries.

These models each have strengths and weaknesses. Both can send price signals to encourage investment in EV network charging networks and favor utilization in off-peak hours. Both need to address problems related to energy poverty and recovery of fixed costs and a "fair return" on investment. However, there is an important difference: the variable charging model measures and charges on the basis of actual use of the network, whereas the fixed charging model does not. In that respect, the variable charging model sends better signals to use the network efficiently. This will matter increasingly as BTM activity becomes more relevant and makes congestion less predictable. The volatility of variable access prices could discourage electrification if it were passed on directly to all consumers. But large consumers will have incentives and the ability to manage this volatility, while retailers and aggregators can decide whether to pass on or smooth the cost variations. Indeed, one would expect these intermediaries to look for opportunities, for instance installing local storage, to enable purchasing electricity in off-peak periods for resale in retail or wholesale markets.

18.6 Establishing local congestion markets

With the growth of DER and multidirectional flows of energy, management of congestion on the distribution network will become more complex. In the past, the distribution network operator could assume that energy would flow in one direction, from the transmission network to the final consumer through the distribution network. Decisions to manage congestion were primarily ones that involved long-term investment in additional capacity.

With the growth of DER, the distribution system operator (DSO) will face significantly greater uncertainty about the volume, timing, and direction of flows on the network. This will require the development of new mechanisms to manage the network, both in the short term and when making investment decisions. There is every reason to use market mechanisms to manage congestion and to include BTM resources in these markets.

Through their BTM decisions, consumers and aggregators can provide the flexibility to help manage congestion on the local distribution network. They need to be given the opportunity and incentives to participate. We have already discussed ways to improve price signals through fiscal reform and through a new design of access tariffs. This section focuses on the creation of new markets for congestion management services.

* *Nodal pricing.* One solution to managing congestion would be to introduce nodal pricing, setting market-based electricity prices for each node on the system. Prices would differ by an amount that reflected the congestion costs between the nodes.

In this way, nodes with high prices would elicit greater supply and reduced demand; and low-priced nodes would have the opposite effect. Although this model is theoretically attractive, and used in some countries, it has three drawbacks. The first is that nodal prices can be technically very complex. The second is that they run into difficulties in countries where regional differences in prices are politically sensitive; this is certainly true in Spain where there is a history of uniform national tariffs. Third, while nodal prices may work and be politically acceptable at a national or regional level, introducing them within a distribution system is more difficult because of the number of nodes. As opposed to transmission that has only a few hundred nodes, distribution has several thousand nodes. The costs and complexity of introducing nodal pricing at distribution level can thus outweigh the benefit.

- *Local flexibility markets.* Congestion management requires flexibility in different timeframes. Drawing once again on the traffic light analogy, here is a proposal that is based on an idea developed by the Spanish market operator (OMIE) in conjunction with IDAE, the Spanish Institute for Energy Diversification and Savings. The green-, yellow-, and red-light conditions would correspond to different levels of congestion. Congestion may be very local, requiring a dynamic local congestion market, whereas access tariffs will, at least initially in Spain, be static, apply across the distribution network and for all distribution networks.[7]
  - *Green-light conditions* exist when there is no congestion on the distribution system. These are fundamentally the same conditions that apply under the green-light access tariffs that were discussed in the last section. In this case, there is no need for a local congestion market; consumers may participate directly in wholesale markets for energy and services. Since the growth of distributed generation will initially reduce the volume of electricity flowing into the distribution network, green-light conditions are likely to apply in most hours.
  - *Yellow-light conditions* reflect temporary congestion, for example, anticipated congestion next Tuesday between 12:00 and 01:00 p.m., in a specific location on the distribution grid. In that case the DSO would request a market operator (which potentially could be controlled by the DSO) to hold a reverse auction to buy the necessary flexibility service. The auction will determine the price for the service and identify the suppliers chosen to provide the service, potentially including BTM providers or their representatives.
  - *Red-light conditions* reflect structural congestion that requires investment to relieve the congestion, either by the distribution company or by alternative providers, such as aggregators with access to a range of BTM resources. In these conditions the DSO would request a market operator—which potentially could be controlled by the DSO—to organize a reverse auction to select the provider for long-term availability and to determine the price for that service. Since overcoming structural congestion is likely to require investment or allocating resources to an asset that will have to be available when needed, the winner of the auction would receive a fixed availability payment for the commitment to provide flexibility, when needed, as well as the variable market price in the flexibility market when the service is called.

---

[7] See also the chapter by Johnston and Sioshansi.

The attraction of this proposal is that it creates local flexibility markets where none now exist. It offers the basis for establishing a price to support efficient investment and operating decisions by consumers with BTM, whether managed by the consumer or by aggregators. However, as always, the devil is in the details, including on auction design and the identity of the market operator. The DSO should only control the market operator if regulation or ownership separation can overcome two conflicts of interest. One is between the DSO and the owner of the distribution network—similar to the conflict of interest between the TSO and the owner of the transmission network. The other, even more complicated, is between the DSO and the market participants—retail, aggregator—belonging to the same vertically integrated group of companies. Spain's market operator (OMIE) is another obvious candidate to run these markets with the advantages of standardization and synergies with access to existing day-ahead and intraday markets. It is also possible to envisage a variety of new local market operators.

18.7 Opening access for behind the meter participation in all markets

While today there are no local markets for energy and flexibility services, wholesale markets do exist. They include financial markets, bilateral physical markets, organized day-ahead and intra-day energy markets, as well as short-term markets to manage congestion on the transmission network, ensure system stability, and balance supply and demand in real time. Fig. 18.4 illustrates many of these markets, including potential local markets and continuous intraday markets. The market operator (OMIE) manages most of the markets until real-time, when the system operator (REE) is responsible for balancing and ancillary services markets used to ensure system stability.

Although existing wholesale markets were designed with large-scale generation in mind, they have, at least in Spain, evolved to facilitate the participation of small-size producers and large consumers, normally through aggregation companies. However, ancillary services and balancing markets have been effectively off limits to prosumers or aggregators wishing to sell energy and flexibility. In these markets a limited number of generators set prices that are passed through to consumers. It is precisely in these markets where demand-side flexibility has an opportunity to compete for relatively attractive margins.

To address these challenges the proposed reform of markets involves at least three changes.

- *Authorization*. The first reform is to authorize consumers, prosumers, and aggregators to participate in all existing markets, subject to meeting certain conditions.
- *Redefine the conditions for participation in existing markets, especially for ancillary services and balancing*. The second and more important reform is to redefine the conditions for participating in these markets so that the door is genuinely open for demand-side participation, including all BTM resources. For instance, current regulations for the balancing market in Spain require suppliers to have at least 10 MW of capacity. Although aggregators could presumably meet that condition, ICT technology is able to cope with suppliers with significantly less capacity. At the time of writing the Spanish regulator is proposing to reduce the required capacity to 1 MW in line with European

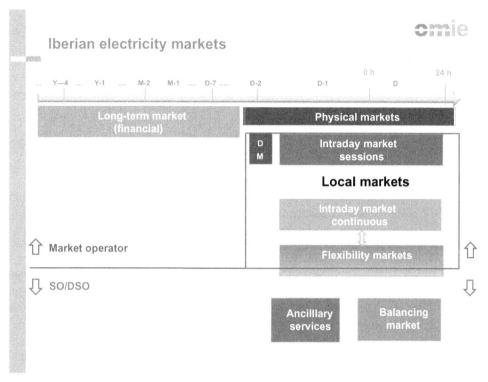

FIGURE 18.4 Electricity markets in Spain and Portugal (Iberia). Source: *With permission from Omie.*

platforms. The system operator may have a natural preference to maintain existing protocols and be able to insist on risks to supply security (resource adequacy) or system stability. However, it should be given strong incentives to promote competition in the provision of balancing and other services. These incentives are the best guarantee that BTM assets will be able to participate in existing and new markets.

- *Establish new markets and services*. A decentralized and decarbonized system will require new kinds of flexibility, in multiple time dimensions. These may include long-term capacity (firm energy) markets, new local markets, as well as new markets to deal with the loss of inertia (resulting from closure of large power stations) and the requirements to respond to frequent short-term fluctuations in output related to intermittent renewables. The regulator should identify the new system needs and provide incentives for the market operators and the system operators to establish new services and markets in which BTM participation is welcomed on a nondiscriminatory basis.

18.8 Rethinking wholesale market design for a decarbonized system

This section looks at a specific proposal for a fundamental reform of the wholesale (energy-only) market. It focuses on consumer preferences and places BTM decisions at its core.

As explained earlier in the chapter, current energy-only electricity markets are broken and the system relies increasingly on governments to determine the mix, location, and quantities of energy resources. There are many proposed reforms, but most aim to solve only one of the problems of energy-only markets, for instance adding capacity markets to overcome the problem of "missing money." This section focuses exclusively on the "two-market" approach that attempts to address all of the problems of the energy-only market (Keay & Robinson, 2017b).

- The two-market approach creates separate markets for two different sorts of power ("on-demand" and "as-available") at both producer and consumer ends. For producers, dispatchable plants would operate in the on-demand market, be dispatched according to merit order when needed, and paid as at present in the "energy-only" model. Intermittent renewable plants would participate in the as-available market; in principle, they would operate when available and, at least initially, be paid a price reflecting the levelized cost of electricity, similar to current auction arrangements in a number of EU countries. The idea is that the differing costs and operation of sources in the two wholesale markets would be reflected in the retail market. Consumers would be able to buy from either of the two markets at retail prices reflecting their respective wholesale prices or buy combinations of the two sources of power. Initially—as at present—it is likely that price support would be needed either at producer or consumer level to make the as-available (renewable) offer attractive to consumers, but over time, as carbon prices increase and renewable costs fall, the support could be removed, creating a potential exit strategy for government subsidies and control over investment decisions. The design is shown schematically in Fig. 18.5.

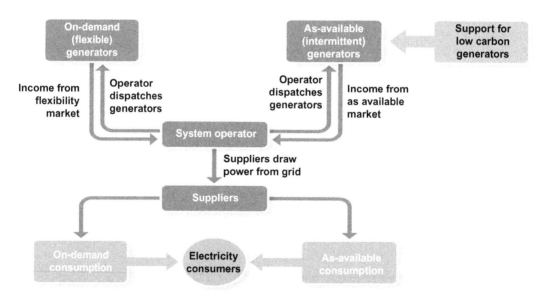

FIGURE 18.5   Schematic of two-market design. Source: Reproduced with permission from Keay, M., & Robinson, D. (June 2017b). The decarbonised electricity system of the future: The 'two market' approach. *Oxford.*

- The benefits of this design would include the following:
  - *Signals for investment in both markets.* By keeping the markets separate, at least in commercial terms, eventually investments in renewables and conventional plants could be remunerated solely from the two markets. Initially, it may be necessary to maintain existing support systems, including auctions for renewables and for firm energy in their respective markets.
  - *Efficient signals for operation in the on-demand market.* This market only includes generation and other resources that can and would be dispatched in merit order. These flexible resources would include demand-side resources from BTM investments, such as batteries and flexible demand.
  - *Incentives for consumers to maximize their use of as-available (renewable) power.* Consumers would now have an understandable and effective choice, along with price incentives, to use renewable power from the system. Markets for demand response, on-site storage, distributed generation and the supply chain that supports these and other services, would develop in response to their preferences.
  - *Meaningful price signals for consumers to contribute to overall system optimization.* In effect, security would be privatized and consumers would be able to decide for themselves how far they were prepared to pay for secure supplies. (System stability is a separate matter and would still be subject to system operator control.) It would be possible for consumers to use their own Value of Lost Load assessments in deciding whether to access the on-demand market. The same ideas could be adapted to enable consumers to reveal their preferences with respect to distributed resources and network access.
  - *Provide an exit strategy.* The financial support for renewables shown in the schematic above could be removed over time; intermittent generators would be able to remunerate their investments from the market once it had developed sufficiently to be understood and used by consumers.
- This model is relevant for the development of BTM activity for at least three reasons.
  - First, consumers facing the option of investing in rooftop solar will have an alternative, namely, to purchase renewable energy produced elsewhere on a short- or longer term contract at a stable price.
  - Second, consumers can potentially contract to sell some of their renewable energy into the AA market at a price that reflects the price in that market. This could be a local market or part of the wholesale AA market and would probably be sold through an aggregator.
  - Third, consumers will have an incentive to use their BTM assets to be flexible in two respects. First, to shift their demand to periods when renewable energy is being produced in the as-available market, thereby avoiding having to purchase electricity in the on-demand market where prices are volatile and likely to be higher. And, second, to manage their own BTM DER, for example, batteries, in order to sell energy and flexibility services into the on-demand market.

This proposal is an effort to reveal consumer preferences and support the development of a supply chain that would respond to those preferences. It should be viewed as a long-term vision, rather than a model to be introduced immediately. If the two-market approach is accepted as a possible long-term vision, there are many steps that could be taken that would lead in that direction, without necessarily ending up in the precise model that is described above. For instance, it might be possible initially to focus the two-markets at the consumer end, finding ways to maintain a single wholesale market, or integrate the two wholesale markets.[8] The initial focus would be to experiment, in a "regulatory sandbox," with tariffs, markets, and regulations that give consumers the opportunity to choose between the two different kinds of energy and that seek to learn about consumer preferences.

18.9 Conclusion

This chapter has argued that investments BTM should provide benefits to society as well as to the individuals investing. Otherwise, there is a risk of wasted resources and an energy transition that is slower and less successful than it could be. It is critical to get the prices right, especially in a liberalized market framework.

On the one hand, regulators and policy makers should make sure that consumers, who move away from the traditional bundled regulated tariffs to more exotic options such as "prosumer" and "prosumager" models, do not avoid paying certain fees and thereby cause higher tariffs for the remaining customers. On the other hand, they should provide incentives for BTM resources that lower the overall costs of the system, for instance by selling energy and flexibility services in competitive wholesale and local markets.

In some cases, it is important to distinguish between price signals sent to final consumers and those sent to intermediaries, like aggregators, traders, and retail companies. For example, network access tariffs should reflect congestion conditions, as suggested by the variable charging model. But it is up to retailers and aggregators to decide how best to manage the difference between the network costs and the final price they charge to consumers. Indeed, this is a business opportunity that arises partly as a result of BTM investments.

Policy makers should recognize the need to think about reforming entire electricity systems, rather than reforming its separate parts. Emphasizing efficient pricing throughout the system—through fiscal policy, regulation, and market design—is one way of ensuring coherent reform. This is also why we recommend system-wide market reform, through the two-market model, rather than partial reforms that address only some of the problems with energy-only markets.

Fundamental changes are under way in the electricity sector. Governments and regulators will continue to play a key role in the new, liberalized electricity system. But their primary responsibility is to provide a framework of markets, regulations, and fiscal policies that send efficient price signals to consumers, aggregators, retailers, and other agents in the system. That framework should be designed to reflect consumer preferences rather than the preferences of central decision-makers and to enable consumers to drive the energy transition process, drawing increasingly on BTM resources.

[8] See Grubb and Drummond (2018), pp. 52–53.

References

EC (2016). *Commission Staff Working Document, Accompanying the document: Report from the Commission to the European Parliament, the Council, the European Economic and Social Committee and the Committee of the Regions: Energy prices and costs in Europe.* European Commission, 30 November 2016, COM (2016) 769 final.

EC (2019). *Commission Staff Working Document, Accompanying the document: Report from the Commission to the European Parliament, the Council, the European Economic and Social Committee and the Committee of the Regions: Energy prices and costs in Europe.* European Commission, COM (2019)1 final.

Grubb, M., & Drummond, P. (February 2018). *UK Industrial Electricity Prices: Competitiveness in a low carbon world.* University College London, Institute for Sustainable Resources.

Joskow, P. (2006). Introduction to electricity sector liberalization: lessons learned from cross- country studies. In Sioshansi, F. and W. Pfaffenberger (Eds.). *Electricity market reform: An international perspective*, pp. 1–32.

Keay, M. (2016). *Electricity markets are broken – Can they be fixed?* Oxford.

Keay, M., & Robinson, D. (2017a). *Managing electricity decarbonisation: Learning from experience – the cases of the UK and Spain.* Oxford.

Keay, M., & Robinson, D. (2017b). *The decarbonised electricity system of the future: The 'two market' approach.* Oxford.

Newbery, D. (2015). *Reforming UK energy policy to live within its means.* Cambridge Working Papers in Economics.

Robinson, D. (2017). *Fiscal policy for decarbonization of energy in Europe.* Oxford.

Robinson, D., Llamas, P. L., López-Otero, X., & Rodrigues, R. (2019). Fiscal policy for decarbonization of energy in Europe, with a focus on urban transport: Case study and proposal for Spain. In M. V. Ezcurra, J. E. Milne, H. Ashiabor, & M. S. Andersen (Eds.), *Environmental Fiscal Challenges for Cities and Transport.* Edward Elgar.

19

Two million plus solar roofs: what's in it for the consumers?

Mike Swanston

The Customer Advocate, Brisbane, QLD, Australia

19.1 Introduction

For the past decade, energy has been the subject of intense public attention and frequent barbeque conversations in Australia.

Originally the conversation focused on the rapidly rising cost of electricity, and what a consumer could or could not do about it. More recently, the discussion has expanded to include the rapid adoption of wind and solar energy; whether it be the consumer benefits of behind-the-meter (BTM) resources in the form of photovoltaic (PV) on the roofs of many Australian households, or batteries in the garage, or in the way renewable energy is becoming a significant proportion of the national generation mix.

These issues are not dissimilar to those in, say, California or Germany, as highlighted in other chapters in this volume. The impact of the PV growth is prominent in Australia when the number of solar roofs—2.2 million and still growing rapidly—is considered against a total population of only 25 million people. In many ways, Australia is the "canary in the coal mine."

Close to one-quarter of Australia's 9 million electricity consumers have chosen to invest in BTM generation in the form of rooftop solar PVs. The predominant incentive for such investment is the attractive payback period of less than 5 years for most consumers with PV (Australian Energy Council, 2019), thanks to an ongoing Federal capital rebate mechanism and, for some years, generous feed-in tariffs (FiTs). This investment not only offered powerful incentives to the consumer in the forms of significantly reduced electricity costs, it provided a perception of independence from mistrusted utilities and the satisfaction of making even a small contribution to a lower carbon future (Romanach, Contreras, & Ashworth, 2013).

Wider benefits for Australian consumers beyond lower energy prices and lower emissions from the power sector are emerging in opportunities for peer-to-peer local energy trading, solar gardens for those in the community without direct access to rooftop generation, and even the efficient grid disconnection for properties in bushfire prone areas; an approach further described by Rai et al. in Chapter 16. The necessary technical, commercial, and regulatory reforms are under consideration and development, in many ways lagging the continued rapid uptake of energy technologies by consumers. It will be some time until these innovations become mainstream, due largely to the complexity and fragmentation of the Australian market.

Once implemented, consumers will be able to "opt-in" to these products and others, such as advanced household demand response, to further reduce their energy costs and realize new commercial opportunities. Not all will seek to engage with the new energy markets, however. Some will be satisfied to support the ever-growing awareness of climate priorities and the imperative of a lower carbon future. Others will reflect the egalitarian nature of the community generally, where the sharing of low-cost energy becomes a community norm.

In parallel with the renewed growth of consumer-owned BTM energy resources in Australia is a record level of investment in utility-scale wind and solar PV generation, complemented by large grid-scale battery storage. The aggressive development of renewable energy sources at both ends of the supply chain has heightened the sensitivity of market and network system operators to topics such as grid strength, load shedding risks, wholesale price impacts, demand response, and a myriad of others in a way that would not have been so prevalent should the growth be in either the utility generation or BTM sector alone. Consumers, too, are well aware of these issues, thanks to regular extensive media coverage of energy-related matters.

Markets, networks, and regulators in Australia have now reached a critical point where the paradigms of industry from the past 50 years are being seriously challenged, topics discussed by Sioshansi in Chapter 1. For consumers, the technical constraints of a two-way local grid are proving to be a limitation, as are the network access pricing mechanisms. Consumer demand response, where consumption needs to be dynamically adjusted to meet the variable nature of solar and wind generation, is emerging as a critical component for the efficient operation of both the wholesale energy market and networks alike. Concerns regarding network stability and the protection of a power system with high levels of intermittent embedded generation are now more prevalent amongst network operators, with market interventions becoming more frequent, and costs to provide grid stability services growing.

In looking forward to the next challenges and opportunities for the energy future in Australia, the response features three key components. First, there are the technical changes needed in network investment, grid optimization and the expansion of interconnections and new market mechanisms needed to prudently and efficiently provide the *more flexible physical platform* to facilitate the new services and capability expected by consumers.

Second, a *renewed market environment* will emerge by upgrading, or perhaps even reinventing, the rules, regulations, and commercial arrangements that oversee the markets and the interaction of distributed energy resources (DER) generally to bring together the physics, the market, and most importantly the consumer to common ground—topics highlighted in the book's Foreword, Preface, and Epilogue.

Importantly, the third aspect of emerging reform relates to Australia's energy consumer landscape, where a new paradigm of *energy-user-concentric thinking* is developing. Consumer protections, affordability, investment efficiency, new price signals, and the influence of split incentives within the supply chain must all be reconsidered, taking a consumer-view of the design. Given the mistrust and sensitivity by consumers toward the energy industry and the broader range of energy perspectives that have been enabled by new energy, there is a risk that the necessary market changes, if not communicated well, will meet resistance; especially as customers see more choices available regarding their energy needs.

It is critical that those in the energy industry—the planners, the policy makers, the operators, and the service providers—put themselves in the consumers' shoes whilst navigating through the changes. The term "disruptive" is used frequently in the energy industry—but as noted by Jeff Bezos, the founder of Amazon, change becomes disruptive only when picked up by consumers and becomes mainstream:

> Invention is not disruptive; only consumer adoption is disruptive.

> At Amazon, we've invented a lot of things that consumers did not care about at all and, believe me, they were not disruptive to anyone. It is only when consumers like the new way that anything becomes disruptive.

This chapter examines what led to Australia's leading position in investment behind and beyond the meter, and extrapolates some of these key factors as influencers, if not prerequisites, for a successful onward journey for both the energy industry and consumers. It takes the consumer's point of view and is organized as follows:

- Section 19.2 profiles the nature of the Australian electricity network and examines the environment that led to Australia's leading position on BTM energy resources.
- Section 19.3 considers five factors that influenced consumers to participate in the PV revolution.
- Section 19.4 outlines the resurgence in DER investment as mid-scale consumers move into an already robust DER market.
- Section 19.5 profiles the Australian prosumer, exploring the nature of a consumer who has embraced change.
- Section 19.6 takes a critical view of the consumer factors that have been evident in the journey so far; and highlights the considerations networks and forecasters must address in planning an efficient and effective way forward for new energy.
- Finally, in light of the drivers of the past adoption of BTM resources, Section 19.7 examines the challenges ahead to continue consumer engagement and participation in the changing energy mix and asks: *"what's in it for the consumers?"*.

19.2 The Australian story, so far

There are approximately 9 million electricity consumers connected to the National Electricity Market system; a long, relatively thin network spanning around 5000 km from the tropical north, along the east coast to the southern island of Tasmania and west to the

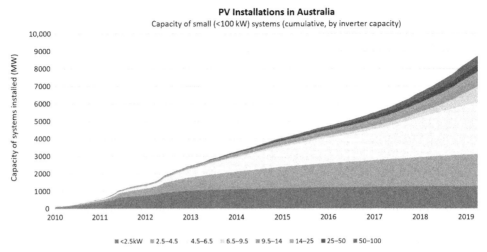

FIGURE 19.1 PV installations in Australia by capacity. *PV*, Photovoltaic. Source: *Data from the Australian PV Institute (APVI).*

arid regions of South Australia. The market is highly fragmented, with both state and privately owned energy retailers, distributors, transmission companies, and generators. New entrants, most notably demand aggregators, are becoming established.[1]

To the west is the South West Interconnected System of Western Australia. The more vertically integrated utilities of Horizon Power and the Power and Water Corporation of the Northern Territory supply electricity to consumers in rural, regional, and mining communities over a highly remote service area of approximately 3.5 million square kilometers through a multitude of advanced microgrids and isolated power systems.

Coal and gas have traditionally formed the base of utility generation in Australia; with no nuclear, no offshore wind; and some hydro generation and pumped hydro storage in Tasmania and the Snowy Mountains. Large solar and wind farms have proliferated in recent years, many with the support of federal incentive schemes.

By mid-2019, Australia had almost 2.2 million small-scale[2] rooftop solar PV installations totaling nearly 9 GW in capacity; installed on almost 24% of all detached and semidetached homes in the country (Fig. 19.1). In the sun-rich states of South Australia and Queensland, around 1-in-3 homes and businesses have become energy prosumers to date (Australian Energy Regulator, 2018, p. 15).

Despite the removal of most generous FiTs and the moderating of the capital rebate incentive, growth in rooftop PV capacity is still a robust 20% pa; with 1.7 GW installed in the last 12 months. The frenetic, almost-unmanageable installation activity seen early in

---

[1] A good overview of the Australian Energy Market from the *Australian Energy Regulator* is—https://www.aer.gov.au/publications/state-of-the-energy-market-reports/state-of-the-energy-market-2018.

[2] Small Scale under the *Renewable Energy (Electricity) Regulations 2001* is a system of less than 100 kW capacity, or generating less that 250 MWh of energy per annum

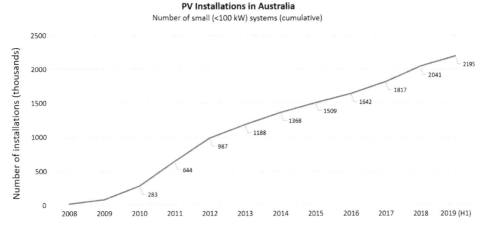

PV Installations in Australia

Number of small (<100 kW) systems (cumulative)

FIGURE 19.2 PV installations in Australia by number. *PV*, Photovóltaic. Source: *Data from the APVI and Australian Clean Energy Regulator (CER).*

the decade has eased however, reflecting the increasing average kW capacity of more recent installations (Fig. 19.2).

Some state jurisdictions continue to test the resilience and capability of the solar PV industry with localized incentive schemes, as discussed in Section 19.4.1.

In conjunction with the 4 GW of large-scale solar generation now in service, the amount of clean electricity consumed in Australia is expected to increase 36% this year and another 25% in the next. Consumer-owned PV generation accounts for 60% of the installed PV capacity in Australia.

Battery uptake is still only moderate, with around 1 in every 40 new PV installations having battery storage included (Australian Energy Council, 2019).

Australia continues to lead the world, per capita, in the installation rate for rooftop solar generation. Renewable generation in Australia is "the new normal."

19.2.1 Electricity hits the headlines

The decade to 2018 was a problematic time for energy consumers, with sharp rises in gas and electricity prices well-outstripping the growth in the cost-price index and wages. Retail electricity prices in Australia rose more than four times that of underlying consumer costs (Fig. 19.3).

The Australian Competition and Consumer Authority (ACCC) (2018) found that in that period retail electricity prices rose overall by 56% in real terms, including a 15% rise in environmental costs and levies, 8% in retail costs, and 13% in retail margins. The ACCC also noted generation market power, retail discounting and penalty charges and disengaged consumers as issues of concern [ACCC, 2018, p. (v)].

Around 2010−13, networks invested heavily in system security infrastructure following several severe weather-related blackouts on the east coast and on concerns of a potential rapid rise in peak demand from the enthusiastic adoption of domestic air-conditioning. These investments led to an underlying increase in network use-of-system (DuoS) prices—which

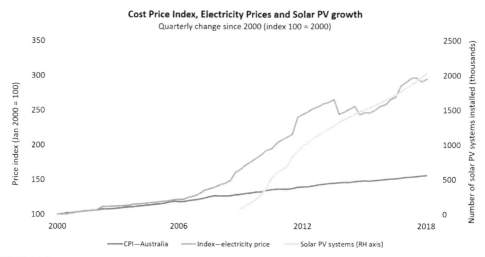

FIGURE 19.3 CPI and solar PV growth in Australia. *CPI*, Australian consumer price index; *PV*, Photovoltaic. Source: *Data from the Australian Bureau of Statistics and the Clean Energy Regulator.*

are around half the consumers' electricity bill—of 38% (Wood, Blowers, & Griffiths, 2018). These are costs that will remain recoverable in utility asset bases for up to 40 years.

At the same time, several other factors were also in play. Retail offers in the market became more confusing, as retailers developed pricing structures that included high pay-on-time discounts, often referred to by consumers as a "pay-late penalty charge." The balance between the fixed and variable components of the consumer bill was shifted significantly toward the fixed connection charge, with little engagement with consumers as to the reason why. Discounts for direct load control (off-peak) tariffs, so effective for many years in agriculture irrigation sector and the residential of storage hot water, were reduced.

Finally, rapid increases in liquified natural gas (LNG) exports from the east coast of Australia and moratoria on onshore gas development in some states stifled the availability of low-cost gas, more than doubling the domestic gas price. As gas is not only a common alternative domestic fuel but also prominent in the electricity generation mix, this price rise impacted all energy consumers through increased average energy prices.

There was a short reprieve in electricity prices in 2014 when the carbon price was repealed, but the respite was brief. More importantly, the price rises raised the profile of energy to a community who were previously largely disengaged from energy issues. A feeling of *disempowerment* emerged amongst consumers, where attempts to reduce or at least manage energy bills through well-understood actions of "turning off the lights" or changing habits to reduce electricity consumption were frustrated by the growing proportion of fixed connection charges, rising kilowatt-hour rates, new metering costs, and less attractive controlled-load tariff discounts.

A similar trend was prevalent in the EU where the levies such as renewables obligations, FiT subsidies, and emission-trading schemes were added on top of tariffs, comprising up to 40% of the bills (European Commission, 2019, p. 2).

It is often quoted that it was not the actual high price of electricity that brought such negative attention to the electricity industry; it was the steep *rate* of change. Whilst that may be so, the media reporting of struggling businesses unable to afford the new energy costs and the impact of the cost increases on vulnerable consumers became almost daily news[3] (Energy Queensland, Powerlink, 2018, p. 13).

Rises in the wholesale and retail price of electricity coincided with mainstream media reporting of closures of coal fired power stations, the rapid rise in gas exports, and even the ecological causes of coral bleaching on the Great Barrier Reef. The community became very aware of the complex array of factors and risks inherent in Australia's energy and environmental policies.

In summary, rapidly rising electricity prices, the reduction in a consumer's control of those prices, and a very public debate about the frailties of the future of low cost, reliable and sustainable electricity in Australia set the scene for the entry of rooftop solar generation.

Moreover, trust in the industry was at an all-time low. The pressure for governments to take action to address "crippling" energy prices was, and to some extent remains today, immense.

19.2.2 The pressure for government intervention

Despite much of the electricity supply chain being fully or partially privatized and networks being regulated by the national competition authority, consumers still see the role of electricity supply as a basic accountability of state governments. This community expectation has its roots in the history of utilities being a state-owned essential service, in a time where energy supply and price could be influenced by the state owners to support wider programs such as regional employment, primary industry efficiency, and contributions to general state revenue. Nowadays, consumers—who are of course, voters—are very much top-of-mind for governments who are keen to maintain environmental credentials, provide a positive influence on household energy budgets, and ensure supply reliability commensurate with the support of regional development.

The Clean Energy Regulator was established in 2012 to administer the federal Small-scale Renewable Energy Target (SRET) scheme.[4] This certificate-based scheme, scheduled to end in 2030, supported the installation of solar panels, solar water heating, and the like. This rebate is most often delivered as a point-of sale discount of up to 30%, based on system size and geographical location, and is set up to decline in value annually.

In parallel, most state governments put in place renewable energy targets, underpinned by very generous solar FiT schemes under the banner of environmental responsibility, with a view to encouraging consumers to install solar PV systems. This was done by providing households with payments for the electricity generated from the solar panels above the market value of this electricity. Prosumers receive payments from their distributor,

---

[3] As an example, see the article in The Conversation, September 2012—http://theconversation.com/the-real-cause-of-electricity-price-rises-in-nsw-8955.

[4] Established in 2012 under the Australian *Clean Energy Regulator Act 2011*.

TABLE 19.1   Premium feed-in tariff schemes, excluding retailer components.

State	Type	Feed-in tariff (c/kWh)	
Victoria	Net	25 and 60	Opened 2009, closed to new entrants 2011, transitional tariff to 2016
New South Wales	Gross	60	Commenced 2009, reduced in 2011 for all participants, closed 2016
Queensland	Net	44	Commenced 2008, closed 2014, continues to June 30, 2028 for legacy participants only
South Australia	Net	44	Commenced 2011, closed 2013, continues to June 30, 2028 for legacy participants only

Note: Retail price of anytime energy at the time was 20−30 c/kWh.
Source: *TCA analysis of utility and government public announcements.*

who recovers these costs through increases in distribution network prices charged to all customers. In addition to the mandated FiT payment, most retailers added a contribution that tended to reflect the wholesale value of the energy itself.

By 2013, consumers were adopting small PV systems almost as quickly as the equipment could be imported and industry could install. A very active and somewhat uncontrolled sales and installation industry emerged almost overnight. The uptake of rooftop solar PV in Australia over this time (2010−13) was around 15% per annum (Australian PV Institute, 2018). Unfortunately, in many cases product quality and service levels fell. Regulators and networks were left to catch up, as product standards, safety inspection processes, consumer protections, and network connection agreements struggled to maintain pace and relevance.

The costs of the schemes increased significantly as a growing number of households and businesses participated in the schemes and received payments, to the point where most schemes were oversubscribed and exceeded all expectations, leading to early closure due to their expense.

The premium schemes were closed to new entrants around 2015. However, most jurisdictions have at least one scheme where households and businesses that joined before they were closed maintain their eligibility and continue to receive these FiTs. The most recent version so the FiT available to most consumers is around the actual value of the wholesale energy, around 10 c/kWh, net[5] (Table 19.1).

Soon after the premium FiT schemes closed, the market stabilized. Due to the nature of the incentive schemes being largely focused on rooftop solar PV, a large proportion of consumers, being renters, residents of multiple occupancy buildings, or owners of premises that did not lend themselves to supporting an efficient rooftop generator, were generally not able to cheaply adopt BTM generation. Energy efficiency incentives were still an option for these consumers, however.

---

[5] State-based feed-in tariff arrangements have been reviewed and changed many times since 2011.

19.3 What sentiment drove the consumers' behind-the-meter investment?

Studies of the time strongly suggested that the main motivation for the decision to install solar technologies was to save money on power bills, with the predominant cohort being owners of detached homes (Romanach et al., 2013).

Clearly, the cost reductions for PV systems through the solar certificate (SRET) scheme in conjunction with the generous FiTs supercharged the take-up rate of rooftop solar, leading to a payback period of around 5 years for most consumers with PV. At the same time, the price of PV was falling rapidly. This has been referred to as an alignment of the *"technology push and the consumer pull."*

In addition to the very attractive payback period, five key considerations supported the rapid investment in solar PV by consumers:

1. *There was a high level of disquiet in the community about energy prices, and a strong desire to explore alternatives.* Electricity prices were climbing steeply; a fact that was frequently highlighted to the wider community by mainstream media with stories of hardship and of how solar was effective at reducing energy bills. Electricity prices and the use of solar PV became a key issue in the community, and the word-of-mouth advice that solar was an effective way of getting the bill down was commonplace.
2. Related to the price rise was *a strong sense of frustration and annoyance with the existing electricity companies.* A perception of disempowerment permeated the community, as attempts to manage power bills were frustrated by considerable rises in fixed connection charges, new metering charges and reductions in the relative discounts associated with off-peak and controlled load tariffs. Trust in the wider industry was at an all-time low, and the desire for many consumers to reduce their reliance on utility energy companies (despite being based more on emotion than fact) was prevalent.
3. *The investment case was relatively simple to understand, seen as low risk, with a strong rate of return.* A competitive market of suppliers and installers quickly emerged, keen to assist consumers understand the benefits of the investment. Through frequent mass-media advertising, price competition was clear to consumers, supporting the concept of "a good deal." The Renewable Energy Target scheme reduced the capital outlay required, and generous FiTs led to a persuasive, simple and relatively low-risk business case for consumers.
4. *"Free money from the government, get in early, don't miss out!"* Legislators from multiple levels of government introduced generous subsidies and FiTs to address the energy price concerns in the community, as well as being seen to address the rising concerns of environmental risks and global commitments. The community reacted enthusiastically.
5. *It was easy—basically "set and forget," with support from trusted advisors from outside the electricity industry.* The marketplace—television, radio, and print—was full of installers and service providers chasing the consumer business, with competitive deals, discounts, and pervasive marketing. The case being put to consumers was simple—one call, quickly installed, save money, and little ongoing involvement and thought for years to come. More importantly, a range of suppliers were generally viewed as "trusted advisors," independent of the legacy electricity industry.

It is useful to look back at the factors behind the success of earlier consumer participation in demand reduction; namely, controlled load water heating and off-peak appliance use that has been available to consumers since the 1980s. Controlled load uptake in the residential sector was effective in many Australian jurisdictions, with well over half of residential electric storage water heaters connected to timeclocks or ripple-control systems. Many of the same features were evident as customers adopted these tariffs—a significant cost reduction, a simple concept for how savings are delivered, and a scheme validated by trusted third parties such as plumbers and electricians. More recently, demand response capabilities in swimming pool filtration and residential air-conditioning have gained momentum for the same reasons.[6,7]

It is this alignment of the *"Consumer pull"* factors—lack of trust in the energy industry, concern about rising prices, a desire for a level of energy independence—with the *"technology push"* of falling prices of BTM technology, clearly subsidized by government to realize a strong and straightforward investment case and supported by trusted advisors from outside the energy industry—is a major contributor to the success of new energy technologies by consumers.

This approach can be extrapolated to many instances of new energy adoption.

19.4 Investment in behind-the-meter photovoltaic generation takes a new turn

By 2016, the heady days of generous FiTs had passed.

Fig. 19.4 illustrates the development of the investment trends in BTM systems. Initially, rooftop systems were generally no greater than 3 kW capacity, reflecting the relative immaturity of the supply and design capability at the time. The "standard" inverter capacity soon rose to 5 kW as the commercial benefits of excess production to the grid through the FiTs became well understood. Many utilities set the maximum capacity of inverters for automatic connection approval at 5 kW for single phase, and 30 kW for three-phase installations. Microinverters were now available for consumers with shaded roofs.

The national market for the "stock standard" 5-kW residential PV system was robust, with installation rates stable at around 12,000 rooftop systems per month.

Within a year, the rate of uptake of solar increased again. Interest intensified within the residential, small businesses, and light industry sectors in the "mid-scale" 6–25 kW BTM installations. With these larger applications become more prevalent, the average installation generation capacity is increasing.

Four factors underpin the growth in systems larger than 5 kW capacity:

1. Despite reduced capital subsidies and moderating FiTs, the *cost to generate a kilowatt-hour of energy in house from renewable sources has now reached a clear tipping point*, falling to the point that it is cheaper than grid-supplied energy. In its first solar report of 2019, the Australian Energy Council (2019) indicates that the levelized cost of energy (LCoE) is now less than the flat anytime tariff offered as a default tariff in most states.

---

[6] Initially, ripple control and timeclock systems provided the demand control. More recently, Australian Standard AS4755 − 2007 provides the framework for demand response capabilities and supporting technologies for electrical products

[7] For example, see the Energex (Queensand) Limited *Peaksmart* and *Positive Payback* initiatives.

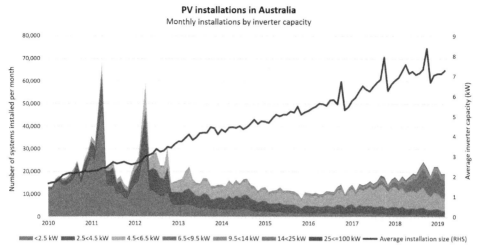

FIGURE 19.4 Installation rate of Australian "behind the meter" inverters, by capacity. Source: *Data from the Australian PV Institute (APVI)*.

2. Second, utilities introduced *advanced connection requirements*, moving from mandating maximum inverter capacity to setting dynamic energy feed-in limits. As more elegant inverter control systems become generally available, customers are now able to install larger generators in premises where the energy is likely to be self-consumed, augmented by smarter controls such as export control, volt–watt, and volt–var settings to reduce the impact of network voltage rise.
3. Australia continues to enjoy some of the *lowest costs worldwide to procure and install BTM PV systems*,[8] as a result of not only the continuing but moderating capital subsidy, but also stable technical and installation standards, progressive connection requirements by utilities, and economies of scale by installers.
4. As the price for new solar PV falls, there is less reliance on the FiT to support the commercial return on investment. Consumers are more aware of demand management practices to increase self-consumption of generated energy, thereby maximizing the return on the PV investment. These consumers also are more ambivalent to the feed-in restrictions imposed by networks in their connection agreements.

Along with larger inverters, there is a tendency nowadays for consumers to install rooftop solar PV systems where the panel capacity exceeds the inverter rating by a factor up to 20%. This oversizing is generally permitted within the inverter specifications and results in a system performance well above the average efficiency of 4–6 kWh/kW inverter capacity per day (based on South-east Queensland performance).

---

[8] International Energy Agency—Trends in Photovoltaic Applications, 2018—http://www.iea-pvps.org/ index.php?id = trends.

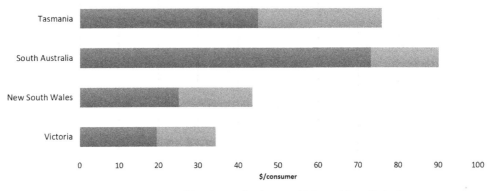

FIGURE 19.5 Environmental costs in electricity bills, 2017. Source: *Based on data from the Australian Competition and Consumer Commission (ACCC).*

19.4.1 The government incentive schemes continue, mostly for the better

The most generous FiT arrangements have expired and are now net energy schemes with the buyback value of around the same cost as the average wholesale energy price. Some states, such as Queensland and Victoria, mandate a FiT based on the wholesale energy cost of approximately around 10 c/kWh. Others, including South Australia, allow the competitive energy retail market to offer energy buyback rates. Many thousands of consumers remain on the generous "grandfathered" schemes. The SRET subsidy scheme remains in place today but is decreasing in value annually.

Environmental policy costs, which include the costs of the renewable energy target and energy savings schemes, comprise approximately 6% of the national average electricity bill in 2017–18, and are expected to increase (AEMC, 2018, p. 61). These costs are embedded in the electricity bills of all consumers and are shown in Fig. 19.5. The exception is Queensland, where a decision was made to carry the cost of the FiT schemes by the state government itself. In Queensland, the electricity distributors are state-owned.

Households that have invested in solar PV have benefited from the solar FiTs and the subsidies for the installation of the system itself through the federal renewable energy scheme. Solar households have reduced consumption of electricity from the grid significantly and are paying, on average, $538 per year less than nonsolar customers. Meanwhile, nonsolar households and businesses carry the "smeared" cost of the cost of premium solar FiT schemes and the Small-scale Renewable Energy Scheme (SRES). While premium solar schemes are closed to new consumers, the costs of these schemes are enduring as most still have thousands of legacy consumers on the premium tariffs (ACCC, 2018, p. 26).

In addition, governments still intervene significantly at regular intervals. Following a state-wide blackout in September 2016 and the closure of a 520 MW coal-fired power station, the South Australian government sponsored investment in renewable generation,

---

BOX 19.1

Excerpt from Renew Economy publication, July 1, 2019.

The boom resumes, as Victoria solar rebate reopens—batteries included

By Sophie Vorrath July 1, 2019 *Renew Economy*

Victoria rooftop solar rebate "sold out" again, with July quota filled in 3 days.

Victoria's residential rooftop solar market is set to take off once again, with the state government's $1.3 billion Solar Home rebate reopening on Monday to "pent-up" demand that has seen one-third of the month's quota snapped up within hours.

The launch of the first full year of the decade-long program follows a short but painful lull in business for the state's solar retailers and installers, after the massively popular scheme—tapped by more than 32,000 in its first 6 months—was closed to new applications for the 3 months to July.

In an effort to prevent this sort of "solar coaster" effect from happening again, Solar Victoria is taking a staggered approach in 2019/20, by offering applications for 3333 rooftop solar systems per month, to deliver a total of 40,000 systems for private homes and community-owned housing in 2019/20 (and another 2000 for rented homes).

Nonetheless, demand appears to be red hot, with nearly 1200 applications already lodged by 3 p.m. on Monday, leaving just 2157 remaining for the month. ■

---

both for large-scale wind and solar, storage through *"the world's largest battery—100 days or it's free"* (ABC News, 2017), and into consumers' premises through subsidies for a proposed 50,000 homes with batteries as part of what was billed as *"the world's largest virtual power plant* (VPP)."[9] In 2018 other states have adopted similar incentives, such as the Victorian residential solar rebate scheme for PV and batteries, and the New South Wales government releasing a zero-interest *Empowering Homes* program with loans to consumers for battery storage systems.[10],[11]

Despite the lessons of the past, the issue of oversubscription remains a concern. The Victorian government's Solar Homes program is being challenged with significant oversubscription due to the popularity with consumers seeking not only a strong return on investment through reduced energy bills but also reflecting the emerging support for environmental imperatives that are generally pervading the wider community.

This excessive level of support is being blamed as generating market distortion and a "boom—bust" cycle for the solar PV industry. Box 19.1 is a typical report from the online media highlighting the problems being experienced by consumers and the solar PV industry itself.

---

[9] Media release, *Premier Steven Marshall, $50 M fund to support new energy storage*, Nov 19, 2018.

[10] Queensland Government interest-free loans: https://www.qld.gov.au/community/cost-of-living-support/concessions/energy-concessions/solar-battery-rebate.

[11] South Australian Government Home Battery Scheme: http://www.renewablessa.sa.gov.au/home-battery-scheme.

19.4.2 Industry and commercial consumers see increasing value

The proportion of BTM activity in commercial and small industrial sites is growing. For most consumers in this sector, the demand pattern is more aligned to daylight hours, meaning a high opportunity for self-consumption. Also, these consumers tend to have a more advanced capability for economic analysis to extract strong return on investment through appropriately sized PV generation that is integrated into building management systems and effective demand shifting with heating, cooling, and process control.

Schools are also a common site for the growth in mid-scale solar PV, where energy consumption is well aligned to daytime PV generation, and opportunities to match generation to demand-controlled air-conditioning are available.

In 2018 approximately 9500 "mid-scale" systems were installed—a 34% increase in number, and a 44% increase in capacity, over 2017 (Clean Energy Regulator, 2019a,b).

Other considerations are at play too. In these situations, the general trend for distributors to apply blanket export (feed-in) limits, sometimes zero, is not a major restriction as the investment case can be made through self-consumption capability alone.

Many small industrial and commercial consumers also find themselves close to the threshold where networks require the consumer to be on a demand tariff, as opposed to an energy-based tariff. For sites with a poor load factor, it is often advantageous and much cheaper to remain on an energy-based tariff. Therefore it is not uncommon for medium-sized commercial and industrial energy users to install on-site PV generation to reduce their overall energy use to below the demand-tariff threshold (often 100- or 160-MWh pa), and therefore qualify to remain on an energy-based tariff.

19.4.3 The story on storage

The uptake of household battery storage is proving variable and difficult to forecast. Expectation is high, with some analysts noting *"Australia to be the largest residential storage market in 2019"* and *"Australian household storage demand to triple in 2019."*[12] Whilst the rooftop solar schemes remain highly subscribed, similar generous schemes for household battery storage are less popular, despite offering a rebate, in some cases up to 50% of the cost of the battery. The reasons for this somewhat lukewarm response are many, and the situation can turn quickly though changes in policy.

In some ways, the alignment of the "technology push−consumer pull" that is evident for solar PV investment is not as prevalent for energy storage. For instance,

1. For consumers without solar PV, a predominance of flat tariffs and a lack of powerful time-varying or demand tariff offerings does not support a strong investment case for arbitrage and therefore not a strong return on the battery investment.
2. Many battery subsidy offers require the consumer entering into contractual arrangements with retailers or aggregators to participate in a VPP; a concept that is not

---

[12] Bloomberg new Energy Finance https://about.bnef.com/blog/australia-largest-residential-storage-market-2019/—Bloomberg Terminal, January 22, 2019.

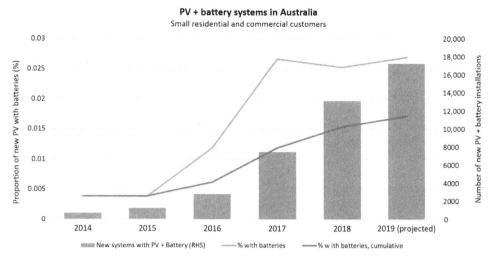

FIGURE 19.6 New PV installations with storage behind-the-meter. *PV*, Photovoltaic. Source: *Based on data from the Australian Clean Energy Regulator (CER).*

well understood by consumers and relies to some extent on a level of trust in the future operation of the customer's equipment by others, in a context of low trust in the energy industry generally.

3. The inverters integrated into the battery systems generally do not offer consumers "islanded" operation mode in the case of blackout or grid failure.
4. Connection agreements with network operators for energy storage systems, especially in the VPP configuration, are not mature.
5. Unlike solar, the individual environmental contribution of energy storage is not as obvious and clear-cut to customers.

In addition, many Australian households have storage electric water heating and access to controlled-load tariffs for swimming pools and air conditioning, providing existing avenues of energy storage through self-consumption that reduces the energy bill. A range of alternative actions that cost much less that batteries are still available and attractive to consumers to make good use of "spare" rooftop energy, offering relatively good value at low capital outlay.

Similarly, many consumers have responded to surveys advising that they see their excess energy positively as *"supporting their neighbors and the community, helping to keep prices down."*[13]

Despite these moderating circumstances, batteries are gaining a foothold in households.[14] Data released by the Clean Energy Regulator and reproduced in Fig. 19.6 shows that 1-in-40 (2.5%) of rooftop solar installations now include batteries.

[13] Queensland Household Energy Survey Insights report, 2017.

[14] Australian Government—Clean Energy Regulator, http://www.cleanenergyregulator.gov.au/RET/Forms-and-resources/Postcode-data-for-small-scale-installations#Smallscale-installations-by-installation-year September 11, 2019.

It is generally accepted that the formal data registered with the Clean Energy Regulator understates the number of battery systems actually being installed by consumers. Anecdotal sales information suggests a stronger uptake of integrated PV plus battery systems, as registration with the regulator is only required to obtain the solar PV rebate. Battery systems installed on their own or in conjunction with an existing PV system do not themselves attract a capital rebate under the SRES and therefore consumers are not incentivized to report their installation.

Under a recent industry rule change sponsored by the market operator AEMO, all battery systems will need to be registered, thereby increasing the visibility of embedded storage for planning and system operation requirements.[15] When the database becomes available, the uptake of battery storage by Australian consumers will be clearer.

Networks remain somewhat neutral toward BTM storage, citing the minimal impact consumer storage has on reducing peak demand. A risk to network performance and congestion exists from the possible undiversified power flows by a group of batteries, such as in VPP configuration, should they be all be called on at once in response to a market requirement.

Installation standards for batteries in residential and small commercial environments also remain relatively immature. Whilst industry bodies have taken great strides to introduce installation guidelines and accreditation processes, the establishment of mandated battery rules and safety guidelines remains a protracted and not always harmonious process, still to be resolved.

At the moment, the numbers for investing in battery storage presently just do not stack up for most Australian energy consumers.

19.4.4 Further growth—the forecast for the next few years

With 2018 being a record year for BTM generation installation, projections are that the strong growth in consumer generation in Australia is expected to continue in the next few years, as more consumers take advantage of the fact that the LCoE from rooftop generation is competitive with that from the grid.

Growth is expected to then moderate a little, reflecting a weakening in retail energy prices with new large- and small-renewable generation entering the market and as the upfront subsidy for new rooftop installations is gradually removed as the SRES closes (Australian Energy Regulator, 2018).

The underlying potential for rooftop solar PV and associated BTM storage and demand response in Australia remains considerable. In its study *"How much rooftop solar can be installed in Australia?"*, the University of New South Wales' Institute for Sustainable Futures suggests that Australia is using less than 5% of its potential capacity for rooftop solar (Roberts, Nagrath, & Briggs, 2019, p. 5), with around half of the unused potential being in residential zones. The market operator, AEMO, in its 2018 forecasts, indicates a two to four times growth of rooftop PV capacity by 2040.[16]

---

[15] Australian Energy Market Operator—https://www.energymagazine.com.au/aemo-to-launch-australias-first-energy-resources-database/—Energy Magazine, September 2019.

[16] Australian Energy Market Operator 2018—https://www.aemo.com.au/Electricity/National-Electricity-Market-NEM/Planning-and-forecasting/Integrated-System-Plan.

Such continued rapid growth will be dependent on appropriate legislative and market rule changes to address dampening effects such as the lack of incentives for landlords to install solar PV and the postage-stamp network transport charges that reduce the attraction of support solar gardens and "community" DER installations.

Mid-scale BTM installations, typically 20−100 kW, will remain a focus as commercial and industrial consumers take advantage of falling system costs and the ability to automate building management systems to optimize self-consumption. Battery uptake is expected to remain subdued, outside government-sponsored schemes, until the mid-2020s (Graham, Wang, Braslavsky, & Reedman, 2018), as energy volume-based tariffs continue to predominate and feed-in limitations become more prevalent. With the expected reforms in retail tariffs in the mid-2020s, the case for battery storage will be more attractive for storing solar energy on site for use at high-cost times.

19.5 Profiling a prosumer

Formal studies undertaken to try to identify the profile of consumers most likely to invest in DER have been, in general, inconclusive, with investigations into financial capacity, socioeconomic rating, education status, and environmental leaning providing conflicting evidence. There is little pattern to the socioeconomic profile for consumers most likely to adopt rooftop solar PV or other forms of DER.

Research suggests that homeowners over 55 years old tended be the most represented demographic for investment in rooftop generation (Sommerfeld and Buys, 2014), with the predominant motivator for adopting embedded generation of reducing electricity bills emerging in 2013 (Romanach et al., 2013).

Anecdotally, uptake has been most prominent in established residential subdivisions close to the coast with a high proportion of "asset-rich, cash-poor" retirees. More recently, rooftop PV has been most popular with consumers in middle socioeconomic regions. Many consumers installing rooftop generation are seeking a "capital-operating cost tradeoff"; utilizing equity in the property to reduce the day-to-day household operating cost.

Fundamentally though, the motivators of becoming a prosumer remain heavily centered on bill reduction and hedging on future energy prices, followed by the positive impact on the environment (Energy Queensland, Powerlink, 2018). There is also strong evidence that concerns about the stability of the industry underpin consumer's desire to seek "grid independence" (Sommerfeld and Buys, 2014).

From the *Queensland Household Energy Survey* 2018:

> The impact of these electricity price concerns is growing levels of interest in alternatives to the grid, such as solar PV, battery storage or to go off grid completely. While in previous years, the main reason for taking up these technologies were economical (e.g. high FiT or rebates), households are now being driven by an additional desire for self-sufficiency, which is related to the above-mentioned pessimism about future price rises.

19.5.1 Distributed energy resources' impact on bills and prices

Savvy owners of DER are focusing on self-consumption, as more stringent access requirements become commonplace and access to the premium feed-tariffs tend to fade away under grandfathering arrangements.

Across the NEM, an average residential consumer pays around $1636 for electricity from the grid annually. However, an average solar consumer will receive a payment of $538 for the electricity they feed back in, which means that they are reducing their overall bill by about a third (ACCC, 2018). In addition, on average, households with solar are typically larger than nonsolar households when including the proportion of consumers who live in apartments. This indicates that solar consumers on average use more electricity than nonsolar households, but this increased usage is offset by their solar PV generation.

When the benefits of self-consumption and the FiT are combined, the households received a benefit equivalent to a 20%−50% discount on their energy as reflected in the average effective unit price for all energy consumed (ACCC, 2018). Some consumers who have remained on the generous FiTs receive a "negative bill," especially in the mid-season periods of Spring and Autumn (Fall) when generation is moderate, but the household demand is not yet dominated by heating and cooling. In these cases, consumers can either accumulate the savings to offset against energy costs in the seasons where household demand is higher than production (generally summer and winter). Otherwise, legislation in most states requires the electricity retailer to refund the excess to the consumer on request.

On the cost side, in 2018 the Renewable Energy Target has accounted for an estimated 6% per annum of the average household electricity bill—about $68.50 per year. This levy, whilst significant, is less than many surcharges and levies attached to electricity bills for consumers in the EU.

There is an expectation however that the wholesale cost of electricity will fall across the country as more renewable energy, along with large-scale storage and grid firming, enter the market (AEMC, 2018). There is debate currently regarding the wider impact of DER may have on wholesale energy prices. Given the rapid growth in the component of utility-scale wind and solar generation, it is difficult to form a view on the impact of the BTM generation on wholesale prices in isolation. Conversely, utilities are seeking new funds to augment networks, information, and automation systems to accommodate increased DER, the cost of which will be embedded in changes to network prices. Therefore it is difficult and somewhat controversial to attempt to take a specific position on the impact DER may have on wholesale energy prices and network charges—costs that affect all consumers, not just those with DER.

19.5.2 The complex subject of cross-subsidies

The issue of cross-subsidies between consumers with solar PV and other consumers is not unique to the Australian context. Regulators, utilities, and consumers have grappled with the unbundling of network charges and allocation of costs for consumers with solar PV in Germany,[17] California,[18] and elsewhere, including Australia.

As noted in Section 19.4.3 of this chapter, the cost of FiTs, green schemes and capital incentives are borne by all energy consumers. In some cases, such as the state of Queensland, some of these costs are funded from government coffers, therefore arguably paid for by all taxpayers. Even less transparent is the shift in contribution to the operating and capital costs of networks by consumers with steep export/import load factors or significant "duck curves" often seen by consumers with solar PV.

The consideration of the imbalance in the contribution of network and infrastructure costs by consumers with or without solar PV are part of the wider current matter of tariff reform and market design in Australia. These issues are explored further in chapters by Tim Schittekatte and David Robinson.

19.6 Industry considerations for a (hopefully) orderly evolution

To efficiently adopt the new energy environment, changes being made to the way markets and networks operate must relate to consumers. It is useful to break down these steps into three areas of activity:

1. Consider the delivery of the infrastructure platform that is needed to support two-way power flow, metering and information provision to consumers, through timely and prudent investment with a strong awareness of the costs and risks for which consumers are prepared to pay.
2. Review the rules, regulations, and market relationships needed to support local area energy trading, consumer protections, cost recovery and the operation of new market entities.
3. Most importantly, take a consumer-focused approach that recognizes and respects community and consumer values such as affordability, trust and a wide range of engagement needs and expectations.

Traditionally, these changes are not fast, reflecting the conservative processes that underpin our regulatory and infrastructure frameworks. Such change is also difficult to consider when forecasts can vary significantly, as evident in the work that has been done by the CSIRO[19] and AEMO[20] in Australia.

---

[17] Energy Transition online, Craig Morris—https://energytransition.org/2015/08/small-german-power-consumers-subsidize-industry/.

[18] Forbes online (2016)—https://www.forbes.com/sites/realspin/2016/01/15/california-solar-subsidy-net-metering/#79f8a2fb722f.

[19] CSIRO—Commonwealth Scientfic and Industrial Research Organisation.

[20] AEMO—Australian Energy Market Operator.

19.6.1 Networks and retailers—part of the solution?

Key to this change is to encourage and reward networks to embrace change. On one level, networks are enthusiastically becoming involved in trials and projects regarding DER, both behind and on the lines-side of the meter. Networks in Australia see change as necessary and inevitable.

The fundamentals to which networks and retailers operate—seeking stable returns from large asset investments or minimizing the cost to serve—remain. Without deep-seated regulatory and market change such as introducing revenue opportunities for "spare" network capacity, or retailer incentives to efficiently undertake local energy trading, the paradigms prevalent in existing utilities and markets will prove hard to change. For distribution system operators (DSOs), the growth in the penetration of rooftop solar PV and DER has not yet delivered opportunities to significantly reduce network augmentation costs and deliver operational productivity. Peak demand, occurring mainly in the late afternoon and evening, is not largely influenced by the existence of solar PV and is not mitigated by household energy storage under current operating practice. Demand may have been limited somewhat by improved appliance efficiency and the price response by consumers, but it remains a driver of network capital investment. Minimum demand levels are also gaining notoriety for complicating network voltage and protection stability. The duck curve— including the "belly of the duck"—has become a significant factor in the technical and commercial operation of networks deep into the local supply system.

Under Australia's revenue-cap regulatory framework, little commercial incentive exists for network owners to improve asset utilization (load) factors, as their revenue is set largely by asset values, not by the amount of energy passing through the wires. This is a core issue for many utilities worldwide. Despite the application of incentive-based regulation, risk is not clearly rewarded, and new revenue streams to encourage the transport of energy by existing assets are very limited. Until networks shareholders see a commercial return from connecting embedded generation and fostering customer BTM resources, the new energy future may not arrive as quickly and efficiently as many consumers would hope.

Like those in Australia, regulators in California and the United Kingdom are insisting on solving many network expansion requirements through so called nonwires alternatives before allowing investment in upgrading the network. This issue is discussed further in the chapter by Johnston and Sioshansi.

A similar issue arises with the retail segment of the industry. Retailers are in a privileged place with a direct relationship with the consumer, holding key information such as consumer name, contact details, consumption, and metering data; and as such are uniquely placed to influence the adoption of new concepts of local energy trading, tariff adoption, and demand response. Yet split incentives exist regarding energy sales incentives, costs to enact demand response and a strong preference to minimize customer interactions. Again, this is a challenge not unique to Australia.

The interaction between the aggregator as a market entity and the retailer is yet to be explored in Australia—and elsewhere as further examined by Poplavskaya and de Vries and De Clercq et al. The recent work done by the Energy Networks Associations in both the United Kingdom and Australia highlight the importance of the retailer and the new

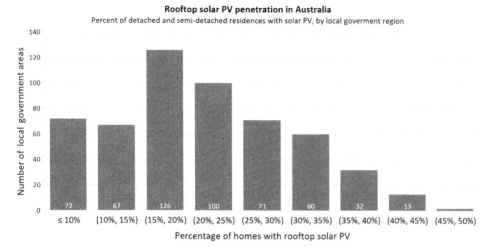

FIGURE 19.7   Frequency of penetration of rooftop PV by local government area, Australia (2018). *PV*, Photovoltaic. Source: *Based on data from the Australian PV Institute (APVI)*.

market actor of aggregator as having a key relationship with the consumer. This critical relationship is still poorly defined, and great care will be needed by the industry to craft the commercial and social operation of the interface between the market and the consumer.[21]

19.6.1.1 Next steps under active consideration in Australia

First, the *voltage rise risk* is central to the ability for the network to accommodate greater levels of energy feed-in, central to the implementation of local energy trading and grid support, including VPPs. Australia has a power network topology much like the United Kingdom and Europe with an extensive low voltage radial supply system forming the "last 500 m" to connect to consumers' premises. The technical constraint of voltage management tends, particularly in long rural lines and built-up areas with PV penetration over 30%, to be the major consideration for networks in permitting more solar PV connections (Fig. 19.7).

Consumers see this grid congestion as a growing tendency for networks to impose "zero export" and "export limited" grid connection. With moderating values of FiTs and the further development of control systems to optimize self-consumption, many consumers seem to understand and reluctantly accept this limitation, as the business case for investment in DER can often remain positive without the factor of FiT earnings.

On a wider scale, operational constraints at a more macro level are emerging. Underfrequency emergency load-shed systems, a critical component of grid security protection, must be reassessed and redesigned to deliver load shaping in times of high embedded generation.

---

[21] https://www.energynetworks.com.au/open-energy-networks-consultation-paper

The emergence of aggregators and VPPs—further covered in chapters by Sioshansi and Lehmbruck et al.—has highlighted the need for a strong working relationship with network operators. VPPs are often operated by retailers or aggregators with a view of responding to wider market signals, such as high pool price, with little awareness of the impact on the local networks of the dispatch of the generation with little diversity. VPPs tend not to have contractual or operating agreements with networks, and the network connection agreement with consumers generally does not consider the risk of undiversified feed-in by multiple VPP sites that are commercially incentivized to operate at maximum export simultaneously.

1. *Tariff development* is a major initiative with the Australian market but is not resonating with consumers as yet. Despite their important role in the new energy environment for equitable cost recovery and customer demand signaling, shifts to dynamic tariffs have a hard road ahead due to consumer wariness and the low penetration of interval meters. Importantly, interval data is needed to assist consumers embrace change when they ask the key question: "if I change tariff, will I be better off?" Tariff reform will also have a large bearing on the return on investment in BTM battery storage.
2. *Cost recovery and equity* is another key consideration in the efficient energy transition. Despite the fixed share of the bill increasing in recent years, consumers transitioning to BTM generation naturally consume less energy from the grid. Under the national electricity legislation, networks can only recover network costs from consumers of energy, not from prosumers feeding energy into the grid. Therefore the cost recovery is distorted, as utilities are restricted by industry conditions, and advise consumer impacts from being able to equitably share network service costs amongst all users.

   The balance of efficiency and fairness in tariff design is further described in chapter by Schittekatte.
3. *Reform to network use-of-system charges* is needed, especially with peer-to-peer trading highlighted as a major opportunity emerging for consumers. A defining characteristic for BTM energy resources is that they can be local—that is, located closely to the site of the energy demand. Therefore the transport arrangements, in the case of networks being the use-of-system charge, needs to be redefined to allow networks to charge to move the power short distances, not the "postage stamp" arrangements that predominate under regulatory cost-recovery requirements today. A key aspect of regulatory reform will be to permit networks to recover use-of-system costs for "short haul," even in the form of an unregulated revenue to unlock the "available capacity" of local networks in times outside peak demand—akin to the "Uber" or "Airbnb" of energy, where spare capacity can be monetized.

   This aspect of network charging and optimization of asset utilization will remain a key opportunity and a regulatory priority.
4. *Customers who cannot or will not take part in new energy* reforms BTM must also be considered. This is a key issue everywhere, and regulators are very sensitive to keep the traditional energy consumers, who will for some time remain the majority of energy consumers, protected from commercial and technical impacts of more adventurous or perhaps even reckless prosumers. Their position will be important to governments who will need to sanction regulatory changes to enable new approaches to the supply of

electricity. One thing about networks is that they do not differentiate significantly between one consumer and the next. The new energy environment will impact *all* consumers, not only those who are in the right situation to embrace new BTM technologies.

Demand management, responses to tariff signals, and adapting forms of energy storage will impact all consumers, not just prosumers, for an efficient, reliable, and sustainable energy supply. The design of markets compatible with BTM investments is examined further in chapters by Schittekatte and Robinson.

Finally, it is important to take care not to overcapitalize and overcomplicate networks, market services, and customer relationships in response to the continued adoption of DER. Customers have highlighted that trust and sensitivity to cost remain the highest priorities in their approach to the electricity industry and are keen to seek ways to distance themselves from the industry wherever possible. All these investments—DSO control systems for consumer equipment, market operator registration requirements, new transmission interconnectors, and the commercial expectations of new market entrants such as aggregators—present a high risk of "eating up" much, if not all, of the potential bill savings and precious consumer goodwill.

So many are long-term investments too, so if the energy world over time takes the turn to become more "local" or a collection of many microgrids (as renewable technology can support this approach), many of these large investments could become stranded but still needed to be paid for by consumers.

19.7 Consumer engagement—the key to a successful energy future

In the move to a new energy environment, renewable energy–related innovations, imperatives, and opportunities abound and are advancing quickly. Many concepts, whilst straightforward on the surface, will rely on regulatory and industry reforms that involve many overlapping and sometimes contradictory objectives.

Policy debates and energy scenarios highlight a number of possible energy futures for consumers. No one is certain what the new energy future will look like; yet the expectation is that it will be more decentralized, decarbonized, digitalized, and more stratified—as described by Sioshansi in Chapter 1—and the level of consumer involvement and requirements will vary greatly. Flexibility, choice, independence, and transparency (leading to trust) will certainly be required. These options will also permit consumers to disengage with the traditional industry.

Knowledge of how consumers are likely to embrace these changes is only emerging and is much less advanced than the understanding of the technical and commercial requirements to deliver the new products and services. As a largely technical industry, we tend to take a risk-adverse view; in this case toward forecasts and scenarios that hold many "what-ifs" and widely varying forecasts, under the banner of a "least regrets" approach. Further in this book, the consideration of uncertainty and customer value is discussed by Smith and MacGill, and consumer limitations in making rational choices in an environment of increasing complexities by Mountain.

Recent studies in the United Kingdom highlight that consumers are generally positive about the need for energy system change, with a level of indifference about utility priorities over BTM investment. Consumers and the wider community are willing and capable of engaging critically on the energy transformation, despite the level of complexity inherent in the tools to deliver change. Social principles such as avoiding waste, the efficient use of resources, and protecting the environment feature in the consumers' expectations (Parkhill, Demski, Butler, Spence, & Pidgeon, 2013).

Network and market operators view the control of consumer's equipment as a priority (AEMO and ENA, 2018), whereas distrust in energy businesses, related organizations, and policymakers is widespread (Nicholls, Arcari, Glover, Martin, & Strengers, 2019). Many consumers see opportunities to become more "grid independent." In an environment where only 39% of consumers trust the energy retail market and only 25% are confident that it works in their interests (Australian Energy Regulator, 2018); it is hard to see that these interests are aligned. Consumer input into the nature, justification, validation, and design of the required network tools is critical for their acceptance.

Price awareness is also a major factor, in terms of cost and affordability. Justification for price rises, or even the failure to deliver the greatest possible price reductions, will need to be clearly explained and understood by consumers. Part of this discussion will include the fairness and equitable access to new energy resources.

The recording, access, and privacy of consumer data in the digital and communication systems inherent in a new energy environment are equally a consideration for consumers. This issue is being addressed by regulators and governments, as is the cyber-security aspects of control systems that connect directly to a consumer's inverter, meter, and appliance. On data, the unregulated access and on-sale of their data by others remains a concern for many consumers.

19.8 Conclusion

Over 2 million consumers, around a quarter of all energy consumers, now own generation capability in Australia. BTM rooftop solar PV systems, batteries, and demand response capability from air-conditioners, pool pumps, and other appliances are the new normal, and significantly changed the way energy is viewed in the country.

Much can be learnt from examining how this situation arose. Rapidly rising prices for grid energy, disempowerment as new charges were introduced and powerful government incentives undoubtedly kick-started the PV revolution in Australia, shifting the role of customer-owned generation and other DER from the premise of visionaries and early adopters into the mainstream.

Strong growth in the investment in rooftop PV is continuing, alongside emerging signs of storage and household energy management systems. Mid-scale rooftop solar PV in commercial and small industrial consumer applications now account for a larger proportion of investment in small-scale, BTM DER capability.

However, growing pains are emerging, creating challenges for regulators, policy makers, and consumers. Network congestion in local low voltage distribution systems is a major point of focus for DSOs, who are developing new tools and controls to facilitate the equitable continued expansion of embedded generation. Demand response is now a necessary component for the efficient future energy landscape. Regulation must move quickly to set the framework to enable further growth and in support of the opportunities offered by the energy future. Unless these challenges are addressed, progress will be inefficient and expensive.

Critical to the successful design and delivery of the changes ahead are, of course, consumers. They are called many things—consumers, customers, stakeholders, prosumers, connections, metering points, and bill recipients. Fundamentally, however, these are the people who make decisions as to how the service will be used, rely intimately on the quality and price of the service, and may not exhibit rational behavior in the eyes of industry experts. Consumers trust the provider to respect and understand their interests and have a critical impact on the success or otherwise of any change initiative the industry, in particular retailers and distributors, may undertake.

The next steps in Australia's energy revolution are upon us, and both consumers and the industry are at the stage when the changes will not happen "in the background." Effective and honest engagement is critical, focusing on affordability, fairness, empowerment, and simplicity—factors for which the energy industry is not always renowned. Only by putting ourselves in the customers' shoes and honestly asking "what's in it for the consumer?" will the full value of our new energy future—behind and beyond the meter—be realized.

References

ABC News. (2017). [Report] *Elon Musk's giant lithium ion battery completed by Tesla in SA's Mid North*. Adelaide: Nick Harmsen.

Australian Competition and Consumer Authority (ACCC). (2018). [Report] *Retail pricing enquiry—Final report*. Canberra: Australian Competition and Consumer Commission.

AEMC. (2018). [Report] *Residential electricity price trends, final report*. Sydney: Australian Energy Market Commission.

AEMO and ENA. (2018). online *Open Energy Networks consultation paper [Report]*. Australia: Australian Energy Market Operator & Energy Networks Australia.

Australian Energy Council. (2019). [Report] *Solar report*. [s.l.]: Australian Energy Council.

Australian Energy Regulator. (2018). [Report] *State of the energy market*. Melbourne, Australia: Australian Competition and Consumer Commission.

Australian PV Institute. (2018). [Report] *APVI/UNSW solar trends report*. Sydney, Australia: Solar Citizens.

Clean Energy Regulator. (2019a). [Report] *Postcode data for small-scale installations (website, spreadsheet)*. Canberra: Clean Energy Regulator.

Clean Energy Regulator. (2019b). [Report] *The acceleration in renewables investment in 2018*. Canberra, Australia: Commonwealth of Australia.

Energy Queensland, Powerlink. (2018). [Report] *Queensland Household Energy Survey*. Queensland, Australia: Colmar Brunton.

European Commission. (2019). [Report] *Report from the Commission to the European Parliament—Energy prices and costs in Europe*. Brussels: European Commission.

Graham, P., Wang, D., Braslavsky, J., & Reedman, L. (2018). [Report] *Projections for small-scale embedded technologies*. Australia: CSIRO, Report for AEMO.

Nicholls, L., Arcari, P., Glover, A., Martin, R., & Strengers, Y. (2019). [Report] *Engaging households towards the future grid: Experiences, expectations and emerging trends*. Melbourne, VIC: Centre for Urban Research, RMIT University.

Parkhill, K. A., Demski, C., Butler, C., Spence, A., & Pidgeon, N. (2013). [Report] *Transforming the UK energy system: Public values, attitudes and acceptability — Synthesis report.* London: UKERC.

Roberts, M., Nagrath, K., Briggs, C., et al. (2019). *How much rooftop solar can be installed in Australia?* [Report] *A report for the Clean Energy Finance Corporation of Australia.* Sydney: University of New South Wales.

Romanach, L., Contreras, Z., & Ashworth, P. (2013). *Australian householders' interest in active participation in the distributed energy market: Survey results* [Report] *Report nt EP13358.* Pullenvale, QLD: CSIRO.

Sommerfeld, J., & Buys, L. (2014). Australian consumer attitudes and decision making on renewable energy technology and its impact on the transformation of the energy sector, [Report] *Open Journal of Energy Efficiency, 3,* 85—91.

Wood, T., Blowers, D., & Griffiths, K. (2018). [Report] *Down to the Wire: A sustainable electricity network for Australia.* [s.l.]: Grattan Institute.

Will behind-the-meter make a difference?

Fereidoon Sioshansi

Menlo Energy Economics, San Francisco, CA, United States

The book started with a chapter asking what lies behind the meter and why it matters—a topic examined in the subsequent chapters. This chapter asks "will behind-the-meter (BTM) make a difference?" The answer, based on the evidence presented, varies depending on where and in what time frame.

In Australia, for example, where a significant number of households have already invested in solar roofs, as described by Swanston, one can argue that BTM matters a lot already and will continue to play a critical role in how electricity is generated, consumed, and potentially shared or traded. In other places, it may not make as big a dent for many years, if ever—for example, in densely populated places such as Hong Kong, Tokyo, or Seoul where most people live in high-rise apartments with little opportunity for investing in distributed generation or storage. In areas where the existing infrastructure is already in place and consumption and the monthly electricity bill by individual consumers is modest, BTM is not likely to make a noticeable impact.

On the other extreme, in places where the delivery network if inadequate, unreliable, or nonexistent, the potential for stand-alone systems that generate, store, and provide electricity service is considerable. In such places, isolated mini networks or micro-grids may provide more reliable service at lower cost. But micro-grids are no longer for remote areas, island or hard to reach rural communities. Many universities in the United States, for example, now rely on such systems, often delivering better service at lower cost.

In all cases, the longer term impact of BTM investments depends on the relative costs, on regulatory policies and—perhaps most important—on the rapidly improved technologies and equally rapidly fall in costs. As more individuals do what Ben Schlesinger has done (Chapter 2) and as more energy communities are formed as described in chapters by Lobbe et al. and Reijnders et al., the notion of producing,

Behind and Beyond the Meter
DOI: https://doi.org/10.1016/B978-0-12-819951-0.00020-7

storing, and consuming electricity in a mostly self-contained system may move main-stream, albeit unevenly in different parts of the world.

What about some of the other BTM topics and associated products or services described in this volume? Will energy using devices be digitalized? Will demand aggregation and optimization or peer-to-peer trading platforms become widespread and profitable?

Here again, the evidence is mixed and it is too early to know the winners and losers based on the limited experience to date. Among the few start-ups featured in this volume, only Next Kraftwerke has grown to size and is profitable. For some of the others, one has to do the 5-year test: wait 5 years or more to see how well they are doing. Many ideas or products launched with great fanfare—think of Segway or 3D printing—have not delivered as promised to date. Electric scooters, for example, have made more of a dent than Segway, which appeals to a narrow niche.

In other areas, say home energy management systems or HEMS covered in chapter by Shaw-Williams—the opportunities are evident but so are the obstacles, including a fragmented market, security and privacy concerns. The jury is still out on whether major players such as Amazon will eventually succeed where others have not.

What about transactive energy where individuals or groups of individuals can trade and share electricity using blockchain and other means that obviates the need for intermediaries or a central clearinghouse. Much excitement exists in future potential of blockchain and distributed ledgers. Only time will tell how soon and how profitable applications will emerge.

One thing, however, is universally agreed and accepted and that is the fact that consumers have more choices in more places and they are—for the most part—exercising their newfound freedom to move away from traditional reliance on a single provider for all their needed services. This is a welcomed development, encouraging service and product innovation in an industry not known for either.

But even here, the evidence in mixed. The research to date suggests that the average consumer is not necessarily well informed or sufficiently motivated to find the best available options or make the best BTM investments. The retailers and vendors of BTM assets make matters worse by false or misleading claims, making it even more difficult for the average consumer to make rational, informed decisions.

Another thing that is widely accepted about BTM, as further explained by Jamme in the book's Preface, is that demand must increasingly play a bigger role in balancing of supply and demand because much of future generation in many regions will be variable renewable energy. Aggregation and management of BTM assets, nearly everyone agrees, will have to be a part of the solution, one way or another.

Should this be a concern to the regulators? Yes and no. Consumers are free to make bad decisions in, say, buying insurance or investing their retirement funds—so why worry about poor BTM decisions? This suggests that aggregators, intermediaries, or orchestrators, topics extensively covered in the book, may be able to provide useful services, not only unbiased advice but actually managing the customers' portfolio of BTM assets, minimizing their bills while enhancing the quality and value of services received. How and how fast such intermediaries may emerge is also subject to the 5-year test.

Reading the book's Foreword and Preface by regulators from Norway and France suggests that they are not only aware of the many complexities of the BTM developments but actively engaged in shaping it in ways that will deliver better value and more service options for future prosumers and prosumagers while protecting the traditional consumers who may be perfectly content with the bundled regulated tariffs.

Some things have already changed, more are likely to change, while some will remain more or less as they have always been.

Epilogue

Since 2017 Fereidoon Sioshansi helps authors and readers to take stock and look ahead by keep pushing his *Innovation and Disruption* discovery agenda *at the Grid's Edge*.[1] Where are we going to, when exiting from this third book? Not less than toward a new electricity system.

We all know the former tectonic shift, when open wholesale markets have been built, from 1990, in Europe and the United States; while being made of open markets, first at their wholesale upstream, and lately at their retail downstream. This sequence of markets did keep the verticality and some of the hierarchical architecture of the formerly integrated utilities. It was not a caricature that the first software running the *England and Wales Electricity Pool* was derived from the earlier software producing the plants' merit order within the integrated CEGB (*Central Electricity Generating Board*). The economic values and ranking found with this software for the Day Ahead market were even used to manage grid constraints in real time. Of course the US nodal pricing does the same differently, but similarly: the equilibrium, the values and ranking are produced and kept coherent from the center of the system, by a "super benevolent agent": the single system and market operator. It is this hierarchical centrality, which is starting to vanish. Sure, only slowly, one little step by little step at a time. But surely. The last wonderful defense of a hierarchical electricity system, rationally and centrally run by a single wholesale market algorithm, was offered us by Thomas-Olivier Léautier at MIT Press in 2019[2] and it has the beauty of a swan song. Why?

Because of DDA: *decentralization, digitalization,* and *activation*, topics covered in this book.

First *decentralization*. Amazing to see that what we did face in the early 1990s with "small" CCGT plants bypassing "large" coal and nuclear plants do happen again, after 2010, at a much smaller scale: with MW-size wind mills or kW-size PV panels. The last large nuclear station undertaken in Western Europe is the coming (2025?) 3200 MW Hinkley Point (£20 billion). My own entry into the Paris very first solar cooperative in March 2019 is under 1 kW, and I invested only 1000 euro.

Second *digitalization*. An older wave of digitalization permitted the first electricity wholesale markets to come alive, by copying the way commodities, stocks and currency markets were revolutionized from the 1980s by computing mainframes and terminals. We all know that new waves of digitalization are permitted today by new types of sensors,

---

[1] Sioshansi, F. (2017). *Innovation and disruption at the grid's edge. How distributed energy resources are disrupting the utility business model.* Academic Press; Sioshansi, F. (2019). *Consumer, prosumer, prosumager. How service innovations will disrupt the utility business model.* Academic Press.

[2] Léautier, T.-O. (2019). *Imperfect markets and imperfect regulation: an introduction to the microeconomics and political economy of power markets.* MIT Press.

servers, computers, algorithms, databases, smart phones, and their new Internet highways, opening a serious future to the Internet of Things.

Third *activation*. In the traditional electricity world, shared by both the vertically integrated utilities of the past and the wholesale market-based systems which followed, "retail-size" units are mainly passive; mainly taking the equilibrium, values, and ranking from the sequence of wholesale markets. But "decentralization" is now opening investment in generation or storage to "retail-size" units—as noted in chapter by Swanston, one-fourth of Australian consumers are prosumers, a world record. And they have become prosumers not by regulatory fiat but primarily by motivation to reduce their electricity bills. What "activation" does is to use digitalization to address the too high transaction costs in traditional "retail-size units" markets, like the one the Nobel Laureate Akerlof did study, in his 1970 *Markets for Lemons*.[3] When Jean Tirole, another Nobel Laureate, published his *Economics for the Common Good*,[4] digital platforms had already become tools to do what was impossible 50 years ago. The "retail-size" units can be activated, and in many ways it is the force which starts transforming the electricity system "as we knew it," with a new ecology of electricity transactions appearing beyond *B2B* (*Business to Business*) and *B2C* (*Business to Consumers*).

In this context, what are these many "activation" novelties in electricity transactions? The very first are the *aggregators* who can target "retail-size" consumption units and pack their active behavior into products tradable into the wholesale market. This is obviously a new type of electricity transaction, where "retail-size" reenters "business-size." That might be termed C2B, but with a strong intermediary—namely, the aggregator—the transaction begins to really look like *C2Aggr2B*.

Then comes a first type of platform—let's call it *Platform1*—which also operates a "single activation" of retail-size units but eliminates the aggregator as a necessary intermediary. It is easy to grasp why, as the buyer within this Platform1, is a "single buyer" [transmission system operator (TSO) or distribution system operator (DSO)], which can then directly pack all the "retail-size" offers to its own particular needs. That transaction is a clear and simple *C2B*. Another story is that various business models are compatible with Platform1. That platform can itself be built and operated by a third party, acting as agent of the "single buyer" DSO or TSO. This "single buyer" can even be a pool of DSOs/TSOs. That platform can also be open to aggregators, keeping an exclusive right on consumption units' activation performed outside the platform.

The next species of transaction comes naturally with another type of platform, let's call it *Platform2*—operating a "double activation": activating both "retail-size" offers *and* "retail-size" demands, as Uber or Airbnb usually do. In such a relation, where both buyers and sellers are "retail-size" units, we find a true "C2C"-like relation but, with one of these two Cs being a producer and a seller—a better term is to call it peer-to-peer or P2P, a topic covered in this volume.

The new ecology of electricity transactions does not stop there. And there are at least three other types of "activated" transactions already working. One is created by *clubs of*

[3] Akerlof, G. (1970). The market for lemons: Quality uncertainty and the market mechanism. *Quarterly Journal of Economics*, *84*(3), 488–500.

[4] Tirole, J. (2017). *Economics for the common good*. Princeton University Press.

blockchains, which are able to eliminate both Platform1 and Platform2 as trading interface. That's because blockchain technologies permit "direct" peer-to-peer transactions by delivering an automatic identification of the product traded, of the trading parties, extended to a self-executing process of delivery and settlement. Of course, to work smoothly, blockchains require an ex ante "certification" of the parties qualified to trade, creating de facto a close "club of peers," closer to a pure *P2P* universe.

When the technologies—tying the "retail-size" parties to trade—are not the key enabler of the new transaction relations, it can be a new type of governance. When and where decentralization is effective enough to bypass the traditional electricity system, but association of several individuals is effective enough to deliver a better outcome than for an isolated individual, there is room for creating *energy communities* as voluntary associations of individuals. Either built on already existing human communities (as Elinor Ostrom did explain to us[5]) or, much more strategic and calculative, by hiring a skilled and professional third party (à la Oliver Williamson[6]) as a manager working for the associated members. Therefore energy communities can act as "self-activation associations," or *P&P*. Of course within such communities, many options—as common aggregation, common platform, common blockchain—can also be performed, all placed under the common governance of the community.

Another type of grouping of individuals can compete with the "communities" as a governance structure for retail-size units' activation. It is where the "third party"—mastering the know-how of individual assets' activation—can make it a business of its own. It is becoming visible as *asset fleets*: the third party coordinates the retail-size assets' behavior, creating portfolios of synchronized assets' activation. It is very intuitive with fleets of electrical vehicles, and tomorrow's fleets of self-driven vehicles, being operated by a central manager controlling the batteries' fleet charging and discharging. It is also coming with "zero-net-consumption" buildings, as in California or the European Union, which are "mini electricity systems" and "mini distribution grids" with their own aggregated management rules and decision-making. Tomorrow, when the main electrical appliances will become controllable as "fleets" within the "Internet of Things," the notion of "electrical asset fleets" could become as mundane as the term of "electrical utilities" has been. It is the promising world of *C2Fleet*, which threatens existing utilities, simple aggregators, and traditional grids operators.

Of course the many conservative players within today's electricity sector are not wrong when saying that some form of centralization will always exist as a key player in the future "decentralized electrical system." In the same way that a transmission grid is better operated as a central tool for managing the wholesale electricity system interactions, the distribution grids will have to be better operated as local tools for managing interactions between decentralized electricity systems. Of course there is no "Amazon's own digitalized distribution network" coming in the electricity sector to bypass all existing electricity grids. It is a jump and a transformation that distribution networks have to undertake on their own, from "brick and mortar" infrastructure operators to enabling digital platforms.

[5] Ostrom, E. (1991). *Governing the commons: The evolution of institutions for collective action.* Cambridge University Press.

[6] Williamson, O. (1985). *The economic institutions of capitalism.* Free Press.

Both the remarkable report at MIT (*Utility of the Future*, 2016[7]) and the many works performed in the Caramanis–Hogan *Distributed Locational Marginal Pricing* research territory[8] show this very clearly. But, as clearly as that, the last survey undertaken by a subpart of the MIT team shows that no convincing comprehensive scheme to centralize interactions between the transmission and the distribution layers of the electricity systems has emerged or been conceived; and nothing really operational has yet started to systematically link the distribution layer to the many "mini grids" or "behind-the-meter" territories.[9,10] Sioshansi, in the last chapter of the book, also refers to some of these ambiguities as we move toward a more decentralized future with different types of consumers, prosumers, prosumagers, traders, aggregators, and smart intermediaries.

Given these complexities, I conclude my epilogue by quoting the 2015 conceptual paper, presented by the US *Gridwise Architecture Council*[11]:

> The whole electricity system is moving from *"heavily centralized"* control to *"decentralized control"* (with *"independent units"* not obeying to any central control); or to a *"distributed control"* (if and where *"decentralized units cooperate to solve a common problem"*).

This world of "distributed control" is a goal that can be reached, if the new components of the electricity systems (self-optimized homes and buildings; more systematic asset fleets; autonomous *campus micro-grids*; virtual power plants; utility-scale mini grids; etc.) enter all in a new interactive *Transactive Energy* system of systems. This conceptual mapping has already reached the *International Energy Agency*, which has launched its own *Observatory of transactive energy, peer-to-peer and collective consumption* in September 2019[12].

Jean-Michel Glachant
Loyola de Palacio Professor in Energy Policy & Director, Florence School of Regulation

---

[7] MIT Energy Initiative (December 2016), *Utility of the future*. MIT Energy Initiative.

[8] Tabors, R., Caramanis, M., Ntakou, E., Parker, G., Van Alstyne, M. W. (2017). Distributed energy resources: New markets and new products. In: *Proceedings of the 50th Hawaî International Conference on System Sciences*.

[9] S.P. Burger, J.D. Jenkins, C. Batlle, and I.J. Pérez-Arriaga., Restructuring revisited part 1: competition in electricity distribution systems. *Energy J.*, 40(3), 31–54. https://www.iaee.org/energyjournal/article/3352.

[10] S.P. Burger, J.D. Jenkins, C. Batlle, and I.J. Pérez-Arriaga., Restructuring revisited part 2: coordination in electricity distribution systems. *Energy J.*, 40(3), 55–76. https://www.iaee.org/energyjournal/article/3353.

[11] GridWise Architecture Council (January 2015). *GridWise transactive energy framework. Version 1.0.*

[12] https://userstcp.org/annex/peer-to-peer-energy-trading/.

Index

A

Access tariffs, redesigning
  fixed charging approach, 369–370
  redesigning, 368–372
  variable charging approach, 370–372
Administered wholesale prices
  National Electricity Market consistency model with, 333–334
Advanced energy communities, 139
Advanced metering infrastructure (AMI), 251–253
AEMC. *See* Australian Energy Market Commission (AEMC)
Aggregator business models in European electricity markets, 285
  behind-the-meter flexibility of residential loads, 288–294
  collective distributed generation in apartment buildings, 294–300
Aggregators, 6, 68, 105, 123–124
  barriers, 110–112
  business models, 112–116
  drivers, 109–110
  new opportunities for, 116–124
    distribution system operators (DSOs), local flexibility for, 121–124
    energy communities, 118–120
    peer-to-peer trading platforms, 120–121
    transformation of regulatory landscape in Europe, 117–118
  roles of, 106–108, 108*f*
AGV. *See* Automated guided vehicles (AGV)
AI. *See* Artificial intelligence (AI)
Airbnb's platform, 62
Alexa-enabled devices, 261
Allocative efficiency, 362
Amazon, 10, 20*b*, 261
Amazon Alexa, 160
Amendment of the Electricity Management and Organisation Act 2010, 294
AMI. *See* Advanced metering infrastructure (AMI)
AMR. *See* Automatic meter reading (AMR)
Apartment buildings, collective distributed generation in, 294–300

Arbitrage value, 315
ARENA. *See* Australian Renewable Energy Agency (ARENA)
Artificial intelligence (AI), 21, 48, 67
As-it-used-to-be-scenario, 348–352
Attention economy, 195
Audio Frequency Load Control signals, 158–159
Australia
  case study. *See* Home energy management systems (HEMS)
  stand-alone power systems (SAPS) in. *See* Stand-alone power systems (SAPS) in Australia
Australian Competition and Consumer Authority, 385
Australian Energy Council, 390
Australian Energy Market Commission (AEMC), 318, 327–328
  preferred model, 335
  review of regulatory framework for SAPS, 327–328
Australian Equipment Energy Efficiency program, 199–200
Australian networks, 171–172
Australian Renewable Energy Agency (ARENA), 139
AutoGrid, 261
Automated connected electric shared (ACES) vehicles, 194–195
Automated guided vehicles (AGV), 0–225
Automatic meter reading (AMR), 251
Autonomy and independence, 315

B

Bain & Company, 203
Balance Responsible Parties (BRPs), 286
Batteries, behind-the-meter self-consumption in combination with, 184–187
  behind-the-meter storage application examples, 185–187
  self-consumption in Germany, 184–185
Battery storage, 36
Behind-the-meter (BTM), 15*b*, 47, 407–409. *See also* Household customers' responses to prices
  aggregation, 11–22
  aggregation, optimization and value creation, 58–71
  assets, 248–249

Behind-the-meter (BTM) (*Continued*)
  digitalization of, 47–48
  optimization of, 48
battery storage capacity, 109–110
  digitalization of, 49–58
distribution network tariff design for.
    See Distribution network tariff design for
    behind-the-meter
  electric vehicles, BTM storage and, 10–11
  flexibility of residential loads, 288–294
  generation, 7–10
  regulating, 24–28
  stand-alone devices, 22–24
  Voltalis (case study), 72–82, 73f, 75f
Behind the meter investments, 361, 389–390
  access tariffs, redesigning, 368–372
    fixed charging approach, 369–370
    variable charging approach, 370–372
  economic efficiency and, 362–363
  fiscal policy, reforming, 365–368
  local congestion markets, establishing, 372–374
  opening access for, 374–375
  rethinking wholesale market design for
    decarbonized system, 375–378
  Spain's changing approach to renewables and,
    363–365
Behind-the-meter PV generation, investment in,
    390–397
  forecast for the next few years, 396–397
  government incentive schemes, 392–393
  industry and commercial consumers, 394
  story on storage, 394–396
Behind-the-meter services, 253, 255–258
BEIS. *See* Business, Energy & Industrial Strategy (BEIS)
Biodiesel, 37–38
BlackRock, 261
Blockchain technology, 51, 267–273, 408
Blockchain use case classification, 271f
Boating, 37–38
BRPs. *See* Balance Responsible Parties (BRPs)
BTM. *See* Behind-the-meter (BTM)
Bundled regulated tariffs, 3
Business, Energy & Industrial Strategy (BEIS), 237–238
  BEIS Energy Entrepreneurs Fund, 241
Business models, 221–226. *See also* Aggregator
    business models in European electricity markets
  for smart meters, 254–259

C

CAISO. *See* California Independent System Operator
    (CAISO)
California Duck Curve, 72
California Independent System Operator (CAISO), 56

California Public Utilities Commission (CPUC), 239
Capacity-based charges, 345–346
Carbon-neutral homes, 31
Carbon neutrality, 32, 40
CEC. *See* Citizen energy communities (CEC)
CEGB (Central Electricity Generating Board), 411
Choptank, 39
Choptank Electric Cooperative, 38, 40
CHP. *See* Combined heat and power (CHP)
Citizen energy communities (CEC), 118–119, 139
  CEC 2019 Building Energy Efficiency Standards, 31
Clean Energy for All Europeans Package, 106
Clean Energy Package, 294–295
Clean Energy Regulator, 387, 395
Climate Change and Energy Transition Law, 364
Collective distributed generation in apartment
    buildings, 294–300
Combined heat and power (CHP), 214, 365
Community-as-a-Service, 274–275, 282–283
Community Energy, 139
Community manager, 87
Competitive market
  barriers to provision of stand-alone power system
    by, 325–327
Connected economy, 195
Consumer engagement, 403–404
Consumer flexibility, 111
Container Terminal Altenwerder (CTA), 224–000
Convoluted flows, managing
  on aging distribution networks, 235–236
Costco, 10
Cost-reflective distribution network tariffs, 343, 345b
CPUC. *See* California Public Utilities Commission (CPUC)
CTA. *See* Container Terminal Altenwerder (CTA)
Customer-oriented aggregators, 116
Customer participation in peer-to-peer (P2P) trading.
    See Peer-to-peer (P2P) trading, customer
    participation in
"Consumer pull" factors, 390
Customers' response to electricity prices, 308–314
  electricity retailers, switching, 308–309
  half-hourly retail charges for households in Great
    Britain, 313–314
  rooftop PV installation in Australia, 311–313
  use tariffs, customers' response to time of, 309–310
Customer values, 203, 206
Cybersecurity weakness, 165

D

D3A energy exchange for transactive grid, 267
  blockchain technology, 268–273
  D3A architecture, 278f
  D3A hierarchical grid structure, 276f

example grid configuration using the D3A user interface, 277f

from simulation to deployment, 273–283

Decarbonized system, rethinking wholesale market design for, 375–378

Decentralized electrical system, 413–414

Decentralized Energy Management toolkit (DEMKit), 151

Deconstruction, 36–37

Demand management (DM) schemes, 158

Demand response (DR), 61, 72–73, 107, 246, 390

Demand Response Enabling Device, 158–159

Demand-side flexibility services, 143

DEMKit. *See* Decentralized Energy Management toolkit (DEMKit)

DERs. *See* Distributed energy resources (DERs)

DG. *See* Distributed generation (DG)

Digital Equipment Corporation (DEC's) "minicomputers", 205–206

Digitalization of behind-the-meter assets, 47, 49–58

Digitalization of electricity sector, 49b, 169f

Distributed energy resources (DERs), 58b, 107, 239, 261, 267–269, 317, 361, 363, 397

  impact on bills and prices, 398

Distributed generation (DG), 6–7, 10–11, 22, 61, 211

Distributed resources (DR), 53b

Distributed storage, 5, 10–11

Distribution companies, 55

Distribution locational marginal pricing (DLMP), 356

Distribution network, 318, 322–323, 344

  platform for trading flexibility on, 233

    managing convoluted flows on aging distribution networks, 235–236

    network upgrades, nonwire solutions to, 236–238

    Piclo flexibility trading platform (case study), 238–247

    trading platforms, 234–235

Distribution network charges, 341

Distribution network operators (DNOs), 55, 97, 236–237, 242–243, 243t, 247, 249

Distribution network tariff design for behind-the-meter, 341

  efficiency and fairness, trade-off between, 348–353

  signaling future grid costs, 343–347

  sunk grid costs, 347–348

  trade-off, breaking, 355–357

    regulatory fixes to remedy fairness concerns without sacrificing efficiency, 356–357

    tools to improve efficiency beyond network tariff design, 355–356

  trade-off, under- or overestimation of, 354

Distribution services, 327

Distribution system operator (DSO), 55, 68, 107, 120, 239, 255, 274, 276, 286, 372, 374, 412

  local flexibility for, 121–124

DLMP. *See* Distribution locational marginal pricing (DLMP)

DM schemes. *See* Demand management (DM) schemes

DNOs. *See* Distribution network operators (DNOs)

DR. *See* Demand response (DR); Distributed resources (DR)

DSO. *See* Distribution system operator (DSO)

Dutch case study. *See* The Netherlands, energy communities in

Dynamic allocation, 281

Dynamic efficiency, 362

Dynamic pricing. *See* Real-time pricing (RTP)

E

Economic efficiency and behind the meter decisions, 362–363

Ecotricity, 229–230

EEG. *See* Energy Source Act (EEG)

Efficiency and fairness, trade-off between, 348–353

Eigenverbrauchsgemeinschaft, 185

Electric cars, 45

Electric energy, 354

Electricity consumption in Australia, 383–388

  electricity prices, 385–387

  government intervention, pressure for, 387–388

Electricity from renewables (RES-E), 188

Electricity markets, 110, 124

Electricity net-neutrality, 40

Electricity retailers, switching, 308–309

Electricity retailing, in European markets, 285

Electricity sector, digitalization of, 49b, 169f

Electricity supply, four models of, 320f

Electric power sector, traditional utility-centric paradigm of, 4f

Electric vehicles (EVs), 5, 12b, 37, 53, 61, 194–195, 221, 226, 267

  battery, 267

  behind-the-meter storage and, 10–11

  growth of, 16b

  solar electric vehicles, 25f

Elektrizitätswerke Schönau eG (EWS) peer-to-peer energy community field test (case study), 84, 88–97, 89b

  field test, 88–95

  peer-to-peer energy trading, 95–96

  preliminary experiences, 96–97

Elektrizitätswerke Schönau eG peer-to-peer energy community field test (case study), 88–97

  field test, 88–95

  peer-to-peer energy trading, 95–96

  preliminary experiences, 96–97

ELEMENTS Gates, 95–96

Elexon, 119

eMotorWerks, 110

EMS. *See* Energy management systems (EMS)

ENA. *See* Energy Networks Association (ENA)

ENERES, 261

Energy2market, 116

Energy Attention, 288–289

Energy awareness, 288–289

  services to increase, 143

  services to increase, 149

Energy Basis, 288–289, 291

Energy blockchain startups

  area of operation, 272f

  location, 272f

Energy cells, 140

Energy Cloud, 59

Energy communities, 84–88, 118–120, 137, 139–144

  current market players, 86–88

  future product development for, 100–102

    individual self-sufficiency, community with focus on, 100–101

    peer-to-peer trading, community with focus on, 102

    virtual power plants, community with focus on, 101–102

  GridFlex concept, extending, 148–151

  GridFlex Heeten, case study of, 144–148, 145f

  preliminary results of case study, 151–153

  regulatory restrictions, 85–86

  research results regarding, 84–85

Energy consumers, 385

Energy management systems (EMS), 183

Energy Networks Association (ENA), 238

"Energy-only" electricity market, 362

Energy price distribution in The Netherlands, 148, 149f

Energy Source Act (EEG), 214

Energy storage systems (ESS), 70

Energy transition, increased acceptance of, 190

Energy Web Foundation (EWF), 268, 271–273

EnerNOC aggregator, 110

Entelios, 122–123

EnyWay, 116

EPEX, 122–123

ESS. *See* Energy storage systems (ESS)

Ethanol fuel, 37–38

EU Clean Energy Package, 118, 120

European electricity markets, aggregator business models in, 285

  behind-the-meter flexibility of residential loads, 288–294

  collective distributed generation in apartment buildings, 294–300

European electricity sector regulation, 124

EVs. *See* Electric vehicles (EVs)

EWF. *See* Energy Web Foundation (EWF)

Experience economy, 195

Explicit demand response, 143

F

Fair merchant mechanism (FMM), 95–96

Federal Energy Regulatory Commission (FERC), 55b, 75

Feed-in tariff (FiT) schemes, 83, 387–388

FERC. *See* Federal Energy Regulatory Commission (FERC)

Financial viability, 195

Fiscal policy, reforming, 365–368

FiT schemes. *See* Feed-in tariff (FiT) schemes

Fixed charging approach, 369–370

Flexibility markets, 122–123, 355–356, 373

Flexibility services, 237–238, 241f, 243, 247

Flex Providers, 246

FMM. *See* Fair merchant mechanism (FMM)

Fossil and nuclear fuels, support the substitution of, 188–189

FRESH project, 224–225

Front- and behind-the-meter, aggregation of, 211

  changing times, changing needs, changing business models, 221–226

  future of VPPs, 226–231

  original VPP business model, 212–221

Future grid costs, signaling, 343–347

G

Gates, Bill, 206

Geothermal energy, 34–36

Geothermal well drilling site, 35f

Geothermal wells and ground-source heat pumps, 34

German Energy Agency DENA, 270

German energy community case study. *See* Peer-to-peer (P2P) trading, customer participation in

German Renewable Energy Sources Act, 83

Germany, self-consumption in, 184–185

GE Solar, 261

Good Energy, 288–294

Google, 20b, 160

Google Home, 160

Google Nest, 261

Government incentive schemes, 392–393

Green-light conditions, 373

Green-light hours, 370

Green Running, 289–290

Green solutions, 109

Grid, exports to, 315

Grid costs, sunk, 347–348

Grid digitalization progress, 167–172

  preparing Australian networks for the transition, 171–172

  smart meter, 169–170

GridFlex concept, extending, 148–151

GridFlex Heeten, case study of, 138, 144–148, 145f

Grid modernization projects, 61
Grid parity, 182
Grid Singularity, 268, 273, 281, 283
Grid stability offerings, 219–220, 219*f*
Grid-to-vehicle (G2V) applications, 57
Groene Mient, 281, 283
Ground-source heat pump systems, 34–36

H

Haezoom, 228
Half-hourly retail charges for households in Great
    Britain, 313–314
Hamburger Hafen und Logistik AG (HHLA), 0–224
HEMS. *See* Home energy management systems
    (HEMS)
HHLA. *See* Hamburger Hafen und Logistik AG
    (HHLA)
Home energy management systems (HEMS), 38,
    157–165
  automation, 163–164
  grid digitalization progress, 167–172
    preparing Australian networks for the transition,
      171–172
    smart meter, 169–170
  optimization potential, 161–163
  smart home appliance fragmentation, potential for,
    166–167
  smart home security and privacy vulnerabilities,
    165–166
  through retrofitting with smart plugs, 164–165
Home energy management systems (HEMSs), 38
Home Innovation Trial, 288–289
  stages of, 289*f*
HomePod, 160
HomeSeer, 159–160
Household customers' responses to prices, 305
  behind-the-meter value, 314–315
    arbitrage, 315
    autonomy and independence, 315
    exports to the grid, 315
    reduced consumption other than supply
      substitution, 315
    supply substitution, 314
  customers' response to electricity prices, 308–314
    electricity retailers, switching, 308–309
    half-hourly retail charges for households in Great
      Britain, 313–314
    rooftop PV installation in Australia, 311–313
    use tariffs, customers' response to time of,
      309–310
Household ecosystems, 167, 167*f*
Household hot water supply, 34–36
Hub Central Controller, 159–160

I

ICEs. *See* Internal combustion engines (ICEs)
ICT. *See* Information and communication technology (ICT)
IFTTT, 164, 166
IIASA, 196–197
Ikea, 10
Independent aggregator, defined, 106
Individual power systems (IPSs), 317–321
Individual self-sufficiency, community with focus on,
    100–101
Industry and commercial consumers, 394
Information and communication technology (ICT), 49
Integrated service delivery model, 333
  with regulated retail prices, 334–335
Intelligent software, 217, 218*f*
Intensive prosumers, 121
Intermediaries, 6
Internal combustion engines (ICEs), 11
International Data Corporation, 160
International Renewable Energy Agency (IRENA),
    323–325
Internet-enabled devices, 307
Internet-of-Things, 271
IPSs. *See* Individual power systems (IPSs)
IRENA. *See* International Renewable Energy Agency
    (IRENA)
Islanded microgrids, 142

J

Jedlix, 226
Job, Steve, 206

K

Kim, Jongkyu, 228
Koch, Guido, 219–220

L

Large electricity generators, 286
Lawn service, 38
LEC. *See* Local energy community (LEC)
Levelized cost of electricity (LCOE), 321*f*
Levelized cost of energy (LCOE), 280–281, 390
Liberalized industry structure, 362
Liberalized markets, 362
Lichtblick, 116
Lithium-ion batteries, capital cost of, 320*f*
LNSP. *See* Local network service provider (LNSP)
Local congestion markets, establishing, 372–374
Local energy community (LEC), 274–275, 280*f*
Local network service provider (LNSP), 318, 336
  barriers to provision of stand-alone power system
      by, 327

Local network service provider-led standalone power system
  regulatory framework, 336–337
    consumer protections and reliability, 337
    new connections and reconnection, 336–337
    planning and engagement, 336
    service classification, 336
  service delivery models for, 330–335
    Australian Energy Market Commission's preferred model, 335
    integrated service delivery model with regulated retail prices, 334–335
    National Electricity Market consistency model with administered wholesale prices, 333–334
    National Electricity Market consistency model with National Electricity Market wholesale spot prices, 333
LOCE generation. *See* Lower levelized cost of electricity (LOCE) generation
Long-run marginal cost (LRMC), 344
Lower levelized cost of electricity (LOCE) generation, 184
LRMC. *See* Long-run marginal cost (LRMC)

M

M2M communication. *See* Machine-to-machine (M2M) communication
Machine learning (ML), 21, 48, 67, 164
Machine-to-machine (M2M) communication, 212–215
McKinsey's technology, 197
Metering point operator (MO), 97
Microgrids, 140, 317–318, 324
Minicomputers, 205–206
ML. *See* Machine learning (ML)
MO. *See* Metering point operator (MO)

N

National Electricity Market (NEM), 318, 334f
  NEM consistency model, 331–332
    with administered wholesale prices, 333–334
    with National Electricity Market wholesale spot prices, 333
National electricity objective (NEO), 328
National Energy and Climate Plan to the European Commission, 364
National energy retail objective (NERO), 328
National Grid ESO, 239, 246
National Institute of Standards and Technologies (NIST), 167
Natural gas, 31–32
NEM. *See* National Electricity Market (NEM)
NEMOCS, 227–229, 230b
NEO. *See* National electricity objective (NEO)

NERO. *See* National energy retail objective (NERO)
The Netherlands
  energy communities in, 137, 139–144
    GridFlex concept, extending, 148–151
    GridFlex Heeten, case study of, 144–148, 145f
    preliminary results of case study, 151–153
  energy price distribution in, 148, 149f
Network tariff, 344
Network upgrades, nonwire solutions to, 236–238
New business models, 49, 60, 61b
New offerings in new markets, 229b
Next Box, 219, 225
Next Grid Singularity, 283
Next Kraftwerke (NK), 212–215, 215f, 217, 225–226, 228–231
  genesis of, 213b
  key data for, 216t
NIST. *See* National Institute of Standards and Technologies (NIST)
NK. *See* Next Kraftwerke (NK)
Nodal pricing, 372–373
NODES platform, 122–123
Nonislanded microgrids, 142
Nonwire alternatives (NWAs), 235–236, 238
Nonwire solutions, 236–238, 239b
Nordpool, 122–123
NWAs. *See* Nonwire alternatives (NWAs)

O

Occupancy certificate, 44
Oekostrom, 294–300, 302
Off Grid Electric, 64
Office for Gas and Electricity Markets (Ofgem), 236
Off-the-shelf residential energy technology, 31–32
Ofgem, 26b, 119, 237–238
OhmConnect, 62–63, 261
OhmHour, 63
Olsen, Ken, 206
OMIE, 374
Open Utility, 61
Operating efficiency, 362
Orchestrators, 6

P

P2P pooling and community, 88
PAYGO off-grid solar + storage systems, 22
PAYGO solar microgrids, 24
Pay-late penalty charge, 386
Peer-to-peer (P2P) trading, 5–6, 61, 68, 143, 149, 267, 271, 408
  community with focus on, 102
  platforms, 120–121
  of renewable electricity, 187–190

fossil and nuclear fuels, support the substitution of, 188−189
overall system cost, reduction of, 189−190
Peer-to-peer (P2P) trading, customer participation in, 83
  customer preferences, 97−99
  Elektrizitätswerke Schönau eG (EWS) peer-to-peer energy community field test (case study), 84, 88−97, 89b
    field test, 88−95
    peer-to-peer energy trading, 95−96
    preliminary experiences, 96−97
  energy communities, 84−88
    current market players, 86−88
    regulatory restrictions, 85−86
    research results regarding, 84−85
  energy communities, future product development for, 100−102
    individual self-sufficiency, community with focus on, 100−101
    peer-to-peer trading, community with focus on, 102
    virtual power plants, community with focus on, 101−102
Photovoltaic installations (PVs), 269
Piclo Flex, 242f, 244, 246, 248−249. See also Open Utility
Piclo flexibility marketplace structure, 240f
Piclo flexibility trading platform (case study), 234, 238−247
  milestone auction result, 248b
Piclo's platform, 62
Postage stamp pricing, 325
Postscarcity economy, 195
Powerboat, 37−38
Power purchase agreements (PPAs), 10
PowerWalls, 10, 36
PPAs. See Power purchase agreements (PPAs)
Price reactiveness, 343
Price-responsive demand, 72
Propane, 37
Prosumage pooling, 87
Prosumagers, 5−6, 48, 86−87, 262, 378
Prosumers, 3−6, 9, 11, 48, 203, 262, 342, 374, 378
  energy profiles, 143, 149−150
  profiling, 397−399
    complex subject of cross-subsidies, 398−399
    DER's impact on bills and prices, 398
  smart meter meeting, 260−262
PVs. See Photovoltaic installations (PVs)

R
Ramsey pricing, 347−348
Rapid supplier switching, 119

Real-time pricing (RTP), 49
REC. See Renewable energy communities (REC)
Red-light conditions, 373
Red-light hours, 370
Reference network tariff, 352
Regulated retail prices, integrated service delivery model with, 334−335
Regulatory sandboxes, 273
Renewable energy communities (REC), 118−119, 139
Renewable green energy, 7−9
REScoop.eu, 141
Réseau de Transport d'Électricité (RTE), 74
Residential loads, behind-the-meter flexibility of, 288−294
Residual grid costs, recuperation of, 349b
Reutlingen Energy Center, 93b
  for Distributed Energy Systems and Energy Efficiency, Reutlingen University, 92
RIIO (Revenue = Incentives + Innovation + Outputs) framework, 236
Rooftop PV installation in Australia, 311−313
Rooftop solar PVs, 309, 313, 316. See also Solar PVs
Royal Decree on Self-consumption (Spain), 118
RTE. See Réseau de Transport d'Électricité (RTE)
RTP. See Real-time pricing (RTP)

S
SAPS. See Stand-alone power systems (SAPS) in Australia
SCAs. See Smart connection agreements (SCAs)
Scottish and Southern Electricity Networks (SSEN), 61
S-curve adoption rates, 197, 198f, 206−207
Self-consumption, 295
  in Germany, 184−185
Self-generation, 4, 9
Self-storage, 5
"Self-sufficiency"-oriented products, 86−87
Sewer system, 38
(Shared) assets, joint purchase and maintenance of, 143, 149
(Shared) energy, supply of, 143, 149
Small-scale Renewable Energy Target (SRET) Scheme, 387
Smart Community, 139
Smart connection agreements (SCAs), 355, 357
Smart home appliance fragmentation, potential for, 166−167
Smart home security and privacy vulnerabilities, 165−166
Smart meter gateway (SMGW), 97
Smart meters, 169−170, 251
  business models for, 254−259
  customer, 259−260

Smart meters (*Continued*)
  deployment, 256*t*
  meeting the prosumer, 260−262
  smart metering system, 252−254
SMGW. *See* Smart meter gateway (SMGW)
Software as a service, 228*b*
Solar electric vehicles, 25*f*
Solar energy, 17*b*
Solar homes, 31
Solar PVs, 7
  in Australia, 8*b*
  panels, 35
Solar renewable energy credits (SRECs), 40
Solar roofs, 381
  behind-the-meter PV generation, investment in,
      390−397
    forecast for the next few years, 396−397
    government incentive schemes, 392−393
    industry and commercial consumers, 394
    story on storage, 394−396
  consumer engagement, 403−404
  consumers' behind-the-meter
      investment, 389−390
  electricity consumption in Australia, 383−388
    electricity prices, 385−387
    government intervention, pressure for, 387−388
  orderly evolution, industry considerations for, 399−403
    networks and retailers, 400−403
  prosumer, profiling, 397−399
    complex subject of cross-subsidies, 398−399
    DER's impact on bills and prices, 398
Sonnen, 70*b*
sonnenFlat tariff, 116
Spain's changing approach to renewables and behind
    the meter investment, 363−365
SRECs. *See* Solar renewable energy credits (SRECs)
SRET Scheme. *See* Small-scale Renewable Energy
    Target (SRET) Scheme
SSEN. *See* Scottish and Southern Electricity Networks
    (SSEN)
Stand-alone devices, 22−24
Stand-alone power systems (SAPS) in Australia, 317,
    326*f*, 338*f*
  barriers to provision of SAPS
    by competitive market, 325−327
    by local network service providers, 327
  as a cost-effective model of supply, 319−325
    customer density, cost-to-serve, and reliability,
        322−323
    falling costs of SAPS, 319−322
    off-grid supply, global research on, 323−325
  designing a regulatory framework for, 327−329
    Australian Energy Market Commission (AEMC),
        327−328

    criteria for assessing potential regulatory
        framework, 328−329
  local network service provider-led standalone power
      system, 330−335
    Australian Energy Market Commission's preferred
        model, 335
    consumer protections and reliability, 337
    integrated service delivery model with regulated
        retail prices, 334−335
    National Electricity Market consistency model
        with administered wholesale
        prices, 333−334
    National Electricity Market consistency model
        with National Electricity Market wholesale spot
        prices, 333
    new connections and reconnection, 336−337
    planning and engagement, 336
    service classification, 336
  SAPS service delivery, 329−330
  third party−led standalone power system,
      regulatory framework for, 337−339
STEAG, 214
Stored energy, 10
Structural energy efficiency, 33−34
SunPower, 38−39
Sun tax, 364, 367
Supply substitution, 314
Swimming pool solar cover, 37

T
Tariff deficit, 367
  limit the potential for, 368
"Technology push and the consumer pull", alignment
    of, 389
Tenant electricity model, 118
Tesla approach, 207
Third Energy Package, 258−259
Third party−led standalone power system, 318
  regulatory framework for, 337−339
Time-of-use tariffs, 289
Tohoku Electric Power Co., Inc., 230
Tohoku EPCO, 230
Trade-off
  breaking, 355−357
    regulatory fixes to remedy fairness concerns
        without sacrificing efficiency, 356−357
    tools to improve efficiency beyond network tariff
        design, 355−356
  under- or overestimation of, 354
Trading platforms, 233−235
Transmission system operator (TSO), 97, 107, 220, 226,
    286, 412
Trilogy 45 system, 34−36
TSO. *See* Transmission system operator (TSO)

U

UK case study. *See* Distribution network, platform for trading flexibility on
Use tariffs, customers' response to time of, 309–310

V

Value added taxes (VAT), 365
Value Pyramid, elements of, 204*f*
Value-stacking, 70
Variable charging approach, 370–372
VAT. *See* Value added taxes (VAT)
VC. *See* Venture capital (VC)
Vehicle to grid (V2G) technology, 57, 248–249
Venture capital (VC), 61
Verve device, 289–291
Virtual power plant (VPP), 70, 107, 140, 211–213, 215–218, 225, 227, 230, 392–393, 401–403
  advantages of, 222*b*
  community with focus on, 101–102
  future of, 226–231
  getting into EV charging business, 226*b*
  original VPP business model, 212–221
  participants in, 217*f*
Voltalis (case study), 72–82, 73*f*, 75*f*
  and traditional DR providers, 77*b*
Voltalis control center, 76*f*
Voltalis control device installation, 74*f*
Volumetric network charges, 352
VPP. *See* Virtual power plant (VPP)

W

Walmart, 10
Water and sewer systems, 38
WECC. *See* Western Electricity Coordinating Council (WECC)
Weightless economy, 195
Western Electricity Coordinating Council (WECC), 56
Wetware, 195–198
Wholesale market design for decarbonized system, 375–378
Wilberts, Onno, 219–220
Working backward from behind the meter, 193
  bumpy look into the consumer's mind, 203–207
  diversity and difference behind the meter, 198–203
  hardware, software, and orgware meet wetware, 195–198

Y

Yellow-light conditions, 373
Yellow-light hours, 370

Z

Zero net energy (ZNE), 31, 201
  "by the way" carbon neutrality, 32
  performance analysis: first year, 38–40
  program defined and implemented, 32–38
  rough-cut economic analysis, 40–44
Zigbee, 166
ZNE. *See* Zero net energy (ZNE)
Z-Wave, 166

Printed in the United States
By Bookmasters